UNCOLLECTED PROSE
BY
W. B. YEATS

UNCOLLECTED PROSE

BY

William Butler

W. B. YEATS

Collected and edited by

JOHN P. FRAYNE

1

FIRST REVIEWS
AND ARTICLES
1886–1896

Columbia University Press

New York 1970

Contents

ARTICLES AND REVIEWS BY W. B. YEATS

CONTENTS

[A general index will be supplied with the second volume of this edition. To locate a book reviewed in this collection, the reader should consult the note before the general bibliography.]

Acknowledgments

PASSAGES from Yeats's letters are quoted with the permission of The Macmillan Company from *The Letters of W. B. Yeats* edited by Allan Wade, copyright 1953, 1954 by Anne Butler Yeats. Passages from Yeats's prose are quoted with the permission of The Macmillan Company from *Essays and Introductions*, copyright 1961 by Mrs. W. B. Yeats and *Mythologies*, copyright 1959 by Mrs. W. B. Yeats. Passages are quoted from Yeats's *Autobiography* with the permission of The Macmillan Company, copyright 1916, 1936 by The Macmillan Company, renewed 1944 by Bertha Georgie Yeats. Passages from Yeats's poems are reprinted with the permission of The Macmillan Company from *The Variorum Edition of the Poems of W. B. Yeats* edited by Peter Allt and Russell K. Alspach, copyright 1903, 1906, 1907, 1912, 1916, 1918, 1919, 1924, 1928, 1931, 1933, 1934, 1935, 1940, 1944, 1945, 1946, 1950, 1956, 1957 by The Macmillan Company, New York, copyright 1940 by Georgie Yeats.

The article "An Exhibition at William Morris's" is reprinted with the permission of *The Providence Sunday Journal* where it first appeared on October 26, 1890. A passage from a letter by Yeats to Horace Reynolds in December, 1932, is reprinted by permission of the Harvard College Library. Quotations from Yeats's early American articles are reprinted by permission of the publishers from Horace Mason Reynolds, editor, W. B. Yeats's *Letters to the New Island*, Cambridge, Mass.: Harvard University Press, copyright 1934 by the President and Fellows of Harvard College, 1962 by Horace Mason Reynolds.

A passage from T. S. Eliot's "Tradition and the Individual Talent" from *Selected Essays* is quoted with the permission of Harcourt, Brace and World, Inc.

Preface

THIS book is the first of a two-volume work designed to gather into book form that prose of W. B. Yeats, in the form of reviews, articles, and letters to newspapers, which has never been or is not now available in prose collections of his work. This book includes material from 1886 to 1896, the period in which the greatest mass of uncollected prose was written. A second volume will gather together the prose from 1897 until the end of Yeats's career.

Books have not only a fate but a conception of their own. This work is the product of a lifelong interest in Yeats and a chance encounter. In the spring of 1964, I was assembling materials for a study of the effect of Swift's writings upon Yeats and other modern Irish writers. While tracing Yeats's review of Richard Ashe King's *Swift in Ireland* (*Bookman*, June, 1896), I learned how large a body of Yeats's prose criticism and propaganda had never been collected. I read much of this material at once, and I was impressed by the excellence of some of the work, and the relevance of all of it to the period of the poet's life most inadequately represented in his collected prose and recalled with bitterness and distortions of his memory in his autobiography.

For many reasons (upon which I speculate in the introductory chapters here) Yeats never gathered this journalistic prose in book form, although he usually displayed a shrewd sense of how to obtain maximum use of his literary property. We are fortunate that Yeats acquired early a bibliographer such as Allan Wade. As early as in the short bibliography appended to the last volume of the 1908 collected works of Yeats, Wade gave an incomplete, but valuable list of Yeats's journalism. This list was considerably expanded by Wade for his bibliography of Yeats's writings (London, Rupert Hart-Davis, in the "Soho Bibliographies" series, 1951, second edition, 1958, third edition, 1968). I need only say in gratitude to the compiler of that book that I know not how many more years this project might have taken were it not for that bibliography.

The Columbia University encouraged this work from its inception, and through the firm of A. P. Watt and Son I requested permission from Mrs. W. B. Yeats to prepare these writings for publication. Permission was quickly granted, and I have had the full cooperation of the Yeats family throughout this project. I wish to thank particularly Mr. Michael B. Yeats for the kind attention he devoted to many aspects of this project. The late Miss Patricia Butler of A. P. Watt and Son was invaluable in helping me trace the ownership of the magazines in which these articles appeared.

A similar project, smaller in scope, was begun during Yeats's lifetime. Mr. Horace Reynolds gathered into a book entitled *Letters to the New Island* (Cambridge, Mass., 1934) only those of Yeats's pieces written for American newspapers. Yeats gave his permission for that book. Although he was indifferent at first, he warmed to the project and even contributed a foreword in which he expressed surprise that much he considered the wisdom gained in old age he had already known as a young man. There is no reason to doubt that he would have welcomed the collection of his English and Irish prose also. He might even have changed some of the pieces, as he wished to do with some of his letters reprinted by Katharine Tynan in her autobiography.

For most of these pieces there was no opportunity to change them and there exist no manuscript versions of the vast majority of his early prose. When we consider that Yeats was not yet a famous man when he wrote these articles, and if we take into account the carelessness, then and now, with which magazine and newspaper editors treat reviewers' manuscripts, it is hardly likely that his manuscripts were ordinarily returned to Yeats. For most of the works in this book, I have taken as my text the version of these reviews which appeared in the newspapers or magazines. Among the manuscripts presented to the National Library of Ireland by the Yeats family, there are two scrapbooks in which Yeats gathered clippings of reviews and made changes in them (MS books 12147 and 12148). In these articles or reviews, I have naturally incorporated Yeats's changes and given the previous readings in footnotes. These scrapbooks have been of the greatest importance to me, since they contained clippings of anonymous reviews, corrected in Yeats's hand. These reviews were attributed to Yeats by Allan Wade, but the reasons for these attributions were not given in Wade's bibliography.

Yeats had great trouble getting his manuscripts accurately printed. The quoted matter in his reviews is frequently only an approximation of the originals. His bad eyesight contributed to what, I suspect, was an innate indifference to accuracy of transcription. Geoffrey Keynes has noted the many curious errors of transcription in the Yeats-Ellis edition of Blake.[1] Yeats's difficult handwriting erected another barrier to accuracy. In one of his early letters, he complained that a typesetter had so mangled his poem as to make him seem a follower of Browning.[2] I

---

[1] Geoffrey Keynes, *A Bibliography of William Blake*, New York, 1921, p. 275.

[2] *The Letters of W. B. Yeats*, edited by Allan Wade, New York, 1955, pp. 55–56. Letter to the editor of the *Gael* (Dublin), November 23, 1887. In subsequent footnotes this book will be cited as *Letters*.

thus realize that many of the questionable points in the text which I have footnoted are possibly the work of a newspaper compositor. But whether the printed versions are more akin to the work of W. B. Yeats or "Compositor X", I have tried to present in my text as close a version as possible to the original magazine versions. In some cases where I have corrected what appear to be typographical errors, I have noted these corrections and the original versions in footnotes. In many cases where the magazine text poses difficulties, I have let the original version stand and indicated amendments in my footnotes, or I have added necessary punctuation in brackets. There are a few instances of "typos" that seemed not the rational choice of Yeats, his editor, or any compositor but rather the mashing of some machine. To these I have applied a silent rule of common sense.

The frequent, lengthy quotations of prose or poems under review offered some difficulty. I have presented the version which Yeats (or his editor) printed. In the footnotes, I have indicated all verbal changes (spelling, changes of words, or changes of word order) and any punctuational changes which seemed to me of major importance. The variorum edition of Yeats's poems shows how much he liked to change the punctuation of his own poems. He took similar liberties with the poetry of others. For one interested in Yeats's practice in punctuation, the original versions of the poems quoted in this collection are available elsewhere for comparison. It has seemed to me that verbal changes are essentially more valuable and worthy to be noted. In the case of Yeats's quotations of a great poet such as Tennyson, I have noted all changes.

In matters of spelling, I have accepted Yeats's usage and I have noted any unusual deviation from accepted usage either in my footnotes or by the use of "*sic*". Yeats's pre-Lady Gregory spelling of Gaelic names is chaotic—and in keeping with the times. Rather than force a norm upon the luxuriance of his orthography, I have instead been content to reproduce that confusion. Perhaps the apex of his tendency to spell according to taste is an early article on Sir Samuel Ferguson, in which he wrote "Dierdre" and "Deirdre" interchangeably.

A good many of these articles were printed in large-circulation British magazines and the text was available in the library of Columbia University or the New York Public Library. Some rare magazine pieces were obtained from the University of Indiana Library, Yale University Library, Harvard University Library, and such New York libraries as those of the Theosophical Society of New York and the American-Irish Historical Society. The holdings of Irish newspapers and magazines in even the greatest of American libraries is notably poor. The University of Illinois Library assisted me by obtaining microfilms of certain important years of *United Ireland* and the *Dublin Daily Express*.

For most of the articles and reviews originally printed in Irish periodicals I would like to thank the exemplary courtesy and service of the staff of the National Library of Ireland in Dublin, and in particular Mr. R. J. Hayes, Mr. Patrick Henchy, and Mr. Alf MacLochlainn.

From the microfilm and photostat copies supplied by the National Library, I prepared a typescript of the articles, largely with the help of my wife, Eva, who copied many of the texts by hand. Some few Irish periodicals were located only in the British Museum, and for Yeats's contributions to the Irish exile publication *Irlande Libre* I would like to thank the Bibliothèque Nationale in Paris. A copy of one American newspaper article not included in *Letters to the New Island* was obtained from the Providence Public Library.

Aside from the anonymous reviews attributed to Yeats by Wade and supported by manuscript evidence, I have included here on my own attribution one review—of Edward Garnett's *An Imaged World*, from the *Speaker*, September 8, 1894. My defense of this one claim of Yeats's authorship is contained in the first chapter of my introduction and also in the headnote to the review itself. I have tried in these headnotes to give some indication of Yeats's relationship, if any, to the author under review, to include any important elements of historical or literary background, and to suggest the relevance of the works reviewed to Yeats's own poetry, prose, or drama. If Irish or English readers find that I have footnoted obvious names or events, let them remember the ignorance of us Americans in these matters, and smile.

Yeats contributed to Irish literary controversies of the nineties in the form of newspaper letters. It is essential, in attempting to understand these letters, to be able to read the letters of Yeats's fellow controversialists. I wish to thank Mr. John Kelly and Mr. Ernest Bates for their assistance in Dublin in tracking down the letters concerned and in obtaining the necessary microfilm copies at the National Library. During a subsequent visit to Dublin I was able to supplement and complete this work.

I would like to thank Professors William Y. Tindall, James L. Clifford, and John Unterecker, who read part of this book when it was submitted and defended as a dissertation at Columbia University in New York. I have profited greatly from their advice and encouragement. My work has been much facilitated by the generous financial grants for the preparation of this book given by the Fellowship Research, Subvention English, at the University of Illinois. A Summer Faculty Fellowship granted by the University of Illinois enabled me to spend part of the summer of 1967 in Dublin, at which time I finished the first volume of this work and gathered the remaining materials for the second volume.

Among my friends who have suffered and toiled vicariously through the past four years, I wish particularly to thank Mr. Ronald Rower for his help and advice and my sister Mary for her manifold assistance in difficult years. Mr. James Sandor Fuss of the New York Public Library has generously given me his help in obtaining xeroxed materials. I am grateful for the advice and information offered by my Illinois colleagues Professors Henry Summerfield, William Curtin, and Klaus Peter Jochum. My typist, Mrs. Patricia Lane, after almost two thousand pages of Yeats, continues to suffer the "Celtic Twilight" patiently. Lastly, whatever is mine to dedicate in this book, I dedicate to the good-humored forbearance of my wife, Eva, my wise and encouraging friend, Dr. Joseph Meiers, and to the memory of my mother, who was of "the indomitable Irishry".

I have consulted as many as possible of the books reviewed by Yeats which are included in the present collection for the purpose of comparing his quotations with the original text. While so doing, I was able to make larger observations about the truth of the book as compared with Yeats's version of the book. In my sometime insistence on the word that kills, I am aware how much I may at times be in variance with the spirit of the great man that lives. Yeats liked to thunder against pedantic scholarship, except for those rare occasions when he attacked other Blake editors for their inaccuracies. Perhaps by repeating the poem which was printed in the first bibliography of his works, I may remove any evil eye from this edition:

Accursed who brings to light of day
The writings I have cast away!
But blessed he that stirs them not
And lets the kind worm take the lot![3]

JOHN P. FRAYNE

[3] Poem contributed to Wade's first bibliography in the 1908 collected edition of Yeats's works, reprinted in *Variorum Edition of the Poems*, New York, 1957, p. 779. Henceforth this book is referred to as *Variorum*.

INTRODUCTION

1. Innisfree and Grub Street

JOURNALISM supplied Yeats with one of his earliest masks. His early articles, reviews, and letters to newspapers were written in the persona of a man who was confident, assured, and even arrogant at times. There is in his early prose little of that "deliberate turning away" which he would find, late in life, to be the shortcoming of his critical prose.[1] As a young man, he attempted to solve great problems in his writings: the conflict of nationalism and art, the future course of literature, and the battle of matter and spirit. For such perennial questions he demanded quick and often simple solutions. Behind this self-assured mask, in his memoirs and—more accurately— in his correspondence with close friends, we see a different Yeats: the frightened provincial, intolerant of Englishmen, journalists, English journalists, editors, men with better educations, and anyone with an entrée to the quality magazines.

Money and the lack of it runs like a somber, but sometimes comical, leitmotif through his letters of the years 1886–1900. His prose, like Milton's, was left-handed and it had a different message from that of his poetry. At the same time that his poetry of the eighties and nineties called for flight, escape, immunity from what he called in his "Into the Twilight" "the nets of wrong and right," his prose, calling for battle with the enemies of Ireland and the spirit, reflected his efforts to survive in a world from which he could not escape. And he stayed and prevailed.

Lack of money and the curse of journalism plagued him, however. His articles, his memoirs, and his private correspondence all express the view that journalism is the most oppressive form of Adam's curse. In addition to worrying about money, Yeats feared that he was taking from his poems invaluable years and giving this time to ephemera. He found in Irishmen a fatal susceptibility to newspaper writing since it appealed to what he considered the Irishman's love of immediate effects without prolonged toil.[2] He need not have fretted so. We will not speculate on how else he would have spent his time; he admitted to Katharine Tynan that he would sometimes lie in bed all day, weaving the garment of his

---

[1] "Introduction, 1937," *Essays and Introductions*, New York, 1961, p. viii.
[2] "The Celt in London, Some Recent Books by Irish Writers," printed in the *Boston Pilot*, April 18, 1891, and reprinted in *Letters to the New Island*, p. 129. The butt of Yeats's attack was *Poems* by John Francis O'Donnell.

reverie. His prose supported him in more than financial ways. The weekly and monthly reviews gave him opportunity to gain new ideas and the scope to develop them. Many of his editorial projects and his reviews of books, particularly of Irish folklore, left their traces in his poems and plays. Some editorial tasks that he started for money, such as his edition of Blake, were to be overwhelmingly important for the remainder of his life's work.

Yeats's first pieces, in prose and poetry, appeared in Irish periodicals of 1886–1887. They have, as might be expected, a heavily nationalistic message. Their tone is either arrogantly overbearing, as was his first piece on Sir Samuel Ferguson, or tentative and uncertain, as if Yeats did not quite know how to address in the name of the muses the readers of the *Irish Fireside*. He was then enthusiastic about the "barbaric truth" of Sir Samuel Ferguson, and he found a reflection of his own awkwardness in the failures of James Clarence Mangan. In the *Irish Fireside* his pieces ran next to Victorian middle-brow articles on cooking, sewing, and all things Irish. He seems to have made a special effort while writing for such magazines to conceal his passion to make the world anew. He complained, with reason, to Katharine Tynan that his ". . . ever-multiplying boxes of unsaleable MSS . . . [were] too strange one moment and too incoherent the next for any first-class magazine and too ambitious for local papers."[3]

As an apprentice, Yeats served many masters. Some like John O'Leary were by choice, others such as his father, John Butler Yeats, by filial necessity. J. B. Yeats preached to W. B. much about the mission of the artist, the superiority of imagination over intellect, and most of all the danger of serving Mammon by taking a steady job. It was J. B.'s financial insecurity which forced W. B. into journalism to begin with, and his father sent him out into the commercial world with attitudes which ensured his discontent there. John Butler Yeats had taught his son that a gentleman was one not exclusively concerned with getting along in the world. Yeats's letters show him perhaps not exclusively but exhaustedly getting along in the world.

Aside from lofty if impractical principles, J. B.'s most important contribution to Yeats's development as a poet was to let his son develop in his own way and at his own pace. Because Yeats's father was against steady employment, he would not let "Willie" take a steady job even when his son had bursts of ambition to support the rest of the family. Reviewing was in J. B.'s estimation the devilish work of the intellect, and so he encouraged his son to earn money by writing stories and novels. The advice was well meant if futile. Yeats spent much time with

---

[3] *The Letters of W. B. Yeats*, edited by Allan Wade, New York, 1955, pp. 74–75. Letter to Katharine Tynan, June, 1888. (Henceforth this volume is referred to as *Letters*.)

little financial result on his novelette, *John Sherman*, and his unfinished novel, *The Speckled Bird*.

As a substitute father, John O'Leary, the old Fenian just returned in 1884 from exile, could give Yeats sound commercial advice. In the *Gael*, the official penny weekly of the Gaelic Athletic Association, O'Leary supervised a literary column, and there he printed some of Yeats's earliest poems and articles. All copies of this paper save one fragment have disappeared. O'Leary not only printed Yeats, he paid him as well (nothing to be taken for granted in Yeats's early days). Along with his function of literary agent, O'Leary exercised a quasi censorship. Yeats had given him his "Ballad of Moll Magee," in which a woman who accidentally killed her child is turned out by her husband to walk the roads. O'Leary thought it too morbid. Yeats withdrew it under the excuse, "It was a mere experiment," as if he were promising to amend his sense of folk tragedy and do better next time.[4] O'Leary may have been right as a literary agent. He had a better sense than Yeats did of what would pass in an Irish newspaper.

O'Leary was an unusual nationalist in that he seldom allowed his patriotism to interfere with his critical judgment. The poems of Thomas Davis had converted him to nationalism, yet he admitted to Yeats that he thought those poems only mediocre in literary qualities. He told Yeats that the Irish character was perhaps not so good as the English character, but that such an imbalance of virtues did not mean that the Irish should try to become Englishmen. He was certainly more liberal than Yeats in this attitude. Yeats left no doubt as to which national character he thought greatly superior.

O'Leary also lent Yeats money and he was very patient in waiting to get it back. Through his influence, Yeats was introduced to another old Fenian, John Boyle O'Reilly, the editor of the *Boston Pilot*, a Catholic weekly. In the years 1888–1891, Yeats regularly contributed articles, reviews, and a few poems to the *Pilot* as well as the *Providence Sunday Journal*. Unlike English and Irish papers, these American papers printed his work immediately and paid him quickly. Yeats's tone in these American pieces was that of St. Paul addressing a not especially bright and rather remote Greek city. The messianic fervor of Gaeldom was there, but Yeats seemed unsure whether those Yankees still knew what it meant to be an Irishman. These pieces, until now, have remained the only collection of Yeats's early reviews to have been reprinted in book form.[5]

There never seems to have been a time in Yeats's life when he was not

---

[4] *Letters*, to John O'Leary (dated by Allan Wade as late May, 1887), p. 38.
[5] *Letters to the New Island*. Reynolds missed one *Providence Sunday Journal* article, which is included in this collection, "An Exhibition at William Morris's" (pp. 182–86).

founding a society or hatching some collective literary scheme. His first society was the "Dublin Hermetical," founded in 1885 with Charles Johnston and Charles Weekes. While barely out of poetical swaddling himself, he was in 1887 masterminding an anthology of the Irish literary revival which had scarcely begun. Yeats seems not to have edited the anthology *Poems and Ballads of Young Ireland* but he publicized it and referred to it in his letters as "our anthology." Of all his fellow contributors, John Todhunter, Douglas Hyde, T. W. Rolleston, and Katharine Tynan, Miss Tynan was his most influential fellow-apprentice.

Katharine Tynan, at first a poetess and later a romancer of over a hundred volumes, was the daughter of a prosperous Clondalkin farmer. J. B. Yeats's portrait of her in the Municipal Gallery of Dublin shows a slight, intense, not pretty young woman whose small face seems lost behind powerful spectacles. She offered Yeats comradeship and sympathy in these early years. It is ironic that her correspondence with Yeats survived and Yeats with Maud Gonne did not, so that the young Yeats is portrayed for us through the friendship with "Katie," certainly less intimate and passionate a friendship than that with Maud Gonne.

She treated Yeats with indulgent affection and a little condescension. Although they were never in love, she was jealous when Maud Gonne entered and took command of Yeats's life. At one time he thought it might be his duty to offer "Katie" marriage, but good sense prevailed. As a devout and conventional Catholic she found his occultism bewildering, and before long his widening interests made them drift apart. In 1887, however, they were two united against a hostile world. Although she was older and had already published a volume of poems, he gave her advice on how to write, tried to get her books reviewed, and was embarrassed when the reviews he obtained were unfavorable. She could supply Yeats with information about fees from American newspapers, and her father lent Yeats money when he was especially poor. Yeats reviewed her books and she wrote articles and profiles of him. One sketch which she contributed to the *Bookman* made the claim that Yeats was born "at his grandfather's residence, Sandymount Castle. . . ."[6] Even though Yeats liked to think himself legitimate heir through the Butlers of the Dukes of Ormonde, he never claimed to have been castle-born.

In 1888 the Yeats family made one of their periodic moves to London in phase with the changing fortunes of J. B. Yeats. This move was crucial, however. W. B. was twenty-three, and this contact with London meant at best a measure of independence but also the threat of failing among strangers in a city which he described to his American

[6] *Bookman*, October, 1893.

audience as "the capital of the enemy."⁷ In his letters to Katharine
Tynan, he enumerated what he detested about London and the English: their placid self-assurance (and his lack of it), their materialism,
their climate, and the habits of English editors. Some of those editors
held on to manuscripts for years before publishing, and sometimes they
rejected his pieces after a year's wait. Yeats wrote about what he knew
best—Irish fairy tales and ballad poetry. From these pieces, he soon
went on to another scheme, his collection of Irish fairy lore, which was
to prove the most enduring of his collections. It is still in print, and
although Yeats rushed through its final stages to save his editor,
Ernest Rhys, from embarrassment, the notes, although inaccurate, were
never changed.

He retold to Katharine Tynan his difficulties in getting payment from
the Dublin weekly *United Ireland* for an article on Wilfred Scawen Blunt.
For the article, which filled two columns of fine print, Yeats expected
£2. (His going rate was still £1 per column for the *Scots Observer* a year
later.) Yeats should have considered himself lucky to get any money at
all from *United Ireland*. He wrote many pieces for it in 1891 after Parnell
had taken the editorial offices by force from his political enemies.
Yeats's work in 1891 was for the glory of the cause alone. Not only for
national causes was an unrecognized writer such as Yeats expected to
produce articles for nothing. Yeats had entered Madame Blavatsky's
circle of theosophists in 1888, and in 1889 he contributed one of his few
attempts at rationalizing the Irish fairies to the theosophical magazine
Lucifer. Contributions to this magazine were not paid, and Yeats's
article, marked "to be continued," was completed in journals whose
rewards were more material.

In 1888 Yeats made an acquaintance more profitable than Madame
Blavatsky. He met William Ernest Henley and began to attend evening
meetings of young authors and wits at Henley's home. Yeats felt an
awkward provincial at first, too frightened to say a word and too
intimidated to leave.⁸ When he met Oscar Wilde there, he was aston-
ished to learn that one could speak in periods as elegant as one could
write. At these Sunday evening gatherings, Yeats became acquainted
with the circle of young bloods Henley had gathered to write for his
new magazine the *Scots*, later the *National, Observer*. Yeats loathed this
group at first and described them as "the shallowest people on the ridge
of the earth."⁹ He kept coming back, however, because Henley was
kind and hospitable, and he printed Yeats.

Henley published many of Yeats's early poems in his magazine, "The
Lake Isle of Innisfree" among them. The political tone of the *Scots*

⁷ "The Irish National Literary Society," *Boston Pilot*, November 19, 1892, reprinted in
Letters to the New Island, p. 153.   ⁸ *Letters*, p. 83.   ⁹ *Ibid*.

Observer was strongly Unionist in its policy toward Ireland and imperialist everywhere else. Yeats went his mournful Celtic way unmolested. He wrote for this magazine some reviews of Irish books and many of the pieces which made up *The Celtic Twilight*. Yeats thought in his memoirs that his writings were apolitical and therefore needed no slanting by Henley. Perhaps Henley was not so innocent. The general tenor of the *Celtic Twilight* pieces would have confirmed in an English reader the prejudice that the Irish were hopeless dreamers and their affairs had best be kept in capable English hands.

Henley did much more for Yeats than print him. He recommended Yeats for various jobs, often unsuccessfully. Yeats tried, through Henley's entrée, to contribute a life of a blind Gaelic bard named Hefernan to the *Dictionary of National Biography*. No such biography appeared. Henley also tried to get Yeats work on *Chambers's Encyclopaedia*, then undergoing revision. If Yeats did do work for *Chambers's* all record of it has disappeared. Matthew Arnold had said that the Irishman was sentimental, "always ready to react against the despotism of fact."[10] Yeats's own uneasiness with facts would have made him a poor writer for encyclopedias.

The turning point of Yeats's career came with the publication of *The Wanderings of Oisin* in January, 1889. With the aid of John O'Leary, he had collected subscriptions for this book the previous year. In his letters to Katharine Tynan he agonized, doubted, speculated, regretted: "I have buried my youth and raised over it a cairn—of clouds." This letter ended with the significant words "Do what you can for it."[11] Despite his case of opening night nerves, Yeats in 1888 saw with deep insight the strength and weakness of his earliest verse:

. . . that it is almost all a flight into fairyland from the real world, and a summons to that flight . . . that it is not the poetry of insight and knowledge, but of longing and complaint—the cry of the heart against necessity. I hope some day to alter that and write poetry of insight and knowledge.[12]

And so he did, but not for almost twenty years.

As the reviews came in early in 1889, Yeats pasted them into a scrapbook. By mid-March he had twenty-two. He discounted the reviews of his friends like Dr. John Todhunter, since he well knew that Todhunter had used the same pair of green tinted glasses Yeats had used when reviewing Todhunter. Only one review annoyed him. A Dublin newspaper reviewer laughed at Yeats's line in "The Indian to his Love" in which "The peahens dance on a smooth lawn. . . ." Yeats replied to

[10] Matthew Arnold, *The Study of Celtic Literature*, London, 1905, p. 85. Arnold attributed this remark to M. Henri Martin in his *Histoire de France*.

[11] *Letters*, to Katharine Tynan, September 6, 1888, p. 84.

[12] *Letters*, to Katharine Tynan, March 14, 1888, p. 63.

Katharine Tynan that peahens danced or all Indian poetry lied. The sum of the remaining reviews were favorable. Oscar Wilde in his two reviews praised Yeats as a still flawed and immature but important talent. After this reception, English editors who had been sitting on Yeats's articles for months and years printed them. A gentleman from Manchester called and offered Yeats a post as literary gossip columnist. Yeats accepted and seems to have contributed tidbits until Oscar Wilde, opportuned for a bit, told Yeats that writing literary gossip was not a job for a gentleman. That magic word awakened Yeats to the horror of his position. Attempts to find Yeats's contributions to any Manchester paper of this period have proved thus far fruitless. Yeats may have mastered journalese so well that the pieces are unrecognizable.

Although it might seem rash to say that Yeats tried all means of making a literary living, an enumeration of all the odd things he tried accounts for almost all possibilities. Even with his bad eyesight, bad handwriting, and worse accuracy, he did copying work at the British Museum and the Bodleian for the publisher David Nutt, until his eyes gave out. He wrote a few doggerel verses to accompany pictures sent to him by the Tract Society. The verses were bad enough to suit, yet there is something distinctively Yeatsian about these lines:

> The sunlight flickering on the pews,
>   The sunlight in the air,
> The flies that dance in threes and twos,
>   They seem to join in prayer.[13]

That Dublin critic of *Oisin* might have said that flies no more than peahens dance.[14]

Along with his book on Irish fairies, Yeats collected an anthology of Irish novelists, a selection of Edmund Spenser, and a fairy tale book especially compiled for children. He could hardly have known when he started his Blake edition with Edwin J. Ellis that it was to be the most important editorial work of his life. He became converted to Blake as he had not before nor would be after to anyone else. The pay was not good. Ellis and Yeats were each promised by the publisher, Bernard Quaritch, thirteen copies of the large paper edition valued singly at £3. Yeats's smaller collection of Blake for the "Muses' Library" paid better, and this edition had a long and useful career, especially in America, where it sold for decades in the Modern Library series. The most spectacular result of Yeats's researches provided Blake with an Irish ancestry.

Part of the reason for Yeats's success in London literary life was the good use he made of his Irishness. Although sincerely and passionately

---

[13] *Letters*, to Katharine Tynan, April 21, 1889, p. 122.
[14] James Joyce, *Finnegans Wake*, New York, 1959, p. 303, footnote to "Doubbllinn-bbayyates"—"When the dander rattles how the peacocks prance!"

a Gael, he knew that he had a valuable commodity to sell. After Gladstone's two unsuccessful attempts to achieve Home Rule, the "Irish Question" took up a regular and large section of British newspapers. The Irishness Yeats exposed in English journals was not the maenad nationalism of Maud Gonne but rather the wisdom of the fairy and folk, which his English readers need not have feared would burn down any landlord's mansion.

He advised Katharine Tynan to develop her Irish Catholicism as a literary speciality. Yeats's own eclectic creed could earn him little, as he soon learned from his experience with Madame Blavatsky's *Lucifer*. His advice to a young poetess to make her verses Irish seems cynical even when one allows that the following remarks were in response to an unsolicited manuscript: "It [Irish settings] helps originality and makes one's verses sincere, and gives one less numerous competitors. Besides one should love best what is nearest and most interwoven with one's life."[15] The stronger reason here seems added as an afterthought. Yeats little suspected that he was creating what he later called scornfully the "Harps and Pepperpots" school.[16] A fictional follower of Yeats's advice was Joyce's character Little Chandler in the *Dubliners* story "A Little Cloud." In case his name gave insufficient indication of Irishness, Chandler "would put in allusions."[17] Max Beerbohm summed up this unsympathetic view of Yeats as a professional Gael in his drawing of Yeats introducing George Moore to the queen of the fairies. On a shelf in the background were books which would have nourished Yeats's *idées fixes*: *Murray's Guide to Ireland*; *Realism Its Causes and Cures*; *Half-Hours with the Symbols*; *Life of Kathleen Mavourneen*; *Erse Without Tears*; *Songs of Innocence*; and *Short Cuts to Mysticism*.[18] Beerbohm recorded his own impression of Yeats as a great mesmerist who in the case of Beerbohm failed to mesmerize. To an Englishman such as Beerbohm it may have seemed as if in Yeats's estimation the Irish could do no wrong. Back in Dublin, however, there were some who suspected that Yeats had stayed so long in London that he was straying from the "grand old cause that never dies."

Yeats never liked London, but he got used to it. Around 1890, he expressed his longing for Sligo in "The Lake Isle of Innisfree" as well as in his novelette *John Sherman*. In this work, Yeats's fictional hero fails in

[15] *Letters*, to Miss L. White, p. 104.
[16] The harp is of obvious origin. The pepperpots were those "shaped to suggest a round tower with a wolf-dog at its feet." The members of this school "would have felt it inappropriate to publish an Irish book that had not harp and shamrock and green cover." W. B. Yeats, *Autobiography*, New York, 1965, p. 136.
[17] James Joyce, *Dubliners*, New York, 1926, p. 90.
[18] This drawing, frequently reprinted, may be seen in S. N. Behrman's *Portrait of Max*, New York, 1960, p. 149.

London and returns to Ballah (Sligo) to marry his true love. The book is not very good fiction although it helped Yeats to write himself out of homesickness. In his letters to Katharine Tynan of these years, one hears hints that Yeats was enjoying London, however much he was reluctant to admit it. He liked the opportunity to study in London certain subjects which interested him (he probably meant magic), and he gave as a mitigating factor "the mere presence of more cultivated people." Lest Miss Tynan think that "Willie" had changed utterly, he lamented the "loss of green field and mountain slope and . . . the tranquil hours of one's own countryside."[19]

In 1891 Yeats revisited Ireland and he was there when Parnell died in October, 1891. This year and the following one mark a transition in Yeats's journalistic career. During this period he contributed many articles to *United Ireland*, six in 1891 and eight in 1892. Although these pieces appeared at the height of the Parnell scandal and the recriminations following his death, Yeats pleaded for a non-political effort to further Irish literature. He was successful in helping to found the Irish Literary Society in London and Dublin but not in avoiding politics. He contributed only one article to *United Ireland* in 1893 and little thereafter to this journal. At the same time as this burst of Irish activity (unpaid, according to Joseph Hone), Yeats's American markets were failing. Alfred Williams, editor of the *Providence Sunday Journal*, had been deeply interested in Irish literature, and he had printed poems and articles by Yeats and many others in the movement.[20] Williams retired in 1891 and his successor changed the policy of the paper. Yeats's work had been printed in John Boyle O'Reilly's *Boston Pilot* from 1889 on. O'Reilly had died in 1890, but Yeats continued to contribute to that paper until 1892.

In the summer of 1892, Yeats began his most productive and enduring relationship with an English journal. Sir William Robertson Nicholl, the publisher of the *British Weekly*, had recently founded the *Bookman*. The tone of this monthly was heavily trade-oriented. Lists of best sellers were reported from London and provincial booksellers, and each issue opened with gossip about the great. From the evidence of the first issues of 1891-1892, the most marketable personalities were Robert Louis Stevenson and Rudyard Kipling. To increase the feeling of engagement on the part of its readers, the *Bookman* published a column of comments by "experts" on manuscripts sent in by beginners, all suitably pseudonymous.

In July, 1892, Yeats was given for review Michael Field's *Sight and*

[19] *Letters*, to Katharine Tynan, October 6, 1890, p. 158.
[20] The whole story is told in Horace Reynolds's pamphlet, *A Providence Episode in the Irish Literary Renaissance*, Providence, 1929.

Song. Yeats ended his reviews for this paper with Lady Gregory's *Poets and Dreamers* in the *Bookman* of May, 1903, although he had really stopped regular reviewing during 1898–1899. All in all he contributed forty-five reviews and articles to the *Bookman*. His peak year for them was 1895 in which he wrote twelve reviews and articles. He acted as their Irish, folk, and poetry specialist. One may judge his quick rise on this magazine by the fact that five months after he started, in November, 1892, he was asked to contribute with other prominent poets to a symposium on the laureateship after Tennyson's death.

Yeats was lucky to get work with new journals such as the *Scots Observer* and the *Bookman*. He never made any headway with the older established critical papers such as the *Athenaeum*, the *Spectator*, or the *Saturday Review*. His friend Lionel Johnson reviewed for the *Academy*, and, perhaps because he did not wish to crowd his friend out, Yeats published but one review and a few articles in that paper. He had better luck with the *Speaker*, founded about the same time as the *Bookman*. A fellow Irishman, Barry O'Brien, was an editor of the *Speaker*, and such friends of Yeats as Katharine Tynan and Lionel Johnson were among Yeats's fellow contributors. The leading literary critic was Arthur Quiller-Couch, and art reviews, dealing largely with the impressionists, were contributed by George Moore. The liberal tone of this weekly does not seem to have affected the literary judgments of the reviewers. To be sure, books on history and politics were given slanted reviews, but Yeats's review of a book on the hairy Ainu was quite reactionary. Most reviews for the *Speaker* were anonymous.

After searching the periodicals that Yeats worked for most, such as the *Scots Observer*, the *Bookman*, and the *Speaker*, I was surprised to see how few unsigned pieces might on strong evidence be attributed to Yeats. Certainly he could sign anything he liked for the *Bookman*. Although he claimed in his memoirs to have signed all his work for the *Scots Observer*, there is a review of William Carleton's *Red-Haired Man's Wife* which is certainly Yeats's and is unsigned. He could hardly have signed that review since it starts with a brief and noncommittal notice of Yeats's own collection of Carleton. In the *Speaker* we know that Yeats signed one article in the series of "Literary Causerie," and we know that Allan Wade on good evidence attributed other *Speaker* reviews to Yeats. One finds in still other reviews traces of Yeats's authorship, sometimes strong and sometimes weak.

The reviews of Edward Garnett's *Poems in Prose* reveal some of the difficulties of tracing Yeats's unsigned work. Garnett was a reader for the publishing firm of T. Fisher Unwin. He had played an important part in Yeats's struggle against Sir C. G. Duffy for the editorship of the "New Irish Library." Yeats told Garnett in a letter dated by Allan Wade

as October, 1892, "How does *The Imaged World* thrive? Please let me
know before any work of yours comes out as I am now reviewing on
the *Bookman* and may be able to be of use."[21] When Garnett's book of
prose poems appeared, it was reviewed in the *Bookman* of August, 1894,
in an article signed G-Y (common initials in the *Bookman*). The review
was unfavorable, largely on the grounds that the prose poem was a
mixed and unsatisfactory form. Such was Yeats's general opinion, but
there are no specific traces of Yeats in this review. Although Yeats
could sign anything he wrote for the *Bookman*, he might have chosen to
hide an unfavorable review of a friend's book under a pseudonym. Such
deviousness on Yeats's part is less likely than the possibility that Yeats
used his influence to have the book reviewed, and that the reviewer did
not like the book. It would not be the first time that Yeats solicited a
review for a friend's book and the review was unfavorable. In any case,
it seems unlikely that Yeats would have offered a review knowing the
book to be prose poems and then give it a bad review because it was
prose poetry. There is a single reference to Celtic nature rhapsodies in
this review but it does not sound like Yeats.

Another review of this book, in the *Speaker* of September 8, 1894,
begins:

When Vaughan the Silurist said that man was a world and had another to
attend him, he but expressed the faith of those medieval mystics who held the
soul to correspond exactly to the universe and its emotions to the stars and
the forest, the seas and the storms.

The cadenced prose and the references to Vaughan the Silurist suggest
Yeats, as do those medieval mystics. Yeats's criticism is not notable for
the range of its literary references. Lionel Johnson[22] could have told
Yeats about medieval mystics, and Yeats surely encountered Henry
Vaughan in the one area where his reading was encyclopedic—magic and
the occult. Later on in the first paragraph Yeats's authorship is suggested by a reference to an alchemist named Dr. Rudd. The general tone of
the review was laudatory although the reviewer complained of the
"vapoury" effect of prose poetry, an opinion which matches Yeats's.
The strongest link with Yeats was the complaint that Garnett "has not
yet amassed them [his impressions] into a coherent image of the world
and marked them round with what Blake called 'the outline of the
Almighty.' " The reviewer had also complained of "a word without

[21] *Letters*, p. 214.
[22] Johnson is most likely, after Yeats, to be the author of the review. Arthur W. Patrick
in his *Lionel Johnson, poète et critique*, Paris, 1939, gave a full listing of Johnson's journalism
and Patrick was able to use Johnson's manuscripts as support. According to Patrick,
reviews by Johnson appeared in the 1894 *Speaker* issues of August 25, September 1, and
September 25, but not September 8.

precision." Yeats said in another Blake review that Blake's great word
had always been "precision." Elsewhere in this review is the complaint
that Garnett struggled between his own originality and "a mannerism
from Walt Whitman or Richard Jefferies, or the peasant poets of
Roumania." Yeats had through his father and Edward Dowden an early
enthusiasm for Walt Whitman but knowledge of Richard Jefferies does
not show in Yeats's other prose. The reference to the peasant poets of
Roumania, puzzling at first, turns out to be a translation by Hélène
Vacaresco (originally into French; the English translation was made by
Carmen Sylva, actually Elizabeth, Queen of Roumania, and Alma
Strettell) called *The Bard of the Dimbovitza*, published in 1891, with a
later volume in 1894. Yeats knew these books, and even quoted from
the second volume as an example of successful prose translation of folk
poetry in his review of Lucy Garnett's *Greek Folk Poesy*.[23] There is one
final note of plausibility in choosing the *Speaker* review as Yeats's
rather than the *Bookman* review. The passages quoted from Garnett in
the *Bookman* review are accurate, a rarity in Yeats, and the passages in
the *Speaker* are full of punctuational and verbal changes in accordance
with Yeats's usual practice.

If the mark of a Yeats review in these years was a Blake reference, it
must be admitted that not every reviewer who cried "Blake, Blake" was
Yeats. One is tempted to see Yeats's hand in a *Speaker* review of March
3, 1894, of David Masson's *In the Footsteps of the Poets*. The fundamental
point of the review, that poets are the instruments of revelation in
modern society, is Yeatsian even though the reviewer showed some
acquaintance with the life and work of Herbert, Cowper, Thomson, and
Wordsworth not apparent in Yeats's other writings. The following
clause is reminiscent of Yeats's style, especially the reference to "woods
and waters":

. . . a chronicle of the gradual elaboration of that religion of poetry which has
taken the spiritualized imagination for its St. John, and the woods and waters
for its Patmos, and which is making the poet seem to many no mere master of
the revels, or at the utmost splendid interpreter of ancient ordinances, but
himself a fountain of truth, a prophet and instrument of revelation.

Yeats agreed so wholeheartedly with these principles that the reviewer's
reservation as to whether this role of the poet is good or bad weakens
the case for Yeats's authorship. There is, to be sure, a Blake reference:
"that purely modern worship of nature which super-spiritual Blake
avowed to be atheism." Yeats knew and quoted the remark of Blake's
that "everything is atheism which assumes the reality of the natural and
unspiritual world."[24] But, and this is the crucial point, would Yeats ever

[23] *Bookman*, October, 1896.
[24] "**Blake's** Illustrations to Dante," *Essays and Introductions*, p. 132.

refer to Blake as "super-spiritual"? For Yeats, Blake's vision was both extraordinary and normal, not excessive. The review closed with an Irish reference which also points to Yeats.

It is true that the poets of ancient Ireland were also the priests; but, then, their duties appear to have been largely confined to the pleasant and comparatively easy one of cursing their enemies.

The note of facetiousness in this remark is unlike Yeats, however. When speaking of the ancient Irish bards, Yeats always magnified their duties and position, never simplified them.

After searching periodicals of the nineties for unsigned Yeats material, one is tempted to claim more such pieces than sober evaluation of the evidence would warrant. My original lists of probable Yeats material were long, but I have narrowed down my attributions to the Garnett review of which I feel reasonably sure. Allan Wade's attributions are solid, and are based on evidence in Yeats's letters and the poet's manuscripts. I have accepted all his attributions but one, a single paragraph notice of a Standish O'Grady romance, a review which is undistinguished in manner and utterly lacking in any important content. I have tried to be wary of identifying reviews as Yeats's on the basis of their style alone. The long, mournful, incantatory sentences with their repetitions of words and phrase were not difficult for Yeats's friends and followers to write after the master became famous. As Katharine Tynan told her daughter, "He showed us the way."

By 1893 Yeats had learned some of the ways to get the most financial good out of his journalism. He had collected some of his fairy and folk pieces under the title *The Celtic Twilight*. Aside from the success of the collection as a book, it gave its name to a sensibility. Other projects to reuse his ephemeral prose were not so successful. He told an interviewer in 1893 that he intended to collect his nationalistic pieces, probably those contributed to *United Ireland*, under the title "The Watch Fire."[25] No such book ever appeared. He started a book on eighteenth-century Ireland for Unwin's "Adventurer" series. The only memento of this project was his *United Ireland* article "Irish Rakes and Duellists." He also wanted to collect his four articles on Irish national literature for the *Bookman* into a shilling pamphlet, without success. His first collection of critical prose, *Ideas of Good and Evil*, was not to appear until 1903, and it contained only one *Bookman* review and fragments of other *Bookman* articles.

Yeats reached his peak of influence as a reviewer in 1895–1896. By then he had lost whatever shyness he ever had in soliciting reviews for friends or even himself. When George Russell's (A.E.'s) first book of

[25] "Interview with Mr. W. B. Yeats" by D. N. D. (Dunlop?), *Irish Theosophist*, October 15, 1893.

poems appeared in 1894, Yeats could say, like those giants of the daily press whom he admired so in 1888, "I think we will be able to organize a reception for it."[26] He had lost his battle in Ireland with Sir Charles Gavan Duffy over the "New Irish Library," but he had the satisfaction of giving Duffy's books bad reviews as they appeared. In his series of articles for the *Bookman* in 1895, his version of Irish national literature appeared and Duffy had no place in it. Under Yeats's influence, almost every month the *Bookman* published notices of Irish books, Irish literary gossip, and profiles of Irish literary personalities, himself included. In these years, Yeats was a member of a happily incestuous group of younger writers who reviewed one another. Yeats reviewed Lionel Johnson, Katharine Tynan, A.E., Arthur Symons, and Oscar Wilde, and they did the same for him. The wonder is that Yeats's reviews of these people were so well balanced in judgment; any remarkable deviation from good fellowship, such as John Davidson's bad review of *The Countess Cathleen*, seems to have been in retaliation, in this case for a bad review by Yeats of a Davidson book.

In the midst of this success, Yeats was unhappy in journalism. His 1895 collected poems started his world-wide fame. After this year he tried to raise his prices for articles and to place them in more exclusive, expensive, and in the case of the *Yellow Book* and the *Savoy*, notorious magazines. His poor eyesight was an even more pressing reason to stop reviewing books. In 1894 he told John O'Leary, "I suppose I shall have to very much drop reviewing and take to stories entirely which will be better artistically at any rate."[27] This turn to fiction produced *The Secret Rose*, and one may question whether this was an improvement artistically over the best of his reviews and articles. But despite his fears for his eyesight, he reviewed more books in 1895 (eight) than in 1894 (five). Maybe he read them less.

Writing fiction was to prove a far more tedious way of supporting himself than journalism. Late in 1896 he signed an agreement with the firm of Lawrence and Bullen to write a novel set in Paris and the Aran islands. Yeats received £2 per week for six months. He told O'Leary that "these arrangements are my attempt to escape from journalism."[28] It was a costly escape. The novel gave him much trouble and was never finished nor published, except posthumously in fragments. To discharge his debt to Lawrence and Bullen he gave them a collection of his despised journalism, which became *Ideas of Good and Evil*.

[26] *Letters*, p. 231. There appeared in Yeats's early letters to Katharine Tynan admiration for such men as Montgomery Ranking, a reviewer on the London *Graphic* (*Letters*, pp. 35ff.).   [27] *Ibid.*, p. 230.

[28] *Ibid.*, p. 268. These "arrangements" also included the collection of stories *The Secret Rose* and a scheme to have his play *The Shadowy Waters* published by Leonard Smithers. The latter project misfired.

His weariness with journalism in 1896–1897 was accompanied by a general change in his way of life, his friends, and his interests. He had met Lady Gregory and George Moore, and his ties with Katharine Tynan (then Mrs. Henry Hinkson) and John O'Leary began to weaken. He had learned as little as he could from Grub Street and he longed to escape. He told Robert Bridges in 1897 that

. . . you must not judge it [his review of Bridges' *Return of Ulysses*] as you would judge an essay meant to be permanent. It is merely . . . journalism like all my criticism so far, and done more quickly than I would like. One has to give something of one's self to the devil that one may live. I have given my criticism.[29]

Yeats's salvation lay finally not in publishers' agreements nor in the increased value of his own work, but in the generosity of Lady Gregory. She gave Yeats the money he would have earned in reviewing and she allowed him more time for his poems and, at the end of the nineties, his dramas. After ten years of journalism and about seventy-five book reviews, Yeats rested. Along with his weariness of journalism and his involvement with the Irish National Theatre, it is hardly surprising that he answered in response to an *Academy* symposium on the best books of 1902: "But for a few works sent me by young authors, I should have read no book published this year, so far as I can recollect, except Lady Gregory's *Cuchullain of Muirthemne*."[30]

Yeats consistently played down his journalistic work in his autobiography. In the introduction to his *Oxford Book of Modern Verse*, one is given the impression that Yeats and the Rhymers would have sooner begged than reviewed.[31] The truth is that most of them were very successful daily or weekly reviewers. In his memoirs he would also have one believe that his projects during the nineties invariably met with failure, and that in his battles over the "New Irish Library" and the Irish Literary Society he had succumbed to the great temptation of the artist, "creation without toil."[32] Certainly his theatrical work of 1900–1910 was more productive in his poetry than his propaganda work of the mid-nineties had been. The propaganda of the nineties, however, is not markedly inferior to his writings on behalf of the Irish National Theatre which he included in his 1908 collected edition.

Yeats condemned his reviews to oblivion himself. They were not collected, as was the case with the reviews of Henley, Wilde, Johnson, Symons, and Le Gallienne, and he gave them scant place in the eight-volume edition of 1908. What is surprising is that they should have

[29] *Letters*, p. 286.
[30] *Academy*, December 6, 1902.
[31] *Oxford Book of Modern Verse*, chosen by W. B. Yeats, Oxford, 1936, Introduction, p. xi.
[32] *Autobiography*, p. 135.

remained uncollected. They exhibit Yeats's mind in his most formative years, and the rashness and arrogance of some of his opinions are refreshing to one who finds his later prose style, although less adorned, more evasive and filled with qualifications. These reviews show how Yeats's ideas changed and also how continuous his major preoccupations were. He was surprised to learn, when Horace Reynolds in 1930 showed him photostats of his early American pieces, that ideas which he thought were acquisitions after long years of meditation were known to him when he was twenty-five.

During a trip to America in 1932, Yeats wrote (on Waldorf-Astoria stationery) to Horace Reynolds about some of the reviews of his youth, and the master reflected upon his apprenticeship.

I am glad to have read those essays of mine after so many years. I find that I am still in agreement with all the generalizations, but not with the examples chosen. I praise Todhunter and others out of measure because they were symbols of generalizations and good friends to my father and myself. The articles are much better than my memory of them, but I knew better than I wrote. I was a propagandist and hated being one. It seems to me that I remember almost the day and hour when revising for some reprint my essay upon the Celtic movement I saw clearly the unrealities and half-truths propaganda had involved me in, and the way out. All one's life one struggles towards reality, finding always but new veils. One knows everything in one's mind. It is the words, children of the occasion, that betray.[33]

I like to think that had Yeats seen again his Irish and English journalism of the nineties, he might have thought these pieces children of the occasion with a special truth of their own.

[33] This letter, dated December 24, 1932, is at the Houghton Library, Harvard University. Yeats may have seen the way out while revising his essay on "The Celtic Element in Literature" for *Ideas of Good and Evil*, but he made no substantial changes in that essay.

2. Twilight Propaganda

On our side is Virtue and Erin,
On *theirs* is the Saxon and Guilt.

Thomas Moore, "The Song of O'Ruark, Prince of Breffni"

IN Yeats's first poetic testament, "To Ireland in the Coming Times" (1892), he claimed his place in that company of poets who sang "to sweeten Ireland's wrong." The wrong which England had done to Ireland was, in Yeats's opinion, cultural and literary as well as political and economic. From the outset of his career, Yeats tried to avenge the neglect of Anglo-Irish literature shown by English critics and Irish intellectuals alike. To achieve this task, Yeats attempted to mold the broken and shattered fragments of a half-forgotten tradition and thereby make the world believe that Ireland possessed an important literature. He did not wait for scholarship to unearth a royal line of bards stretching back to Ossian—he created his pedigree. It was not an easy task to establish a royal line in Irish letters: certain pretenders had to be exposed, some contemporary claimants had to be rejected, and as Yeats developed his style from peasant simplicity to aristocratic obscurity the patents of nobility were changed continually.

It would not be fair to judge Yeats as a critic by his early pronouncements on his own Irish contemporaries and on Irish writers of the past. We shall examine later his more consistently literary judgments. When he appraised works of Irish literature, he wrote as a propagandist, and in his desire to produce an Irish literature he often forgot his dictum that "the true ambition is to make criticism as international, and literature as National, as possible."[1] As a propagandist, Yeats became skilled in the art of making a little go a long way. If Homer did not begin Irish literature, then Yeats was able to make Sir Samuel Ferguson do instead.

In the first stage of Yeats's work as a propagandist for the Irish literary cause, during the late eighties and early nineties, his main effort went into distinguishing between which literature he considered true and which false to his national ideal. By the mid nineties, Yeats's exhortations had produced some books on Irish subjects for him to praise. No longer did he have to argue what a hypothetical Irish literature of the future would be like. Instead he could devote his reviews to

[1] *Letters*, "To the Editor of *United Ireland*," November 10, 1894, p. 239.

praising the members of his own school. By the turn of the century, Yeats gave up active journalism and ceased his propagandizing for the general Irish literary cause. At this time, he devoted his energies more to the specialized task of setting up an Irish national theater. By then, modern Irish literature was well under way, and the movement was mature enough to have produced a split between the followers of Douglas Hyde, who wanted a Gaelic literature, and men such as Yeats and George Russell, who wanted a compromise solution: a literature Irish in subject matter and manner but still in the English language. Although Yeats stopped his active propaganda early in life, he never ceased his efforts to define an Irish literary tradition. In the late 1920s and early 1930s he rediscovered those stones which he had scorned to use in the 1890s for the grand edifice—Burke, Goldsmith, and Swift. By his death, he had created in his own life and work as resplendent a literary tradition as he had ever discovered in the past.

If the reputations of certain neglected Irish writers of the past had to be established, certain idols had to be destroyed. The Irish image had to be remolded in English as well as Irish opinion. At the same time, the nostalgic sentimentality of the Irish-American had to be exposed for what it was. The effort on the part of writers to change the popular image of their people is commonplace in many times and countries. As the Negro American writer of today rejects the sentimental condescension behind the portrayal of the Negro in Harriet Beecher Stowe and DuBose Heyward, so Yeats rejected the image of the stage-Irish buffoon created for an English audience in the novels of Charles Lever and Samuel Lover. Even if the Irish themselves enjoyed such clowning, Yeats regarded the stage Irishman as slander on a national scale.

In other matters, Yeats was to find most of his literary enemies within the Irish camp itself. Because sentimental patriotism was his worst enemy, Yeats devoted much of his energies to dethroning Thomas Moore as Ireland's national poet and to undermining the literary reputation of Thomas Davis and the "Young Ireland" movement which Davis had led.

If there was only one Irish book in an English household in the late nineteenth century, it was sure to be Thomas Moore's *Irish Melodies*. Moore stood for the convivial Ireland of the tear and the smile, a manageable, Unionist Ireland that need not be taken seriously. Yeats did not have to downgrade Moore as a serious poet; English criticism had already done that. Nevertheless, Moore's position as a great popular poet was still high. Yeats, however, even excluded Moore from the ranks of the popular Irish balladeers. In his article, "Popular Ballad Poetry of Ireland," Yeats had examined what the poetry of the people had to say about "Ireland poetic, passionate, remembering, idyllic, fanciful and always patriotic." Near the end of the article, Yeats supposed that an English reader may have wondered at the absence of Moore, Samuel Lover, and Charles Lever. Yeats scornfully replied:

They were never poets of the people. Moore lived in the drawing-rooms, and still finds his audience therein. . . . Ireland was a metaphor to Moore, to Lever and Lover a merry harlequin, sometimes even pathetic, to be patted and pitied and laughed at so long as he said "your honour," and presumed in nowise to be considered a serious or tragic person.[2]

Yeats ignored Moore's obvious charms as a song writer because he thought Moore was a baneful influence. Moore's Irishman was an emotional weathercock. Yeats's Irishman, on the other hand, had to be capable of high tragedy. Yeats fought against the conventional picture of the Irishman in an early article on Sir Samuel Ferguson: "We are often told that we are men of infirm will and lavish lips, planning one thing and doing another. . . ."[3] In contrast to the boastful Irish orator of his own time, Yeats found a different national character in the ancient heroic legends of Ireland.

The mind of the Celt loves to linger on images of persistence; implacable hate, implacable love, on Conor and Deirdre, and Setanta watching by the door of Cullan, and the long waiting of the blind Lynott.[4]

Tom Moore talked much of these qualities in his verse, but they are not embodied in his writing. Yeats was hardly consistent in his criticisms; there were occasions when he considered implacability not a virtue.[5] Among the Irish peasantry of more recent times, Yeats might have allowed some emotional variability. Among the ancient heroes, Yeats could only see pure extremes of love and hate. Poor Tom Moore had turned the bardic heroes into boudoir drama. He had no past to reveal to Yeats, and had to be discarded.

Moore was not to be moved from the Irish pantheon with impunity. Yeats tells in his autobiography how D. J. O'Donoghue, the author of a dictionary of Irish poets containing two thousand names, was thrown out of a tombstone maker's house for slandering Moore's name.[6] During the mid-nineties, Yeats was a prolific compiler of reading lists of the best Irish books. Upon occasion, such as a proposal to set up local reading rooms in conjunction with the Young Ireland League,

[2] W. B. Yeats, "Popular Ballad Poetry of Ireland," *Leisure Hour*, November, 1889, p. 38.
[3] W. B. Yeats, "The Poetry of Sir Samuel Ferguson," *Dublin University Review*, November, 1886, p. 940. [4] *Ibid.*
[5] In a review of Douglas Hyde's *Love Songs of Connacht* for the *Bookman*, October, 1893, Yeats quoted with approval Hyde's description of the Irish peasant: "The same man who will today be dancing, sporting, drinking, and shouting, will be soliloquizing by himself to-morrow, heavy and sick and sad in his poor lonely little hut, making a croon over departed hopes, lost life, the vanity of this world and the coming of death. There is for you the Gaelic nature. . . ." [6] "Ireland after Parnell," *Autobiography*, p. 140.

Yeats suggested stocking Moore's *Irish Melodies* among the essential books.[7] In other lists of best Irish books, however, such as those contributed to the Dublin *Daily Express* of February 27, 1895, and to the *Bookman* of October, 1895, Moore is omitted. In Yeats's 1895 *Book of Irish Verse*, intended "not at all for Irish peasants," Yeats included only two Moore poems with many misprints, and one howler.[8]

Although Moore could be safely ignored as a vital literary influence, the prestige of Thomas Davis, the long-dead editor of the *Nation* newspaper, was strong, and, according to Yeats, destructive of real poetic talent. Davis had led the "Young Ireland" movement until his death in 1845. His patriotic, rhetorical ballads, such as "Lament for the Death of Eoghan Ruadh O'Neill" and "The Sack of Baltimore," had remained up to Yeats's day the model for those who would vaunt the shamrock over the rose. Davis was one of that triad, "Davis, Mangan, Ferguson," which Yeats had proclaimed in 1892 to be part of his poetic pedigree. It is difficult to justify the choice of Davis unless one supposes that Yeats was choosing tribal gods rather than expressing his poetic taste.

In the first flush of patriotic enthusiasm, Yeats had found romance in lives which he later confessed to be most dull and prosaic.[9] Davis's life, however, never seems to have fascinated Yeats. He liked to contrast Davis on many occasions with the decadent Mangan: "the one absorbed, moody, and morbid, in penury, one of the people, wilful and self-trained, wasted by routine [Mangan]; the other university trained, a man of action, patient and gay, one of the gentry, surrounded by friends."[10] Of the two masks, the bohemian Mangan or the respectable Davis, Yeats in 1887 chose to identify himself with the former. In his article on "Popular Ballad Poetry of Ireland" in 1889, Yeats praised Davis as one whose ballads were sung by children in the street. On Davis's political poetry, Yeats found it politic to remain silent in an English magazine. Just as he dismissed Lionel Johnson's patriotic poems a decade later, Yeats said of Davis's jingoism, "Suffice it to say it still goes on, whether for good or evil, serving its purpose, making opinion."[11]

Yeats's opinion of Davis steadily declined until, by the middle nineties, Yeats found that the followers of Davis, led by Sir Charles Gavan Duffy, were the most important opposing camp in the Irish literary revival. By 1895 Davis's poetry had become part of "that interesting, unsatisfactory, pathetic movement which we call in Ireland 'the poetry

[7] Yeats, "The Young Ireland League," *United Ireland*, October 3, 1891.
[8] Moore's line "The cheerful hearts now broken!" was printed by Yeats as "The cheerful homes now broken!"   [9] "Reveries," *Autobiography*, p. 67.
[10] Yeats, "Popular Ballad Poetry of Ireland," *Leisure Hour*, November, 1889, p. 36.
[11] *Ibid.*, p. 37.

of Young Ireland.' "[12] Yeats considered the "Young Ireland" movement abortive and passé because it had roots only in Irish politics and
not in the heroic Irish past. The writers of this school had not learned
their craft from the great writers of the world but rather from those
Scottish models, Macaulay, Campbell, Sir Walter Scott, and Carlyle,
whom Yeats considered the ideals of self-educated clerks in the 1840s.[13]
For the followers of Davis all genres were rooted in politics. Love
poems were not written by them out of deep emotion but rather,
claimed Yeats, "by a patriot who wanted to prove that we did indeed
possess, in the words of Daniel O'Connell, the 'finest peasantry upon
earth.' "[14] When Davis needed a tragedy written, he simply asked a
friend to write one, upon the presumption that tragedy should be
within the range of every Irish patriot.[15]

The greatest danger from the *Nation* group was that some of its
leading lights were still active. Lady Wilde, Oscar Wilde's mother, had
been famous in her youth as a contributor of fiery patriotic poems to the
Nation under the pseudonym of "Speranza," and she still published
folklore. Many older men who remembered their youth and the *Nation*
with equal affection were horrified to hear Yeats at Irish Literary Society
meetings criticize the poetry of Davis in public. Sir Charles Gavan
Duffy, an old comrade and biographer of Davis, had returned from
Australia and had become an important rival of Yeats for the leadership
of the Irish literary movement.

In 1892 Yeats and T. W. Rolleston had instituted a scheme to
publish a series of popular, low-priced books on Irish subjects in conjunction with the other activities of the Irish Literary Society. Rolleston
was to strike the proper opening note with a biography of Wolfe Tone,
one of the heroes of the 1798 uprising. Such a choice of subject may
have been intended to capitalize on the interest in the coming centenary
of '98. Yet, however much Rolleston was to wave the green flag, it was
Yeats's intention to have Tone's life presented with scholarly accuracy.
Yeats projected for a second volume a consecutive history of Ireland
told in popular ballads, edited and arranged by himself. Lady Wilde
was to contribute a life of Patrick Sarsfield, one of the heroes of James
the Second's war in Ireland, and Lionel Johnson was willing to start a
work on Irish educational problems.[16]

[12] Yeats, "Irish National Literature, From Callanan to Carleton," *Bookman*, July, 1895,
p. 106.   [13] Yeats, "Ireland after Parnell," *Autobiography*, p. 136.
[14] *Ibid.*, p. 137.
[15] Yeats, Review of Sir Charles Gavan Duffy's *Young Ireland* in the *Bookman*, January,
1897, p. 120.
[16] *Letters*, to Sir Charles Gavan Duffy, dated by Wade as July, 1892, p. 212. Most of these
projects are listed in this letter. Some of these books were suggested in other letters of this
year.

All was going well until Duffy became interested in the project, to be called the "New Irish Library." Some members of the Irish Literary Society, such as Rolleston, thought that Duffy would make a splendid head of the publishing company. Yeats was not alarmed at first since he thought that Duffy would serve as a figurehead. He soon learned that Duffy had his own ideas on what to publish—books which Yeats felt sure would be publishing disasters. Yeats made anguished appeals to the projected publisher, T. Fisher Unwin, to his friend Richard Garnett, Unwin's reader, and to his protector, John O'Leary. In the heat of battle, Yeats was not afraid to boast of "a somewhat considerable experience of the editing of cheap books—I have edited five, some of which were sold in thousands. . . ."[17] Yeats's expertise enabled him to foresee ruin for the project under Duffy's editorship. Yet all was in vain; Yeats was defeated. Duffy, with his eyes on the past, opened up the series with his edition of a pamphlet by Thomas Davis on the patriot parliament of 1689. Although the book sold well, Yeats claimed that the peasantry found it so dull that they would have nothing to do with the later numbers in the series.[18]

Yeats's first opportunity to discuss Duffy's project came in August, 1894, when he reviewed three of the "New Irish Library" volumes for the *Bookman*. Aside from the "Patriot Parliament" volume, Duffy had chosen for publication a volume of old-fashioned jingoistic verses called *The New Spirit of the Nation*, and an awkward adaptation of a poor Balzac novel turned into an agricultural treatise titled *A Parish Providence*, signed with a pseudonym, " E. M. Lynch," which Yeats believed, perhaps erroneously, to conceal Sir Charles himself. Yeats was severe in his criticisms. He was interested in two extremes of literary consciousness: one was to be a simple literature based on peasant life and themes which would complement, on the other hand, a sophisticated, aristocratic literature derived from the remote Celtic past. The first would satisfy a Gaelic-speaking peasantry, and the second could rival English literature for the attention of the educated class in Ireland. What Davis gave and what Duffy served up cold again was a literature which appealed, in Yeats's opinion, to an urbanized, non-peasant, half-literate, shopkeeper class. In his *Bookman* review of August, 1894, Yeats gave a horrible example of the poetry of "Young Ireland":

[17] Letter to the *Freeman's Journal*, September 6, 1892. By this year, Yeats had edited *Fairy and Folk Tales of the Irish Peasantry, Stories from Carleton, Representative Irish Tales, Irish Fairy Tales* (for children), and he may have considered himself as editor of a fifth, the 1888 collection, *Poems and Ballads of Young Ireland*. His Blake edition was not yet finished.

[18] Letter to *United Ireland*, September 1, 1894. Yeats's pessimism was unfounded. After a bad start, the New Irish Library issued volumes which Yeats found praiseworthy.

Come, Liberty, come! We are ripe for thy coming;
Come, freshen the hearts where thy rival has trod;
Come, richest and rarest! Come, purest and fairest!
Come, daughter of science! Come, gift of the god!

Although this is certainly jingling doggerel with its echoes of Schiller's "Ode to Joy," Yeats must have known that the tree of nationalism can bear such crab apples as well as

> *The silver apples of the moon,*
> *The golden apples of the sun.*

If young Irish writers among Yeats's contemporaries had bad models in Tom Moore and Thomas Davis, Ireland's great institutions had also proven inadequate guides. For Yeats, the Anglo-Irish intellectual establishment was symbolized by Trinity College, Dublin, an institution which Yeats had never attended but which often received his criticisms. In 1892, the Parnell controversy had so exacerbated all tensions in Ireland, political and religious, that Yeats's natural antipathy to organized higher learning led him to attack Trinity College, which had the previous year celebrated its three-hundredth anniversary. He wrote in the Parnellite journal, *United Ireland*:

As Dublin Castle with the help of the police keeps Ireland for England, so Trinity College with the help of the schoolmasters keeps the mind of Ireland for scholasticism with its accompanying weight of mediocrity.[19]

As he wrote the article, Yeats sat among students grinding for examinations in the reading room of the National Library. Looking upon what he thought an imaginative desert, he lamented the absence of almost any books on the Irish language or upon Celtic literature in the library's collection. Times have changed in some ways.

Yeats always seems to have thought that English education was superior to Irish. When he remembered his own experiences in English and Irish schools, he compared the fostering of independent intellectual interests in England with the strenuous preparation for examinations in Irish schools. In one of his few favorable mentions of Matthew Arnold, Yeats quoted him on Oxford: "She has given herself to many causes that have not been my causes, but never to the Philistines." Yeats thought that Trinity College, on the other hand, was a Philistine encampment.

Trinity College's indifference to nationalistic goals was embodied for Yeats in Trinity's Professor of English, Edward Dowden. Yeats was at a very young age when he first met Dowden, since Dowden was an old friend of his father's. In his *Autobiography*, Yeats admitted an adolescent devotion to Dowden, to the point of hero-worship. Yeats would speak

[19] Yeats, "Dublin Scholasticism and Trinity College," *United Ireland*, July 30, 1892.

to Dowden of his youthful enthusiasms and ambitions and "he would put the question away with good-humored irony; he seemed to condescend to everyone and everything and was now [1884–1885] my sage."[20] Yeats seemed to learn soon that he was among those who were condescended to, and his subsequent rancor at Dowden may have been increased by the memory of the youthful follies at which Dowden had smiled.

Dowden himself had come very early to fame. He had been appointed Professor of English at Trinity four years after his graduation from the college, and his famous study of Shakespeare (still in print) was published when he was thirty-two. He subsequently wrote less successful books on Shelley and Browning, and he collected in book form his articles on such then avant-garde figures as his good friend, Walt Whitman. To John Butler Yeats such a conventionally successful career was the price of Dowden's having betrayed his creative faculties to the development of his critical faculties. Poor Dowden, a quiet scholar amid a din of awakening Gaels, seems always to have been kindly disposed to W. B. Yeats; he had expressed his admiration for *The Wanderings of Oisin* at a time when such praise was crucial to Yeats's career.

Dowden had maintained a cosmopolitan aloofness from the revival of interest in Celtic literature. In one of his first articles, "The Poetry of Sir Samuel Ferguson," Yeats made the accusation that Irish critics, with Dowden as the chief offender, had betrayed Ferguson by allowing English critics to treat him with contumely. Dowden, a close friend of Ferguson's, had praised (but in a letter, not in public print) Ferguson's short epic, *Conary*, but Dowden had never used his great prestige as a critic to spread Sir Samuel's fame.[21] With the harsh judgment of youth, Yeats could not see how Dowden may have been faced with a genuine dilemma. The Trinity professor may have regarded Ferguson highly as a scholar and antiquarian but he may have thought that Ferguson's poetic talents were negligible. Dowden was a minor poet himself. For an intellectual like Dowden, the pressures to praise all things Irish were irrelevant, and the nationalistic clamor of young writers such as Yeats may have antagonized him against a native Irish literature.

In 1886, Yeats would accept no compromise. Dowden's attitude of neutrality toward the Irish literary revival was "West Britonism," and typical of the professorial classes who, Yeats rashly claimed, "appear at no time to have thought of the affairs of their country till they first

[20] "Reveries," *Autobiography*, p. 57.
[21] Dowden's letter of praise to Ferguson was reprinted in part in Lady Ferguson's biography of her husband, *Sir Samuel Ferguson in the Ireland of his Day*, London, 1896, Vol. II, pp. 270–71.

feared for their emoluments. . . ."[22] Although Dowden seems to have remained silent in response to Yeats's 1886 charges, within a decade he had become sufficiently angered by the young Irish group to denounce them in public. Yeats had to answer in newspaper letters Dowden's charges that the writings of the Irish Literary Society suffered from rhetorical failures, sentimentality, and bad technique. Yeats defended his contemporaries in his newspaper letters by cataloguing works in which a distinctive Irish quality could be isolated, and by calling an honor roll of younger Irish writers. The list, containing such names as T. W. Rolleston, Douglas Hyde, A. P. Graves (an older man), and Lionel Johnson, is not very impressive today and it would seem to have borne out Dowden's point. Yeats, the only major talent of the group, could not praise himself, and Dowden indeed never doubted the quality of Yeats's writings. Dowden's attitude of exasperated neutrality was not without its distinguished successors. James Joyce attacked the young Irish Literary Theatre in his early article, "The Day of the Rabblement," on the grounds that independent criticism was lost among the nationalistic furor of 1901 Ireland.[23]

Although Yeats liked to quote the Gaelic proverb "Contention is better than loneliness," the bulk of his early prose did not consist of negative or destructive criticism. He thought that he had powerful allies among Irish writers of the past, men whom he considered worthy (at least for a time) of his discipleship. Yeats had not discovered the Celtic past unaided. The credit for giving the first impulse to the Irish literary revival is usually given to Standish O'Grady, historian and romancer. O'Grady, like Yeats, of Protestant background, was a passionate Celt whose unorthodox ideas on Irish history helped him create in his two-volume *History of Ireland* (*Heroic Period*, 1878, *Cuculain and his Contemporaries*, 1880) a fictionalized version of the Irish past. Scorning the traditional history of names, dates, and catalogs of visible archaeological remains, O'Grady felt that the historian should first of all bring the figures of the past vividly to life before his readers. The result resembled more Sir Walter Scott's pictures of the Scottish Highlands than the Bronze Age in Ireland. As MacPherson a century earlier had moved Ossian, Fingal, and their companions out of their hill forts and animal skins into palaces and armor, so O'Grady gave a Homeric élan to Cuchulain, Conor, and Fergus.

But even with the inspiration O'Grady afforded, there would have been no literary revival in Ireland without a poet of genius such as

[22] Yeats, "The Poetry of Sir Samuel Ferguson," *Dublin University Review*, November, 1886, p. 941.

[23] James Joyce, "The Day of the Rabblement," reprinted in *The Critical Writings of James Joyce*, ed. Ellsworth Mason and Richard Ellmann, New York, 1959, pp. 68–72.

Yeats. In his autobiography, Yeats gave credit to O'Grady's *History of Ireland* as a motive force, but Yeats seldom singled out O'Grady for praise in his early writings.[24] Although he reviewed most of O'Grady's books favorably in the nineties, Yeats did not think him one of those who could transmute the heroic wealth of the past into great art. O'Grady had provided only the first necessary step in making available to modern English readers the Irish past. O'Grady (who, ironically enough, seems to have known as little Gaelic as Yeats[25]) was the first of a long line of Yeats's guides through the Irish past. The line culminated in Lady Gregory, who at the turn of the century revealed the matter of Ireland all over again in what Yeats considered its finest translation.

"Some old half-savage bard chanting to his companions at the forest fire" was Yeats's imaginative description of the quiet, mild-mannered poet and antiquarian, Sir Samuel Ferguson.[26] Of those who opened up the Celtic past to Yeats, Ferguson received the first and loudest praise from Yeats, and yet he was one of the first to be forgotten. Ferguson followed O'Grady in exposing to Yeats what he could not read in Gaelic, and, what was more important than mere information, he could show Yeats the poetic possibilities of the old legends. During Ferguson's ascendancy, he was Yeats's Homer, and the quiet scholar's work was flaunted as a banner by Yeats against all those who doubted the Irish literary cause. Although Ferguson was well enough known as an antiquarian to be knighted for his achievements, his poetry had been dismissed by English critics as the work of an amateur. This neglect seemed to Yeats in 1886, writing upon the occasion of Ferguson's death, to be a deliberate insult to Irish honor. Aside from questions of national pride, however, Yeats looked upon Ferguson as one of his literary masters. Ferguson's work offered Yeats a way out of the ideological perplexities of the nineteenth century and an opportunity to retreat to a primitive literature, to what Yeats offered as the basic quality of Ferguson's poetry, "barbarous truth."[27]

Yeats was disturbed by the psychological complexity of the nature poetry of Wordsworth, Tennyson, and Matthew Arnold. Ferguson, on the other hand, had that noble simplicity which Matthew Arnold had ascribed to Sophocles, "who saw life steadily, and saw it whole."[28] In 1886 Yeats could look back upon the Victorians and the romantics and say:

At once the fault and the beauty of the nature-description of most modern poets is that for them the stars, and stream, the leaves, and the animals, are

[24] Yeats, "Ireland after Parnell," *Autobiography*, p. 148.   [25] *Ibid*.

[26] Yeats, "Popular Ballad Poetry of Ireland," *Leisure Hour*, November, 1889, p. 37.

[27] Yeats, "The Poetry of Sir Samuel Ferguson," *Irish Fireside*, October 9, 1886. Yeats quotes the phrase as "the words of Spencer." He probably meant the philosopher, Herbert Spencer.   [28] Matthew Arnold, Sonnet, "To a Friend."

only masks behind which go on the sad soliloquies of a nineteenth century egoism. When the world was fresh they gave us a clear glass to see the world through, but slowly, as nature lost her newness, or they began more and more to live in cities or for some other cause, the glass was dyed with ever deepening colours, and now we scarcely see what lies beyond because of the pictures that are painted all over it. But here is one who brings us a clear glass once more.[29]

However much Yeats admired such simplicity, he could not imitate this manner in his most characteristic early poems. "The deep wood's woven shade" of "Who Goes with Fergus" was still the sad soliloquizing of a nineteenth-century escapee. Yeats was to succeed better in achieving a simplicity of natural description in his later poetry, although certain sympathetic English readers (among them Dorothy Wellesley) had never thought his rendering of external nature visually convincing.[30]

To the young Yeats, Ferguson's simplicity was Homeric. A few years later, when he was less anxious to demonstrate the excellence of all things Irish, what once might have seemed Homeric became that conventional stiffness which Yeats thought characteristic of the eighteenth century. One does not have to wait long to see a change in Yeats's opinion of Ferguson. In an article printed in 1889 but written more than a year earlier, Yeats thought that "an antique coldness" had prevented Ferguson from reaching popularity. Yeats, however, felt guilty in criticizing Ferguson: "If we long, while listening, for the more elaborate music of modern days, the fault is in us and in our time."[31] Ferguson's steady view of nature, like that of the popular ballad poets of Ireland, had precluded any insight on their part into what Wordsworth saw in nature—"the types and symbols of eternity." Yeats claimed that "the grass was merely green to them and the sea merely blue. . . ."[32] For the young Yeats, the greenness of the grass was in itself a declaration of nationalistic faith.

However little poetic technique Ferguson could teach Yeats, he could give to Yeats an enthusiasm for the poetic possibilities of the old Celtic legends. Yeats's summaries of Ferguson's narrative poems frequently throw more light on Yeats's own poems than the notes written for his own collected editions. In his character and conduct, Ferguson served as a model which Yeats seemed to follow in his own

[29] Yeats, "The Poetry of Sir Samuel Ferguson," *Dublin University Review*, November, 1886, p. 940.
[30] Dorothy Wellesley thought that Yeats's lack of interest in the visible, external world was due partly to his poor eyesight and partly to a general failure among Celtic poets in this matter. *Letters on Poetry from W. B. Yeats to Dorothy Wellesley*, London, 1964, pp. 172–74.
[31] Yeats, "Popular Ballad Poetry of Ireland," *Leisure Hour*, November, 1889, p. 37.
[32] *Ibid.*

old age. He described Ferguson as "one who, among the somewhat sybaritic singers of his day, was like some aged sea-king sitting among the inland wheat and poppies—the savour of the sea about him, and its strength."[33]

Ferguson long remained a standard of the primitive quality which Yeats thought modern Irish literature should have. Yet with each repeated mention of Ferguson, Yeats found a new fault: "At his worst he is monotonous in cadence and clumsy in language; at his best a little like Homer in his delight in savage strength, in tumultuous action, in overshadowing doom."[34] When it came time to review Lady Ferguson's life of her husband in May, 1896, Yeats had much praise for the man, little for the poetry, but he treated scornfully the society of Unionist bishops and civil servants which surrounded him.

In Ferguson Yeats found a Homer, and in James Clarence Mangan he found an Irish Baudelaire and Poe. If Ferguson was to give the new Irish literature heroic simplicity, James Clarence Mangan offered the new school a continental tone by his disordered life, his consumption of alcohol and opium. Mangan, a contributor to Davis's *Nation*, did many translations from the German, Gaelic, and other languages in his sober intervals, and wrote one great patriotic poem, "Dark Rosaleen." His life, however, did not illustrate for Yeats the patriotic virtues. The early biographical articles of Yeats on Mangan do not have a strongly nationalistic tone. They were intended to illustrate the immortal enmity between the children of genius and the sons of men. Mangan, like Shelley, Blake, and Yeats, was persecuted as a child by vulgar boys because of his genius. "If you tie a red ribbon to the leg of a sea-gull the other gulls will pick it to death."[35] Such, thought Yeats, was the penalty of not joining the flock. Mangan's long alcoholic decline as a cataloguer in Trinity College Library was for Yeats an example of the baleful effect of a routine job upon the poet. Yeats admired the outpourings of intimate despair in Mangan's poems, and he included several of them along with "Dark Rosaleen" in his Irish anthology. He did not, however, rate Mangan as high as James Joyce did. In a conversation with Padraic Colum, Joyce claimed that there was more intensity in a single passage of Mangan than in all of Swift's writings.[36] Joyce's two

[33] Yeats, "The Poetry of Sir Samuel Ferguson," *Dublin University Review*, November, 1886, p. 940. Yeats described himself in old age as "A weather-worn, marble triton/ Among the streams . . ." ("Men Improve with the Years," *Variorum Edition of the Poems*, New York, 1957, p. 329).

[34] Yeats, "Irish National Literature. From Callanan to Carleton," *Bookman*, July, 1895, p. 106.

[35] Yeats, "Clarence Mangan's Love Affair," *United Ireland*, August 22, 1891. This statement, apparently a favorite with Yeats, is quoted in the introduction to Yeats's *Poems of William Blake*, New York, n.d., p. xv.

[36] Mary and Padraic Colum, *Our Friend James Joyce*, New York, 1958, p. 149.

laudatory magazine articles on Mangan prove that this statement was no momentary perversity.

Yeats's efforts to further the cause of Irish literature were not only prompted by patriotic considerations but also in part by a desire to defend his choice of subject matter for his own poetry. In his earliest poems, which he collected in his 1895 volume under the appropriate title *Crossways*, he had experimented with Indian themes and had considered classical Greek themes long enough to inform his readers that "the woods of Arcady are dead,/ And over is their antique joy. . . ."[37] Although his sympathies for Indian philosophy and religion were deep and to prove lifelong, he soon realized the foolhardiness of following cultural patterns so exotic and alien to him. What other choices remained? He could have unburied the woods of Arcady and written poems inspired by classical myths and themes in the manner of Swinburne, Tennyson, and Arnold. Yeats, however, unlike the leading English poets of his own and the previous generation, had not received a sound classical education. Although he was to call upon the name of Homer as often as Matthew Arnold, it was Homer in translation, not in Greek. Although Yeats studied a little Latin in school, he seems never to have shown much enthusiasm for Roman literature.[38]

Yeats needed an independent body of undeveloped myth close to English and Irish experience yet sufficiently strange to his contemporary readers so as to seem novel and original. These factors conditioned his choice of the Fenian and Cuchulain cycles of ancient Celtic legends, but the choice itself was free and deliberate. He did not have to use these myths in his poetry, in the sense that they were not an essential part of his culture or upbringing. He had not encountered them during his sentimental education in Howth and Sligo, a lack which he lamented in later life.[39] Yeats could not have discovered these legends as part of his own independent scholarly inquiry, for although he repeatedly attempted Gaelic, he could not have read those tales in their

---

[37] Yeats, "The Song of the Happy Shepherd," *Variorum*, p. 64.

[38] "Teach nothing but Greek, Gaelic, mathematics, and perhaps one modern language. I reject Latin because it was a language of the Graeco-Roman decadence, all imitation and manner and other feminine tricks; the much or little Latin necessary for a priest, doctor or lawyer should be part of professional training and come later. . . . No passing beggar or fiddler or benighted countryman has ever trembled or been awe-struck by nymph-haunted or Fury-haunted wood described in Roman poetry. Roman poetry is founded upon documents, not upon belief." "Ireland after the Revolution," from "On the Boiler," *Explorations*, New York, 1962, pp. 438–39.

[39] "When I was a child I had only to climb the hill behind the house to see long, blue, ragged hills flowing along the southern horizon. What beauty was lost to me, what depth of emotion is still perhaps lacking in me, because nobody told me, not even the merchant captains who knew everything, that Cruachan of the Enchantments lay behind those long, blue, ragged hills!" Preface to Lady Gregory's *Cuchulain of Muirthemne*, London, 1903, p. xvii.

original form. He chose Celtic mythology because it was fresh, un-exploited, non-Christian, and remote, as well as because it had, to use his favorite phrase, "stirred his imagination."

These legends carried Yeats and his readers away from the pressing and impossible divisions of modern Ireland. Although Oisin and St. Patrick, the two speakers in his first long poem, touched upon the potentially sensitive theme of a pagan versus Christian view of life, their quarrel did not allude to the inflammatory conflict of Catholic and Protestant Ireland. In his youth Yeats was neutral, and he wished to lure Ireland away from what he called the "nets of wrong and right."[40] If Catholic Ireland could not forget Cromwell and Protestant Ireland James II and the Pope, then Yeats would try to divert his country's attention away from "the mystery play of devils and angels which we call our national history. . . ."[41] Rather than brood upon the past seven centuries of confusion and defeat, the Irish could escape into a remoter past of everlasting victory—all sentiments, to be sure, not very different from those expressed in Tom Moore's patriotic songs ("Let Erin remember the days of old . . ."). In spite of this superficial resemblance to the metaphor which Ireland had been to Moore, for Yeats Ireland was to be a symbol of remote, tragic solitude.

One great advantage of Celtic mythology for Yeats was that its resemblance to other mythological systems made it seem strange to modern readers and yet at the same time familiar. The name Cuchulain was unknown to most English readers, yet his personality and deeds were close enough to those of Achilles and Siegfried to mitigate the novelty. Deirdre could be treated by Yeats as a composite of the queenly heroines of Greek tragedy, a mixture of Elektra, Ariadne, and Antigone. That all mythologies and folklores had a common spiritual basis was sound theosophical doctrine, and Yeats had learned this conviction from Madame Blavatsky's books and from the lady herself.

One cannot absolve Yeats from much chauvinism and a certain degree of obscurantism in his choice of Irish mythological subjects. By insisting upon a certain essential Irishness in the legends which he treated, he was able to warn non-Irish poets to keep off (although it was not difficult to achieve Irishness by adoption, as did Lionel Johnson). Yeats may have been obscure in that his entire body of poetry and his plays do not contain in themselves a coherent account of Celtic legend. He was always dependent upon other writers to clarify his legendary system, and his exaggerated praise of Lady Gregory's two books of

[40] "Into the Twilight," *Variorum*, p. 147.
[41] Yeats, Review of John Todhunter's *The Life of Patrick Sarsfield*, *Bookman*, November, 1895, p. 59.

Irish heroic cycles may have been due to his gratitude that she had at last provided the common reader with the necessary equipment to read Yeats. Although he seems to have intended *The Wanderings of Oisin* as a first part of a lengthy imitation of Hugo's *Légende des siècles*, the project was soon discontinued. His cycle of Cuchulain plays came closest to an attempt to "explain" his mythology. For Yeats, mythologies did not exist to clarify but to symbolize and idealize a national past.

It was an extremely fortunate historical accident that placed Irish legends at the young Yeats's disposal. He was not immune to intellectual fashions, and, born a generation earlier, he might have ignored Celtic mythology. Not only the naturally partial Irish, however, but also such neutral critics as Ernest Renan and Matthew Arnold were awed by the achievements of the early Celts. The grand dimensions of the Celtic past were being surveyed by such non-Irish scholars as Kuno Meyer and H. D'Arbois de Jubainville. John Rhys, in the Hibbert Lectures of 1886, had examined the mythology of the ancient Celts in the context of nineteenth-century archaeology and anthropology. Rhys helped refute the literalism of older writers on pre-history who believed that the divinities in mythologies were ultimately based on real characters. The "solar myth" theory was used by a mythographer such as Rhys to account for the myths of primitive peoples as imaginative explanations of natural phenomena—the cycle of the seasons, of sowing and harvest, and the eclipses of the sun and moon. With all the joy of a young man possessing a new intellectual weapon, Yeats liked to use such quasi-scientific rationalizations of Celtic mythology against those old-fashioned literalists who believed that the ancient races of Ireland, the Fomorians, the Tuatha de Danaan, and the Milesians, had really existed. Even though the "solar myth" gave intellectual respectability to the study of bardic tales, Yeats could not wholly subscribe to such rationalizations. Treating Cuchulain as a solar hero took some epic grandeur and mystery from those early tales. Yeats wanted profound revelations of the nature of the cosmos, not explanations intended to reconcile the mysteries of the primitive mind to nineteenth-century reason.

Some remote mythology was essential for Yeats, for he regarded the modern life of cities as hopeless materials for poetry. The recent Irish past also was for Yeats largely barren as subject matter for literature. Except in the rural districts, where the folk still believed in the primacy of supernatural forces, a steady vulgarization had taken place. Bad English doggerel had usurped the splendid Gaelic poetry of ten centuries. Instead of rejecting the recent Irish past, a writer of another kind of genius might have thought otherwise. For an Irish Sir Walter

Scott, the wars of William and James II, the uprising of 1798, the Union and Catholic Emancipation crises, and the great famine of the late 1840s might have seemed invaluable matter for a national literature. With certain notable exceptions such as the short play *Cathleen Ni Houlihan*, these events enter only incidentally into Yeats's work. Under his guidance, an Irishman, crushed by a long series of defeats, had to retreat at least a millennium before reaching an entirely satisfactory past. There, in that past which he loved to call "dim," one could discover the rudiments of a great literature. Yeats had to admit that it had been an incomplete literature. After a splendid start, Ireland had been cheated by history of its rightful place as a world leader in art and the things of the spirit. A simple solution offered itself to Yeats in the early nineties as a means to redress this balance. The modern Irish poet must return to that ancient body of legend and finish it as a work of art. Such a decision was prompted by both Yeats's theory of literature and his own interpretation of Irish history.

What might be called Yeats's own myth of the Irish past was an amalgam of standard scholarly accounts and his spiritualized account. Although Yeats far preferred pagan Ireland to Christian Ireland, he loved to dwell upon those centuries when Irish missionaries had gone to convert the European continent to Christianity. But even this prodigal outpouring of spiritual energy, Yeats thought, had its tragic effect in weakening Ireland in preparation for the invaders. The most durable conquerors, the English, had their own views of the Irish past in the form of slanders, which Yeats asserted were proven false by the evidence of ancient Celtic civilization. The true Irish character was to be found among Oisin, Deirdre, and Cuchulain, not among the impoverished tillers of a ruined countryside nor among the unfortunate Irish immigrants who had, after the great famine, crowded into the slums of New York and Boston.

In the characters of the ancient bards, Yeats found a proper poetic mask for himself. The lofty, distant, proud bards were all that the "sybaritic singers" of his own day were not. As Yeats described them, "The bards, kept by the rules of their order from wars and the common affairs of men, rode hither and thither gathering up the dim feelings of the time, and making them conscious."[42] To Yeats, who had never fully accepted the doctrine of "art for art's sake," the ancient bards were enviable for the political and religious power which they had exercised. He retold with obvious envy the tale of a bard who asked for a king's eye and had it plucked out for him. Another bard had created a state of famine in the land by his curse alone.

Some of Yeats's views on Ireland in ancient times seem more

[42] Review of Sophie Bryant's *Celtic Ireland*, in *Scots Observer*, January 4, 1890, p. 182.

Tennysonian than historical. His mythical Ireland was self-conscious in a distinctly modern way:

The warriors were not simply warriors, the kings simply kings, the smiths merely smiths; they all seem striving to bring something out of the world of thoughts into the world of deeds—a something that always eluded them.[43]

In the midst of the literary dilettantism of London, Yeats looked back with longing to the Fenian militia, a band of men who harked back to an even more primitive period, living in the forest, marrying only for love, and rejecting all those who did not understand the art of poetry. Whether the bardic histories of ancient Ireland had any basis in fact was immaterial to Yeats. He admitted the possibility that all that splendid ancient history might be fiction: "Indeed Cuchulain, Finn, Oisin, St. Patrick, the whole ancient world of Erin may well have been sung out of the void by the harps of the great bardic order."[44] Such a prodigious effort of the imagination, more valuable to Yeats than mere facts, had its parallel in Yeats's own efforts to create a heroic world out of his contemporary Ireland.

The efforts of the ancient bards had been in vain, however. When other nations were reaching a sufficiently high degree of civilization to impose a deliberate literary culture on its ancient sagas, Ireland had been too harried by foreign invaders to achieve anything but monstrous and incoherent forms: "but Ireland was doomed to have no rest, no peace, no leisure for students to labour in: the bees were too hard pressed by the wasps to make any honey."[45] First the Danes and then the Normans had torn the fabric of Irish culture, and the final blow—the long centuries of English rule—had all but destroyed Gaelic culture. Yet the substance of a great literature was still there in heroes like Cuchulain, "some epic needing only deliberate craft to be scarce less than Homer."[46] Yeats and his circle would supply the deliberate craft, however unlikely that possibility might seem in the "Mauve Decade." History, which had so badly abused Ireland, would now give her a harvest one hundred fold. The tables of the law might yet be finished, even in the language of the conqueror. That main characteristic of the Celt according to Yeats, the persistence of his passion, would see its reward: "A man loves or hates until he falls into the grave. Years pass over the head of Conchubar and Finn: they forget nothing."[47]

Yeats promulgated a theory of nationalism and literature which accorded with his hopes that the hour of the Celt had come at last. In a lecture delivered to the National Literary Society in Dublin in May, 1893, Yeats explained the growth and decline of national literature in terms of the organic development of a tree, certainly one of his favorite

[43] *Ibid.*   [44] *Ibid.*   [45] *Ibid.*, p. 183.   [46] *Ibid.*   [47] *Ibid.*

symbols. Like the tree, a literature passed through different stages and exhibited different characteristics, all determined by laws of growth external to the plant or literature. In a national literature, the three main periods were marked by the predominance of a genre which matched a major stage in the national life. The first period, the epic stage, was characterized by a concern on the part of poets with vast themes which affected the entire national destiny. This stage was followed by a narrowing of focus, an exclusive concern with great individual characters in the form of heroic drama. Last of all came a lyric phase in which the poet was concerned with the communication in highly sophisticated forms of his own evanescent moods. As the forms grow shorter, the mode of expression becomes more complex.

Yeats drew his examples from Greek and English literature, since he assumed that they were best known to his listeners. It was characteristic of him to ignore Latin literature, which he studied in school and disliked ever aftèr. In Yeats's theory, the Homeric stage of Greek literature was paralleled with the periods of Chaucer and Malory in English literature, and the Attic dramatists with Shakespeare and his contemporaries. The lyric age of Greek literature for Yeats was the period of the Greek Anthology rather than that of Sappho, Alcaeus, and Pindar. A Hellenist might have objected that the golden age of Greek lyric poetry came in the early fifth century B.C. and hence before the great period of Greek drama. The English equivalent of the Greek lyric stage was the romantic period, a standard judgment for Yeats's generation, before the great Donne revival.

Some of Yeats's ideas on literary history are sufficiently individual to be noted. Yeats found Chaucer "simple," where a modern medievalist might find him complex. For Yeats, there was no literary continuity between the ancient and modern world. After the barbarian invasions silenced Greece, ". . . there came a long blank until the next great creative period, when the literature of England arose and went through the same stages. . . ."[48] Yeats was to supplement this curious view of literary history in many ways during the next thirty years, not least through the guidance of Ezra Pound, his future secretary, whose own version of literary history gave prominence to those periods, medieval and renaissance Italian, and Provençal, ignored by Yeats.

The propaganda value of this theory is obvious. In another context, Yeats put the conclusion very bluntly: "England is old and her poets must scrape up the crumbs of an almost finished banquet, but Ireland has still full tables."[49] Ireland was still in her ballad or epic stage, as was

---

[48] Yeats, "Nationality and Literature," *United Ireland*, May 27, 1893.
[49] *Letters to the New Island*, in section entitled, "The Rhymers' Club," which first appeared in the *Boston Pilot* of April 23, 1892.

obvious from the works of Ferguson, Aubrey de Vere, and others among Yeats's immediate elders. England, on the other hand, was at the last, decadent end of its lyric phase. (Yeats's own problem was whether he himself was in his epic or lyric or even dramatic phase.) He admitted the possibility that what he considered a separate Irish literature might in fact only be a small eddy of "the advancing tide of English literature" and be doomed to a common decline and old age with English literature.[50] The suggestion was advanced only to be rejected as highly unlikely by all true patriots.

The Irish, then, were only rank beginners in 1893 with all the advantages of a new and fresh literature, but also with some of the disadvantages of inexperience. Along with the virtue of epic simplicity, the Irish had the vices of the near-primitive, carelessness with form, and impatience with technique. Before English and European literatures reached the coming doom, Yeats advised the improvisatory Irish to learn the virtues of style and complexity. Here again is Yeats's paradoxical balance: literature as national as possible, criticism and the literary education of the poet as international as possible.

We may ask what Yeats, the herald of a new literary dawn, was doing among the decadents of the Rhymers' Club. Yeats himself saw the contradiction, and, in a *United Ireland* article, "Hopes and Fears for Irish Literature," he attempted to balance his association with the decadents in England with his position in Ireland as a founder of a new literature. In England, such Rhymers as Arthur Symons, Ernest Dowson, and Lionel Johnson before his double conversion to Rome and Tara were interested in poetic form to the exclusion of Yeats's favorite topics of race and nationality, questions which they regarded as extra-literary. In Ireland, there was ample nationalistic conviction but little or no interest in questions of literary form. The Irish of his own and the previous generation seemed to Yeats to have too great a faith in the spontaneous effort and a corresponding distrust of careful composition.

In his autobiography Yeats told how he used to preach of the glories of nationalism to bored, silent Rhymers who were anxious to hear Arthur Symons talk of absinthe and music hall dancers. In his 1892 article, closer to the event than his autobiographical account, this is how he told the story:

I well remember the irritated silence that fell upon a noted gathering of the younger English imaginative writers once, when I tried to explain a philosophy of poetry in which I was profoundly interested, and to show the dependence, as I conceived it, of all great art and literature upon conviction and upon heroic life.[51]

[50] "Nationality and Literature," *United Ireland*, May 27, 1893.
[51] "Hopes and Fears for Irish Literature," *United Ireland*, October 15 1892.

If Yeats, on the one hand, held the conviction that the Irish writer needed a profound sense of involvement with the destiny of his country and the life of its country people, on the other hand, Yeats believed along with Verlaine and "the school of the sunset"[52] that the writer must exercise the greatest devotion to his craft and its techniques. Against the Irish love of facility in expression, Yeats preached a monastic code of devotion to perfection:

Yet, he who would write a memorable song must be ready to give often days to a few lines, and be ready, perhaps, to pay for it afterwards with certain other days of dire exhaustion and depression, and, if he would be remembered when he is in his grave, he must give to his art the devotion the Crusaders of old gave to their cause and be content to be alone among men, apart alike from their joys and their sorrows, having for companions the multitude of his dreams and for reward the kingdom of his pride.[53]

Already in 1892, Yeats had that love of strange, proud, lonely things which was to be reflected in his choice of personal heroes, in John O'Leary, Parnell, Red Hanrahan, and Jonathan Swift. The poet, in Yeats's imaginings, was to retreat in inner exile, and, rather than a triumphant return, Yeats seemed to anticipate an eternal sojourn amid the poet's Luciferan pride ("and learn to chaunt a tongue men do not know"[54]). The Irish are a convivial and gregarious people, and there were to be deep conflicts between Yeats's ideal of the withdrawn poet and the demands which Irish public life made upon him.

Such were the abstract historical principles which gave Yeats hopes for an Irish literary revival. In descending from abstractions to individual authors, he immediately encountered difficulties. He did not wholly approve of the previous Irish literature of the nineteenth century and an Irish literature written to his own prescription could not be produced fast enough to make believable his own exaggerated claims for it. Yeats's main hopes depended, however, not upon individual talents but upon racial types.

What were the characteristics of the Celt which Yeats idealized in his newspaper articles? The Celt was young and vigorous in contrast to his effete though successful Saxon neighbors. He was sociable and spiritual instead of dour and practical like the Saxon. Yeats could find support for such an allegation even in Matthew Arnold's writing on Celtic literature. The Irish could be praised for abstraction, usually a term of reproach for Yeats. John O'Leary's book of recollections was in 1897 for Yeats "a new example of that sense of abstract ideas, of

[52] Although Yeats did not meet Verlaine until February, 1894, he quoted early in October, 1892, Verlaine's description of the decadents as "a school of the sunset." Yeats probably learned of these matters through Symons.
[53] "Hopes and Fears for Irish Literature," *United Ireland*, October 15, 1892.
[54] "To the Rose upon the Rood of Time," *Variorum*, p. 101.

abstract law, which I believe the Celtic peoples have preserved, together with a capacity for abstract emotion, longer than more successful and practical races."[55] One may perhaps feel what Yeats meant by an "abstract emotion" even though the ideational content of the phrase is elusive.

Much of Yeats's Celticizing was based upon the assumption that the conquered are morally superior to their conquerors. In an 1897 article on the poetry of A.E., Nora Hopper, and Lionel Johnson, Yeats began with the claim that "it is hardly an exaggeration to say that the spiritual history of the world has been the history of conquered races."[56] His only example was "and has not our Christianity come to us from defeated and captive Judea?" If the common reader were to make the next logical step—to the second coming, and the immediate expectation of a Celtic messiah—he would not have been far behind Yeats. During the mid-nineties, Yeats, assisted by Maud Gonne, had planned to found a castle of the heroes in the west of Ireland, and there to revive the ancient Druidic religion of the Celts by combining it with a blend of Rosicrucianism.[57]

Although Yeats did not indifferently extol all Irish writing of the nineties, a writer could be reasonably sure of his praise if he followed Yeats's general directions on subject matter (peasant or mythic) and manner (twilit and spiritual). Yeats's own example as a poet was more powerful than his literary precepts in that his poems and plays were the most undoubted proof that there was an Irish literary revival. Great critical gifts do not always go with creative gifts. Whether great critic or not, the power of Yeats's praise was formidable.

The Irish poets of the nineties whom Yeats could offer as proof of a national literary ferment belonged in the main to his own generation. The careers of such contemporaries as A.E., Katharine Tynan, and Lionel Johnson ran parallel to his own, and, although they may have profited by Yeats's example, their careers as poets initiated from forces other than his inspiration. In his autobiography, Yeats said that one is never satisfied with the maturity of those whom one knew in youth.[58] With Katharine Tynan, Yeats was pleased as long as she followed his advice to write on Irish subjects. Even when her simplicity, which he had originally praised, began to pall for him, he always found something to praise in her work. When A.E. published his first volume of

<hr/>

[55] In Yeats's review of O'Leary's *Recollections of Fenians and Fenianism* in the *Bookman* of February, 1897.
[56] In a special supplement, "A Celtic Christmas," to the *Irish Homestead*, December, 1897.
[57] "Hodos Chameliontos," *Autobiography*, p. 169.
[58] "Ireland after Parnell," *Autobiography*, p. 165. In the passage cited, Yeats discusses George Russell (A.E.).

verse, in 1894, Yeats had sufficient influence to act as impresario. A.E. pleased Yeats by his mysticism, although he later fell from favor because he was not a sufficiently careful craftsman.[59]

Lionel Johnson had been a valuable convert to Gaeldom from without. Yeats had much sympathy with Johnson's hieratic and latinate Catholicism and Johnson was able to supply him with classical learning during his "Rosa Alchemica" period. But it was precisely in Johnson's most Irish poems, his fire-breathing patriotic verses, that Yeats sensed a hysterical note which displeased him.

If Yeats was less successful in finding a body of Irish prose writers than poets, his failure was matched by his own lack of success as a novelist. To match Ferguson in verse, Yeats had early discovered in William Carleton a prose writer who had given a masterful picture of the Irish peasant. Carleton, however, had followed the usual Irish literary practice of collapsing in mid-career. With a defective artistic consciousness, Carleton, under the influence of Davis's *Nation* movement, had been lured into didactic hack work. In a nation hypersensitive to religious differences, Carleton had changed from Catholicism to Protestantism and hence was sometimes a liability as a literary model.

Yeats had much to say of the Irish novelists of the nineteenth century during the period when he was compiling his anthology of *Representative Irish Tales* (1891). Although he seems to have quickly forgotten his reading of them, in his list of the best Irish books for the *Bookman*[60] Yeats recommended more novels and romances than books of poetry. To show how the best novels of Irish writers were neglected in Ireland, Yeats listed four novels which were then out of print.

Yeats had much greater difficulty in promoting non-folklore Irish prose, partly because he had placed too narrow restrictions on the Irish prose tradition. In a controversy in 1895 with Edward Dowden, he had rejected the notion that the works of Bishop Ussher, Bishop Berkeley, Jonathan Swift, and Laurence Sterne were Irish literature on the grounds that they were not about Irish subjects.[61] Shortly thereafter, he learned enough about Swift to respect him as an example of great literature as the expression of a merely human temperament.[62] Even though his reconciliation with the eighteenth century had to wait for thirty more years, Yeats, on the information that Goldsmith's "Deserted Village" was based on Listowel in Ireland, included a passage from this poem in his 1895 Irish poetry anthology.

[59] Yeats's later opinions of A.E. were tempered by the somewhat hostile attitude of A.E. toward the sophisticated directions the Irish National Theatre was taking under the direction of Yeats and Lady Gregory.

[60] Yeats's list was included in the fourth, and last, article on "Irish National Literature" for the *Bookman*, October, 1895.   [61] Letter to the *Dublin Daily Express*, March 8, 1895.

[62] In a review of Richard Ashe King's *Swift in Ireland*, in the *Bookman*, June, 1896.

Most of Yeats's criticisms of Irish prose was devoted to praising such now-forgotten novelists and romancers as Emily Lawless, Julia Barlow, and Nora Hopper. In the work of these writers Yeats found worthy of praise a kind of anti-naturalistic writing about peasant life which was out of the main currents of the best work then being done in fiction. When the great prose writers came, one of them, James Joyce, in his first prose collection, treated the life of urban Dublin in the spirit of the French and Russian naturalists, and Synge's prose dramas were to reveal the non-supernatural life of rural Ireland. In the meanwhile, Yeats thought that he had found in Fiona Macleod a prose writer who embodied an ideal blend of twilight and myth, and it was to take some time before he realized her style was as false as her identity.

In all areas of literature, Yeats wished the Irish writer to study the finest models of English literature as guides. The central assumption behind this oft-repeated advice—that English was to remain the literary language of Ireland—was not to go unchallenged. Douglas Hyde, whom Yeats admired as the first of Irish folklorists (before he met Lady Gregory), advanced in a famous lecture before the National Literary Society in 1892 a proposal to de-Anglicize Ireland.[63] Douglas Hyde urged the re-establishment of Gaelic as a national language, the continuance of the revival of Irish sports, and the substitution of ancient Irish customs for English in every possible area of life. In his reply to Hyde, Yeats objected that Hyde himself had admitted that the hope of a complete revival of Gaelic was hopeless. Why not then a de-Anglicizing process in English, asked Yeats: "Can we not build up a national tradition, a national literature, which shall be none the less Irish in spirit from being English in language?"[64] Yeats's example of a successful cultural break with England was American literature, which reflected a distinct national characteristic in such authors as Walt Whitman, Henry David Thoreau, Bret Harte, and George Washington Cable. The language itself of a culture could be dispensed with in Yeats's estimation. "When we remember the majesty of Cuchulain and the beauty of sorrowing Deirdre we should not forget that it is that majesty and that beauty which are immortal, and not the perishing tongue that first told of them."[65] Perhaps Yeats's shortcomings as a linguist and his dependence upon translations made him indifferent to a particular and unique expression of a culture in a given language.

By 1900 Yeats had ample opportunity to realize how far he had underestimated Hyde's Gaelic revival, which by then had grown into a

[63] Douglas Hyde's speech, "The Necessity for De-Anglicizing Ireland," was reprinted in a collection of speeches, *The Revival of Irish Literature*, London, 1894.
[64] Letter to *United Ireland*, December 17, 1892.   [65] *Ibid.*

mighty political force, and much to Yeats's regret had removed Hyde from literature into the politics of the market place. Yeats then foresaw some future generation which might be completely Gaelicized, but for his generation such a transition was impossible, "for no man can write well except in the language he has been born and bred to, and no man, as I think, becomes perfectly cultivated except through the influence of that language."[66]

As a program of reform, Yeats's propagandistic writings of the nineties, formed by his solitary reverie and by the pressures of real controversies, bore uneven fruit. A race of literary geniuses did not spring from the dragon's teeth which he sowed. He failed to achieve a lasting revival of interest in those Irish writers of the past, such as Ferguson and Mangan, whom he promoted. All this activity was not without its achievements, however. Through a constant stream of articles by himself and his friends, Yeats held the attention of British journals and convinced the English reading public that a "Celtic Renaissance" was actually in progress. He once more made it intellectually respectable to be Irish. He created a national image which was all the more powerful for being, in most places, the opposite to the realities of Irish life. To the facile Irish, he preached the labor of the file; to a nation of easy talkers, he opened the tragic road; and to a nation of dreamers cast out into a world of hard labor, he resurrected a past in which they could, for better or worse, dream on in an endless country of the young.

If he remembered little of his literary agitation of the nineties, save its bitterness,[67] it was far different with his next great project—the Irish Literary Theatre. Yeats collected in book form very little of his propaganda of the nineties, but of his theater propaganda a considerable portion was reprinted in his 1908 collected edition. Some great poems came out of his theatrical and political battles of the first decade of this century, while his propaganda of the previous decade seemed in retrospect to Yeats to be the supreme temptation of the artist—creation without toil.[68]

Perhaps the basic conflict in Yeats's literary position of the nineties was too extreme to be encompassed in his own work or in the techniques he advised to others. That literature should be as national as possible, criticism as international as possible, is a neat rhetorical balance, but more difficult to achieve than to state. Yeats preached to others the practice of literary simplicity but he could not achieve this goal in his poetry of the nineties. In his criticism of Irish literature in this decade, he could not switch adroitly enough from a conviction that

---

[66] Letter to the *Leader*, September 1, 1900.
[67] "Ireland after Parnell," *Autobiography*, p. 157.
[68] *Ibid.*, p. 135.

the hour of the Gael was at hand to a dispassionate appraisal of the literary faults of his friends. However much he may have proclaimed that his heart was with Mangan, Davis, Ferguson, it was to Shelley, Blake, and William Morris that he went for his literary apprenticeship.

3. Yeats as Critic-Reviewer

YEATS was, at least in theory, an unwilling critic. He regarded the function of criticism as a suspicious and hostile one to the creation of imaginative art. However, he needed quick money from his writings in the nineties and reviewing was and is the readiest means of making such money. In spite of his low opinion of the critic as a man of intellect, he evidently enjoyed preaching his ideas about literature. His own poetry of the eighties and nineties was based on the set of firmly held convictions which is consistent in his criticism, however much the expression of these ideas may have changed as he formulated them from review to review. More accurate than his autobiographical memories and more public than the private comments of his letters, Yeats's reviews clarify the growth and development of his ideas at that stage of his life.

First and foremost in his prose writings, he said that the function of poetry was the revelation of a better world and not the reflection of the present imperfect world. If literature could be demeaned by having a purpose, and his method of defining literature was to divest it of all unnecessary or trivial purposes, it was to bring again the golden age—the phrase was borrowed from Blake.[1] The means of achieving this golden age were never practical. In Ireland Yeats had fought against the use of poetry as an instrument of political agitation. On the broader scope of English literature, Yeats wished to see poetry purged of all but spiritual essences. Irrelevant things, persons, and ideas such as had cluttered the poetry of Tennyson and Browning had to be removed. What remained was symbol, and the symbol established a correspondence with the finer world of the spirit.

Yeats's theory of the function of poetry resembled that of Shelley rather than that of Matthew Arnold. He took from Shelley's "Defence of Poetry" his conviction that poetry existed to enlarge the mind and imagination and not to preach a moral which might be only the reflection of a transient conventional opinion. In Shelley, Yeats also found corroboration for his "Immortal Moods" as permanent archetypes of the emotions. Shelley had said that a poem is "the creation of actions according to the unchangeable forms of human nature, as existing in

[1] Yeats attributed the phrase to Blake in the review of Richard Ashe King's *Swift in Ireland, Bookman*, June, 1896.

the mind of the creator, which is itself the image of all other minds."[2] Yeats took this Platonic notion and, as he did with other ideas, turned the word into flesh. From Swedenborg and Blake, Yeats had learned how to bridge the gap between soul and matter. Angels did not like butter, according to Swedenborg (see p. 190), and in Blake the process of imagination was understood by the image of a lark ascending into heaven and meeting a lark descending. Shelley's notion of a poem as an idea existing in the *Anima Mundi* became in Yeats an angelic reality, "because every emotion is in its hidden essence, an unfallen angel of God, a being of uncorruptible flame."[3] In his descriptions of the immortal moods or archetypal emotions, Yeats kicks away the ladder of analogy or correspondence. Assertion replaces suggestion: "These moods are the labourers and messengers of the Ruler of All, the gods of ancient days still dwelling on their secret Olymp the aus,ngels of more modern days ascending and descending upon their shining ladder . . ."[4] and again, "when the external world is no more the standard of reality, we will learn again that the great passions are angels of God. . . ."[5]

His earliest idea about literature was that it was a divine revelation. In 1885 he had preached to the Dublin Hermetic Society the doctrine "that the poets were uttering, under the mask of phantasy, the old revelations. . . ."[6] His source in 1885 for this revelation was Shelley; it was later to become Blake. Matthew Arnold had suggested that imaginative literature would steadily replace the old religions as a source of ethical inspiration. Yeats, however, wanted the old religions as well as literature as the medium of their expression. It is not clear how much of Matthew Arnold's critical writings Yeats knew or how much of them he understood. He never tired of deriding Arnold's dictum that literature should be a criticism of life. But Yeats did not want a literature the opposite of a criticism of the ever-present age of lead, but rather one which would be a summons "to the waters and the wild . . . For the world's more full of weeping than you can understand."[7] For Yeats, poetry was not a criticism but a reproach to life.

In these reproaches, the poet must never argue about social problems

[2] Shelley, "A Defence of Poetry," reprinted with Peacock's "Four Ages of Poetry," and Browning's "Essay on Shelley," as no. 3 of *The Percy Reprints*, ed. H. F. B. Brett-Smith, Oxford, 1937, p. 30.

[3] Review of Arthur Symons's *London Nights*, in the *Bookman*, August, 1895.

[4] This passage first appeared in the second part of Yeats's series on Irish national literature for the *Bookman* (August, 1895). Yeats later included it under the title, "The Moods," in *Ideas of Good and Evil*, London, 1903.

[5] This passage is from part three, "Contemporary Irish Poets," September, 1895, of Yeats's series on Irish national literature for the *Bookman*. He included it in *Ideas of Good and Evil* as "The Body of Father Christian Rosencrux."

[6] Review of *Homeward Songs by the Way* by A.E., *Bookman*, August, 1894.

[7] "The Stolen Child," *Variorum*, p. 87.

or about the shortcomings of the contemporary world. He must never dispute with the profane about what they mistakenly describe as the real world, for his sense revealed to him a world finer than that known to grosser senses. If the Philistines wish to follow him to the Tir-nan-og, then he would lead, but he must not struggle directly. This quietism seems strange for a man who felt elected to lead Irish poetry into a promised land. His struggles as a propagandist were in prose, and he wished his poetry to be unsullied by mere political opinions. His verse after 1910 showed an obvious change of heart and head. Poetry then joined in the struggle in the pit as well as in the search for a golden age.

Yeats's general statements on literature made in the nineties were an attempt to purify it of mere distractions. His negatives ring impressively in a way which he would have been ashamed to admit as rhetorical: "For poetry is not an amusement and a rest, but a fountain of ardour and peace, whither we must force our way even through briar and bramble."[8]

Yeats knew that fountains may be also amusing and restful, but when he made that remark he was forcing his way through the briars and brambles of Edwin J. Ellis's poetry. The opposite of poetry as "an amusement and a rest" was didacticism, which was continually attacked by Yeats as the most sinister form of practical purpose for poetry. In a review of a book on Jonathan Swift, he may have had in mind Swift's famous remark about making two blades of grass grow where only one grew before:

imaginative literature wholly, and all literature in some degree, exists to reveal a more powerful and passionate, a more divine world than ours; and not to make our ploughing and sowing, our spinning and weaving, more easy or more pleasant.[9]

That "more divine world than ours" is here as elsewhere left undefined either as a golden age of the present world or the ideal hereafter. The extremes of this distinction—divine world and ploughing—are typically wide. Yeats leaves the reader still wondering what literature has to say about the vast area of experience between the divine world and ploughing.

As well as avoiding a concern with social problems, the poet must guard against the distractions of too exclusive a concern with aesthetic questions: "Great literature is always great because the writer was thinking of truth and life and beauty more than of literary form and literary fame."[10] When Yeats made this remark, he was fighting against

---

[8] Review of E. J. Ellis's *Fate in Arcadia, Bookman*, September, 1892.
[9] Review of Richard Ashe King's *Swift in Ireland, Bookman*, June, 1896.
[10] Review of Robert Buchanan's *The Wandering Jew, Bookman*, April, 1893.

the decadents' attempt to divorce literature and philosophy, and so he may have then slighted form and fame more than his wont. Poetry might dispense with all other impurities but not philosophy. Had he been pressed to define philosophy he might have replied that it was what the poets in their moments of highest inspiration had uttered. Literature as a mere container or conveyor of philosophical principles, his persistent criticism of Browning and Tennyson, was strongly to be avoided.

Much of Yeats's general theory of literature had rhetoric as its villain. Rhetoric was for Yeats defined by its function, didactic, rather than its techniques, which he freely used in his own poetry and prose; in short, this science was "the triumph of the desire to convince over the desire to reveal."[11] Again, in one of his negative definitions, literature was not

an exposition of certain opinions about which they [the "Young Irelanders"] were agreed and hoped to make others agree, and [not] of a certain type of character which all men might be expected to admire [but rather] a capricious inspiration coming with an unforseen message out of the dim places of the mind.[12]

Irish oratory had provoked Yeats into a hatred of rhetoric, yet his Irishness doomed him to a rhetorical expression of his own ideas.

Although Yeats was Arnoldian enough to have critical touchstones, those he most often used were philosophical statements rather than examples of perfect art. On the one occasion when he did mention three perfect things (against which he thought Villiers's *Axël* imperfect), one was a painting, one an experience, and the third an unspecified passage of poetry:

a certain night scene long ago, when I heard the wind blowing in a bed of reeds by the border of a little lake, a Japanese picture of cranes flying through a blue sky, and a line or two out of Homer.[13]

All impressionistic and all revelations. Among his more literary touchstones were Bacon's remark (as quoted by Yeats), "There can be no great beauty without some strangeness," and Thomas Nashe's line, "Brightness falls from the air . . ." as well as an entire set of principles from Blake.

Yeats could hardly have escaped the influence of Walter Pater, the most admired literary philosopher of the Rhymers' Club. If Yeats had not read *Marius the Epicurean* with great pleasure,[14] he might have heard Pater's principles at second hand after Lionel Johnson or Arthur

[11] Review of William Morris's *The Well at the World's End, Bookman*, November, 1896.
[12] Review of Sir C. G. Duffy's *Young Ireland, Bookman*, January, 1897.
[13] Review of Villiers de l'Isle-Adam's *Axël, Bookman*, April, 1894.
[14] Yeats found in Pater's "jewelled paragraphs" Platonic support for a belief in the Irish fairies. "A Ballad Singer," *Letters to the New Island*, pp. 137–38.

Symons returned from one of their visits to the master in Oxford. Certainly Pater left his mark on the involved cadences of the stories in *The Secret Rose*. Yeats also might have found in Pater's insistence on an art removed from ordinary life support for his own disdain for didactic or politically oriented art. Oddly enough, there are few mentions of Pater as a source of aesthetic wisdom in Yeats's critical prose of the nineties. Perhaps Pater was too skeptical in his attitude toward the supernatural. Since Yeats thought that the nineteenth century had suffered from too intermittent a belief in the divinity of the imagination, then Pater, in separating art from other cultural and spiritual forces, would have come under Yeats's general proscription. Although Yeats used impressionistic devices to convey the emotional experience of having read a book, he was too dogmatic in his own philosophical opinions to be an impressionistic critic. Perhaps the critic who would follow Pater's example usurped too much in Yeats's estimation the role of the poet.

Yeats's criticism and reviewing were the work of a poet condescending to use the inferior and alien tools of the intellect. His work as a reviewer is much better than one would be led to believe from his own estimation of the role of the critic. His distinction between intellect and imagination was absolute: "The work of the poet is revelation, and the work of the reader is criticism."[15] Yeats also wanted a gulf between prose with its analytic method and the synthetic method of poetry, a distinction borrowed from Shelley and applied rigorously by Yeats to all deviations such as prose poems. Along with their separate methods, poet and critic had different personalities. Yeats readily accepted the "romantic" Shelleyan mantle of the wild and unpredictable artist and he expected the intellectual critic to be sober and decorous. The Lancelots of history had been the poets and the King Arthurs had practised criticism and lesser arts.[16] In the review where he stated this opposition, he placed alongside Tennyson the poet, the sober, good-natured, and merely prudent (albeit profound in his criticism) Arthur Henry Hallam. Even farther down the tree of life than critics were scholars, dismissed in an epigram so clever that one hardly believes it to be Yeats: "For there is all the difference in the world between the man who finds one thing in everything and him who finds everything in one thing—between the pedant and the artist."[17]

Yeats realized that the English public had selected Shelley as its ideal figure of the poet for reasons not complimentary to poets or poetry.

[15] Review of Ibsen's *Brand, Bookman*, October, 1894.
[16] Review of *The Poems of Arthur Henry Hallam*, in the *Speaker*, July 22, 1893.
[17] Review of J. D. Hosken's *Verses by the Way* and Fenil Haig's *The Questions at the Well*, *Speaker*, August 26, 1893.

The public wished to have its prejudices about the impracticality of poets reinforced by the presence of impractical poets. Yeats found in the life and works of William Morris a better ideal of the poet, "for he more than any man of modern days tried to change the life of his time into the life of his dream."[18] Morris's dream, as expressed in his major works, was sufficiently golden and removed from possibility to preclude the danger of poets stooping to plough or spin. What Yeats made of Morris's spinning and weaving, of his practical efforts to improve the life of his day, we know from his review of the arts and crafts exhibition in 1890, where he described Morris (with no conscious irony) as "Poet, Socialist, romance-writer, artist and upholsterer. . . ."[19]

The set of ideas woven together from Shelley and Blake which served Yeats as basic critical principles found support in an unexpected source. In Arthur Henry Hallam's essay on the early poems of Tennyson, Yeats thought that the principles of the "aesthetic school" (Keats, Tennyson, Rossetti, Swinburne, and ultimately himself) had been best set forth. Hallam asserted that the senses of the poet gave him a more complex and refined picture of the world than that available to the gross carnality of the vulgar. If the poet is to remain true to the complexity of his vision in expressing this fine frenzy, he cannot communicate his images in any way for the vulgar to understand. True art is therefore unpopular art. The implied opposite of this, which Yeats eagerly welcomed, was that popular art is false art. Yeats thought so highly of Hallam's words that he put them in italics and then called attention to his italicization: *"Whatever is mixed up with art, and appears under its semblance, is always more favourably regarded than art free and unalloyed."*[20] Such a principle is so broad that it was difficult to apply, especially since the term "art" is left undefined. Yeats thought he knew what was meant by it:

teaching us to rank such 'reflections' [Hallam's words are put in single quotation marks in Yeats's statement] of the mind as rhetorical and didactic verse, painted anecdotes, pictures 'complicated with ideas' that are not pictorial ideas, below poetry and painting that mirror the 'multiplied' and 'minute' and 'diversified' 'sensations' of the body and the soul.[21]

Under such a principle, Michael Field's poetic descriptions of great paintings were inferior to the web of one's reveries, and Lionel Johnson's poems celebrating the sorrows of Catholic Ireland were thrown into a patriotically useful dustbin. But what of Yeats's own poems which use Irish mythology as a means of escape from the soul sickness of a modern sensibility? Is it not easy to value them for their exotic

[18] Review of William Morris's *The Well at the World's End*, *Bookman*, November, 1896.
[19] "An Exhibition at William Morris's," *Providence Sunday Journal*, October 26, 1890.
[20] Review of *The Poems of Arthur Henry Hallam*, in the *Speaker*, July 22, 1893.   [21] *Ibid.*

mythology, and hence make of the Irish past a cultural distraction? Yeats might have replied that his early Irish poems taught no moral, but they indeed taught a powerful political moral. In the later "rose" poems, one reads of the "diversified sensations of the body and the soul," yet it remains a problem how much of Yeats's mystical reading his poetry could absorb without being damaged by the pollution of an alien substance. Yeats's critical principles more often represent what he wanted to achieve than what he had successfully accomplished. The most dutiful listener to his literary sermons was himself.

The poet's finer sensibilities made him an outcast from society. Yeats thought that the most dangerous path for such an outcast was a good, steady job. In this conviction he luckily found an ally in his father. Thomas Davis was his Irish example of a poet forgetting his job of revelation in an effort to become socially useful, and Clarence Mangan was his paradigm of a great talent crucified by routine. He gave solemn warning against those writers "buried in those heterogeneous occupations which Arthur Hallam believed more dangerous to a writer than the most immoral of lives."[22] Yeats was far from recommending an immoral life by his own example. His circle of friends in the Rhymers' Club were to give him such an example of the toll of immoral lives that he was to call them "the Tragic Generation."

After the past forty-seven years, in which the official doctrine has been that, in T. S. Eliot's words, "poetry is not a turning loose of emotion, but an escape from emotion; it is not the expression of personality, but an escape from personality . . . ,"[23] Yeats's own reliance on temperament makes his critical writings seem of another age: "All good literature is made out of temperaments."[24] In later life Yeats knew that he was on the defensive, and, as in many other areas of thought, he maintained that his Irish isolation made him immune to the worst ravages of romanticism: "And why should I, whose ancestors never accepted the anarchic subjectivity of the nineteenth century, accept its recoil; why should men's heads ache that never drank?"[25] Not only temperament was needed, but fine, aristocratic temperament, usually brooding in solitude over the bog-wisdom of an unspoiled peasantry. Of the shop-keeping class with its exaggerated respect for the rhetoric of Carlyle and Macaulay, Yeats said, "Out of the ideas and emotions of the average man you can make no better thing than good rhetoric."[26] So much for L. Bloom.

[22] Review of Sir C. G. Duffy's *Young Ireland, Bookman*, January, 1897.
[23] Eliot, "Tradition and Individual Talent," *Selected Essays*, New York, 1950, p. 10.
[24] Review of Sir C. G. Duffy's *Young Ireland, Bookman*, January, 1897.
[25] From his introduction to J. M. Hone's and H. M. Rossi's *Bishop Berkeley*, reprinted in *Essays and Introductions*, p. 407.
[26] Review of Sir C. G. Duffy's *Young Ireland, Bookman*, January, 1897.

If the method of the poet was synthesis, the force which allowed him to fuse the elements of this experience was imagination—that most splendid, most indefinable of nineteenth-century words, to which Yeats added his own special confusion of terminology. "Imagination is God in the world of art," he annunciated with majestic ambiguity in a folk-lore article of 1893.[27] It is more probable that he meant that imagination is divine power manifested in art rather than that imagination holds a place in art analogous to that of God in creation. Yeats's tradition of imagination was certainly a divine one, more mystical than Coleridge's even though both men were deeply influenced by the writings of the German mystic Jacob Boehme. There, in a compilation of Boehme's writings called *The Way to Christ*, Yeats says he found the discovery of imagination as a great power in modern literature. The definition given was actually by William Law, one of Boehme's commentators. Although neither Law nor Boehme meant the term "imagination" to be used in a strictly literary sense, Law's definition of imagination—"the magia or power of raising and forming such substances, and the greatest power in nature . . ."[28]—gave Yeats a divine sanction for the poetic imagination. In Blake rather than in Boehme's work Yeats found the doctrine of the divine source of the imagination fully developed. Blake's main message, said Yeats, was "that the imagination is the means whereby we communicate with God."[29] This knowledge of the divine power of imagination was for Yeats the great key to poetry and indeed all life. Blake had done for him what Remy de Gourmont claimed Villiers de l'Isle-Adam had done for his generation in France: he had "opened the doors of the beyond with a crash that our generation might pass through them."[30]

According to this view of the imagination, the images formed by our minds have a reality as messengers from the beyond, and we have no moral right to assume that the reality of our imagination is inferior in importance to the palpable world apprehended by the senses. Since the world of sense denied the world of spirit, Yeats did not merely assert the equal importance of both but raised the world of spirit to a far higher plane of value than the mere world of things. Yeats liked to pronounce Blake's ringing phrases as an anathema upon materialism: "Everything is atheism which assumes the reality of the natural and unspiritual world."[31] So much for the lake poets. Blake had supplied

[27] "The Message of the Folk-lorist," *Speaker*, August 19, 1893.
[28] Review of Richard Garnett's *William Blake*, *Bookman*, 1896. The edition Yeats used was Jacob Behmen's *The Way to Christ*, Bath, 1775, pp. 425–26. The quotation is therein cited as taken from "*Law's* appeal to all that doubt, etc., p. 169."
[29] *Ibid.*; the words quoted are Yeats's.
[30] Review of Maeterlinck's *Aglavaine and Sélysette*, *Bookman*, September, 1897.
[31] "William Blake and His Illustrations to the *Divine Comedy*," *Essays and Introductions*, p. 132.

him with a metaphysic of the imagination, and Swedenborg gave him a cosmology. Our imaginations may be governed by angels of God or by lower spirits as Swedenborg described in his diary, and our lesser ideas might be inspired by damned spirits. Such a distinction saved Yeats from the conviction that he was continually in touch with the Almighty. His Hermetic initials, D. E. D. I. (*Demon est Deus Inversus*), implied such a duality of spiritualistic communication.

The generation previous to Yeats, with its paltry criticism of life, had failed to reach the highest peaks of art in that it "had no constant and tranquil belief in the divinity of imagination."[32] Yeats derived his own constant and tumultuous, not tranquil, belief from Blake. He used Blake's allegorical description of the imagination to embody his own beliefs, that it was a lark ascending from earth to heaven which met halfway a lark descending from heaven. The two larks touched wings and the vital impulse was transferred. Such divinity in poetry did not mean that Yeats neglected the struggle to develop craftsmanship. He liked to warn his Irish contemporaries against the dangerous view that inspiration precluded technical proficiency.

He [the poet] must go on perfecting earthly power and perception until they are so subtilized that divine power and divine perception descend to meet them, and the song of earth and the song of heaven mingle together.[33]

Given such a theory of inspiration, how did Yeats apply it as a reviewer-critic? One would think that he had left himself the task of deciding whether the larks of his contemporaries, Johnson, Dowson, Symons, Davidson, had ever encountered anything on their heavenward flight. Fortunately for his criticism, Yeats had, aside from his grandiose theories, a good nose for poetry, and despite a weakness for the nebulous, he was a good judge of fakery. Literature which seemed to announce the grand truth had a special appeal for Yeats. As a negative measure, below which there can be no poetry or great literature, he adapted Maeterlinck's words about that polemical writing which goes to "one of those infirmaries of the human mind, where . . . all truths which are not truths come out of a solitary and mysterious ideal, go at last and to die."[34] What was the essential quality of great literature for Yeats is hard to define although his remark about the essence of great plays, which Maeterlinck lacked, might suffice: "that continual revery about destiny that is, as it were, the perfect raiment of beautiful emotions."[35] In his most exasperated and least rational mood, he could

---

[32] Review of Fiona Macleod's *Spiritual Tales, Sketch*, April 28, 1897.

[33] Review of *The Life of William Carleton, Bookman*, March, 1896.

[34] Review of Sir C. G. Duffy's *Young Ireland, Bookman*, January, 1897. As might be expected, Duffy did not meet this standard.

[35] Review of Maeterlinck's *Aglavaine and Sélysette, Bookman*, September, 1897.

denounce all bad poems as crab apples from the Tree of Knowledge and all good poems as apples from the Tree of Life.[36]

Yeats's criticism in the nineties adheres consistently to a small set of basic convictions—that intellect opposes the imagination, that poetry reveals the spiritual world, and that modern life is worthless as a subject for poetry. Despite this seeming consistency, or monotony, of his opinions, one may observe, when looking at his writings of the nineties as a whole, the rise and fall of certain basic interests. The year 1893 was the loudest in folklore, not surprisingly, since that was the year in which he published *The Celtic Twilight*. In 1895, with the printing of his articles on Irish national literature, he was most involved in saving Irish literature from Sir Charles Gavan Duffy. The intensity of his interest waned somewhat after this year, only to take other, later forms. By 1897 he had been to Paris and talked with Verlaine, he had watched "the trembling of the veil of the temple"[37] at the première of *Axël*, and he had come under the spell of Maeterlinck. For a year or so after 1897, Yeats annunciated the passing of realism, naturalism, atheism, and Victorianism, and a second coming which would be the coming of symbolic art. This belief too passed away when Yeats realized that instead of a neo-romantic art, he and the friends of his youth had been the last romantics.

The choice of 1893 as the peak year of his interest in folklore is not to deny his lifelong interest in that subject. When his devotion to the folk began to wane in the late nineties, Lady Gregory helped to revive it (and Yeats) by touring the peasant cottages near her estate and gathering the lore into notebooks. The year 1893, however, did see Yeats offering, at his loudest and most insistent, folklore as the universal remedy for tired moderns. In his "causerie" for the *Speaker*, he found that the great poets, "Homer, Aeschylus, Sophocles, Shakespeare, and even Dante, Goethe, and Keats, were little more than folk-lorists with musical tongues."[38] Never was so much owed to that word "little." When this conviction of a Celt was transferred to his practice as a critic, it followed that not much of a musical tongue could convince him that folklore had been raised to the rank of Homer and the others. Even admitting that his prejudice in favor of folklorists and folk- and myth-inspired poets was a weakness, it is refreshing to hear Homer and Sir Samuel Ferguson mentioned in the same breath. It is better for the critic to see no essential gap between the good and the great than for the critic to set up a series of unapproachable literary gods. Yeats was

[36] Review of Lady Gregory's *Poets and Dreamers*, *Bookman*, May, 1903.

[37] This phrase, remembered from Stéphane Mallarmé, was used by Yeats as the title of the second (1922) volume of his autobiography.

[38] "The Message of the Folk-lorist," *Speaker*, August 9, 1893.

always against inflated praise of the mediocre, especially when done by
Thomas Davis or other fellow Irishmen. He knew that hyperbole was
the national disease. On the other hand, Yeats was open to the possibility that his contemporaries were creating immortal masterpieces. His
love for folklore led him to believe that Douglas Hyde's *Love Songs of
Connacht* was such a masterpiece. In retrospect, his praise for this book
seems both excessive and justified. It was in evaluating Lady Gregory's
folklore and popularizing of myth that Yeats became unhinged. The
same or similar matter as was in Homer was there, the tongue was
musical, and hence great literature was present. His praise of Lady
Gregory seems so determined by personal loyalty and affection that
such eulogy, unlike his criticism of Hyde, errs on the side of indulgence.

Although the folklorist, no matter what his or her talents, always
received an attentive hearing from Yeats, his first principle of literary
inspiration—that a man's work must grow out of his life and experience—allowed him to praise even realistic art. The postman-poet,
J. D. Hosken, should have written of the London docks which he
knew rather than compose Elizabethan sonnets beginning "In vain
my teardrops fall for thee, dead Imogen."[39] Buried in Yeats's criticism
there is even a favorable mention of Kipling as a writer who used the
life around him with all its ugliness and brutality.[40] To the neophyte
Fenil Haig (Ford Madox Ford in his earliest manifestation) Yeats
preached out of Emerson, "To thine orchard's edge belong,/all the
brass and plume of song. . . ."[41] Yeats may have allowed to other
men other experiences but he seemed sure that his own orchard was
the folk imagination. Any attempt to create a poetic tradition away
from it he thought doomed to failure.

Yeats envied the spontaneous inspiration of those unknown makers
of Hyde's *Love Songs of Connacht*. For a fallen angel like himself, such
ease in writing was not possible. The very difficulty in writing as a
modern made him more acutely aware of the beauty of folk poetry than
the folk who had created it. He had read the prose of Fiona Macleod on
the deck of an Aran island fishing boat and its style was enhanced by
the view. The fisherman made replies to Yeats's questions that satisfied
him as to the wisdom of the folk. Late in life, in his talk on Eliot and
modern poetry, Yeats implied that efforts to turn Paddington Railway
Station into poetry were futile if not sacrilegious.[42] Shelley had made

[39] "Two Minor Lyrists," Review of *Verses by the Way* of J. D. Hosken and *The Questions
at the Well* by Fenil Haig, *Speaker*, August 26, 1893.

[40] Review of Fiona Macleod's *Spiritual Tales*, *Sketch*, April 28, 1897.

[41] See footnote 39.

[42] Essay on "Modern Poetry," reprinted in *Essays and Introductions*, p. 499. Yeats may be
heard making these remarks on a *Spoken Arts* record, a dubbing of his BBC talk of October
11, 1936.

the mistake of using a dead mythology; the poets of his generation were trying to make the modern city and its squalor into a poetic tradition. Yeats doubted.

No conscious invention can take the place of tradition, for he who would write a folktale, and thereby bring a new life into literature, must have the fatigue of the spade in his hands and the stupors of the fields in his heart.[43]

Yeats had neither spade nor stupor but watched from afar. Certainly, the writer of *A Vision* did attempt to create a tradition by means of conscious (or unconscious) invention. If a high degree of involvement in a subject could make great poetry, then Yeats had to admit, and did so, that Symons and Dowson could gain the music hall, absinthe, and skirt-dance equivalent of "the fatigue of the spade in his hands and the stupors of the fields in his heart."

By the later nineties, Yeats's conviction that folklore was the key to great literature had hardened into a mythological method. Unlike the later use of mythological underpinning by Eliot and Joyce, Yeats's method did not attempt a reconciliation with modern life but escaped from it. Eliot and Joyce juxtapose. Yeats translates.

Emotions which seem vague or extravagant when expressed under the influence of modern literature, cease to be vague and extravagant when associated with ancient legend and mythology, for legend and mythology were born out of man's longing for the mysterious and the infinite.[44]

By this method, Yeats is transformed into Fergus, or Aengus, or Oisin, and his emotions ceased to be vague or extravagant. At his best use of this method, the transformation of Yeats into Oisin preceded the poetic act and his involvement in primitive myth was profound. Yeats's lesser followers substituted ancient names for modern ones, and only the typography was altered thereby.

Yeats found Ernest Rhys's rendering of Welsh ballads mere prettiness when not held down by some "old legend or ballad":

legends are the magical beryls in which we see life, not as it is, but as the heroic part of us, the part which desires always dreams and emotions greater than any in the world, and loves beauty and does not hate sorrow, hopes in secret that it may become.[45]

One does Yeats, the magus, injustice if one understands the term "magical beryls" as a mere metaphor. The process of transforming ancient legend into modern life had at its foundation the mystical unity of all experience. By the process of metempsychosis, Yeats's identification with the Irish bards was no loose inspiration. Yeats was Oisin,

[43] "Message of the Folk-lorist," *Speaker*, August 19, 1893.
[44] Review of Fiona Macleod's *From the Hills of Dream*, *Bookman*, December, 1896.
[45] Review of Ernest Rhys's *Welsh Ballads*, *Bookman*, April, 1898.

Fergus, and Aengus. For better or worse, the above principles, to love beauty and not to hate sorrow, served as guide for the prose of *The Secret Rose* and the poetry of *The Wind Among the Reeds*.

The flaws of this mythological method are to be seen not only in Yeats's second-rate work but in the works of the lesser writers whom he praised for practising this method. The writing of Fiona Macleod was Yeats's model for mythologizing.

Other writers are busy with the way men and women act in sorrow or in joy, but Miss Macleod has re-discovered the art of the myth-maker, and gives a visible shape to joys and sorrows and makes them seem realities and men and women illusions.[46]

Maurice Maeterlinck was praised for this same facility in replacing character with symbol. A reader bewildered at seeing the real world fade into the forest dim of symbol might be reassured to learn that even Yeats's taste for the nebulous was limited. Certain vapors in Miss Macleod disturbed him.

When Miss Macleod writes of "the white Peace" which "lies not on the sunlit hill," nor "on the sunlit plain," nor "on any running stream," but comes sometimes into the soul of man as "the moonlight of a perfect Peace," I find her thought too vague greatly to move or impress me.[47]

One welcomes such judgments as evidence of a keen sense in Yeats for the fraudulent. But alas, look what he liked:

When she writes of "the four white winds of the world, whose father the golden sun is, whose mother the wheeling moon is, the north and the south and the east and the west," and of "the three dark winds of the world; the chill breath of the grave, the breath from the depths of the sea," and "the breath of tomorrow," I am altogether moved and impressed.[48]

The addition of myth has certainly made a difference between the two passages, but one wonders whether the difference is in quality or in wind. The writings of Fiona Macleod serve as a test case of Yeats's soundness as a critic. If a writer were creating what Yeats considered a necessary kind of literature, Yeats would praise him or her (in the case of Fiona Macleod both sexes in one) until the novelty wore thin and all that remained was his sober judgment. His final opinion of Fiona Macleod, even before he learned that she was William Sharp, was not a flattering one.

Like other leaders of a new order in poetry, Yeats was much surer of what he wanted to change in existing poetic styles than of what

[46] Review of Fiona Macleod's *The Dominion of Dreams, Bookman,* July, 1899.
[47] Review of Fiona Macleod's *From the Hills of Dream, Bookman,* December, 1896.
[48] *Ibid.*

principles of composition he advocated. We now look upon the decade of the nineties as transitional—a period following the great Victorians, filled with a number of literary curiosities (Wilde, Sharp, Johnson, Dowson), and waiting for the Eliot-Pound stylistic revolution. It was Yeats's ill fortune to give marching orders to a transition. To present-day readers it may seem that Yeats exaggerated the differences between the work of his contemporaries and the poetry of the previous generation, but to Yeats, writing under the declining shadows of Tennyson and Browning, even the smallest gestures of freedom were momentous.

He rejected the Victorians because their poetry was too full of the merely laudable and praiseworthy, too concerned with social causes and irrelevant psychologizing. By his continual announcements of the coming of symbolic art, he meant to remove all matters from poetry except emotion and passion. Whatever was allowed to remain must never stand for itself alone. Any real or imagined thing in a poem must symbolize or correspond to something in the emotive life or the spiritual realm. This belief, no literary conviction only, embodied a whole set of ideas, and was "an insurrection against everything which assumes that the external and material are the only fixed things, the only standards of reality."[49] Since those believers in an external reality denied the existence of the spiritual world, it was only fair for Yeats and his fellow believers to deny the material world. In 1897 it was too early for a compromise with real things, "grey eighteenth-century houses," which he later achieved. With all external reality swept away, what remained was symbol: "A movement which never mentions an external thing except to express a state of the soul, has taken the place of a movement which delighted in picturesque and bizarre things for their own sake."[50] Such intensity carries its own dangers. Without "rocks and stones and trees" the air near the mystical rose might be too rarefied for the reader to breathe. Once again, Arthur Henry Hallam supplied for Yeats the answer that the public enjoys only the impurities of art, not its essential excellence.

Yeats's excitement about the coming of symbolic art reached messianic intensity about 1897 and remained so until the end of the century. This rise in intensity is not apparent if one reads only the criticism which Yeats collected in book form. From *Ideas of Good and Evil*, one would believe that Yeats had always believed that a new symbolic day was dawning, but such a conviction had developed steadily over a decade. In 1897 the second coming was to be a new order of art which revealed "invisible and impalpable things" instead of the "rough beast" of two decades later. The leading examples Yeats offered of this new

[49] Review of Maeterlinck's *The Treasure of the Humble, Bookman*, July, 1897.
[50] Review of Maeterlinck's *Aglavaine and Sélysette, Bookman*, September, 1897.

art, Maeterlinck and Fiona Macleod, were most successful in strange
and dim effects, and, in the latter case, in little else.

This anti-Victorian reaction was not only stylistic but also political
in its rejection of enlightenment and progress. In a 1900 review of a
folklore collection, Yeats said that civilized man was an outcast from
nature and that primitive man, who sees visions, is the natural and
healthy one.[51] At times, however, not even the return of the visionary
man could console Yeats enough to read any modern poetry at all:

there are moods in which one cannot read modern poetry at all; it is so full of
eccentric and temporal things, so gnarled and twisted by the presence of a
complicated life, so burdened by that painful riddle of the universe, which
never seems inexplicable till men gather in crowds to talk it over.[52]

At such moments of pique, Yeats hardly seems to have changed his
opinions since he had, in 1886, defended Sir Samuel Ferguson against
the "sad soliloquies of a nineteenth-century egoism."

Yeats could not always be sure who was on his side in his battles with
Victorianism and the external. In his effort to form an anti-Victorian
school among his contemporaries, he formed strange alliances, and
defended these alliances by even stranger twistings of thought. One
unexpected corollary of the new symbolic art was "a franker trust in
passion and in beauty."[53] At times this trust in passion became so frank
that it provoked the bourgeoisie to call it decadent.

Yeats equivocated on the erotic element in literature. He demanded
little license himself since he preferred in his early poetry to hide his
impulses behind extravagant imagery. His own formulation of the
aesthetic ideal was "that art which resembles the sun is smiling alike
upon the just and the unjust, the excellent and the inferior, the laudable
and the blameworthy."[54] Arthur Symons, Yeats's main source of
French literary doctrines, had so frank a trust in passion and beauty that
Yeats's skills as a defender were strained. Since the poet by definition
is a man of finer sensibilities than the mass of mankind, the vulgar had
no right to call decadent "a poetry which is personal and solitary, and
must therefore be judged by poetical instinct alone."[55] Symons's re-
counting of his café-dancer loves had for Yeats at least the merit of
giving a realistic portrayal of the passions. To suffer in love was only
given to the truly enlightened such as Yeats and Symons, and so the
latter's "Mundi Victima" was "a long ecstasy of sorrow, a long revery
of that utter wisdom which comes only to those who have certain

[51] Review of Daniel Deeney's *Peasant Lore From Gaelic Ireland*, *Speaker*, July 14, 1900.
[52] Review of Lady Gregory's *Poets and Dreamers*, *Bookman*, May, 1903.
[53] Review of Fiona Macleod's *From the Hills of Dream*, *Bookman*, December, 1896.
[54] Review of *The Poems of Arthur Henry Hallam*, *Speaker*, July 22, 1893.
[55] Review of Arthur Symons's *Amoris Victima*, *Bookman*, April, 1897.

emotional distinction."[56] Even though Yeats could find excuses for Symons's sinning in public, he thought Symons faulty in not writing passionately enough, with not finding the true inner beauty of his experiences. The critics who had branded Symons as a decadent were called by Yeats, with a cleverness usually beneath him, decadents themselves since they insisted upon a moral or literary standard of propriety so long out of date.

Naturalists and realists were near to atheism in Yeats's esteem because they denied imagination or God in the world of art. However, he did not like poets who were celibate in their spirituality. To A.E.'s moods of patient resignation to the consequences of human love, Yeats replied, "Some passionate temperaments, amorous of the colour and softness of the world, will refuse the quietism of the idea . . ." [of A.E.'s "Our Throne's Decay"].[57] Doubtless Yeats was a possessor of that more passionate temperament. His general criticism of A.E.'s verses, like those reviews of his other friends, is in a tone of praise. The qualifications given in A.E.'s case—rhymes repeated too often and stanzas needlessly obscure—mark in Yeats the successful blend of the skillful propagandist and the sharp-eyed critic.

Lionel Johnson also received from Yeats a good measure of praise, yet with the continual qualification that Johnson's mysticism was too thin-blooded. Johnson was a member of that company who "renounced the joy of the world without accepting the joy of God."[58] Yeats's abhorrence of the ordinary and the everyday as subjects for poetry led him to hate naturalism, but even for Yeats there were limits of remoteness. Lionel Johnson's *Ireland and Other Poems* was a disappointment for Yeats:

it mirrors a temperament so cold, so austere, so indifferent to our pains and pleasures, so wrapped up in one lonely and monotonous mood that one comes from it wearied and exalted, as though one had posed for some noble action, in a strange *tableau vivant*, that casts its painful stillness upon the mind instead of upon the body.[59]

Yeats was very skilful in making his boredom appear hieratic and extraordinary. One cannot but suppose that such a review must have strained his friendship with Johnson.

With Lionel Johnson as well as with other friends, Yeats encountered their work first in manuscript long before these poems reached public print. The reviews of the work of his intimates show Yeats as a faithful but not indulgent friend. At times loyalty and critical honesty clashed,

[56] *Ibid.*
[57] Review of A.E.'s *Homeward Songs by the Way, Bookman*, August, 1897.
[58] Review of Lionel Johnson's *Ireland and Other Poems, Bookman*, February, 1898.
[59] *Ibid.*

and in such cases Yeats equivocated. He apparently could make very little of Ellis's long symbolic poem, *Seen in Three Days*. He put off reviewing it, and in his *Bookman* article he did little more than summarize a very difficult scenario. While he shared lodgings with John O'Leary, he saw the old Fenian working painfully over his memoirs. The completed work, *Recollections of Fenians and Fenianism*, disappointed Yeats. His review of the book became a paean for O'Leary, the man, and in the noise of praise the work goes unobserved. Only his loyalty to Lady Gregory swayed Yeats's critical sense. Her financial support which enabled him to leave reviewing has spared us more reviews such as that of *Poets and Dreamers*.

Yeats thought that book reviewing distracted him from higher matters and he left it with great relief. Such work exposed him to a great variety of books and some strange subjects. He seldom approached any book with an unbiased attitude, nor did he leave a book without drawing from it some observation, profound or not. His strangest assignment was to review a book on the hairy Ainu. The style and ideas are distinctively Yeatsian—primitive man and his joys compared to modern confusion. The Ainu and the Galway peasant were brothers under the hair: "He has his spear and his supple-bow, and the delight of the long-followed trail, and love, and the talk about the fire, and at the end of all the heaven of stars or the heaven of cloud."[60]

Unlike a university-trained critic such as Lionel Johnson, Yeats did not bring to a book a large knowledge of literary history, but rather a small set of deeply held convictions. What Yeats knew, he made distinctly his own, even if he distorted names, dates, and quotations in the process. The seriousness of his convictions precluded any witty displays of malice. Compared to the reviews by Oscar Wilde, Yeats's articles are very sober, yet they have more to say. His critical judgments of individual books can surprise when one compares them to the prevailing current of his thought. Although he deplored the influence of the later realistic, prose dramas of Ibsen and his followers on the English stage, he enjoyed Ibsen's *Brand* in a verse translation and he looked upon Ibsen as a great poet gone wrong. However much Yeats might have been expected to praise Tennyson in 1892, the year of Tennyson's death, his criticism of *The Death of Oenone* is balanced and judicious even so close to the poet's death.

Yeats never failed to praise greatness. He also found merit in much poetry that only readers of his reviews will remember—the verse of Sarah Piatt, James Dryden Hosken, and Charles Weekes. He could not

[60] Review of B. Douglas Howard's *Life with Trans-Siberian Savages*, *Speaker*, October 7, 1893.

choose his subjects for review, at least in the early nineties, and chance did not throw many masterpieces his way.

Although Yeats took the opportunity of the review to preach immortal truths, he took the short view of the weekly or monthly reviewer. He left it to the future to pronounce masterpieces. His view, he knew, would only be a preliminary judgment. He was too avid a reader of the reviews of his own books to practice any self-deception about the reviewer's deciding final questions of taste, indifferent to the commercial effects of his decision. In his reviews of poetry, he operated on the general assumption that most books of verse were rather good things. A book was seldom damned entirely, and he always balanced any fault finding with an enumeration of some good points. Perhaps the only exception to his generally charitable attitude was Sir Charles Gavan Duffy, and there was much more than abstract truth at stake here.

In kindness to poetic amateurs, Yeats liked to describe as "pretty" any poetry which he did not know what else to do with. On matters of technique, he was a strict reader. A poet need not have shared Yeats's views on the universe if he was a careful craftsman. Yeats disliked prose poems and he never found much merit in metrical experiments. Such deviations could draw from him the very uncharacteristic, pedantic rebuke: "The best critics are not convinced that wild and irregular measures are perfectly legitimate."[61]

Yeats's reviews are valuable as a reflection of his own temperament and ideas during a period of his life not otherwise covered by his prose and distorted in his memoirs. As a journalist, Yeats achieved much. By his prose propaganda as well as by his poetry he created the Irish literary revival. He helped Blake's influence and fame to grow, and by his continual denunciation of the Victorian virtues he helped poetry to reform itself, even though the poetry of the future was not what he had prophesied. As examples of his art, his reviews are filled with beautiful passages, albeit too poetic for the best prose, and lacking the intensity he could and did give his ideas in verse form. Even so, this prose is too good to be neglected in forgotten magazines or to moulder in newspaper archives. Yeats made a suggestion in another context which may serve for his own uncollected prose:

When we have banqueted let Learning gather the crumbs into her larder, and welcome. She will serve them up again in time of famine.[62]

---

[61] Review of Fiona Macleod's *From the Hills of Dream, Bookman,* December, 1896.
[62] Review of Douglas Hyde's *Beside the Fire, National Observer,* February 28, 1891.

UNCOLLECTED PROSE BY
W. B. YEATS

The Poetry of Sir Samuel Ferguson—I

BY W. B. YEATS

This article—the first published prose piece by Yeats which has survived—appeared under the heading "Irish Poets and Irish Poetry" in the *Irish Fireside* of October 9, 1886. For Yeats's other contributions to this series, see the two-part article on R. D. Joyce later in this collection. This article may have been occasioned by the death of Sir Samuel Ferguson on August 9, 1886. The next article in this collection, a much longer piece on Ferguson contributed to the *Dublin University Review* of November, 1886, was clearly meant as obituary and eulogy. The *Irish Fireside* article reads like a summary of the *Dublin University Review* piece and may have been composed after it, for Yeats refers here to the later article as one in which ". . . I have written somewhat copiously elsewhere." (See footnote 16 to the present article.)

Yeats complained in a letter to Katharine Tynan that he had great difficulty in writing on a low enough level to suit the editors of popular papers and magazines (*Letters*, p. 74). The condescending tone of the present article was one solution to Yeats's problem. Solecisms are frequent in this piece, and the *Irish Fireside* typesetters seem to have made less than usual of Yeats's difficult handwriting.

In the second Ferguson article, Yeats emphasized Ferguson's role as a great national poet, one who exemplified the virtues of linking "fatherland and song." In this article, Yeats offered Ferguson's primitivism as one means of escape for the individual from his adulthood or for a nation from modern times.

> *Of old, unhappy, far-off things,*
> *And battles long ago.*[1]

IN the garden of the world's imagination there are seven great fountains. The seven great cycles of legends—the Indian; the Homeric; the Charlemagnic; the Spanish, circling round the Cid; the Arthurian; the Scandinavian; and the Irish—all differing one from the other, as the peoples differed who created them. Every one of these cycles is the voice of some race celebrating itself, embalming for ever what it hated and loved. Back to their old legends go, year after year, the poets of the earth, seeking the truth about nature and man, that they may not be lost in a world of mere shadow and dream.

[1] William Wordsworth, "The Solitary Reaper."

Sir Samuel Ferguson's special claim to our attention is that he went back to the Irish cycle, finding it, in truth, a fountain that, in the passage of centuries, was overgrown with weeds and grass, so that the very way to it was forgotten of the poets; but now that his feet have worn the pathway, many others will follow, and bring thence living waters for the healing of our nation, helping us to live the larger life of the Spirit, and lifting our souls away from their selfish joys and sorrows to be the companions of those who lived greatly among the woods and hills when the world was young.

It was in Ferguson's later poems that he restored to us the old heroes themselves; in his first work, "Lays of the Western Gael," he gave us rather instants of heroic passion, as in "Owen Bawn," and "Dierdre's[2] Lament for the Sons of Usnach," or poems in which character is sub-ordinated to some dominant idea or event, as in the "Welshmen of Tirawley," and "Willy Gilliland," or tales round which is shed the soft lustre of idyllic thought, as the "Fairy Thorn."

In other words, he was more lyrical and romantic than dramatic in this first and best known of his books, "The Fairy Thorn."[3] Does the whole range of our rich ballad literature contain a more beautiful ballad of "the good people" than this? I will quote almost the whole of it:

> *"Get up, our Anna dear, from the weary spinning-wheel,*
> *For your father's on the hill, and your mother's asleep;*
> *Come up above the crags, and we'll dance a highland-reel*
> *Around the fairy thorn on the steep."*
>
> *At Anna Grace's door 'twas thus the maidens cried—*
> *Three merry maidens fair, in kirtles of the green;*
> *And Anna laid the sock[4] and weary wheel aside,*
> *The fairest of the four, I ween.*
>
> *They're glancing through the glimmer of the quiet eve,*
> *Away, in milky wavings of neck and ankle bare;*
> *The heavy sliding stream in its sleepy song they leave,*
> *And the crags in the ghostly air;*
>
> *And linking hand in hand, and singing as they go,*
> *The maids along the hillside have ta'en their fearless way,*
> *Till they come to where the rowen trees in lonely beauty grow*
> *Beside the fairy hawthorne grey.*

·   ·   ·   ·   ·

---

[2] *Dierdre*: usually written "Deirdre," but written "Dierdre" throughout this article.

[3] Ferguson's first and best-known book was *Lays of the Western Gael*. The title "The Fairy Thorn" should go with the next sentence.

[4] *sock*: Ferguson reads "rock."

But solemn is the silence of the silvery haze
  That drinks away their voices echoless repose,[5]
And dreamily the evening has still'd the haunted braes,
  And dreamier the gloaming grows.

And sinking one by one, like lark-notes from the sky
  When the falcon's shadow saileth across the open shaw,
Are hushed the maidens' voices, as cowering down they lie
  In the flutter of their sudden awe.

For from the air above, and the grassy ground beneath,
  And from the mountain ashes, and the old whitethorn between,
A power of faint enchantment doth through their beings breathe,
  And they sink down together on the green.

                    .   .   .   .

Thus clasped and prostrate all, with their heads together bow'd,
  Soft on[6] *their bosoms beating—the only human sound—*
They hear the silky footsteps of the silent fairy crowd,
  Like a river in the air, gliding round.

No scream can they raise, nor prayer can they say,[7]
  But wild, wild, the terror of the speechless three—
For they feel fair Anna Grace drawn silently away—
  By whom they dare not look to see.

They feel their tresses twine with her parting locks of gold,
  And the curls elastic falling, as her head withdraws;
They feel her sliding arms from their tranced arms unfold,
  But they may not look to see the cause.

For heavy on their senses the faint enchantment lies
  Through all that night of anguish and perilous amaze;
And neither fear nor wonder can ope their quivering eyes,
  Or their limbs from the cold ground raise.

Till out of night the earth has rolled her dewy side,
  With every haunted mountain and streamy vale below;
When, as the mist dissolves in the yellow morning tide,
  The maidens' trance dissolveth so.

Then fly the ghastly three as swiftly as they may,
  And tell their tale of sorrow to anxious friends in vain—
They pined away, and died within the year and day;
  And ne'er was Anna Grace seen again.

You must go to the book itself for that ringing ballad, "Willy
Gilliland," or that other, "The Welshmen of Tirawley," which I am

[5] *voices echoless repose*: Ferguson reads "voices in echoless repose."
[6] *Soft on*: Ferguson reads "Soft o'er."
[7] This line reads in Ferguson, "No scream can any raise, nor prayer can any say . . . ."

told the English poet Swinburne considers the best Irish poem, for I cannot do them justice by short quotations. I could give no idea of a fine building by showing a carved flower from a cornice.

His well-known poem, the "Lament of Dierdre," is a version from the Irish. It is one of "the things of the old time before." The name of him who wrote it has perished, his grave is unknown; and she in whose mouth it is put beheld the dawn from her tent door, and heard the long oars smiting the grey sea, and beheld the hills and the forest, and had her good things long ago, and departed. Well then, perhaps, some one will say, if it has come from so far off, what good can it do us moderns, with our complex life? Assuredly it will not help you to make a fortune, or even live respectably that little life of yours. Great poetry does not teach us anything—it changes us. Man is like a musical instrument of many strings, of which only a few are sounded by the narrow interests of his daily life; and the others, for want of use, are continually becoming tuneless and forgotten. Heroic poetry is a phantom finger swept over all the strings, arousing from man's whole nature a song of answering harmony. It is the poetry of action, for such alone can arouse the whole nature of man.[8] It touches all the strings—those of wonder and pity, of fear and joy. It ignores morals, for its business is not in any way to make us rules for life, but to make character. It is not, as a great English writer[9] has said, "a criticism of life," but rather a fire in the spirit, burning away what is mean and deepening what is shallow.

Sir S. Ferguson's longest poem, "Congal," appeared in 1872. Many critics held this to be his greatest work. I myself rather prefer his "Dierdre," of which more presently. "Dierdre" is in blank verse, which, I think, sustains better the dignity of its subject than the somewhat ballad metre of "Congal." Nevertheless, "Congal" is a poem of lyric strength and panther-like speed.

It is the story of the death in the seventh century, at the battle of Moyra (or Moira) of Congal Claen. Congal was a heathen; his enemy, the arch-King Ardrigh,[10] was a Christian. This war was the sunset of Irish heathendom. Across Ireland, eager for the battle, march Congal and his warriors. The demons of field and flood appear to them and prophesy their destruction. Defying heaven and hell, on march the heathen hosts. One morning, in the midst of the ford of Ullarvu, they

[8] These sentences presage some lines from Yeats's "To a Friend Whose Work Has Come to Nothing":

> *And like a laughing string*
> *Whereon mad fingers play*
> *Amid a place of stone,*
> *Be secret and exult* . . . .

[9] Matthew Arnold, of course. Yeats was continually refuting his dictum.

[10] Congal's enemy was King Domnal. The name "Ardrigh" which Yeats gives is the Gaelic word for "high king."

behold that gruesomest of Celtic demons, "the Washer of the Ford"—a grey hag, to her knees in the river, washing the heads and the bodies of men. Congal fearlessly questions her.

> *"I am the Washer of the Ford," she answered; "and my race*
> *Is of the Tuath de Danaan line of Magi; and my place*
> *For toil is in the running streams of Erin; and my cave*
> *For sleep is in the middle of the shell-heaped Cairn of Maev,*
> *High up on haunted Knocknurea,*[11] *and this fine carnage-heap*
> *Before me, in these silken vests and mantles which I steep*
> *Thus in the running water, are the severed heads and hands,*
> *And spear-torn scarfs and tunics of these gay-dressed gallant bands*
> *Whom thou, O Congal, leadest to death. And this," the Fury said,*
> *Uplifting by the clotted locks what seemed a dead man's head,*
> *"Is thine head, O Congal!"*

Still on they go, these indomitable pagans. Surely nothing will resist their onset. Will they not even shake the throne of God in their sublime audacity? No; Congal when he has accomplished deeds of marvellous valour is slain by the hand of an idiot boy who carries a sickle for sword, and the lid of a cauldron for shield. Ah, strange irony of the Celt.

Notice throughout this poem the continual introduction of the super-natural. I once heard a great English poet,[12] in comparing two existing descriptions of the battle of Clontarf, the Irish and the Danish, say that the Irish narrator turns continually aside to discuss some great problem, or describe some supernatural event, while the Dane records only what affects the result of the battle. This was so, he said, because the Celtic nature is mainly lyrical, and the Danish, mainly dramatic.

The lyrical nature loves to linger on what is strange and fantastic.

In 1880, was published Ferguson's last volume, "Poems."

In England it received no manner of recognition.[13] Anti-Irish feeling ran too high. "Can any good thing come out of Galilee," they thought.[14] How could these enlightened critics be expected to praise a book that entered their world with no homage of imitation towards things Anglican?

Sir Samuel Ferguson himself, declares the true cause of this want of recognition in English critical centres in a letter published the other day in the *Irish Monthly*. He sought to lay the foundation of a literature

[11] *Knocknurea*: Ferguson wrote "Knocknarea." This mountain, the burial place of Queen Maeve, is an important part of what was for Yeats the symbolic landscape of Sligo. See "The Hosting of the Sidhe."
[12] William Morris. Yeats retold this anecdote, supplying Morris's name, in the preface to Lady Gregory's *Cuchulain of Muirthemne*, p. xii.
[13] Yeats recounts in his next article with greater detail how poorly Ferguson's *Poems* were reviewed in the *Academy* magazine in 1880.
[14] For Yeats, the messianic overtones of this remark were not fortuitous.

for Ireland that should be in every way characteristic and national, hence the critics were against him.

In this last book of his are his two greatest poems, "Conary," which De Vere[15] considers the best Irish poem, and "Dierdre."

In "Conary," thus is the king of Ireland described by a pirate's spy—

> One I saw
> Seated apart: before his couch there hung
> A silver broidered curtain; grey he was,
> Of aspect mild, benevolent, composed.
> A cloak he wore, of colour like the haze
> Of a May morning, when the sun shines warm
> On dewy meads and fresh-ploughed tillage land;
> Variously beautiful, with border broad
> Of golden woof that glittered to his knee
> A stream of light. Before him, on the floor,
> A juggler played his feats; nine balls he had,
> And flung them upward, eight in air at once,
> And one in hand: like swarm of summer bees
> They danced and circled, till his eye met mine;
> Then he could catch no more; but down they fell
> And rolled upon the floor. "An evil eye
> Has seen me," said the juggler.

Of this poem's splendid plot, which I have no space to describe here, I have written somewhat copiously elsewhere.[16]

Dierdre is the noblest woman in Irish romance. Pursued by the love of King Conar,[17] she flies with her lover and his brethren and his tribe. Who has not heard of their famous wanderings? At last peace is made; but she who has been like a wise elder sister to the sons of Usnac[18] knows that it is treacherous, and warns Naise,[19] her lover. He will not believe her. Sadly she sings upon her harp, as they leave their refuge in Glen Etive—

> Harp, take my bosom's burthen on thy string,
> And, turning it to sad, sweet melody,
> Waste and disperse it on the careless air.
>
> Air, take the harp-string's burthen on thy breast,
> And, softly thrilling soul-ward through the sense,
> Bring my love's heart again in tune with mine.

---

[15] *De Vere*: Aubrey de Vere (1814–1902), Anglo-Irish poet. He was a member of the Oxford Movement, and he became a Catholic in 1851. In the 1860s and 1870s he produced a series of poems on Irish subjects.

[16] In the article on Ferguson that appeared in the November, 1886, issue of the *Dublin University Review*, which is the next article in this collection.

[17] *Conar*: written "Conor" in Ferguson, and so written in Yeats's other article on Ferguson.

[18] *Usnac*: written "Usnach" in Ferguson.   [19] *Naise*: written "Naisi" in Ferguson.

Albu, farewell! Farewell, fair Etive bank!
Sun kiss thee; moon caress thee; dewy stars
Refresh thee long, dear scene of quiet days!

Slowly they are meshed about and entrapped; the sons of Usnac are slain, and she kills herself that she may escape the power of King Conar.

Sir Samuel Ferguson, I contend, is the greatest Irish poet, because in his poems and the legends, they embody more completely than in any other man's writings, the Irish character. Its unflinching devotion to some single aim. Its passion. "The food of the passions is bitter, the food of the spirit is sweet," say the wise Indians. And this faithfulness to things tragic and bitter, to thoughts that wear one's life out and scatter one's joy, the Celt has above all others. Those who have it, alone are worthy of great causes. Those who have it not, have in them some vein of hopeless levity, the harlequins of the earth.[20]

One thing more before I cease; if I were asked to characterize, as shortly as may be, these poems, I should do so by applying to them the words of Spencer, "barbarous truth."[21]

The Poetry of Sir Samuel Ferguson—II

This article appeared in the *Dublin University Review* of November, 1886. The death of Sir Samuel Ferguson, the Ulster-born poet and antiquary, on August 9, 1886, called forth a number of appreciations of the man's life and work. The two principal articles, one by J. P. Mahaffy in the *Athenaeum* and the other by Margaret Stokes in the *Academy*, had stressed Ferguson's loyalty to the British crown. Yeats's article was a reply that Ferguson, whether he meant to or not, was a "true member of that company/That sang to sweeten Ireland's wrong . . ." and hence was a nationalist whether he wanted to be or not.

Although this article is Yeats's second known published prose piece, it is his first major statement of his literary philosophy. In choosing a national literature embodying the ideals of "fatherland and song," Yeats declared war on the Anglo-Irish ("West-Briton" as he called it) literary establishment in

---

[20] Cf. . . . *Being certain that they and I*
       But lived where motley is worn . . .
                "Easter, 1916".
[21] The philosopher Herbert Spencer, in the first part of his *Principles of Sociology*, examined how primitive man formed his ideas, folk beliefs, and superstitions. Although Yeats disliked the scientific rationalism of men such as Spencer, he might have found congenial Spencer's ability to make folk beliefs seem, for primitive intelligence, a convincing interpretation of nature. I have not found where Spencer uses the phrase "barbarous truth."

their chief institution—Trinity College—and its chief spokesman—Professor Edward Dowden.

Yeats declared for an epic literature, one based on ancient Irish saga which would enable him to escape what he here called the "sad soliloquies of a nineteenth-century egoism." Although Yeats as frequently changed his opinions as his poems, he here expresses some of the central forces of his long career: his love of convictions rather than intellectual reservations, his primitivism, and even a foreshadowing of his self-images in old age. The "aged sea-king" he admired in Ferguson, he was to aspire to himself.

One may doubt whether Yeats's enthusiasm for Ferguson is supported by the passages he quotes from Ferguson's poems. The appeal to national loyalties is here more powerful than reasons offered to the literary judgments. The arrogant and defiant opening to this essay and its concluding clarion call to a rebirth of the Gael are magnificent and a fitting opening for a man who would sing the "indomitable Irishry."

I N the literature of every country there are two classes, the creative and the critical. In Scotland all the poets have been Scotch in feeling, or, as we would call it, national, and the cultured and critical public read their books, and applauded, for the nation was homogeneous. Over here things have gone according to an altogether different fashion.

It has not paid to praise things Irish, or write on Irish subjects; but the poet, who is, as far as he is a poet at all, by the very nature of his calling a man of convictions and principle, has gone on remaining true to himself and his country, singing for those who cannot reward him with wealth or fame, who cannot even understand what he loves most in his work. This he has done while the Irish critic, who should be a man of convictions, but generally becomes, by the force of circumstances a man of tact, industry, and judgment; who studies the *convenances* of the literary world and praises what it is conformable to praise, has remained with his ears to the ground listening for the faintest echo of English thought. Meanwhile the poet has become silent or careless, for everywhere the supply ultimately depends on the demand. If Ireland has produced no great poet, it is not that her poetic impulse has run dry, but because her critics have failed her, for every community is a solidarity, all depending upon cach, and each upon all. Heaven and earth have not seen the man who could go on producing great work without a sensitive and exacting audience. Why did a writer like Sir Samuel Ferguson publish in a long life so little poetry, and after he had given evidences of such new and vivid power, become no longer vocal, and busy himself mainly with matters of research?

The greatest of his faculties was killed long ago by indifference.

It is a question whether the most distinguished of our critics,

Professor Dowden,[1] would not only have more consulted the interests of his country, but more also, in the long run, his own dignity and reputation, which are dear to all Irishmen, if he had devoted some of those elaborate pages which he has spent on the much bewritten George Eliot, to a man like the subject of this article. A few pages from him would have made it impossible for a journal like the *Academy* to write in 1880, that Sir Samuel Ferguson should have published his poetry only for his intimate friends, and that it did not even 'rise to the low water-mark of poetry.'[2] Remember this was not said of a young man, but one old, who had finished his life's labour. If Sir Samuel Ferguson had written to the glory of that, from a moral point of view, more than dubious achievement, British civilization, the critics, probably including Professor Dowden, would have taken care of his reputation.

Lately another professor[3] of Trinity appears to have taken most pleasure in writing, not that the author of *Congal* was a fine poet, nor that he was a profound antiquarian, but in assuring us that he was an 'orderly citizen'; which, if it means anything, means, I suppose, that unlike Socrates, he never felt the weight of the law for his opinions.

'I would,' said one of the most famous of living English poets[4] to the author of this article, 'gladly lecture in Dublin on Irish literature, but the people know too little about it.'

The most cultivated of Irish readers are only anxious to be academic, and to be servile to English notions. If Sir Samuel Ferguson had written of Arthur and of Guinevere, they would have received him

---

[1] Edward Dowden (1843–1913) was Professor of English at Trinity College, a post he was given four years after his graduation from that same college. His best known work of criticism is his study of Shakespeare. Since Dowden was a friend of John Butler Yeats, William had met Dowden some years before this article appeared. In his autobiography Yeats said that he first worshiped Dowden but was soon repelled by the older man's detachment as a scholar. Dowden admired Ferguson's poems but he had said so only in private letters. During the nineties Yeats and Dowden quarreled frequently over literary politics and critical matters but Dowden always had a high regard for Yeats's poetry.

[2] Ferguson's poems were reviewed in the *Academy* of July 24, 1880. The anonymous critic made the remark about "low water-mark" in reference to Ferguson's "Hymn of the Fisherman." The critic also said of his "Hymn" that "we would suggest that it would be more reverent if persons who have not the gifts necessary for composing poetry would confine themselves entirely to secular subjects."

[3] In an anonymous obituary in the *Athenaeum* of April 14, 1886 (p. 205), the eulogist said of Ferguson that despite the poet's knowledge of the "real grievances of his country . . . yet there was never a more loyal or orderly British citizen, or one who felt more deeply the mistakes that are made, and the crimes that are committed, under the guise of demanding justice for his country. He never lent his poetic talent to increase the volume of Irish discontent." Lady Ferguson in her biography *Sir Samuel Ferguson in the Ireland of His Day* identified the author of the *Athenaeum* article as the Rev. J. P. Mahaffy (1839–1919), the famous professor of Latin and Greek at Trinity College.

[4] Yeats retold this anecdote in his preface to Lady Gregory's *Cuchulain of Muirthemne*, p. xii, and there he identified the English poet as William Morris.

gladly; that he chose rather to tell of Congal and of desolate and queenly Deirdre, we give him full-hearted thanks; he has restored to our hills and rivers their epic interest. The nation has found in Davis a battle call, as in Mangan its cry of despair; but he only, the one Homeric poet of our time, could give us immortal companions still wet with the dew of their primal world.

To know the meaning and mission of any poet we must study his works as a whole. Sir Samuel Ferguson has himself pointed out how this may best be done in his own case. He tells us that the main poems in his first volume and his last should be read in the following order:— *Twins of Macha* ('Poems,') *The Naming of Cuchullin* ('Poems,') *Abdication of Fergus* ('Lays of the Western Gael,') *Mesgedra* ('Poems,') *Deirdre* ('Poems,') *Conary* ('Poems,') *Healing of Conall Carnach* ('Lays,') *The Tian[5] Quest* ('Lays.')

The Twins of Macha and *The Naming of Cuchullin* give us the keynote of his work—that simplicity, which is force. He is never florid, never for a moment rhetorical. We see at once that he has the supreme gifts of the story-teller—imagination enough to make history read like romance, and simplicity enough to make romance read like history.

The boy Setanta approaching at night the house of the great smith, Cullan, is attacked by the smith's gigantic watch dog and kills it. The old man laments the loss of his faithful hound:—

> *Boy, for his sake who bid[6] thee to my board*
> *I give thee welcome: for thine own sake, no.*
> *For thou hast slain my servant and my friend,*
> *The hound I loved, that, fierce, intractable*
> *To all men else, was ever mild to me.*
> *He knew me; and he knew my uttered words,*
> *All my commandments, as a man might know;*
> *More than a man he knew my looks and tones*
> *And turns of gesture, and discerned my mind*
> *Unspoken, if in grief or if in joy.*
> *He was my pride, my strength, my company,*
> *For I am childless; and that hand of thine*
> *Has left an old man lonely in the world.*

The boy declares that till he has trained the watchdog's whelp to take the place of the dead hound, he himself will guard the house, remaining at his post by day and by night. Those who are standing by cry out that henceforth his name shall be Cuchullin, the 'Hound of Cullan.' All this is told with such simplicity and sincerity that we seem to be no longer in this modern decade, but listening to some simple

[5] *Tian*: elsewhere spelled "Tain."
[6] *who bid*: Ferguson reads "who bade."

and savage old chief telling his companions round a forest fire,[7] of something his own eyes have seen. There is not much fancy, little of the subtler forms of music. Many a minor English poet whom the world will make haste to forget, has more of these; but here are the very things which he has not, the germinal thoughts of poetry.

The *Abdication of Fergus* follows next in the cycle. The poet-king, who loves hunting and the freedom of the great wood, far better than the councils is delighted by the wisdom with which his stepson who sits beside him on the judgment seat, arrays in some most tangled case argument against argument—

> *As a sheep-dog sorts his cattle,*
> *As a king arrays his battle.*

He takes from his head the crown and lays it beside him on the bench. Let Fergus tell his own tale.

> *And I rose, and on my feet*
> *Standing by the judgment-seat,*
> *Took the circlet from my head,*
> *Laid it on the bench and said:—*
>
> *'Men of Uladh, I resign*
> *That which is not rightly mine,*
> *That a worthier than I*
> *May your judge's place supply.*
>
> *Lo, it is no easy thing*
> *For a man to be a king,*
> *Judging well, as should behove*
> *One who claims a people's love.*
>
> *Uladh's judgment-seat to fill*
> *I have neither wit nor will.*
> *One is here may justly claim*
> *Both the function and the name.*
>
> *Conor is of royal blood:*
> *Fair he is; I trust him good;*
> *Wise he is we all may say*
> *Who have heard his words to-day.*
>
> *Take him therefore in my room,*
> *Letting me the place assume—*
> *Office but with life to end—*
> *Of his counseller[8] and friend.'*

---

[7] In his article on "Popular Ballad Poetry of Ireland," *Leisure Hour*, November, 1889, Yeats described Ferguson as "some old half-savage bard chanting to his companions at a forest fire."   [8] *counseller*: in the Ferguson poem spelled "councillor."

So young Conor gained the crown;
So I laid the kingship down;
Laying with it as I went
All I knew of discontent.

In *Mesgedra*, Conall Carnach, after Cuchullin the greatest of the Red-Branch chieftains, finds his enemy, Mesgedra, with one arm disabled, taking sanctuary under a sacred tree, and, in order that they may fight on equal terms, binds one of his own arms to his side, and when a chance blow releases it, binds it again.

We now come to *Deirdre*, which I hold to be the greatest of Sir Samuel Ferguson's poems. It is in no manner possible to do it justice by quotation. There is an admirable, but altogether trivial, English poet called Edmund Gosse.[9] If fate compelled me to review his work, and to review also some princely ancient Homer or Aeschylus, and to do this by the method of short quotations, the admirable Londoner, in the minds of many readers, would rule the roost. For in his works grow luxuriantly those forms of fancy and of verbal felicity that are above all things *portable*; while the mighty heathen sought rather after breadth and golden severity, knowing well that the merely pretty is contraband of art. With him beauty lies in great masses—thought woven with thought—each line, the sustainer of his fellow. Take a beauty from that which surrounds it—its colour is faded, its plumage is ruffled—it is dead.

In this Sir Samuel Ferguson was like the ancients; not that he was an imitator, as Matthew Arnold in *Sohrab and Rustum*, but for a much better reason; he was *like* them—like them in nature, for his spirit had sat with the old heroes of his country. In *Deirdre* he has restored to us a fragment of the buried Odyssey of Ireland.

In Scotch Glen Etive, Naïsi, Son of Usnach, lives in exile with his two brothers and his bride—his Deirdre, for he has carried her off from a little lonely island in a lake where the king, Conor, had hidden her away in charge of her nurse and an old Druid, that he might make her his mistress when her beauty had grown to full flower. Deirdre is entirely happy, for love is all-sufficient for her; not so her lover—he longs for war, and to sit once more in council with his peers. Suddenly

[9] At this point in the *Dublin University Review* printing, the following footnote, signed "Ed. *D.U.R.*," appeared: "Mr. Gosse is now in so much trouble about other matters than his poetry, that it may seem unkindly at the present juncture to add a stone, or even a pebble, to the cairn of his reputation. It is right then to say that Mr. Yeats' remarks were in type before the appearance of the last *Quarterly Review*." Edmund Gosse (1849–1928), better known as a literary historian and biographer than as poet, later became an acquaintance of Yeats's. Yeats considered Gosse, Andrew Lang, and Austin Dobson, taken as a group, to be his immediate predecessors, and rivals, in English poetry. Gosse's book *From Shakespeare to Pope* had been given a devastating review by J. Churton Collins in the *Quarterly Review*, October, 1886. Collins collected that review in his *Ephemera Critica*, London, 1901.

is heard through Glen Etive the hunting-call of ex-king Fergus. He brings a pardon.

Of all those who return with him Deirdre alone is sad, she knows the peace is treacherous, that Conor is only seeking to bring her once more into his power. None believes her. Are they not safe under the protection of Fergus? But no; she will not place trust in one who gave up his kingdom so lightly. They reach land. Fergus is enticed away by a ruse of King Conor. Their protectors now are the two young sons of Fergus. How beautiful, as they ride across the country, is that talk between Deirdre and the youngest of the two, who afterwards dies for her. He does not love the company of warriors:—

> I[10] *would rather, if I might,*
> *Frequent the open country, and converse*
> *With shepherds, hunters, and such innocents.*

Then they talk of love, these two, so young, and yet so different; the one on the threshold of life, the other, who has known wandering and weariness. He loves all the world, for in her whom he loves are all the world's perfections. There is something maternal in her reply:

> *Long be thou happy in believing so.*

Then turning to the other son, who afterwards betrays her, she seeks to sound his nature also. He is one of those who apply to all the moral obligations of life the corrosive power of the intellect, and she, who knows only how to feel and believe, murmurs sadly, half to herself:

> *Oh yonder see the lake in prospect fair,*
> *It lies beneath us, like a polished shield.*
> *Ah, me! methinks I could imagine it*
> *Cast down by some despairing deity*
> *Flying before the unbelief of men.*

Close by this lake is the 'Red-Branch' house, where their journey ends. I have not space to tell how, point by point, she sees fate drawing near them—how to the very end Naisi, the simple soldier, sits calmly playing chess[11] even when they are surrounded—how Conor comes with his magic shield that was hammered in the sea by fairy smiths, and how there was between it and the seas of Ireland a strange sympathy, so that when it is smitten they all surge. I have not space to tell how the sons of Usnach are slain, but I cannot resist quoting in full the beautiful lament of Deirdre:

> *The lions of the hill are gone*
> *And I am left alone—alone—*
> *Dig the grave both wide and deep,*
> *For I am sick, and fain would sleep!*

[10] This "I" is supplied by Yeats and is not in Ferguson.
[11] The game of chess between Naisi and Deirdre is the central episode of Yeats's own play, *Deirdre*.

The falcons of the wood are flown,
And I am left alone—alone—
Dig the grave both deep and wide,
And let us slumber side by side.

The dragons of the rock are sleeping,
Sleep that wakes not for our weeping;
Dig the grave and make it ready;
Lay me on my true[-]love's body.

Lay their spears and bucklers bright
By the warriors' sides aright;
Many a day the three before me
On their linkèd bucklers bore me.

Lay upon the low grave floor,
'Neath each head, the blue claymore;
Many a time the noble three
Redden'd these blue blades for me.

Lay the collars, as is meet,
Of their greyhounds at their feet;
Many a time for me have they
Brought the tall red deer to bay.

Sweet companions ye were ever—
Harsh to me, your sister, never;
Woods and wilds and misty valleys
Were, with you, as good's a palace.[12]

Oh! to hear my true-love singing,
Sweet as sound of trumpet ringing;
Like the sway of ocean swelling
Roll'd his deep voice round our dwelling.

Oh! to hear the echoes pealing
Round our green and fairy sheeling,
When the three, with soaring chorus
Pass'd the silent skylark o'er us.

Echo, now sleep, morn and even—
Lark alone enchant the heaven!—
Ardan's lips are scant of breath,
Neesa's tongue is cold in death.

[12] This stanza is not in the version of the poem reprinted in standard Ferguson editions. As Yeats notes below, he got this stanza from an earlier version of the poem, to be found in Justice O'Hagan's *The Poetry of Sir Samuel Ferguson*, Dublin, 1887. Yeats omitted a stanza immediately before this seventh one, which is included in *Lays of the Western Gael* and reprinted by O'Hagan. It goes as follows:

> In the falcon's jesses throw,
> Hook and arrow, line and bow;
> Never again by stream or plain
> Shall the gentle woodsmen go.

Stag exult on glen and mountain—
Salmon, leap from loch to fountain—
Herons in the free air warm ye—
Usnach's sons no more will harm ye!

Erin's stay no more you are,
Rulers of the ridge of war;
Never more 'twill be your fate
To keep the beam of battle straight.

Woe is me! By fraud and wrong,
Traitors false and tyrants strong,
Fell Clan Usnach, bought and sold,
For Barach's feast and Conor's gold!

Woe to Emain, roof and wall!—
Woe to Red Branch, hearth and hall!—
Tenfold woe and black dishonour
To the foul and false Clan Conor!

Dig the grave both wide and deep,
Sick I am, and fain would sleep!
Dig the grave and make it ready,
Lay me on my true-love's body!

This is not the version in the text but an earlier and more beautiful one—a version from the Irish, which I have followed Judge O'Hagan's lead in quoting from the *Lays of the Western Gael*. I know not any lament so piercing.

No one will deny excellence to the Idylls of the King; no one will say that Lord Tennyson's Girton[13] girls do not look well in those old costumes of dead chivalry. No one will deny that he has thrown over everything a glamour of radiant words—that the candelabras shine brightly on the fancy ball. Yet here is that which the Idylls do not at any time contain, beauty at once feminine and heroic. But as Lord Tennyson's ideal women will never find a flawless sympathy outside the upper English middle class, so this Deirdre will never, maybe, win entire credence outside the limits—wide enough they are—of the Irish race.

There is a great gap that Sir Samuel Ferguson never filled up between this poem and the next. Here should have come the record of the foiled vengeance of Fergus.

In *Conary*, a pirate fleet is shown us, lying off Howth, commanded by the banished foster brothers of King Conary and the British pirate Ingcel. Spies have been sent on shore. They return. 'What saw ye?'

[13] *Girton*: a woman's college, founded in 1869 and moved in 1873 to Cambridge, although it had at that time no official connection with the university.

They have seen a line of seventeen chariots—in the first, reverend men, judges or poets; in the second heralds; in the third an aged man, 'full-grey, majestical, of face serene;' in the others a numerous household. 'What heard ye?' They have heard one within a guest-house lighting a fire for the reception of a king. The pirates land; a spy is sent before them—he approaches the guest-house and hears within—

> *A hum as of a crowd of feasting men.*
> *Princely the murmur, as when voices strong*
> *Of far-heard captains on the front of war,*
> *Sink low and sweet in company of queens.*

On his return he describes one by one the great chiefs of Ireland that he saw within, and Ferragon, foster brother of Conary, declares their names. There is Cormac Condlongas, son of Conor, who in rage for the betrayal of the sons of Usnach, made war on his father and his kin.

> *The nine he sat among,*
> *Were men of steadfast looks, that at his word,*
> *So seemed it me, would stay not to inquire*
> *Whose kindred were they he might bid them slay.*

> *'I knew them also,' answered Ferragon.*
> *'Of them 'tis said they never slew a man*
> *For evil deed, and never spared a man*
> *For good deed; but as ordered, duteous slew*
> *Or slew not. Shun that nine, unless your heads*
> *Be cased in caskets*[14] *made of adamant.'*

There too is Conall Carnach:

> *Fair-haired he is,*
> *And yellow-bearded, with an eye of blue.*
> *He sits apart and wears a wistful look,*
> *As if he missed some friend's companionship.*
> *Then Ferragon, not waiting question, cried:*
> *Gods! all the foremost, all the valiantest*
> *Of Erin's champions, gathered in one place*
> *For our destruction, are assembled here!*
> *That man is Conall Carnach; and the friend*
> *He looks for vainly with a wistful eye*
> *Is great Cuchullin: he no more shall share*
> *The upper bench with Conall; since the tomb*
> *Holds him, by hand of Conall well avenged.*

One by one the great chieftains are re-created for us in words like the clang of hammer on anvil in fashioning a sword. The arch-king Conary is there.

[14] *caskets*: Ferguson reads "casquets."

THE POETRY OF SIR SAMUEL FERGUSON—II

> *One I saw*
> *Seated apart: before his couch there hung*
> *A silver broidered curtain; grey he was,*
> *Of aspect mild, benevolent, composed.*
> *A cloak he wore of colour like the haze*
> *Of a May morning when the sun shines warm*
> *On dewy meads and fresh ploughed tillage land*
> *Variously beautiful, with border broad*
> *Of golden woof that glittered to his knee*
> *A stream of light. Before him on the floor*
> *A juggler played his feats; nine balls he had*
> *And flung them upward, eight in air at once,*
> *And one in hand! Like swarm of summer bees*
> *They danced and circled, till his eye met mine;*
> *Then he could catch no more; but down they fell*
> *And rolled upon the floor. 'An evil eye*
> *Has seen me,' said the juggler.*

The spy has observed others who were not warriors:

> *I saw three slender, three face-shaven men*
> *Robed in red mantles and with caps of red.*
> *No swords had they, nor bore they spear or shield,*
> *But each man on his knee a bag-pipe held*
> *With jewelled chanter flashing as he moved,*
> *And mouthpiece ready to supply the wind.*
>
> *'What pipers these?'*
>
> > *These pipers of a truth*
> *If so it be that I mistake them not,*
> *Appear not often in men's halls of glee:*
> *Men of the* Sidhe[15] *they are.*
>
> .   .   .   .   .
>
> *To-night their pipes will play[16] us to our ships*
> *With strains of triumph; or their fingers' ends*
> *Shall never close the stops of music more.*

The attack is sounded. Conary sends one troop of his warriors against them, bidding one of the strange pipers sound a pibroch for the onset:

> *'Yea, mighty king,' said one,*
> *'The strain I play ye shall remember long,'*
> *And put the mouthpiece to his lips. At once*
> *It seemed as earth and sky were sound alone,*
> *And every sound a maddening battle-call,*
> *So spread desire of fight through breast and brain.*

[15] *Sidhe*: Ferguson reads "*Sidhs*."
[16] *will play*: Ferguson reads "shall play."

They drive all before them and force a way through the enemy, but fainter and fainter to the ears of Conary comes the sound of the music and the swords. For the treacherous piping has led them far away into the darkness by an irresistible spell; and now the king bids another troop go out against the pirates:

> *And let another piper play you on.*

Again the sound of the music and the swords comes fainter and fainter. Conall Carnach must seek them with a third troop, and to these is appointed the third piper:

> *'Trust not these pipers, I am but a child,'*
> *Said Ferflath; 'but I know they are not men*
> *Of mankind, and will pipe you all to harm,'*
> *'Peace, little prince,' said Conall, 'trust in me.*
> *I shall but make one circuit of the house.'*

They sally out, and those within first hear the sound of 'legions over-thrown,' but soon 'clamour and scream' grow fainter in the distance. Now that it is too late they see the truth:

> *The gods*
> *Have given us over to the spirits who dwell*
> *Beneath the earth.*

The great arch-king himself prepares for 'battle long disused,' and with his household, 'steward and butler, cup-bearer and groom,' goes out against his besiegers.

In the moment of victory he is attacked by a terrible thirst, and cries out for water. Cecht, the only great warrior who remains with him, sets out with the child Ferflath to find it in a distant well. Twice it is spilt, and when at last in the gray of the morning they return, the arch-king is slain, and the three strayed troops stand round him:

> *As men who doubted did they dream or wake,*
> *Or were they honest, to be judged, or base.*

These things are supposed to have happened near the spot where Donnybrook bridge now stands, and there, a few years ago, some workmen found a sword and spear-head of immense antiquity, and a mass of headless skeletons.

I have not space to do much more than mention the next two poems. Though lucid and beautiful, they are of much less importance than Deirdre or Conary. In these latter the wave of song reaches its greatest volume of sound and strength. In the *Healing of Conall Carnach* it ebbs with soft notes that are almost idyllic, and with a half regretful prophecy of change.

The Tain Quest tells how in the course of ages the poem in which Fergus had recorded the previous stories is lost, and the bards have sought it everywhere in vain. At last Murgen, the chief bard's son, resting in a lonely valley find[s] written on the stone on which he leaned, that there Fergus was buried. He calls upon the ghost of the dead warrior to rise and give the Tain once more to the world. Vainly he conjures him by the name of Love, by his Nessa's eyes, by the heroic deeds of his son. At last he conjures him by the sacred name of Song:

> *In dark days near[17] at hand*
> *Song shall be the only treasure left them in their native land.*

Fergus rises:

> *. . . . A mist and a flush*
> *Of brazen sandals blended with a mantle's wafture green.[18]*

So the song is recovered, but Murgen has to give his life in exchange.

There is a wonderful incident full of Celtic irony in the epic of *Congal*. The great chief, from whom the poem takes its name, having driven all his enemies before him, finds himself suddenly face to face with an idiot boy with a bill-hook for sword and the head of a cauldron for a shield. Congal turns away half in scorn and half in pity, but as he turns the idiot wounds him mortally with the bill-hook, and seeking out his king, reports what he has done. The king, in gratitude, promises him great gifts:

> ' 'Tis good,' said Cuanna, and sat down, and from the gravelly soil*
> *Picking the pebbles smooth, began to toss with patient toil*
> *The little stones from hand to hand, alternate back and palm,*
> *Regardless of the presence round, and lapsed in childish calm.*

Meanwhile a notorious coward seeing Congal faint from loss of blood, resolves to win the glory of having killed him. He severs Congal's wrist with a sword-cut, and the hand is driven far over the ground grasping, but he who gave the sword-cut has fled without waiting to see the effect of his blow. So the most famous warrior of his time bleeds to death, slain by the hands of an idiot boy and a coward.

In thus describing these poems I have not sought to convey to my readers, for it were hopeless, their fine momentum, the sign manual of the great writers. I am in every way satisfied if I have made plain the personality of the work.

I must now speak of the slighter poems. To these it is more possible to do justice by quotation.

---

[17] *near*: Ferguson reads "hard."
[18] This quotation reads in Ferguson as follows:
> *. . . a mist ascended with him, and a flash was seen*
> *As of brazen sandals blended with a mantle's wafture green . . . .*

It is a long cry from the days of Congal to those of Davis:—

> *I walked through Ballinderry in the springtime,*
>   *When the bud was on the tree;*
> *And I said, in every fresh-ploughed field beholding*
>   *The sowers striding free,*
> *Scattering broadcast forth the corn in golden plenty*
>   *On the quick seed-clasping soil,*
> *Even such, this day, among the fresh-stirred hearts of Erin,*
>   *Thomas Davis is thy toil.*

> .   .   .   .   .

> *O brave young men, my love, my pride, my promise,*
>   *'Tis on you my hopes are set*
> *In manliness, in kindliness, in justice,*
>   *To make Erin a nation yet;*
> *Self-respecting, self-relying, self-advancing,*
>   *In union or in severance, free and strong—*
> *And if God grant this, then, under God, to Thomas Davis*
>   *Let the greater praise belong.*

Thus wrote Sir Samuel Ferguson at the time of his friend's death. Of the sincerity of the national feeling running through this and all his other poems he gave earnest by being at one time an ardent politician. Towards the last, however, when he had exchanged poetry for antiquarian studies, his Nationalism (in the political sense), though not his patriotism, became less ardent, 'Years robbed him of courage,' as Wordsworth said of himself in a moment of melancholy insight.[19]

Beautiful with their desire for some stronger life, one with the rapture of the sea and the stars, are those opening lines from *Grace O'Malley*—[20]

[19] "In her obituary notice of Ferguson in the *Academy*, Miss Stokes gravely errs in asserting that after Davis's death he 'severed himself wholly' from the national movement. Her subsequent statement that he 'always' cherished the hope—'the fulfilment of which was cut short by his friend's early death'—that Davis would eventually turn into a kind of West Briton, is a still more flagrant violation of biographical truth. *Two years after Davis's death*, Ferguson was chairman of the Protestant Repeal Association, and delivered in that capacity a speech so national in tone that Emmet might have owned it. See Sir C. G. Duffy's *Four Years of Irish History*, Book III, ch. 1. True it is that he afterwards suppressed some of his patriotic poems, 'lest, by any means, the Nationalists should claim him for their own.' But the suppression was not carried far enough. We claim him through every line, Irish singers, who are genuinely Irish in thought, subject and style, must, whether they will or no, nourish the forces that make for the political liberties of Ireland." (Yeats's footnote)

Margaret Stokes (1832–1900), archaeologist and illustrator of Ferguson's poems, wrote an obituary of Ferguson for the *Academy* issue of August 21, 1886. She also wrote a long article on Ferguson for the *Blackwood's* issue of November, 1886.

The reference to Duffy's *Four Years of Irish History*, London, 1883, is to pp. 578–79.
[20] Ferguson's title is "Grace O'Maly."

She left the close-air'd land of trees
And Proud MacWilliam's palace,
For clear, bare Clare's health-salted breeze,
Her oarsmen and her galleys:
And where, beside the bending strand
The rock and billow wrestle,
Between the deep sea and the land
She built her Island Castle.

The Spanish captains, sailing by
For Newport, with amazement
Behold[21] *the cannon'd longship lie*
Moored to the lady's casement;
And, covering coin and cup of gold
In haste their hatches under,
They whispered, ' 'Tis a pirate's hold;
She sails the seas for plunder!'

But no; 'twas not for sordid spoil
Of barque or sea-board borough
She plough'd, with unfatiguing toil,
The fluent-rolling furrow;
Delighting, on the broad-back'd deep,
To feel the quivering galley
Strain up the opposing hill, and sweep
Down the withdrawing valley

Or, sped before a driving blast,
By following seas uplifted,
Catch, from the huge heaps heaving past,
And from the spray they drifted,
And from the winds that toss'd the crest
Of each wide-shouldering giant,
The smack of freedom and the zest
Of rapturous life defiant.

Almost all the poetry of this age is written by students, for students. But Ferguson's is truly bardic, appealing to all natures alike, to the great concourse of the people, for it has gone deeper than knowledge or fancy, deeper than the intelligence which knows of difference—of the good and the evil, of the foolish and the wise, of this one and of that—to the universal emotions that have not heard of aristocracies, down to where Brahman and Sudra[22] are not even names.

The following lines from the poem to Brittany, are very different, with their love of peace and their regret for the past. Those who

[21] *Behold*: Ferguson reads "Beheld."
[22] Brahman is the highest and Sudra the lowest of the four great Hindu castes.

remember that last year's address of Renan's[23] on the same subject will notice how like it they are in temper and substance:

> *Leave to him—to the vehement man*
> *Of the Loire, of the Seine, of the Rhone,—*
> *In the Idea's high pathways to march in the van,*
> *To o'erthrow, and set up the o'erthrown:*
>
> *Be it thine in the broad beaten ways*
> *That the world's simple seniors have trod,*
> *To walk with soft steps, living peaceable days,*
> *And on earth not forgetful of God.*
>
> *Nor repine that thy lot has been cast*
> *With the things of the old time before,*
> *For to thee are committed the keys of the past,*
> *Oh grey monumental Arvôr!*

Of all the lesser poems of Sir Samuel Ferguson there is none more beautiful than that on the burial of Aideen, who died of grief for the death of Oscar, and whose grave is the cromlech at Howth:—

> *They heaved the stone; they heap'd the cairn,*
> *Said Ossian. 'In a queenly grave*
> *We leave her, 'mong the fields of fern,*
> *Between the cliff and wave.*
>
> *'The cliff behind stands clear and bare,*
> *And bare, above, the heathery steep*
> *Scales the clear heaven's expanse, to where*
> *The Danaan Druids sleep.*
>
> *'And all the sands that, left and right,*
> *The grassy isthmus-ridge confine,*
> *In yellow bars lie bare and bright*
> *Among the sparkling brine.*
>
> *'A clear pure air pervades the scene,*
> *In loneliness and awe secure;*
> *Meet spot to sepulchre a queen*
> *Who in her life was pure.*
>
> *'Here, far from camp and chase removed,*
> *Apart in Nature's quiet room,*
> *The music that alive she loved*
> *Shall cheer her in the tomb.*

---

[23] Yeats may have been referring to an address given by Ernest Renan at a "Celtic feast" ("*Fête celtique*") at Quimper on August 17, 1885. This speech, like many another delivered at these feasts, is in praise of Brittany and the Celtic race in general. The speech may be found in Renan's *Discours et conférences*, Paris, 1887.

'The humming of the noontide bees,
  The larks loud carol all day long,
And borne on evening's salted breeze,
  The clanking sea-bird's song

'Shall round her airy chamber float,
  And with the whispering winds and streams,
Attune to Nature's tenderest note
  The tenor of her dreams.

'And oft, at tranquil eve's decline,
  When full tides lip the old Green Plain,
The lowing of Moynalty's kine
  Shall round her breathe again.

'In sweet remembrance of the days
  When, duteous, in the lowly vale,
Unconscious of my Oscar's gaze,
  She filled the fragrant pail.

              .   .   .   .   .

'Farewell! the strength of men is worn;
  The night approaches dark and chill;
Sleep, till perchance an endless morn
  Descend the glittering hill.'

Of Oscar and Aideen bereft,
  So Ossian sang. The Fenians sped
Three mighty shouts to heaven; and left
  Ben-Edar to the dead.

At once the fault and the beauty of the nature-description of most modern poets is that for them the stars, and streams, the leaves, and the animals, are only masks behind which go on the sad soliloquies of a nineteenth century egoism. When the world was fresh they gave us a clear glass to see the world through, but slowly, as nature lost her newness, or they began more and more to live in cities or for some other cause, the glass was dyed with ever deepening colours, and now we scarcely see what lies beyond because of the pictures that are painted all over it. But here is one who brings us a clear glass once more.

The author of these poems is the greatest poet Ireland has produced, because the most central and most Celtic. Whatever the future may bring forth in the way of a truly great and national literature—and now that the race is so large, so widely spread, and so conscious of its unity, the years are ripe—will find its morning in these three volumes of one who was made by the purifying flame of National sentiment the one man of his time who wrote heroic poetry—one who, among the some-what sybaritic singers of his day, was like some aged sea-king sitting among the inland wheat and poppies—the savour of the sea about him, and its strength.

In these poems and the legends they contain lies the refutation of the calumnies of England and those amongst us who are false to their country. We are often told that we are men of infirm will and lavish lips, planning one thing and doing another, seeking this to-day and that tomorrow. But a widely different story do these legends tell. The mind of the Celt loves to linger on images of persistance [*sic*]; implacable hate, implacable love, on Conor and Deirdre, and Setanta watching by the door of Cullan,[24] and the long waiting of the blind Lynott.[25]

Of all the many things the past bequeaths to the future, the greatest are great legends; they are the mothers of nations. I hold it the duty of every Irish reader to study those of his own country till they are familiar as his own hands, for in them is the Celtic heart.

If you will do this you will perhaps be saved in their high companionship from that leprosy of the modern—tepid emotions and many aims. Many aims, when the greatest of the earth often owned but two—two linked and arduous thoughts—fatherland and song. For them the personal perplexities of life grew dim and there alone remained its noble sorrows and its noble joys.

I do not appeal to the professorial classes, who, in Ireland, at least, appear at no time to have thought of the affairs of their country till they first feared for their emoluments—nor do I appeal to the shoddy society of 'West Britonism,'—but to those young men clustered here and there throughout our land, whom the emotion of Patriotism has lifted into that world of selfless passion in which heroic deeds are possible and heroic poetry credible.

W. B. Yeats

The Poetry of R. D. Joyce

BY W. B. YEATS

Yeats's article on Robert Dwyer Joyce appeared in the *Irish Fireside* in two installments, on November 27 and December 4, 1886, under the heading "Irish Poets and Irish Poetry." R. D. Joyce was the brother of the Gaelic scholar and compiler of *Ancient Celtic Romances*, Patrick Weston Joyce. James Joyce was no relation to these men. R. D. Joyce, a doctor, had gone to Boston

[24] For this episode, see Yeats's earlier summary of Ferguson's poem "The Naming of Cuchullin."

[25] In Ferguson's "Welshmen of Tirawley," the blinded Emon Lynott raises up his son Emon Oge to avenge his father's blindness on the Barrett clan of Tirawley.

to practice medicine. Like Blackmore, the doctor-writer of epics in the eighteenth century, Joyce composed his epics while in his carriage on the way to visit his patients.

Unlike some of Yeats's early enthusiasms—Mangan, Ferguson, Allingham—R. D. Joyce was never after recommended by Yeats to Irish readers. Joyce is missing from Yeats's longest reading list, that one compiled for the *Bookman* in October, 1895. Of all the forgotten versifiers on whom Yeats lavished his youthful praises, Joyce was probably the poorest. These articles contain interesting matters, however. Yeats here distinguished between the esoteric, coterie poet and the simple bard who sings for the common man. Yeats wished to be ranked among the school of Burns, Scott, and even Joyce, but his best early verse resembles more that of Coleridge and Shelley, whom Yeats here characterizes as writing for a coterie and leaving a school.

Yeats himself does not fit either category. Despite the esoteric roots of his verse, Yeats's total effect is close to what he here considered the subjects of the bard: "the universal emotions, our loves and angers, our delight in stories and heroes, our delight in things beautiful and gallant."

PART ONE

POETS may be divided roughly into two classes. First, those who—like Coleridge, Shelley, and Wordsworth—investigate what is obscure in emotion, and appeal to what is abnormal in man, or become the healers of some particular disease of the spirit. During their lifetime they write for a clique, and leave after them a school. And second, the bardic class—the Homers and Hugos, the Burnses and Scotts—who sing of the universal emotions, our loves and angers, our delight in stories and heroes, our delight in things beautiful and gallant. They do not write for a clique, or leave after them a school, for they sing for all men.

Both classes are necessary; yet these, though they have not, as the first often have, a definite teaching intention, are perhaps more valuable to mankind, for they speak to the manhood in us, not to the scholar or the philosopher. They are better for a nation than savan[t]s or moralists, or philosophers. Such may teach us to know the good from the evil, the true from the false, the beautiful from the ugly and the coarse; but only the poets can make us love what they please—and that which makes men differ is not what they know, but what they love.

To this latter class belongs Joyce, and, indeed, almost all our Irish poets. He is essentially a bard. He sought to give us whole men, apart from all that limits; therefore he went for his subjects to that simple and legendary past, whither every hill in his own many-fabled Limerick must have appeared to beckon him.

What an effect they must have had on a sensitive boy—those hills
and valleys, with their memories of heroic wars—those ruined castles,
where lovers had pined for each other's footsteps, and been befooled
of fate—that cave, wherein men thought if you wandered far enough
you crossed a stream, and came to the flowers and the fields of fairyland,
when you might wed a fairy princess, and never return to your native
village.

In this book, "Ballads, Romances, and Songs," published in '61, as I
turn over the leaves I see legend after legend of Limerick, and the
counties most immediately about it, embodied in verse—not great,
yet such as will sweeten the hills and streams for many a long day with
memories; and without memories, the most wonderful scenery is like
a beautiful and soulless face. The aim of a ballad writer is not character
or passion—the story is everything with him. He chooses simple words
that, when they have served their purpose, step aside and efface
themselves. The old Fenian story of the Black Robber[1] is a beautiful
instance:

I

By Mumhan's mountain,[2] airy and stern,
A well lies circled by rock and fern,
And fiercely over a precipice near
Rusheth a waterfall brown and clear.

II

In a hollow rent by that bright well's fount,[3]
A mighty robber once made his home;—
A man he was full sullen and dark
As ever brooded on murder stark.

III

A mighty man of a fearful name,
Who took their treasures from all who came,
Who hated mankind, who murdered for greed,
With an iron heart for each bloody deed.

IV

As he went[4] by the torrent ford one day,
A weird-like beldame came down the way:
Red was her mantle, and rich and fine,
But toil and travel had dimmed its shine.

---

[1] "Romance of the Black Robber."
[2] *By Mumhan's mountain*: Joyce reads "By a Numhan mountain."
[3] *fount*: Joyce reads "foam."
[4] *As he went*: Joyce reads "As he sat."

V

A war axe in his red hand he took,
And he killed the beldame beside the brook,
And when on the greensward in death she rolled,
In her arms, lo! a babe, clad in pearls and gold!

VI

He buried the beldame beside the wave,
And he took the child to his mountain cave,
And the first jewel his red hand met,
A Fern and a Hound on its gem were set.

VII

Yet darkly he raised his hand to kill,
But his fierce heart smote him such blood to spill;
Oh! the rage for murder was then[5] delayed
By the innocent smile of that infant maid!

VIII

He made it a bed of the fern leaves green
And he nursed it well from that evening sheen,
And day by day, as the sweet child grew,
The heart of tho robber grew softer too.

IX

Ten long years were past and gone,
And the robber sat by the ford's grey stone,
And there on the eve of a Springtide day
A lordly pageant came down the way.

X

Before them a banner of green and gold
With a Fern and a Hound on its glittering fold,
Behind it a prince with a sad pale face,—
A mighty prince of a mighty race.

XI

The robber looked on the Fern and Hound,
Then sprang towards the prince with an eager bound,
And "Why art thou sad, O King?" said he,
["]In the midst of that lordly companie!["]

XII

His kindly purpose they all mistook,
For though wan and worn yet fierce his look,
And sudden a noble drew out his glaive,
And cleft his skull on the beldame's grave!

5 *then*: Joyce reads "there."

XIII

"Sad," said the pale prince "my fate has been,
Since the dark enchanters have ta'en my queen,
Since they bore my child from the nurse's hand
And keep her away[6] in th'enchanted land."

XIV

The dying robber half rose by the wave,
"Oh! enter," he cried, "yon lonely cave!"
They entered,—the pale prince found his child,
And all was joy in that mountain wild.

Altogether too long for quotation are some of the best ballads, such as the "Baron and the Miller," or "Murgal and Garmon,"[7] that story of a lover who, touching on the phantom shores of Hy Brasil,[8] returns for his betrothed, that they may dwell together where the birds are like "the children of the rainbow." Legend dear to the Celtic heart, sung of in a thousand ways—surely this love of shadowy Hy Brasil is very characteristic of the Celtic race, ever desiring the things that lie beyond the actual; dreamy and fanciful things, unreal if you will, as are all the belongings of the spirit from the point of view of the body, that loves to cry "dreamer, dreamer," to its hard task-master the spirit.

Of songs and ballads of the homely type, such as "The Spalpeen," there are several fine examples, reminding us that though we have perhaps no poet equal to the best of the English, we have a poetry of the people, altogether different to those vulgar ballads of modern England, that I sometimes fear will invade us; those stories of impossible street boys sentimentalising about heaven, those half Police News half didactic poems so popular as penny readings, or those still lower songs of the London streets. When we have touched pathos we have redeemed it with beauty, when we have touched the familiar we have set it to music.

We now come to the songs, altogether inferior to the ballads.

I

The cock and the sparrow

One morn, at the sack of Cragnour,
    A cock and a sparrow were speaking,
While neath where they sat on the tower
    The crop-ears their fury were wreaking—
Were wreaking in blood, fire and smoke.
    "Ah! the castle is ta'en, bone and marrow,
And my poor Irish heart it is broke,"
    Said the brave jolly cock to the sparrow.

[6] *away*: Joyce reads "alway."
[7] This title in Joyce reads "Romance of Meergal and Garmon."
[8] Hy Brasil is a legendary phantom island west of the Aran Islands.

II

"For the crop-ears will have us full soon,
    And our bed will be no bed of roses;
They will starve us right dead to the tune
    Of a psalm that they'll twang thro' their noses.
Never more shall I crow in the hall,
    For the gloom there my bosom would harrow,
May the fiend whip them off, psalm[9] and all,"
Said the brave jolly cock to the sparrow.

III

" 'Tis certain the castle they've got,
    And 'tis sure that they'll slay all that's in it;
But as victory's theirs and what not,
    You're expected to crow like a linnet,"
Cried the sparrow with voice sad low.[10]
    "But I'd[11] rather my grave cold and narrow,
Than at Puritan triumph to crow,"
Said the brave jolly cock to the sparrow.

. . . . .

We must say farewell to the songs and ballads, their virtues are simplicity and strength, the faults occasional baldness and a lack of finish in the style—a besetting sin of the Irish poets; though indeed the poets of what I have called the bardic class are often less careful than the others about finish; not heeding, I suppose, so sensitive an instrument of expression, having to deal with things large and simple rather than subtle. In a later edition were added other poems, including the "Blacksmith of Limerick," a fine ballad, far too well known for me to quote it. It is in nearly all the "collections."

PART TWO

In 1866 Joyce settled in Boston, U.S.A., as a doctor, and, in 1876, appeared "Dierdre,"[12] by far his finest work, written, as his brother, Professor Joyce, tells us, in his carriage, going from patient to patient.

Founded on one of those romances, called by the old Celtic bards "The Three Sorrows of Song," it has all the essentials for a popular poem—a fine story, swiftness of narration, richness of colouring, typical character, a hero for its centre—that is to say, it was, before all things, bardic. In three or four days ten thousand copies were sold.

9 *psalm*: Joyce reads "psalms."
10 *sad low*: Joyce reads "sad and low."
11 *"But I'd*: Joyce reads—But "I'd . . . ."
12 *Dierdre*: Joyce wrote it the usual way, i.e., "Deirdre." In this article it is spelled both ways.

In the first canto warriors are feasting at the house of the king's story-teller, Feilemid,[13] who, finding himself sad—he knew not why—had given a great feast, and invited the king, his master; and now—

> *Full soon the old man felt his soul restored,*
> *As laugh and jest were bandied round the board,*
> *As the king smiled upon him, kind and gay,*
> *As songs were sung, and harps began to play,*
> *And cups were kissed by many a bearded lip.*

In the midst of the feast comes the news that a daughter has been born to Feilimid. The feasters are all silent—

> *As[14] from the door, in solemn slow array,*
> *A bevy of old beldames, two by two,*
> *Paced rustling up the hall.*
>
> .   .   .   .   .
>
> *First of all there came*
> *Old Lavarcum,[15] the conversation dame*
> *Of the great king, who told him all the sport,*
> *And loves, and plots, and scandals of the court.*
> *A pace before them walked she mincingly,*
> *And to each great lord bent the pliant knee;*
> *Sharp eyes she had, each speck and fault that saw,*
> *And face as yellow as an osprey's claw,*
> *And wrinkled, like tough vellum, by the heat,*
> *As moved she toward the monarch's golden seat,*
> *Smirking and smiling on the baby bright.*

Cuffin,[16] the Druid, rises, and prophesies that in times to come this child shall be a woman so beautiful that mighty queens shall long for her destruction, and kings fall down before her, and her face shall kindle war through the whole land,

> *Led by one aged lord[17]*
> *Now unto all things callous grown.[18]*

The warriors agree that the child shall be slain at once.

> *As when, mid Allen's bogs, some sunny day*
> *The wild geese with their offspring are at play,*
> *And as they gambol by the lakelet's edge,*
> *The hunter's arrow shears the rustling sedge*

[13] *Feilemid*: spelled in Joyce "Feilimid," and thus correctly spelled by Yeats later in this article.   [14] *As*: Joyce reads "And."
[15] *Lavarcum*: Joyce spells this name "Levarcam."
[16] *Cuffin*: Joyce spells this name "Caffa."
[17] This line is Yeats's, not Joyce's.
[18] This line reads in Joyce, "Now unto all things was he callous grown . . . ."

And splashes in the shallow marsh there by,[19]
At once the wild fowl raise their signal cry
Of danger, and, loud cackling in their fear,
Some hide in reeds, some seek the middle mere;
So at the grisly warriors' words of doom,
The aged dames 'gan rustling round the room,
Some fled the hall, some gathered round the child,
And shrieking, clapped their hands with clamour wild.

But the king decides that the child shall be hidden in a lonely palace, in the charge of Lavarcum, and when old enough, he will make her his wife.

The second book, dealing with the childhood of Deirdre, is perhaps the most beautiful in the poem. At first she is happy, but gradually a sadness, a foreshadowing, falls on her, and she begins to ask questions about everything in a beautiful child-like way.

Oh, Lavarcum,
Come, tell me!—oh, come tell me what I am!
Did I come here just like the summer fly
To sparkle in the sun, and then to die?
I've asked the flies full oft, but murmuringly
They said they were too full[20] of present glee
To give me answer, and they passed away;
And once unto the streamlet did I say
"What am I?" for in grove or garden walk,
I oft feel lonely and perforce must talk
To all things round that creep, or walk, or fly,
And well I know their speech. And "what am I?"
I asked the stream; and it is curlish[21] too,
And would not speak, but from its weeds upthrew
A great brown frog puffed up with too much pride,
And ugly! ugly! ugly![22] hoarse he cried;
And then from off the streamlet's grassy brim
He made great mouths at me, and I at him.

At first she knows nothing of the world but the palace garden. Years go by, and at last one day she climbs a tree, and sees over the high walls

The great world spread out.

One day, as I sat neath the beechen bough,
I saw a little squirrel climb the tree,
Sit on a branch and eye me roguishly.
These were my glad times, and the squirrel gay,
Amid the branches[23] did it seem to say,

[19] *there by*: Joyce reads "thereby."
[20] *full*: Joyce reads 'filled.'
[21] *is curlish*: Joyce reads "was churlish."
[23] *branches*: Joyce reads "branches green."
[22] This phrase is printed in Joyce as "Ugly! Ugly! Ugly!"

With wild bright eyes, and bushy tail upcurled,
Come up! Come up! come up, and see the world!
And up I clomb the green tree after him,
Higher and higher still, from limb to limb.

From this tree she sees the young warrior and is seen by him; hence all the trouble.

They escape, and then begin their wanderings, their odyssey of love, the beauty of Dierdre kindling war everywhere. By land and sea they go, flying the wrath of the king. When they reach the shores of Alba, they have been so long at sea that "many an old dame's tongue wagged voluble" with joy, and the warriors "shook their spears with gladness."

They are enticed home to Eman by treacherous promises from the king, from a beautiful island in the sea, where at last they had found peace. For a time the tent of Dierdre is guarded by Manahun,[24] the sea god. He stands by the door, unseen by any but Dierdre and her child. There is a beautiful passage where the child—with all the fearlessness of infancy—asks the giant phantom for his jewelled dagger. Soon their death is planned. Naide[25] and all his tribe are treacherously slain, and Dierdre falls dead on the body of her lover.

What gives the poem its especial excellence, after its unlingering narrative, are the descriptions and the little touches of character. There is no vapour of the study about them; they come direct from nature—earth touches.

In 1879 appeared his last work, "Blanid." The dedication is lovely, and sad with that Celtic sadness that is half tenderness.

O Thou, to come, though yet perchance unborn,
  My country's poet, prince of bards, sublime
'Mongst those who in the future's gleaming morn
  Will make great music, in thy manhood's prime
And day of fame, remember me, and climb
  My hill of rest, and take thy musing way
Unto the place of tombs, and with sweet rhyme
  Stand thou beside my headstone lone and gray,
And strike thy sounding harp and sing no little lay!

For I am of the race of those longsyne,
The maker[26] of heroic minstrelsy.[27]

· · · · ·

But the poem itself is much inferior to Dierdre. It is more literary; there is more of the study, less of the earth in it. It has less of that barbaric

[24] *Manahun*: Joyce spells this name "Mananan."
[25] *Naide*: Joyce spells this name "Naisi."   [26] *maker:* Joyce reads "makers."
[27] The irony of Yeats, at twenty-one, quoting this address to "My country's poet, prince of bards" is touching. It is not unlikely that Yeats was aware of the prophetic irony.

simplicity that makes Dierdre so delightful. The characters have
lingered in the vestibules of modern thought, and have learned to talk
like this:—

> *Where the vapours thicken*
> *Through the city's ways,*
> *And the people sicken*
> *In the poisoned blaze*
> *Of the sun that rots the swamp,*
> *There beside the failing lamp*
> *Of the lowly and the stricken,*
> *He hath stood to cheer and quicken,*
> *With his harp life's dying rays.*

And so on. This is modern, with its cities and its philanthropy. The old
heroes were as simple as children who had never been to school.

There is a slight hint of Swinburne in the rhythm of one or two of
the lyrics that is startling after the originality of all the rest of Joyce's
work. Not that the poem does not contain many original things, such
as this description of how a harper finds his fairy sweetheart:

> *And now he touched his harp, and soft and low*
> *The strings spoke to his fingers, and anear*
> *The kine drew in the ever-brightening glow*
> *Of the calm dawn, while one, unknown to fear,*
> *The infant of the herd, with footsteps slow*
> *Came nigher still, and stood with raptured ear,*
> *As if she ne'er again cared to behold*
> *The buttercups that turned her teeth to gold.*
>
> *And still the sweet strings spoke, and nearer yet*
> *To the green tree the large-eyed listener drew,*
> *With dainty footsteps that scarce seemed to fret*
> *From the young flowers and grass the diamond dew.*
> *Then stooped the player; down his harp he set*
> *Beside the tree, and from his ambush flew*
> *And grasped the bright-backed offspring of the morn*
> *By one pink ear, and by one budding horn.*
>
> *A hurrying by the lakelet, and a cry,*
> *A sparkle in his eyes—no more, no more*
> *He held his little captive; with a sigh*
> *He turned, and on the meadow's blossomed floor,*
> *His love stood near the stream-bank, bright and shy*
> *As a young seagull on some sunny shore* [. . . .]

In this poem Joyce kept much less close to the original story than in
Dierdre. I think this was a mistake, for no one knew better than an old

bard what moved men, for he was taught in a bitter school—the school of fierce dissent and applause. He was like a great orator, who only when he feels all hearts beat in unison with his, rises to his best, and becomes alone with the universe and his own voice. Therefore, the bardic work ever human and living.

I hold Joyce to be the poet of all the external things that appertain to the barbaric earth—the earth of hunters and riders, and all young people; the poet of armour and hunting, of hounds and horses. That he was in no way a singer, also, of man's inner nature, of the vague *desires*, though it takes from his stature as a poet, makes him so much the dearer to many worn with modern unrest. In seeking to restore the young world, long faded, he has restored to us for an instant our childhood.

Clarence Mangan
(1803–1849)

This article on Clarence Mangan appeared under the title "Irish Authors and Poets" in the *Irish Fireside* of March 12, 1887. Yeats previously contributed articles on Sir Samuel Ferguson and R. D. Joyce to this same series on "Irish Authors and Poets." During these years Yeats seems to have carried out much research into Mangan's life. He was quite proud of the announcement in print for the first time of the name of Mangan's love, Frances Stackpoole.

Much of the information and opinions of this piece were repeated in an article entitled "Clarence Mangan's Love Affair," which appeared in *United Ireland* on August 22, 1891. It is apparent from this second article that Yeats's identification of Mangan's beloved had not gone unchallenged. However, by 1891 Yeats had the corroboration of Sir Charles Gavan Duffy, who knew both Mangan and Miss Stackpoole. Of the three poets—Davis, Mangan, Ferguson—whom Yeats claimed as his literary forebears in "To Ireland in the Coming Times," Mangan was admired the most for his literary, nonnationalistic qualities. James Joyce "discovered" Mangan again about 1900 without being aware of, or perhaps not caring about, Yeats's and others' efforts on Mangan's behalf during the intervening decade. It has been Mangan's fate to be often discovered.

All my Divinities have died of grief,
And left me wedded to the Rude and Real.[1]
MANGAN

O NE thing is to be remembered concerning Mangan. Unlike most
poets, his childhood was not spent among woods and fields, with
Nature's primitive peace and ancient happiness. He had no early dream
—no treasure-house of innocent recollection: his birthplace sooty
Fishamble-street—his father a grocer, who boasted that his children
would run into a mouse-hole to escape him. His school, round the
corner in Saul's-court, in those days given over to clothes-lines and
children and sparrows, and now abolished to make room for Lord
Edward-street. From here he was transferred to a scrivener's office, his
family having come down in life and now depending in the main on
him. Concerning his office companions, he himself has left something
on record in that strange fragment of autobiography prefixed to the
"Poets of Munster":[2]—

My nervous and hypochondriacal feelings almost verged on insanity. I
seemed to myself to be shut up in a cavern with serpents and scorpions, and
all hideous and monstrous things, which writhed and hissed around me, and
discharged their slime and venom upon my person.

Yet, likely enough, these office companions were by no means bad
fellows. From time immemorial the children of genius have got on ill
with the children of men. King Alfred let the cakes burn, and the
housewife did her best to lead him a life of it; for her the smoke and
smother of her burnt cakes, for him the fiery dream and the tremendous
vision. Seven years Mangan spent in this office, three more as an
attorney's clerk; yet acquired, after his day's work, much polyglot
knowledge of foreign tongues, loving especially to read about the
strange and mysterious—contributed largely to the *Dublin Penny Journal*
and other papers poems, acrostics, &c. Meanwhile the cloud had drawn
closer and closer about him; already he had written "The Dying
Enthusiast" and "The One Mystery," all but the saddest of his songs.
His style was fully developed, with its energy and old-fashioned directness. Of late the muse has left her ancient ways, and is now a lady of

---

[1] These lines are from a Mangan translation entitled "The Unrealities" of Schiller's *Die
Ideale*. Mangan improved upon these lines of Schiller:
            . . . *Er ist dahin, der süsse Glaube*
            An Wesen, die mein Traum gebar,
            Der rauhen Wirklichkeit zum Raube,
            Was einst so schön, so göttlich war.
Mangan's translation read "welded to the Rude and Real," not "wedded."

[2] *The Poets and Poetry of Munster*, an anthology of Mangan's translations of Gaelic songs
and ballads, was gathered shortly before his death by John O'Daly and published in his
edition in 1849.

fashion, learned in refined insincerities and graceful affections, smiling behind her fan—*ça ira*.

Whatever fragment of inbred happiness remained to his spirit, that had asked all things and was given routine and ill health, was lost now; he loved and was jilted; concerning the object of his love, rumour has contradictory voices, beautiful and *spirituelle*, says Mitchel, by no means so, says my informant. One thing alone seems pretty certain, she was a Miss Stackpoole (now for the first time named) of Mount Pleasant-square, one of three sisters.

A short dream this love affair of Mangan's. Before long between him and his Eden was the flaming cherub and the closed gate. I have heard a curious story, which I give for what it is worth, of his rushing with drawn knife at one who had spoken ill of his faithless "Frances;" now, if not before, he sought the comfort of rum, and some say also, opium—

> *And when the inanity of all things human,*
> *And when the dark ingratitude of man,*
> *And when the hollower perfidy of woman*
> *Comes down like night upon the feelings—*[3]

What cure for this? Why, rum and water. So writes he in one of his strange latter poems.

About this time he is described as follows, by Mitchel, who saw him in the library of Trinity College, when Mangan was employed compiling a catalogue—

An acquaintance pointed out to me a man perched on the top of a ladder, with the whispered information that the figure was Clarence Mangan. It was an unearthly and ghostly figure, in a brown garment, the same garment (to all appearance) which lasted till the day of his death. The blanched hair was totally unkempt; the corpse-like features still as marble; a large book was in his arms, and all his soul was in the book. I had never heard of Clarence Mangan before, and knew not for what he was celebrated, whether as a magician, a poet, or a murderer; yet took a volume and spread it on a table, not to read, but with pretence of reading, to gaze on the spectral creature upon the ladder.[4]

Towards the last Mangan commenced his autobiography, or "confession," as he called it. But, haunted by apparitions, as he believed, and overpowered by his ever-growing misery, he could no longer at all do that which was so difficult to calm Goethe—distinguish between fact and illusion. When this was pointed out to him he bid them destroy what he had written. Fortunately this was not done, and it remains not so much a record of his early life as a wonderful piece of the sorrow of his latter, that had stained even memory its own colour.

[3] From "Broken-Hearted Lays."
[4] From Mitchel's biographical introduction to Mangan's *Poems*, New York, 1859, p. 13.

For days he would disappear, living in a barn or some such place, drinking and brooding. His haunts were ever the lowest taverns. I read in Mrs. Atkinson's "Biography of Mary Aikenhead,"[5] that once he was brought to St. Vincent's Hospital. "Oh! the luxury of clean sheets!" he exclaimed. The man with the "face handsome in outline, bloodless, and wrinkled, though not with age," and the "blue eyes, distraught with the opium eater's dreams," and the "heavy lids," appears to have proved a somewhat troublesome patient. Said one of the sisters—"These poets have nerves in every pore."[6] Yet, withal, he does not seem to have been so much a weak character as a man fated. He had powerful convictions, political and other; and convictions bear the same relation to the character as thoughts do to the intellect. In all he wrote there was a sort of intensity, not merely of the intellectual or of the aesthetic nature, but of the whole man; and supreme misery, like supreme happiness, or supreme anything, seems only given to the world's supreme spirits.

At last death released him from his misery. He died of cholera in the Meath Hospital. I have it from one who had it from the doctor in attendance, that when he was dead his face became beautiful and calm. When the contorted soul had gone, the muscles relaxed, and the clay returned to its primal innocence.

Other poets have found refuge from their unhappiness in philosophic subtleties and aeriel turnings and pirouettings of the spirit. But this man, Mangan, born in torpid days in a torpid city, could only write in diverse fashions, "I am Miserable." No hopes! No philosophy! No illusions! A brute cry from the gutters of the earth! and for solace or rather for a drug—this—

> *No more, no more, with aching brow,*
> *   And restless heart, and burning brain,*
> *We ask the When, the Where, the How,*
> *   And ask in vain.*
> *And all philosophy, all faith,*
> *   All earthly—all celestial lore,*
> *Have but one voice, which only saith—*
> *   Endure—adore.*[7]

His work is divided into translations from the German, the Irish, and poems from apocryphal Persian or other sources, and original poems in the main personal. Pages there are abundantly wearying and hollow, but whenever there are thoughts on the littleness of life or the short time its good things stay with us, or the vanity of all subtile and sad longings, or if there be any fragment of ghostly pageantry, then

[5] *Mary Aikenhead, Her Life, Her Work, and Her Friends,* by "S.A.," Dublin, 1879.
[6] This quotation reads in the biography "those poets have nerves at every pore."
[7] From "The One Mystery."

from beneath the pen of this haunted (for so he believed) and prematurely aged man, the words flowed like electric flashes. I do not find as much beauty in his oriental poems as others do, though they, like his Irish poems, have a certain radiant energy. Of these last, "My Dark Rosaleen," is quite wonderful with the passionate self-abandonment of its latter stanzas. But powerful and moving more than anything else that he has done are his few personal poems "Twenty Golden Years Ago," with its beautiful ending—

> *Soon thou sleepest where the thistles blow,*
> *Curious anti-climax to thy dreams,*
> *Twenty golden years ago* [. . .]

"Nameless,"[8] and, may[9] say "Siberia," for that Siberia where the White Tzar sends so many of his wisest and best, seems a sort of type of that Siberia within, where his thoughts wandered and murmured, like outlaws cast from the world's soft places for some unknown offence—

> *Pain as in a dream,*
> *When years go by,*
> *Funeral paced*[10] *yet fugitive,*
> *When man lives and doth not live,*
> *Doth not live nor die.*

But far the strongest of all his poems is "Nameless."[11] He who has once learnt this poem will never forget it; it will stay with him with something of the eternity of painful things. Many poems as delicate and fragrant as rose-leaves we soon forget—they vanish with the coquetry of joy. All the great poems of the world have their foundations fixed in agony—not that this is, in the highest sense, a great poem; it is a great lyric, an altogether different thing.

I know not whether I may not seem to have over-valued Clarence Mangan. No, I am not impartial—who is? Under even the most philosophic utterance is a good dose of personal bias. There is no impartial critic save Time, and he only seems so, maybe, because there is no one to accuse him.

Plainly, this scrivener's clerk brought one thing into the world that was not there before, one new thing into letters—his misery—a misery peculiar in quality. He never lost belief in happiness because he was miserable, or faith in goodness because his life was spent among the taverns. He had not that solace.

He can never be popular like Davis, for he did not embody in clear

---

[8] Despite the period at the end of the previous quotation, these names of poems evidently continues the above sentence.

[9] "May" is a misprint, perhaps for "many" or "one may."

[10] Mangan's "Siberia" reads "Funeral-paced."

[11] Mangan's title is "The Nameless One."

verse the thoughts of normal mankind. He never startles us by saying beautifully things we have long felt. He does not say look at yourself in this mirror; but, rather, "Look at me—I am so strange, so exotic, so different."

W. B. Yeats

Miss Tynan's New Book

Katharine Tynan's *Shamrocks*, London, 1887, was reviewed by Yeats in the *Irish Fireside*, July 9, 1887.

Miss Tynan (1861–1931), Irish poet and novelist, was the first of a long and distinguished series of feminine confidants from whom Yeats sought advice and sympathy. Yeats first met her in 1885, and when he went to London in 1887 they wrote to each other regularly. Their correspondence during the period of their warmest friendship, 1887–1892, contains, in the letters of Yeats which have survived, the most accurate account of this period of his life. Since Miss Tynan had published a volume of poems in 1885, four years before Yeats's *Wanderings of Oisin* appeared in 1889, Yeats treated her as his superior in literary experience. He lectured her on the importance of Irishness and other matters, and, it is clear from her memoirs, she treated the young genius, then in his "cloud and foam" period, with affectionate indulgence. Roger McHugh, the editor of the Yeats-Tynan correspondence, and Joseph Hone, Yeats's biographer, both claim, on the basis of Yeats's first and unpublished draft of his autobiography, that he seems to have convinced himself that it was his duty to propose to Miss Tynan. There are signs in the correspondence that she reacted jealously to Yeats's account of his first meeting with Maud Gonne. No matter what their feelings toward one another, the rules of Victorian propriety were adhered to in their letters. They had corresponded for about two and a half years before Yeats presumed to ask to address her by her Christian name; thereafter, she was "My dear Katey."

After Miss Tynan married Henry Hinkson in 1893, she and Yeats corresponded less frequently, and rarely wrote to each other after 1895. Yeats's spiritualism had always been repugnant to her deep Catholic convictions, and with his widening intellectual interests Yeats soon had less and less in common with his old friend. To earn money, Miss Tynan had to turn her attention away from the Irish literary movement to the writing of novels, an activity in which she was prolific, producing more than one hundred romances for the circulating libraries.

In her 1913 volume of memoirs, *Twenty-five Years: Reminiscences*, she quoted extensively and haphazardly from Yeats's early letters to her. Yeats was angry, partly because she had been indiscreet and partly because she had not given him an opportunity to "improve" the letters. Perhaps because of this difference of opinion, she is mentioned but once in the published version of Yeats's *Autobiography*. Although they drew apart as friends, Yeats's high opinion of some of her verse was enduring; he edited a selection of her poems for the Dun Emer press in 1907.

Miss Tynan's first volume of poems, *Louise de la Vallière*, 1885, was heavily influenced by Christina Rossetti. Her second volume, *Shamrocks*, 1887, although dedicated to William Michael and Christina Rossetti, showed the effects of Yeats's injunctions to be as Irish as possible. Her mild-mannered cheerfulness is well summed up in her epigraph to *Shamrocks*: "'Tis always Morning somewhere in the world."

Only one other review of her work by Yeats has survived. The *Evening Herald* for January 2, 1892, contained a review by Yeats of her *Ballads and Lyrics*, which Roger McHugh has reprinted in part in *W. B. Yeats, Letters to Katharine Tynan*, pp. 181–83.

VERSES mainly simple, always sensuous and passionate—the year will hardly see a pleasanter book. The pre-Raphaelite[1] mannerism and alien methods of thought that obscured the nationality of Miss Tynan's first volume are here almost entirely absent; and in the finding [of] her nationality she has found also herself, and written many pages of great truthfulness and simplicity. Considering the small space allowed me, it is only possible to say concerning "Dermot and Grania—The Fate of King Fergus and the Story of Aibhric,"[2] that there can be no better companions these summer afternoons than those ancient warriors and star-crossed lovers, and pass on with less regret—having given several columns elsewhere to the longer[3]—to the shorter poems.

"I now," said the youthful Goethe, "write of the metaphors of things; some day I shall write of the things themselves."[4] This, in its

[1] *Irish Fireside* text read "pro-Raphaelite." Yeats's lifelong struggle with typesetters was the result of his poor eyesight, which made him a poor copyist of other writers, and his own difficult-to-decipher handwriting. See the early letter of November 23, 1887, to the editor of the *Gael* in which Yeats complained that the *Gael*'s compositor had so mangled his poem that it seemed to be written by an imitator of Browning (*Letters*, pp. 55–56).

[2] Yeats here referred to three separate poems: "The Pursuit of Diarmuid and Grainne," the first and longest poem of the collection, "The Fate of King Feargus," and "The Story of Aibhric."

[3] The treatment elsewhere of the longer poems may have been in the review of *Shamrocks* in the now-lost *Gael* which Yeats mentioned in a letter to Miss Tynan, dated by Wade as April, 1887 (*Letters*, pp. 33–34).

[4] Yeats may have had in mind a description of the young Goethe by August Kestner, one of Goethe's companions of the period: "*Er hat sehr viel Talente, ist ein wahres Genie, und ein Mensch von Character, besitzt eine ausserordentlich lebhafte Einbildungskraft, daher er sich meistens in Bildern und Gleichnissen ausdrückt. Er pflegt auch selbst zu sagen, dass er sich immer uneigentlich audrücke, niemals eigentlich ausdrücken könne: wenn er aber älter werde, hoffe er die Gedanken selbst, wie sie wären, zu denken und zu sagen.*" (*Goethe und Werther. Briefe Goethe's*, A. Kestner, editor, Stuttgart and Augsburg, 1855.) Yeats read no German, but he may have encountered the passage in Lewes's famous *Life and Works of Goethe*, where Kestner's remarks were translated

most verbal sense, is true of the difference between Miss Tynan's first book and her second. In the first we have "The sun and his good knights" riding "Up the eastern field of the cloth of gold," and the dead spring "Like Elaine, with small dead hands on her resting heart," and many more such lines—the mind drawn off from the thing to the metaphor; while in the second the things themselves are often painted with passionate and careful fidelity, as in these lines from "The Sick Princess":—

> Outside, the peacocks on the terraces
>   Flash to the sun their green and purple eyes,
>   And doves are wheeling, and the dragon-flies;
> The garden all one bower of beauty is—
> So still, so still, the sun dreams in the blue,
>   A midday silence brooding over all;
>   The city's bells sound faint and musical—
> The leaves thirst for the dew.[5]

> The Roman de la Rose[6] lies on the ground,
>   Face downward, as she cast it yesterday;
>   Her palfrey calls with far, impatient neigh—
> Her hawk goes with his jesses still unbound—
> Though kites fly low, and trembling doves are mute.
>   Her needle rusts in her embroidery—
>   Her half-done missal fades, her paints run dry;[7]
> The string snaps[8] of her lute.

Not that the first method is not beautiful in its degree, but the second must ever be the main thing. This I say dogmatically, believing there are no two sides to the question; but the next criticism is a mere personal predilection possibly. I wish the sick princess ended differently, even though she were to die of some common sickness—of something, at any rate, not operatic and literary.[9] I object to the motive, not because it is fanciful, but because it is a kind of motive becoming more and more conventional.

"The metaphors of things" and "The things themselves!" There is

---

by Lewes as follows: "He has a great deal of talent, is a true genius and a man of character; possesses an extraordinarily vivid imagination, and hence generally expresses himself in images and similes. He often says, himself, that he always speaks figuratively, and can never express himself literally; but that when he is older he hopes to think and say the thought itself as it really is." (George Henry Lewes, *The Life and Works of Goethe*, Boston, 1856, p. 173, and many later editions.)

[5] *Shamrocks*' printing has no punctuation after "dew."
[6] *Shamrocks* reads "The Roman de la Rose."
[7] *Shamrocks* reads "paints are dry."   [8] *Shamrocks* reads "strings snap."
[9] In "The Sick Princess," the heroine runs away in peasant costume and recovers her health. At the ending which Yeats objected to, the princess and her lover, also in disguise, meet years later and go off into the enchanted forest to live in a fairy palace.

I imagine, this same difference in the religious poems, "the things themselves" becoming more numerous as time goes on. In the first, the religion of symbol and metaphor, as in "A Tired Heart," "The Two Way-farers," and "Faint Hearted;" in the second book, besides many poems in the first manner, like that rich and beautiful "Angel of the Annunciation":—

> *None saw as he passed their way;*
> *But the children paused in their play,*
> *And smiled as his feet went by;*
> *A bird sang clear from the nest,*
> *And a babe on its mother's breast*
> *Stretched hands with an eager cry.*
>
> *The women stood at*[10] *the well,*
> *Most grave, and the laughter fell,*
> *The chatter and gossip grew mute;*
> *They raised their hands to their eyes—*
> *Had the gold sun waxed in the skies?*
> *Was that the voice of a lute?*
>
> *All in the stillness and heat,*
> *The angel passed in*[11] *the street,*
> *Nor pausing nor looking behind,*
> *God's finger-touch on his lips;*
> *His great wings fire at the tips,*
> *His gold hair flame in the wind.*

may be found such mingling of earthly love and unearthly resignation as in the "Heart of a Mother," and such naive and ancient piety as "St. Francis to the Birds"—as I take it, the most faultless poem in the book. Be sure they will do more to give the mind a holy and temperate thought than a great number of poems of the symbols and metaphors of religion—of the "viols and lutes," and the "harp playing," and the "jasper gates."

W. B. Yeats

The Prose and Poetry of Wilfred Blunt

BY W. B. YEATS

This review of Wilfred Scawen Blunt's *Love Sonnets of Proteus*, London, 1885, appeared in *United Ireland*, January 28, 1888.

Wilfred Scawen Blunt (1840–1922), poet, horseman, and traveler, was a champion at various times in his life of the causes of nationalism in Egypt,

[10] *Shamrocks* reads "stood by." [11] *Shamrocks* reads "passed through."

India, and Ireland. In 1887 he became involved in that peasant agitation against absentee landlordism which he was later to call "the Land War in Ireland." As the result of holding a forbidden meeting in the West of Ireland, Blunt was arrested, tried, and sentenced to two months' imprisonment in Galway. While in prison, he wrote the sonnets which made up his volume *In Vinculis* (1889). His journal of this period served as the basis for his *Land War in Ireland* (1912).

To the nationalist journal *United Ireland*, Blunt was a martyr, and to the young Yeats he served as a model of heroic manhood rather than an example of poetic craftsmanship. The probable reprinting of Blunt's *Love Sonnets of Proteus* served as pretext for an article of more political than literary inspiration.

Yeats does not seem to have known Blunt at the time of this article. Lady Gregory, a lifelong friend of Blunt, introduced Yeats to Blunt on April 1, 1898. On that occasion, they talked of "the coming doom of England," and Yeats experimented magically upon Blunt, a performance which Blunt called "imperfect, not to say dull" (Blunt, *My Diaries*, London, 1919, Part One, pp. 358–59). Although Yeats included some poems of Blunt in his *Oxford Book of Modern Verse*, he implied in his introduction that he was not, in his youth, very familiar with Blunt's work:

To the generation which began to think and read in the late eighties of the last century the four poets whose work begins this book were unknown, or, if known, of an earlier generation that did not stir its sympathy. . . . [The four poets were Hopkins, Hardy, Bridges, and Blunt.] Wilfred Blunt one knew through the report of friends as a fashionable amateur who had sacrificed a capacity for literature and the visible arts to personal adventure. Some ten years had to pass before anybody understood that certain sonnets, lyrics, stanzas of his were permanent in our literature. (Introduction to *Oxford Book of Modern Verse*, pp. v–vi.)

The Yeats who wrote the above passage hardly remembered that he had written as a young man a review of Blunt's work in which Blunt appeared as anything but "a fashionable amateur." Those ten years which had to pass neatly spanned the period between this review and Yeats's first meeting with Blunt. It was, however, extravagant of Yeats to say that no one in the early nineties thought Blunt's work permanent. In 1891 William Morris printed at the Kelmscott Press a selection of Blunt's "Proteus" poems.

Yeats and Blunt became well acquainted after 1900. Blunt attended meetings of the Irish Literary Society in London as well as performances of Irish plays. In 1902 he finished a drama on an episode of the Cuchulain legend, *Fand of the Fair Cheek*. Yeats and Lady Gregory were enthusiastic about the play, but the performance which they promised never seemed to take place. Blunt had given up hope when, in 1907, he read an announcement that his play had been performed by the Abbey Players. He had been given no prior warning, and he remarked, "It is only in Ireland, I suppose, that a play could be performed for the first time and the author know nothing about it" (Edith Finch, *Wilfred Scawen Blunt, 1840–1922*, London, 1938, p. 317).

In 1914, on the occasion of Blunt's seventieth birthday, Yeats took part in a dinner of homage to him at which a peacock was served in full plumage and an address in verse form delivered by Ezra Pound.

MR. WILFRED BLUNT has asked for pen and paper that he may edit a volume of his poems[1]—believed to be the Love Sonnets of Proteus (1880), now out of print—a book as daring and unconventional as his own life of adventure; not with the self-conscious originality of so many modern books, but with the barbaric sincerity of one who has not time for conventions.

A Brahman philosopher[2] said once to the author of this—"I see in Europe members of society and members of professions, but no men." But here, in these Proteus sonnets at any rate are the poems of one who is man first, not even poet or thinker or artist first—scarcely artist at all unhappily. He writes always like a man of action—like one who is intent on living his life out.

They are so frank and personal—these sonnets—that the reader thinks more of the writer than the writing. The book was anonymous for three editions, but to the fourth[3] was added this preface—"No life is perfect that has not been lived—youth in feeling—manhood in battle—old age in meditation. Again, no life is perfect that is not sincere. For these reasons I have decided to add my name to the title-page."

Many of his best poems are not love poems at all, but lookings forward into that manhood to be spent in battle, and protests against that life of domestic ease and public indifference most men wish for, and against love itself.

" If I could live without the thought of death,
    Forgetful to Time's waste, the soul's decay,
I would not ask for other joy than breath,
    With light and sound of birds and the sun's ray.
I could sit on untroubled day by day
    Watching the grass grow and the wild flowers range
From blue to yellow and from red to gray
    In natural sequence as the seasons change.

[1] Blunt more likely asked for pen and paper to compose the sonnets which make up the collection *In Vinculis* (1889). The date of *Love Sonnets of Proteus* is given in reference works and studies of Blunt as 1880 and 1881.
[2] The Brahman philosopher was Babu Mohini Chatterji (so spelled by Hone and Madame Blavatsky), an Indian Theosophist whose visit to Dublin in 1885 was described by Yeats in "The Way of Wisdom," in the *Speaker*, April 14, 1900, an article reprinted as "The Pathway" in the eighth volume of Yeats's 1908 collected works. Yeats also wrote a poem about him, entitled "Mohini Chatterjee."
[3] The fourth edition of *Love Sonnets of Proteus* appeared in 1885.

> *I could afford to wait, but for the hurt*
> *Of this dull tick of time which chides my ear.*
> *But now I dare not sit with loins ungirt*
> *And staff unlifted, for Death stands too near.*
> *I must be up and doing—ay, each minute.*
> *The grave gives time for rest when we are in it."*

As in the writings of all strong natures, whether men of thought or men of action—of men of action more than any, perhaps—there is much melancholy, very different from the ignoble, self-pitying wretchedness—with a whimper in it—of feeble natures.

"Laughter and Death" is a fine contemplative sonnet without the false rhymes that mar so many of the others:—

> *" There is no laughter in the natural world*
> *Of beast or fish or bird, though no sad doubt*
> *Of their futility to them unfurled*
> *Has dared to check the mirth-compelling shout.*
> *The lion roars his solemn thunder out*
> *To the sleeping woods. The eagle screams her cry.*
> *Even the lark must strain a serious throat*
> *To hurl his blest defiance at the sky.*
> *Fear, anger, jealousy has found a voice—*
> *Love's pain or rapture the brute bosoms swell.*
> *Nature has symbols for her nobler joys,*
> *Her nobler sorrows. Who had dared fortell*
> *That only man, by some sad mockery,*
> *Should learn to laugh who learns that he must die."*

In 1874 was made the first of his many Arabian journeys. I know not to which these lines on the oasis of Sidikhaled must be referred:—

> *" How the earth burns! Each pebble under foot*
> *Is as a living thing with power to wound.*
> *The white sand quivers, and the footfall mute*
> *Of the slow camels strikes but gives no sound,*
> *As though they walked on flame, not solid ground.*
> *'Tis noon, and the beasts' shadows even have fled*
> *Back to their feet, and there is fire around.*
> *And fire beneath, and overhead the sun.*
> *Pitiful heaven! what is this we view?*
> *Tall trees, a river, pools, where swallows fly,*
> *Thickets of oleander where doves coo,*
> *Shades, deep as midnight, greenness for tired eyes—*
> *Hark, how the light winds in the palm-tops sigh—*
> *Oh, this is rest. Oh, this is paradise."*

On his third Arabian journey he was accompanied by Lady Blunt, who chronicled it in her "Bedouins of the Euphrates,"⁴ a most interesting book, wherein may be learned many things concerning the life and religion, or non-religion, of the Bedouins. How they do not believe in the immortality of the soul, because they never think of death, being always busy with matters of the moment. How they believe in God, and do not pray. How as a race they are brave, but do not reprove the coward. "God has not made me courageous," one will say.⁵ How they are virtuous without law;⁶ and acquire in old age a look of fierceness from contracting their eyebrows, because of the sun as they look out over the desert. Children of nature who age rapidly, but live their short lives without care or regret—taking everything in the day's work. In the "Sonnets of Proteus" they are addressed thus:

> *"Children of Shem. First born of Noah's race,*
> *But still for ever children; at the door*
> *Of Eden found, unconscious of disgrace,*
> *And loitering on, while all are gone before;*
> *Too proud to dig; too careless to be poor;*
> *Taking the gifts of God in thanklessness,*
> *Not rendering aught, nor supplicating more,*
> *Nor arguing with Him when He hides His face.*
> *Yours is the rain and sunshine, and the way*
> *Of an old wisdom by our world forgot,*
> *The courage of a day which knew not death.*
> *Well may we sons of Japhet in dismay*
> *Pause in our vain mad fight for life and breath,*
> *Beholding you I bow and reason not."*

1878–1879 were the years of the notable "Pilgrimage to Nejd," recorded in Lady Blunt's second book of travels.⁷ The motive was romantic. Mohammed, son to the chief of Palmyra—Soloman's "Tadmour in the Wilderness"⁸—had been their guide in the Euphrates expedition. On their return Mr. Blunt gave him his choice between a large sum of money or becoming, according to Bedouin custom, his brother. He chose the last. Now, this young Bedouin was the descen-

---

⁴ *Bedouin Tribes of the Euphrates*, by Lady Anne Blunt, "edited, with a preface and some account of the Arabs and their horses, by W.S.B., in two volumes," London, 1879.

⁵ Yeats misquotes. Lady Blunt wrote, " 'God has not given me courage,' they will sometimes say, 'and I do not fight,' just as an English hunting man will admit having 'lost his nerve' " (Vol. 2, pp. 202–03).

⁶ Lady Blunt did not claim that the Bedouins were virtuous without law. She rather said that they have a strict respect for their own tribal law, but none for European or Turkish law (Vol. 2, p. 205).

⁷ *A Pilgrimage to Nejd, The Cradle of the Arab Race*, two volumes, London, 1881.

⁸ In II Chron. 8:4, it is stated that Solomon founded Tadmor. The modern spelling, used by Lady Blunt, is Tudmur.

dant of one of three brothers who fled, during a time of political trouble
a hundred years before, on one camel from Nejd. The event was still
preserved in a popular Arabian ballad, the three brothers having been
great men in their day. One settled in the oasis of Jôf. The other two
quarrelled—one going one way, one the other. Mohammed's fore-
father settled in Palmyra and in the end became its chief. Then he
married a woman not of the noble or Bedouin blood like himself, but
one of the townspeople. Thereupon his descendants were looked down
upon. Bedouin fathers would not give them their daughters. They had
ceased to be thought of as nobles. This was a secret trouble to the
young Mohammed. Mr. Blunt offered in his capacity of brother to go
with him to Nejd and find a wife for him from his own relations if any
remained, and so redeem the race. After a long journey through places
unknown to Europe they reached Nejd, with its shepherd kings as in
Bible days. But word reaching them of a rising in Palmyra, the young
chief hurried home, where he was imprisoned by the Turkish authori-
tics on some charge or other. Mr. Blunt succeeding in getting him
released, however, and so acted out his part of brother.

After this journey the well-known Arabian articles began in the
"Nineteenth Century," and "The Fortnightly Review"—"The Sultan's
Heirs in Asia," "Recent Events in Arabia," and the notable series,
"The Future of Islam," with their continual cry against the Turk and
their showing how England put him on his legs again once upon a
time, and filled his wallet and sent him on his way with a blessing to
tyrannise and brutalise. But according to Mr. Blunt he is not to last
always. Cairo or Mecca is to be the Islamitish capital, and the Arab the
heir of the Tartar. Neither is Mahomedism a decaying power, but the
most living and growing thing in Asia. In "The Egyptian Revolution"[9]
he described the diplomacy that led up to the Egyptian War. This is
what he said of Arabi:[10]—

It was evident that he believed he had a mission to restore good Mussulman
government in his country. On the other hand, he was as evidently the
reverse of a fanatic. When informed that my wife, Lady Anne Blunt, who
was with me, was a granddaughter of Lord Byron the poet "who had fought
for the Greeks," he showed great interest and satisfaction, a sign by which I
judged him more than all else to have a true love of Liberty. Indeed, the
universal sympathy we have received from Mussulmans in Egypt, because we

9 "The Egyptian Revolution" appeared in the *Nineteenth Century*, September 1882, XII,
324-46. The following quotation is from p. 332.
10 Arabi Pasha (c. 1839–1910), Egyptian soldier-politician, led in 1881–1882 a revolt
against European rule in Egypt. He was defeated by the British at Tel-el-Kebir in September, 1882, and put on trial for rebellion, W. S. Blunt aided in his defense, and after pleading
guilty, Arabi was sentenced to exile in Ceylon for twenty years. He was pardoned and
returned to Egypt in 1901.

are connected with one who died in arms against the Turks, seems to me a most convincing proof of the national and liberal character of the movement.

And again:

He understands that broader Islam which existed before Mohammed, and the bond of a common worship of the one true God, which unites his own faith with that of Judaism and Christianity. I have but once heard this idea more clearly expressed. He disclaims all personal ambition, and there is no kind of doubt the army and the country are devoted to him. . . . Of his own position he speaks with modesty. 'I am,' he says, 'the representative of the army, because circumstances have made the army trust me; but the army is but the representative of the people, its guardian, till such time as the people shall no longer need it. At present, we are the sole National force standing between Egypt and its Turkish rulers. . . . We have won for the people their right to speak in the assembly of notables, and we keep the ground to prevent their being cajoled or frightened out of it. In this we work not for ourselves, but for our children and those who trust us.' 'We soldiers,' he once said to me, 'are for the moment in the position of those Arabs who answered the Caliph Omar, when in old age he asked the people whether they were satisfied with his rule, and whether he had walked straightly in the path of justice. 'Oh, son of El Khattab,' said they, 'thou hast, indeed, walked straightly, and we love thee; but thou knewest that we were at hand and ready, if thou hadst walked crookedly, to straighten thee with our swords.'[11]

It is still fresh in men's memory how he saved Arabi from probable shooting or hanging, paying £5,000 for his defence, if I remember rightly. Terrible disastrous wars, in which once more God was on the side of the big battalions—for a time. Meanwhile, the Right can but register its protest and its prophecy. He did both in an impassioned poem, "The Wind and the Whirlwind."[12]

[11] This passage, from pp. 332–33 of the *Fortnightly Review* article, was taken by Blunt from a letter written by him to Gladstone on December 20, 1881. Since Yeats made considerable alterations in this quotation, I give the original below: "He understands that broader Islam which existed before Mohammed, and the bond of a common worship of the one true God which unites his own faith with that of Judaism and Christianity. I have never but once heard this idea more clearly expressed. He disclaims, and I believe him, all personal ambition; and there is no kind of doubt that the army and the country are devoted to him. . . . Of his own position he speaks with modesty. 'I am,' he says, 'the representative of the army, because circumstances have made the army trust me; but the army itself is but the representative of the people, its guardian till such time as the people shall no longer need it. At present, we are the sole national force standing between Egypt and its Turkish rulers. . . . We have won for the people their right to speak in an assembly of notables, and we keep the ground to prevent their being cajoled or frightened out of it. In this we work not for ourselves but for our children, and for those who trust us.' 'We soldiers,' he once said to me, 'are for the moment in the position of those Arabs who answered the Caliph Omar, when in old age he asked the people whether they were satisfied with his rule, and whether he had walked straightly in the path of justice. 'O son of El Khattab,' said they, 'thou hast indeed walked straightly, and we love thee; but thou knewest that we were at hand and ready, if thou hadst walked crookedly, to straighten thee with our swords.' "

[12] Published in 1883.

In 1884 were printed in the "Fortnightly" his articles, "Ideas about India,"[13] being his statement of the grievances he found most complained against in that country, where it is officially stated that 40 per cent. of the natives go through life on insufficient food, and where, according to his calculations, the peasant of the Deccan pays 40 per cent off the produce in taxation, and where, to quote the "Ideas,"

It is a perpetual astonishment to travellers to note the scale of living of every Englishman employed in India, in however mean a capacity. The enormous palaces of governors and lieutenant-governors, their country houses, their residences in the hills, their banquets and entertainments, their retinues of servants, their carriages and horses, their special trains on their journeyings, their tents, their armies of retainers and camp followers—these are only samples of the universal profusion; an equally noble hospitality reigns in every bungalow on the plains; and endless dinners of imported delicacies, with libations of imported wines, tempt, night after night, the inhabitants of the most solitary stations to forget the dismal fact that they are in Asia, and far from their own land.[14]

The Viceroy during Mr. Blunt's visit was Lord Ripon;[15] in the light of whose Irish action it is interesting to know how they thought of him in that perhaps other Ireland:—

No Viceroy, [says Mr. Blunt,] Lord Canning possibly excepted, ever enjoyed such popularity as Lord Ripon did in the early part of last winter. Wherever I went in India I heard the same story—from the poor peasants of the South, who for the first time, perhaps, had learned the individual name of the ruler; from the high caste Brahamans of Madras and Bombay; the Calcutta students; from the Mohammedan divines of Lucknow; from the noblemen of Delhi and Hyderabad; everywhere his praise was in all men's mouths, and moved the people to surprise and gratitude. 'He is an honest man,' one said, 'and one who fears God.'[16]

[13] His series, "Ideas about India," was published in the *Fortnightly Review* in five parts: (1) "The Agricultural Danger," (2) "Race Hatred," (3) "The Mohammedan Question," (4) "The Native States," and (5) "The Future of Self-Government."
[14] This passage is from "The Agricultural Danger," in the *Fortnightly Review*, 1884, XLII, N.S. XXXVI, 175.
[15] George Frederick Samuel Robinson, 1st Marquess of Ripon (1827–1909), served as Viceroy of India from 1880 to 1884. What Yeats called his "Irish action" was Lord Ripon's contribution as Lord President of the Council during the first Gladstone ministry (1868–1874) to the disestablishment of the Anglican Church of Ireland and the enactment of an Irish land bill.
[16] "Race Hatred," *Fortnightly Review*, 1884, XLII, N.S. XXXVI, 454–55. Yeats changed this passage considerably. The original is as follows: "No Viceroy, Lord Canning possibly excepted, ever enjoyed such popularity as Lord Ripon did in the early part of last winter. Wherever I went in India I heard the same story; from the poor peasants of the south who for the first time had learned the individual name of the ruler, from the high caste Brahmins of Madras and Bombay; from the Calcutta students; from the Mohammedan divines of Lucknow; from the noblemen of Delhi and Hyderabad, everywhere his praise was in all men's mouths, and moved the people to surprise and gratitude. 'He is an honest man,' men said, 'and one who fears God.'"

But from the officials, it seems, he earned a hatred in equal measure. In Hyderabad, a protected State, there had been going on among the English officials, to quote the "Ideas" again, a general scramble at the expense of the Treasury. Lord Ripon announced his intention of investigating the matter in person.

There was a scare of cholera raised and the Viceroy's camp was fixed twelve miles from the city. It was given out that the Viceroy wished to see no one, and a kind of quarantine cordon was established. The camp itself was put in the enemy's keeping, and intimidation was to my knowledge used to prevent the Nizam speaking all his mind, and a huge body of officials surrounded the Viceroy day and night.[17]

Nevertheless the Viceroy did get to the bottom of the matter, and made that part of the Empire a little cleaner any way—washed that particular sucker of the octopus somewhat.

Irish Fairies, Ghosts, Witches, etc.

This article is a relic of Yeats's association with Madame Blavatsky's London Theosophical Society. It appeared in the theosophical magazine *Lucifer* in the issue dated January 15, 1889. The work was unpaid and the sequel promised at the end of this article never appeared. By the end of 1890, Yeats was asked to resign from the inner circle of the Theosophical Society because he wrote in another magazine articles critical of *Lucifer*.
   This discussion is the closest Yeats ever came to "explaining" the Irish fairies. The explanation is here theosophical, not scientific in the skeptical, rationalizing sense. The information Yeats gave in this article parallels closely the introductory material in Yeats's compilation *Irish Fairy and Irish Folk Tales*.

I T has occurred to me that it would be interesting if some spiritualist or occultist would try to explain the various curious and intricate spiritualistic beliefs of peasants. When reading Irish folk-lore, or listening to Irish peasants telling their tales of magic and fairyism and witchcraft, more and more is one convinced that some clue there must be. Even if it is all dreaming, why have they dreamed this particular dream? Clearly the occultist should have his say as well as the folk-

---

[17] "The Native States," *Fortnightly Review*, 1885, XLIII, N.S. XXXVII, 247.

lorist. The history of a belief is not enough, one would gladly hear about its cause.

Here and there an occult clue is visible plainly. Some of the beliefs about ghosts are theosophical; the Irish ghost or *thivish*, for instance, is merely an earth-bound shell, fading and whimpering in the places it loved. And many writers, from Paracelsus to d'Assier,[1] have shed a somewhat smoky light on witches and their works, and Irish witches do not differ much from their tribe elsewhere, except in being rather more harmless. Perhaps never being burnt or persecuted has lessened the bitterness of their war against mankind, for in Ireland they have had on the whole, a very peaceable and quiet time, disappearing altogether from public life since the "loyal minority" pilloried and imprisoned three and knocked out the eye of one with a cabbage stump, in 1711, in the town of Carrickfergus.[2] For many a long year now have they contented themselves with going out in the grey of the morning, in the shape of hares, and sucking dry their neighbour's cows, or muttering spells while they skimmed with the severed hand of a corpse the surface of a well gathering thereon a neighbour's butter.

It is when we come to the fairies and "fairy doctors," we feel most the want of some clue—some light, no matter how smoky. These "fairy doctors," are they mediums or clairvoyants? Why do they fear the hazel tree, or hold an ash tree in their hands when they pray? Why do they say that if you knock once at their doors they will not open, for you may be a spirit, but if you knock three times they will open. What are these figures, now little, now great, now kindly, now fierce, now ugly, now beautiful, who are said to surround them—these fairies, whom they never confuse with spirits, but describe as fighting with the spirits though generally having the worst of it, for their enemies are more God-fearing? Can any spiritualist or occultist tell us of these things? Hoping they can, I set down here this classification of Irish fairyism and demonology. The mediaeval divisions of sylphs, gnomes, undines and salamanders will not be found to help us. This is a different dynasty.

FAIRY DOCTORS

Unlike the witch, who deals with ghosts and spirits, the fairy doctor is never malignant; at worst, he is mischievous like his masters and

[1] Adolphe d'Assier, author of *Essai sur l'humanité posthume et le spiritisme, par un positiviste*, Paris, 1883. (English translation by H. S. Olcott: *Posthumous Humanity, A Study of Phantoms*, London, 1887.)

[2] Yeats wrote an article on the contrast between Irish and Scots treatment of witches which he reprinted in *The Celtic Twilight* as "A Remonstrance with Scotsmen for having Soured the disposition of their Ghosts and Faeries."

servants the fairies. Croker,[3] in the "Confessions of Tom Bourke," said by Keightly,[4] of the "Fairy Mythology," to be the most valuable chapter in all his writings, describes the sayings and doings of such a man. Each family has its particular adherent among the "good people," as the fairies are called, and sometimes when a man died the factions of his father and mother would fight as to the grave-yard he was to be buried in, the relations delaying the funeral until Tom Bourke told them one party or other had won. If they buried in the wrong grave-yard all kinds of ill luck would follow, for fairies know how to kill cattle with their fairy darts, and do all kinds of mischief.

The fairy doctor is great with herbs and spells. He can make the fairies give up people they have carried off, and is in every way the opposite of the witch.

Lady Wilde,[5] in her "Ancient Legends," thus describes one who lived in the Island of Innis-Sark: "He can heal diseases by a word, even at a distance, and his glance sees into the very heart and reads the secret thoughts of men. He never touched beer, spirits or meat in all his life, but has lived entirely on bread, fruit, and vegetables. A man who knew him thus describes him: Winter and summer his dress is the same, merely a flannel shirt and coat. He will pay his share at a feast, but neither eats nor drinks of the food and drink set before him. He speaks no English, and never could be made to learn the English tongue, though he says it might be used with great effect to curse one's enemy. He holds a burial-ground sacred, and would not carry away so much as a leaf of ivy from a grave; and he maintains that the people are right in keeping to their ancient usages—such as never to dig a grave on a Monday, and to carry the coffin three times round the grave, following the course of the sun, for then the dead rest in peace. Like the people, also, he holds suicides accursed;[6] for they believe that all the dead who have been recently buried turn over on their faces if a suicide is laid amongst them.

"Though well off, he never, even in his youth, thought of taking a wife, nor was he ever known to love a woman. He stands quite apart from life, and by this means holds his power over the mysteries. No money will tempt him to impart this knowledge to another, for if he did he would be struck dead, so he believes. He would not touch a hazel

---

[3] Thomas Crofton Croker (1798–1854) compiled *Fairy Legends and Traditions of the South of Ireland*, three volumes, London, 1826–1828.

[4] Thomas Keightly (1789–1872) helped Croker edit *Fairy Legends*. Keightly published his *Fairy Mythology* anonymously in 1828.

[5] Jane Francesca, Lady Wilde (1826–1896) was the mother of Oscar Wilde and an author of note in her own right. Her *Ancient Legends, Mystic Charms and Superstitions of Ireland*, London, 1887, was followed by *Ancient Cures, Charms and Usages of Ireland*, London, 1890, a book which Yeats reviewed favorably.

[6] *suicides accursed*: Lady Wilde reads "suicides as accurst."

stick, but carries an ash wand, which he holds in his hand when he prays, laid across his knees, and the whole of his life is given[7] to works of grace and charity.

"Though an old man,[8] he has never had a day's sickness; no one has ever seen him in a rage, nor heard an angry word from his lips but once, and then, being under great irritation, he recited the Lord's Prayer backwards as an imprecation on his enemy. Before his death he will reveal the mystery of his power, but not till the hand of death is on him for certain," and then we may be sure he will reveal it only to his successor.

THE SOCIABLE FAIRIES

These are the Sheogues[9] (Ir. *Sidheog*, "a little fairy,"), and are usually of small size when first seen, though seeming of common human height when you are once glamoured. It sometimes appears as if they could take any shape according to their whim. Commonly, they go about in troops, and are kind to the kindly and mischievous to the evil and ill-tempered, being like beautiful children, having every charm but that of conscience—consistency.

Their divisions are sheogue, a land fairy, and merrow Ir. *moruadh*,[10] or "sea maid" (the masculine is unknown), a water fairy. The merrow is said not to be uncommon. I asked a peasant woman once whether the fishermen of her village ever saw one. "Indeed, they don't like to see them at all," she answered, "for they always bring bad weather." Sometimes the merrows come out of the sea in the shape of little, hornless cows. When in their own shape, they have fish tails and wear a red cap usually covered with feathers, called a *cohullen druith*. The men among them have green teeth, green hair, pigs' eyes and red noses, but their women are beautiful, and sometimes prefer handsome fishermen to their green-haired lovers. Near Bantry, in the last century, lived a woman covered with scales like a fish, who was descended from such a marriage.

All over Ireland are little fields circled by ditches, and supposed to be ancient fortifications and sheep folds. These are the raths or forts. Here, marrying and giving in marriage, live the land fairies. Many a mortal have they enticed down into their dim world. Many more have listened to their fairy music, till all human cares and joys drifted from their hearts, and they became great fairy doctors, or great musicians, or poets like Carolan,[11] who gathered his tunes while sleeping on a fairy rath; or else they died in a year and a day, to live ever after among the fairies.

---

[7] *given*: Lady Wilde reads "devoted."
[8] *Though an old man*: Lady Wilde reads "Though now an old man."
[9] Throughout this article *Lucifer* (indeed!) spelled this word "sheoques."
[10] *Lucifer* printing had read *moruada*. Yeats corrected it in a clipping in MS 12147 (National Library of Ireland).   [11] Turlogh Carolan (1670–1738), called the "Last of the Bards."

These sociable fairies are in the main good, but one most malicious habit have they—a habit worthy of a witch. They steal children, and leave a withered fairy a thousand, or may be two thousand years old, for the matter of that, instead. Two or three years ago a man wrote to one of the Irish papers, telling of a case in his own village, and how the parish priest made the fairies deliver up again the stolen child.

At times full grown men and women have been carried off. Near the village of Ballisodare, Sligo, I have been told, lives an old woman who was taken in her youth. When she came home, at the end of seven years, she had no toes, for she had danced them off.

Especially do they steal men, women and children on May eve, Midsummer eve, and November eve, for these are their festivities.

On May eve, every seventh year, they fight for the harvest, for the best ears of corn belong to them. An old man told me he saw them fighting once. They tore the thatch off a house in the battle. Had you or I been there we had merely felt a great wind blowing; the peasantry know better than to mistake the fairies for the wind. When a little whirlwind passes, lifting the straws, they take off their hats and say: "God bless them," for the fairies are going by.

On Midsummer eve, Bonfire Night, as we call it, the sheogues are very gay, and on this night more than any other do they steal beautiful mortals to be their brides.

On November eve, according to the old Gaelic reckoning the first night of winter, the fairies are very gloomy, and in their green raths dance with the ghosts, while abroad in the world witches make their spells, and a solitary and wicked fairy, called the Pooka, has power, and girls set tables with food in the name of the devil, that the fetch of their future lovers may come through the window and eat.

The sociable fairies are very quarrelsome.

Lady Wilde tells about one battle in which, no stones being at hand, they stole butter and flung it at each other. A quantity stuck in the branches of an alder-tree. A man in the neighbourhood mended the handle of the dash of his churn with a branch of this tree. As soon as he began churning, the butter, until now hanging invisible in the alder branches, flowed into his churn. The same happened every churning-day, until he told the matter to a fairy doctor, which telling broke the spell, for all these things have to be kept secret.

Kennedy describes a battle heard by a peasant of his acquaintance. The sheogues were in the air over a river. He heard shots and light bodies falling into the water, and a faint sound of shouting, but could see nothing. Old Patrick Kennedy,[12] who records this, was a second-hand bookseller in Dublin, and claimed in one of his works to know

---

[12] Patrick Kennedy (1801–1873), author of *Legendary Fictions of the Irish Celts*.

spells for making the fairies visible, but would not tell them for fear they might set dangerous forces in action—forces that might destroy the user of the spell. These battles are often described by Irish fairy seers. Sometimes the sociable sheogues, dressed in green coats, fight with the solitary red-coated fairies.

THE SOLITARY FAIRIES

The best known of these is the Lepracaun (Ir. *Leith bhrogan, i.e.,* the "one shoe maker")[.] He is seen sitting under a hedge mending a shoe, and one who catches him and keeps his eyes on him can make him deliver up his crocks of gold, for he is a rich miser; but if he takes his eyes off him, the creature vanishes like smoke. He is said to be the child of a spirit and a debased fairy, and, according to MacNally,[13] wears a red coat with seven rows of buttons, seven buttons in each row, and a cocked hat, on the point of which he sometimes spins like a top.

Some writers have supposed the Cluricaun to be another name of the same fairy, given him when he has laid aside his shoe-making at night and goes on the spree. The Cluricaun's one occupation is robbing wine-cellars.

The Gonconer or Gancanagh (Ir. *Gean-canagh i.e.,* "Love talker")[14] is a little creature of the Lepracaun type, unlike him, however, in being an idler. He always appears with a pipe in his mouth in lonely valleys, where he makes love to shepherdesses and milkmaids.

The Far Darrig (Ir. *Fear-Dearg i.e.,* red man) plays practical jokes continually. A favourite trick is to make some poor mortal tramp over hedges and ditches, carrying a corpse on his back, or to make him turn it on a spit. Of all these solitary, and mainly evil, fairies there is no more lubberly wretch than this same Far Darrig. Like the next phantom, he presides over evil dreams.

The Pooka seems to be of the family of the nightmare. He has most likely never appeared in human form, the one or two recorded instances being probably mistakes, he being mixed up with the Far Darrig. His shape is that of a horse, a bull, goat, eagle, ass and perhaps of a black dog, though this last may be a separate spirit. The Pooka's delight is to get a rider, whom he rushes with through ditches and rivers and over mountains, and shakes off in the grey of the morning. Especially does he love to plague a drunkard—a drunkard's sleep is his kingdom.

The Dullahan is another gruesome phantom. He has no head, or

[13] David Rice McAnally, whose name Yeats spelled variously, was the author of *Irish Wonders,* Boston, 1888.
[14] Yeats's short novel *John Sherman* was published in 1891 under the pseudonym "Ganconagh."

carries it under his arm. Often he is seen driving a black coach, called the coach-a-bower (Ir. *Coise-bodhar*), drawn by headless horses. It will rumble to your door, and if you open to it, a basin of blood is thrown in your face. To the houses where it pauses it is an omen of death. Such a coach, not very long ago, went through Sligo in the grey of the morning (the spirit hour). A seaman saw it, with many shudderings. In some villages its rumbling is heard many times in the year.

The Leanhaun Shee (fairy mistress) seeks the love of men. If they refuse, she is their slave; if they consent, they are hers, and can only escape by finding one to take their place. Her lovers waste away, for she lives on their life. Most of the Gaelic poets, down to quite recent times, have had a Leanhaun Shee, for she gives inspiration to her slaves. She is the Gaelic muse, this malignant fairy. Her lovers, the Gaelic poets, died young. She grew restless, and carried them away to other worlds, for death does not destroy her power.

Besides these, we have other solitary fairies, such as the House Spirit and Water Sheerie, a kind of Will-o'-the-Wisp, and various animal spirits, such as the Anghiska, the water-horse, and the Pastha (*Piast bestea*)[15] the lake dragon, a guardian of hidden treasure, and two fairies, the Far-gorta and the Banshee, who are technically solitary fairies, though quite unlike their fellows in disposition.

The Far-gorta (man of hunger) is an emaciated fairy that goes through the land in famine time, begging, and bringing good luck to the giver of alms.

The Banshee (*Bean-sidhe*) seems to be one of the sociable fairies grown solitary through the sorrow or the triumph of the moment; her name merely means woman-fairy, answering to the less common word Farshee [*Fear-sidhe*], man fairy. She wails, as most people know, over the death of some member of an old Irish family. Sometimes she is an enemy of the house, and wails with triumph; sometimes a friend, and wails with sorrow. When more than one Banshee comes to cry, the man or woman who is dying must have been very holy or very brave. Occasionally she is undoubtedly believed to be one of the sociable fairies. Cleena, once an ancient Irish goddess, is now a Munster sheogue.

O'Donovan,[16] one of the very greatest of the Irish antiquarians, wrote in 1849 to a friend, who quoted his words in the Dublin University Magazine: "When my grandfather died in Leinster, in 1798, Cleena came all the way from Tonn Cleena, at Glandore, to lament him; but she has not been heard ever since lamenting any of our race, though I

---

[15] *Lucifer* printing had read "(*Piast-vestea*)." Yeats corrected it in a clipping in MS 12147 (National Library of Ireland).
[16] John O'Donovan (1809–1861) edited *The Annals of the Four Masters*, in seven volumes, 1848–1851.

believe she still weeps in the mountains of Drumaleaque in her own country, where so many of the race of Eoghan More are dying of starvation."

The Banshee who cries with triumph is often believed to be no fairy, but the ghost of one wronged by an ancestor of the dying. Besides these are various fairies who fall into none of the regular groups, such as "Dark Joan of the Boyne." This fairy visits houses in the form of a hen with a lot of chickens, or a pig with a litter of banyans. Several now living say thay have fought with this fairy pig. This taking the appearance of several animals at one time is curious, and brings to mind how completely a matter of whim, or symbolism the form of an enchanted being must be thought. Indeed, the shape of Irish fairies seems to change with their moods—symbolizing or following the feelings of the moment.

When we look for the source of this spirit rabble, we get many different answers. The peasants say they are fallen angels who were too good to be lost, too bad to be saved, and have to work out their time in barren places of the earth. An old Irish authority—the Book of Armagh[17]—calls them gods of the earth, and quite beyond any kind of doubt many of them were long ago gods in Ireland.

Once upon a time the Celtic nations worshipped gods of the light, called in Ireland Tuath-de-Danan and corresponding to Jupiter and his fellows, and gods of the great darkness corresponding to the Saturnian Titans.[18] Among the sociable fairies are many of the light gods; perhaps, some day, we may learn to look for the dark gods among the solitary fairies. The Pooka we can trace, a mysterious deity of decay, to earliest times. Certainly, he is no bright Tuath-de-Danan. Around him hangs the dark vapour of Domnian[19] Titanism.

W. B. Yeats

(To be continued.)[20]

---

[17] The Book of Armagh is a manuscript book compiled during the late eighth and early ninth century and contains many writings concerning Saint Patrick.

[18] Yeats's authorities for this parallel between Greek and Celtic mythology were John Rhys in his *Lectures on the Origin and Growth of Religion as Illustrated by Celtic Heathendom*, London, 1888, and Henri D'Arbois de Jubainville's *Le Cycle Mythologique Irlandais et la Mythologie Celtique*, Paris, 1884.

[19] "Domnian" from "Domnu," whom Rhys identified as the goddess of the deep. Her sons, the "Fir Domnann" along with other Titans—the Firbolgs, the Formorians—war with the Tuatha de Danaan, the gods of light.

[20] The sequel to this article never appeared.

Irish Wonders

David Rice McAnally Jr.'s book, *Irish Wonders, The Ghosts, Giants, Pookas, Demons, Leprechawns, Banshees, Fairies, Witches, Widows, Old Maids and Other Marvels of the Emerald Isle*, Boston and New York, 1888, was reviewed by Yeats in two journals. Aside from the review below, printed in the *Scots Observer* of March 30, 1889 (not 1890 as stated by Allan Wade in his Yeats bibliography), Yeats wrote an article on McAnally's book for the *Providence Sunday Journal* of July 7, 1889 (reprinted in *Letters to the New Island*, edited by Horace Reynolds in 1934). Yeats's American review was rather more severe on McAnally's "stage-Irish" language than his English one. Both reviews repeat the same stories from McAnally—the fairy ball and Darby O'Hooligan whose wife returns to the land of fairy. The two reviews, however, are by no means identical.

The previous summer, during Yeats's compilation of his own *Fairy and Folk Tales of the Irish Peasantry*, he had gone to considerable trouble to locate *Irish Wonders* in the hope of using some of its material. Some of the severity of Yeats's review may have stemmed from his disappointment when he finally located the book. It is a cloying example of Blarney Stone Irish, hardly improved by trite, comic illustrations. Whatever Yeats's reservations about McAnally's methods, the author of *Irish Wonders* was included in Yeats's list of authorities on Irish folklore at the end of *Fairy and Folk Tales of the Irish Peasantry*.

A clipping of this anonymous review is contained in MS 12147 (National Library of Ireland) along with other Yeats articles, some of them corrected in the author's hand. It was reprinted by Horace Reynolds in January, 1942, in *The Tuftonian*, magazine of Tufts College, Medford, Massachusetts, with a note explaining why Reynolds then thought it to be Yeats's work.

I N the matter of folk-tales, the scientific-minded wish for the very words they are told in. Others would allow some equivalent for the lost gesture, local allusions, and quaint manners of the story-tellers— some concentrating of humour and dialect. They consider that a folk-tale told by Carleton[1] gives a truer impression of what it sounds like when some old voice is reciting in the turf smoke, than any word-for-word version. Carleton has never added anything untrue, anything incongruous: no other man ever knew the Irish peasantry as he did; none other ever touched Irish folk-lore with like genius. But because

---

[1] William Carleton (1794–1869), Irish novelist and storyteller, whose *Traits and Stories of the Irish Peasantry* served Yeats well as source for his folklore compilation. Yeats published in 1889 a collection of *Stories from Carleton*, and in October, 1889, he reviewed Carleton's *Red-Haired Man's Wife* for the *Scots Observer* (see pp. 141–46).

genius is justified of all her children, that does not prove Mr. M'Anally[2] right in leaving the accurate, reverent way, to dress up his fine tales in a poor slatternly patchwork of inaccurate dialect and sham picturesqueness. Had he told them word for word, or even in common literary English, he might have produced a book that students would turn to for years to come. Instead, he has made his whole work smack of the tourist's car. The dialects of north and south, and east and west, are all rolled into one ridiculous mixture. Why, the village children in Ireland laugh at the speech of the next county, almost at that of the next village. Mr. M'Anally is an Irish-American. In his feelings for the old country there is a touch of genuine poetry. But the Ireland he loves is not the real Ireland: it is the false Ireland of sentiment. He strains to make everything humorous, according to the old convention, pretty according to the old prepossession. From his desperate search for the pretty and humorous, he has brought home some strange baggage. He fathers, or rather mothers, the following on a 'knowledgable woman' of Coloney, Sligo. The matter discussed is a fairy ball, 'seen by her grandmother's aunt': 'It was the 'cutest sight alive. There was a place for thim to shtand on, an' a wondherful big fiddle av the size ye cud slape in it, that was played be a monsthrous frog, an' two little fiddles that two kittens fiddled on, an' two big drums baten be cats, an' two trumpets, played be fat pigs. All round the fairies were dancin' like angels, the fire-flies givin' thim light to see by, an' the moon-bames shinin' on the lake, for it was be the shore it was; an' if ye don't belave it, the glen's still there, that they call the Fairy Glen to this blessed day.'

The writer of this article, though he has not gathered folk-tales in Coloney, has done so within two miles of it, as well as reading most, if not all, recorded Irish fairy tales, but never has he heard anything like this. Even if the fire-fly were forgiven, this would remain the worst-invented piece of folk-lore on record. These fiddling and trumpeting beasts are quite alien to Celtic myth; for Celtic fairies are much like common men and women. Often the fairy-seer meets with them on some lonely road, and joins in their dance, and listens to their music; and does not know what people they are till the whole company melts away into shadow and night. On those occasions when it pleases them to take on diminutive size, and so be known at once, they are still, in well-nigh all their works and ways, like human beings. This fiddling fancy may be German; good Celtic it cannot be. The whole surroundings of the *deenee shee* (fairy people) are simple and matter-of-fact. The peasant credits them with what he himself admires. 'They have,' said

---

[2] *M'Anally*: This name is usually spelled McAnally, but here as elsewhere in the review it was given as "M'Anally."

one old peasant to the writer, 'the most beautiful parlours and drawing-
rooms.' By saying it was the poor 'knowledgable woman's' grandmother's aunt that saw the fiddling, Mr. M'Anally means, we suppose,
to suggest the old calumny that nobody but somebody's distant relation
ever saw a spirit. There is probably not a village in Ireland where a
fairy-seer or two may not be found. As to the last sentence of Mr.
M'Anally's amusing nine lines, there is, of course, not a peasant in
Ireland who would use such an argument.

It is sincerely to be regretted that Mr. M'Anally has not the convincing art: one often really wishes to believe him, as in the leprechawn
chapter—the most full of detail of anything ever written about that
goblin shoemaker.[3] It sounds for the most part like honest folk-lore; but
then that fire-fly! There is one tale in the chapter too good, however,
to have been changed in any essential. There was a child who was
stolen at birth by the fairies of Lough Erne. When she began to grow
up, they gave her a dance every night down under the lake. The queen
meant to find her a good husband among the fairies, but she fell in love
with an old leprechawn. Thereupon the queen, 'to circumvent her,'
gave her leave to walk on the shore of the lake, where she met Darby
O'Hoolighan, and loved him. They married, and the queen gave them
cattle and household things, but told her to tell her husband she would
return to the fairies if he struck her three blows. For seventeen years
they lived happily, and had two big sons. At last, one day they were
going to a wedding, and she was very slow. Darby struck her on the
shoulder with his hand, and she began to cry, and said it was the first
of the three blows. A year later he was teaching his boy to use a
shillaly, and she got behind and was struck. That was the second blow.
'Divil take the stick,' he cried, and flung it against the wall. The stick
bounced back and struck her, and made the third blow. She kissed her
sons, and went and called the cows in the fields, and they quit grazing
and followed her; and the oxen in the stalls heard her, and stopped
eating and followed. She spoke to the calf they had killed that morning,
and it came down from where it was hanging in the yard and followed
her. The lamb that was killed the day before, and the pigs that were
salted and hung up to dry, went after her in a string. Next she called the
things in the house. The chairs and tables, and the chest of drawers, and
the boxes, and the pots and pans and grid-irons, and buckets, and
noggins, all put out legs 'like bastes,' and walked after her; and the
house was left bare and empty. They came to the edge of the lake, and
all went under, down again to fairy-land. After this she used sometimes
to come close to the shore to see her two sons. One day there was seen

---

[3] Yeats gave some of McAnally's information on leprechauns as authoritative in his notes
to *Fairy and Folk Tales of the Irish Peasantry*.

'a little atomy of a man along wid her, that was a leprechawn'; therefore it got about that the real reason she left her husband was to get
back to the old leprechawn she was in love with before she married
Darby.

Mr. M'Anally's stories are nearly all good in themselves. His sentences, too, have often an Irish turn in them, though the pronunciation
is written anyhow. It is mainly his isolated assertions that trouble. He
says the most momentous things in the most jaunty, careless way. He
tells us, for instance, that, of the spirits of the bad, 'some are chained at
the bottom of the lakes, others buried under ground, others confined
in mountain gorges; some hang on the sides of precipices, others are
transfixed on the tree-tops, while others haunt the houses of their
ancestors: all waiting till the penance has been endured, and the hour
of release arrives.' There is a fine gloomy suggestion about the ghosts
swinging on the tree-tops which we feel sure that Mr. M'Anally has
honestly reported. But why is there not some authority reverently
given for so strange a thing? In what part of Ireland was it said, this
saying recalling *Mahabharata* and *Divine Comedy*?[4] We believe it to be
honest folk-lore and defy that shining insect circling and flickering
before us, anxious to remind us of another name for the God of Flies.[5]

William Carleton

This review of Yeats's compilation *Stories from Carleton*, London, 1889, and
William Carleton's *The Red-Haired Man's Wife*, Dublin, 1889, appeared in
the *Scots Observer*, October 19, 1889.

Although this review was printed anonymously, the style and opinions of
the reviewer mark it as Yeats's as well as does the evidence of a letter of Yeats
to Katherine Tynan on April 21, 1889: "The *Scots Observer* people have asked

[4] *Mahabharata and Divine Comedy*: the *Mahabharata*, an Indian epic poem of great length,
is one of the chief sources for Vedic myth. It is best known in one of its parts, the *Bagavad-
Gita*. Yeats was probably referring generally to the Hindu doctrine of reincarnation. See
his poem, "Fergus and the Druid":
> . . . *I have been many things—*
> *A green drop in the surge, a gleam of light*
> *Upon a sword, a fir-tree on a hill.* . . .
The Dante reference is to Canto 13 of the *Inferno*, where the souls of suicides are imprisoned
within trees.

[5] Another name for the God of the Flies is Beelzebub, which is literally translated as
"lord of the flies." The *O.E.D.* gives as a definition of "fly"—"a familiar demon."

me to write an article on him [Carleton] apropos of the *Red-Haired Man's Wife*, the posthumous tale of his discovered somewhere and printed the other day by Sealy, Bryers & Walker" (*Letters*, p. 121; see also a letter to Fr. Matthew Russell of July 13, 1889, in *Letters*, p. 129).

Somewhat incoherent as a review, this article was more a product of Yeats's current interests than a critical examination of the works at hand. Yeats was then in the midst of an extensive reading of Carleton's works, an effort which was to supply him with short excerpts for his *Fairy and Folk Tales* book as well as his two volumes of *Representative Irish Tales*, and all the materials for his *Stories from Carleton* (1889).

The few sentences noticing his *Stories from Carleton* at the beginning of the review were probably not by Yeats. Even if they were, their tone is too perfunctory to consist of self-praise. The body of the article consists of opinions which closely parallel his introduction to his Carleton selection. To save editor from embarrassment, he had rushed through his introduction to his *Stories from Carleton*. He therefore must have welcomed the opportunity for a more leisurely exposition of his ideas.

His advocacy of Carleton, who had turned from Catholicism to the Church of Ireland early in life, got Yeats into difficulties in Ireland. As in so many other instances in his life, Yeats's universalist notions about religion led him to underestimate the force of Irish sectarian prejudice. Yeats had to defend Carleton's religion even to the liberal Fr. Matthew Russell, S.J., the editor of the *Catholic Monthly* (*Letters*, pp. 130–31). The *Nation* of Dublin, in reviewing Yeats's selection, called Carleton a "renegade" to be placed in the "literary pillory" for his stories attacking Catholic rites and practices. Yeats replied in a strongly worded letter of January 11, 1890, that in his works taken as a whole Carleton showed a predominant affection for the church of his fathers (see pp. 116–69). When Carleton's autobiography was published in 1896, Yeats reviewed it for the *Bookman* in March, 1896 (see pp. 394–97).

Like many other of Yeats's early passions, his admiration for Carleton waned quickly. In a copy of *Stories from Carleton*, presented to John Quinn in 1904, he wrote, "I thought no end of Carleton in those days & would still I dare say if I had not forgotten him" (quoted in Allan Wade's *A Bibliography of the Writings of W. B. Yeats*, London, 1958, p. 220).

OF Mr. Yeats's selection from Carleton's *Traits and Stories* it will be enough to say that it is good and representative, and that the prefatory matter is judicious and well written. Of the second number on our list, it is proper to note that, the last of Carleton's novels, it was published a few years ago—(do the publishers know this?)—in the *Carlow College Magazine*, under the editorship of that Father Kavanagh who was killed by the fall of an image while celebrating mass, after a series of incidents that made the awe-struck peasantry see in his death an event unearthly and tremendous. It is at last re-issued in a flaring red cover. From the preface about a 'serious mishap' and 'a literary

friend,' and from internal evidence, we gather that only a portion is by
Carleton; the first two-thirds are his any way. It is not possible to
determine the line of cleavage, for never was Carleton so little like
himself and so like a score of others, and the *Carlow College Magazine* is
long dead and vanished even from the book-stalls;[1] and when he wrote
he was old and feeble. Once he apologises for his many repetitions by
saying he has passed his seventieth year, and that old men love to be
repeating. The manner is all the more pathetic in its feebleness from
the whimsical Carletonian matter. There was a family of peasants who
never could make up their minds; they decided everything by a toss-up.
The had of the family head settled the amount of dowry he got with his
wife by 'heads or harps,' and when he died he left his land to be tossed
for by his two sons. His strong-souled wife, who always knew her own
mind, had made him very miserable; so his son was to avenge his father
on all women-kind. This son became a haunter of fairs on the look-out
for hearts to trouble; and, being good-looking and supposed to be
rich, found many. He was nicknamed 'Sthagan Varagy,' or 'The Market
Stroller,' and a Gaelic song was made about him. It goes in English:

> '*As I was one day going through the town,*
> *Whom did I meet but Sthagan Varagy?—*
> *Sthagan Varagy, the beloved of the girls,*
> *Horo! fare you well.*'

He had a merry time, till one day the people drove him from the fair
with sticks.

There are three distinct periods in the life of Carleton. First, the
period that followed his conversion to Protestantism: a time of short
stories, beginning with *Lough Derg*, and ending with the *Traits and
Stories* and *Irish Life and Character*. Then, after his heart at any rate had
returned to Catholicism, he wrote a series of long stories of peasant
life, beginning with *Fardorougha* and ending with *The Black Prophet*.
And last of all there was his twenty years' decadence: a time mainly of
bad historical novels. When, about 1820,[2] his short stories began
appearing, there was no Irish public taking Irish things seriously, and
the general reading world had agreed to find certain attributes of Irish
peasant life more marketable than others. They wanted to laugh a great
deal, and they did not mind weeping a little, but they wished all
through to retain their sense of superiority. Carleton could not help
being a little conscious of this; and hence these short stories, full as
they are of abundant youthful vigour, are less perfect as works of art
or as social history than the best of the long stories—as *Fardorougha* and

---

[1] The *Carlow College Magazine* ran from May, 1869, to April, 1870.
[2] Carleton's first important story, *The Lough Derg Pilgrim*, appeared in the *Christian Examiner* in 1828.

The Black Prophet, written when a true Irish public had gathered for a brief while round the *University Magazine*.[3]

In *Fardorougha* there is none of the fierce political feeling that degraded some of Carleton's later novels into caricature. The book has a perfect unity: the scene is filled by a single character, the miser Fardorougha, and by the battle between his love for his money and his love for his son. That son is falsely charged with murder. Though half-dead of a broken heart, the old man tries to cheapen the defence. He is robbed of his money by a fraudulent county treasurer; and having delivered himself of one of those superb Irish curses, he falls sick and dies of sorrow. Before his death he turns to his son—having been commanded by his priest to warn him against miserliness—and bids him to be careful not to give the Church as much as it asks for the masses. He himself, he says, saved enough to buy a new pair of boots by beating it down over the masses for his father's soul; and with these words he passes away. He is one of the strangest figures in literature, and yet there is no caricature. The wrinkle of almost any old Irish farmer might harbour an identical soul. Miserliness, according to Carleton, is more often than people think an Irish peasant sin. They who take their notions from Lever's descriptions of his own very different class think of him rather as a spendthrift. As for *The Black Prophet*, it describes a local famine in one of the early decades of the century: the gradual perishing of the crops, the long period of rain, the supernatural terror of the people, the slow decay of well-to-do folk, the bargaining with a thieving meal-seller, the fever slaying what the famine has spared. From the first to last it is full of a mournful fervour strange to those who know Carleton merely as a humourist; and through all its mournfulness there runs a kind of unhuman fatalism that makes one think of barren moors at moonlight and leaden sunsets over sea.[4] He has never used the dialect to such purpose elsewhere. It serves him for everything, from grotesque humour to intense lyricism.

Carleton would have been strangely puzzled had he known that the Irish public, which loves tales of nobles and rapparees and beautiful women, would finally take most of all to one of the novels of his decadence and read forty editions of such rubbish as *Willy Reilly*; for he

[3] *Fardorougha the Miser, or the Convicts of Lisnamona* was serialized in the *Dublin University Magazine* in 1837–1838, and *The Black Prophet, a Tale of the Famine* in the same magazine in 1846. Other contributors to this journal were John and Michael Banim and James Clarence Mangan.

[4] Yeats expressed the same idea, perhaps more beautifully, in his introduction to *Stories from Carleton*: "When I read any portion of the 'Black Prophet,' or the scenes with Raymound the Madman in 'Valentine M'Clutchy,' I seem to be looking out at the wild, torn storm-clouds that lie in heaps at sundown along the western seas of Ireland; all nature, and not merely man's nature, seems to pour out for me its inbred fatalism."

knew well he had written himself out. He would have been a little comforted to learn that his humourous tales contributed to the 'National Library'—that series of blue-covered sixpennies which has done so much for Ireland—his *Paddy go Easy*, and the three volumes of extracts from *Traits and Stories* and *Irish Life and Character*, are on the counter of every little stationer's shop in the island. The stories that won him the name of the 'Prose Burns of Ireland' are popular as ever, but his two best novels can only be had from the second-hand book-stalls. Only one novel of his good period, *Valentine M'Clutchy*, is still published; but the artist has passed, and only the politician remains. Carleton had every passion of the peasant; to him a bad landlord, a process server, an agent or a gauger were persons of demoniac wickedness. It is the same feeling that starts the stories, so common in Ireland, of squires and squireens carried off by the devil in person. 'How fast they are going,' said an onlooker at a funeral a while since, 'the Devil is dragging at him.' *Valentine M'Clutchy*, where half the characters are devils, would be intolerable but for its wild humour and the presence of the village madman, in whose half-inspired and crazy oratory Carleton seems to pour himself out. Among the things that have helped the book to its great popularity is perhaps the satire on a rich proselytising vicar of the Established Church—a satire coming strangely from a new convert like Carleton. He wrote against the Scarlet Woman in the *Christian Examiner*, but his whole heart was northern Catholic—was Catholic made stubborn by the near neighbourhood of Orangeism.[5] At no time could he refrain from commending his heroines for their devotion to their creed; and when the father of one of them dies he wills that his body be laid in a certain graveyard where a Protestant was laid but once, and then a thorn-bush sprang from his body. Perhaps he was thinking of himself when he makes two converts fight about their new creeds, and before it is over unconsciously return to their old ones: the new-made Catholic 'bloody-ending' the Pope, the new-made Protestant abusing the Hero of the Boyne.

The great thing about Carleton was that he always remained a peasant, hating and loving with his class. On one point he was ever consistent, was always a peasant moralist; that is the land question. Almost every story he wrote deals with it; and in *The Red-Haired Man's Wife*, written just before his death in 1870,[6] he makes a curious prophecy. Then Fenianism was everywhere; but this, he said, was not the movement to be dreaded, but a new one that was coming—a land war that would prove the greatest movement Ireland had seen. He says this several times in different parts of the book. A few years later a now

---

[5] Carleton was born in Co. Tyrone in Ulster.
[6] Yeats erred somewhat; Carleton died in January, 1869.

famous agitator called on an old Fenian (since dead) and asked him, Would the people take up a land cry? 'I am only afraid,' was the answer, 'they would go to the gates of hell for it,' and the event has shown how far he was right.[7]

Popular Ballad Poetry of Ireland

Although this article first appeared in the *Leisure Hour* (London) in November, 1889, it was written long before. Yeats first mentioned it in a letter to Katharine Tynan on July 1, 1887: "I am writing on Irish poets for *Leisure Hour*, also on Irish Fairies" (*Letters*, p. 43). On March 14, 1888, he told Miss Tynan of two long articles awaiting the decision of editors. Finally, in a letter which Wade dates as November 6, 1889, he told Miss Tynan that he was sending along a copy of the *Leisure Hour* with the article in it, and he added: "It is very incomplete—you are not mentioned at all—the reason is that when I wrote I intended to deal with contemporary writers in a separate article. The *Leisure Hour* people, however, having an Irish story and other Irish things running, were afraid of so much Ireland" (*Letters*, p. 140).

Like much else in Yeats's career, this article had to wait for the publication early in 1889 of *The Wanderings of Oisin and other Poems* to push editors into publishing his articles. The article on Irish fairies mentioned in July, 1887, was finally published by the *Leisure Hour* in October, 1890. Yeats made some early attempts in such poems as "The Ballad of Moll Magee" and "Down by the Salley Gardens" to emulate the simple directness of the Irish balladeer, but without great success. He was too self-consciously searching for a subtler, deeper tone than used by poets, as he says at the end of this article, for whom "the grass was merely green . . . and the sea merely blue." Crazy Jane is closer to the old Gaelic poets than Moll Magee.

For biographical information on Gaelic poets, Yeats seems to have used John O'Daly's edition of Mangan's *The Poets and Poetry of Munster*, Dublin, 1849 and later editions, as well as the second edition of Edward Walsh's *Irish Popular Songs*, Dublin, 1883.

---

[7] Yeats told the same story in his autobiography (p. 238), with names supplied, and apparently under the impression that he had never told the story before: "O'Leary had told me the story, not I think hitherto published. A prominent Irish American, not long released from the prison where Fenianism had sent him, cabled to Parnell: 'Take up Land Reform side by side with the National Question and we will support you. See Kickham.' What had Parnell, a landowner and a haughty man, to do with the peasant or the peasant's grievance? And he was indeed so ignorant of both that he asked Kickham, novelist and Fenian leader, if he thought the people would take up land agitation, and Kickham answered: 'I am only afraid they would go to the Gates of Hell for it'; and O'Leary's comment was, 'and so they have.' "

B EHIND Ireland fierce and militant, is Ireland poetic, passionate, remembering, idyllic, fanciful, and always patriotic. With this second Ireland only have I to do in this article, and what it writes and reads. I have here a row of little blue-paper-poem books—a whole ballad literature as foreign from all modern English ways as though it were of farthest Iceland and not of neighbouring Ireland, and unknown in name even to most Anglo-Saxon households.

Every now and then the world may read in the accredited organs of enlightenment that the ballad or dramatic poem, or something else, is obsolete. The writers of these little blue books wrote on regardless; but then, perhaps, the accredited organs of enlightenment never reached them or their barbarous mountains, or their readers, who read and sang, and delighted in what they wrote, as men delighted in poetry of old before organs of enlightenment were even heard of. It is centuries since England has written ballads. Many beautiful poems in ballad verse have been written; but the true ballad—the poem of the populace —she has let die; commercialism and other matters have driven it away: she has no longer the conditions.

For a popular ballad literature to arise, firstly are needful national traditions not hidden in libraries, but living in the minds of the populace. These Ireland has. Every ivy-matted tower carries its legend of stormy feud or love-lorn lady; every little round rath earth-piled its story of leprehaun[1] and pooka;[2] and over all broods the one great dominant thought, love of country, while around that thought gather the long-remembered names of exiles.

Secondly, it is needful that the populace and the poets shall have one heart—that there shall be no literary class with its own way of seeing things and its own conventions. This condition Ireland has long had— whatever the people were the poets have been more intensely; were the people poor, they were poorer; did the people suffer, they suffered also. Did the people love their country, did not the poets keep alive that love through years of misfortune? They were one with the people in their faults and their virtues—in their aims and their passions.

Hence, long before the days of these little blue-paper-poem books, in the more Gaelic-speaking days, was a copious ballad literature going from mouth to mouth, for few could read. Since the time of Elizabeth (when English ballad literature began to die) have arisen in Ireland

---

[1] *leprehaun*: this shoe-making fairy, the best known member of the Irish fairy pantheon, is usually spelled "leprechaun."

[2] Yeats in his article "Irish Fairies, Ghosts, Witches, Etc." for *Lucifer* (January 15, 1889) defines the pooka as ". . . of the family of the nightmare. He has most likely never appeared in human form. . . . His shape is that of a horse, a bull, goat, eagle, ass and perhaps of a black dog. . . ."

twenty-six Gaelic-speaking poets of fame, no less; and many a fameless one-song man, like the author of that old seventeenth-century song so popular in Galway and Mayo, with its pathetic ending, as it goes in a translation now old itself:

> *"'Tis my grief that Patrick Loughlin is not Earl of Irrul still,*
> *And that Brian Duff no longer rules as lord upon the hill;*
> *And that Colonel Hugh McGrady should be lying dead and low,*
> *And I sailing, sailing swiftly from the county of Mayo."*[3]

In the last century there gathered in Munster a most notable group of Gaelic poets, some of them strolling ne'er-do-weels of genius, like that O'Tuomy,[4] who wrote over the door of his inn, when he had a door to write over, much to the indignation of his wife—

> *"Should one of the stock of the noble Gael—*
> *A brother bard who is fond of good cheer—*
> *Be short of the price of a tankard of ale,*
> *He's*[5] *welcome to O'Tuomy a thousand times here."*

Others were hedge schoolmasters, who, when to educate was penal, taught for a living in the hedges and ditches, and while the thing was forbidden seem to have aroused among the ploughboys of whole country-sides quite a furore for Latin, ay, and even Greek. Men like that Macnamarah,[6] who, banished by poverty brought on by his own love of frolic and imprudent satire, wandered away into foreign lands far from mirth and boon companions, and composed the "Fair Hills of Earie [*sic*] 'O;" or like him who, exiled at Homburg [*sic*], wrote the more famous "Hills of Holy Ireland." Thus beautifully has Fergusson[7] translated this exile song of a nation of farmers:

> *"A plenteous place is Ireland for hospitable cheer,*
> *Uileacan dubh O!*[8]
> *Where the wholesome fruit is bursting from the yellow barley ear,*
> *Uileacan dubh O!*
> *There is honey in the trees where her misty vales expand,*
> *And her forest paths in summer are by falling waters fanned;*
> *There is dew at high noontide there, and springs i' the yellow sand,*
> *On the fair hills of Holy Ireland.*

---

[3] This poem is attributed to Thomas Flavell. The translation is by George Fox.

[4] John O'Tuomy (1706–1775) kept a public house in Limerick.

[5] The version printed by John O'Daly in *The Poets and Poetry of Munster* reads "He is welcome. . . ."

[6] Donough Mac Con-Mara (1738–1814) spent some years in Newfoundland. Yeats below seems to be confusing Mac Con-Mara who taught school at Hamburg and there composed "The Fair Hills of Eire O!" with the unknown seventeenth-century poet who composed "The Hills of Holy Ireland," best known in the translation of Sir Samuel Ferguson.

[7] *Fergusson*: usually spelled "Ferguson" but so spelled throughout this article.

[8] "*Uileacan dubh O!*" is usually translated "O sad lament!"

Curled he is, and ringleted, and plaided to the knee,
          Uileacan dubh O!
Each captain who comes sailing across the Irish Sea,
          Uileacan dubh O!
And I will make my journey, if life and health but stand,
Unto that pleasant country, that fresh and fragrant strand,
And leave your boasted braveries, your wealth and high command,
          For the fair hills of Holy Ireland.

Large and profitable are the stacks upon the ground,
          Uileacan dubh O!
The butter and the cream do wondrously abound,
          Uileacan dubh O!
The cresses on the water and the sorrels are at hand,
And the cuckoo's calling daily his note of music bland,
And the bold thrush sings bravely his song i' the forests grand,
          On the fair hills of Holy Ireland."

Beautiful as some of their poems were, the hedge schoolmaster's work was often pedantic in manner and tepid in matter, far inferior to the mere peasant poetry. The hedge schoolmaster indeed, with his zeal for learning, and his efforts, not often successful, to do creative work, was a not uninteresting forerunner of the modern man of letters.

The poets of those days would make a long list[9]—Andrew Macgrath, surnamed "The Merry Pedlar;" O'Sullivan the Red, pious and profligate; John MacConnell, of vision-seeing memory; John O'Cullen, who lamented in such famous words over the Abbey of Timoleaque;[10] and Hefferman [*sic*],[11] the blind, who in his old age loved to stand listening while the ploughboys in the hedge school droned out some Greek poet; and many another.

Twice a year, in the earlier portion of last century, they held what were called sessions of the bards. Young poets used to recite their verse against each other, the victors being crowned. These meetings were finally suppressed by the penal laws.

The political poetry of these men was no light matter in its day. Because of it they were hated and pursued by the powerful and the rich,

---

[9] John O'Daly gave biographical sketches of some of these men in *The Poets and Poetry of Munster*. The full names and dates are: Andrew Magrath (c. 1723–1790); Owen Roe O'Sullivan (c. 1748–1784) (Yeats has wrongly attributed the piety and profligacy of Timothy O'Sullivan, "The Simple," to Owen Roe O'Sullivan); John MacDonnell, "Clarach" (1691–1754).

[10] Sir Samuel Ferguson translated "Lament over the Ruins of the Abbey of Timoleague," and in Ferguson's *Lays of the Western Gael* the Gaelic original is attributed to "John Collins, died, 1816."

[11] Yeats was preparing a biographical article on Heffernan, "The Blind," for the *Dictionary of National Biography*, but no such article ever appeared (*Letters*, p. 96). Heffernan wrote the Gaelic original of Mangan's "Kathleen Ny-Houlahan."

and loved by the poor. They disguised their meaning in metaphor and symbol. The poet goes out in the morning and meets a beautiful spirit weeping and lamenting, a "banshee" with "a mien of unearthly mildness." On her he lavishes all his power of description, and then calls her Ireland. Or else he evades the law by hiding his sedition under the guise of a love-song. Then Ireland becomes his Kathleen, Ny-Houlahan, or else his Roisin Dubh,[12] or some other name of Gaelic endearment. To her he sings:

> "Oh! the Erne shall run red
>   With redundance of blood,
> The earth shall rock beneath our tread,
>   And flames wrap hill and wood,
> And gun-peal and slogan cry
>   Wake many a glen serene,
> Ere you shall fade, ere you shall die,
>   My dark Rosaleen!
>   My own Rosaleen!
> The judgment hour must first be nigh,
> Ere you can fade, ere you can die,
>   My dark Rosaleen!"

As it goes in Mangan's version.[13]

So things went on, until some two or three decades before the printing of these little blue books men began to look for a national poetry printed in English. A new literature commenced. The stock of originals at first was scanty; the new movement depended for a time mainly on translations. At the beginning of this new movement were Walsh and Callanan.

Callanan[14] crowded much capricious incident into his short life, beginning in 1795 and ending at Lisbon—whither he had gone as a tutor, in hopes of recovering his health—in 1829. After training for the priesthood he enlisted as a soldier, and was bought out by his friends as his regiment was on the point of sailing for Malta. Subsequently he wandered through the country collecting old legends to dress up in verse or prose for magazine or newspaper, and translating old Gaelic peasant songs.

It is interesting to know that shortly before his death the old passion came uppermost, and he began collecting songs and legends among the Spanish peasantry.

His friends found him, I fear, a great ne'er-do-weel, and yet he asked not much—no man's wealth—only food to eat and a little leisure to

---

[12] "*Roisin Dubh*" is Gaelic for "the little black rose."
[13] Mangan's version is entitled "Dark Rosaleen."
[14] James Joseph (sometimes given as Jeremiah) Callanan.

hunt out and meditate on the stories he loved. Maybe in some distant time the poets will no longer gather together in cities, but stay, as he did, in their own country-sides, content to write of the people about them, and so shall poetry sweeten the lives of even the simplest of folk, for assuredly the legends of the hills that we see in childhood and age from our own doors, so far as we are simple and natural, are more to us than the legends of any other place on earth. Such a poetry would go deeper into men's lives than any verses of the cities, no matter how full these be of the passion of intellectual attainment.

Callanan, like his successor, Edward Walsh, has left a few original poems—passionate, sincere, and simple verses, celebrating the scenes and legends of his native Munster.

Edward Walsh, born in Londonderry in 1805, a militiaman's son, had all along a hard time of it—first overworked schoolmaster of Cork, afterwards overworked schoolmaster of Spike Island.[15] Nevertheless, he did manage to bring out two small collections of translated popular songs, Gaelic and English side by side. "We remember,"[16] writes his latest editor, "(though now forty years since),[17] following Walsh in the twilight of an autumn evening, drinking in the odd chords that came from the little harp that lay on his left arm as he wandered, lonely and unknown, by the then desert Jones's Road, or reposed himself on one of the seats that at the[18] time were outside the walls of Conliffe House." Passionate, wild songs were they, well-nigh Oriental in their ardour, that he loved to sing to the little harp on his left arm.

A simple and spontaneous thing was this peasant poet-craft. The man who wrote love-songs really was in love. The man who wrote laments really was unhappy. Poor dead Gaelic men, how many centuries ago did they sing the funeral song above you, and here are your passions and sorrows crying from Edward Walsh's little harp!

The troubled year of '48 found him still schoolmaster to the convicts at Spike Island. When John Mitchell[19] was sent there on the way to his Bermuda hulk, Walsh approached him reverently, and stooping, kissed the famous rebel journalist's hand, and said, "You are now the man in all Ireland most to be envied." That night John Mitchell meditated

---

[15] Spike Island is in the bay outside Cork, near present-day Cobh.

[16] Yeats quoted from the preface by "J. S. S." to the second, 1883, edition of Edward Walsh's *Irish Popular Songs*.

[17] In the *Leisure Hour* printing, this parenthetical phrase was incorrectly left outside the quotation marks.

[18] *the*: Walsh's *Irish Popular Songs* reads "that."

[19] *Mitchell*: usually spelled "Mitchel." John Mitchel (1815–1875) was the assistant editor of the *Nation* newspaper, and in 1848 he founded the *United Irishman*. For his articles in that journal he was tried and convicted on a charge of "treason-felony." During his five years of penal servitude he kept a famous *Jail Journal*, which was published in New York in 1854 after his escape from Van Diemen's Land.

over it all in his journal, thus: "Poor Walsh, he has a family of young children; he seems broken in health and spirits. Ruin has him in the wind at last;[20] there are more contented galley-slaves toiling[21] at Spike than the schoolmaster. Perhaps this man does really envy me, and most assuredly I do not envy him."

His death was not so far off now, for the schoolmaster, having got little good of his five-and-forty years, died in 1850; but lived long enough to see in his last decade the rise of a literary movement that gathered his and his fellow-workers' poems from old newspapers and magazines or readerless volumes, and printed them in thousands with new and worthy companions.

This movement began with the founding in 1842 of the "Nation," a powerful and seditious sheet in those days. Everything was considered Irish that embodied Irish passion and thought. In the ballad collections that began in 1845 with Gavan Duffy's[22] "Ballad Poetry of Ireland"—a volume with a larger circulation than any other published in Ireland—and the first of these little blue books—a few Orange ballads even found place.

An Irish poet[23] was to write on his title-page later on:

"We are one at heart if you be Ireland's friend,
Though leagues asunder our opinions tend;
There are but two great parties in the end."

In Duffy's ballad book what was to grow plainer as years went on was already plain—that three men, Davis, Fergusson, and Mangan, stood above all other Irish writers of that day.

Not one of those I have heretofore discussed could have been called a prosperous or happy man, and Clarence Mangan, the greatest, it will be seen, was also the most miserable. The others were poets of the farm and the hills. The lover in the old ballad laments because he has no riches for his beloved, no cattle "to drive through the long twilight." In the earliest poems of seven hundred years ago, as in the latest, the singer's sweetheart has lips the colour of the berries of the quicken-tree (the mountain ash). In his more sentimental moods he

---

[20] Mitchel's *Jail Journal* reads: "Ruin has been on his traces for years, and I think has him in the wind at last."

[21] *toiling*: Mitchel reads "moiling."

[22] Sir Charles Gavan Duffy (1816–1903) helped to found the *Nation* newspaper. He was exiled to Australia where he had a distinguished political career, becoming finally Prime Minister there. Within five years of this article Yeats became involved with Duffy in a struggle for the editorship of a publishing venture called "The New Irish Library." Duffy won, and Yeats took his revenge by giving bad reviews to some of the volumes of this series, particularly Duffy's works.

[23] William Allingham.

sings like the lover in the Munster peasant song, whereof I make this version:[24]

> *"My love, we will go, we will go, I and you.*
> *And away in the woods we will scatter the dew,*
> *And the salmon behold and the ousel too.*
> *My love, I and you, we will hear, we will hear,*
> *The calling afar of the doe and the deer,*
> *And the bird in the branches will cry for us clear,*
> *And the cuckoo unseen in his festival mood.*
> *And death, O my fair one! will never come near*
> *In the bosom afar of the fragrant wood."*

Than which same pastoral aspiration I know nothing more impossibly romantic and Celtic. Nature with these men was a passion, but in the poetry of Mangan are no beautiful descriptions. Outer things were only to him mere symbols to express his own inmost and desperate heart. Nurtured and schooled in grimy back streets of Dublin, woods and rivers were not for him. His father boasted that his children would run into a mousehole to escape him; afterwards shut up in a scrivener's office, the amenity and beauty of human intercourse was not for him. Sensitive in an extreme degree, persecuted and solitary, in this scrivener's office he spent seven years; three more years he laboured as an attorney's clerk to support father, brother, and sisters, then wholly depending on him; for the father, when Mangan was quite a young lad, finding him of working age, appears to have struck work. Hard drudging it was year in year out. No wonder he wrote—

> *"All my divinities have died of grief,*
> *And left me wedded to the rude and real."*[25]

And yet he found time to read many an out-of-the-way book and to teach himself German, Spanish, Italian, French, Latin, and maybe some smattering of Oriental tongues, though this is not certain, and to write several strange and pessimistic poems.

But already from his ever-growing misery he seems to have sought solace in opium and gin. In Mount Pleasant Square, Dublin, lived three

---

[24] Yeats adapted a translation by Edward Walsh (p. 78 of the 1883 edition of *Irish Popular Songs*) of a stanza from the song "Edmund of the Hill" by Edmund O'Ryan. Walsh's version is as follows:

> *My hope, my love, we will proceed*
> *Into the woods, scattering the dews,*
> *Where we will behold the salmon, and the ousel in its nest,*
> *The deer and the roe-buck calling,*
> *The sweetest bird on the branches warbling,*
> *The cuckoo on the summit of the green hill;*
> *And death shall never approach us*
> *In the bosom of the fragrant wood!*

[25] These lines are from Mangan's translation of Schiller's poem *Die Ideale*.

sisters, of higher social position than he. With Frances,[26] the youngest of these, he fell in love madly, hopelessly. She encouraged him; and then, when the novelty wore off, sent him about his business. Whatever of brittle happiness had staid with him was quite gone now. More and more did he seek to blot out memory with gin and opium.

His father was dead, but his ghost, as he believed, with other phantoms, haunted him day and night. In his latter days some one found him a post in the Library of Trinity College, more congenial then scrivening.

"An acquaintance pointed out to me," wrote Mitchell [sic], "a man perched on the top of a ladder, with the whispered information that the figure was Clarence Mangan. It was an unearthly and ghostly figure, in a brown garment (the same garment to all appearance which lasted to[27] the day of his death). The blanched hair was totally unkempt; the corpse-like features still as marble; a large book was in his arms, and all his soul was in the book. I had never heard of Clarence Mangan before, and knew not for what he was celebrated, whether as a magician, a poet, or a murderer, yet took a volume and spread it on the table, not to read, but with pretence of reading, to gaze at[28] the spectral creature upon the ladder."[29]

Many of his earlier poems had been printed in the "Nation;" but now he transferred his allegiance to Mitchell's [sic] "United Irishman," contributing thereto much verse, original or translated, from Gaelic song or German ballad. But gradually he became useless for any good purpose. For days together he would disappear. A priest, I have heard said, brought him once before a looking-glass, and pointed to his haggard face and tattered clothes therein reflected. "Ah!" cried Mangan, "it is nothing to the state of the inner man."

In the end he fell a victim to cholera (he always believed he would die of cholera), at the Meath Hospital, in 1849, he being in his forty-seventh year. After death his face was sketched by the present head of the National Gallery of London, and the sketch hangs now in the Irish National Gallery. In the beautiful profile there is visible no mark of his life's struggle. The poor crazed soul, as it seemed, had left the clay to the ancient innocence of dead things. Few more pitiful stories are on record. But who will say anything about his life, momentous as he himself has said, under the symbol of Siberia:

> "*In Siberia's wastes*
> *The ice-wind's breath*
> *Woundeth like the toothèd steel;*

[26] Yeats identified her as Frances Stackpoole in his article on Mangan for *Irish Fireside*, March 12, 1887.   [27] *to*: Mitchel reads "till."   [28] *at*: Mitchel reads "on."
[29] This quotation is from the biographical sketch which Mitchel prefixed to his edition of Mangan's poems.

Lost Siberia doth reveal
  Only blight and death.

Blight and death alone—
No summer shines.
Night is interblent with day.
In Siberia's wastes alway
  The blood blackens, the heart pines.

In Siberia's wastes
  No tears are shed,
For they freeze within the brain.
Nought is felt but dullest pain—
  Pain acute, yet dead;

Pain as in a dream,
  When years go by
Funeral-paced, yet fugitive;
When man lives and doth not live—
  Doth not live—nor die.

In Siberia's wastes
  Are sands and rocks;
Nothing blooms of green or soft,
But the snow-peaks rise aloft,
  And the gaunt ice-blocks.

And the exile there
  Is one with those;
They are part and he is part—
For the sands are in his heart,
  And the killing snows.

Therefore in those wastes
  None curse the Czar.
Each man's tongue is cloven by
The north blast, who[30] heweth nigh
  With sharp scymitar.

And such doom he[31] drees
  Till, hunger-gnawn
And cold-slain, he at length sinks there;
Yet scarce more a corpse than ere
  His last breath was drawn.''

Where among your drawing-room bards of fashionable pessimism
are any verses regal and terrible as these? Be it noted they do not
arraign Heaven; nor here nor elsewhere does he excuse or luxuriously
pity and fondle himself, this poet of the depths.

[30] *who*: Mangan reads "that."   [31] *he*: Mangan reads "each."

Of his translations the most often printed in the ballad books are those from the Gaelic: The "Testament of Catheir Mor," "Dark Rosaleen," "Lament for the Princess of Tyrone and Tyrconnell," and "The Woman of Three Cows."

> "Oh! think of Donnell of the ships, the chief whom nothing daunted;
> See how he fell in distant Spain, unchronicled, unchanted!
> He sleeps the great O'Sullivan, where thunder cannot rouse;
> Then ask yourself, should you be proud, good woman of three cows?"

And many more. Instead of giving any of his ballads—for to quote at length is not possible, and to quote piecemeal is scant justice to any poem with a story—I give a few stanzas of his version of those curious rhymes by King Alfred of Northumberland descriptive of Ireland, whither he had gone in youth to be educated:

> "I found in Innisfail the Fair,
> In Ireland, while in exile there,
> Women of worth, both grave and gay men—
> Many clerics and many laymen.
>
> .   .   .   .   .
>
> Gold and silver I found, and money,
> Plenty of wheat and plenty of honey;
> I found God's people rich in pity,
> Found many a feast and many a city.
>
> .   .   .   .   .
>
> I found the good lay monks and brothers
> Ever beseeching help for others;
> And in their keeping the Holy Word
> Pure as it came from Jesus the Lord.
>
> I found in Munster, unfettered of any,
> Kings, and queens, and poets a many—
> Poets were skilled in music and measure—
> Prosperous doings, mirth, and pleasure.
>
> .   .   .   .   .
>
> I found in Ulster, from hill to glen,
> Hardy warriors, resolute men—
> Beauty that bloomed when youth was gone,
> And strength transmitted from sire to son.
>
> .   .   .   .   .
>
> I found in Leinster, the smooth and sleek,
> From Dublin to Slewmargy's peak,
> Flourishing pastures, valour, health,
> Long-living worthies, commerce, wealth.
>
> .   .   .   .   .

> *I found strict morals in age and youth,*
> *I found historians recording truth.*
> *The things I sing of in verse unsmooth*
> *I found them all; I have written sooth."*

A very different ancient Ireland from the barbarous place some have imagined. To almost everything he gave a rueful and visionary tinge. You must not go to his work for delicate grace or tender pity, for such are the expressions of the happy moments of usually happy men, but for desolation and sympathy with whatever is barbaric in men's hearts.

It is not possible to imagine two men more different than Clarence Mangan and Thomas Davis—the one absorbed, moody, and morbid, in penury, one of the people, wilful and self-taught, wasted by routine; the other, university trained, a man of action, patient and gay, one of the gentry, surrounded by friends. The one wrote because he was miserable, the other wrote because he was happy and noble and wished to make others so. Thomas Osburne[32] Davis, Ireland has no name more widely loved, no more potent maker of opinion. At college in no way different from his fellows save in his contempt for the oratorical honours of the Debating Society, few would have imagined him destined to lead a rebel party. He was twenty-seven before he made a single verse, and then only because his "young Irelanders" felt the need of ballads for the "Nation" newspaper, started in 1842; and all he wrote was done within the limits of a year and a half. In 1845 he died. Diverse parties—the O'Connellites whose power he had broken, and they to whom his ideals were a veritable fire-pillar, and they who held them the merest Jack-o'-lantern flickerings—all trooped to his funeral. Fergusson wrote his burial ode:

> "I walked through Ballinderry in the spring-time,
>   When the bud was on the tree;
> And I said, in every fresh-ploughed field beholding
>   The sowers striding free,
> Scattering broadcast forth the corn in golden plenty
>   On the quick seed-clasping soil,
> 'Even such, this day, among the fresh-stirred hearts of Erin,
>   Thomas Davis, is thy toil![']
>
> I sat by Ballyshannon in the summer,
>   And saw the salmon leap;
> And I said, as I beheld the gallant creatures
>   Spring glittering from the deep,

---

[32] *Osburne*: usually spelled "Osborne."

Through the spray, and through the prone heaps striving onward
  To the calm clear streams above,
'So seekest thou thy native founts of freedom, Thomas Davis,
  In thy brightness of strength and love! [']

. . . . . .

Young husbandmen of Erin's fruitful seed-time,
  In the fresh track of danger's plough!
Who will walk the heavy, toilsome, perilous furrow,
  Girt with freedom's seed-sheets now?"

Many a fine war-ballad has he left us, many a fine war-song. Of the first, the most notable being "The Sack of Baltimore," a history of a descent by Algerian pirates on the Irish shore, written just before his death; of the last, the song, "Oh, for a sword and a rushing steed." Yes, Ireland has no name more beloved. Often have I heard the children of the people singing his songs, putting their whole soul therein. There are concerts where all the singers are children and all the songs are his —their beloved. Here is one I have heard well rendered:

"Oh! the marriage, the marriage!
  With love and mo bhuachaill[33] *for me;*
The ladies that ride in a carriage
  Might envy my marriage to me.
For Eoghan is straight as a tower,
  And tender and loving and true;
He told me more love in an hour
  Than the squires of the county could do.
        Then, oh! the marriage! etc.

His hair is a shower of soft gold,
  His eye is as clear as the day,
His conscience and vote were unsold
  When others were carried away.
His word is as good as an oath,
  And freely 'twas given to me;
Oh! sure 'twill be happy for both
  The day of our marriage to see.
        Then, oh! the marriage! etc.

His kinsmen are honest and kind,
  The neighbours think much of his skill,
And Eoghan's the lad to my mind,
  Though he owns neither castle nor mill.
But he has a tilloch of land,
  A horse, and a stocking of coin,
A foot for a dance, and a hand
  In cause of his country to join.
        Then, oh! the marriage! etc.

[33] "*Mo bhuachaill*" means "my bridegroom" in Gaelic.

We meet in the market and fair,
  We meet in the morning and night;
He sits on the half of my chair,
  And my people are wild with delight.
Yet I long through the winter to skim—
  Though Eoghan longs more, I can see—
When I will be married to him,
  And he will be married to me.
            Then, oh! the marriage, the marriage!
              With love and mo bhuachaill *for me;*
            The ladies that ride in a carriage
              Might envy my marriage to me."

Of his political poetry I cannot speak; suffice it to say it still goes on, whether for good or evil, serving its purpose, making opinion.

Perhaps reading and reasonable Irishmen should put Fergusson where they put Mangan, at the head of their poets. He has not the other's lyrical intensity, but his power is more serene and lofty. His ballad, "The Vengeance of the Welshmen of Tirawley,"[34] is admittedly the best of Irish ballads, and in some ways the most Homeric poem of the century. His "Conary" is the most perfect equivalent for the manner of the ancient Celtic bards in modern literature. The very breadth and serenity of Fergusson has robbed him of popularity—there is an antique coldness about him. I heard him discussing a few months before his death some recent decorative architecture. To him it seemed florid and unimpressive. He preferred the plain buildings of earlier times. This severity of mind is in all he wrote. When reading the "Welshmen of Tirawley," or his more recent "Conary," one seems to be listening to some old half-savage bard chanting to his companions at a forest fire. If we long, while listening, for the more elaborate music of modern days, the fault is in us and in our time. The lives of Mangan and Davis were short and crowded with incident. The life of Fergusson was long and uneventful. He died some three years since, full of years and honours. A collected edition of his poems and prose writings—he was a noted antiquarian and old-fashioned romance writer—has been coming out in shilling volumes since his death.

In the little blue ballad books there is many another name dear wherever the Irish are—Griffin[35] with his "Gille Machree," and Banim,[36] truer to peasant nature and mother earth, with his famous and typical "Soggarth aroon" (priest dear).

---

[34] Ferguson's title is "The Welshmen of Tirawley."
[35] Gerald Griffin (1803–1840), best known as a novelist.
[36] John Banim (1798–1842) collaborated with his brother Michael on many novels dealing with Irish life.

"*Am I the slave they say,*
  Soggarth aroon?
Since you did show the way,
  Soggarth aroon,
Their slave no more to be,
While they would work with me
Ould Ireland's slavery,
  Soggarth aroon?

Why not her poorest man,
  Soggarth aroon,
Try and do all he can,
  Soggarth aroon,
Her commands to fulfil
Of his own heart and will,
Side by side with you still,
  Soggarth aroon?

Loyal and brave to you,
  Soggarth aroon,
Yet be not slave to you,
  Soggarth aroon.
Nor out of fear to you—
Stand up so near to you—
Och! out of fear to you!
  Soggarth aroon!

Who in the winter's night,
  Soggarth aroon,
When the cold blast did bite,
  Soggarth aroon,
Came to my cabin door,
And, on my earthen-flure,[37]
Knelt by me, sick and poor,
  Soggarth aroon?

Who on the marriage day,
  Soggarth aroon,
Made the poor cabin gay,
  Soggarth aroon—
And did both laugh and sing,
Making our hearts to ring,
At the poor Christening,
  Soggarth aroon?

Who as a friend only met,
  Soggarth aroon,
Never did flout me yet,
  Soggarth aroon?

[37] *flure*: Banim reads "floor."

And when my hearth[38] *was dim*
Gave, while his eye did brim,
What I should give to him,
    Soggarth aroon?

Och! you, and only you,
    Soggarth aroon!
And for this I was true to you,
    Soggarth aroon.
In love they'll never shake
When for ould Ireland's sake
We a true part did take,
    Soggarth aroon!"

And Keegan,[39] the farm-labourer, and Frazer, the weaver, and Florence McCarthy, whose work was more of the fancy than the heart, and Darcy Magee [*sic*], afterwards assassinated, and rebel Doheny, with his one memorable song, written as he lay in hiding, and Gavan Duffy, and Ingram with his famous "Memory of the Dead;" and later on in Fenian times, Casey, with his "Rising of the Moon," and Kickham, Fenian leader and convict, most rambling and yet withal most vivid, humorous, and most sincere of Irish novelists, with his ballad of "Blind Sheehan," and his "Irish Peasant-girl;" and Joyce, with his many ballads, also author of a national epic, that reached, it is said, a sale of ten thousand copies in a few days, mainly among Irish Americans; and in our own times Alfred Percival Graves, with his

"Little red lark
Like a rosy spark,"

and his "Father O'Flynn;" and many more besides these, anonymous and named. Others again whose work is in the main written for the few, have yet occasionally reached the people, like Allingham, with his "Fair Maid of Ballyshannon," by the help of music, or, like De Vere, through the ballad books.

The English reader may be surprised to find no mention of Moore,[40] or the verses of Lever and Lover.[41] They were never poets of the

---

[38] *hearth*: Banim reads "heart."

[39] The full names and dates of the poets in this list are as follows: John Keegan (1809–1849); John Frazer (1804–1852); Denis Florence McCarthy (1817–1882); Thomas D'Arcy McGee (1825–1868); Michael Doheny (1805–1863), whose one famous song was "A Cushla Gal Mo Chree" (Bright Vein of My Heart); Sir Charles Gavan Duffy (1816–1903); John Kells Ingram (1823–1907); John Keegan Casey (1846–1870); Charles Joseph Kickham (1826–1882); Robert Dwyer Joyce (1830–1883); Arthur Percival Graves (1846–1931); William Allingham (1824–1889); Aubrey DeVere (1814–1902).

[40] Thomas Moore (1779–1852), the author of the best known book of Irish songs, *Irish Melodies*.

[41] Charles James Lever (1806–1872), Samuel Lover (1797–1868), both primarily known as novelists.

people. Moore lived in the drawing-rooms, and still finds his audience therein. Lever and Lover, kept apart by opinion from the body of the nation, wrote ever with one eye on London. They never wrote for the people, and neither have they ever, therefore, in prose or verse, written faithfully of the people. Ireland was a metaphor to Moore, to Lever and Lover a merry harlequin, sometimes even pathetic, to be patted and pitied and laughed at so long as he said "your honour," and presumed in nowise to be considered a serious or tragic person. Yet the poetry of the men I write of is above all things tragic and melancholy. We must not seek, however, from these, or any other makers of popular song and ballad, the same things we love in more studious writers. The grass is merely green to them and the sea merely blue, and their very spontaneity has made them unequal. But a wonderful freshness and sweetness they have, like the smell of newly-ploughed earth. They are always honest companions; no one of them wrote out of mere vanity or mere ambition, but ever from a full heart.

W. B. Yeats

Bardic Ireland

Yeats reviewed Sophie Bryant's *Celtic Ireland*, London, 1889, in the *Scots Observer* of January 4, 1890.

   Mrs. Bryant (1850–1922), Irish-born educator, wrote on biblical and historical subjects (such as *Celtic Ireland*). She made another contribution to the background literature of the Irish Literary Revival in 1913 with her *Genius of the Gael, A Study in Celtic Psychology and its Manifestations*, in which she praised the dramas of Synge and Yeats as masterpieces of Gaelic psychology.

   Yeats's review of her book contains one of his most impassioned laments over the tragic incompleteness of Irish history. His identification of the Celtic race with the sea is certainly a reflection of his own practice in using the sea as symbol and image in much of his poetry. Yeats was much given to assigning symbolic properties to the four elements, and in a late classification, in 1934, he told Olivia Shakespear that water stood for "the blood and the sex organs" and "passion."

A GOOD deal has been written about the first few centuries of Irish history both for the specialist and the general reader. He who cannot be persuaded to dip into the *Senchus Mor*[1] and *The Book of the Dun*

   [1] *Senchus Mor*: the *Law of Distress*, a compilation of ancient Gaelic law.

Cow[2] for himself, can turn to the histories of Mr. Standish O'Grady, or to Lady Fergusson's *Irish Before the Conquest*, or to Mrs. Bryant's *Celtic Ireland* (London: Kegan Paul). Sir Samuel Fergusson's[3] ballads and Mr. Aubrey de Vere's *Legends of St. Patrick*, and the retrospective poems in his *Innisfail*—these more than the *Legends*—are full, too, of the spirit of these stormy centuries. Mrs. Bryant runs over what is known of the eleven hundred years from the Nativity to the landing of Strongbow. She does not take it king by king and saint by saint like Lady Fergusson, but picks out facts that seem to her of moment and comments on these. Thus, she has chapters on the influence of ancient Ireland and England on each other, on the bardic order, on St. Patrick and his clerics, on the working in precious metals and the missal-painting of the Irish, and so forth; and the general effect is good.

In those ages the genius of the Gael seems to have found its most complete expression. From the monasteries of Ireland Europe learned to illuminate its bibles and psalters, and therewith the manner of working beautifully in metals. Irish music, also, was widely heard of; and some believe that the modern harp came thus from Ireland. Celtic conquest poured out too, one Irish *ard-reigh*[4] meeting his death by lightning as he crossed the Alps; and when St. Patrick had Christianised the country another kind of conquest began, and England, Scotland, Iceland, Germany, and France owed their Christianity mainly to the Irish missions. In these first centuries the Celt made himself: later on Fate made him. It is in his early history and literature that you must look for his character: above all in his literature. The bards, kept by the rules of their order apart from war and the common affairs of men, rode hither and thither gathering up the dim feelings of the time, and making them conscious. In the history one sees Ireland ever struggling vainly to attain some kind of unity. In the bardic tales it is ever one, warring within itself, indeed, but always obedient, unless under some great provocation, to its high king. The *Tain Bo*,[5] the greatest of all these epics, is full of this devotion. Later, when things were less plastic, men rose against their *ard-reigh* for any and everything: one because at dinner he was given a hen's egg instead of a duck's.[6]

The bards were the most powerful influence in the land, and all manner of superstitious reverence environed them round. No gift they

---

[2] *The Book of the Dun Cow: Lebor na Huidre*, a codex, dating from the early twelfth century, which contains an important compilation of bardic tales.

[3] The name of this poet is usually spelled Ferguson. His wife's name, Lady Ferguson, is also misspelled ("Fergusson") in this article.

[4] The *ard-reigh*, or high king, who met his death crossing the Alps was King Dathi.

[5] *Tain Bo Cuailgné: The Cattle Raid of Cooley*.

[6] The incident of the hen's egg plays an important part in Yeats's late play, *The Herne's Egg* (1938), in which Congal, King of Connacht, kills Aedh, King of Tara, because he is served a hen's egg instead of a herne's.

demanded might be refused them. One king being asked for his eye by
a bard in quest of an excuse for rousing the people against him plucked
it out and gave it. Their rule was one of fear as much as love. A poem
and an incantation were almost the same. A satire could fill a whole
country-side with famine. Something of the same feeling still survives,
perhaps, in the extreme dread of being 'rhymed up' by some local
maker of unkindly verses. This power of the bards was responsible, it
may be, for one curious thing in ancient Celtic history: its self-conscious-
ness. The warriors were not simply warriors, the kings simply kings,
the smiths simply smiths: they all seem striving to bring something
out of the world of thoughts into the world of deeds—a something
that always eluded them. When the Fenian militia were established in
the second century they were no mere defenders of coast-line or
quellers of popular tumult. They wanted to revive the kind of life lived
in old days when the Chiefs of the Red Branch gathered round Cuchullin. They found themselves in an age when men began to love rich
draperies and well-wrought swords, to exult in dominion and the lord-
ship of many flocks. They resolved to live away from these things in
the forest, cooking their food by burying it under a fire; and passing
such laws as that none of their order should take a dowry with his wife,
but marry her for love alone. Nor would they have among them any man
who did not understand all the several kinds of poetry. In the end they
grew proud and tyrannical, and the people rose and killed them at
Gavra.[7] Old Celtic Ireland was full of these conscious strivings—unless[8]
her whole history be fiction. Indeed Cuchullin, Finn, Oisin, St.
Patrick, the whole ancient world of Erin may well have been sung out
of the void by the harps of the great bardic order.

Almost certainly a number of things taken most literally by Mrs.
Bryant are in no sense history. She supposes it a matter proven and
indisputable that the primeval races, Fomorians, Tuatha dé Dananns,[9]
Milesians and the rest mentioned in *The Book of Invasions*, were historic
peoples; and Rhys, Joubainville,[10] and others have made it certain that
they were merely bardic myths. Their present was not their ancient
shape. The monks amused themselves by humanising these old gods,

[7] Battle of Gavra, A.D. 293, at which Oscar, son of Oisin, was supposedly killed by
King Carbi.
[8] Yeats changed the wording of this phrase in a clipping contained in MS 12147 (National
Library of Ireland). The *Scots Observer* printing read "unless, indeed, her whole history...".
[9] Yeats usually spelled this phrase "Tuath" or "Tuatha de Danaan." Later in this article
the spelling varies further.
[10] This name is usually spelled Jubainville. Sir John Rhys was author of *Lectures on the
Origin and Growth of Religion as Illustrated by Celtic Heathendom*. H. D'Arbois de Jubainville
was author of a twelve-volume series, *Cours de littérature celtique*. The second volume, *Le
Cycle mythologique irlandais, et la mythologie celtique*, 1884, was translated into English by
Richard Irvine Best and published in Dublin in 1903.

turning them into pious early colonisers, and tracing their descent to Noah. It has been found possible, however, to pick out something of their old significance, and discern in them the gods of light warring on the spirits of darkness—on the Fomorians who had but one leg under them and one arm in the middle of their breasts, and lived under the sea: creatures who turned under the monkish touch into common two-armed and two-legged pirates. Some few of the divine races, indeed—the Tuath dé Danann chiefly—preserved a parcel of their ancient dignity, and, becoming the fairies, dwell happily near their deserted altars. The monks were sad spoilers of things pagan. The old warlike centuries bored them. On the margin of a Latin history of the early days of Finn Ma Cool, the scribe has written in Gaelic: 'Holy Virgin, when will brother Edmund come home from the meeting?'

Mrs. Bryant takes this hurly-burly of gods quite seriously, and tries to identify them with Iberian, Ugrian, Belgae, and other races. She does not seem to have heard even of the mythologic view. Other portions of her book are excellent. Her chapter on the Brehon Laws could scarce be better. She shows how Ireland was above all things democratic and communistic—all lands belonging to the tribe. It was just such a system that a sociable people full of restless energies would make themselves; and, as might be said of Greece, it turned out good for the world, bad for the nation. When other countries were bowed under military despotism, missions poured forth over Europe from the schools of Ireland, but when the day of battle came she could not combine against the invader. Each province had its own assembly and its own king. There was no focus to draw the tribes into one. The national order perished at the moment when other countries like Germany and Iceland were beginning to write out their sagas and epics in deliberate form. The trappings of the warrior ages had not yet passed away, yet modern thought was near enough to give them a certain remoteness, so that the artist could detach himself from his material. The moment had come to write out old tales in *Nibelungenlieds* and *Eddas*; but Ireland was doomed to have no rest, no peace, no leisure for students to labour in: the bees were too hard pressed by the wasps to make any honey. Her passionate bardic inspiration died away, leaving nothing but seeds that never bore stems, stems that never wore flowers, flowers that knew no fruitage. The literature of ancient Ireland is a literature of vast, half-dumb conceptions. The moment when the two worlds, ours and theirs, drew near to speak with each other was wasted in flight. No sooner were the Danes expelled than Strongbow came in. The shaping of bardic tales, the adornment of missals, the working in precious metals, all came to an end. The last-wrought gold shrine was done in 1166, three years before the landing of the Norman. Instead of the well-made poems we might have had, there remains but a wild anarchy of legends—a vast pell-mell of monstrous shapes: huge demons driving swine on the hill-tops; beautiful shadows whose hair has a peculiar life and moves responsive to their thought; and here and there some great hero like Cuchullin, some epic needing only deliberate craft to be scarce less than Homer. There behind the Ireland of to-day, lost in the ages, this chaos murmurs like a dark and stormy sea full of the sounds of lamentation. And through all these throbs one impulse—the persistence of Celtic passion: a man loves or hates until he falls into the grave. Years pass over the head of Conchobar and Finn: they forget nothing. Quinet has traced the influence of the desert on the Israelitish people.[11] As they were children of the earth, and as the Parsees are of the fire, so do the Celtic Irish seem of the fellowship of the sea: ever changing, ever the same.

W. B. Yeats

Carleton as an Irish Historian

Yeats's collection of *Stories from Carleton* had been reviewed by the *Nation* (Dublin) on December 28, 1889. The reviewer had praised the book and he had said of Yeats's introduction that it was "a model of interpretative and sympathetic criticism." He continued: "But it is criticism by a poet. The 'faint idealizing haze' has flowed round Carleton, and hid his defects." Yeats had said in his introduction that Carleton was a great Irish historian in that his books were true pictures of that essential history of a people, their common everyday life.

Much of the *Nation* review was devoted to a long quotation from the story "Shane Fadh's Wedding," in which are described the comic antics of drunken priests at an Irish peasant wedding. The review concluded with the statement: "We thought we had passed the day when his envenomed caricature would be accepted as portraiture. But it seems not. But till that day passes the slanderous Carleton should be kept by Irish critics in the literary pillory."

After the printing of Yeats's letter, the editor of the *Nation* added a para-

[11] Edgar Quinet (1803–1875) in his *Génie des Religions*, (1842) Book V, "La Religion Hébraïque," section one, "Jéhovah—La Révélation Par le Désert." Quinet contrasted the effect of the unchanging desert on Judaic monotheism with the effects of the everchanging sea upon the polytheism of Greece and India. Yeats repeated this idea in "Earth, Fire and Water," a short piece printed in the *Speaker*, March 15, 1902, and reprinted in *The Celtic Twilight*, 1902. By that time, he had become considerably more vague in his memories: "Some French writer that I read when I was a boy said that the desert went into the heart of the Jews in their wanderings and made them what they are" (*Mythologies*, London and New York, 1959, p. 80).

graph in which he claimed that Yeats had distorted the review, that the critic had praised Carleton's stories and Yeats's work as an editor, and had only condemned the "slanderous Carleton." The editor concluded that Yeats's letter "is only another instance of how a man of genius may sometimes err in zeal." The description in January, 1890, of Yeats as a "man of genius" shows either considerable critical foresight or ironic flattery. In this exchange, Yeats had a strong point in his favor. The *Nation* review, while appearing to give a balanced judgment, would have had the effect of warning all Catholics off the Carleton volume because it was an example of Protestant bigotry.

January 11, 1890

"CARLETON AS AN IRISH HISTORIAN"

TO THE EDITOR OF *THE NATION*

3 Blenheim-road, Bedford Park, Chiswick,
London, January 3rd, 1890.

DEAR SIR—I have only just read your criticism of my "Stories from Carleton," in THE NATION of the 28th ult. I wonder does your critic know his Carleton well. I fear he scorned to read so "envenomed" a writer. He much preferred to cry "renegade," to take up the old calumny and pass it on. Carleton came up to Dublin a young man, at the age when opinions change. What literature Ireland then had was Protestant; proselytism and letters, too, had just come together in most unnatural marriage. The tradition of the great Protestant orators of Ireland was still new. The young Northern peasant's mind was still unformed, and brilliancy, culture, enlightenment, all seemed to have made alliance against his old Faith. He changed his creed. There is not one fragment of evidence to prove he did so other than honestly, or that "he wrote for the market," as your critic puts it. For a few, a very few years, he was full of zeal for his new opinions—an ever-lessening zeal. As time went on, he crossed out zealous passage after passage from his stories, as their turn came to be reprinted—the more wrong-headed he never republished at all; and, by the time his powers had climaxed, found himself most fierce against proselytising of all kinds, Protestant kinds more than any. He showed by book after book that his heart was wholly with the Faith of his childhood. The "Irish Established Church" has only once been satirised since Swift by a man of genius; that man was William Carleton.

I have here beside me, gathered from the *Christian Examiner*, and bound into one volume the anti-Catholic tales of his childhood. I and not Carleton have gathered them together. Had he written for the market he would not have left them sleeping in the dusty pages of an old magazine, for they have power of a kind in plenty. They make, after all, but a slim volume; it does not weigh much in genius or avoirdupois. Besides, there are a few scattered passages in "Shane Fadh,"[1] a story of almost Chaucerian breadth and power, and in one or two others of "The Traits and Stories."[2] Into the other scale of the balance, Carleton threw all the works of his prime—the fierce advocacy of "M'Clutchy,"[3] the many impassioned scenes of entirely Catholic life of "The Black Prophet" and "Ahadara [sic]."[4] From some years before the publication of "M'Clutchy," in 1846, until his death in 1870- book after book came from him in only too great profusion, and almost all contains some eulogy, defence, or tender description of the Faith of his childhood. Yet your good critic has no word for him but "renegade;" no other mention of his genius than to call it "envenomed." Scotland left Burns in the Excise; the world has mocked her for it. The coming century would find it a strange thing to look back on, if we, many years after our great prose Burns had been rotting in his grave, and when all other reading folk had learned to honour him, if we in his own country should find nothing more for his memory than what your critic is pleased to call "the Literary Pillory." It would think us wholly given over to never-lifting night and ignorance. And yet Catholicism can well afford to be generous; no Catholic need show the bigotry of some poor sectary. Enough now of your critic. I feel wholly saddened to think that any countryman of Carleton's should make this letter needful at all.

There is no fear, however, of Carleton's name among our people. They are more generous than some who would teach them, and will not forget this one great peasant writer of their country, the man who remained ever a peasant, one of themselves, full of all their passion, all their feelings. Quite close to me, here in London, lives an old seamstress, very poor and pious, who remembers how he used to dine in her father's cabin—a peasant among peasants. It is too late to cry "renegade" now, and fortunately the "literary pillory" is at no articlewriter's command. It were much better work for Irish journalists to do what they can to get his great novels into print again. It is the fault of the Catholic publishers of Ireland that the "Black Prophet" and "Fardorougha the Miser"—making, together with Miss Edgeworth's

---

[1] "Shane Fadh's Wedding" was included in Yeats's volume. The *Nation* reviewer had excerpted a passage from this story as an example of Carleton's anti-Catholic bias.

[2] *Traits and Stories of the Irish Peasantry* (first series, 1830; second series, 1833) was the collection of Carleton's early stories.

[3] *Valentine M'Clutchy, the Irish Agent: or, Cronicles of Castle Cumber*, Dublin, 1845.

[4] *The Emigrants of Ahadarra*, Belfast, 1847.

[5] Carleton died in 1869. Yeats gives 1870 as the date of Carleton's death also in his *Scots Observer* review of *The Red-Haired Man's Wife*, in the issue of October 19, 1889.

"Castle Rackrent," our greatest fiction—should be out of print, while the early tales sown thinly with anti-Catholic passages and the Catholic, but feeble novels of his decadence, are for sale in countless bookshops. One can buy only at second-hand bookstalls the great works of his maturity wherein he shed the light of immortality on peasant and Catholic Ireland.—Yours, &c.,

W. B. Yeats

Tales from the Twilight

This review of Lady Wilde's *Ancient Cures, Charms, and Usages of Ireland*, London, 1890, appeared in the *Scots Observer*, March 1, 1890.

Jane Francesca, Lady Wilde (1826–1896), the mother of Oscar Wilde, enjoyed considerable fame of her own as poet, propagandist, translator from the German and French, and as folklorist. Under the pseudonym "Speranza" she was an important contributor to the *Nation* magazine between 1845 and 1848. Her inflammatory article "Jacta alea est" resulted in the suppression of the *Nation* and the unsuccessful prosecution of Charles Gavan Duffy, its editor, for sedition. During the trial, she admitted in open court her authorship of the article. In 1851 she married the noted Dublin surgeon, William Wilde, a man with wide interest in literature, folklore, and ethnography. After Sir William's death in 1876 she moved to London, and in the late 1880s she presided over a salon at her lodgings in Chelsea. Since old age had ravaged her once famous beauty, she held her gatherings in almost total darkness.

Lady Wilde published a two-volume set of folk tales in 1887, *Ancient Legends, Mystic Charms, and Superstitions of Ireland*. This venture was successful enough to be followed by a one-volume edition the following year, and, in 1890, by the collection *Ancient Cures, Charms . . .*, which Yeats reviewed.

Yeats has recorded in his autobiography the kindness which Oscar Wilde showed to him in his early years in London, a kindness which is very evident in Wilde's reviews of Yeats's *Fairy and Folk Tales of the Irish Peasantry*, and *The Wanderings of Oisin*. Yeats, in his turn, frequently praised Lady Wilde's books and defended her against an unfavorable review in the *Academy* magazine by writing a letter, "Poetry and Science in Folk-Lore," printed in the *Academy* issue of October 2, 1890. In his reviews of Lady Wilde's books as well as Douglas Hyde's, Yeats makes no allusion to the ardent nationalistic sentiments she expressed. The politics of Henley's *Scots Observer*, strongly Unionist and imperialist, inhibited Yeats's nationalism.

The point Yeats made in this review, that the Irish fairies were mild and benign, had been the main point of an earlier piece for the *Scots Observer*,

"Scots and Irish Fairies" (March 2, 1889), which Yeats reprinted in *The Celtic Twilight* as "A Remonstrance with *Scotsmen* for Having Soured the Disposition of their Fairies."

The end of this review makes clear that for Yeats the "Celtic Twilight" was the transition from darkness to dawn more than the twilight of evening.

T HIS new book of Lady Wilde's —*Ancient Cures, Charms, and Usages of Ireland* (London: Ward and Downey)—is a collection of folklore mainly from the western islands, the most unpuritan places in Europe. Around and northward of Dublin no small amount of gloom has blown from overseas, though not more than a few miles from Dublin—at Howth, for instance—the old life goes on but little changed. But westward the second century is nearer than the nineteenth, and a pagan memory is more of a power than any modern feeling. On Innismurray, an island near my own district, the people look reverently on the seals as they lie in the warm, shallow water near the shore; for may they not be the spirits of their forebears? Even in their social customs they do not recognise our century; for two peasants, hereditary king and queen of the island, control disputes and deal out laws as occasion demands. From these remote parts Sir William Wilde collected a vast bulk of tales and spells and proverbs. In addition to the peasants he regularly employed to glean the stubble of tradition for him, he got many things from patients at his Dublin hospital; for when grateful patients would offer to send him geese or eggs or butter, he would bargain for a fragment of folk-lore instead. He threw all his gatherings into a big box, and thence it is that Lady Wilde has quarried the materials of her new book: a farrago of spells, cures, fairy-tales, and proverbs— these last beyond price—the districts seldom specified and the dates of discovery never. I heartily wish they had been better and more scientifically treated, but I scarce know whom to blame: Lady Wilde, Sir William Wilde, his collectors, or the big box. However that may be, and in spite of these defects, my author's two volumes of *Ancient Legends* and this new collection are the fullest and most beautiful gathering of Irish folk-lore in existence. Mr. Douglas Hyde may some day surpass it—no one else can. In the 'Spells and Cures' section Lady Wilde has lighted on a subject which, so far as Ireland is concerned, has hitherto been almost ignored. Well-nigh all prove with how little gloom the Irish peasant looks on death and decay, but rather turns them to favour and to prettiness. For madness he would give you 'three things not made by the hand of man'—salt and honey and milk, to be drunk out of a sea-shell before sunrise; for the falling sickness he would hang about your neck three hairs of a milk-white greyhound; for almost any minor evil he would prescribe an ointment made of cowslip roots or red berries of rowan, unless indeed you have chanced on one of those desperate ailments that require a plaster of spiders or a draught of water from the skull of a man.

For we too have our horrors, but all are so fancifully self-conscious that they are in no wise burdensome. For instance, if you love and love in vain, all you have to do is to go to a grave-yard at midnight, dig up a corpse, and take a strip of skin off it from head to heel, watch until you catch your mistress sleeping and tie it round her waist, and thereafter she will love you for ever. Even our witches are not so horrible as other peoples'. Sometimes they do things wicked as weird:[1] such, for instance, as burying a sheaf of corn and leaving it to rot away while some hated life rots with it. But the witches themselves are countrywomen of ours, and so we try to forget and forgive. Mostly, too, they are guilty of nothing worse than stealing corn or milk, or making their own fields flourish in unnatural abundance. We have not soured their temper with faggot and stake. Once, it is true, we knocked out a witch's eye with a cabbage-stump, but that was long ago and in the north. Lady Wilde gives a good witch-tale of one of the western islands. There was a man, one Flaherty, who was greatly suspected by his neighbours of foregathering with the Evil One, because with little land he had always much corn. Turns and turns about they watched by night, until one morning a watcher saw something black moving in the field and carrying a grain of corn. That grain the something planted. Then it brought another and did the same, and then another, and yet another, and many hundreds of others; and the man drew near and found it a hideous insect. So he stooped and caught it, and put it in a horn snuff-box, and shut down the lid, and went off home; and presently there was great commotion and excitement, for Flaherty's wife had disappeared. The man happened to mention the black thing in the snuff-box; and 'How do you know,' said his friend, 'but it may be Flaherty's wife?' Flaherty heard the tale, and begged the man to go with him, and carry the snuff-box into the house, and open it in his presence. The man went home with him, and some neighbours likewise; and when the box was opened out crawled a great black insect, and made straight into Mrs. Flaherty's room as hard as it could go; and after a little Mrs. Flaherty came out, and she was very pale and one finger was bleeding. 'What means the blood?' asked the man of the snuff-box; and says Flaherty: 'When you shut down the lid you snapped off a little bit of the beetle's claw, and so my wife suffers.' After this Flaherty was shunned, and one day he and his wife sailed for another

---

[1] *weird*: probably in the sense *Oxford English Dictionary* gives as "an evil fate inflicted by supernatural power, especially by way of retribution."

island. There was no trial, no punishing, no 'swimming.' The people did not even throw stones.

Not only witches but the whole demoniac nation is surrounded with fancies that show almost an affection for its terrors: an affection made possible, perhaps, by a sense that he that pays his chapel-dues and has a good heart and does not pull up a sacred hawthorn may get through the world secure, nor find a need for hate. One evil spirit of very murderous habits was accustomed to take the shape of a bag of wool and go rolling along the road; and Death himself at Innisshark comes down and stands by the dying in the form of a black cock, and has been pleased into harmlessness by the blood of a crowing hen. Once by mischance a woman caught not a common barn-door bird but the son of the King of the Cats, who was taking the air in that shape. Then two huge black cats came in and tore her face until they were tired; but her sick child got well, for Death had leave to take but one life, and the son of the King of the Cats was dead. Lady Wilde thinks these stories may be relied on, because the western islanders are an accurate people, who never exaggerate but tell only the simple truth, and are too homely to invent. At Hollandtide[2] they are much troubled by the dead from their graves, who return to ride the sea's white horses, so that no wise fisherman will push out that night. A man once did so, and just as he reached the shore he heard the noise of the breakers behind him, and turning round saw a dead man upon every wave. One came close to him, and he recognised a neighbour drowned the year before; and the neighbour leaned over and bade him hasten home, for the dead were seeking him. He left boat and ca go and fled, and never again put out at Hollandtide.

In Ireland this world and the other are not widely sundered; sometimes, indeed, it seems almost as if our earthly chattels were no more than the shadows of things beyond. A lady I knew once[3] saw a village child running about with a long trailing petticoat upon her, and asked the creature why she did not have it cut short. 'It was my grandmother's,' said the child; 'would you have her going about yonder with her petticoat up to her knees, and she dead but four days?' Lady Wilde tells a story of a woman whose ghost haunted her people because they had made her grave-clothes so short that the fires of purgatory burned her knees. And to them the truth is that beyond the grave they will have houses much like their earthly homes, only there the thatch will never grow leaky, nor the white walls lose their lustre, nor shall the dairy be at any time empty of good milk and butter. But now and then a landlord

---

[2] *Hollandtide*: All Hallows Eve, November 1.

[3] Yeats repeated this story in *The Celtic Twilight* under the title "Concerning the Nearness Together of Heaven, Earth, and Purgatory."

or an agent or a gauger will go by begging his bread, to show how God divides the righteous from the unrighteous.

Irish legends and Irish peasant minds, however, have no lack of melancholy. The accidents of Nature supply good store of it to all men, and in their hearts, too, there dwells a sadness still unfathomed. Yet in that sadness there is no gloom, no darkness, no love of the ugly, no moping. The sadness of a people who hold that 'contention is better than loneliness,' it is half a visionary fatalism, a belief that all things rest with God and with His angels or with the demons that beset man's fortunes. 'God is nearer than the door,' they say; 'He waits long; He strikes at last.' They say too that 'Misfortune follows fortune inch by inch'; and again, 'It is better to be lucky than wise'; or, 'Every web as it is woven, every nursling as it is nursed.' Shakespeare's witches are born of the Teuton gloom; our Irish sadness grows visible in other shapes. Somewhere I have read a tale that is touched with its very essence. At the grey of dawn an Irish peasant went out to the hills, to shoot curlew or what not. He saw a deer drinking at a pool, and levelled his gun. Now iron dissolves every manner of spell, and the moment he looked along the barrel he saw that the deer was really an old man changed by wizardry; then, knowing him for something wicked, he fired, and the thing fell, and there upon the grass, quite dead, lay the oldest man he ever set eyes on; and while he stood watching a light wind rose, and the appearance crumbled away before his eyes, and not a wrack was left to tell of what had been. The grey of the morning is the Irish witches' hour, when they gather in the shapes of large hares and suck the cattle dry; and the grey morning melancholy runs through all the legends of my people. Then it is that this world and the other draw near, and not at midnight upon Brockens amidst the foul revelry of evil souls and in the light of the torches of hell. At the dawning the wizards come and go and fairy nations play their games of hurley and make their sudden journeys. Nations of gay creatures, having no souls; nothing in their bright bodies but a mouthful of sweet air.

W. B. Yeats

Poetry and Science in Folk-Lore

This letter, published October 11, 1890, in the *Academy*, was in response to a review of Lady Wilde's *Ancient Cures, Charms, and Usages of Ireland* by Percy Miles in the *Academy*, September 27, 1890. Myles had objected to the carelessness with which Lady Wilde had treated her folk tales. In Yeats's review of this same book (*Scots Observer*, March 1, 1890), he had also complained about the complete absence of any documentation for the folklore. Myles, in his review, had said that Yeats's *Irish Fairy and Folk Tales*, although charming in a literary way, had shown the same anti-scientific bias. Yeats was replying directly to a passage in the review in which Myles said, ". . . the editor [of *Irish Fairy and Folk Tales*] goes out of his way to gibe at the honest folk-lorist who tells what he had actually heard, not what he thinks he might have heard, or what he thinks his audience would like to hear."

The slighting reference to the *Folk-lore Journal* at the end of Yeats's letter drew a reply from Alfred Nutt, the editor of the *Journal* and the publisher of much folklore (but not Yeats's). In this letter, dated October 15, 1890, Nutt reminded Yeats that one of the stories in *Irish Fairy and Folk Tales* was culled from the pages of the *Folk-lore Journal*. Nutt also said that ". . . it is hardly fair to compare the Transactions of a learned society, which are in duty bound to collect and print much that is fragmentary and of value only to experts, with a volume intended for the public at large."

[London: Oct. 2, 1890]

THE Rev. Percy Myles, in a review of Lady Wilde's *Ancient Cures, Charms, and Usages* (*Academy*, Sept. 27), makes complimentary mention of my little compilation, *Fairy and Folk Tales of the Irish Peasantry*. He misunderstands, however, what I said about scientific folk-lorists in the Introduction. I do not want the fairy-tale gatherer to tell us "what he thinks he might have heard, or what he thinks his audience would like to hear." But I deeply regret when I find that some folk-lorist is merely scientific, and lacks the needful subtle imaginative sympathy to tell his stories well. There are innumerable little turns of expression and quaint phrases that in the mouth of a peasant give half the meaning, and often the whole charm. The man of science is too often a person who has exchanged his soul for a formula; and when he captures a folk-tale, nothing remains with him for all his trouble but a wretched lifeless thing with the down rubbed off and a pin thrust through its once all-living body. I object to the "honest folk-lorist," not because his versions are accurate, but because they are inaccurate, or rather incomplete. What lover of Celtic lore has not been filled with a sacred rage when he came upon some exquisite story, dear to him from childhood, written out in newspaper English and called science? To me, the ideal folk-lorist is Mr. Douglas Hyde. A tale told by him is quite as accurate as any "scientific" person's rendering; but in dialect and so forth he is careful to give us the most quaint, or poetical, or humorous version he has heard. I am inclined to think also that some concentration and elaboration of dialect is justified, if only it does not touch the fundamentals of the story. It is but a fair equivalent for the gesture and voice of the peasant tale-teller. Mr. Hyde has, I believe, done this in his marvellous Teig O'Kane, with the result that we have a story more full of the characteristics of true Irish folk-lore than all the pages given to Ireland from time to time in the *Folk-lore Journal*.

W. B. Yeats

Irish Fairies

"Irish Fairies" first appeared in the October, 1890, issue of the *Leisure Hour* (London). This article is probably the one on Irish fairies which, along with an article on Irish popular ballad poetry, Yeats told Katharine Tynan he was working on all the way back in July, 1887. The article on ballads finally reached print in November, 1889, after Yeats's first book of poems, *The Wanderings of Oisin*, gave him some reputation. This article had to wait another year, perhaps because, as Yeats told Miss Tynan (*Letters*, p. 140), the *Leisure Hour* people were afraid of too much Ireland.

Soon after the composition of this article Yeats became busy with his compilation of *Fairy and Folk Tales of the Irish Peasantry*, London, 1888. Three of the stories in "Irish Fairies," those of the Sligo servant girl who disappeared, of the three O'Byrnes, and of Michael Hart and the corpse, also appeared in *The Celtic Twilight*, London, 1893. In telling fairy and ghost stories, Yeats was successful in avoiding a bogus stage-Irish charm on the one hand and a ponderous scientific air on the other hand. Oscar Wilde described this quality well (allowing for the exaggerations) in his review of *The Wanderings of Oisin*: "He is very naive and very primitive and speaks of his giants with the air of a child" (*A Critic in Pall Mall*, London, 1919).

WHEN I tell people that the Irish peasantry still believe in fairies, I am often doubted. They think that I am merely trying to weave a forlorn piece of gilt thread into the dull grey worsted of this century. They do not imagine it possible that our highly thought of philosophies so soon grow silent outside the walls of the lecture room, or that any kind of ghost or goblin can live within the range of our daily papers. If the papers and the lectures have not done it, they think, surely at any rate the steam-whistle has scared the whole tribe out of the world. They are quite wrong. The ghosts and goblins do still live and rule in the imaginations of innumerable Irish men and women, and not merely in remote places, but close even to big cities.

At Howth, for instance, ten miles from Dublin, there is a "fairies'

path," whereon a great colony of other-world creatures travel nightly
from the hill to the sea and home again. There is also a field that ever
since a cholera shed stood there for a few months, has broken out in
fairies and evil spirits. The last man I have heard of as seeing anything
in it is an industrious fisherman of great strength. He is a teetotaler; his
sister indeed has told me that his wife and wife's sister often sit and
talk of him and wonder "what he would do if he drank." They half
regret that sobriety should make so strong a man hide his light under a
bushel. One night he was coming home through the field, when he saw
in front of him a small white cat. While he looked at it the creature
began to swell bigger and bigger, and as it grew in size he lost in
strength, as though it sucked out his vitality. He stood for a time
motionless with terror, but at last turned and fled, and as he got
further away his strength came back. It was, a peasant would tell you,
a fairy animal, for not all the fairies have human shapes.

Everyone has heard of changelings, how a baby will be taken away
and a miserable goblin left in its stead. But animals, it is not generally
known, run the same risk. A fine fat calf may be carried off, and one of
the fairies of animal shape left in its stead, and no one be the wiser until
the butcher tries to kill it; then it will rush away and vanish into some
green hillside. The fairy kingdom has everything we have, cats, dogs,
horses, carriages, and even firearms, for the sounds of unearthly
volleys fired by troops of spirits embattled on the winds have been
heard by a Munster seer who lived about twenty years ago.

It is, however, further afield than Howth, down westward among
the deep bays and mountains valleys of Sligo, that I have heard the best
tales and found the most ardent belief. There, many a peasant dreams
of growing rich by finding a fairy's crock of gold, and many a peasant's
daughter trembles as she passes some famous haunted hillside, and
goes over in her mind the names of men and women carried off, as
tradition will have it, to the dim kingdom. Only very recently one of
these fabled robberies is reported to have been attempted. A little girl,
who is at service with a farmer in the village of Grange, suddenly
disappeared.[1] There was at once great excitement in the neighbourhood, because it was rumoured that the fairies had taken her. A
villager was said to have long struggled to hold her from them, but at
last they prevailed, and he found nothing in his hands but a broomstick. The local constable was applied to, and he at once instituted a
house-to-house search, and at the same time advised the people to burn
all the *bucalauns* (ragweed) on the field she vanished from, because

[1] This story of the girl who disappeared was told in *The Celtic Twilight* in the chapter
entitled "Belief and Unbelief." In *The Celtic Twilight* Yeats said that the girl "was" at
service, and he placed the story "about three years ago."

bucalauns are sacred to the fairies. They spent the whole night burning
them, the constable repeating spells the while. In the morning the little
girl was found, the story goes, wandering in the field. She said the
fairies had taken her away a great distance, riding on a fairy horse. At
last she saw a big river, and the man who had tried to keep her from
being carried off was drifting down it—such are the topsy-turvydoms
of fairy glamour—in a cockle-shell. On the way her companions had
mentioned the names of several people who were about to die shortly
in the village. Such is the story. I will not pretend to find out what
really did happen. I at any rate have not the heart to break upon the
wheel so quaint a butterfly.

Sligo is, indeed, a great place for fairy pillaging of this kind. In the
side of Ben Bulben is a white square in the limestone.[2] It is said to be
the door of fairyland. There is no more inaccessible place in existence
than this white square door; no human foot has ever gone near it, not
even the mountain goats can browse the saxifrage beside its mysterious
whiteness. Tradition says that it swings open at nightfall and lets pour
through an unearthly troop of hurrying spirits. To those gifted to hear
their voices the air will be full at such a moment with a sound like
whistling. Many have been carried away out of the neighbouring
villages by this troop of riders. I have quite a number of records beside
me, picked up at odd times from the faithful memories of old peasants.
Brides and new-born children are especially in danger. Peasant mothers,
too, are sometimes carried off to nurse the children of the fairies. At
the end of seven years they have a chance of returning, and if they do
not escape then are always prisoners. A woman, said still to be living,
was taken from near a village called Ballisodare, and when she came
home after seven years she had no toes—she had danced them off. It is
not possible to find out whether the stolen people are happy among
"the gentry," as the fairies are called for politeness. Accounts differ.
Some say they are happy enough, but lose their souls, because, perhaps,
the soul cannot live without sorrow. Others will have it that they are
always wretched, longing for their friends, and that the splendour of
the fairy kingdom is merely a magical delusion, woven to deceive the
minds of men by poor little withered apparitions who live in caves and
barren places. But this is, I suspect, a theological opinion, invented
because all goblins are pagans. Many things about fairies, indeed, are
most uncertain. We do not even know whether they die. An old
Gaelic poem says, "Death is even among the fairies," but then many
stories represent them as hundreds of years old.

There are a number of Gaelic songs and ballads about them, and

[2] Some of the material in this paragraph appeared in altered form in the "Kidnappers"
chapter of *The Celtic Twilight*.

about the people they have stolen. Some modern Irishmen also have
written beautifully on the same matter. An Irish village schoolmaster,
named Walsh,[3] wrote the following. It is supposed to be sung by a
fairy over a child she has stolen:[4]

> "*Sweet babe! a golden cradle holds thee,*
> *And soft the snow-white fleece enfolds thee;*
> *In airy bower I'll watch thy sleeping,*
> *Where branchy trees to the breeze are sweeping.*
>   *Shuheen, sho, lulo, lo!*
>
> *When mothers languish, broken-hearted,*
> *When young wives are from husbands parted,*
> *Ah, little think the keeners[5] lonely,*
> *They weep some time-worn fairy only.*
>   *Shuheen, sho, lulo, lo!*
>
> *Within our magic halls of brightness*
> *Trips many a foot of snowy whiteness;*
> *Stolen maidens, queens of fairy,*
> *And kings and chiefs a* sluagh shee[6] *airy.*
>   *Shuheen, sho, lulo, lo!*
>
> *Rest thee, babe! I love thee dearly,*
> *And as thy mortal mother, nearly;*
> *Ours is the swiftest steed and proudest,*
> *That moves where the tramp of the host is loudest.*
>   *Shuheen, sho, lulo, lo!*
>
> *Rest thee, babe! for soon thy slumbers*
> *Shall flee at the magic* koel shee's[7] *numbers;*
> *In airy bower I'll watch thy sleeping,*
> *When[8] branchy trees to the breeze are sweeping.*
>   *Shuheen, sho, lulo, lo!"*

The poor schoolmaster has perfectly given the fascination of the
mysterious kingdom where the fairies live—a kingdom that has been
imagined and endowed with all they know of splendour and riches by
a poor peasantry amid their rags. As heaven is the home of their
spiritual desires, so fairyland has been for ages the refuge of their earthly
ideals. In its shadow kingdom they have piled up all they know of
magnificence. Sometimes there is a quaint modernness in the finery.

[3] Edward Walsh (1805–1850), the compiler and translator of *Irish Popular Songs*.

[4] This song, "The Fairy Nurse," is somewhat similar to Yeats's poem "The Unappeasable
Host," which begins (in its original version), "The fairy children laugh in cradles of wrought
gold. . . ."

[5] The keeners are those who raise the funeral cry over the dead. [Yeats's note]

[6] *A* sluagh shee means "fairy host," and "airy" is the peasant's way of saying "aery."
[Yeats's note]

[7] *Koel shee*, fairy music. [Yeats's note]

[8] *When:* Walsh reads "Where."

One old man said to me, "It is full of beautiful drawing-rooms and parlours."

The fairies are of course not merely feared as robbers, they are looked up to and respected for their great wealth. If a man always speaks respectfully of them, and never digs up one of their sacred thorn bushes, there is no knowing but he may some day dream of a crock of gold and the next day go and find it, and be rich for ever. A man once confessed to me that he had gone at midnight into my uncle's garden and dug for a treasure he had dreamed of, but there was "a power of earth" in the place, and so he gave up the search and went home.

The finest treasure tale[9] I have, however, comes from Donegal. A friend was once at a village near Sleive League. One day he was straying about a rath called "Cashel Nore." (Raths are small fields encircled by earth fences; they were inhabited by the ancient races, and are now great haunts of fairies.) A man with a haggard face and unkempt hair, and clothes falling in pieces, came into the rath and began digging. My friend turned to a peasant who was working near and asked who the man was. "That is the third O'Byrne," was the answer. A few days after he learned this story: A great quantity of treasure had been buried in the rath in pagan times, and a number of evil fairies set to guard it; but some day it was to be found and belong to the family of the O'Byrnes. Before that day three O'Byrnes must first find it and die. Two had already done so. The first had dug and dug until at last he got a glimpse of the stone coffin[10] that contained it, but immediately a thing like a huge hairy dog came down the mountain and tore him to pieces. The next morning the treasure had again vanished deep into the earth. The second O'Byrne came and dug and dug until he found the coffer, and lifted the lid and saw the gold shining within. He saw some horrible sight the next moment, and went raving mad and soon died. The treasure again sank out of sight. The third O'Byrne is now digging. He believes that he will die in some horrible way the moment he finds the treasure, but that the spell will be broken, and the O'Byrne family made rich for ever, and become again a great people, as they were of old. A peasant of the neighbourhood once saw the treasure. He found the shin-bones of a hare lying on the grass. He took it up; there was a hole in it; he looked through the hole, and saw the gold heaped up under the ground. He hurried home to bring a spade, but when he got to the rath again he could not find the spot where he had seen it through the spell-dissolving bone.

---

[9] This tale was included in *The Celtic Twilight* as "The Three O'Byrnes and the Evil Faeries."

[10] *The Celtic Twilight* version in the collected edition of Yeats's works (1908) has "coffin" changed to "coffer."

     IRISH FAIRIES

This tale of the O'Byrnes is right full of Celtic intensity. The third O'Byrne, at this moment in all likelihood digging, digging, with ragged hair blown in the wind, and growing old amid his resolve, deserves some more permanent record than this ephemeral article and will perhaps find it some day. Some poet looking for tales in Donegal, long decades hence, may hear the story of the life and death of the third O'Byrne. Tradition is sure to make him find the treasure.

There is one well-known Cork family, all of whose riches are traced back by the people to the days when an old henwife dreamed of a certain field where an iron pot full of gold lay hidden. She is well remembered, because a Celtic poet of the last century, who had come down in the world through the great quantities of whisky he had given away to other Celtic poets, was employed in minding her hens and chickens. He wrote a well-known Gaelic song about her, called "The Dame of the Slender Wattle."[11]

I have spoken, so far, entirely of the malice or kindness of the fairies, and said nothing of their mere wantonness. They are as little to be trusted as monkeys and jackdaws. The worst among them may be known, however, by their going about singly or in twos and threes, instead of in tumultuous troops like the more harmless kinds. The best known among the solitary fairies is the Lepricaun.[12] He is something of a dandy, and dresses in a red coat with seven rows of buttons, seven buttons on each row, and wears a cocked-hat, upon whose pointed end he is wont in the north-eastern counties, according to McNally,[13] to spin like a top when the fit seizes him. His most common pursuit, as everyone knows, is cobbling. The fairies are always wearing out their shoes and setting him to mend them. At night he sometimes rides shepherds' dogs through the country, leaving them muddy and panting at the dawn. He is constantly described as peevish and ill-natured. His mischief, for all that, is much less gruesome than that of the Fir Darrig[14] or Red Man, the most unpleasant joker of all the race. I heard a grim story from a one-armed Sligo man that is probably a chronicle of one of his practical jokes.[15] It is a type of story always told in the first person:

[11] John O'Tuomy (1706–1775) ran a public house in Limerick, where he dispensed free drinks to sessions of the bards, who revered his memory.

[12] *Lepricaun*: Yeats spelled this word variously. The most common spelling is "leprechaun."

[13] *McNally*: Yeats so spelled the name of David Rice McAnally, Jr., the author of *Irish Wonders, The Ghosts, Giants, Pookas . . . and Other Marvels of the Emerald Isle*. Yeats reviewed this book twice, unfavorably, but often quoted McAnally as an authority.

[14] *Fir Darrig*: Yeats elsewhere spells this "Far Darrig."

[15] Yeats used this story four times. It first appeared under the title "Columkille and Rosses" in the *Scots Observer*, October 5, 1889. Aside from the present article, Yeats also included it in *Irish Fairy Tales*, London, 1892, and, under the title "Drumcliffe and Rosses." in *The Celtic Twilight*. In its *Celtic Twilight* form, the teller is referred to as "Michael H——" and no mention is made of his having only one arm.

"In the times when we used to travel by canal," said the one-armed man, "I was coming down from Dublin. When we came to Mullingar the canal ended, and I began to walk, and stiff and fatigued I was after the slowness. I had some friends with me, and now and then we walked, now and then we rode in a cart. So on till we saw some girls milking a cow, and stopped to joke with them. After a while we asked them for a drink of milk. 'We have nothing to put it in here,' they said; 'but come to the house with us.' We went home with them and sat round the fire talking.

"After a while the others went, and left me, loth to stir from the good fire. I asked the girls for something to eat. There was a pot on the fire and they took the meat out and put it on a plate and told me to eat only the meat that came from the head. When I had eaten, the girls went out and I did not see them again.

"It grew darker and darker, and there I still sat, loth as ever to leave the good fire; and after a while two men came in, carrying between them a corpse. When I saw them I hid behind a door. Says one to the other, 'Who'll turn the spit?' Says the other, 'Michael Hart, come out of that and turn the meat!' I came out in a tremble, and began turning the spit. 'Michael Hart,' says the one who spoke first, 'if you let it burn we'll have to put you on the spit instead!' and on that they went out. I sat there trembling and turning the corpse until midnight. The men came again, and the one said it was burnt, and the other said it was done right. But having fallen out over it, they both said they would do me no harm that time; and, sitting by the fire, one of them cried out, 'Michael Hart, can you tell us a story?' 'Never a one!' said I, on which he caught me by the shoulders and put me out like a shot.

"It was a wild, blowing night; never in all my born days did I see such a night—the darkest night that ever came out of the heavens. I did not know where I was for the life of me. So when one of the men came after me and touched me on the shoulder, with a 'Michael Hart, can you tell a story now?' 'I can,' says I. In he brought me, and, putting me by the fire, says, 'Begin!' 'I have no story but the one,' says I, 'that I was sitting here, and that you two men brought in a corpse and put it on the spit and set me turning it.' 'That will do,' says he; 'you may go in there and lie down on the bed.' And in I went, nothing loth, and in the morning where was I but in the middle of a green field!"

In spite of such horrible doings as this, the fairies are in the main innocent and graceful and kindly. The English peasantry have forgotten their fairies. The Irish peasant remembers and believes—and the Scotch, too, for the matter of that.

We will not too severely judge these creatures of the imagination. There are worse things after all than to believe some pretty piece of unreason, if by so doing you keep yourself from thinking that the earth under your feet is the only god, and that the soul is a little whiff of gas, or some such thing.

The world is, I believe, more full of significance to the Irish peasant than to the English. The fairy populace of hill and lake and woodland have helped to keep it so. It gives a fanciful life to the dead hillsides, and surrounds the peasant, as he ploughs and digs,[16] with tender shadows of poetry. No wonder that he is gay, and can take man and his destiny without gloom and make up proverbs like this from the old Gaelic—"The lake is not burdened by its swan, the steed by its bridle, or a man by the soul that is in him."

W. B. Yeats

An Exhibition at William Morris's

This review of the 1890 Arts and Crafts Exhibition appeared in the *Providence Sunday Journal*, October 26, 1890. If education and training are necessary prerequisites for a critic of any art, then Yeats was better prepared by his years as an art student in Dublin and his father's tutelage to be an art critic rather than a literary critic. Nevertheless, Yeats's art criticism is minimal and whatever exists is devoted, like his essays on Blake's illustrations for Dante's *Commedia*, to the literary aspects of pictorial art. The present piece is the only art review by Yeats, and the only prose piece for an American newspaper not included by Horace Reynolds in his compilation, *Letters to the New Island*.

Yeats had been closer to the Morris family around 1890 than at any other time. He attended French classes for a time at Kelmscott House and sat in on some of the meetings of the Socialist League at Morris's home. His sister Lily was studying embroidery under Miss May Morris. William Morris had told Yeats that *The Wanderings of Oisin* was his kind of poetry but a review promised by Morris in his magazine, *Commonweal*, never appeared.

The title of this article contains a considerable distortion, which may, after all, have been the fault of the American newspaper editor rather than Yeats. The exhibition under review was not "at William Morris's" but rather was the third annual showing of the Arts and Crafts Exhibition Society at the New Gallery in Regent Street. William Morris was only one of several guiding spirits of the organization since its first exhibition in 1888. Morris was elected president of the society in 1891 and continued in that office until

[16] In a clipping of this article, contained in MS 12147 (National Library of Ireland) Yeats added commas before and after the phrase "as he ploughs and digs."

his death. In the lecture series which sometimes accompanied the exhibition, Morris spoke on the printing of books, and he contributed a preface to a collection of these essays, which was printed in 1893.

The interest which Yeats took in the displays of book bindings and printing matches the care he showed in how his own works appeared in the public eye. In his reviews, hardly a book passed under his notice without Yeats passing judgment on whether it was "comely to look upon."

THE movement most characteristic of the literature and art and to some small extent of the thoughts, too, of our century has been romanticism. We all know the old formal classicisms gave battle to it and was [*sic*] defeated when Hernani's horn rang out on the French stage.[1] That horn has been ringing through the world ever since. There is hardly a movement in which we do not hear its echo. It marked the regained freedom of the spirit and imagination of man in literature. Since then painting in its turn has flung aside the old conventions. The arts of decoration are now making the same struggle. They have been making it for some years under the leadership of William Morris, poet, Socialist, romance writer, artist and upholsterer, and in all ways the most many-sided man of our times. But for these "arts and crafts" exhibitions[2] of which this is the third year, the outer public would hardly be able to judge of the immense change that is going on in all kinds of decorative art and how completely it is dominated by one man of genius. Last Saturday was the private view. The handsome room of the new art gallery[3] with their white pillars and leaping fountain were crowded by much that is best and most thoughtful of London Society—above all with whatever is "advanced" in any direction—literature, politics, art. It was this future paying homage to one man who had turned aside for a little from his dreams of a Eutopia of Socialism for the poor, to create a reality of art scarcely less beautiful for any rich man who cares for these heavy tapestries and deep-tiled fireplaces, for these hanging draperies and stained-glass windows that all seem to murmur of the middle ages, and the "olden times long ago." Only a small part of the exhibits are from Morris & Co., and yet all the numberless people who send work from the well-known firm that made the huge fireplace in the north gallery to the lady who illuminated the copy of Coventry

[1] Victor Hugo's drama, *Hernani*, was first produced in Paris on February 25, 1830, under riotous circumstances.

[2] These showings were officially sponsored by the Arts and Crafts Exhibition Society, founded in 1888. After the 1890 exhibition, there were two more events, in 1893 and 1896.

[3] *new art gallery*: The New Gallery in Regent Street. Yeats gives the impression that the gallery was a new wing of William Morris's home.

Patmore's poems in the balcony are under the same spell. The melancholy beauty of "The Earthly Paradise"[4] is everywhere. "The Idle Singer of an Empty Day"[5] has neither sung nor wrought idly.

The south gallery is chiefly notable for the cartoons for stained glass and for Cobden Sanderson's[6] book binding. Along the south wall goes a huge design by Burne-Jones for a window at Jesus College, Cambridge. The window itself is to be executed by Morris & Co. The subject is the ninefold "Hierarchy" of angels, archangels, cherubim, seraphim, thrones, dominions, principalities, powers and virtues. It is full of medieval symbolism difficult for modern ignorance to remember and understand. The figures are of course full of that peculiar kind of subtle expression and pensive grace runs through all Burne-Jones's work, but it is hard to judge of the final effect with its blazing and jewel-like color from these uncolored drawings. One can but remember the windows from the same hand at Oxford and fill in the reds, and gold, and blues out of one's head; but then the Oxford windows I have in mind were done when Burne-Jones was young,[7] and his manner almost indistinguishable from that of Rossetti, whereas these angels and archangels are in his most recent and decorative style. They have not the intensity of feeling of the early work, but are, on the other hand, much less crabbed in drawing and crowded in composition. In the same room are other window designs from the same hand—would that they were colored—of subjects like "The Annunciation of the Shepherds," "Lazarus and Mary," "Rachel and Jacob." The windows themselves in each instance being the work of Morris & Co. The case of artistic book covers is charming. In few handicrafts has there been greater need of reforms, the book covers of this century have been for the most part pretentious and foolish, with their gilding smeared hither and thither in purposeless and conventional forms. These Cobden Sanderson books are, however, simple and artistic, but also not cheap. One expects illuminated pages like G. E. Renter's six specimen sheets of Morris's romance, "The Roads of the Mountains" to be as dear as you please, but there seems to be no reason why the covers of books should not be designed by good artists and yet remain not altogether beyond the purse of the poor student for whom, after all, books chiefly exist. In comparison to the immense bills for paper,

[4] *The Earthly Paradise*: Morris's collection of Greek, medieval, and Norse tales in the Chaucerian manner, published between 1867 and 1870.

[5] "The Idle Singer of an Empty Day"— a phrase Morris used to describe himself in "An Apology" prefacing *The Earthly Paradise*.

[6] T. B. Cobden-Sanderson (1840–1922), a printer and bookbinder, had been one of the founders of the Arts and Crafts Exhibition Society. He started the Doves Press in 1900, where the famous Doves Bible was printed.

[7] Burne-Jones did many windows at Oxford. His best known early work there is the east windows of Christ Church, done in 1859, which depicted the story of St. Frideswide.

and printing, publishing, illustrating, and writing, the expense of the cover designer should count for little.

The feature of the west gallery is distinctly a huge green marble mantel piece, with a sculptured figure of Fouque's [*sic*] "Undine"[8] in the centre. In some ways, perhaps, the most interesting exhibit of all. It is the work of Messrs. Farmer and Brindsley. In the same room is Mr. Parnell's[9] contribution, the Irish national banner, designed by Walter Crane.[10] The subject is the "Sunburst," breaking into a Celtic cross, enclosed by an Irish harp, surrounded with the motto "Children of the Gael shoulder to shoulder," the four quarters of the banner contain the shields of the four provinces. In the right hand is Mr. Parnell's now familiar autograph. The banner may look fine enough when blown out in the wind but it certainly looks over-glaring in color and formal in design among the soft greens and rich golds of estheticisms.

In the north gallery is the furniture, oaken and cushioned alcoves, deep fireplaces pannelled with every kind of form and colors, heavy curtains, carved writing tables and desks and all stamped with the same signet of romanticism and medievalism. There is nothing to remind one that the formal classicism of the eighteenth century, with its legacy to the nineteenth, of dismal mahogany and pallid coloring ever existed anywhere.

Upstairs in the balcony are more bookbindings and book illumination, too, to make us remember that the art of the old world has been revived in our day. There is also an etching from Madox Brown's "Dream of Sardanapalus,"[11] a picture seldom seen, though among the finest he has painted, and to my mind much more interesting than his big cartoons in the south gallery. "The Baptism of Eadwins,"[12] a picture that I cannot persuade myself to like chiefly, I think, because I have taken a violent hatred for "Eadwins" himself, with his clerical

---

[8] Friedrich, Baron de la Motte-Fouqué (1777–1843), German romancer. For evidence that Yeats had read Fouqué's *Undine* (1811) see Yeats's review of Robert Buchanan's *The Wandering Jew* (*Bookman*, April, 1893).

[9] Charles Stewart Parnell (1846–1891), the "uncrowned king" of Ireland, head of the home rule faction in the House of Commons, and one of the idols of Yeats's early manhood. By October, 1890, Parnell was already involved in the divorce suit brought by Captain O'Shea which caused Parnell's political downfall and death the following year.

[10] Walter Crane (1845–1915) was, aside from a painter and book illustrator, a member of the socialist league which met at William Morris's home every Sunday. The Irish banner was executed by Miss Una Taylor.

[11] "*Dream of Sardanapalus*": the title of this painting is usually given as "Sardanapalus and Myrra."

[12] "*Baptism of Eadwins*": name is usually spelled "Eadwine." There probably should be a comma or the connective "of" before the phrase "The Baptism of Eadwins." Yeats here refers to one of the frescoes Ford Madox Brown had designed for the Manchester Town Hall. The purpose of the series was to display the history of the Manchester area since Roman times. Eadwine, or Edwin, was the king of Northumbria in the seventh century in whose reign Christianity was introduced to that area of England.

beard, and because I do not know what he has done with his feet in that very small fount they have immersed him in. Not that the cartoon is not full of that curious realism of pose and fullness of light that marks the Father of Prae-Raphaelites [*sic*].

On the whole, then, we have in this exhibition the last echo of Hernani's horn—the long-waited-for deliverance of the decorative arts.

W. B. Yeats

Irish Folk Tales

Beside the Fire: A Collection of Irish Gaelic Folk Stories, with English translation by Douglas Hyde, London, 1890, was reviewed by Yeats in the *National Observer* of February 28, 1891.

Douglas Hyde (1860–1949) was born in County Roscommon in the province of Connacht. He was responsible as much as any single man for the revival of the Gaelic language in Ireland. At the time of the founding of the Gaelic League in 1893, Hyde, in a famous speech, called for "the de-Angliciz-ing of Ireland." Yeats then replied to Hyde that the language in which a culture was expressed was not so important as the great ideas and myths of that culture. Yeats later admitted that he was amazed at the political forces released by Hyde's Gaelic League. He also mourned the loss of Hyde as another Irish sacrifice of genius to politics. Hyde was President of Eire from 1938 to 1945.

Yeats did not mention in his review the fiery anti-English sentiments Hyde expressed in his introduction. Hyde was a harsh critic of folklorists, such as Lady Wilde, who revealed a large ignorance of common Gaelic words. Yeats was sometimes guilty in this respect.

This review was included in the 1893 *The Celtic Twilight* under the title "The Four Winds of Desire," but it was omitted from the 1901 edition and never after reprinted.

IN the notes at the end of *Beside the Fire* (London: Nutt) Dr. Hyde contrasts with certain tales of Indian jugglery[1] an old Gaelic account of a magician who threw a rope-ladder into the air and then sent climbing up it all manner of men and beasts. It reads like an allegory to explain the charms of folk- and fairy-tales: a parable to show how man mounts to the infinite by the ladder of the impossible. When our narrow rooms, our short lives, our soon-ended passions and emotions,

---

[1] Hyde had heard the story of the Indian juggler from Colonel Henry Olcott, one of the founders of the Theosophical Society of America, who had visited Ireland at that time to examine Irish fairy lore from a theosophic standpoint.

put us out of conceit with sooty and finite reality, we have only to read some story like Dr. Hyde's 'Paudeen O'Kelly and the Weasel,' and listen to the witch complaining to the robber, 'Why did you bring away my gold that I was for five hundred years gathering through[2] the hills and hollows of the world?' Here at last is a universe where all is large and intense enough to almost satisfy the emotions of man. Certainly such stories are not a criticism of life[3] but rather an extension, thereby much more closely resembling Homer than that last phase of 'the improving book,' a social drama by Henrik Ibsen. They are an existence and not a thought, and make our world of tea-tables seem but a shabby penumbra.

It is perhaps, therefore, by no means strange that the age of 'realism' should be also the harvest-time of folk-lore. We grow tired of tuning our fiddles to the clank of this our heavy chain, and lay them down to listen gladly to one who tells us of men hundreds of years old and endlessly mirthful. Our new-wakened interest in the impossible has been of the greatest service to Irish folk-literature. Until about three years ago the only writers who had dealt with the subject at any length were Crofton Croker,[4] a second-hand bookseller named Kennedy[5] and an anonymous writer in *The Dublin and London Magazine* for 1825 and 1828. Others, it is true, had incorporated (like Gerald Griffin) odd folk-tales in the pages of long novels, or based on them (like Carleton and Lover) stories of peasant-life. Croker was certainly no ideal collector. He altered his materials without word of warning, and could never resist the chance of turning some naïve fairy tale into a drunken peasant's dream. With all his buoyant humour and imagination he was continually guilty of that great sin against art—the sin of rationalism. He tried to take away from his stories the impossibility that makes them dear to us. Nor could he quite desist from dressing his personages in the dirty rags of the stage Irishman. Kennedy, an incomparably worse writer, had one great advantage: he believed in his goblins as sincerely as any peasant. He has explained in his *Legendary Fictions* that he could tell a number of spells for raising the fairies, but he will not—for fear of putting his readers up to mischief. Years went by, and it seemed that we should never have another gathering. Then about three years ago came Lady Wilde's two volumes[6] and David Fitzgerald's contributions

---

[2] *through*: Hyde reads "throughout."   [3] *criticism of life*: Yeats's favorite Arnoldian echo.

[4] Crofton Croker was the author of *Fairy Legends and Traditions of the South of Ireland*. Croker and the other folklorists mentioned in this review were Yeats's sources for his compilation *Fairy and Folk Tales of the Irish Peasantry*.

[5] Patrick Kennedy was the author of *Legendary Fictions of the Irish Celts* and *The Fireside Stories of Ireland*.

[6] *Ancient Legends, Mystic Charms, and Superstitions of Ireland* and *Ancient Cures, Charms, and Usages of Ireland*. Yeats wrote a notice of the second volume for the *Boston Pilot*, and his review of this same volume for the *Scots Observer* is reprinted in this collection.

to the *Revue Celtique*; with M'Anally's[7] inaccurate and ill-written *Irish Wonders* and Curtin's[8] fine collections a little later; and now appears Dr. Hyde's incomparable little book. There has been published in three years as much Irish folk-lore as in the foregoing fifty. Its quality, too, is higher. Dr. Hyde's volume is the best written of any. He has caught and faithfully reproduced the peasant idiom and phrase. In becoming scientifically accurate, he has not ceased to be a man of letters. His fifteen translations from traditional Gaelic originals are models of what such translations should be. Unlike Campbell of Islay,[9] he has not been content merely to turn the Gaelic into English; but where the idiom is radically different he has searched out colloquial equivalents from among the English-speaking peasants. The Gaelic is printed side by side with the English, so that the substantial accuracy of his versions can always be tested. The result is many pages in which you can hear in imagination the very voice of the sennachie,[10] and almost smell the smoke of his turf fire.

Now and then Dr. Hyde has collected stories which he was compelled to write out in his own Irish through the impossibility, he tells us, of taking them down word for word at the time. He has only printed a half of one story of this kind on the present occasion. One wishes he had not been so rigorous in the matter, especially as it is for this reason, I conclude, that *Teig O'Kane*,[11] still the weirdest of Irish folk-tales, has been omitted. He has printed it elsewhere, but one would gladly have had all his stories under one cover. He is so completely a Gael, alike in thought and literary idiom, that I do not think he could falsify a folk-tale if he tried. At the most he would change it as a few years' passing from sennachie to sennachie must do perforce. Two villages a mile apart will have different versions of the same story; why, then, should Dr. Hyde exclude his own reverent adaptions? We cannot all read them in the Gaelic of his *Leabhar Sgeulaighteachta*.[12] Is it the evil communications of that very scientific person, Mr. Alfred Nutt[13] (he contributes learned notes), which have robbed us of the latter pages of *Guleesh na Guss Dhu*? We might at least have had some outline

[7] *M'Anally*: David Rice McAnally, Jr.'s book *Irish Wonders, The Ghosts, Giants, Pookas . . . and Other Marvels of the Emerald Isle* was reviewed by Yeats in the *Scots Observer* for March 30, 1889.

[8] Jeremiah Curtin, collector of *Myths and Folk-lore of Ireland* (1889) and *Hero-tales of Ireland* (1894). He was also known as a translator of Polish and Russian literature.

[9] *Campbell of Islay*: John Francis Campbell (1822–1885), whose researches were published in four columes as *Popular Tales of the West Highlands Orally Collected* (1890–1893).

[10] *sennachie*: Gaelic word for chronicler or bard.

[11] *Teig O'Kane*: Yeats included Hyde's English translation of this tale in his *Fairy and Folk Tales of the Irish Peasantry*.

[12] *Leabhar Sgeulaighteachta*: Hyde spelled these words *Leabhar Sgeuluigheachta*.

[13] *Mr. Alfred Nutt*: publisher and folklorist. For more information, see headnote to Yeats's review of Nutt's *Voyage of Bran* (*Bookman*, September, 1898).

of the final adventures of the young fairy seer and the French princess. After all, imaginative impulse—the quintessence of life—is our great need from folk-lore. When we have banqueted let Learning gather the crumbs into her larder, and welcome. She will serve them up again in time of famine.

Dr. Hyde has four tales of hidden treasure, five stories of adventure with a princess or a fortune at the end, a legend of a haunted forest, and a tale of a man who grew very thin and weakly through swallowing a hungry newt, which was only dislodged when made wildly a-thirst by a heavy dinner of salt pork and the allurement of a running stream. Love, fortune, adventure, wonder—the four winds of desire! There is also a chapter of quaint riddles in rhyme. The whole book is full of charming expressions. The French princess is described as 'the loveliest woman on the ridge of the world. The rose and the lily were fighting together in her face, and one could not tell which would get the victory.'[14] Here and there, too, is a piece of delicate observation, as when Guleesh na Guss Dhu waits for the fairies listening to 'the cronawn (hum) of the insects,' and watching 'the fadoques and fibeens (golden and green clover) rising and lying, lying and rising, as they do on a fine night.'[15] The riddles also have no lack of poetry. Here is a description of a boreen or little country lane:

'*From house to house he goes,*
A messenger small and slight,
And whether it rains or snows
He sleeps outside in the night.'

And here is one of the lintel on a wet day:

'*There's a poor man at rest*
With a stick beneath his breast,
And he breaking his heart a-crying.'

These riddles are the possession of children, and have the simple fancifulness of childhood.

It is small wonder that this book should be beautiful, for it is the chronicle of that world of glory and suprise imagined in the unknown by the peasant as he leant painfully over his spade. His spiritual desires ascended into heaven, but all he could dream of material well-being and freedom was lavished upon this world of kings and goblins. We who have less terrible a need dream less splendidly. Mr. Hyde bids us know that all this exultant world of fancies is passing away, soon to exist for

[14] This passage in Hyde reads, ". . . and there he saw the loveliest woman that was, he thought, upon the ridge of the world. The rose and the lily were fighting together in her face, and one could not tell which of them got the victory."

[15] In Hyde this passage reads, ". . . the sharp whistle of the fadogues and flibeens (golden and green plover), rising and lying, lying and rising, as they do on a calm night."

none but stray scholars and the gentlemen of the sun-myth. He has
written on his title-page this motto from an old Gaelic poem: 'They are
like a mist on the coming of night that is scattered away by a light
breath of wind.' I know that this is the common belief of folk-lorists,
but I do not feel certain that it is altogether true. Much, no doubt,
will perish—perhaps the whole tribe of folk-tales proper; but the fairy
and ghost kingdom is more stubborn than men dream of. It will perhaps,
in Ireland at any rate, be always going and never gone. I have talked
with men who believe they have seen it. And why should Swedenborg
monopolise all the visions? Surely the mantle of Coleridge's 'man of
ten centuries'[16] is large enough to cover the witch-doctors also. There is
not so much difference between them. Swedenborg's assertion, in the
Spiritual Diary,[17] that 'the angels do not like butter,' would make
admirable folk-lore. Dr. Hyde finds a sun-myth in one of his most
ancient stories. The sun and the revolving seasons have not done
helping to draw legends from the right minds. Some time ago a friend
of mine talked with an old Irish peasant who had seen a vision of a great
tree amid whose branches two animals, one white and one black,
pursued each other continually; and wherever the white beast came
the branches burst into foliage, and wherever the black one, then all
withered away. The changing of the seasons, among the rest, is here
very palpable. Only let it be quite plain that the peasant's vision meant
much more than the mere atmospheric allegory of the learned. He saw
within his tree the birth and death of all things. It cast a light of imagination on his own dull cattle-minding and earth-turning destiny, and gave
him heart to repeat the Gaelic proverb: 'The lake is not burdened
by its swan, the steed by its bridle, nor a man by the soul that is in him.'

W. B. Yeats

Plays by an Irish Poet

BY W. B. YEATS

This review of performances of John Todhunter's plays *A Sicilian Idyll* and
The Poison Flower appeared in the Parnellite weekly, *United Ireland*, on July 11,
1891. In Yeats's prefatory remarks to the collection of his American news-

---

[16] Coleridge had much to say of Swedenborg, both complimentary and critical, but I
have not traced such a remark.

[17] Yeats learned this in *The Spiritual Diary of Emanuel Swedenborg . . . Translated from the
Original by J. H. Smithson*, Vol. I, London, 1846. Diary entry no. 1161 (p. 354) reads: "That
the spiritual angels, or such as constitute the spiritual class dislike butter, was made evident
from this circumstance:—that although at other times I relished butter, yet [when in their
society] I did not for a long while, even for some months, desire it; and when I tasted it,
it wanted its agreeable flavour, and consequently its relish, such as I had before enjoyed."

paper articles, *Letters to the New Island*, he admitted to having overpraised Todhunter, a neighbor of the Yeats family in London and an old friend of Yeats's father. Yeats claimed that he praised Todhunter not out of friendship but because such poetic dramas as *A Sicilian Idyll* were worthy reactions to oratorical, rhetorical dramas such as Tennyson's *Becket* and all realistic plays. In all, *A Sicilian Idyll* received four notices from Yeats. He had puffed this play in his *Boston Pilot* article of June 14, 1890. The same production as the one reviewed in the present *United Ireland* article was noticed by Yeats in another *Boston Pilot* piece of August 1, 1891, and in the *Providence Sunday Journal* of July 26, 1891.

The style of much of this piece is Yeats's journalese at its most fatigued, e.g., "the land so loved by Browning." The prophetic conclusion attests to his early intention of creating a golden age of the Irish theater. This early concern for the theater surprised Yeats when he read his American journalism in his old age.

I R I S H readers know Dr. Todhunter's name from the modern versions of old legends he published two years ago in a volume called "The Banshee," and from his contributions to "The Poems and Ballads of Young Ireland."[1] The Londoner knows him, however, from a series of dramatic experiments, beginning with "Helena in Troas," some five years ago, and ending for the time being in the reproduction of "A Sicilian Idyll" and "The Poison Flower" at the Vaudeville a few days ago. He has also published two long dramas that as yet have not been tried upon the stage. "Helena," the most ambitious of his acted plays, was performed on the only exact reproduction of an old Greek theatre the modern world has seen. Many of the audience afterwards said that the whole gave them a curious religious feeling, singularly unlike the impression made by the modern stage. The sonorous, if somewhat elaborate, verse, with its continuous burden of imminent Fate, was well suited to prolong the feeling, and stamp it with the rhythmical form needed to give it permanence in the memory. Day after day the theatre was crowded with all that was most fashionable or most cultured in London society. The first matinee alone produced, I believe, three hundred pounds. The success of "A Sicilian Idyll" at the little playhouse in Bedford Park[2] last year was more clearly a triumph of drama; for much of the vogue of "Helena" was undoubtedly due to the curiosity aroused by its strange surroundings. "The Idyll," a much more dramatic play

[1] The title of this collection had no definite article. *Poems and Ballads of Young Ireland* appeared in 1888. Aside from Todhunter's, it contained contributions by Yeats, Katharine Tynan, Douglas Hyde, and T. W. Rolleston.

[2] *Bedford Park*: The Yeats family and Todhunter were living in this pre-Raphaelite suburb of London. Yeats had encouraged Todhunter to write a pastoral drama for the clubhouse theater in Bedford Park.

than its forerunner, was beautifully staged, and, as far as one of the performers was concerned,[3] beautifully acted it is true; but still there was nothing in either to bring people for its own sake. We see good acting and good scene-painting every day. The play itself was the main thing this time at any rate. The little theatre was crowded from end to end during the whole of the short run. Twice the number of performances originally intended were given, and almost everyone who loved poetry managed to put in an appearance. The play, charmingly printed by the Chiswick Press and introduced by a frontispiece by Walter Crane, is now to be had in the distinctive white and grey of Mr. Elkin Mathew's[4] publications. It is a pastoral romance suggested by Theocritus and written in the elaborate verse which we expect to find in plays of Arcadia ever since Fletcher[5] sang of the grove's "pale passion lover." There is one scene of incantation which was delivered the other day at the Vaudeville by Miss Florence Farr with astonishing power and effect—a scene that has the very stateliest qualities of dramatic verse. When the poem was revived a week ago it was preluded by a new drama called "The Poison Flower," founded on a story by Hawthorne. In it Dr. Todhunter again went to magic for his strangest effects, but laid the scene of the story in medieval Italy instead of classical Sicily. He has off and on seen a good deal of Italian life, and has laid the scene of no small number of his poems in the land so loved by Browning.

This gives him a certain advantage over Hawthorne, who had never been there.[6] Hawthorne's story, "Rappacini's Daughter," as he called it, is exquisite, but I have always felt that it is a little over fanciful. It seems to have no meaning of sufficient weight to justify its great sadness. Even the folk-tale, when it becomes sad, grows full of some spiritual significance like our Irish story, "The Countess Kathleen."[7] Hawthorne's beautiful story is fantastic, and a little arbitrary. A great writer should have shown more lofty intention than to make your flesh creep. Dr. Todhunter's play, on the other hand, seems to me to improve on Hawthorne in this matter. He has given an allegorical significance to the garden of poisonous flowers, in which the magician's daughter lives, until she, too, has grown as deadly for all her gentleness and beauty as the dreadful flowers she tends. The magician is seeking,

---

[3] *One of the performers*: Florence Farr.   [4] *Mathew's*: should be Mathews'.
[5] Yeats probably referred to John Fletcher's *The Faithful Shepherdess*, 1610. The phrase "pale passion lover" may be a paraphrase of the lines
"Fountain heads, and pathless groves,
Places which pale passion loves."
(*The Nice Valour*, Song, iii, iii).
[6] Hawthorne visited Italy, but after he wrote "Rappacini's Daughter."
[7] Yeats had been working on his play *The Countess Kathleen* for two years. He changed the spelling of the title to "Cathleen" in 1895.

by his mysterious art, to change her into the Eve of a new race, to whom the poison of the world—its sins and diseases—shall be harmless; for this new race will have in its blood the essences of every poison all tempered into harmlessness and health. Just such a dream for the physical redemption of the world was dreamed the other day by that new Italian Rappacini who thought he had discovered the *bacillus* of old age, and that it was only necessary to inoculate people with it to bring about for all men an eternal youth. A happy dream that would, if fulfilled, have made unnecessary the prayers of the heroine in the French play, "Oh, Lord, confine my wrinkles to my heels." Dr. Todhunter, too, in making the magician a Kabalist has given him historical reality and made it much more easy to believe in him. The copy of the Kabala, here in front of me on my own table, pleads for him, and tells me that such men have lived and dreamed such dreams for the bettering of the world. They dreamed them even in Dublin itself, as a certain record I have close to my hand sets forth.[8] He has brought Hawthorne's beautiful story down from no man's land and set it on the common earth of Italy, and realised all the characters until it moves before one with that vivid life of noble drama which makes faint as mist the poor crippled existence we all live. It is a very long time since any play has given me the same kind of pleasure, and I here record my gratitude. What can the prose drama do at its very best compared to that elevation of the whole mind caused by dramatic poetry?

When our political passions have died out in the fulfillment of their aim[9] shall we, I wonder, have a fine native drama of our own? It is very likely. A very great number of the best playwrights who have written for the English stage, from Sheridan and Goldsmith to our own day, have been Irishmen. We are a young country, and still care, I think, for the high thoughts and high feelings of poetry, if in a somewhat uncultivated fashion. We love the dramatic side of events and have too much imagination to think plays which advertise "a real locomotive engine" or "a real fire engine" as the chief attraction to be a better form of drama than the heroic passions and noble diction of the great ages of the theatre. We have never yet been fairly tested. Our playwrights have been poor men who were forced to write for an English public in the very last stages of dramatic decadence. I should very much like to see what Dr. Todhunter could do with an Irish theme written for and acted before an Irish audience. Surely, they would not find the mere fact of its being poetry the very great difficulty English audiences seem

[8] Yeats may have been alluding to evidence of sorcery in Dublin which he found in the memoirs of Dr. Adam Clarke. He mentions this evidence in *United Ireland*, Dec. 30, 1893.

[9] In the summer of 1891 Yeats and many another Irishman expected the quick passage of home rule. In his autobiography, he said that the fall of Parnell and the failure of home rule turned Ireland's attention to literature and the theater.

to find it. We have had the only popular ballad literature of recent days. Does not that prove the poetic capacities of our uneducated masses? Or has English influence and "the union of hearts" made us as prosaic as our neighbours?

Clarence Mangan's Love Affair

This article, Yeats's second piece on Mangan, appeared in *United Ireland* on August 22, 1891. Much of the biographical information is repeated from Yeats's earlier piece, which appeared in *Irish Fireside* on March 12, 1888. The first article included a discussion of Mangan's poetry as well as his miserable life. In the years between 1888 and 1891, Yeats added Blake and Swedenborg to his authorities.

In the 1888 piece Yeats had claimed to have named Frances Stackpoole for the first time as Mangan's beloved. Some admirers of Mangan had objected to this identification, but by 1891 Yeats thought that he had stronger evidence in the testimony of Sir Charles Gavan Duffy. In her 1897 edition of Mangan's works, Louise Imogen Guiney said that Miss Susan Gavan Duffy, the daughter of Yeats's expert, told her that Mangan's beloved was Margaret, not Frances, Stacpoole [*sic*].

Yeats looked back in later life with amusement on his literary pilgrimages to the birthplaces of forgotten Irish poets. His interest in the small points of Mangan's life may seem to be misplaced enthusiasm. However, a poet as autobiographical as Yeats might be assumed to take a similar interest in the lives of other poets. He had no illusions about the separation of life and art.

I DO not now busy myself with the poetry of Clarence Mangan, but with the making and marrying[1] of the man, and with the kind of soul he had, and with the fashion in which he lived. I write mainly to put on record one or two new facts that have come to my knowledge with the thought that they may interest the biographer who at some time, near or distant, must gather up all the threads and weave them into a coherent life.

Mangan was born in Fishamble-street, then somewhat less shabby and smoke-discoloured than it has been for many a day now. His father was a grocer, who did well in business, retired, spent what he had made to the last halfpenny in extravagant living, went bankrupt,

[1] *marrying*: this word must be a printer's error since Mangan never married. Yeats probably used the expression "making and marring."

and died of a broken heart. Apart from this we know little of his character except that, according to Mangan himself, he boasted that his children would run into a mouse-hole to escape him. He seems to have possessed that curious but not unknown combination—the flint heart and the open hand. The shadow of his thriftless gaiety was Clarence Mangan's life-long agony. Upon his death the poet, full of endless desire for a life of joy and freedom, found himself in a scrivener's office, left thus to drudge on, the sole support of a penniless family of young brothers and sisters. Life seemed to promise him nothing except that he might cover with his pen numberless sheets of paper, as the Wandering Jew covers the earth with his feet. He asked "more than any understood," and was given routines, the saddest of things upon this old, dirty planet. Nor was he happy with his office companions. "My nervous and hypochondriacal feelings almost verged on insanity," he wrote in later life. "I seemed to myself to be shut up in a cavern with serpents and scorpions and all hideous and monstrous things, which writhed and hissed around me, and discharged their slime and venom on my person." I have been told that Mangan could not have been unhappy with these fellow-clerks, because one of them afterwards became a bishop. When you have a flaming heart, and it has been plunged down into commonplace, it does not redeem everything to have a future bishop among your companions. Yet these clerks were probably no worse than others. The children of genius have got on badly in all ages with the children of men. The old woman in the story saw nothing more in King Alfred than a careless, good-for-nothing loon, who let her cakes burn, and accordingly did her best to lead him a life of it. Shelley was so tortured at school that he thrust a knife through the hand of a schoolfellow. The great mysterious poet and artist, William Blake, was when a boy so ill-treated by the Westminster students that he flung one of them from a scaffolding where he was at work copying cornices or inscriptions. The abstracted ways and unusual opinions of the man of thought are deadly offenses to commonplace people. The exceptional is ever persecuted. If you tie a red ribbon to the leg of a sea-gull the other gulls will pick it to death. To the soul of Clarence Mangan was tied the burning ribbon of genius.

Mangan had now reached manhood. He had grown up amid penury, cut off from education and refinement. The few poems written during these years, acrostics and other dismal puzzles with words, have no value whatever. They are as sordid as his life. The man needed one thing before he should be ready to deliver his message. He had to love hopelessly—to look out of his "cavern" to a brighter and more beautiful world and then turn his eyes upon the darkness and keep them there for the rest of his life. This love affair is the first of my new facts.

Mangan met—between his twentieth and twenty-fifth year apparently
—a Miss Stackpoole, one of three sisters, who lived in Mountpleasant-
square. She was a fascinating coquette, who encouraged him, amused
herself with his devotion, and then "whistled him down the wind."
Mitchel[2] knew of her, but did not know her name, with the result that
many, Father Meehan[3] for instance, have since doubted her existence
and set the whole story down to Mangan's imagination. She was real
enough—a handsome girl, with a tint of red in her hair, a very fashionable colour in our day, whatever it was then. When I first published her
name some time ago[4] I received a letter from a well-known Mangan
enthusiast denying the whole story point blank. I had then no proof
except the word of an eccentric Protestant clergyman who remembered
both her and Mangan. He might readily have been mistaken. Sir Charles
Gavan Duffy has since, however, corroborated the story, and stated to
me that he lent a dozen or more unpublished letters of Mangan's,
giving, I understand, Mangan's own account of it, to the Irish Exhibition at Earl's Court, but has never been able to recover them, owing to
the scandalous neglect of the committee. My old clergyman also told
me an anecdote, which Sir Charles Gavan Duffy had never heard, of
Mangan's rushing with knife or dagger at one who spoke ill of his faithless "Frances." This, then, is the truth, and I fear all the truth we are
ever likely to know, about that mysterious beauty whom Mangan saw
"a little while—and then no more."[5] His world had flamed up and then
died down into grey ashes—and ashes henceforth it remained. When a
man's love affair goes bankrupt, romance-makers assure us, a little
devil gets into the soles of his feet and drives him hither and thither,
on into his heart and makes him seek out some exciting activity, but
for Clarence Mangan there was nothing but scrivening—scrivening;
he could only watch his labouring quill travelling over ream after ream
of paper.

It was after this that we begin to hear of Mangan's rum-loving and,
if Mitchel speaks truth, opium-eating habits. He became a member of
"The Comet Club," a gathering of journalists and writers of whom the

---

[2] John Mitchel, the famous editor of the *United Irishman*, published in 1859 a collection of
Mangan's poems, to which he contributed a biographical introduction.

[3] The Rev. C. P. Meehan (1812–1890) was a close friend of Mangan's, collected his poems,
and officiated at his funeral.

[4] Yeats named her in his article for *Irish Fireside*, March 12, 1888.

[5] This quotation is from Mangan's translation of a poem by Friedrich Rückert entitled
"Und dann nicht mehr." Mitchel quoted some stanzas of it in his biographical introduction
to Mangan's poems. The following is a sample:

> *I saw her once, one little while, and then no more.*
> *Earth looked like Heaven a little while, and then no more.*
> *Her presence thrilled and lighted to its inner core*
> *My desert breast a little while, and then no more.*

most important was Samuel Lover. He [there] seems to have first drunk deeply. In "The Nameless One" he certainly implies that misery drove him to it. He yet found time to learn several foreign tongues, and to begin the long series of translations from the German, published in 1845, as the "Germanica Anthologia."[6] He contributed much to the *Dublin Penny Journal*, *The Comet*, the newspaper from which the club took its name, *The Dublin University Review*[7] and finally to the *Nation* and *United Irishman*. As times went on he passed from scrivening to an attorney's office, and from that through a period of irregular employment on the *Nation* to a small post in the College Library, where he was employed compiling a catalogue. Here Michel saw him for the first time: "An acquaintance pointed out to me a man perched on the top of a ladder, with the whispered information that the figure was Clarence Mangan. It was an unearthly and ghostly figure in a brown garment[8] (to all appearances) which lasted till the day of his death. The blanched hair was totally unkempt, the corpse-like features still as marble; a large book was in his arms, and all his soul was in the book. I had never heard of Clarence Mangan before, and knew not for what he was celebrated, whether as a magician, a poet, or a murderer; yet took a volume and spread it on a table, not to read, but with pretense of reading, to glare on the spectral creature on this ladder."

The unearthly something that made Mitchel compare him to a magician had its justification in a strong visionary bent that lay deep in the man. He describes himself as "one whom some have called a seer," and seer he was if visions can make man such. One who remembers him has told me of his devotion to Swedenborg's "Heaven and Hell," and another how he would see, like the great Swede, a sphere of light about men's souls. He himself has asserted that he was continually haunted by this persecuting phantom of his follies. It sometimes happens to a man that when this outer world has grown utterly blank there exists within a spiritual illumination. Such seems to have come to Mangan, but only dimly and fitfully, and bearing with it visions of terrible things more often than of joyous and beautiful. One good thing it brought him—an infinite faith in man's destiny. He never denied happiness because he was miserable, or goodness because his own life was in the gutter.

When the internal eye grows bright the outward gaze sometimes is bleared and uncertain, and we confuse the real and the unreal, and see men as trees walking. It was thus with Mangan. He wrote at this latter

[6] This title is usually given as *Anthologia Germanica*.

[7] The *Dublin University Review* did not begin until the 1880s. Yeats meant the *Dublin University Magazine*.

[8] In Mitchel's edition of Mangan's poems this passage reads as follows: ". . . in a brown garment; the same garment (to all appearance) which lasted. . . ."

end of his life an autobiography called a "Confession," full of terrible, untrue things that he believed. Thus he asserts that he was brought to an hospital when a boy for some broken bones or other, and put into a bed with a leper, from whom he caught leprosy, but as an inward, spiritual disease, invisible to all, but none the less eating his soul away. Once (before he came there to die) he really was brought to an hospital, but in late life. It was St. Vincent's, and his visit is described in Mrs. Atkinson's biography of Mary Aikenhead.[9] "Oh, the luxury of clean sheets," he exclaimed. His face is described in this book from the words of an eye-witness as "handsome in outline, bloodless and wrinkled," with "heavy lids" and "blue eyes, distraught with the opium-eater's dreams." Clean sheets may well have been a wonder to him, for he had long now been haunting the lowest taverns, disappearing often for days to live in some barn, drinking and brooding, turning over in his mind, perhaps, some one of those wild songs of his "The Nameless One," "Siberia," "The Dying Enthusiast," or some other; or watching phantoms coming and going amid the straw, or listening to unearthly voices whispering in the air. Once after one of these disappearances, the late Father Meehan, I have been told, brought him before a looking-glass and made him look at his own worn and ragged form. "Ah, but the state of the outer man is nothing to the state of the inner," was the answer.

At last he died, and journeyed elsewhere. He died in the Meath Hospital of cholera. Some say he had foretold his own death from the epidemic some time before. I have it from one who had it from the doctor in attendance, that when he was dead his face became beautiful and calm. When the contorted soul had gone the muscles relapsed, and the clay returned to its primal innocence; or, if you prefer it, when life had fallen away the departing soul shed some of the light of its new peace upon the body. The dawn touched it, and the lustre of the dawn was reflected into the valley of the shadow it had fled from.

W. B. Yeats

A Reckless Century.
Irish Rakes and Duellists

BY W. B. YEATS

This article appeared in *United Ireland* on September 12, 1891. Yeats's researches into Irish rakes of the eighteenth century were part of his preparation of a volume for the "Adventure Series" published by T. Fisher Unwin.

[9] *Mary Aikenhead, Her Life, Her Work, and Her Friends*, by Sarah Atkinson, Dublin, 1879.

In about October of 1892, Yeats told Edward Garnett, a reader for Unwin, that he had finished the introduction to the "Adventurers" volume. For some reason or other, the volume never appeared and this article is the only relic of that research. In Yeats's letters of the early nineties there is some talk of a projected romance on eighteenth-century Ireland, but that project never came to fruition.

Many of the anecdotes in this article are taken, as Yeats admitted, from *Ireland Sixty Years Ago*, Dublin, 1847, a volume attributed to John Edward Walsh. A few stories came from Sir Jonah Barrington's *Personal Sketches of His Own Times*, London, 1869.

Yeats mentions this article in a piece on Oscar Wilde for *United Ireland* (September 26, 1891). The ferocious energy of the old rakes had been channeled, in Yeats's opinion, into the intellectual wit of such Irishmen as Oscar Wilde and Bernard Shaw. The present article is a good example of Yeats's use of the past for propaganda purposes. The Hellfire Club, Power of Daragle, and Brian Maguire were all, whether they knew it or not, preparing the way for the Celtic Revival.

O N the top of Mount Pelier, one of the Dublin hills, stands the building of the Hellfire Club, upon its stone roof a few tufts of grass resembling hair, and in its front dark openings reminding one of sightless eyes—the whole like a grinning skull, hideous symbol of an age without ideals, without responsibility, without order, without peace. About it the winds howl unceasing, as though they keened for a violence that was as theirs is, for an age in whose unbridled life there was something elemental, something of the winds and floods. The neighbourhood still mutters with tales of deeds done within their grey walls. Here the devil came often, the story is, and feasted among these eighteenth-century worshippers of his, leaving on one notable night his hoof-mark on the hearthstone; here a number of the gentry of Ireland were wont to drink to the toast "May we be all damned," and to go through the ceremony of the Mass with obscene accompaniments; and here, to show their contempt for that eternal flame thought to be their lot, did they set fire to the building in a drunken spree, and sit on mocking the flames until they were driven out half stifled. Murders too, the peasants will have it, were not unknown; and now a hundred years after the last of its frequenters has brawled himself into the grave it is haunted, the tale goes, by drunken phantoms, who feast and gamble, with their master in the midst of them. For all this copious tradition not much is known for certainty of this Hellfire Club. There is something in Walsh[1]—the anonymous author of "Ireland Sixty Years Ago"—

[1] John Edward Walsh (1816–1869). *Ireland Sixty Years Ago* first appeared in Dublin in 1847.

something in Barrington,[2] something in old magazines, and something in popular tradition; but it is not much at best, and little reliable. We know more of the "Cherokees," whose iniquitous rules and regulations have been preserved by a contemporary writer. No man was eligible for membership unless he gave clear evidence of a debauched life, and no man could be president until he could swear to having killed his man in a duel. This club became a terror in Dublin, and had many encounters with the authorities, beating them on every occasion. It was wont to march through the streets dressed as a military corps, and no power was found to cope with it.

There were also the "Hawkabites," the "Sweaters," and "Pinkin-dindies," who took an inch or so off the point of their scabbards, and went about prodding people out of sheer high spirits, and now and then killing a barber or two who had made them late for ball or dinner party by not turning up in time to powder and pomatum their empty heads. Sometimes they would stand at cross roads, notably at the College end of Dame-street, and prod the passers-by.

The wild passion for duelling that past through the country in that age is somewhat more worthy of sympathy. The destruction of the national forces at the battle of the Boyne had filled the land with Catholic gentlemen who had no defence against insult but their own unaided swords, and from their contests with their supplanters spread through the country a habit of fighting for anything and everything. Men lived for it, and pistol practice became a consuming passion. Swaggering swashbucklers though they were, they did after all hold their lives lightly and risk them for a song. A little conviction would have made them good rebels. We hear of a certain Fitzgerald fighting a duel across a table, and when his opponent's pistol missed fire going over and priming it himself, and then returning to his place to receive the shot; nor can one help giving sympathy to Power of Daragle, when two Englishmen at an English inn bribed the waiters to give him for dinner, in mockery of his nationality, a dish of potatoes, and he replied by eating the potatoes, and then having served two dishes, one for himself and one for the Englishmen, which proved when the covers were lifted to contain pistols. Nor do we sympathize less because the Englishmen, much shocked at the notion of anything so foolish and Irish as a duel, fled hurriedly from the room leaving an unsettled bill which Power of Daragle paid charitably. The bragadocio [*sic*] of Brian Maguire—huge, whiskered bully that he was—standing at a narrow crossing and daring the passerby to jostle him, is not so pleasant an object even though his skill was so great that he always rang his bell with a bullet and could snuff a candle held in his wife's hand with a pistol

[2] Sir Jonah Barrington (1760–1834), author of *Personal Sketches of His Own Times*.

shot; nor does the statement of a certain contemporary pamphleteer that his ancestors were once kings in Ireland, but that "the infamous invader had been impoverishing Mr. Maguire for centuries," make us feel any the more anxious to see his like again.

This reckless and turbulent spirit was by no means confined to the upper classes, but spread to the shopkeepers and artisans to a considerable extent. Poor men, when condemned to death, would spend the night before their hanging gambling upon the lids of their own coffins, making amends for a life without dignity by a death without fear. During all the early part of the eighteenth century the nation had little or no sense of national duty and public responsibility, the proper chiefs of the people were dead or exiled with foreign armies, the bards had passed away—the last bardic college came to an end in 1680—and the ballad-makers had only just begun to take their place. The Anglo-Irish gentry who had succeeded to the defeated chiefs held allegiance only to England, and were responsible to no man. They had not yet awakened to the temporary patriotism of the Volunteer[3] movement, nor listened as yet to the terrible raillery of Swift. The contemporary life of England was reckless enough, but its recklessness, never at all equal to that of Ireland, was tempered by some sense of public welfare. The gentry of Ireland thought only to eat, drink, and be merry, for tomorrow might come rebellion and confiscation. Almost the only sense of national duty was, for long, among the poor. They were driven to their excesses often enough by patriotic hope. With what different feelings do we look back at the irresponsible turbulence of the gentry and at that storm of popular indignation when the mob attacked the Parliament House and made the members swear truth to Ireland one after another, and then, to show their contempt of England, set an old woman with a pipe in her mouth upon the throne of the Viceroy.

Such were the thoughts and stories brought to my mind the other day by that grinning skull at Mount Pelier. All the four winds of heaven seemed to be howling at once upon the green hilltop, and telling to each other tales of forgotten violence and dead recklessness. What message of hope did they bring me? What judgment are we to pronounce upon that eighteenth century? What should it make us expect from the future? I find nothing but fortunate prophesies in that dead century. I see there the Celtic intensity, the Celtic fire, the Celtic daring wasting themselves, it is true in all kinds of evil, but needing only the

[3] The Volunteers were a force, raised in part by Henry Flood, to repel a possible French invasion during the American Revolution. Their number grew to 40,000 and they were able to demand, with success, such concessions as the opening of the British colonies to Irish trade.

responsibility of self-government and the restraint of a trained public opinion to have laboured devotedly for the public weal. The vast energy that filled Ireland with bullies and swashbucklers will some day give us great poets and thinkers. It is better to be violent and irresponsible than full of body-worship and money-grubbing. The duellist Whaley going off for a bet to play ball against the ramparts of Jerusalem is a nobler sight than the railway king putting his millions together. Those eighteenth-century duellists, at any rate, tried to really live, and not merely exist. They took their lives into their hands and went through the world with a song upon their lips; and if a curse was mingled with the song they are none the less better to think of than had they grown rich and much-esteemed, and yet lasted on no more than half alive, toadstools upon the state. The energy that filled them is still in our veins, but working now for public good. If a man or a people have energy all is well with them, and if they use it for ill to-day they will turn it to good to-morrow. When the devil is converted, goes the old proverb, he will be the first of the sons of God.[4] If the sword be strong it will make so much the better ploughshare when the day of peace is at hand. Their swords were strong, at any rate, though they were not turned often enough, or persistently enough, towards the enemies of their country.

Oscar Wilde's Last Book

BY W. B. YEATS

This review of Oscar Wilde's *Lord Arthur Savile's Crime and Other Stories,* London, 1891, appeared in *United Ireland,* September 26, 1891.

From the beginning of their acquaintance, Yeats regarded Oscar Wilde more highly as a wit and figure of legend than as an author. He met Wilde at the soirées of William Ernest Henley, one of the first magazine editors to print Yeats's poetry. Wilde was kind to him, invited Yeats to his home for Christmas dinner (probably in 1889), and had Yeats tell fairy tales to Wilde's son, whom Yeats thoroughly frightened by mentioning a giant. Burdened by a sense of his provincial awkwardness, Yeats was awed by the splendor of Wilde's personality and ménage, but in retrospect Yeats thought Wilde's address contained too much artifice.

Before their meeting, Wilde had reviewed Yeats's book of fairy tales for *Woman's World* (February, 1889), and he had helped the reception of Yeats's

---

[4] Yeats's name within the secret Order of the Golden Dawn was "*Demon est Deus Inversus*" (a demon is an inverted god).

first volume, *The Wanderings of Oisin*, with two reviews (*Woman's World*, March, 1889, and *Pall Mall Gazette*, July 12, 1889). He was kind to Yeats's poems although he found "strange crudities and irritating conceits" in them.

Neither this review nor Yeats's later review of Wilde's drama *A Woman of No Importance* was wholly favorable. Although not conspicuously stained by Ibsenism, Wilde's dramas lacked that poetry which Yeats most loved in the theater, and his somewhat negative reaction to "Lord Arthur Savile's Crime" may have been caused by Wilde's satire on palmistry.

Yeats thought that the true basis for Wilde's fame lay in his willingness to stay in England and face judicial vengeance and public disgrace. In *A Vision*, Yeats placed Wilde in the nineteenth phase of the moon, that of the assertive man, a phase which marked the beginnings of "the artificial, the abstract, the fragmentary, and the dramatic" (*A Vision*, London, 1937, New York, 1956, p. 148).

W E have the irresponsible Irishman in life, and would gladly get rid of him. We have him now in literature and in the things of the mind, and are compelled perforce to see that there is a good deal to be said for him. The men I described to you the other day under the heading, "A Reckless Century,"[1] thought they might drink, dice, and shoot each other to their hearts' content, if they did but do it gaily and gallantly, and here now is Mr. Oscar Wilde, who does not care what strange opinions he defends or what time-honoured virtue he makes laughter of, provided he does it cleverly. Many were injured by the escapades of the rakes and duellists, but no man is likely to be the worse for Mr. Wilde's shower of paradox. We are not likely to poison any one because he writes with appreciation of Wainwright[2]—art critic and poisoner—nor have I heard that there has been any increased mortality among deans because the good young hero of his last book tries to blow up one with an infernal machine; but upon the other hand we are likely enough to gain something of brightness and refinement from the deft and witty pages in which he sets forth these matters.

"Beer, bible, and the seven deadly virtues have made England what she is," wrote Mr. Wilde once; and a part of the Nemesis that has fallen upon her is a complete inability to understand anything he says. *We* should not find him so unintelligible—for much about him is Irish of the Irish. I see in his life and works an extravagant Celtic crusade against

[1] See the previous article in this collection.

[2] Wainwright: usually spelled "Wainewright." Thomas Griffiths Wainewright (1794-1847) wrote art criticism for the *London Magazine* and exhibited paintings at the Royal Academy. He committed forgery in 1822 and 1824, and then he was thought to have poisoned several of his relatives. Convicted of forgery, he was exiled to Tasmania, where he died. Wilde's memoir of Wainewright is contained in "Pen, Pencil and Poison," printed in *Intentions*, London, 1891.

Anglo-Saxon stupidity. "I labour under a perpetual fear of not being misunderstood," he wrote, a short time since, and from behind this barrier of misunderstanding he peppers John Bull with his pea-shooter of wit, content to know there are some few who laugh with him. There is scarcely an eminent man in London who has not one of those little peas sticking somewhere about him. "Providence and Mr. Walter Besant have exhausted the obvious," he wrote once, to the deep indignation of Mr. Walter Besant;[3] and of a certain notorious and clever, but coldblooded Socialist,[4] he said, "he has no enemies, but is intensely disliked by all his friends." Gradually people have begun to notice what a very great number of those little peas are lying about, and from this reckoning has sprung up a great respect for so deft a shooter, for John Bull, though he does not understand wit, respects everything that he can count up and number and prove to have bulk. He now sees beyond question that the witty sayings of this man whom he has so long despised are as plenty as the wood blocks in the pavement of Cheapside. As a last resource he has raised the cry that his tormentor is most insincere, and Mr. Wilde replies in various ways that it is quite an error to suppose that a thing is true because John Bull sincerely believes it. Upon the other hand, if he did not believe it, it might have some chance of being true. This controversy is carried on upon the part of John by the newspapers; therefore, those who only read them have as low an opinion of Mr. Wilde as those who read books have a high one. "Dorian Grey" [sic] with all its faults of method, is a wonderful book. "The Happy Prince" is a volume of as pretty fairy tales as our generation has seen; and "Intentions" hides within its immense paradox some of the most subtle literary criticism we are likely to see for many a long day. To this list has now been added "Lord Arthur Savile's Crime and other Stories" (James R. Osgood, M'Ilvaine, and Co.). It disappoints me a little, I must confess. The story it takes its name from is amusing enough in all conscience. "The Sphinx without a Secret" has a quaint if rather meagre charm; but "The Canterville Ghost" with its supernatural horse-play, and "The Model Millionaire," with its conventional motive, are quite unworthy of more than a passing interest.

In "Lord Arthur Savile's Crime: A Study of Duty," a young aristocrat is told by a cheiromantist that he is fated to commit a murder. At first he is very miserable, because he is engaged to be married, for he considers it would be a great crime to marry with such a doom hanging

---

[3] Walter Besant (1836–1901), voluminous romancer and writer of novels advocating social reform. Wilde's famous epigram on Besant is from part two of "The Critic as Artist," reprinted in *Intentions*.

[4] *Coldblooded Socialist*: Bernard Shaw. Yeats met Shaw at one of William Morris's gatherings. Their dislike was mutual.

over him. Presently he sees his duty. He does not hesitate a moment, being a young man of principle. He must commit the murder at once, and get it over. He postpones his engagement, and picks out an old aunt to be the victim. She had no money to leave him, so there would be no sordid motives. He gives her a box containing a piece of aconite which she is to take when she next gets an attack of heartburn she is subject to. It is an American cure he assures her. Presently he hears of her death, and grows quite happy making preparations for his wedding. Alas, one day, he finds the aconite untasted among her papers. She died of the heartburn, not of the poison. Again he postpones his marriage and chooses a victim—the Dean of Chichester. He sends him an infernal machine in the form of a clock. The clock, however, goes off with a whizz and a puff of smoke, and the dean thinks it must be a kind of alarm clock sent him by an admirer of his sermons, and gives it to his children, who take it to the nursery, and make explosions all day long by putting a little powder under a clapper they find among the works. The good young aristocrat is in despair. He had tried to do his duty in vain. Fate, however, is kind to him; and as he is pacing up and down the Thames Embankment he comes upon the cheiromantist leaning against the parapet, and with a vigorous shove sends him into the river, and watches him drown with satisfaction at this accomplishment of his duty. "Did you drop anything, sir?" says a policeman.[5] "Nothing of importance, sergeant," he answers, as he hailed a hansom. After this he marries and lives out his life in perfect happiness, and with a proud sense of duty done against much temptation to have done otherwise.

Surely we have in this story something of the same spirit that filled Ireland once with gallant, irresponsible ill-doing, but now it is in its right place making merry among the things of the mind, and laughing gaily at our most firm fixed convictions. In one other Londoner, the socialist, Mr. Bernard Shaw, I recognize the same spirit. His account[6] of how the old Adam gradually changed into the great political economist Adam Smith is like Oscar Wilde in every way. These two men, together with Mr. Whistler,[7] the painter—half an Irishman also, I believe—keep literary London continually agog to know what they will say next.

---

[5] "Lord Arthur Savile's Crime" reads: " 'Have you dropped anything, sir?' said a voice behind him suddenly."

[6] *His account*: in "The Economic Basis of Socialism" from *Fabian Essays*, London, 1889.

[7] James McNeill Whistler, the American painter, was descended on his father's side from an old British family with an Irish branch. His mother was of Scots origin. For Yeats in 1891, very little Irish blood indeed made a man "half an Irishman." By finding an O'Neill in William Blake's ancestral closet, Yeats made his master half an Irishman, to a storm of English protest.

The Young Ireland League

This article was printed in *United Ireland* on October 3, 1891, three days before the death of Charles Stewart Parnell. Yeats had then high hopes for the passage of a Home Rule bill, but the scandal over Parnell's affair with Kitty O'Shea and the sudden death of "the Chief" had doomed such hopes. The occasion for this article was the banding together of local Young Ireland Societies into a literary society. Such a project was for Yeats only a prelude to a larger undertaking. At the end of December, 1891, he founded with T. W. Rolleston the Irish Literary Society of London, and on May 24, 1892, he helped to found the National Literary Society in Dublin. Maud Gonne helped Yeats in the attempt to establish local libraries. Indeed, some commentators have explained Yeats's enthusiasm for the whole project as an effort to impress Maud Gonne with his abilities as a man of action.

THE newspapers have not been able to make out the meaning of this League of ours. That a number of literary societies should wish to band themselves together and sing Irish ballads instead of the songs of the music halls, and recite Irish poems at their meetings, and help each other to the possession of good books seems the last thing likely to the great wisdom of the Press. Anything else seems more worthy of belief. We are coming forth, the English papers tell us, trying to trouble the peace of nations with our pikes. We are Fenians coming to take care of Mr. Parnell. Nor is the wisdom of our Irish Press much more equal to the occasion, for no matter how they vary the minor notes the old hurdy-gurdy can play but one tune—the wickedness of Mr. Parnell. It really seems needful to say that our aim is to help to train up a nation of worthy men and women who shall be able to work for public good, whether we are about to win an Irish Parliament or whether the old war against English dominion is still to go on. The general election,[1] or the coming of Home Rule itself, will not do away with the need for our work, for our enemies are ignorance and bigotry and fanaticism, the eternal foes of the human race which may not be abolished in any way by Acts of Parliament.

To do this work of ours we seek to revive certain educational instruments—the young Ireland societies—that proved effective in the past and at the same time to do away with various defects which we have learned to remedy by experience. The old societies were started in 1880, and spread all over the country, setting everywhere groups of

---

[1] In the general election of July, 1892, Gladstone's Liberal Party won a majority. In 1893, a Home Rule bill was passed by the House of Commons, but it was rejected by the House of Lords.

young men working and thinking. For six years there were twenty or thirty branches in active existence, and there might be as many still if the central body in Dublin had not come to an end in 1885, but had gone on feeding them from its central life. We now seek to pour new life into those branches which are still living, to revive those which have died, and to make new societies where there were none before, and to bring all under the influence of an elective council of fifty members. These members are to be elected yearly and will be independent of any particular branch and its varying fortunes. The old branches and members are promising their support. In Dublin the Leinster Literary Society, the Rathmines National League Literary Society, the Arran-quay National League Literary Society, the National Club Literary Society, and probably the Ninety Club Literary Society will join with us; and in the country the Passage West, Maryborough, and Thurles Young Ireland Societies will shortly affiliate. Groups of young men in Cork, Belfast, Clonmel, Macroom, Kingstown, Kilmailock, Waterford, Glasgow, Bray, Middleton, Limerick, Tralee, Cavan, and Bruff, promise to form branches; and there are [*sic*] also some hope of help from the Irishmen in England. The Belfast and Cork Young Ireland Societies still hold aloof from us, but they will be drawn in when they find that we are really neutral in the present political dispute, that we welcome Parnellite and M'Carthyite[2] equally, that our League holds out the flag of truce to all Nationalists, and that, perhaps, in ours alone of national organizations may they find the peace that comes from working for distant purposes. We desire to make the fanatic, on which side soever he be found, less fanatical, and to make the rankerous [*sic*] heart, wheresoever it be, less bitter. In no other sense have we to do with parties.

The actual work before the League is definite enough. Classes will be organized to teach the history and language of Ireland, lectures will be given upon Irish subjects, and most important of all, reading-rooms will be started in connection with the various branches. They need not cost much. It has been calculated that a reading-room, where the papers of all sides and the best magazines are taken, can be kept going in a country village for 4s. or 5s. a week. This includes the rent of a room. No caretaker would be required, for each member might have his own key. For four or five pounds additional such a room could be stocked with a library containing, not only the best Irish books, but the masterpieces of other countries as well. It is proposed that the council draw up a list for the guidance of the local members, and that the organization as a whole bear a portion of the cost. The Irish books in these

---

[2] After the split in the Irish Home Rule faction, those men who rejected Parnell's leadership were led by Justin McCarthy (1830–1912).

reading-rooms should be before all else (though by no means excluding all else) the books that feed the imagination. They should include Mitchel, Mangan, Davis, both prose and verse, all the Irish ballad collections, the radiant and romantic histories of Standish O'Grady, the "Celtic Romances" of Joyce,[3] the poems of Sir Samuel Ferguson, the poems of William Allingham, the best novels of Carleton, Banim, Griffin, and Lever, three or four of the Irish stories of Miss Edgeworth, the folk-lore writings of Hyde, Croker, and Lady Wilde, Moore's Melodies, and some of the best translations from the old Celtic epics. Most of these books are very cheap, and when they are at all dear they can be got secondhand. The best hundred Irish books, as set forth in the *Freeman* some time ago,[4] would be both far too many and quite of the wrong kind. Imagination, and not learning, is the centre of life, and from the direction it takes spring thought and conduct, and in books like those I have mentioned dwells the best imagination of National Ireland. Irish writers of equal or greater merit there have been whom I have not mentioned, because they did not make Ireland their subject matter, but united with the main stream of English literature. They have no special claim upon us, but must be read when, like Goldsmith, they are important enough to make a needful part of general knowledge. But those writers who have made Ireland their study have a peculiar claim on our affections. An article in the *National Press*, in which I recognize a hand worthy of a better cause, has assured us that we have no literature except a few songs and stories, and that the sooner we of the Young Ireland League find it out the better. I, at any rate, found it out long ago, and was well pleased, for songs and stories are no inconsiderable things when the men who wrote them loved the grass under their feet and the flying Irish clouds over their heads, and the blue mountains, and the bowed forms of the ploughing and reaping people among whom they lived, and when they know how to fill others with the same love.

W. B. Yeats

A Poet We Have Neglected

Yeats reviewed the six-volume collected edition of the poems of William Allingham, London, 1887–1891, in the December 12, 1891, issue of *United Ireland*.

Although not included by Yeats before this article in the holy trinity of "Davis, Mangan, Ferguson," William Allingham was a powerful influence

[3] Patrick Weston Joyce, compiler and translator of *Old Celtic Romances*.   [4] See note 1, p. 383.

upon the early fairy and peasant ballad poems of Yeats. "The Stolen Child" of Yeats, for instance, is full of echoes of Allingham's "Fairies" and "Twilight Voices."

Three years before the present article, Yeats had written as his first prose contribution to an American newspaper the account of Allingham that was printed in the *Providence Sunday Journal* of September 2, 1888. The critical judgments are similar in both articles, even the phrasing at times, although in 1888 Yeats had been more severe on Allingham's lack of a strong Irish nationalism. He had even then found absent in Allingham a unified sense of life. Yeats's phrasing as early as 1888 had a strongly Blakean tone: "Nothing is an isolated artistic moment; there is unity everywhere; everything fulfills a purpose that is not its own; the hailstone is a journeyman of God; the grass blade carries the universe upon its point." Aside from such flashes of eloquence, the 1888 piece contained flowers of rhetoric which Yeats had by 1891 learned to avoid. Of Allingham's "Fairies'" in 1888 Yeats said, ". . . such songs, the heart covers them with its ivy."

In 1892 Yeats contributed a sketch on Allingham to Miles's anthology *The Poets and the Poetry of the Century*, and in 1905 he prepared for the Dun Emer Press an edition of *Sixteen Poems by William Allingham*. Not all of Yeats's enthusiasms lasted so long.

O F all recognized Irish poets, William Allingham is at once the most delicate and the least read on this side of the water. To most Irishmen and women he is merely the author of "Fairies," or of some other stray lyric which has drifted into our ballad collections. In England he is becoming better known, and now, two years after his death, Messrs. Reeves and Turner have completed the collected edition of his works by the addition of "Thought and Word" and "Black-berries." These six little books, with their vellum backs and illustrations by Dante Rossetti, and Millais, and their advertisement of more expensive editions on luxe paper, have all the signs of being addressed to an assured public, who will both read their Allingham and pay for him too. It is time for us over here to claim him as our own, and give him his due place among our sacred poets; to range his books beside Davis and Mangan, and Ferguson; for he, too, sang of Irish scenes and Irish faces.

He was the poet of Ballyshannon,[1] though not of Ireland; perhaps that is the reason why we have not known more of him. His feeling was local and not national, and we have now[2] such dire need for all our national fire that we have had but little time or thought for any

---

[1] *Ballyshannon*: port town in County Donegal, on the west coast of Ireland only twenty miles northeast of Sligo town.

[2] *United Ireland*, in which this article appeared, was then a Parnellite journal. The "now" Yeats referred to was only two months after Parnell's death and a time of continued political wrangling between Parnell's followers and those Irishmen who had voted him out as leader of the Home Rule faction.

narrower inspiration. Yet, certainly, we have been wrong to neglect this man. "Irish Songs and Poems," the first volume of his collected works, should be on all Irish bookshelves. In it is enshrined that passionate devotion that so many Irishmen feel for the little town where they were born, and for the mountains they saw from the doors they passed through in childhood. It should be dear to our exiles, and grow a new link in the chain that binds them to their native land. Some day, when copyrights have lapsed, it will be reprinted for a few pence, I doubt not, and grow dear and familiar to many of our sea-wandering and land-traversing people. Its author will take his place among that band of poets whose swift shuttles weave about us a web of tender affection and spirited dreams. He will always, however, be best loved by those who, like the present writer, have spent their childhood in some small Western seaboard town, and who remember how it was for years the centre of their world, and how its enclosing mountains and its quiet rivers became a portion of their life for ever. How kindly in their ears will ever sound Allingham's lines—

> *"A wild west coast, a little town*
> *Where little folk go up and down,*
> *Tides flow and winds blow.*
> *Human wile and human fate,*
> *Night and tempest and the sea,*
> *What is little, what is great?*
> *Howsoe'er the answer be*
> *Let me sing of what I know."*[3]

The greater part of his life was spent there "where little folk go up and down," and for them he printed many of his poems on broad sheets that had so wide a circulation that the Government gave him a small pension on the ground of their value as education for the people.[4] It is well to remember these broad sheets, for they prove his genuine wish to be considered an Irish poet, and not a mere cosmopolitan choosing his themes from Ireland, as he might choose them in another way from Kamskchatka. One song of his, "Kate of Ballyshannon,"[5]

---

[3] These lines are the opening section of "A Stormy Night. A Story of the Donegal Coast," from *Irish Songs and Poems*. Yeats reversed the fourth and fifth lines as well as making one verbal change—on line five, Yeats wrote "Human wile" for "Human Will." The first five lines should read as follows:

> *A Wild west Coast, a little Town,*
> *Where little Folk go up and down,*
> *Tides flow and winds blow:*
> *Night and Tempest and the Sea,*
> *Human Will and Human Fate. . . .*

[4] In 1864.

[5] This title is usually given in Allingham editions as "Kate O'Bellyshanny."

was often sung by the peasantry. It is one of the deftest of Irish mock serious songs—

> *"One summer's day, the banks were gay,*
>   *The Erne in sunshine glancin' there,*
> *The big cascade its music play'd*
>   *And set the salmon dancin' there.*
> *Along the green my joy was seen;*
>   *Some goddess bright I thought her there;*
> *The fishes, too, swam close to view*
>   *Her image in the water there.*
>   *From top to toe, where'er you go,*
>   *The loveliest girl of any, O,*
>   *Ochone! your mind I find unkind,*
>   *Sweet Kate O'Ballyshannon, O!*
>
> *"My dear, give ear!—the river's near,*
>   *And if you think I'm shammin' now,*
> *To end my grief I'll seek relief*
>   *Among the trout and salmon now;*
> *For shrimps and sharks to make their marks,*
>   *And other watery vermin there;*
> *Unless a mermaid saves my life,*
>   *My wife and me her merman there.*
>   *From top to toe," etc.*

The Ballyshannon poems contain many much more serious and beautiful things than these dancing verses, such as the well-known "Fairies" and "The Winding Banks of Erne" which is known through being included in Sparling's Irish Minstrelsy[6] and "Lovely Mary Donnelly," which has found its way into the ballad books. Two hundred years hence those songs of his may have turned Ballyshannon into one of the spots' held sacred by literary history, and travelling Germans and Americans will think it would "discredit their travel" to have come to Ireland and not gone there. A mild light of imagination will shine upon its streets such as shines where a Herbert, or a Crashaw, or a Herrick lived and laboured.

When I wrote· a while since that Allingham's poems should be included in the books[7] recommended by the Council of the Young Ireland League to the projected village libraries,[8] I had the first volume, "Irish Poems," in my mind. Those who care to know his genius more perfectly should add to it the third volume, "Flower Fancies," for the

---

[6] H. Halliday Sparling's collection of Irish ballads, *Irish Minstrelsy*, 1887. *United Ireland* printed "sparkling Irish minstrelsy," and indeed it may be that as well.

[7] *books: United Ireland* read "book."

[8] Yeats contributed a letter on "The Young Ireland League" to *United Ireland*, October 3, 1891. In the letter Yeats had referred generally to "poems of William Allingham."

sake of the poems called "Day and Night Songs." A few of them have
to do with Ireland, but most are expressions of personal feeling, like
that most exquisite of all his lyrics, "Twilight Voices,"⁹ wherein he
sings of the coming of old age, and of the mysterious voices that call to
him "out of the dimness, vague and vast," of the unknown world
beyond the tomb. They need not concern themselves—unless they be
very ardent readers—with the other volumes; for, though they contain
one or two fine things, they were written for the most part either after
Allingham had left Ballyshannon for London, and lost his inspiration,
or before he had found it, or are merely reprints of long poems like
"Laurence Bloomfield," and for long poems he had no faculty. When
he had to deal with a large subject, the inherent limitation of his mind
marred all. He is essentially a poet of the accidental and fleeting—of
passing artistic moments. The pilot's daughter in her Sunday frock,
the sound¹⁰ of a clarionet through the ruddy window of a forge, the
fishers drawing in their nets with a silver wave of salmon—these are his
true subject matter. He had no sense of the great unities—the relations
of man to man, and all to the serious life of the world. It was this that
kept him from feeling Ireland as a whole; from writing of the joys and
sorrows of the Irish people, as Davis, and Ferguson, and Mangan have
done, and from stirring our blood with great emotions. Had he felt the
unity of life, he, with his marvellous artistic faculty, could have given
us long poems that would be really alive; but, not feeling it, the best he
could do was "Laurence Bloomfield," with its fine pictures of detached
things, and its total failure as an Irish epic of the land troubles. But let us
be grateful for what he has given us. If he was no national poet, he was,
at any rate, no thin-blooded cosmopolitan, but loved the hills about
him and the land under his feet.

W. B. Yeats

The New "Speranza"

This article, from *United Ireland*, January 16, 1892, was the first of two pieces
which Yeats wrote during that month in support of Maud Gonne's nationalistic activities in Paris. As all the world knows, Yeats was deeply in love with
Maud Gonne. She served as the inspiration for his drama *The Countess
Cathleen* and for most of his early love poems. What Yeats did not know at
this time was that Miss Gonne was in love with a French journalist, Lucien

⁹ "Twilight Voices" was included in Yeats's *A Book of Irish Verse*, London, 1895.
¹⁰ *sound of a clarionet*: this and the succeeding phrase about salmon are almost identical with
Yeats's 1888 *Providence Sunday Journal* article.

Millevoye. Part of her influence upon the French press may have been Mille-voye's work. A few years after this, she bore Millevoye two children, one of whom died, and the other, named Iseult, was publicly acknowledged as Maud's niece. (See Elizabeth Coxhead, *Daughters of Erin*, for this gossip, and also Joyce's *Ulysses*, p. 43 (Modern Library Edition).)

At about this time, Millevoye became editor of the newspaper *La Patrie*, and Maud Gonne founded a small paper for Irish propaganda called *L'Irlande Libre*. Later in this decade, Yeats contributed two pieces to this paper, one on Fiona Macleod and one on John O'Leary.

By the title of this article Yeats intended to draw a parallel between the new "Speranza" and the old "Speranza," Lady Wilde, who had signed the name "Speranza" to her fiery pieces for the *Nation* magazine in the 1840s. An article very similar to this one appeared in the *Boston Pilot* on July 30, 1892, and was included in the collection of Yeats's American newspaper pieces, *Letters to the New Island*.

O NE little colony of Irishmen and women has ever stood outside the National organization. No Irish leader of recent days has ever given a thought to the little community of Irish people living in Paris, and yet the good will of Europe is of moment to us, and they might help to answer that ceaseless stream of calumny England has sent forth against us through continental nations. To have the ear of Paris would be to have the ear of Europe, and no oppressed nation can well spare any friend. Miss Maud Gonne has set herself the task of organizing this community and has founded an *"Association Irlandais"* to bring the Irish of Paris into touch with one another, and to keep France informed of the true state of the Irish Question. She began her work by presiding at a dinner given by French sympathizers with the cause of Ireland, and made a great stir by her eloquent statement of the case for Ireland. The French papers are loud in her praise; the *Figaro* has interviewed her, and described her speech as having made a sensation. *L'Etendard Nationale* cannot find words strong enough to describe its effect. "Pathetic and persuasive, sweet and passionate, full of truth and indig-nation," it writes; "now dwelling on the past and now prophetic, she was soon absolute mistress of her audience. While speaking, the Celtic Druidess looked at no one, her great black eyes, full of flame, gazed out into the future full of hope of better days. In a kind of wild ecstasy this Irish patricien [*sic*] seemed to address legions of adherents visible on the horizon to her mystical fore knowledge [*sic*]; and one knew that upon that mysterious horizon she could divine her defenders—her avengers, also, perhaps.

"Before her speech had closed the women were all in tears and the men seeking in vain to hide their emotion. Colonel Chareton, the

Marquis de Castellane, Jean Dupuis, the Prince de Lusignan, the Baron de Chambourg, Charles Joller, the Comte of Susini d'Ariscia, the Duc de Chatre, and the Marquis of Villeneuve were the first to furtively brush away their tears. The example was contagious, and I affirm that I have never seen an audience of the elite of Paris so moved." *Le Bien Public* is no less enthusiastic. "Very singular," it says, "Was the emotion that seized upon that audience of politicians," and then goes on to describe the great beauty and the marvellous voice of the young orator.

The speech itself is given by one paper in its entirety, to the complete exclusion of the speeches of Clovis Huges[1] and the other eminent politicians who were present. Shorn of the marvellous delivery of the speaker, it has yet many beautiful passages, and has throughout the wild sweetness of an Aeolian Harp upon which the winds play, a little fitfully perhaps, but ever musically. "I have given all my heart to Ireland," she began, "and I will give her my life also if events permit me. If I could tell to France, the great country of noble and generous ideas, all that I have seen in Ireland of heroism and patriotism, of misery that never flinched, and of invincible national faith, and if I can make pass into your hearts and consciences the indignation which fills my soul against the oppressors of my country, I shall have fulfilled my mission as a patriot and a woman.

"Ah, how can I make you see, how can I make you feel, the marvellous past which lives eternally in the heart and in the memory of my race? Our illustrious dead, our heroes, our martyrs, all that world of memories, of examples, of glories, of immortal actions which England would bury in the tomb, but which shall rise one day against her!

"Gentlemen, the tyranny of England towards Ireland for many centuries has been a crime against God and against the whole of humanity. She made us first a vassal and then a slave. We cannot tread upon any sod of our country without passing above the trace of a crime. Your great poet, Victor Hugo, has called hunger 'a public crime,' and that crime England has carried out against Ireland by cold premeditation and calculation. For centuries she has reached forth her arms to seize Ireland and to strangle her, but she has forgotten that the blood of martyrs is the eternal seed of liberty.

"Do you ask us what we are seeking for? I will tell you. We are three things—a race, a country, and a democracy—and we wish to make of these three a nation."

Miss Gonne then went on to describe the ancient civilization of Ireland, and how England came to destroy it. She ran swiftly through the history of Ireland, and told how in modern days we had shrunk

---

[1] *Clovis Huges*: should be spelled "Hugues." For information on this man, see the article "Clovis Huges on Ireland," below.

from twelve millions to nine, and then from nine to four, with the rare tact of the orator. She dwelt much on the brigades and on the battles they won for France—"always dying, always living"—and told them that if Ireland was to be separated from France "twenty pages of our common history would have to be torn out," and then concluded amid great enthusiasm.

What a singular scene—this young girl of twenty-five addressing that audience of politicians, and moving them more than all their famous speakers although she spoke in a language not her own. What does it mean for Ireland? Surely, that here is the new "Speranza" who shall do with the voice all, or more than all, the old "Speranza" did with her pen. Surely there is here a new orator who adds the power of beauty to the power of the golden tongue, and who shall be a marvellous standard-bearer for that better Future that is dawning for our race.

W. B. Yeats

Dr. Todhunter's Irish Poems

This review of *The Banshee and Other Poems* by John Todhunter appeared in *United Ireland*, January 23, 1892. Yeats had reviewed the first edition of *The Banshee* for the *Providence Sunday Journal* on February 10, 1889. For the American newspaper Yeats had concentrated on Todhunter's translations of Irish bardic tales.

Yeats reviewed many of Todhunter's books during this period. He explained why in the preface to the collection of his American newspaper pieces, *Letters to the New Island*, pp. viii, ix:

In these articles I overrated Dr. Todhunter's poetical importance, not because he was a friendly neighbor with a charming house, a Morris carpet on the drawing-room floor, upon the walls early pictures by my father painted under the influence of Rossetti, but because a single play of his, the *Sicilian Idyll*—I did not overrate the rest of his work—and still more its success confirmed a passion for that other art [poetic drama opposed to realism].

Yeats's one-act play *The Land of Heart's Desire* was produced in 1894 with Todhunter's *The Comedy of Sighs*. After Todhunter's play failed, Yeats's piece was continued with Shaw's *Arms and the Man*.

THE alliance of politics and literature that marked the " '48 movement"[1] resulted in so great a popularity for the poets and prose writers who taught the doctrine of nationality that we are accustomed

---

[1] This movement, better known as the "Young Ireland movement," was led by Thomas Davis. Its chief vehicle was the *Nation* magazine.

ever since to think of those years as our one period of literary activity. The writers who came after, lacking the great wind of politics to fill their sails, have lived and wrought almost forgotten of the nation. Allingham found English audiences, but won few listeners this side of the Channel, and De Vere is to-day more noted as a poet of the English Catholics than as an Irish writer, despite his "Innisfail," and his "Children of Lir," and "Fardiar," and "Legends of St. Patrick." When time has removed this century into the dimness of the past it will be seen that Ireland, like England, has had a literary development of her own, and that "48" was not a mere isolated outburst. "The king is dead; long live the king." Davis, and Carleton, and Mangan passed, away, but Allingham, and De Vere, and O'Grady and the Ferguson of "Conaire"[2] and "Deirdre," came to take their places, and to find, alas! the ear of the people closed. Among these later writers who took up the golden chain of Irish literature, we should, I think, place Dr. Todhunter, by right of his book of Irish legendary verse, called "The Banshee and other Poems." It has just been republished at 1s. by Seeley, Bryers, and Walker, of Dublin, and Dr. Todhunter promises a "Deirdre" as its successor. "The Library of Ireland" when first issued was more expensive, and yet I wonder will this artistically bound shilling's worth win half the success of the least able volume in the famous "Library."[3] The time he lives in, and not Dr. Todhunter, is to blame if this be so, for it should be incumbent on all good Irishmen to know something of their old legends, and it has been well said that a better idea of what that renowned old legend of the *caoine* of Lir must have sounded like to the folk who gathered about the old bards who chanted it can be got from the version in this "Banshee and other Poems" than from any translation. The name-poem, too, should be widely known. It is a noble chant over the sorrows of Ireland. How well the wild, irregular verses —something between Walt Whitman and the Scotch Ossian—would go in recitation:

> Green in the wizard arms
> Of the foam-bearded Atlantic,
> An isle of old enchantment,
> A melancholy isle,
> Enchanted and dreaming lies;
> And thou,[4] by Shannon's flowing,
> In the moonlight, spectre-thin
> The spectre Erin sits.

[2] The title of Ferguson's poem is "Conary."
[3] The "Library of Ireland" was published by James Duffy around 1845–1846. Works by Charles Gavan Duffy and Thomas Davis appeared in this series.
[4] *thou*: Todhunter's poem reads "there."

An aged desolation,
She sits by old Shannon's flowing,
A mother of many children,
Of children exiled and dead,
In her home, with bent head, homeless,
Clasping her knees she sits,
Keening, keening!

    .   .   .   .   .

How[5] the nations hear in the void and quaking time of night,
Sad unto dawning, dirges,
Solemn dirges,
And snatches of bardic song;
Their souls quake in the void and quaking time of night,
And they dream of the weird of kings,
And tyrannies moulting, sick
In the dreadful wind of change.

Wail no more, lonely one, mother of exiles, wail no more,
Banshee of the world—no more!
Thy sorrows are the world's, thou art no more alone;
Thy wrongs the world's.

"The Sons of Turann" is a fine version of another of "The Three Sorrows of Story-Telling," as the bards called "Deirdre," "The Children of Lir," and "The Sons of Turann," and "Agadoe" must be well known to many through its inclusion in "Poems and Ballads of Young Ireland."[6] All the poems are extremely simple and almost rough in their strain for primeval utterance. They are so far removed from conventional poetic diction as to be at times too matter-of-fact and bald, like the old stories themselves.

The twenty pages of poems on other than Irish subjects bound up with them are, I cannot help thinking, a mistake. They are in quite a different manner, and as full of poetic diction as the others are free of it. "Methinks I saw these sixteen things of storm"—the opening of one of the sonnets—is a strong line, and little the worse for its conventional "methinks," but certainly it is in a very different style to the clear utterance of the Celtic poems. These "other poems" were, I believe, added to please an English publisher who seemed sceptical of his chance of making English readers take to anything with an Irish subject. They might have been left out of the present Irish edition with advantage to the unity of the book.

Gradually as Irish readers begin to understand that they have a

---

[5] *How*: Todhunter's poem reads "And the . . . ."
[6] Yeats and his friends Katharine Tynan, T. W. Rolleston, and John O'Leary arranged for the publication of this volume in 1888.

literature which is racy of the soil, and that it goes on decade by decade, and was not a strange spirit of a unique period, they will begin to look for and study books like this. Miss Tynan's new volume, "Poems and Lyrics," Dr. Hyde's stories, the humor of F. J. Allan,[7] and volumes like the one here noticed, will gradually, I believe, convince them that it is a literature various enough for many tastes. Gavan Duffy's projected new "Library of Ireland"[8] also, if it be not too exclusively a basket to gather up the fragments that remained after the feast of the old "Library," may do much to foster a reading public in Ireland.

W. B. Yeats

Clovis Huges on Ireland

This piece, from *United Ireland* of January 30, 1892, was a sequel to Yeats's article of two weeks before, "The New 'Speranza,' " and a continuation of his efforts to support Maud Gonne's nationalistic agitation in Paris.

Clovis Hugues (not "Huges" as Yeats spelled it) (1851–1907) was a French poet and politician of the far left. He was imprisoned for his support of the Paris Commune of 1871, and he killed a rival journalist in a duel in 1877. His wife shot and killed a court official in the *Palais de Justice* in 1884 and was acquitted after a sensational trial. Hugues was, like Lucien Millevoye, a follower of General Boulanger. His poetry, as one may observe from the example in this article, was oratorical. It is amusing to see Yeats struggling, in the name of Ireland and Maud Gonne, to praise this sorry poem. As Yeats put it, it was some time before Hugues "got into the full stream of inspiration with the winds of poetry in his sails."

THE French papers have not yet ceased to celebrate both the beauty and eloquence of our new "Speranza", and divers English papers have followed suit, notably Mr. Stead's *Review of Reviews*,[1] which gives a bad portrait of Miss Maud Gonne, and explains that she is a Parnellite, or Separatist—a luminous definition very suggestive of the kind of Home Rule Mr. Stead believes the seceders to be looking for—and that

[7] F. J. Allan wrote *Aids to Sanitary Science* (1891). It is more likely that Yeats meant F. M. Allen, the pen-name of Edmund Downey (1856–1937), an author of many humorous works.

[8] This series was called the "New Irish Library." Yeats later thought that his fears here expressed were realized.

[1] The *Review of Reviews* (New York edition) had a paragraph on Maud Gonne on p. 6 of its February, 1892, issue. The magazine was edited by W. T. Stead.

her mission to Paris is to win armed help for Ireland, in which, it adds, although "one of the most beautiful women in the world," she will hardly succeed. Now, in spite of the *Review of Reviews*, Miss Maud Gonne is not only no Separatist under present conditions, but is succeeding beyond all expectations in her perfectly practical business-like, and unsensational project of organising the Irish people of Paris and the Parisians of Irish descent into a society which will be able to serve Ireland by bringing politicians at home into touch with distinguished continental statesmen, should the need arise, by helping the home organization with funds in the event of the society spreading widely; by keeping the continental Press well posted in the matter of our Irish wrongs; and by generally cultivating good relations between Ireland and her old ally, France. The most charming of the many marks of the sympathy it has already awakened, is a poem which the distinguished poet and politician, Clovis Huges [*sic*], has dedicated to Miss Maud Gonne. My friend, Mr. Edwin J. Ellis,[2] himself a poet, whom the world will receive gladly some day, has made for me a translation no less charming than the original poem. I do not think that any thought or any beauty has been missed:

A Toast to Ireland

(Dedicated to Miss Maud Gonne.)

The Masters, in derisive laurel crowned,
With Death for President, are sitting round
At a most monstrous banquet: see them here,
Decked out with crimes, ready to drink a tear,
Or blood, or wine unto the brim high poured!
Yet while they toast the horror of the sword,
Insult the vanquished, mock the sad ones more,
I, in the waves name and the long, low shore,
Drink to the form of dreaming Ireland, where
Along the salt wind blows her level hair.

From bearded Celts the shipmen from afar
Have stolen their fields, and stolen their guiding star;
Yet, though these go, the tempest in their shrouds
Planting their poles and canvas home like clouds
Around the marshes where the rushes bend,
A dawn will clear the coast from end to end.

[2] Edwin J. Ellis was co-editor with Yeats of the works of William Blake, a project then nearing completion. Yeats reviewed Ellis's *Fate in Arcadia* in the September, 1892, *Bookman* (see below).

A star will flower again in heaven more bright,
Oh, ancient bards, leap up with new delight!
I drink to Ireland, kissing the earth green,
Where sleep in peace her great ones that have been.

The peaks were looking far beyond the hills:
"What sight is this that your sad seeing fills?"
Cried all the waves. "Murder and rape," they said,
"And storm-wind on the rafterless homestead,
And Women vainly weeping as they go."
I, too, have seen and known a land in woe,
And heard sad secrets from the burial place.
Up on thy feet! Up, up, oh! thou lost race!
I drink to Ireland, bidding her prepare,
While on the stones they drag her by the hair.

"What see you now?" Again the blue wave speaks.
"All-powerful Evil!" answered the high peaks.
"Youth and sweet love have no more time to flower,
But fortune-gilded thieves are gods in power—
Gilded with gold of barley ripe, and rye,
And wheat-ears pillaged as they wandered by."
The thunder growls behind the reddening cloud,
Those whom the darkness knows I name aloud;
I drink to Ireland, Ireland hungry grown,
Amid the yellow corn herself has sown.

By her dead hearths and troubled soul, where through
The winged hopes were song-birds in the blue,
Green Erin is made now in all her space
Like one great tear, sad on the heaven's face,
Where palely shine reflected woods and shore.
Do nations die, and is a race no more
Because her torn and ragged cloak is sold?
The days go by. Right keeps her dwelling old.
I drink to Ireland, while I see outpour
Tears on the doorstep of a tomb's white door.

At moments, tired of the scythe, so vain
When held by her, she arms herself again,
Starting with joy, a people's king to hear,
When some O'Connell rises without fear.
Oh, bid your flute-players guard you on the moor,
Landlords, who make men poor and gibe the poor!
Beware, for those who rise more high shall see
A greater fall in the near days to be.
I drink to Ireland, who wrestles now
Even with the thorns bound close around her brow.

Ah, though a hideous blank be the grave's word,
Let us be Ireland's brother. Never heard
From our lips, by her, be this sad news.
That never more the branch with heavenly dews
The holy dove shall now be seen to bring.
For fallen is our dream with broken wing.
Faith smiles on her, to whom St. Patrick brought
This treasure, therefore now in reverent thought
I drink to Ireland, praying with bent head,
For prayer is still the strong man's daily bread.

She, too, but lately saw her hopeful day
When France, my mother, cast her kings away,
And sent her sons to render Ireland free.
But destiny betrayed us, and the sea
More bitter proved than ills endured or tears.
But bronze is reddened e'er the statue rears—
Who thinks on all those evil days again?
For life gone past is even with the slain.
I drink to Ireland, who disaster knew
On the same day when we were conquered, too.

The poem is a little vague, perhaps, as is indeed inevitable in the work of a man writing of a country he has never seen, and of history of which he has but a very general knowledge; but there is a great beauty, especially in the later stanzas. It was an improvization made at the dinner of the *Union Mediterraneenne* [*sic*] after Miss Maud Gonne's speech, and I think the slightly conventional opening, with its banquet, when the masters of Ireland's destiny drink blood and tears, is evidence that the *improvisar* took time—a very short time certainly—before he got into the full stream of inspiration with the winds of poetry in his sails. The last stanza, with its allusion to the day when France, no less than Ireland, was conquered, is very touching in the mouth of a Frenchman. The poem when published in a French newspaper was marked with the French equivalent for "please copy," and has, no doubt, been widely quoted throughout France; and even if it were less fine as a poem it would be still of importance both as an evidence, and, in some slight degree, as a cause even, of sympathy between Ireland and her ancient ally. The stars of destiny shall have to bring several things about before we can finally say that such sympathy is no longer needed, and that a movement to bring the men at home into bonds of friendship with their fellow-countrymen in Paris and with the decendants [*sic*] of the old brigade, is a movement without good right to exist.

W. B. Yeats

The Irish Intellectual Capital: Where Is It?

This letter, printed in *United Ireland* on May 14, 1892, was Yeats's contribution to a controversy waged in that paper during April and May of 1892 over whether London or Dublin was the Irish intellectual capital. In December, 1891, Yeats and T. W. Rolleston had founded the London Irish Literary Society. This action must have stirred up resentment in Dublin for it held the implication that the Irish exiles in London were the leaders in matters of the intellect.

United Ireland of April, 1892, contained a notice of a dinner given in London in honor of David J. O'Donoghue upon the publication of his *Dictionary of Irish Poets*. Yeats offered a toast in which he predicted an Irish intellectual awakening. No one said anything about Irish intellectual capitals. But apparently the implication was there, for the editor of *United Ireland* in a following paragraph served notice to such exiled intellectuals that Dublin was the Irish intellectual capital and one day soon they should all come home.

Battle was joined in the April 9 issue by John Augustus O'Shea, the chairman of the London banquet, who replied that Dublin booksellers and the Dublin public refused to support literature. By the time Yeats joined the controversy, the main tenor of the letters had been to bewail the indifference to literature by Dubliners and, by extension, all the Irish.

In the issue following Yeats's letter (May 21, 1892), John T. Kelly suggested the founding of an Irish literary society in Dublin, and he advised readers of *United Ireland* to get in touch with him or W. B. Yeats. On May 24, 1892, the National Literary Society was founded in Dublin.

The scheme to publish Irish books, mentioned in this article, was to bring Yeats much grief, as will be apparent from the following letters and articles in this collection. In brief, Yeats's plans for books to be published were foiled when Sir Charles Gavan Duffy was chosen as chief editor of the project. Yeats strenuously objected to the choice of Duffy because he believed that Duffy's notions of literature were formed by the Young Ireland movement of 1845 and were thus hopelessly out of date. Duffy won the battle, but Yeats had the pleasure of giving bad reviews to some of the books issued by what became known as "The New Irish Library."

United Ireland, May 14, 1892

THE PUBLICATION OF IRISH BOOKS

TO THE EDITOR OF *UNITED IRELAND*

SIR—One windy night I saw a fisherman staggering, very drunk, about Howth Pier and shouting at somebody that he was no gentleman because he had not been educated at Trinity College, Dublin.

Had he been an Englishman he would have made his definition of "gentleman" depend on money, and if he had been not only an Englishman, but a Cockney, on the excellence of the dinner he supposed his enemy to have eaten that day. My drunken fisherman had a profound respect for the things of the mind, and yet it is highly probable that he had never read a book in his life, and that even the newspapers were almost unknown to him. He is only too typical of Ireland. The people of Ireland respect letters and read nothing. They hold the words "poet" and "thinker" honourable, yet buy no books. They are proud of being a more imaginative people than the English, and yet compel their own imaginative writers to seek an audience across the sea. Surely there is some cause for all this and some remedy if we could but find it. I do not believe we are a nation of hypocrites.

Is not the cause mainly the great difficulty of bringing books, and the movements and "burning questions" of educated life, to the doors of a people who are scattered through small towns and villages, or sprinkled over solitary hillsides, and of doing so persistently enough to win a hearing amid the tumult of politics? The people have never learned to go to the book-shop, nor have they any brilliant literary journals and magazines to awaken their interest in thought and literature; nor would they read them if they had. Yet surely some method of reaching them can be found. The *Nation*[1] found a method, and "brought a new soul into Ireland," and to-day the need is almost greater. Ireland is between the upper and the nether millstone—between the influence of America and the influence of England, and which of the two is denationalizing us more rapidly it is hard to say. Whether we have still to face a long period of struggle, or have come to the land of promise at last, we need all our central fire, all our nationality.

It was with the desire to do what we could to arrest this denationalisation that we founded the "Irish Literary Society, London,"[2] and not to do anything so absurd and impossible as to make London "the intellectual centre of Ireland," and it is with this desire in my mind that I now appeal to the four or five Dublin literary societies to do what they can to help us. The third object of our society, the first two being of purely local interest, is "to assist towards the publication in popular form of approved works on Irish subjects." We intend to do this by organizing a circulation, "and not by incurring," to quote the prospectus again, "the liabilities of a publishing enterprise." We have, however, a definite scheme which will be put forward in good time, and are appealing to all the Irish literary societies in America to

[1] The *Nation* was founded in 1842 by Thomas Davis, Charles Gavan Duffy, and John Dillon. It served as the main literary organ of the Young Ireland movement.
[2] Yeats had founded, with T. W. Rolleston, this society in late December, 1891.

communicate with us in view of this scheme. Let the Dublin societies unite together in some fashion among themselves—the proposed constitution of "The Young Ireland League"[3] a little altered will serve right well—not of necessity sinking their separate individuality, and then put themselves into communication with the societies through the country. When they have done so we and they will see what can be done to create and circulate a library of Irish books like the old "Library of Ireland," Duffy's ballads, "The Spirit of the Nation," Mitchel's "O'Neill,"[4] and all that noble series which spread themselves through Ireland by the help of the Repeal Reading Rooms; and there seems to be no reason why the Young Ireland societies and literary societies of the day may not serve a like purpose. The periodical appearance of such books would give new interest to their debates, and new subjects for their lectures, and make them feel they were part of a great body of fellow-workers and not mere local debating clubs.

Eminent writers have offered their help. I have here before me a list of promised books on subjects ranging from Fenianism to the Education Question, from Oisin to Robert Emmet—and with a little energy and organization we shall be able to circulate through Ireland a series of books which will be no mere echo of the literature of '48,[5] but radiant from the living heart of the day. Irish authors who have been compelled to make their pens the servants of a foreign literature, and foreign inspirations, will come gladly to our help, and in so doing they will themselves rise to greater status, for no man who deserts his own literature for another's can hope for the highest rank. The cradles of the greatest writers are rocked among the scenes they are to celebrate. Ireland has no lack of talent, but that talent is flung broadcast over the world, and turned to any rather than Irish purposes. Until it has been gathered together again and applied to the needs of Ireland it will never do anything great in literature. "He who tastes a crust of bread," wrote Parocelsus at Hoenheim,[6] "tastes all the stars and all the heavens," and he who studies the legends, and history, and life of his own countryside may find there all the themes of art and song. Let it be the work of the literary societies to teach to the writers on the one hand, and to the readers on the other, that there is no nationality without literature, no literature without nationality. In the old days when Davis sang there

[3] In the fall and winter of 1891 Yeats had attempted to consolidate various Young Ireland societies into a league with the object of opening local reading rooms.

[4] Yeats referred to *The Ballad Poetry of Ireland*, edited by Charles Gavan Duffy, *The Spirit of the Nation*, a collection of songs and ballads from the *Nation* magazine, also edited by Duffy, and *The Life and Times of Aodh O'Neill, Prince of Ulster* by John Mitchel.

[5] By the "literature of '48," Yeats meant the Young Ireland movement, usually associated with the names of Mitchel, Davis, and Duffy.

[6] This is a misprint for "Paracelsus at Hohenheim." Yeats used this quotation as an epigraph to *Poems*, 1895.

was no need to teach it, for then Apollo struck his lyre with a pike-head, but now he has flung both pike-head and lyre into the sea.—
Yours, &c.,

                                                                    W. B. Yeats

London, May 1892

Sight and Song

Yeats's review of Michael Field's book of poems *Sight and Song*, London, 1892, appeared in the *Bookman* in July, 1892. It was the first of a long series of reviews by Yeats for this magazine. The early dramas of Michael Field, the composite pseudonym of Katherine Harris Bradley and Edith Emma Cooper, had been a youthful passion of Yeats's. According to Allan Wade, among Yeats's papers there are parts of a manuscript review of Michael Field's plays *The Father's Tragedy*, *William Rufus*, and *Loyalty in Love*, but the place of publication of the review, if any, is unknown.

By the time of this review, Yeats's enthusiasm had evidently waned. Yeats's disillusionment with Michael Field was not permanent, however, for he included nine poems by them in his *Oxford Book of Modern Verse*. Nor was Yeats always so dogmatically opposed to works of art serving as inspiration for poetry, at least for his own later poems.

There is a long, rather unsympathetic reminiscence of Yeats in *Works and Days, From the Journal of Michael Field*, London, 1933. The ladies found Yeats to be ". . . not one of us— he is a preacher. He preaches some excellent things and some foolish things." In 1903 Yeats refused their play *Deirdre* for production at the Abbey Theater.

THIS interesting, suggestive and thoroughly unsatisfactory book is a new instance of the growing tendency to make the critical faculty do the work of the creative. "The aim of this little volume is, as far as may be," says the preface, "to translate into verse what the lines and colours of certain chosen pictures sing in themselves; to express not so much what these pictures are to the poet, but rather what poetry they objectively incarnate." That is to say, the two ladies who hide themselves behind the pen-name of Michael Field have set to work to observe and interpret a number of pictures, instead of singing out of their own hearts and setting to music their own souls. They have poetic feeling and imagination in abundance, and yet they have preferred to work with the studious and interpretive side of the mind and write a guide-book to the picture galleries of Europe, instead of giving us a book full

of the emotions and fancies which must be crowding in upon their
minds perpetually. They seem to have thought it incumbent upon them
to do something serious, something worthy of an age of text-books,
something that would have uniformity and deliberate intention, and
be in no wise given over to that unprincipled daughter of whim and
desire whom we call imagination.

We open the book at a venture, and come to a poem on Benozzo
Gozzoli's 'Treading the Press.'

> *"From the trellis hang the grapes*
> *Purple deep;*
> *Maidens with white, curving napes*
> *And coiled hair backward leap,*
> *As they catch the fruit, mid laughter,*
> *Cut from every silvan rafter.*
>
> *Baskets, over-filled with fruit,*
> *From their heads*
> *Down into the press they shoot*
> *A white-clad peasant treads,*
> *Firmly crimson circles smashing*
> *Into must with his feet's thrashing.*
>
> *Wild and rich the oozings pour*
> *From the press;*
> *Leaner grows the tangled store*
> *Of vintage, ever less:*
> *Wine that kindles and entrances*
> *Thus is made by one who dances."*[1]

The last couplet has some faint shadow of poetry, perhaps, but as
for the rest—well, it is neither more nor less than 'The Spanish Gypsey'[2]
again. It is impossible not to respect it, impossible not to admire the
careful massing of detail, but no man will ever feel his eyes suffuse with
tears or his heart leap with joy when he reads it. There are scores of
other verses in the book which are as like it as one pea is to another.
None of them have any sustained music, for music is the garment of
emotion and passion, but all are well put together with carefully
chosen rhymes, out of the way adjectives and phrases full of minute
observation. Having looked in vain for anything conspicuously better
or worse than the lines we have quoted, we open the book again at a

---

[1] This poem is quoted correctly—sufficient cause for comment.

[2] *Gypsey*: should be "Gipsy." Yeats's dislike for George Eliot was persistent. The first
letter in Allan Wade's edition of Yeats's letters contains an enumeration of Yeats's reasons
for dislike.

venture,[3] and find a poem on Cosimo Tura's 'St. Jerome.' We quote the first two stanzas:—

> "*Saint Jerome kneels within the wilderness;*
> *Along the cavern's sandy channels press*
> *The flowings of deep water. On one knee,*
> *On one foot he rests his weight—*
> *A foot that rather seems to be*
> *The clawed base of a pillar past all date*
> *Than prop of flesh and bone;*
> *About his sallow, osseous frame*
> *A cinder-coloured cloak is thrown*
> *For ample emblem of his shame.*
>
> *Grey are the hollowed rocks, grey is his head*
> *And grey his beard, formal and as dread*[4]
> *As some Assyrian's on a monument,*
> *From the chin is sloping down.*
> *O'er his tonsure heaven has bent*
> *A solid disc of unillumined brown;*
> *His scarlet hat is flung*
> *Low on the pebbles by a shoot*
> *Of tiny nightshade that among*
> *The pebbles has maintained a root.*"

These stanzas do not contain a single commonplace simile or trite adjective, the authors even prefer "osseous" to "bony" in their search for the unexpected. There is intellectual agility in every sentence, and yet of what account are these verses, or any number like them? They are simply unmitigated guide-book.

One regrets the faults of this book the more because they are faults which have for some time been growing on "Michael Field." 'Callirhoë'[5] had imagination and fancy in plenty, and we hoped its authors would in time get more music and less crudity and at last create a poem of genius. A few years later 'Brutus Ultor' came and almost crowned our hopes, but now we have watched and waited for a long time in vain. 'Sight and Song,' following as it does 'The Tragic Mary,' is enough to make us turn our eyes for ever from the "false dawn" we believed to be the coming day.

W. B. Yeats

---

[3] Had Yeats opened the book on page 81, he would have seen a poem on "A Pen Drawing of Leda, by Sodoma."

[4] The original of this line reads, "And grey his beard that, formal . . . ." Yeats, or the *Bookman's* compositors, ignored the elaborate indentation scheme of the original.

[5] *Callirrhoï*, *Brutus Ultor*, and *The Tragic Mary* are early verse plays by Michael Field.

Some New Irish Books

This review of the collected works of George Savage-Armstrong, London, 1891–1892; *Fand* by William Larminie, Dublin, 1892; and *Songs of Arcady* by Robert J. Reilly, Dublin, 1892, appeared in *United Ireland*, July 23, 1892.

The review was printed anonymously. However, Yeats admitted the authorship of the Armstrong and Larminie portion in a letter to John O'Leary, dated by Allan Wade (on the basis of this review) as written during the week of July 23, 1892. Yeats told O'Leary, "I have Armstrong's collected works—nine volumes—to review for *Bookman*, and have given them a preliminary notice, mainly hostile, in this week's *United Ireland*, also like treatment to Larminie" (*Letters*, p. 211). It seems evident that the Reilly review was written by the author of the Armstrong and Larminie portion. Some miscellaneous historical volumes were included in the same column, but Allan Wade thought them not the work of Yeats and this editor agrees with him.

George Savage-Armstrong (1845–1906) was Professor of History and English at Queen's College, Cork. His English loyalties are evident in his "Victoria Regina et Imperatrix, a Jubilee Song from Ireland," 1887. In his *Bookman* review of September, 1892 (see below), Yeats was less caustic and even quoted a part of Armstrong's dialogue atop Lugnaquilla. He had made an enemy, however, and in 1898 Yeats recounted to Lady Gregory a public quarrel with Armstrong. The latter had denounced the Irish literary movement in a public lecture, and had claimed that the work of dissenters from Gaeldom like himself was boycotted. Yeats replied with the charge that Armstrong, a West Briton, was ignorant of contemporary Ireland in and out of literature. (*Letters*, pp. 300–301.)

William Larminie (1849–1900) was better known as a folklorist than as a poet; Yeats gave high praise to Larminie's *West Irish Folk Tales* in a review in the *Bookman* of June, 1894. Yeats's quotation in this review hardly does Larminie justice as a poet.

The name of the author of *Songs of Arcady* given in *United Ireland*, "W. O'Reilly," is inaccurate. This volume was the work of Robert James Reilly (1862–1895), doctor and poetaster who occasionally contributed poems to the *Irish Monthly*, *Irish Fireside*, and *United Ireland*. For the identification of Reilly and other forgotten versifiers, I am indebted to D. J. O'Donoghue's *The Poets of Ireland*, Dublin, 1912.

W E have here before us, bound in solid blue covers and printed on thick paper, the most substantial edition of the collected works of any Irish poet which has appeared for many years. Mr. Allingham's slim vellum-backed volumes, and Aubrey de Vere's three or four big green ones, cannot compete with Mr. Armstrong's nine, some of which have more than four hundred pages apiece. What public they are intended for it is hard to imagine, for there is little, indeed, in "The Tragedy of Israel," or "Ugone," or in the prolonged rhetoric of "Poems: Lyrical¹ and Dramatic," to stir the soul of man. Mr. Armstrong has cut himself off from the life of the nation in which his days are passed, and has suffered the inevitable penalty. He has tried to be an Englishman and to write as an Englishman, instead of reflecting the life that is about him, the history of which every hillside must remind him, and the legends the women murmur over the fire in the cabins by the roadside. An Irishman might possibly succeed in writing and thinking as the best Englishmen do if he left Ireland in his childhood and threw himself wholly into the life of his adopted country; but if he lives here he must choose between expressing in noble forms the life and passion of this nation, or being the beater of the air all his days. Despite his very genuine poetic feeling and obvious intellectual forces Mr. Armstrong has, we believe, written but one volume with which the future will feel any concern whatever, and that is his one book upon an Irish theme—"Stories of Wicklow." Despite an obvious unfamiliarity with the Celtic feeling and the Celtic traditions of this country he has written in this one book many pages for which we feel heartly [*sic*] grateful. Even at his best in blank verse he has made the dialogue on the top of Lugnaquilla entirely moving, glowing, and beautiful. The more humorous parts of the book are a little touched with that conventionality of feeling which seems inseparable from West Britonism.

Mr. Larminie is, on the other hand, Irish enough, and, so far as his metres go, quite unconventional, but then he does not show at present the same innate poetic faculty as that which Mr. Armstrong has thrown away through a false philosophy of life. At the same time Mr. Larminie may do better when he has either abandoned or perfected the experimental rhythmic metres he has invented. He will probably find they are a mistake, for a metre is the slow growth of time and is evolved as blank verse was evolved in the last two or three centuries, to meet some practical need. That he can do fairly well now and then, despite his metres, is plain enough from the following:—

> "*Ghosts of day's thoughts are dreams,*
> *Beautiful shapes benign,*
> *Or hateful, hideous, and evil;*
> *Phantom growth of the seeds*
> *That are sown in the hours of our waking;*
> *Blossoms of brightest hue and scent most sweet—*
> *Or airs—odorous, poison-laden.*
> *Therefore, if death be night and life be day,*
> *Take heed unto day's thoughts that they be fair,*

¹ *Lyrical: United Ireland's* printing read "Lyricus."

And fair shall be the shapes that haunt thy sleep:
A garden of sweet flowers thy soul shall be:
Let thy dreams come!
Thou shalt have fear of none."

The thought in these lines is poetical; but it loses rather than gains from the metre into which it is thrown. There are plenty of passages of equal or greater interest in the two long legendary poems, "Fand" and "Moy Tura," which make up the bulk of the volume.

Mr. O'Reilly's songs of Arcady are anything but experimental in their metres. He prefers the oldest and the simplest forms of verse, and for the most part uses them with admirable effect. Simple, sincere, and lucid, his poetry will delight its little class of readers and delight them all the more because it is wholly without ambition and as quiet and unobtrusive as the tasteful brown paper cover in which Messrs Sealy, Bryers, and Walker have bound it up. If we were writing at any other time than now, when election news and election gossip treads into even smaller compass the narrow space a newspaper can allow to the reviews of verse, we would gladly quote a poem or two, but can do no more as things are than dismiss the little book with a hearty God-speed.

The Irish Literary Society, London

This letter, printed in *United Ireland* of July 30, 1892, was Yeats's attempt to forestall a controversy over some remarks by his colleague T. W. Rolleston. *United Ireland* had already sponsored a controversy, to which Yeats contributed a few letters, over whether Dublin was the intellectual center of Irish life. The main rival for that distinction was London. Rolleston's remark that the Irish Literary Society, London, planned to open branches in "England, Ireland, America, and the Colonies" would have provoked a storm of injured pride in Dublin. Yeats's mild rebuke seems to have headed off a second round to the controversy.

United Ireland
July 30, 1892

THE IRISH LITERARY SOCIETY, LONDON
TO THE EDITOR OF *UNITED IRELAND*

SIR—Mr. Rolleston, unless indeed, it be a slip of the reporters, stated at the inaugural meeting of the Irish Literary Society, London, last Saturday, that his society hoped to have branches in "England, Ireland,

America, and the Colonies." I find that this statement has caused a certain amount of dissatisfaction among the members of the National Literary Society, as they wish it to be kept perfectly plain that their society is wholly distinct from the London one. I am sure that Mr. Rolleston, under the circumstances, will forgive my saying that the centre of Irish literary activity can only be had in Ireland, and that whatever body may undertake the starting of "branches" in Ireland, the London Society is, of necessity, incapacitated from doing so. When at the close of last autumn I proposed the foundation of the "Irish Literary Society, London," it was with the direct object of federating it with a central body in Ireland, and it was neither my fault nor the fault of the provisional committee that circumstances made the intention of no avail. —

Yours very truly,

W. B. Yeats

53 Mountjoy-square, Dublin.

Dublin Scholasticism and Trinity College

This article appeared in *United Ireland*, July 30, 1892. Yeats had not attended Trinity College, Dublin, although his father was a graduate and had wanted his son to go there. Yeats's lifelong hostility to learned institutions was particularly intense in his youth, although in old age he lamented his lack of a knowledge of the Greek language.

Yeats's disdain for Trinity in 1892 was partly caused by the hostility of the professor of English literature, Edward Dowden, toward the Irish literary movement. In the previous year Trinity had celebrated its three-hundredth anniversary, and Yeats's article is something of a belated and sour birthday greeting.

His opinions changed with the years. When Edward Dowden's illness in 1910 made his retirement seem imminent, Yeats was considered for the post of professor of English, and he was then eager to accept. In 1922, after he won the Nobel Prize, he was given an honorary degree by Trinity.

I AM writing in the National Library, and as I look around me I see a great number of young men reading medical, mathematical, and other text-books, many of them with their note-books open before them. Opposite me is a student deep in medical diagrams, and on my right is another with an algebraical work on the bookrest in front of him. And as the readers are to-day, so were they yesterday, and the day before, and the day before that again, and back as far as the memory of any frequenter of the library can carry him. The glacial weight of scholasticism[1] is over the room and over all the would-be intellectual life of Dublin. Nobody in this great library is doing any disinterested reading, nobody is poring over any book for the sake of the beauty of its words, for the glory of its thought, but all are reading that they may pass an examination; no one is trying to develop his personal taste, but all are endeavoring to force their minds into the mould made for them by professors and examiners. What wonder is it that publishers complain that no book is bought in Dublin unless it be the text-book for some examination, that alone among the great cities of the United Kingdom Dublin is deaf to the voice of genius—deafened by the roar of politics on the one hand and lulled into the deadly sleep of scholasticism upon the other.

Let it be admitted that we are a poor nation, and must seize upon every chance of making "an honest penny" out of intermediate examinations and college scholarships, even at the expense of much travail of the soul, much blinding and deafening of the personal inspiration that is or should be in every one of us, and of most dire delution [sic] of the whole man. Let this be admitted, and yet the explanation does not lie here, for half the energy we have given to covering the roads with bicycles and to all manner of muscular occupations would have made us both a reading and reasonable people. I know poor clerks in London who read the best books with entire delight and devotion, while here in Dublin countless numbers of fairly-leisured and well-to-do men and women hardly know the very names of the great writers of the day. Nay, further, they do not know the commonest legends or the most famous poems of their own land. Here in this very library, called National, there are Greek grammars in profusion and an entire wilderness of text-books of every genera and species, and but the meagrest sprinkling of books of Irish poetry and Irish legends. The library authorities are little if at all to blame, for they would get them if they were asked for. The blame is upon the teaching institutions which have given us scholasticism for our god.

I was four or five years at an English school and then four or five years at an Irish one,[2] and I found in the contrast much to ponder and remember. In England every clever boy had his hobby—literature,

---

[1] As is obvious from the context, Yeats meant by "scholasticism" not the philosophy of Scotus or Aquinas but rather all formalized higher education.

[2] Yeats attended the Godolphin School, Hammersmith, London, from 1877 to 1880. He attended the Erasmus Smith High School in Dublin from 1881 to 1883. After graduation he refused to go to Trinity College and went instead to the Metropolitan School of Art in Dublin.

entomology, or what not. In Ireland every energy of the kind was dis-
couraged and trampled upon, for the shadow of scholasticism was over
all and the great god of examinations ruled supreme. But the worst
blame does not lie at the door of the schools, but rather at the door of
the university which gives them their tone and is the very centre of
their life. As Dublin Castle with the help of the police keeps Ireland
for England, so Trinity College with the help of the schoolmasters
keeps the mind of Ireland for scholasticism with its accompanying
weight of mediocrity. All noble life, all noble thought, depends
primarily upon enthusiasm, and Trinity College, in abject fear of the
National enthusiasm which is at her gates, has shut itself off from every
kind of ardour, from every kind of fiery and exultant life. She has gone
over body and soul to scholasticism, and scholasticism is but an
aspect of the great god, Dagon of the Philistines. "She has given herself
to many causes that have not been my causes, but never to the Philistines," Matthew Arnold wrote once of Oxford. Alas, that we can but
invert the sentences when we speak of our own University—"Never
to any cause, but always to the Philistines," is written over her chimneys.
She has piped to us, and we have danced at her bidding, and flung our
caps into the air; but let us not refrain from saying, even with the
Tercentenary uproar still in our ears, that she has no great part in the
higher life of the people. Let us not sentimentalize over her, but let us
grant her all that she has, her mathematics, and her metaphysics, and
then acknowledge that a tractarian movement,[3] or a single poet of the
rank of Arnold or of Clough even, were more than all these things, for
not out of any logic mill, but out of prolonged and fiery ardour and an
ever present consciousness of the overshadowing mysteries of life,
emerges the soul of man and the heroic heart.

In that attempt to bring a true cultivation into the minds of the
people of Ireland, which was sketched out by Sir Charles Gavan Duffy
in his speech last Saturday,[4] we will have to reckon with the apathy of
all the Trinity College personages, and with the certain apathy and the
probable hostility of all scholastic persons outside its walls, and with
the antagonism of the shallow persiflage which passes for wit among
those who have not even the perverted convictions of which Blake
speaks when he says that the foolish man has been compelled by God

[3] Tractarianism was the principles set forth in a series of pamphlets issued at Oxford
(1833–1841) by members of what came to be known as the Oxford Movement. It was
generally a movement within the Church of England toward older and more traditional
doctrines and liturgical forms. Its most famous member, John Henry Newman, eventually
became a Catholic.

[4] Duffy had made a speech to the Irish Literary Society, London, in which he had
suggested the publication of books on Irish subjects at popular prices. The speech was
printed in the same issue of *United Ireland* as this article.

"to defend a lie that enthusiasm and life may not cease." We have more to expect from the Orangemen of the North who "defend" their "lie" than from the West Britons of the South who have not fire enough to defend even a falsehood.

W. B. Yeats

A New Poet

Yeats reviewed Edwin J. Ellis's *Fate in Arcadia*, London, 1892, in the *Bookman* of September, 1892.

Ellis was an old friend of John Butler Yeats, and from 1889 he had been collaborating with W. B. on their edition of Blake. With all this, Yeats could hardly play the objective critic—as he himself admitted. There are enough reservations about Ellis's book to save Yeats's honor.

Ellis contributed to the *Bookman* an article on Bernard Quaritch (July, 1893), the publisher of the Yeats-Ellis edition of Blake, and an article on Blake by Ellis appeared in February, 1893. For Yeats's private opinion of Ellis as a poet, see his autobiography, pp. 107–109 (Macmillan-Collier paperback edition). Yeats also reviewed Ellis's *Seen in Three Days* (*Bookman*, February, 1894), and he was then less successful in concealing his inability to follow Ellis's symbolism.

THE majority of books of verse impress the reader with the conviction that the feeling and thoughts they contain have been invented for the sake of the poems. It is rare to come across a book where the poems have all been written obviously for the sake of the feelings and thoughts, where the verses seem to come out of a great depth of emotion which exists for itself alone, where every beautiful image and simile is but, as it were, the embroidered hem of the garment of reverie which wraps its author's life about. When we do meet with such books we make them our continual companions, and admit them into the secret fellowship of the soul. Such a book is Mr. Edwin Ellis's 'Fate in Arcadia.' Exquisite as the verse constantly is, it is almost impossible to criticise it as verse alone, "for he who touches this book touches a man," as Whitman puts it,[1] and one is tempted to write rather of the beliefs and fancies and moods that are in it as one would of the spoken words

[1] The Whitman quotation is from "So Long!" in *Leaves of Grass*.
Camerado, this is no book,
Who touches this touches a man. . . .

of some deep thinking and much experienced person. Most books of poetry are collections of isolated poems which gain little from each other, but here every verse seems the deeper because of the all-pervading personality of the writer. The very defects of the book, its occasional obscurity, and the careless way in which the stanzas are built every now and then, come from excess, and not, as is commonly the case, from lack of personality—everything is vitalised, though often vitalised awry. In drawing attention to such a book for the first time, however, it is the duty of the reviewer to praise its excellences, and leave the discussion of its defects to those coming years whose more considerate judgment it is destined to challenge.

The name-poem, an Arcadian drama of about thirty pages, though full of beautiful things, is not, I think, so good as several of the lyrics, notably, "The Hermit Answered," "The Maid Well Loved," "The Maid's Confession," "Thrice Lost," "Outcast," and that strange poem, perhaps the most powerful in the book, "Himself." "Himself" is the lament of the selfhood of Christ, the outcry of that portion of humanity which is perpetually sacrificed for great causes and great faiths. The poet comes to Golgotha, and sees there a phantom Christ upon a phantom cross, and listens to the terrible cry, "Eli, Eli, thou hast forsaken me." Thus the phantom complains in the night:—

> " 'Where is the life I might have known
>   If God had never lit on me?
> I might have loved one heart alone,
>   A woman white as chastity.
>
> I might have hated devils, and fled
>   Whene'er they came. I might have turned
> From sinners, and I might have led
>   A life where no sin-knowledge burned.
>
> But between voice and voice I chose,
>   Of these two selves, and clave to this—
> Who left me here, where no man knows,
>   And fled to dwell with light in bliss.
>
> Oh, you who still have voice and deed,
>   Call Eli! Eli call, my soul;
> But if He comes to thee and plead
>   That thou shalt let him have the whole
>
> Of all thy will and life, and be
>   Christ come again by flesh of thine;
> Thou, too, shalt know what came to me
>   Then, when I bound my selfhood fine,

And called it Satan for His sake,
  And lived, and saved the world, and died
Only for Him, my Light, to make
  His joy, who floated from my side,

And left me here with wound of spears,
  A cast-off ghostly shade, to rave
And haunt the place for endless years,
  Crying, "Himself He cannot save." '

So spake the ghost of Joseph's son,
  Haunting the place where Christ was slain:
I pray that e'er this world be done,
  Christ may relieve his piteous pain."

Is not this poem one of those startling imaginations which illuminate thought and emotion with their strange light, and which, when once known, can never be forgotten? I find something of the same curious depth of feeling in the little lyric called "Outcast"—

"When God, the ever-living, makes
  His home in deathly winter frost,
And God, the ever-loving, wakes
  In hardening eyes of women lost,
Then through the midnight moves a wraith:
Open the door, for this is Faith.

Open the door, and bring her in,
  And stir thy heart's poor fires that shrink.
Ah, fear to see her pale and thin.
  Give love and dreams to eat and drink;
For Faith may faint in wandering by—
In that day thou shalt surely die."

The lyrics on lighter themes and in lighter manner are a great contrast to those I have just quoted. Could anything be prettier and brighter than the following poem, called "Thrice Lost"?—

"First his parents said they lost him,
No one knew where to accost him,
  Though his loss had made no showing,
  He was there, and yet no knowing
  Where he was—he was but growing.
Yet his parents said they lost him
And the secret to accost him.

Then his friends found out they missed him
It was since a maid had kissed him.
  And with no great outward seeming
  He went through the world of dreaming,
  And this loss had no redeeming.

No one knew the maid had kissed him;
Quite in vain they said they missed him.

Now the world of busy men
Cannot find him once again,
While he seeks in vain to nerve them
To high duty, and to serve them.
He can make, not break, nor curve them;
For, outgrowing busy men,
Like a child, he's lost again."

I have quoted enough from this book to prove its varied power and its constant possession of that greater beauty which, according to the Elizabethan, cannot be without strangeness.[2] He who buys it will have obtained a wise comrade and an ever-fascinated friend.

W. B. Yeats

"Noetry" and Poetry

Yeats's review of the nine volumes of George Savage-Armstrong's verse and drama appeared in the *Bookman* of September, 1892. Yeats had reviewed these volumes previously in *United Ireland* of July 23, 1892, and there he had accused Savage-Armstrong of the literary treason of "West-Britonism." The *Bookman* review finds fault on purely literary grounds. Yeats's quotation of Savage-Armstrong at his best sounds like third-rate Wordsworth. Happily Yeats seems to have been incapable of writing such discursive blank verse himself in spite of his admiration for Savage-Armstrong "in the full dress of blank verse."

A FRIEND of mine[1] is accustomed to say that there is poetry and there is prose, and a something which, though often most interesting, and even moving, is yet neither one nor the other. To this he applies the curious term "noetry"; a word ingenious persons derive from the Greek word nous, and consider descriptive of verse which though full of intellectual faculty, is lacking in imaginative impulse. I do not know my friend's own derivation of his word, but find "noetry," whatever its derivation be, a term of most constant utility. Mr. Savage

---

[2] *Elizabethan*: Francis Bacon, in his essay "Of Beauty." "There is no excellent beauty that hath not some strangeness in the proportion." This is one of Yeats's favorite quotations.

[1] It would be tempting to identify the author of this distinction as Lionel Johnson, the source of most of Yeats's Latin and, one presumes, of his Greek as well.

Armstrong[2] has published nine volumes, of which seven are "noetry" pure and simple, and the remainder a compound of "noetry" and authentic poetry itself, and these nine volumes he has just gathered into "a collected edition" (Longman [*sic*] and Co.). There are first his early verses, "Poems Lyrical and Dramatic," which are rhetoric and nothing better; and then there are "Ugone" in one, and the "Tragedy of Israel" in three volumes, and of these plays be it said that they are of the kind that neither gods nor men nor booksellers can tolerate,[3] and after these come "The Garland of Greece"[4] and "Stories of Wicklow," two very readable and pleasant works, especially in their blank verse parts, and "Mephistopheles in Broadcloth," a rather crude satire; and last of all, "One in the Infinite," a work more or less religious, in not very musical lyric stanzas.

When one has flung by the board the seven volumes of "noetry,' one finds that after all there does remain in the Greek and Irish poems a very fairly bulky collection of more or less interesting verse—all the more interesting because Mr. Armstrong takes the world and his own mission very seriously. The trifler is too much with us, and it is a pleasure to find a poet who is best when writing of the most weighty themes and in the most lofty metrical forms. In an age of lyrical poets, it is good, by way of change, to meet with one who is most at home in the full dress of blank verse, and evidently uncomfortable in the *deshabille* of lighter measures. "The Oracle" in the Greek book and "Lugnaquilia"[5] in the Wicklow book, are typical of his power over great themes and great metres. In the first, three old priests of Apollo lament together the decay of the old faith and the coming in of the new, and in the second a circle of Irish students, who have climbed to the top of Lugnaquila [*sic*] to see the sunrise, discourse of faith and immortality in cadences not wholly unworthy of the beauty of the scene and of the solemn hour. One talks of doubt, and one of earth and its pleasures in which he finds sufficient joy without seeking a life beyond. A third bursts forth in lofty affirmation of immortality:

> *"And if you ask me what the vision is*
> *That lures my heart I answer, 'Tis a dream*
> *Of life unending and invulnerable;*
> *A life of tranquil joy; communion close*
> *With Godlike spirits in untroubled love;*
> *Glad operance in the labours infinite*
> *Of the dread Mind that shapes the infinite worlds;*

[2] This name is usually written Savage-Armstrong.

[3] The phrase "neither gods nor men nor booksellers can tolerate" is a translation of line 372 of Horace's *Ars Poetica*.

[4] The title of this book is *A Garland from Greece*.

[5] *Lugnaquilia*: spelled "Lugnaquilla" in Armstrong.

> *Of ever-widening knowledge of the cause,*
> *And birth and growth of the innumerable,*
> *Immeasurable products of that Mind;*
> *A life of motion and of rapturous toil*
> *That fevers not nor strains; of ministering help*
> *In angel-errands on from orb to orb;*
> *Of painless conflict with the powers confused*
> *Of Chaos and of Darkness; and the shaping*
> *Of Light, of Beauty, Order, Peace and Law.*"[6]

We have here Mr. Armstrong at his best, and it is a best more than once reached in other parts of the volume. The whole book is full of Wicklow scenes and Wicklow memories, and may well prove a companionable friend to many a Wicklow scholar, and stand on his shelves side by side with the local history, and commemorate for a generation or two Mr. Armstrong's name and keep him a king among his own people. Some may even grow curious enough to turn over the pages of the Greek book, and they shall have their reward. As for the other volumes—well, time takes heavy toll from the best, and for "noetry" in all its shapes and fashions, has neither mercy nor tolerance.

W. B. Yeats

New Irish Library Controversy

Soon after the founding of the Irish Literary Society, Dublin, in the spring of 1892, a project was begun to organize a small publishing company which would issue out-of-print Irish classics and new books on Irish subjects. This project was suggested by the founding of local reading rooms throughout Ireland under the auspices of the various Young Ireland societies.

Yeats had many ideas for books which would be prepared by himself and his friends. It is obvious from Yeats's correspondence of this year that he considered the publishing scheme his own in inception and execution. He had assured the English publication of the books by the firm of T. Fisher Unwin through his friendship with one of Unwin's readers, Edward Garnett. All went well until, in the summer of 1892, Sir Charles Gavan Duffy became interested in the project. Sir Charles, then in his seventies, had returned some years before to Ireland after a distinguished political career in Australia and was then living most of the year in the south of France. Duffy was closely identified with the "Young Ireland" movement which had found its chief expression in the *Nation* magazine of the 1840s. Yeats thought that Duffy's ideas on what books should be published were hopelessly out of date. Duffy

---

[6] Yeats made some punctuational changes in this passage but no verbal changes.

liked history, oratory, and politics and Yeats wished to distract Irish attention from these obsessions. Apparently there was wide support for Duffy as an eminent figure above party or cabal.

In these letters, published in the *Freeman's Journal* September 6, 8, 10, 1892, Yeats struggled against Duffy's editorship and lost. His main adversary was John F. Taylor, the orator. Taylor's powers of brutal sarcasm are evident in his replies to Yeats. His great gifts as an orator may be seen in the paraphrase of his "Tables of the Law" speech given in the Aeolus chapter of Joyce's *Ulysses*. Yeats gave a weaker version of the same speech in his unsympathetic picture of Taylor in his autobiography. John O'Leary, who was a good friend of both Taylor and Yeats, tried to mediate the dispute. O'Leary himself did not care for Duffy's editorship.

On the previous August 8, Duffy had set forth the book publishing scheme in a lecture. On August 16 the inaugural meeting of the Irish Literary Society took place. A meeting dealing with the publishing company was convened on August 20. According to the newspaper reports, Yeats (usually spelled "Yeates") was present at all these meetings.

The Freeman's Journal
September 6, 1892

THE NATIONAL PUBLISHING COMPANY
SHOULD THE BOOKS BE EDITED?
Mr. W. B. YEATS' OPINION

IT is now almost certain that "The National Publishing Company" will get £3,000 it has asked for. The question is now, not will it be able to publish at all, but will it publish the right books on the right subjects, and if it does so, will it be able to put them into the hands of a sufficient number of Irish readers? Whether it does or does not succeed in doing these things must largely depend on whether or not it keeps itself in touch with the young men of Ireland whom it wishes to influence, with those who represent them, and with the various organizations which they have formed or are forming through the country.

It would be easy for men of position and of literary knowledge to publish an excellent series of books which would be quite unfitted for the Ireland of to-day, and it should be the business of the shareholders of this company to guard against this danger. No one man, however profound his knowledge of the Ireland of forty years ago, however eminent be his name, should have all the power thrust upon him. Ireland is a complex nation and has many needs and many interests, and no man, above all no man who has lived long out of Ireland, can hold the threads of all these needs and interests within his hands. Sir Charles Gavan Duffy has asked to be made editor-in-chief of the proposed new "library of Ireland," that we may guarantee the freedom of the books from any sectarian or sectional colour, but zeal for a great name and a great career should not induce the shareholders to press upon an old man, somewhat weary, as he has told us, of this world and its cares, a greater burden of responsibility and power than he has felt compelled in the interest of the company to ask for. Sir Gavan Duffy has expressed his willingness to work with an editorial committee situated in Dublin, and this committee should be constituted as soon as possible, that the writers may be chosen and set to work, for good books cannot be written in a day. The instructions should mainly rest with this committee, for it should know best its generation and what that generation needs and is capable of. It is probable that only a small proportion of the books published in such a "library" will be spontaneously offered, at least during the first few months. Writers will have to be sought out and started writing on the subjects they are most fitted for. Sir Gavan Duffy himself found out John Mitchel in this way, and set him to write the life of Hugh O'Neill,[1] and at this moment there may be men as obscure as Mitchel was when the editor of *The Nation* chanced upon him, who could do as picturesque and moving histories and biographies.

A somewhat considerable experience of the editing of cheap books— I have edited five,[2] some of which were sold in thousands—and of the editors and writers of such books and of the methods used by the editors of the various "libraries" and "series" they appear in, has convinced me that it would mean certain failure were the shareholders to persuade Sir Charles Gavan Duffy, living as he is forced to do out of Ireland, to become sole editor. A committee, say, of five should be formed, and this committee should be selected from men like Mr. Richard Ashe King,[3] Dr. Douglas Hyde,[4] Dr. Sigerson,[5] Mr. Robert Donovan, Count Plunkett,[6] Mr. Magrath,[7] Mr. George Coffey,[8] whose archaeological knowledge would be of the first importance, and Mr. John O'Leary, whose unequalled familiarity with the Irish literature of

---

[1] A later letter to the *Freeman's Journal* corrected Yeats and claimed that Thomas Davis, not Duffy, had discovered Mitchel.

[2] Yeats had edited *Fairy and Folk Tales of the Irish Peasantry, Representative Irish Tales* and others. It is difficult to make the total come to five. Yeats may have counted books which were completed by 1892 but had not yet appeared.

[3] Richard Ashe King (1839–1932) contributed *Swift in Ireland* to the *New Irish Library.* Yeats reviewed this book in the June, 1896, issue of the *Bookman.*

[4] Douglas Hyde (1860–1949) was the founder of the Gaelic League; his *Story of Early Gaelic Literature* appeared as part of the New Irish Library in 1895.

[5] George Sigerson (1839–1925) collected and translated *Bards of the Gael and Gall* (London, 1897).

[6] George Noble Plunkett (1851–1948), a Papal Count, was a minor poet and the father of the 1916 leader Joseph Mary Plunkett.

[7] John McGrath succeeded Edmund Leamy during the nineties as editor of *United Ireland.*

[8] George Coffey (1857–1916) was the author of several works on Irish archaeology.

the past would help greatly if the question of reprints arose. A "library" so edited would be truly national, and would command the confidence of all sections and parties of the Irish race. We have now a great opportunity, and we must tread warily for it may not occur again. If we fail now to interest the people of Ireland in intellectual matters by giving them books of the kind they seek for, if we fail to enlist the sympathy of the young men who will have the building up of the Ireland of to-morrow, we may throw back the intellectual development of this country for years.

W. B. Yeats

The Freeman's Journal
September 8, 1892

TO THE EDITOR FREEMAN AND NATIONAL PRESS.

September 7th

Dear Sir—I find by this morning's *Freeman* that you consider "that the shareholders of the proposed Irish Publishing Company do not take to Mr. Yeats's proposal of a committee to assist Sir Charles Gavan Duffy in his task as editor." You forget, at any rate, one very distinguished shareholder—I refer to Sir Charles Gavan Duffy himself—who explained to a representative of the *Evening Telegraph* some weeks ago that he would gladly accept such assistance, nor did he express any alarm less [*sic*] "the new company should be used as a propagandist machine for sectional ideas and principles." He evidently considered that his position as "editor-in-chief" would be ample guarantee of the innocuous nature of the books. The rest of your leader deals with matters of opinion rather than matters of fact, and needs no comment from me, except that free discussion of the question must of necessity do good and help the right opinion to prevail. I am sorry to see by the tone of Mr. Taylor's letter that the discussion is less welcome to him than to me, and I very genuinely regret, for the sake of his own reputation, that he should have felt impelled to write such a letter—a letter which certainly calls for no further answer than that I have met several shareholders who assure me that he had no mandate from them. I have tried in vain to understand what bearing his extraordinary last paragraph[1] has upon the question at issue, or why he has dragged such

[1] Taylor accused Yeats of attempting to make the publishing company into a house organ for Yeats's coterie. The last paragraphs of Taylor's letter, printed in the September 7, 1890, issue of the *Freeman's Journal*, ran as follows:

"It is not an edifying spectacle to see A reviewing B, and B in turn reviewing A, and both going into raptures of admiration. Such things have happened, even in modern times. A poet, not of the Della Cruscan school, has commemorated such things in moving verse—

matters into a discussion which I, at any rate, have carried on with courtesy and good temper.—Yours sincerely,

W. B. Yeats

Taylor had replied to Yeats in a letter printed in the *Freeman's Journal* of September 9, 1892. He said that Yeats and his group had done all they could "to thwart, obstruct, retard, and wreck all that he [Duffy] undertakes." He also claimed that the success of such a venture as the publishing company depended upon the efforts of average men, not men of genius, and if a man of genius should appear, he would approach Duffy rather than "the freaks of any coterie of select and kindred spirits." Taylor's last charge was that the men named by Yeats in his September 6 letter as suitable for a committee were by no means willing to serve.

John O'Leary, a friend of both Taylor and Yeats, came to Yeats's defense in this same September 10 issue. Like Yeats, O'Leary said that this controversy involved private and confidential matters and hence it was difficult to counter Taylor's slurs.

The Freeman's Journal
September 10, 1892

TO THE EDITOR FREEMAN AND NATIONAL PRESS.

September 9th

Dear Sir—I am beset by two difficulties in answering Mr. Taylor. I can neither descend to the weapons which he has thought it compatible with his dignity to make use of, nor can I enter like him into the discussion of what was said and done at committee meetings and private conferences. In order to make the fabric of personalities and insinuations which he has built up crumble, it is only necessary for me to say that I have taken no single step in this matter of the company except offer consultation with my friends and fellow-workers, and that my whole endeavour has been to arrange a compromise between those who object altogether to the predominance of Sir Charles Gavan Duffy and those who wish to make that predominance absolute. But now enough of Mr. Taylor. I will answer him no more.

You ask in your Thursday's issue for an assurance that I and my friends are not seeking to make the company the mouthpiece of party.

> You'll praise and I'll praise,
> We'll both praise together, O!
> What jolly fun we'll have
> Praising one another, O!

It will be gratifying to Mr. Yeats to know that Sir Charles, as editor, will be able to restrain such 'log rolling' and to work the enterprise in an earnest and honest way."

I give that assurance most[1] heartily, and I am glad to add that the question I raised had [sic] been solved in the way I suggested, Sir Charles Gavan Duffy having consented to act with a committee which will consult with him and offer advice without in any way overriding his decisions.—Yours sincerely,

W. B. Yeats

Libraries Scheme

This letter, printed in *United Ireland*, September 24, 1892, was part of Yeats's campaign in support of a project to establish reading rooms and libraries in the smaller Irish towns. The project was sponsored by the National Literary Society, which had been founded the previous spring.

United Ireland
September 24, 1892

TO THE EDITOR OF UNITED IRELAND

SIR—Would you kindly publish the enclosed circular, which I am issuing in connection with the Libraries Scheme of the Literary Society,—Yours truly, W. B. Yeats.

"Dear Sir,—In the small towns of Ireland are few bookshops and few books. Here and there are literary societies, some of which have started reading-rooms where in most cases there is nothing to read except the newspapers and in the few cases where there is every book has been read three or four times over. The National Literary Society hopes to remedy all this and set up small lending libraries wherever a reading-room already exists, or wherever a local committee is willing to start one. The number of cheap series of standard books have made it possible to buy for four or five pounds a fairly representative collection of books of both Irish and general literature. The society proposes to organise lectures in connection with the scheme and to send lecturers at stated intervals to every local society which is ready to work with it in the way described and to begin at once to carry out its programme. A sufficient amount of money has been subscribed to enable it to make a beginning; but much more is needed if the work is to be carried out on any considerable scale. Small donations, either in books or money, can

---

[1] *most*: *Freeman's Journal* printed "must."

be sent to the Hon Treasurer of the Library Committee, Count Plunkett, 25 Upper Fitzwilliam-street, Dublin; or to myself, at 2 Russell-street, Dublin.—I remain, yours sincerely,

W. B. Yeats Hon Secretary.

Invoking the Irish Fairies

This article appeared in the first issue (October, 1892) of the *Irish Theosophist.* The initials signed at the end, "D.E.D.I.," represent the Latin phrase "Demon est deus inversus," or in English, "A demon is an inverted god." These initials are known to have been those assumed by Yeats when he joined the Order of the Golden Dawn in March, 1890, a short time before he was expelled from the Esoteric Section of Madame Blavatsky's Theosophical Society in London.

This account of a trance is filled with learning which Yeats would have been acquiring as he passed through the first stages of initiation in the Golden Dawn. His companion, "D.D.," may have been either Florence Farr ("S.S.D.D." in the Golden Dawn) or Maud Gonne (whose initials were "P.I.A.L." in this society).

The *Irish Theosophist* was the magazine of the Dublin Theosophical Society. A.E. was the guiding spirit of this branch of the society, and the magazine was edited by David M. Dunlop. Yeats, though never formally a member, took part in some of their activities. For another account of a trance attended by Yeats, see "The Sorcerers" in *The Celtic Twilight.*

THE Occultist and student of Alchemy whom I shall call D. D. and myself sat at opposite sides of the fire one morning, wearied with symbolism and magic. D. D. had put down a kettle to boil. We were accustomed to meet every now and then, that we might summon the invisible powers and gaze into the astral light; for we had learned to see with the internal eyes. But this morning we knew not what to summon, for we had already on other mornings invoked that personal vision of impersonal good which men name Heaven, and that personal vision of impersonal evil, which men name Hell.[1] We had called up likewise, the trees of knowledge and of life, and we had studied the hidden meaning of the Zodiac, and enquired under what groups of stars, the various events of the bible story were classified by those dead Occultists who held all things, from the firmament above to the waters

---

[1] Yeats liked the phrase "which men name. . . ." See "The Secret Rose":—". . . heavy with the sleep/men have named beauty."

under the Earth, to be but symbol and again symbol. We had gone to ancient Egypt, seen the burial of her dead and heard mysterious talk of Isis and Osiris. We had made the invisible powers interpret for us the mystic tablet of Cardinal Bembo,[2] and we had asked of the future and heard words of dread and hope. We had called up the Klippoth[3] and in terror seen them rush by like great black rams, and now we were a little weary of shining colours and sweeping forms. "We have seen the great and they have tired us," I said; "let us call the little for a change. The Irish fairies may be worth the seeing; there is time for them to come and go before the water is boiled."

I used a lunar invocation and left the seeing mainly to D. D. She saw first a thin cloud as though with the ordinary eyes and then with the interior sight, a barren mountain crest with one ragged tree. The leaves and branches of the tree were all upon one side, as though it had been blighted by the sea winds. The Moon shone through the branches and a white woman stood beneath them. We commanded this woman to show us the fairies of Ireland marshalled in order. Immediately a great multitude of little creatures appeared, with green hair like sea-weed and after them another multitude dragging a car containing an enormous bubble. The white woman, who appeared to be their queen, said the first were the water fairies and the second the fairies of the air. The first were called the Gelki and the second the Gieri (I have mislaid my notes and am not quite certain if I give their names correctly). They passed on and a troop who were like living flames followed and after them a singular multitude whose bodies were like the stems of flowers and their dresses like the petals. These latter fairies after a while, stood still under a green bush from which dropped honey like dew and thrust out their tongues, which were so long, that they were able to lick the honey-covered ground without stooping. These two troops were the fairies of the fire and the fairies of the earth.

The white woman told us that these were the good fairies and that she would now bring D. D. to the fairies of evil. Soon a great abyss appeared and in the midst was a fat serpent, with forms, half animal, half human, polishing his heavy scales. The name of this serpent was Grew-grew and he was the chief of the wicked goblins. About him moved quantities of things like pigs, only with shorter legs, and above

[2] Pietro, Cardinal Bembo (1460–1547), Italian Renaissance historian and man of letters. I have not located any mystical writings of Cardinal Bembo. Yeats may have meant an eleventh-century Cardinal Benno who was interested in diabolism. Benno claimed that between Popes John XII (965–972) and Gregory VII (1073–1085) there had been an unbroken line of eighteen popes who had practiced black magic (E. M. Butler, *The Myth of the Magus*, London and New York, 1948).

[3] "Klippoth" is the Hebrew word for demons. Literally "the world of shells," in Kabalistic cosmology it is formed from emanations of the Yetzirah or world of the gods.

him in the air flew vast flocks of cherubs and bats. The bats, however flew with their heads down and the cherubs with their foreheads lower than their winged chins.— I was at the time studying a mystic system that makes this inversion of the form a mark of certain types of evil spirits, giving it much the same significance as is usually given to the inverted pentegram [*sic*]. This system was unknown to D. D. whose mind was possibly, however, overshadowed for the moment by mine; the invoking mind being always more positive than the mind of the seer.—Had she been invoking the conditions would have been reversed.

Presently the bats and cherubs and the forms that a moment before had been polishing the scales of Grew-grew, rushed high up into the air and from an opposite direction appeared the troops of the good fairies, and the two kingdoms began a most terrible warfare. The evil fairies hurled burning darts but were unable to approach very near to the good fairies, for they seemed unable to bear the neighbourhood of pure spirits. The contest seemed to fill the whole heavens, for as far as the sight could go the clouds of embattled goblins went also. It is that contest of the minor forces of good and evil which knows no hour of peace but goes on everywhere and always. The fairies are the lesser spiritual moods of that universal mind, wherein every mood is a soul and every thought a body.[4] Their world is very different from ours, and they can but appear in forms borrowed from our limited consciousness, but nevertheless, every form they take and every action they go through, has its significance and can be read by the mind trained in the correspondence of sensuous form and supersensuous meaning.

D. E. D. I.

Hopes and Fears for Irish Literature

This article, from *United Ireland*, October 15, 1892, presents with great clarity the dilemma that faced Yeats in the early 1890s. In London he was a founder and active member in the "Rhymers' Club," a group of aesthetes notably indifferent to politics who met at the "Cheshire Cheese," to read and discuss each other's poems. In Dublin his rhymer's aestheticism was exchanged for the patriotic fervor of a man committed to the expression of Irish culture in literary form. He tried to combine the best of both cities and thus pleased neither. His London literary friends thought that he was wasting his poetic gifts on Irish literary politics. In Dublin his view of life was considered too

[4] By 1895 this doctrine of the moods as spiritual emanations of the world soul was to become an essential part of Yeats's aesthetic. See "Irish National Literature, II," p. 367 in this book.

remote and delicate for nationalistic struggles. Though he did not succeed in uniting such extreme views, he was successful in mitigating the faults of both. He lured the aesthete Lionel Johnson into supporting the Irish cause, and in Dublin he made it increasingly difficult for patriotic fervor alone to pass for poetic genius.

WHEN I come over here from London or cross over to London I am always struck afresh by the difference between the cultivated people in England and the cultivated people—alas! too few—here in Ireland. They could not differ more if they were divided from each other by a half score of centuries. I am thinking especially of the men of my own age, though not entirely of them. In England amongst the best minds art and poetry are becoming every day more entirely ends in themselves, and all life is made more and more but so much fuel to feed their fire. It is partly the influence of France that is bringing this about. In France a man may do anything he pleases, he may spend years in prison even, like Verlaine,[1] and the more advanced of the young men will speak well of him if he have but loved his art sincerely, and they will worship his name as they worship Verlaine's if he have but made beautiful things and added a little to the world's store of memorable experiences. The influence of France is every year pervading more completely English literary life. The influence of that school which calls itself, in the words of its leader, Verlaine, a school of the sunset, or by the term which was flung at it "as a reproach, and caught up as a battle cry," Decadants [*sic*] is now the dominating thing in many lives. Poetry is an end in itself; it has nothing to do with thought, nothing to do with philosophy, nothing to do with life, nothing to do with anything but the music of cadence, and beauty of phrase. This is the new doctrine of letters. I well remember the irritated silence that fell upon a noted gathering[2] of the younger English imaginative writers once, when I tried to explain a philosophy of poetry in which I was profoundly interested, and to show the dependence, as I conceived it, of all great art and literature upon conviction and upon heroic life. To them literature had ceased to be the handmaid of humanity, and become instead a terrible queen, in whose services the stars rose and set, and for whose pleasure life stumbles along in the darkness. There is a good deal to be said in favour of all this. Never before, perhaps, were men so anxious to write their best—as they conceive that best—and so entirely loth to bow to the prejudices of the multitude. There is much to be said even for Verlaine, for he who writes well and lives badly is

---

[1] Paul Verlaine served a two-year prison sentence at Mons for the crime of having wounded Arthur Rimbaud in a quarrel at Brussels, in July, 1873.
[2] The Rhymers' Club.

usually of more service to the world at large than he who writes badly and lives well, and he is always better than the crowd who do both indifferently. But one thing cannot be said. It is not possible to call a literature produced in this way the literature of energy and youth. The age which has produced it is getting old and feeble, and sits in the chimney-corner carving all manner of curious and even beautiful things upon the staff that can no longer guide its steps. Here in Ireland we are living in a young age, full of hope and promise—a young age which has only just begun to make its literature. It was only yesterday that it cut from the green hillside the staff which is to help its steps upon the long road. There is no carving upon the staff, the rough bark is still there, and the knots are many upon its side.

When I talk to people of literary ambition here in Ireland, I find them holding that literature must be the expression of conviction, and be the garment of noble emotion and not an end in itself. I found them most interested in the literary forms that give most opportunity for the display of great characters and great passions. Turning to our literature I find that such forms are plenty, often absolutely crude and uninteresting, as in the case of M'Carthy's "Fardiah," and Joyce's "Blanid;" occasionally crude and interesting, like Joyce's "Deirdre," and Ferguson's "Congal;"[3] and once or twice beyond all praise and all imitation like Ferguson's "Conary," and his better known "Vengeance of the Welshmen of Tirawley." But side by side with this robustness and rough energy of ours there goes most utter indifference to art, the most dire carelessness, the most dreadful intermixture of the commonplace. I have before me a letter from a young man in a remote part of Ireland asking an opinion about some verses and telling me, as if it was a special merit, that he did them at great speed, two columns in an hour, I think. I have not yet read his poems; but it is obvious that good poetry cannot be done in this fashion. There is a printed letter of John Francis O'Donnell's,[4] in which he claims to have written I know not how many columns of verse and prose in two or three days. Yet, he who would write a memorable song must be ready to give often days to a few lines, and be ready, perhaps, to pay for it afterwards with certain other days of dire exhaustion and depression, and, if he would be remembered when he is in his grave, he must give to his art the devotion the Crusaders of old gave to their cause and be content to be alone among men, apart alike from their joys and their sorrows, having

[3] Yeats referred to "Ferdiah: an episode from the Táin Bó Chuailgne" by Denis Florence MacCarthy, the two epics *Blanid* and *Deirdre* by P. W. Joyce, and Sir Samuel Ferguson's epic *Congal*.

[4] John Francis O'Donnell (1837–1874), Irish poet and journalist. Yeats gave a bad review to O'Donnell's collected poems in an article for the *Boston Pilot*, April 18, 1891 (collected in *Letters to the New Island*).

for companions the multitude of his dreams and for reward the kingdom of his pride. He who would belong to things eternal must for the most part renounce his allotted place amid the things of time. Here in Ireland the art of living interests us greatly, and the art of writing but little. We seek effectiveness rather than depth. We produce good correspondents, good journalists, and good talkers, and few profound and solitary students. "You Irish people," said a witty woman to me once, "will never have a future because you have a present." "We are," said a famous Irishman[5] to me, "too poetical to be poets, we are the greatest talkers since the Greeks, we are a nation of brilliant failures." I no more complain of this absorption in mere living than I complain of the narrow devotion to mere verbal beauty of the newest generation of literary men in France and England. We have the limitations of dawn. They have the limitations of sunset. We also in the coming centuries will grow into the broad noon and pass on at last into twilight and darkness.

Can we but learn a little of their skill, and a little of their devotion to form, a little of their hatred of the commonplace and the banal, we may make all these restless energies of ours alike the inspiration and the theme of a new and wonderful literature. We have behind us in the past the most moving legends and a history full of lofty passions. If we can but take that history and those legends and turn them into dramas, poems, and stories full of the living soul of the present, and make them massive with conviction and profound with reverie, we may deliver that new great utterance for which the world is waiting. Men are growing tired of mere subtleties of form, self-conscious art and no less self-conscious simplicity. But if we are to do this we must study all things Irish, until we know the peculiar glamour that belongs to this nation, and how to distinguish it from the glamour of other countries and other races. "Know thyself" is a true advice for nations as well as for individuals. We must know and feel our national faults and limitations no less than our national virtues, and care for things Gaelic and Irish, not because we hold them better than things Saxon and English, but because they belong to us, and because our lives are to be spent among them, whether they be good or evil. Whether the power that lies latent in this nation is but the seed of some meagre shrub or the seed from which shall rise the vast and spreading tree[6] is not for us to consider. It is our duty to care for that seed and tend it until it has grown to perfection after its kind.

W. B. Yeats

[5] Oscar Wilde.

[6] Yeats developed at great length the metaphor of the growing tree compared to the growth of a national literature in his lecture "Nationality and Literature," reprinted in *United Ireland* on May 27, 1893. See pp. 266–75 of this book.

The Death of Oenone

Yeats's review of *The Death of Oenone, Akbar's Dream, and Other Poems*, London, 1892, appeared in the *Bookman* of December, 1892.

Alfred, Lord Tennyson had died on October 6, 1892. The *Bookman*, along with many other literary journals of the English-speaking world, was full of retrospective notices and appreciations. This magazine held a symposium of four letters from poets on the question of Tennyson's successor in the laureateship. The second letter was from Yeats, as he admitted in a letter to John O'Leary (*Letters*, pp. 220–21). In his statement (*Letters*, pp. 218–20), he pleaded for a broader interpretation of the office of the laureate, and he put forward the names of William Morris and Swinburne although he admitted that neither poet could accept the office as it was then defined. That Yeats was given Tennyson's last book to review marks his arrival as foremost poetry reviewer for the *Bookman*.

Yeats saw a reflection of his own dilemma in Tennyson's failure to write a *magnum opus*. Yeats feared that the modern poet tended to diffuse his inspiration in a series of beautiful lyrics. In his lecture on nationalism and literature (*United Ireland*, May 27, 1893), Yeats saw his own epoch as the third and last phase of English literature, a period of lyric moods without any great epic or drama. It was his hope that he, unlike Tennyson, belonged to a separate Irish tradition and hence could escape the coming doom of English letters.

This review could hardly give Yeats's whole mind on the subject of the great Victorians. In the introduction to his *Oxford Book of Modern Verse* he offered a catalog of Victorian faults, which included ". . . irrelevant descriptions of nature, the scientific and moral discursiveness of *In Memoriam* . . ., the political eloquence of Swinburne, the psychological curiosity of Browning, and the poetical diction of everybody" (p. ix). At a banquet honoring Wilfred Blunt in January, 1914, Yeats said, "We are now at the end of Victorian romance—completely at an end. One may admire Tennyson, but one can not read him . . ." (quoted in *A Poet's Life* by Harriet Monroe, New York, 1938). How complete an end of Victorianism in January, 1914, Yeats and his friends had reached, they had no way of knowing.

MODERN writers, the great no less than the small among them, have been heavily handicapped by being born in a lyrical age, and thereby compelled for the most part to break up their inspiration into many glints and glimmers, instead of letting it burn in one steady flame. A hundred years hence their work will seem to lack largeness and simplicity when compared with the work of an earlier time. It is true that they have their compensations, for the glints and glimmers find their way into many a corner and cranny that never could be reached by

the great light of a Divine Comedy or an Iliad, for lyrics are very easy
to read and remember when compared to the long masterpieces into
which men put their whole lives and their whole beings. It is true also
that while a writer lives men are too near him to judge him as a whole,
and that it takes generations before he sinks far enough into the distance for his palace of art to stand clear against the heavens. Let the
lyric poet eat, drink, and be merry for some to-morrow his work in its
totality will be compared with those great buildings of the past which
were built out of so great stones and upon so magnificently simple a
plan, and beside them it may seem like a phantastic and flimsy pagoda.
Lord Tennyson seems to have felt this with ever-increasing intensity,
for despite the discouragement of critics, who long would have it that
he was a lyrist and nothing else, and the disappointment of the public,
who cried out for ever-new lyrics, he attempted great work after great
work, now triumphing with 'The Idylls of the King,' and now failing
dismally with 'Queen Mary' and 'Harold,' and battling between failure
and victory with 'Beckett.' For long it seemed as though his latter years
were to be given wholly to such experiment and the lyrical outburst of
the volume called 'Tiresias' was a distinct surprise. It is well, perhaps,
that this last book of his, his farewell volume, should contain a little
fleet of the lyrics that the people love, and no great argosy of drama or
epic, built expressly for the high seas of Time. It is well, too, that it
should contain, as it does, an epitome of his latest manner, alike in its
faults and its virtues, and so bring him the nearer to us. The new
OEnone is, indeed, but a feeble ghost of the old, and the account of his
refusal to cure Paris but mere scene-painting beside the haunting
rhythms and lofty melancholy of Mr. Morris' account thereof in 'The
Earthly Paradise'; but then 'Churchwarden and Curate' is no less a
masterpiece than the 'Northern Farmer,' and the verse of 'Akbar's
Dream,' 'Telemachus,' 'The Wanderer,' and 'Silent Voices'[1] is shining
with that vivid personal exaltation which only attained complete
development long after he had reached his prime; while 'The Dawn,'
'The Making of Man,' 'God and the Universe,' are charged with that
sense of the travail of the world which came to him in its full imaginative
significance only when he had dulled with gathering years the too com-
fortable optimism of the first 'Locksley Hall,' and cast angrily away in
the second his once great faith in material progress and in that coming
day when "the heavens" would "fill with commerce, argosies of magic
sails, pilots of the purple twilight," and learned to base his dreams alone
upon the regeneration of the heart of man. As years passed over him
the poet grew not less and the man grew incomparably greater, and this

[1] Some of these titles are inaccurate. Yeats referred to "The Churchwarden and the
Curate," "St. Telemachus," and "The Silent Voices."

growth was accompanied ever by a shedding off of hopes based upon
mere mechanical change and mere scientific or political inventiveness,
until at the last his soul came near to standing, as the soul of the poet
should, naked under the heavens. In early days a too great sense of the
mere corporeal bigness of the universe and of the infinity of its trans-
formations had interfered with his sense of spiritual vastness and of the
momentousness of spiritual change, but in his latter days he seems to
have grown conscious of this interference. In 'God and the Universe'
in the present book, he asks—

> "*Will my tiny spark of being wholly vanish*
> *in your deeps and heights?*
> *Must my day be dark by reason, O ye Heavens,*
> *of your boundless nights,*
> *Rush of suns, and roll of systems, and your*
> *fiery clash of meteorites?*"—

and then bids himself be of good cheer, for God is in all. Tennyson's
attitude towards material things reminds one of the astronomical person
with whom Blake quarrelled.[2] The astronomical person bored Blake by
talking of the immense distance of the fixed stars until Blake would hear
no more, but burst out with, "I tell you that it is not so, for I touched
the heavens with my stick at the end of a dark lane the other night."
To Blake the only real world was the mental world, and the rest was of
the stuff that dreams are made of. The heavens were to him merely the
limit of the world of thought and feeling, which limit is now near, now
far. That they should have seemed so very different, so very real, to
Lord Tennyson is made the more strange by his being scarce less of a
visionary in some ways than Blake himself, for has he not told us of
visions and trances obtained by meditating on the letters of his own
name, and how in these visions and trances the spiritual world became
"the clearest of the clear, the surest of the sure"? And has not Mr. Stead
just made known to us the startling fact that Lord Tennyson believed
himself, like Blake, to be in constant communication with unseen
intelligences?[3]

This observation on outer things has its good side, for in it lies the
secret of that marvellous picturesque power, that wonderful gift of
sight into the world about him. Had he been more Blake-like, or even

---

[2] The anecdote about Blake and the astronomer is from Alexander Gilchrist's *Life of
William Blake*, London, 1880, Vol. 1, p. 371: "Some persons of a scientific turn were once
discoursing pompously and, to him, distastefully, about the incredible distance of the
planets, the length of time light takes to travel to the earth, etc., when he burst out, ' 'Tis
false! I was walking down a lane the other day, and at the end of it I touched the sky with
my stick!' " A good example of Yeats's creative memory.

[3] This story is told in William T. Stead's article "Tennyson the Man: A Character
Sketch" in *Review of Reviews*, December, 1892 (American edition, pp. 568–69).

more Shelley-like, he could never have turned from work so subjective as 'The Silent Voices,' 'The Wanderer,' 'The God and the Universe',[4] to the miraculous observation and penetrating satire of 'The Churchwarden and the Curate.'

From his penetration into outer things, and his never-ceasing interest in every movement of his age, came too, I doubt not, that exalted reason and inspired temperance which made him kin to Plato. "Victor Hugo," said Carlyle once to an acquaintance of mine, "is the greatest poet of the day, for he has most music"—he meant by music, I take it, no mere verbal harmony—"but Tennyson has the most reason." 'Akbar's Dream' is a supreme instance of this reason, and even Tennyson has written nothing wiser than Akbar's remonstrance with the warring sects:

> *"He knows Himself, men nor themselves nor Him,*
> *For every splinter'd fraction of a sect*
> *Will clamour, 'I am on the Perfect Way,*
> *All else is to perdition.'*
>   *Shall the rose*
> *Cry to the lotus, 'No flower thou'? the palm*
> *Call to the cypress, 'I alone am fair'?[5]*
> *The mango spurn the melon at his foot?*
> *'Mine is the one fruit all made for man.'"[6]*

                                              W. B. Yeats

The De-Anglicising of Ireland

Douglas Hyde delivered on December 2, 1892, a speech to the Irish Literary Society, Dublin, entitled "The De-Anglicising of Ireland." More than any other single event, it marks the beginning of the effort to revive the Gaelic language. In the following year, the Gaelic League was founded with Hyde as its first president.

Hyde recommended in his speech the substitution of Gaelic sports, dress, manners, customs as well as language for all things English. It was only by such drastic measures, Hyde thought, that Ireland could cease to be a shoddy, second-rate imitation of England.

It is understandable that such a man as Yeats, engaged in an effort to create an Irish literature in English, should have suspected that such a language movement would draw much energy from the literary movement. Yeats

[4] Tennyson's title is "God and the Universe."
[5] Original has no comma after "cypress."
[6] Tennyson's line reads "one fruit alla [Allah] made for man."

admitted later that he had underestimated the potential political force of the Gaelic language movement and he also lamented the loss of Douglas Hyde to the cockpit of linguistic politics.

Hyde's speech was reprinted in 1894, along with speeches by George Sigerson and Sir Charles Gavan Duffy, in *The Revival of Irish Literature*.

December 17, 1892

TO THE EDITOR OF *UNITED IRELAND*

DEAR SIR—I agree with every word you said last week about Dr. Hyde's lecture, and, like many another, am deeply grateful to you for your reprint of it in the current number. Without going as far as some enthusiastic members of Dr. Hyde's audience, whom I heard call it the most important utterance of its kind since '48,[1] I will say that it seems to me the best possible augury for the success of the movement we are trying to create. Its learning, its profound sincerity, its passionate conviction, are all pledges that the President of the National Literary Society, at any rate, will go the whole journey with us, come foul or fair weather. At the same time there was a good deal in Dr. Hyde's lecture which would have depressed me had I agreed with it. He seemed to have the bulk of his hopes for the "de-Anglicising" of Ireland upon the revival, or, at any rate, the preservation, of the Gaelic language, and at the same time to pronounce it "impossible to find either men or money" to carry out the one scheme he held capable of doing this. Alas, I fear he spoke the truth, and that the Gaelic language will soon be no more heard, except here and there in remote villages, and on the wind-beaten shores of Connaught.

Is there, then, no hope for the de-Anglicising of our people? Can we not build up a national tradition, a national literature, which shall be none the less Irish in spirit from being English in language? Can we not keep the continuity of the nation's life, not by trying to do what Dr. Hyde has practically pronounced impossible, but by translating or retelling in English, which shall have an indefinable Irish quality of rythm [*sic*] and style, all that is best of the ancient literature? Can we not write and persuade others to write histories and romances of the great Gaelic men of the past, from the son of Nessa to Owen Roe,[2] until there has been made a golden bridge between the old and the new?

America, with no past to speak of, a mere "parvenue" among nations, is creating a national literature which in its most characteristic products

[1] 1848, the height of the Young Ireland movement.
[2] The son of Nessa was Conchubar, who replaced Fergus as king of Ulster. Owen Roe O'Neill (1590–1649) was a famous Irish general during the mid-seventeenth-century wars in Ireland.

differs almost as much from English literature as does the literature of France. Walt Whitman, Thoreau, Bret Harte, and Cable, to name no more, are very American, and yet America was once an English colony. It should be more easy for us, who have in us that wild Celtic blood, the most un-English of all things under heaven, to make such a litera- ture. If we fail it shall not be because we lack the materials, but because we lack the power to use them. But we are not failing. Mr. Hyde, Lady Wilde in her recent books, and Mr. Curtin, and the editor of the just- published "Vision of M'Comaile,"[3] are setting before us a table spread with strange Gaelic fruits, from which an ever-growing band of makers of song and story shall draw food for their souls. Nor do we lack creative artists either. Has not Miss Tynan given us her "Legends and Lyrics," Miss Barlow her "Irish Idylls," Miss Lawless her "Grania," and Mr. O'Grady his wonderful and incomparable "Fin and his Com panions,"[4] within the last year or two? Let us make these books and the books of our older writers known among the people and we will do more to de-Anglicise Ireland than by longing to recall the Gaelic tongue and the snows of yester year. Let us by all means prevent the decay of that tongue where we can, and preserve it always among us as a learned language to be a fountain of nationality in our midst, but do not let us base upon it our hopes of nationhood. When we remember the majesty of Cuchullin and the beauty of sorrowing Deirdre we should not forget that it is that majesty and that beauty which are immortal, and not the perishing tongue that first told of them.—

Yours, &c., W. B. Yeats.

Ellen O'Leary

Yeats contributed this introduction to a selection of Ellen O'Leary's poetry to Alfred Miles's anthology *The Poets and the Poetry of the Century*, London, 1892.

MISS O'LEARY, the Fenian[1] poet, belongs to a type of writers better known in Ireland than in England. Her verses are songs and ballads in the old sense of the word rather than poems and lyrics.

[3] Yeats may have meant *The Vision of MacConglinne* edited by Kuno Meyer (London, 1892), a book which Yeats was to review in the *Bookman*, February, 1893 (see below).

[4] The original title is "Finn and his Companions."

[1] Fenianism, named after the ancient Irish warrior brotherhood, was an Irish and Irish American movement which attempted in the later 1860s to liberate Ireland. Yeats, in his youth, was for a time a member of one of its branches, the Irish Republican Brotherhood.

Living in a country where the populace are strongly moved by great fundamental passions, she was able to find an audience for her tender and simple rhymes. The streets of her native Tipperary have echoed more than once to some ballad of hers about emigrants and their sorrows, or like theme, sung by the ballad-singers from their little strips of fluttering paper. *The Commercial Journal, The Irishman,* and the Fenian organ *The Irish People,* helped also to spread her verse through the country. Her poetry, and the poetry of Casey, and Kickham's "Sally Kavanagh" and his three or four ballads, made up, indeed, the whole literary product of the Fenian agitation. "Young Ireland" days had brought their reaction of silence. Simple verse could still, however, find an audience; as it, indeed, always can in Ireland, where the ballad age has not yet gone by. It may be that a troubled history and the smouldering unrest of agitation and conspiracy are good for the making of ballads. If this be so, Miss O'Leary lived amid surroundings of an ideal kind, for all her life she was deep in the councils of Fenianism. Her brother, Mr. John O'Leary, is now the most important survivor of the company of men who led the forlorn hope of 1864. O'Leary, Kickham, and Luby formed what was known as the Triumvirate under James Stephens, who bore the singular title of "Chief Executive." In 1864 Stephens, O'Leary, Luby, and Kickham were arrested. The escape of Stephens was at once planned, and carried out successfully. Miss O'Leary was the only woman told of the project. From this on she was constantly employed by Stephens carrying messages. While her brother was awaiting trial, she obeyed without murmur a command that sent her to Paris. Her brother might have been condemned to penal servitude in her absence, but she put her cause before all else. She was back in time, however, to hear the sentence pronounced, and to listen to his characteristic speech: "I have been found guilty of treason or treason felony. Treason is a foul crime. The poet Dante consigned traitors, I believe, to the ninth circle of hell; but what kind of traitors? Traitors against king, against country, against friends, against benefactors. England is not my country, and I have betrayed no friend, no benefactors. Sidney and Emmet were legal traitors."

It is impossible to describe Miss O'Leary's life without touching on that of her brother, for he was the most powerful influence she met with. His imprisonment did not, however, abate her political activity. She hid more than one rebel for whom the Government was searching; and when it became necessary to get James Stephens out of the country, raised £200 by a mortgage on some small property she had, to charter a vessel. In 1867, the movement having failed, she went to her native town, and lived there until her brother's return in 1885. He had been five years in prison and fifteen in banishment, but returned still hopeful for Ireland, still waiting the day of deliverance. From 1885 until her death she lived with her brother in Dublin, and their house became a centre of literary endeavour. A little circle of writers who have sought to carry on the ballad literature of Ireland according to the tradition of 1848 drew much of their inspiration from the teaching of Mr. O'Leary and his sister, and many of their facts and legends from the books that filled every corner and crevice of Mr. O'Leary's rooms. Indeed, no influence in modern Ireland has been more ennobling that that of these two Fenians. Driven by the force of events into hostility to all the dominant parties in Irish politics, they concentrated their influence upon giving to all they met a loftier public spirit and more devoted patriotism. Unionist or Nationalist, Conservative or Liberal, it was nearly all one to them, if they thought you loved Ireland and were ready to seek her prosperity by setting the moral law above all the counsels of expediency. On this last they ever dwelt with most uncompromising insistence.

Miss O'Leary died in 1889, just when she had completed the correction of a collected edition of her poems. It is from this volume, published in 1890 by Sealey, Bryers, and Walker (Lower Abbey Street, Dublin), that the selection has been made.

Poetry such as hers belongs to a primitive country and a young literature. It is exceedingly simple, both in thought and expression. Its very simplicity and sincerity have made it, like much Irish verse, unequal; for when the inspiration fails, the writer has no art to fall back upon. Nor does it know anything of studied adjective and subtle observation. To it the grass is simply green and the sea simply blue; and yet it has, in its degree, the sacred passion of true poetry.

W. B. Yeats

William Allingham
(1824–1889)

This introductory sketch, contributed to Alfred Miles's anthology *The Poets and the Poetry of the Century*, London, 1892, is very similar to Yeats's piece on Allingham for *United Ireland*, December 12, 1891 (see below). What Yeats says of Allingham in the last paragraph points up the difference between the two men as well as showing how much Yeats's vision of the world was being molded by his study of William Blake.

WILLIAM ALLINGHAM was born in 1824 in Ballyshannon, a little Donegal town, where his ancestors had lived for generations. Here he grew up, filling his mind with all the quaint legends and fancies that linger still in such odd corners of the world, and with that devotion for the place where he was born, felt by few people so intensely as by the Irish. When he was old enough, a small post in the Customs was found for him, and there seemed every likelihood of his spending an obscure life in

> *"a little town*
> *Where little folk go up and down."*

In his twenty-sixth year his first volume, "Poems," was issued, and, four years later, in 1854, the first series of those "Day and Night Songs," which contain so many of his best lyrics. "The Music Master" and a new series of "Day and Night Songs" followed in 1855. From 1848 it had been his custom to cross over to London every summer. In one of these visits he had met Rossetti, and been introduced by him to Millais and the rest of the pre-Raphaelites. Rossetti and Millais now illustrated "The Music Master" with the fine drawings reprinted in the collected edition of Allingham's works. It was followed by "Laurence Bloomfield"— an agrarian epic—and "Fifty Modern Poems," containing his last Ballyshannon verse, in 1864 and 1865 respectively. During these years he had also published poems in Ballyshannon itself, by means of broadsheets, which had a wide circulation among the peasantry. The Government considered this local popularity of his verse useful to education, and rewarded him with a pension of £60 a year.

He now left Ballyshannon for London, and either because his imagination flagged among the London crowds, or because he had said all that was in him to say, or for some other reason not so easy to trace, he ceased to write any poetry as good as the old, and little poetry of any kind. He busied himself with revising, not always happily, his earlier verses, and republishing them from time to time. In 1874 he was appointed editor of *Frazer*, and printed in its pages his one prose book, "The Rambles of Patricius Walker," an account of his journeys through English country places. In the same year he married Miss Helen Paterson, the well-known artist. Among his few poetical ventures in these later years were "Ashby Manor," a play written in alternate prose and verse, limpid and graceful, but quite lacking in true passion and dramatic energy; and "Evil May Day," a heavy argumentative experiment in philosophic poetry. He had almost quite lost the light touch and flying fancy of his younger days, and but seldom gave any echo of the old beauty in stray lyric or haphazard snatch of rhyme. The last years of his life were spent mainly at Whitby, where he died in 1889, after a somewhat long illness, brought on by a fall when riding.

To feel the entire fascination of his poetry, it is perhaps necessary to have spent one's childhood, like the present writer, in one of those little seaboard Connaught towns. He has expressed that curious devotion of the people for the earth under their feet, a devotion that is not national, but local, a thing at once more narrow and more idyllic. He sang Ballyshannon and not Ireland. Neither his emotions nor his thoughts took any wide sweep over the world of man and nature. He was the poet of little things and little moments, and of that vague melancholy Lord Palmerston considered peculiar to the peasantry of the wild seaboard where he lived. In one of the rare moments of quaint inspiration that came to him in recent years, he wrote—

> "Four ducks on a pond,
> A grass-bank beyond,
> A blue sky of spring,
> White clouds on the wing;
> What a little thing
> To remember for years—
> To remember with tears."

and in the words summed up unconsciously his own poetic personality. The charm of his work is everywhere the charm of stray moments and detached scenes that have moved him; the pilot's daughter in her Sunday frock; the wake with the candles round the corpse, and a cloth under the chin; the ruined Abbey of Asaroe, an old man who was of the blood of those who founded it, watching sadly the crumbling walls; girls sewing and singing under a thorn tree; the hauling in of the salmon nets; the sound of a clarionet through the open and ruddy shutter of a forge; the piano from some larger house, and so on, a rubble of old memories and impressions made beautiful by pensive feeling. Exquisite in short lyrics, this method of his was quite inadequate to keep the interest alive through a long poem. "Laurence Bloomfield," for all its stray felicities, is dull, and "The Music Master" and "The Lady of the Sea" are tame and uninventive. He saw neither the great unities of God or of man, of his own spiritual life or of the life of the nation about him, but looked at all through a kaleidoscope full of charming accidents and momentary occurrences. In greater poets everything has relation to the national life or to profound feeling; nothing is an isolated artistic moment; there is a unity everywhere, everything fulfils a purpose that is not its own; the hailstone is a journeyman of God, and the grass blade carries the universe upon its point. But, then, if Allingham had had this greater virtue, he might have lost that which was peculiar to himself, and we might never have had the "Twilight Voices" or "Mary Donnelly," or that bitter-sweet exile ballad "The Winding Banks of Erne."

W. B. Yeats

The Vision of MacConglinne

The Vision of MacConglinne or *Aislinge Meic Conglinne*, edited by Kuno Meyer, was reviewed by Yeats for the *Bookman* of February, 1893. Yeats borrowed the plot of this "Vision" for his story "The Crucifixion of the Outcast" included in *The Secret Rose*. The successful and victorious medieval bard of the legend is replaced in Yeats's modern version by the outcast artist who is crucified at the end of the story. Yeats gave no indication in his review that Meyer's book was a formidable, scholarly, facing-page translation of this middle-Irish wonder tale, with copious notes.

THIS certainly is one of the most singular and suggestive Irish books I have ever come across. It brings before one with very startling vividness that strange mixture of extravagant asceticism and extravagant indulgence, mystical aspiration and gross materialism which we call the Middle Ages. It is a romance, in prose and verse, written down first, according to the surmise of its editor and translator, about the end of the twelfth century. It is the work of a gleeman, or strolling story-teller and juggler, and gets its greatest interest from the fierce attacks upon the monks, and upon the very symbols of religion itself, in which the author avenges the sufferings of his persecuted tribe. The law made the gleemen outlaws, and the Church denied them salvation, and against this double persecution they had but one weapon —satire. 'The Vision of MacConglinne' exists to prove that the weapon was both sharp and glittering. The gleeman MacConglinne is described upon the one hand as wise and learned, and such beautiful phrases are put in his mouth as my "treasure is only in heaven or on earth, in wisdom or in poetry"; while the best that can be said of the monks is, "Ye curs, and ye robbers, and dunghounds, and unlettered brutes, ye shifting, blundering, hang-head monks of Cork." The whole story, too, is but a description of the gradual rout of the monks and the slow triumph of the gleeman, until it leaves him sitting at the right hand of the king.

The plot is a masterpiece. MacConglinne arrives one night at the Guest House of Cork, and finds the fire out and the blanket alive with vermin, "numerous as the sands of the sea, as sparks of fire, or dew on a May morning, or the stars of heaven."[1] He makes a great noise singing hymns that he may attract attention, and succeeds at last in awaking the bishop himself, who sends his servant to bring him his "rations." These rations are but two lumps of turf and a little straw to make a fire, and some whey water for his supper. MacConglinne is so filled with wrath that he indites a satire upon the bishop and the monks. The bishop, when he hears this, is filled with a great rage, and declares that "little boys will sing those verses, unless the words are avenged on him who made them." Accordingly he bids them strip the clothes off the gleeman, beat him almost to death, and dip him in the river Lea,[2] and then put him back into the guest house, naked as he was, and leave him thus until the morning, and in the morning he must be crucified for reviling the Church. He is beaten and dipped in the river accordingly, and in the morning taken to be crucified. He is made to cut down his "passion-tree" himself, but manages to delay his execution by various ruses, until it is so late that the monks plead with the bishop to postpone it until the next day, for they are hungry and tired. MacConglinne is accordingly tied to a pillar-stone and left there for the night, when he has a vision of a land of plenty, where the lakes are of milk and the houses built of various kinds of food. This vision is told in such a way as to parody those religious visions of monks and saints which were so common at the time. In the morning he tells his tormentors of his vision, reminds them that Cathar,[3] the King of Munster, is tormented by a devouring demon so that he is eating up the whole produce of the land, and declares that it has been revealed to him that the revelation of this vision will cure him. The bishop also, it appears, has had a revelation telling him that MacConglinne can deliver the king. MacConglinne is accordingly released, and sent to the court of Cathar. He explains his mission to Pican,[4] a great nobleman with whom the king was staying, and begins work by inducing the king to fast for two days by trapping him into an oath to grant him what he will. At the end of the two days he induces Pican to have the king seized and tied to a pillar. He then spreads great quantities of food before him, and tantalizes Cathar and the demon that possesses him by holding pieces of meat just in front of his mouth, but beyond his reach, and by repeating his vision of plenty the while. At last the demon can bear it no longer, but rushes out to

[1] Meyer reads ". . . numerous as the sand of the sea, or sparks of heaven . . . ." In Yeats's version, "The Crucifixion of the Outcast," this sentence becomes, in part, ". . . and are not the fleas in the blanket as many as the waves of the sea and as lively?"

[2] *Lea*: in Meyer, the river "Lee."   [3] *Cathar*: in Meyer, spelled "Cathal."
[4] *Pican*: in Meyer, spelled "Pichan."

seize a piece of meat, and is caught under an inverted cauldron. Every one then leaves the house, and it is set fire to, and the demon rushes out of it, and after sitting for a while upon the roof of the next house, flies "into the air among the people of Hell." The king is now cured and full of gratitude, but the bishop and the monks of Cork still seek to take their prey. The king bids them lodge in court a large sum of money, and he himself will lodge an equal sum in the name of the gleeman, and when the judges have tried the case the money shall go to the winner. The judges decide for the gleeman, and the monks beget them to their monastery discomfited, while their victim remains at court as the guest and friend of the king, and receives for reward "a cow out of every close in Munsterland, and an ounce for every householder, and a cloak for every church, and a sheep for every house from Carn to Cork."

Besides the interest of its curious story, the work is crowded with picturesque details of mediaeval manners and customs, and will be a treasure to the writer of historical romance and to the student of history.

W. B. Yeats

The Wandering Jew

Yeats reviewed Robert Buchanan's poem *The Wandering Jew*, London, 1893, in the *Bookman* of April, 1893.

The literary controversy involving this book was three months old by the time Yeats's review appeared. The book had been reviewed adversely by Richard Le Gallienne in the *Daily Chronicle* of January 11 and in the *Star* of January 12, 1893. Buchanan replied by letter to the *Daily Chronicle*, and a long public controversy followed, largely on the question of whether Christianity was "played out." Le Gallienne capitalized on his position of *defensor fidei* by publishing that same year his *Religion of a Literary Man*.

Buchanan was a seasoned literary gladiator. In 1871, under the name of Thomas Maitland, he had provoked a storm of abuse by his article in the *Contemporary Review*, "The Fleshly School of Poetry: Mr. D. G. Rossetti." Oddly enough, Buchanan and Yeats had in common a contempt for the poetry of Thomas Moore. In an article in his *Look Round Literature* (1887) on "The Irish 'National' Poet," Buchanan had rejected Moore because Moore "lacked simplicity, that one unmistakable gift of all great national poets. . . ."

It may also seem odd to hear Yeats invoking "precision of thought and phrase" and lamenting that "the intellect has nothing to ponder over."

Yeats's ideas on intellect, borrowed from Blake, involved precision and accuracy of imagination, not the analysis of ideas. In his last paragraph, Yeats repeated what he had been preaching unsuccessfully to the Rhymers' Club—that literature and philosophy cannot be separated.

DE LA MOTTE FOUQUÉ in one of his romances describes the Father of Evil as having a face that no man could remember and a name that sounded "Greek and noble," but passed out of men's minds as soon as it was uttered.[1] I find Mr. Buchanan's new poem well-nigh as hard to remember now that I take it up a month after first reading it. I have a vague recollection of something vehement, insistent, eloquent, and chaotic, with here and there a touch or two of serener beauty. I recollect also that while I was reading it Mr. Buchanan was hurling no less vehement, insistent, eloquent, and chaotic expostulations at the head of one who liked him not, and that he was explaining—I remember no more—that the bulk of English literature, from the 'Faery Queen' [sic] and 'Paradise Lost' to our own day, was quite ineffective because "mere literature."[2] Poem and expostulations alike were no doubt "Greek and noble," or some modern equivalent for these things, but they are, so far as I am concerned, with the snows of yester year. But I must try and bring this 'Wandering Jew' back into memory again.

The poet meets in the streets of the city, late one night, an old man, weak and forlorn. This old man reveals himself to be the Wandering Jew. Then by various signs, the control of the elements, the stigmata on his hands, the Wandering Jew makes himself known as Christ. Finally the poet sees a vision of a vast Golgotha amid a sea of human souls, and upon this Golgotha "the Spirit of Humanity" sits as judge. Christ is brought before him and is accused by a skeleton-like figure, who is apparently Death, and by a cloud of witnesses from all periods and nations. Among these witnesses are Buddha, Nero, Galileo, Bruno, Montezuma, Petrarch, De Gama [sic], Columbus and countless others. Christ, they say, was a noble but self-deluded enthusiast who misled the world and cheated it of present happiness by fatal dreams of happiness hereafter, by the persecution of his clergy, and by a feverish asceticism. They talk, no matter what their period or nation, as though they came fresh from a study of the *National Reformer*, and the publication of a certain Fleet Street house, and all agree with Mr. Buchanan that Christianity "is played out." In despair of getting anything but "mere

---

[1] In Fouqué's *Undine*, Chapter 10.
[2] In the *Daily Chronicle* for January 12, 1893, Buchanan said of *The Wandering Jew*, "As to the literary quality of the poem, I am indifferent. I have no respect whatever for mere art or mere literature. . . ."

literature" from the witnesses, we turn to the symbolism itself, and
find a very well-arranged "grand valley" of the Last Judgment, and
nothing more. I do not wish to be flippant, or to be guilty of that
easiest of shallow things, "smart writing," but I can find no other
phrase. This "valley" affects the nerves and the senses certainly, but the
heart and the intellect—no. Blake painted a Last Judgment, but how
different his method was can be seen by his own description. "I entreat
that the spectator," he wrote, "will attend to the hands and feet, to the
lineaments of the countenance. They are all descriptive of character,
and not a line is drawn without intention, and that most discriminate
and particular. As poetry admits not a letter that is insignificant, so
painting admits not a grain of sand or a blade of grass insignificant,
much less an insignificant blur or blot."³ Let us look to the "lineaments"
of Mr. Buchanan's personages. Here is his "Spirit of Humanity":—

> "Then my soul was 'ware
> Of One who silent sat in judgment there,
> Shrouded and spectral; lonely as a cloud
> He loomed above the surging and shrieking crowd.
> Human he seemed, and yet his eye-balls shone
> From fleshless sockets of a skeleton,
> And from the shroud around him darkly roll'd
> He pointed with a fleshless hand and cold
> At those who came."

Compare this admirable fragment of rhetoric with the no less admirably
rhetorical description of the accuser, Death or whatever he be:—

> "Then calmly amid the shadows of the throne
> Another awful shrouded skeleton,
> Human, yet more than human, rose his height,
> With baleful eyes of wild and wistful light."

There is surely no "discriminate and particular" intention in these
vague and commonplace affrightments. Does Mr. Buchanan think that
"the Spirit of Humanity" and "Death" have no distinct identity? If he
thinks that they have not, then why not make this plain? and if he thinks
they have—and surely even Mr. Buchanan would not make them
different personages unless he saw a difference—why not give some
outer sign of opposing function and nature, for "poetry admits not a
letter that is insignificant"? He seems anxious alone to make a vague
impression of sublimity by piling up indefinite words and pictures,
veritable offspring of the void, and by uttering sonorous words that,

³ Blake's description of his Last Judgment: in "Blake's sequel to his description of the
Picture of the Last Judgment," Vol. 2 of Yeats-Ellis edition of *The Works of William Blake*,
London, 1893, p. 400.

howsoever "Greek and noble," have make[4] them stick in the heart and the memory. He fails, as most moderns fail when they attempt long poems; he has no real sublimity because no precision of thought and phrase. When once the vague shock to the nerves has gone by, the intellect has nothing to ponder over and to recall the impression by.

Mr. Buchanan is perhaps hardly to blame except in his choice of subject, for he is neither mystic, metaphysician, or theologian, and you cannot write to any purpose about human hope and human fate— Christ and Golgotha—without being one or other of these three things. He has in fact given us "mere literature," when we had a right to expect not only high literature, but high philosophy. I say this with the more regret because I am heartily at one with much of Mr. Buchanan's disgust at the worship of "mere literature." Great literature is always great because the writer was thinking of truth and life and beauty more than of literary form and literary fame. The belief of the typical literary man of the time, that you can separate poetry from philosophy and from belief, is but the phantasy of an empty day. Dante, who revealed God, and Shakespeare, who revealed man, must have spent their days in brooding upon God and upon man, and not upon the technique of style and the gossip of literary history. When philosophy and belief have gone out of life, then, and then only, shall they be gone out of literature. Let us certainly, if we will, hold with Mr. Buchanan that "mere literature" is accursed; but do not let us trumpet, as Mr. Buchanan does, "mere literature," which is also "mere journalism" set to rhyme, as never-to-be-forgotten revelation, but let us remember always that Providence has provided a place for it and a use in the journals of the day. So long as it keeps to that place and that use we should give thanks for whatever of "Greek and noble" it may have, but let us not encourage it to revolt like him who fell into pride of old time.

W. B. Yeats

Nationality and Literature

W. B. YEATS

This account of a lecture given on May 19, 1893, was reprinted in *United Ireland*, May 27, 1893. It is the most candid and developed expression of Yeats's hopes for Irish literature in the early nineties.

One may read this lecture as an answer to two groups of adversaries: the

---

4 *have make:* this clause is incoherent. Yeats may have meant, ". . . words that, howsoever 'Greek and noble,' have [no precision to] make them stick in the heart and memory."

first, represented by John F. Taylor, believed that oratory and rhetorical and polemical poetry were the supreme Irish literary arts. Yeats disliked oratory and he believed that such indulgence in rhetoric had destroyed the Young Ireland movement of 1848. The second group were those Irish literary patriots who believed that Irish writing should be judged by Ireland alone and hence English or continental criticism was irrelevant. Yeats also thought that Irish writing should be the product of as intense a national or local feeling as possible, but that only a study of great works of literature by foreigners such as Homer and Balzac could save the Irish writers of his own time from becoming locally revered mediocrities. Although he wanted young Irish writers to study other literatures, he tried to separate Irish from English literature, especially since he implies that English literature was in its death throes—an assertion which would make true Irish patriots forgive Yeats for censuring native literary slovenliness.

The division of the development of a literature into epic, dramatic, and lyric was one which Yeats tried to follow himself. He began with epic—*The Wanderings of Oisin*—and he soon attempted a drama of heroic character as described in this lecture, in *The Countess Cathleen*. But Yeats realized, assisted by his critics, that the subtle delineation of lyric moods was his genius (at least in the Mauve Decade) and not national epic or heroic drama. The result of this disparity between intention and performance was a confusion on Yeats's part whether he was in an Irish, epic, phase or an English, lyric, decadent (Rhymers' Club) phase. Yeats resolved this dilemma by founding the Irish National Theatre and so Ireland moved into its dramatic phase. The still-to-be-completed epic phase was abandoned, at least by Yeats.

The literary history in this lecture is somewhat sketchy. Nor is the argumentation very logical. Yeats first suggests an analogy of tree and literature and then continues as if the organic development of literature were a necessity. That Yeats chose the tree for his analogy will not surprise the reader of his poetry familiar with the many tree images and symbols. The following poem from December, 1910, shows such symbolism at its most concise and powerful, and Yeats might here be commenting on his earlier literary prophecies:

> *Though leaves are many, the root is one;*
> *Through all the lying days of my youth*
> *I swayed my leaves and flowers in the sun;*
> *Now I may wither into the truth.*

THE May lecture of the National Literary Society was given on Friday night last in the Molesworth Hall, Dublin, by Mr. W. B. Yeats.

Mr. Yeats having in his opening remarks compared mere oratory to the fiery and fleeting patterns which children make upon the night air with a burning stick, and having said that even if he could achieve this kind of speech-making, exciting though it was, he would prefer careful criticism, proceeded as follows— I am going to talk a little philosophy. If I were addressing an English audience I would not venture to even use the word philosophy, for it is only the Celt who cares much for ideas which have no immediate practical bearing. At least Matthew Arnold has said so,[1] and I think he is right, for the flood-gates of materialism are only half-open among us as yet here in Ireland; perhaps the new age may close them before the tide is quite upon us. Remembering those but half-open gates, I venture into criticism of the fundamentals of literature, and into the discussion of things which, I am proud to say, have never made two blades of grass grow where one did before,[2] or in any other fashion served the material needs of the race. Criticism has been defined as the separation and isolation of some literary tendency, mood, or impression, until we can look at it separated from all other tendencies, moods, or impressions. I wish to separate the general course of literary development and set it apart from mere historical accident and circumstance, and having so done, to examine the stages it passes through, and then to try and point out in what stage the literature of England is, and in what stage the literature of Ireland is. I will have to go far a-field before I come to the case of Ireland, for it is necessary, in the first instance, to find this general law of development. But first let us see if there is an analogy in external nature for this development. Is there any object which we can isolate and watch going through its growth and decay, and thereby perhaps discover a law of development which is common alike to it and to literature. Any tree or plant is just such an object. It grows from a simple seed, and having sent up a little green sprout of no great complexity, though much more complex than its seed, it develops a complex trunk at[3] last and all innumerable and intricate leaves, and flowers, and fruits. Its growth is from unity to multiplicity, from simplicity to complexity, and if we examine the method of this growth, we find that it takes place through a constant sub-division of the constituent cells. I hope to show you that a literature develops in an analogous way, and that this development takes place by a constant sub-division of moods and emotions, corresponding to the sub-division of the cells in the tree. In its youth it is simple, and in its mid-period it grows in complexity, as does the tree when it puts forth many branches, and in its mature age it is covered by an innumerable variety of fruits and flowers and leaves of thought and

[1] Matthew Arnold said so, at large, in *The Study of Celtic Literature*.

[2] Yeats is paraphrasing Swift, *Gulliver's Travels*, Voyage to Brobdingnag: "And he gave it for his opinion, that whoever could make two ears of corn, or two blades of grass, to grow upon a spot of ground where only one grew before, would deserve better of mankind, and do more essential service to his country, than the whole race of politicians put together."

[3] *United Ireland* printed "and last," but clearly "at last" was meant.

experience. I will show you, too, that it must go through these periods no matter how greatly we long for finality, no matter how much we desire to make this or that stage permanent. I wish to show you, too, that all these stages are beautiful in their various fashions, and that our desire should be to make each perfect after its kind, and not to try and make one imitate another quite different one, or even a corresponding one to itself in some quite different literature. For all such endeavours will fail, and, perhaps, stunt the tree. If I succeed I will show that not only is this literature of England different in character from the literature of Ireland, as different as the beach tree from the oak, but that the two literatures are in quite different stages of their development. I wish to show you also what it is that we can learn from English and other literatures without loss of national individuality; how, we can learn from their complex and mature literature to carry to perfection our own simple and immature one. We are gardeners, trying to grow various kinds of trees and flowers that are peculiar to our soil and climate; but we have to go for the art of gardening to men who grow very different flowers and trees in very different soils and climates. But now to apply in detail the analogy of the tree or plant and of its growth by sub-division from simplicity to complexity.

Let us take for our examples the literatures we all know something of, the literatures of Greece and England, though the literature of any other country would, I believe, serve as well. In both you find three clearly-marked periods:—First, the period of narrative poetry, the epic or ballad period; next the dramatic period; and after that the period of lyric poetry. In Greece the first period is represented by Homer, who describes great racial or national movements and events, and sings of the Greek race rather than of any particular member of it. After him come Aeschulus [*sic*] and Sophocles, who subdivide these great movements and events into the characters who lived and wrought in them. The Siege of Troy is now no longer the theme, for Agamemnon and Clytemnestra and Oedipus dominate the stage. After the dramatists come the lyric poets, who are known to us through the Greek anthology. And now not only have the racial events disappeared but the great personages themselves, for literature has begun to centre itself about this or that emotion or mood, about the Love or Hatred, the Hope or Fear which were to Aeschulus and Sophocles merely parts of Oedipus or Agamemnon or Clytemnestra, or of some other great tragic man or woman. The poets had at the beginning for their material the national character, and the national history, and the national circumstances, and having found an expression of the first in the second, they divided and sub-divided the national imagination, for there was nought else for them to do. They could not suddenly become Turks, or Englishmen, or Frenchmen, and so start with a new character and a new history. They could but investigate and express ever more minutely and subtly the character, and history, and circumstance of climate and scenery, that they had got. When they could subdivide no more, or when the barbarian had defeated them into silence there came a long blank[4] until the next great creative period, when the literature of England arose and went through the same stages, and set to music its very different national character, national history, and national circumstance of climate and of scenery.

In England the first period was represented by the poems of Chaucer, by Mallory's "King Arthur," [sic] and by the ballad writers. England was not to carry this period to the same perfection as did Greece, for her genius inclined her rather to dramatic and lyric expression. In the writings I have named there is no lack of characterization, but every character exists rather as a part of some story, or for the sake of some action, than for its own sake. England had no great epic tales, and so we find this early literature dealing, not with some tale of Troy, or the like, but with innumerable stories and incidents, expressing the general bustle of the national life. As time passed on, men became more and more interested in character for its own sake, until at last they were ripe for the great dramatic movement of Queen Elizabeth's reign. Poetry now no longer reflected the general life, but gave us Lear, Hamlet, and Macbeth,[5] isolated colossal characters, dominating the whole life about them, and deafening into silence the general bustle of the world. But this dramatic period could not last, for literature can never repeat itself and the human spirit must ever go on analyzing itself further and further, and expressing[6] more and more minutely and subtly its own profound activity. The dramatic gave way to the lyrical, and the poets took for their themes the passions and moods that were once but parts of those great characters, and again the part drove out the whole. The great personages fell like immense globes of glass, and scattered into a thousand iridescent fragments, flashing and flickering in the sun. Men ceased to write of Romeo and sang of Love. They thought no more of Iago but sang of Hatred. When the time was ripe the English spirit cast up that lyrical outburst of which Byron, Shelley, and Keats were the most characteristic writers. Character, no longer

[4] Since Yeats considered only Greek and English literature, this "long blank" is explainable. In the entire context of Western literature Yeats omitted Roman, medieval Provençal, German, and French literatures as well as Dante. Yeats was later to learn about some of these literatures, in particular of Provençal, through Ezra Pound.

[5] Yeats changed this sentence in a clipping in MS 12148 (National Library of Ireland). The original *United Ireland* printing read ". . . and Macbeth, making silent isolated colossal characters. . . ."

[6] Yeats changed this phrasing (see footnote 5 above). The *United Ireland* printing read ". . . expressing ever more and more. . . ."

loved for its own sake, or as an expression of the general bustle of life, became merely the mask for some mood or passion, as in Byron's "Manfred" and in his "Don Juan." In other words, the poets began to write but little of individual men and women, but rather of great types, great symbols of passion and of mood, like Alastor, Don Juan, Manfred, Ahasuerus,[7] Prometheus, and Isabella of the Basil Pot.[8] When they tried, as in Byron's plays, to display character for its own sake they failed.

In the age of lyric poetry every kind of subtlety, obscurity, and intricate utterance prevails, for the human spirit has begun to look in upon itself with microscopic eyes and to judge of ideas and feelings apart from their effects upon action. The vast bulk of our moods and feelings are too fine, too subjective, too impalpable to find any clear expression in action or in speech tending towards action, and epic and dramatic poetry must deal with one or other of these. In a lyric age the poets no longer can take their inspiration mainly from external activities and from what are called matters of fact, for they must express every phase of human consciousness no matter how subtle, how vague, how impalpable. With this advancing subtlety poetry steps out of the market-place, out of the general tide of life and becomes a mysterious cult, as it were, an almost secret religion made by the few for the few. To express its fine shades of meaning, an ever more elaborate language, an ever more subtle rhythm has to be invented. The dramatic form, and the ballad and epic forms exist still, of course, but they do so, as the lyric form existed in the age of drama and of epic, and their whole burden is lyrical. The old simplicity has gone out of them, and an often great obscurity has come in its stead. The form of Browning is more commonly than not dramatic or epic, but the substance is lyrical. Another reason why the poetry of the lyric period steps aside further and further from the general life is, that in order to express the intricate meaning and subtle changes of mood,[9] it is compelled to combine external objects in ways never or seldom seen in nature. In other words, it is compelled more and more to idealize nature. But the most obvious distinction between the old and the new is the growing complexity of language and thought. Compare, for instance, the description of nature in almost any old ballad, description in which the sea is simply blue and the grass simply green and the flowers simply sweet-smelling, with such a description as that contained in Tennyson's famous line, "A

[7] Ahasuerus, the Wandering Jew in Shelley's play *Hellas*. Yeats once aspired to Ahasuerus' solitary contemplation, and a lengthy passage from Shelley's play is quoted in Yeats's autobiography.

[8] John Keats: "Isabella or the Pot of Basil."

[9] Yeats changed this word in MS 12148 (National Library of Ireland). *United Ireland* printing read "word."

roaring moon of daffodils,"[10] or compare the simple thought of Chaucer or of the ballad writers, or the writers of the miracle plays with the elaborate thought of modern poems like "In Memoriam," the "Paracelsus" and "Sordello" of Browning; the sonnets of Rossetti, "The Atalanta in Caledon," [sic] or the "Tristan and Iseult" of Swinburne, or with any of the poetry of George Meredith. The very names of these writers and of these poems are enough to prove my case. The tree has come to its greatest complexity of leaf and fruit and flower. And what is true of England is true also of all the older literatures of Europe. I need but mention to you the name of Goethe, having in my mind more particularly his "Faust," and of Hugo, having in my mind more particularly his later and more oracular song. Everywhere the elaborate luxuriance of leaf and bud and flower.

Now, I want to notice especially one peculiarity of all these poets. They more often than not go to foreign countries for their subjects; they are, in fact, citizens of the world, cosmopolitans. It is obvious that a story like that of the Siege of Troy or stories like those in Chaucer cannot be separated from the countries they happened in, and that characters like Macbeth and Lear, like Oedipus and Agamemnon, cannot be separated either from the world about them. But tell me to what nations do Hatred, Fear, Hope, and Love belong? The epic and the dramatic periods tend to be national because people understand character and incident best when embodied in life they understand and set amid the scenery they know of, and every man knows and understands his own country the best. They may now and then permit their poets to fare far afield even unto the seacoast of Bohemia,[11] but they soon call them home again. But the lyric age, upon the other hand, becomes as it advances towards an ever complete lyricism, more and more cosmopolitan; for the great passions know nothing of boundaries. As do the great beasts in the forest, they wander without let or hindrance through the universe of God.

Granted fit time and fit occasion, I could apply the same law of division and sub-division and of ever increasing complexity to human society itself—to human life itself—and show you how in the old civilizations an endless sub-division of society to trades and professions, and of human life to habits and rules, is making men every day more subtle and complex, less forcible and adaptable. The old nations are like old men and women sitting over the fire gossiping [sic] of stars and planets, talking of all things in heaven and earth and in the waters

[10] The phrase "in this roaring moon of daffodil" is from Tennyson's prefatory sonnet, contributed to the first number of *The Nineteenth Century*, March, 1877.

[11] Yeats refers to Shakespeare's famous solecism in *A Winter's Tale*, in which the stage direction for Act III reads "Bohemia. A desert Country near the Sea."

under the earth, and forgetting in a trance of subtlety the flaming heart of man.

If time and fit occasion offered, I could take you upon that path, beaten by the feet of the seers, and show you behind human society and human life the causal universe itself, "falling," in the words of my master, William Blake, "into division," and foretell with him "its resurrection into unity." But this is not fit time or fit occasion. And already the fascination of that beaten path has taken me further than I would. I wished merely to show you that the older literatures of Europe are in their golden sunset, their wise old age, that I might the better prove to you, in the closing parts of my lecture, that we here in Ireland who, like the Scandinavian people, are at the outset [of] a literary epoch, must learn from them but not imitate them, and by so doing we will bring new life and fresh impulse not only to ourselves but to those old literatures themselves. But are we really at the outset of a literary epoch? or are we not, perhaps, merely a little eddy cast up by the advancing tide of English literature and are we not doomed, perhaps, to its old age and coming decline? On the contrary, I affirm that we are a young nation with unexhausted material lying within us in our still unexpressed national character, about us in our scenery, and in the clearly marked outlines of our life, and behind us in our multitude of legends. Look at our literature and you will see that we are still in our epic or ballad period. All that is greatest in that literature is based upon legend—upon those tales which are made by no one man, but by the nation itself through a slow process of modification and adaption, to express its loves and its hates, its likes and its dislikes. Our best writers, De Vere, Ferguson, Allingham, Mangan, Davis, O'Grady, are all either ballad or epic writers, and all base their greatest work, if I except a song or two of Mangan's and Allingham's, upon legends and upon the fortunes of the nation. Alone, perhaps, among the nations of Europe we are in our ballad or epic age. The future will put some of our ballads with "Percy's Reliques" and with the "border" ballads, and at least one of our epic songs, the "Conary" of Ferguson, among the simple, primitive poems of the world. Even the "Spirit of the Nation"[12] belongs to the epic age, for it deals with great National events. Our poetry is still a poetry of the people in the main, for it still deals with the tales and thoughts of the people. The little foreign criticism of Irish literature which I have seen speaks of it as simple and primitive. They are right. There is a distinct school of Irish literature, which we must foster and protect, and its foundation is sunk in the legend lore of the people and in the National history. The literature of Greece and India

[12] *The Spirit of the Nation*, an anthology of songs and poems from *The Nation* magazine, was edited by Thomas Davis, Dublin, 1845.

had just such a foundation, and as we, like the Greeks and the Indians, are an idealistic people, this foundation is fixed in legend rather than in history. But, we must not imitate the writers of any other country, we must study them constantly and learn from them the secret of their greatness. Only by study of the great models can we acquire style, and this, St. Beuf[13] says, is the only thing in literature which is immortal. We must learn, too, from the old nations to make literature almost the most serious thing in our lives if we would understand it properly, and quite the most serious thing if we could write it well. How often do I hear it said that such and such a poet is obscure and therefore bad, as if obscurity had anything to do with greatness, as if obscurity was not inevitable unless much that is most profound in thought and feeling is to be left out of poetry. All poetries in their lyrical age get into obscurity. We in this country go to literature to be rested after our day's work, we must go to it on the other hand that we may be made the stronger for that work. How often do I not hear in this country that literature is to be achieved by some kind of mysterious visitation of God, which makes it needless for us to labor at the literary art, and hearing this long for one hour among my books with the great Flaubert, who talked of art, art and again art, or with Blake, who held that life itself became an art when wisely lived. When I hear this kind of talk I am inclined to say that being inspired by God is a profession that is full, so many men have I met who have held themselves to be thus visited. Alas, the inspiration of God, which is, indeed, the source of all which is greatest in the world, comes only to him who labours at rhythm and cadence, at form and style, until they have no secret hidden from him. This art we must learn from the old literatures of the world. We have hitherto been slovens, and even our best writers, if I except Allingham, have put their best thoughts side by side with the most contemptible commonplaces, and their most musical lines into the midst of the tritest rhythms, and our best prose writers have mingled their own gold dust with every kind of ignoble clay. We have shrunk from the labour that art demands, and have made thereby our best moments of no account. We must learn from the literatures of France and England to be supreme artists and then God will send to us supreme inspiration. There is still much to say, but I have already passed the time I allotted to myself, and in conclusion I must apologise to you for not having spoken from a more familiar and therefore more generally interesting point of view, by repeating the words of the crow who was asked why he went to a wedding in a black suit, "I had no other."

Mr. George Casey occupied the chair. Amongst those present were the following:—

[13] Charles-Augustin Sainte-Beuve.

Dr. Ffrench-Mullen, Dr. G. Sigerson, F R U T; Rev. J. F. Hogan, Mr. J. Larminie, Mrs. Pierce Mahony, Miss Dora Sigerson, Miss Mary Fitzpatrick, Miss Esther Sigerson, Miss Mary Furlong, Miss Alice Furlong, Mr. J. P. Quinn, Mr. Dunlop, Mr. O'Leary Curtis, Mr. George Russell, Mr. M'Call, Mr. T. P. O'Carroll, Mr. John M'Grath, Miss Murray, Miss Dickenson, Mr. J. O'Mahony, etc.[14]

The Chairman briefly opened the proceedings, and introduced the lecturer.

Rev. J. F. Hogan, in proposing a vote of thanks to the lecturer, said that Mr. Yeats had made his mark in Irish literature, and he was likely to make his mark much deeper in the future (applause). The energies of a people might be applied to painting, architecture, industry, or commerce, but the most perfect expression of life and thought and intellectual power of a people was to be found in its literature, and they should pay all possible honour to those who were distinguished in literature in Ireland in the past, especially to those who were faithful to the country (applause). Speaking of the important part which literature had played in other countries, he said that, when Hungary was making a struggle for National independence, similar to that which they were making in Ireland, they had three literary men who did more, perhaps, for their country than any three generals who led the army to battle (applause).

Mr. J. Larminie seconded the vote of thanks, and said that if some primitiveness was observable in a good deal of their poetry produced in the present century, it might be explained by the fact that there was a good deal of isolation especially in certain of their poets.

The Chairman, in putting the resolution, said that art and literature seemed to run through several phases—first, simplicity and directness, then expression, and afterwards a return to the older simplicity, produced by an over decorative period. If they produced anything really great in art or literature, no matter to what period it belonged, it would command the attention of the world. He had great pleasure in putting the vote of thanks.

The resolution having been adopted,

Mr. Yeats, in replying, said the work they hoped to do in Ireland was part of the new impulse; of the new literary enthusiasm of the new kind of racial character. They had exceptional opportunity in the great mass of legendary lore by which they were surrounded. They could add a new beauty to their legends by bringing to bear upon them their experience of the literature of other countries (applause).

The proceedings then terminated.

[14] Among these worthies, one recognizes Doctor George Sigerson, the translator of Gaelic poetry; his daughter Dora, a poet; D. N. Dunlop, the editor of *Irish Theosophist*; George Russell, better known as "A.E.," and John McGrath, the editor of *United Ireland*.

A Bundle of Poets

This is an anonymous review, from the July 22, 1893, *Speaker*, of the following books: *The Poems of Arthur Henry Hallam, Together with his Essay on the Lyrical Poems of Alfred Tennyson*, London, 1893; *Anne Boleyn: A Historical Drama in Five Acts*, London, 1893; Charles Sayle's *Musa Consolatrix*, London, 1893; and Sarah Piatt's *An Enchanted Castle*, London, 1893.

The evidence for Yeats's authorship of this review is a clipping of it in MS 12148 (National Library of Ireland) which contains other reviews of Yeats, corrected in the author's hand. Judging from the content of the review, one may say that it is certain that Yeats knew Hallam's essay on Tennyson. A month after this review, in a notice of Laurence Housman's selection of Blake, Yeats was echoing Hallam's statement that the sensitivity of the artist precluded easy public acceptance of true poetry and the banality of bad poetry assured its acceptance by a public which adores images of itself. Yeats quoted Hallam frequently thereafter (see Yeats's review of Sir C. G. Duffy's *Young Ireland, Bookman*, January, 1897).

Of the other authors in this review, Charles Sayle was also an editor of Sir Thomas Browne, and Sarah Piatt was acquainted through her brother, the American consul at Queenstown, with the circle of young Irish writers.

Yeats was active on the liberal weekly, the *Speaker*, at this time. Barry O'Brien, an editor of this magazine, was a friend of his, and John Davidson, a fellow Rhymer not always on good terms with Yeats, was in charge of a column of short notices of new books. Most of the book reviews in the *Speaker* were, like the present one, unsigned.

MESSRS. MATHEWS and Lane have done altogether well in reissuing some of the prose and poetry of Arthur Hallam, and in getting Mr. Le Gallienne to write the introduction, but by no means well in omitting a portrait of the author. We do not get such a great deal for our five shillings in their slender volume that we can pardon the lack of any visible presentment of one who was so much more remarkable than his work. We turn over page after page of fluid and graceful if cloudy verse, of subtle and serene if academical prose, and come to nothing to bring visibly before us the inspirer of the most famous friendship of the century. Arthur Hallam seems to have been ever deliberate, conscious, and reasonable, with nothing of that wilful and incalculable temperament out of which comes self-portraiture. The very things, perhaps, which made him a loyal and valuable friend made him of no account as an artistic personality. He seems, if one can judge by this book, to have been so preoccupied with excellent reasons and laudable purposes that he had no time for those unconscious feelings and bitter protests through which men express themselves, and out of which they create beautiful things. Since time out of mind the world has looked to its Lancelots and not to its King Arthurs to sing it songs and tell it stories. It expects obviously deliberate, conscious, and reasonable natures to give it critical rather than creative work, and will find, in the present book at any rate, criticism which is of the best and rarest sort. If one set aside Shelley's essay on poetry[1] and Browning's essay on Shelley,[2] one does not know where to turn in modern English criticism for anything so philosophic—anything so fundamental and radical—as the first half of Arthur Hallam's essay "On some of the Characteristics of Modern Poetry and on the Lyrical Poems of Alfred Tennyson." We have plenty of criticism in which a stray passage out of one poet is compared with a stray passage out of another, but all mere impressionism of this kind is easy and superficial in comparison to such an exposition of the first principles of a school—and that the least philosophically articulate because the most entirely instinctive of all schools—as is contained in this essay. Writing long before the days of Rossetti and Swinburne, Arthur Hallam explained the principles of the aesthetic movement, claimed Tennyson as its living representative, and traced its origin to Keats and Shelley, who, like Wordsworth, made beauty the beginning and end of all things in art. Any who adopt their principles, he explained, share their unpopularity, and "How should they be popular whose senses told them a richer and ampler tale than most men could understand; and who constantly expressed, because they constantly felt, sentiments of exquisite pleasure or pain which most men were not permitted to experience?" "And yet,"[3] he went on, "every bosom contains the elements of those complex emotions which the artist feels, and every head can, to a certain extent, go over in itself the process of their combination, so as to understand his expressions and sympathise with his state. But this requires exertion. . . . Since then the[4] demand on the reader for activity, when he wants to peruse his author in a luxurious passiveness, is the very thing that moves his bile: it is obvious that those writers will be always most popular who require the least degree of exertion. *Hence, whatever is mixed up with art, and appears under its semblance, is always more favourably regarded than art free and unalloyed.* Hence, half the fashionable poems in the world are mere rhetoric, and half the remainder are perhaps not liked by the generality for their substantial merits." The passage we have put in italics is the best explanation we have seen of the popularity of the didactic poets and

[1] Shelley's "A Defence of Poetry."
[2] Browning's "Essay on Shelley" was prepared to be printed in 1852 with a collection of Shelley's letters. Since the letters proved to be forgeries, the essay did not appear at that time but was published by the Shelley Society, London, in 1888.
[3] The phrase "And yet" is not Hallam's but Yeats's.   [4] *the*: Hallam wrote "this."

of the anecdotists of all ages. The whole criticism is indeed so admirable that our one complaint against Mr. Le Gallienne is that he does not give us some other of those essays of which he speaks in his graceful introduction. The poetry is of little account, and many pages might well have been spared to make room for them.

The writer of "Anne Boleyn," who is an evident Roman Catholic, with a brief against Henry and Cranmer, has precision of thought and phrase and some facility for writing dignified blank verse, and with more developed sense of character might write a readable if not an actable play. The present writer has read every word of "Anne Boleyn," and got pleasure out of it; but then he can read almost anything which is written in dramatic form.

Mr. Charles Sayle quotes Verlaine, and has sent forth his book, after the Parisian fashion, in a paper cover. One reads it with a vague sense of instruction, as though one were reading a foreign language; and yet the thing is naught. Mr. Sayle has, however, humility, and in a poem— "To Modern Rhymers"[5]—puts it into verse not without a touch of music—

> *"I have no strength to blow a blast to fill*
> *This England glutted with the healthy bread*
> *Of Liberty and Equal Right. I tread*
> *A lowlier, silent, older path alone,*
> *And, challenged, hardly dare to raise my head.*
> *I sit apart and watch you."*

Both Mr. Sayle and the author of "Anne Boleyn" have not a little of Arthur Hallam's fatal love for the laudable and the excellent, and show as yet no clear mastery over that art which resembles the sun in smiling alike upon the just and the unjust, the excellent and the inferior, the laudable and the blameworthy. Turning from them with pleasure to one who has a pure aesthetic ideal, and is a master in her sphere, we take up with relief Mrs. Piatt's delicate, if somewhat mannered, reveries over old buildings and dead celebrities.[6] They are all perhaps a little obviously American, a little too plainly the tribute of a new nation to an old, a pleasant and comely expression of that instinct which impels a certain Boston gentleman to spend all his days at the British Museum, working up old English genealogies. But, after all, is not our complaint against America's self-assertiveness upon the one hand, and her profound interest in ourselves upon the other, a trifle contradictory. Mrs. Piatt has sung only of this latter feeling, and we have no cause to complain of our flatterer. She is neither profuse nor grudging, and, but for

---

[5] "To Modern Rhymers" was dedicated to Arthur Symons.
[6] The subtitle of Sarah Piatt's book was *Pictures, Portraits and People in Ireland.*

a too copious use of epithets like "Old World," would pay her homage with admirable skill. "In the Round Tower at Cloyne" is surely perfect after its kind—

> "*They shivered lest the child should fall;*
> *He did not heed a whit.*
> *They knew it were as well to call*
> *To those who builded it.*
>
> "*'I want to climb it any way*
> *And find out what is there;*
> *There may be things—you know there may—*
> *Lost in the dark somewhere.'*[7]
>
> "*He made a ladder of their fears*
> *For his light, eager feet;*
> *It never, in its thousand years,*
> *Held anything so sweet.*
>
> "*The blue eyes peeped through dust and doubt,*
> *The small heads*[8] *shook the Past;*
> *'He'll find the Round Tower's secret out,'*
> *They, laughing, said at last.*
>
> "*The enchanted ivy that had grown,*
> *As usual, in a night*
> *Out of a legend, round the stone,*
> *He parted left and right.*
>
> "*And what the little climber heard*
> *And saw there, say who will,*
> *Where Time sits brooding like a bird*
> *In that grey nest and still.*
>
> "*. . . About the Round Tower tears may fall;*
> *He does not heed a whit.*
> *They know it were as well to call*
> *To those who builded it.*"[9]

Mrs. Piatt has not written many pages altogether, and even the present little book is not all new. She seems anxious to constantly remind us, by making the best of her old poems a large part of each new book, of how light a burden she has fashioned for the wallet of Father Time. She knows him to be a lazy porter who loves best the lightest load.

[7] Mrs. Piatt's line reads "Lost, in the dark somewhere."   [8] The original poem reads 'hands" instead of "heads."   [9] Mrs. Piatt had apparently read Yeats's "The Stolen Child."

The Writings of William Blake

This review of Laurence Housman's *Selections from the Writings of William Blake*, London, 1893, appeared in the *Bookman* of August, 1893. Usually scornful of mere scholarship, Yeats is here seen in a rare guise of a defender of scholarly accuracy. After he finished his collaboration with Edwin J. Ellis on an edition of William Blake in 1893, Yeats took a proprietary interest in the text of Blake. After all, his and Ellis's edition was designed to forestall such hasty compilations as Housman's. The Yeats-Ellis edition had run into heavy fire from critics who found their interpretation of Blake's prophetic writing unconvincing, if not useless.

THE attitude of Blake's editors towards his text and his thought has long been a cause of blaspheming to the few earnest students of his work. These editors appear to hold him to have had so much either of the spoilt child or of the crazy enthusiast in him, that it was their veritable duty to improve his text and warn the unwary not to take his deepest convictions seriously. At first the "improvement" and warning alike were intelligible, and perhaps excusable, for the first editors, Messrs. Dante Gabriel and William Rossetti, had to introduce him for the first time to a public which hates the unusual and the obscure with a bitter personal hatred based largely upon the notion that he who is either unusual or obscure claims to be more distinguished in some way than it is itself, perhaps even to have senses and faculties which it does not possess. The public loves writers that are magnified reflections of itself, but abhors all who claim to belong to some special community, some special cult, some special tribe which is not of its kin. What wonder, then, that Blake's first editors said in substance to their readers, "Do tolerate this strange friend of ours; he is really very nice, though he does talk nonsense at times about inspiration and about seeing visions, and that kind of thing. If you will be civil to him we will smooth his hair, and put him into a coat as like your own as possible, and hide quite out of sight his own outlandish one." It is, however, wonderful and again wonderful, and no less inexcusable than wonderful, that any later editor should accept this dressed and brushed Blake for the real man, and do this without any word about the men who did the brushing and the tailoring, or without even mention that such a thing had been done. Yet Mr. Dante Rossetti was frank enough. In printing from Blake's MS. he found it necessary, he said, "to omit, transpose, or combine" in order to lessen "obscurity" or to "avoid redundance."[1] He also made many corrections of metre and grammar in poems which had been printed before, and avowed doing so, and against this little can be said, for the originals were in print and posterity could judge. Nor would even his doctoring of the poems from MS. have been a very serious falsification had he but taken care to preserve the originals from the vicissitudes of an already fading manuscript. He was wise in his generation, and to his wisdom perhaps Blake owes something of his popularity.

But what excuse can be offered for a publisher, for I do Mr. Housman the credit of supposing that publishers' reasons prevailed over the dictates of scholarship, who, months after the correct text has been printed in 'The Works of William Blake' (B. Quaritch), re-issues the old doctored text not only without a word of explanation or excuse, but without a single sentence to warn the reader that this is not Blake's own text? Would that the fiery mystic who taught that "The tigers of wrath are wiser than the horses of instruction," could shake the dust of Blundel[2] Fields from his old bones, and, dropping in upon editor and publishers, explain in person that "improvement makes straight roads, but the crooked roads without improvement are roads of genius."[3]

Mr. Housman's book is only a book of selections, and some among the most "improved" verses are therefore left out, but certainly enough of them are included in all conscience. A comparison of "Broken Love," to use the misleading title which Mr. Housman adopts from Gilchrist, as given here with Blake's own manuscript, shows not only that there are five stanzas of great importance left out without a word, but that certain other stanzas which Blake put separately, with no clue to their proper place are inserted at the places chosen by Mr. Rossetti, and that the remaining stanzas are put into an order not Blake's. The version of "The Grey Monk" is quite as arbitrary, for Mr. Housman has simply reprinted Rossetti's text in which Blake's second stanza is made the third, his third the fourth, his fourth the fifth, his fifth the seventh, his seventh the ninth, and in which one whole stanza of his, the ninth, is left out altogether, and a stanza which he wrote for a different poem imported to go second. Then, too, Mr. Housman reproduces Mr. W. M. Rossetti's version of "The Garden of Love" in all its formlessness, and has not a word to tell us that the first two stanzas were never printed by Blake in any known copy of "The Songs of Experience," but left in manuscript and as an entirely different poem. Again, we have

---

[1] Dante Gabriel Rossetti edited a selection of Blake's poems in the second volume of Gilchrist's *Life and Works of William Blake*. The remarks Yeats quotes are from the introductory note to *Ideas of Good and Evil*, Vol. 2 of Gilchrist, p. 85 (1880 edition).

[2] *Blundel Fields*: Blake is buried in Bunhill Fields.

[3] This quotation and the one above, "The tigers of wrath . . .," are both "Proverbs of Hell" from Blake's *The Marriage of Heaven and Hell*.

"The Vision of the Last Judgment" in the arbitrary order and incomplete form in which it appears in Gilchrist's 'Life of Blake.' And all the while there is not a single word to show that the editor is even aware that he is uttering other people's false coin.

I turn from the text to the introduction, and I find it equally typical of the kind of thing which has been accepted these last twenty years for Blake scholarship. It is fairly well written, it is highly intelligent, and it is now and then eloquent, but besides one or two old errors of no great importance, such as the statement that the Peckham Rye vision was Blake's first, and one new error, the statement that "The Island of the Moon" has hitherto remained wholly in manuscript—it treats "the prophetic books" with the amused patronage, and dismisses them with the shallow remark about their formlessness, which we all know so well, and chatters about their unintelligibility. "They are too large and too sad a ground[4] to be searched for any sound result," Mr. Housman explains; though how "sadness" and "largeness" can cause obscurity is a statement more obscure to my ears than anything in "the prophetic books" themselves. "It matters little," however he assures us, "whether the meaning can ever be wrung out that is there; the process must always be unlovely and partial and artificial in its results," though he omits to tell us how he can possibly know until he has given the books a much deeper study than this introduction gives evidence of. A man has a perfect right, even before he has read them, to think "the prophetic books" nonsense, but if he think this, then let him, in the name of the nine gods, keep from editing Blake; or if an importunate publisher or his own enthusiasm for song or picture drive him on to do so, let him, having apologised for his lack of knowledge, write with all diffidence upon even the painter and the poet, and keep from commenting at all upon the mystic. Even if he have read 'the prophetic books,' and have no sympathy for mysticism of any kind, he should turn aside from all comment upon them, or confine himself to those moments in which, in Mr. Housman's words, "clean fury[5] of temperament" and several other strange things comes through "in some recall of lyric thought, when prophecy is relinquished and the decorative hand with its sense of gold restored."

Blake was a great poet and a great painter, but he was a great mystic also, and cast his mysticism into a form which, however chaotic when compared with his lyrics and his painting, was in every way more beautiful than the form chosen by Swedenborg or Boehme. It was even

[4] Housman's sentence began "The prophetic books have seemed, therefore, too large . . . ."

[5] *Bookman* printing had originally read "clear Fury." In a clipping in MS 12148 (National Library of Ireland) Yeats changed it back to Housman's own phrase—"clean fury."

less chaotic in many ways than the 'Mysterium Magnum' and 'Aurora.'[6] And what would we think of an editor who had no more to say of Swedenborg or of Boehme than that their literary style was objectionable?

I say these hard things about Mr. Housman's 'Blake' with deep regret, for I have the most profound respect, or rather admiration, for his work as a book illustrator, and would gladly have left him alone were it not necessary for the sake of the great causes of poetic mysticism and of good scholarship to speak the truth about the way Blake has been treated by his editors. Mr. Housman is less to blame than the tradition, and would be ashamed, if left to his own devices, to dismiss in a few patronising words books which he has never pretended to understand, and probably never read more than a few lines of, and to reprint an "improved" text without warning or explanation. I have done my best to put the tradition in the pillory, and would let him go free. It is time that Blake should cease to be a theme of endless eloquence without knowledge, and for the board, with the inscription "fine sentences may be shot here," to be taken down from the doorway to his House Beautiful.

W. B. Yeats

The Message of the Folk-lorist

This article, printed in the *Speaker* issue of August 19, 1893, under the title "A Literary Causerie," is actually an enlarged review of T. F. Thistelton Dyer's *The Ghost World*, London, 1893.

Yeats had been long waiting to write this "causerie." In a letter to John O'Leary dated by Wade as July, 1892, Yeats asked, "When am I to do that 'Causerie' for the *Speaker*? I have waited to hear from Barry O'Brien but have not done so" (*Letters*, p. 209). If Wade's dating is correct, Yeats waited a full year and more before O'Brien, a fellow member of the London Irish Literary Society, printed this piece. The *Speaker*'s steadiest writer of "causeries" was Arthur Quiller-Couch. The usual "causerie" was not an expanded review as Yeats's piece is but informal literary chatter.

In his earlier pieces on folklore, Yeats advised Irish writers to produce a simple ballad literature. By 1893 Yeats wanted a sophisticated poetry in the manner of Keats, based upon folklore. This article contains one of the earliest uses of the term "the moods," which Yeats was later to develop into an aesthetic doctrine to account for divine inspiration of poetry. His allusion

[6] Yeats refers to Jacob Boehme's *Mysterium Magnum, Erklärung über das Erste Buch Mosis* (1623) and his *Aurora, oder Morgenröthe im Aufgang* (1612).

to "the poetry of cigarettes and black coffee, of absinthe, and the skirt dance . . ." reflects his difficulty in convincing his fellow Rhymers—Symons, Dowson, Davidson—that every grass blade asserted the existence of God.

There exists in MS 12148 (National Library of Ireland) a galley proof of this article, corrected in Yeats's hand. Some of the corrections were incorporated in the printed version in the *Speaker* but many others were not. I have changed the text in accordance with Yeats's corrections, and I have given the *Speaker* version in the footnotes. Since Yeats waited for a year for this article to appear (see above), it is possible that he corrected *two* sets of page proof, the copies in MS 12148 and another copy, whose changes were reflected in the *Speaker* printing.

I N one of his unpublished watercolour illustrations to Young's "Night Thoughts," William Blake has drawn a numberless host of spirits and fairies affirming the existence of God. Out of every flower and every grass-blade comes a little creature lifting its right hand above its head. It is possible that the books of folk-lore, coming in these later days from almost every country in the world, are bringing the fairies and the spirits to our study tables that we may witness a like affirmation, and see innumerable hands lifted testifying to the ancient supremacy of imagination. Imagination is God in the world of art, and may well desire to have us come to an issue with the atheists who would make us naught but[1] "realists," "naturalists," or the like.

Folk-lore is at once the Bible, the Thirty-nine Articles, and the Book of Common Prayer, and well-nigh all the great poets have lived by its light. Homer, Aeschylus, Sophocles, Shakespeare, and even Dante, Goethe, and Keats, were little more than folk-lorists with musical tongues. The root-stories of the Greek poets are told to-day at the cabin fires of Donegal; the Slavonian peasants tell their children now, as they did a thousand years before Shakespeare was born, of the spirit prisoned in the cloven pine; the Swedes had need neither of Dante nor Spenser to tell them of the living trees that cry or bleed if you break off a bough; and through all the long backward and abysm of time, Faust, under many names, has signed the infernal compact, and girls at St. Agnes' Eve have waited for visions of their lovers to come to them "upon the honeyed middle of the night." It is only in these latter decades that we have refused to learn of the poor and the simple, and turned atheists in our pride. The folk-lore of Greece and Rome lasted us a long time; but having ceased to be a living tradition, it became both worn out and unmanageable, like an old servant. We can now no more get up a great[2] interest in the gods of Olympus than we can in the stories

[1] Yeats added "naught but" to a page proof of this article in MS 12148 (National Library of Ireland).   [2] The phrase "up a great" was added by Yeats in page proof.

told by the showman of a travelling waxwork company. And[3] for lack of those great typical personages who flung the thunderbolts or had serpents in their hair, we have betaken ourselves in a hurry to the poetry of cigarettes and black coffee, of absinthe, and the skirt dance, or are trying to persuade the lecture and the scientific book to look, at least to the eye, like the old poems and dramas and stories that were in the ages of faith long ago. But the countless little hands are lifted and the affirmation has begun.

There is no passion, no vague desire, no tender longing that cannot find fit type or symbol in the legends of the peasantry or in the traditions of the scalds[4] and the gleemen. And these traditions are now being gathered up or translated by a multitude[5] of writers. The most recent of books upon the subject—"The Ghost World" (Ward & Downey)—is neither a translation nor a collection of tales gathered among the people by its author, but one of those classifications and reviews of already collected facts of which we stand in great need. Its author, Mr. T. F. Thistelton Dyer [sic], treats as exhaustively as his four hundred odd pages permit him with the beliefs about ghosts held in every part of the world. The outside of the book is far from comely to look at, and the inside is that mixture of ancient beauty and modern commonplace one has got used to in books by scientific folk-lorists. Mr. Dyer collects numbers of the most entirely lovely and sacred, or tragic and terrible, beliefs in the world, and sets them side by side, transfixed with diverse irrelevancies—in much the same fashion that boys stick moths and butterflies side by side upon a door, with long pins in their bodies. At other times he irritates by being hopelessly inadequate, as when he follows a story of priceless beauty with the remark that "these folktales are interesting as embodying the superstitions of the people among whom they are current."[6] But then no one expects the scientific folk-lorist to have a tongue of music, and this one gives us a great deal less of himself than the bulk of his tribe, and has the good taste to gird at no man—not even the poor spiritualist.

He deals in thirty-one chapters with such subjects as "The Soul's Exit," "The Temporary Exit of the Soul," "The Nature of the Soul," "Why Ghosts Wander," "Phantom Birds," "Animal Ghosts," "Phantom Music," and the like. The pages upon the state of the soul after death are particularly interesting and have as much of the heart's blood of poetry as had ever Dis or Hades. Jacob Boehme held that every man

[3] Yeats added "And" in page proof.

[4] *Speaker* printing read "scolds," which Yeats changed in page proof to "scalds."

[5] *multitude*: *Speaker* printing read "whole army." Yeats changed this in page proof.

[6] This remark by Thistelton Dyer follows the Swedish ballad about the shroud and the rose leaves quoted below by Yeats.

was represented by a symbolic beast or bird,[7] and that these beasts and birds varied with the characters of men, and in the folk-lore of almost every country, the ghosts revisit the earth as moths[8] or butterflies, as doves or ravens, or in some other representative shape. Sometimes only voices are heard. The Zulu sorcerer, Mr. Dyer says, "hears the spirits, who speak by whistlings, speaking to him," while the Algonquin Indians of North America "could hear the shadow souls of the dead chirp like crickets."[9] In Denmark, he adds, the night ravens are held to be exorcised evil spirits who are for ever flying towards the East, for if they can reach the Holy Sepulchre they will be at rest; and "In the Saemund Edda it is said that in the nether world singed souls fly about like swarms of flies." He might have quoted here the account in the old Irish romance called "The Voyage of Maeldune"[10] of that[11] great saint who dwelt upon the wooded island among the flocks of holy birds who were the souls of his relations, awaiting the blare of the last trumpet. Folk-lore often[12] makes the souls of the blessed take upon themselves every evening the shape of white birds, and whether it put them into such charming shape or not, is ever anxious to keep us from troubling their happiness with our grief. Mr. Dyer tells, for instance, the story of a girl who heard a voice speaking from the grass-plot of her lover, and saying, "Every time a tear falls from thine eyes, my shroud is full of blood. Every time thy heart is gay, my shroud is full of rose leaves."

[7] The editor has been unable to find such an assertion in the works of Jacob Böhme. Here, as elsewhere, Yeats may have confused Böhme's word with William Law's interpretation of Böhme. In Law's explanations of his symbolic drawings which illustrate Böhme's principles, he had this to say of a peacock representing man: "On the Right Side is a Peacock, as a Signature and Character of Man, in the State represented here, even in his most glittering Appearance But if everyone should set down his own peculiar Signature and Character, there would appear as many Figures, as there are Beasts and other Animals in the World; nay truly many more. Because the manifold Combinations and Mixtures whereby three or four or more of those Beasts, which in outward Nature have all but one single Body, jointly concurring, and entering as it were into one compound Body, make up but one Bestial Nature or Property, in one Person after this, and in another after another Manner. For no one that ever came from Adam and Eve can here except himself." (On p. 28 of "An Illustration of the Deep Principles of Jacob Behmen, the Teutonic Theosopher, in Figures, Left by the Reverend William Law, M.A." This section is bound at the end of volume two of *The Works of Jacob Behmen*, in four volumes, London, for G. Robinson, 1772.)

[8] *moths*: *Speaker* printing read "horses." Yeats changed it in page proof.

[9] The statement about the Algonquin Indians is not Thistelton Dyer's, but is quoted by him from Sir Edward Tylor's *Primitive Culture*, New York, 1883, vol. I, p. 452. The Zulu passage quoted above is a paraphrase of Tylor, vol. I, pp. 452–53.

[10] *Maeldune*: *Speaker* printing read "Maclunds." Yeats changed this in page proof to "Maeldune," the hero of a romance translated by P. W. Joyce in his *Old Celtic Romances*. Tennyson's poem on this subject, "The Voyage of Maeldune," served Yeats and other early Celtic revivalists as an example of what a great poet could do with Celtic materials.

[11] *that*: *Speaker* printing read "this." Yeats changed it in page proof.

[12] *often*: Yeats added this word in page proof.

All these stories are such as to unite man more closely to the woods and hills and waters about him, and to the birds and animals that live in them, and to give him types and symbols for those feelings and passions which find no adequate expression in common life. Could there be any expression of Nature-worship more tender and lovely than that tale of the Indians who lived once by the river Pascajoula, which Mr. Dyer tells in his chapter on "Phantom Music"? Strange musical sounds were said to come out of the river at one place, and close to this place the Indians had set up an idol representing the water spirit who made the music. Every night they gathered about the image and played to it sweet tunes upon many stringed instruments, for they held it to love all music. One day a priest came and tried to convert them from the worship of this spirit, and might have succeeded; but one night the water was convulsed, and the convulsion drew the whole tribe to the edge of the river to hear music more lovely than the spirit ever sang before. They listened until one plunged into the river in his ecstasy and sank for ever, and then men, women and children—the whole tribe—plunged after him, and left a world that had begun to turn from the ancient ways.

The greatest poets of every nation have drawn from stories like this, symbols and events to express the most lyrical, the most subjective moods. In modern days there has been one great poet who tried to express such moods without adequate[13] folk-lore. Most of us feel, I think, no matter how greatly we admire him, that there is something of over-much cloud and rainbow in the poetry of Shelley, and is not this simply because he lacked the true symbols and types and stories to express his intense subjective inspiration?[14] Could he have been as full of folk-lore as was Shakespeare, or even Keats, he might have delivered his message and yet kept as close to our hearthstone as did the one in

[13] *Speaker* printing read "adequate knowledge of folk-lore."

[14] From this point until the end of the article, Yeats revised his galley proofs extensively. I have printed the result of Yeats's revisions. The printed version in the *Speaker* was as follows: "Could he have been as full of folk-lore as was Shakespeare, or even Keats, he might have delivered his message and yet kept as close to our hearthstone as did the one in 'The Tempest' and 'Mid-summer Night's Dream,' or as did the others in 'The Eve of St. Agnes;' but as it is, there is a world of difference between Puck and Peasblossom and the lady who waited for 'The honeyed middle of the night' upon the one hand and the spirits of the hour and the evil voices of Prometheus upon the other. Shakespeare and Keats had the folk-lore of their own day, while Shelley had but mythology; and a mythology which has been passing for long through literary minds without any new influx from living tradition loses all the incalculable instructive and convincing quality of the popular traditions. No conscious invention can take the place of tradition, for he who would write a folk tale, and thereby bring a new life into literature, must have the fatigue of the spade in his hands and the stupors of the fields in his heart. Let us listen humbly to the old people telling their stories, and perhaps God will send the primitive excellent imagination into the midst of us again. Why should we be either 'naturalists' or 'realists'? Are not those little right hands lifted everywhere in affirmation?"

"Mid-summer Night's Dream" or as did the other in "The Eve of St. Agnes;" but as it is, there is a world of difference between Puck [,][15] Peasblossom and the lady who waited for "The honeyed middle of the night" upon the one hand and the spirits of the hour and the voices of Prometheus "The Unbound" upon the other. Shakespeare and Keats had the folk-lore of their own day, while Shelley had but mythology; and a mythology which had been passing for long through literary minds without any new inflow from living tradition loses all the incalculable instructive and convincing quality of the popular traditions. No conscious invention can take the place of tradition, for he who would write a folk tale, and thereby bring a new life into literature, must have the fatigue of the spade in his hands and the stupor of the fields in his heart. Let us listen humbly to the old people telling their stories, and perhaps God will send the primitive excellent imagination into the midst of us again. Why should we be either "naturalists" or "realists" alone? Are not those little right hands lifted everywhere in affirmation?

Two Minor Lyrists

This review of *Verses by the Way* by James Dryden Hosken and *The Questions at the Well* by Fenil Haig (Ford Madox Ford's earliest pseudonym) appeared anonymously in the *Speaker*, August 26, 1893. A clipping of this article, corrected in Yeats's hand, may be found in MS 12148, a manuscript volume of press clippings in the National Library of Ireland.

The praise given to a slim volume by the then unknown Ford Madox Ford attests to Yeats's critical powers. Ford said that despite praise from *The Times*, the *Daily News*, and the *Academy*, the public bought only fourteen copies of his first book of poems (in his *Collected Poems*, London, 1914).

"Q"[1] INTRODUCES "Verses by the Way" with an admirable account of how their author was driven from pillar to post through a good ten years, being now an "extra outdoor" Customs officer at the Albert Docks—whither "half the wild adventures and floating wickedness of this planet find their way at one time or other"[2] —now a "super" at a theatre, and now a postman at a little town in West Cornwall, besides several other things between-whiles. One reads

---

[15] *Speaker* printing read "Puck and Peasblossom." In the page proofs, Yeats crossed out the "and" but added nothing. A comma is clearly indicated.

[1] "Q" was Arthur Quiller-Couch (1863–1944), novelist, poet, and editor of the *Oxford Book of English Verse*. He was then the principal literary critic of the *Speaker*.

[2] "Q" said "at one time or another."

these matters and thinks what strange impressions, what unique experiences, what a salient turn of thought, must needs have come to
Mr. Hosken amid the obscure places of the earth; and when, on first
turning over the pages of the poems themselves one finds that he really
does know how to write, hope grows ardent indeed. He must have
found new symbols of emotion, new forms of thought! He has been
down in the waters above the pearl-beds, and must needs have his hands
loaded with the glimmering merchandise. "The indolent reviewer"
thinks these things for a moment and is happy; but, alas! here is no new
Burns, but one who makes sonnet sequences, and sings "In vain my
teardrops flow for thee, dead Imogen"[3] in the way we all know so well.
How gladly one would have heard of those "wild adventures" and of
that "floating wickedness;" for in such things human energy finds ever
new expression for itself, and the record could not be other than radical
and original also. The present indolent reviewer, at any rate, is ever a-
thirst for a new sensation, and forgives but slowly one who sells a
unique experience for a mess of Elizabethan phrases, however pretty
and musical. For a single noble or beautiful reflection wedded to the
incidents and symbols of the docks or the postman's beat he would
gladly let all Mr. Hosken's Imogens go pack. He still keeps alive a
smouldering fit of anger against the late Mr. Allingham for having in
his latter days renounced Ballishannon[4] and Ballishannon songs, and
thereby watered his good grain until it became a kind of cosmopolitan
water-gruel. Emerson's admirable saying—

> "*To thine orchard's edge belong*
> *All the brass and plume of song*"—

should be writ over the mantelpiece of every poet. The spirits in
Blake's "Milton" are shut up within eggs of light, that they may be
forced "to live within their own energy."[5] Till Mr. Hosken has got
such an egg of light, either from the events of his own life or from some
other and less likely quarter, one can but say of him that he has done
better than Capern,[6] the Devon postman, and not so well as Mr.

---

3 The name of Hosken's character was "Imogene."
4 The name of the town is usually spelled "Ballyshannon."
5 William Blake *Milton*, Book 1, section 27, p. 343 (Vol. 2) in *The Writings of William
Blake*, ed. Geoffrey Keynes, London, 1925.
> "*For in every Nation & every Family the Three Classes* [the Elect,
>   the Reprobate, and the Redeemed} *are born,*
> "*And in every Species of Earth, Metal, Tree, Fish, Bird & Beast.*
> "*We* [Los and the Labourers of the Vintage] *form the Mundane*
>   *Egg, that Spectres coming by fury or amity,*
>   "*All is the same, & every one remains in his own energy* . . . .
6 Edward Capern (1819–1894) was known as "the rural postman of Bideford." His
works include *Wayside Warbles* and *Sungleams and Shadows*.

Skipsey,[7] the northern miner, despite a better mastery over metre and rhythm; for Mr. Skipsey has sung the blackness of the pit and the loves and tragedies of the pit-mouth. Mr. Hosken writes often, however, with real force and beauty, and all would be well but for the great masters who have sung of like things before him. He is quite at his best in "Robin Hood," and to take it apart by itself is almost to forget one's desire for a more personal song:—

> *"I read 'A Lytell Geste of Robyn Hode'*
>   *Within an ancient forest far withdrawn:*
> *The story rapt me in a wondrous mood,*
>   *And I outread the dawn.*
> *There was a trembling light upon the page,*
>   *The meeting of the morning and the day;*
>   *The dewdrops[8] shook not on the silent spray;*
> *The world forgot its age—*
>   *The silent golden world that morn in May.*
>
> *"The fever and the dust of this worn time*
>   *Passed like a dream from me, and left me free*
> *Musing on that antique dramatic rime*
>   *Beneath an old-world tree.*
> *I looked and saw a merry company*
>   *Down a green avenue with laugh and song*
>   *And little joyful noises come along;*
> *Then died the tyranny*
>   *Of this grey world in me, with hoary wrong.*
>
> *"There saw I—Robin, with his fearless brow*
>   *And eye of frolic love; Maid Marian;*
> *The moon-faced Tuck; and, sporting 'neath a bough,*
>   *John, Robin's master man.*
> *Scarlet, and Much, and all the outlaw clan,*
>   *With polished horn and bow, in Lincoln green,*
>   *Moved ceaselessly between the leafy screen.*
> *A natural freedom ran*
>   *Through every spirit on that sylvan green.[9]"*

The two remaining verses are well nigh as good.

The temptation to preach "thine orchard's edge" to Mr. Fenil Haig is not quite so strong, though strong withal. His "Questions at the Well" is one of the few first[10] books of promise which come to a reviewer in a season; nor is the promise the less evident because one

---

[7] Joseph Skipsey (1832–1903) was a coal miner turned poet. For most of his later life he was caretaker of Shakespeare's house at Stratford on Avon.

[8] The *Speaker* printed "dewdroops."   [9] Hosken reads "sylvan scene."

[10] In MS 12148, National Library of Ireland, Yeats changed "few new books" to "few first books."

does not quite know what it promises. It would be a work of remarkable achievement as well if Mr. Fenil Haig had only staked and hedged his orchard about and been careful never to stray beyond the boundary. His apples of knowledge are of his own growing, but he has let them get mixed up with sticks and stones from over the way. In other words, he is yet but little of an artist, for art is before all other things the finding and cleaving to one's own. The best of his longer poems is a queer realistic idyll beginning—

> "*Down there near the Gare du Nord,*
>   *At the corner of the street,*
>   *Where the double tram-lines meet,*
> Bonhomme *Simon Pierreauford,*
>   *And his nagging wife, Lisette,*
> *Kept their café, he and she;*
> *He lets life slip carelessly,*
>   *She a sleepless martinet.*
>
> "*He in posing, portly rest,*
>   *Stands for ever at the door,*
>   *Glancing at his waiters four,*
> *Or chatting with a well-known guest;*
>   *She, with tongue that never stops,*
> *Scolds the sweating cooks for waste,*
> *Makes the panting waiters haste,*
>   *Wipes the marble table-tops.*"

There is a right lyrical vehemence in most of his shorter verses too—notably in "The Wind's Guest":[11]

> " '*O where shall I find rest?*'
> *Sighed the Wind from the West,*
>   '*I've sought in vale, o'er dale and down,*
>   *Through tangled woodland, tarn and town,*
> *But found no rest.*'
>
> " '*Rest, thou ne'er shalt find,*'
> *Answered Love to the Wind;*
>   '*For thou and I, and the great grey sea,*
>   *May never rest til eternity*
>   *Its end shall find.*' "

But really he must hedge and stake that orchard with more care. No man is an artist until he has made his orchard, even though it be but an orchard in Cloud-Cuckoo-Land. This hedging and staking by no means involves any narrow specialism; for there is all the difference in the world between the man who finds one thing in everything and him who finds everything in one thing—between the pedant and the artist.

[11] Fenil Haig's title was "The Wind's Quest."

Old Gaelic Love Songs

Yeats reviewed Douglas Hyde's translation of *Love Songs of Connacht* (in Gaelic and English, London, 1893) in the *Bookman* issue of October, 1893.

This review marks the apex of Yeats's opinion of Douglas Hyde as a translator and folklorist. Never again did he find Hyde's work to be quite so flawless. Yeats had always suspected that the scholar in Hyde would overcome the artist. As events turned out, Hyde's Gaelic League drew him from both books and poems into the center of Irish nationalistic politics. Lady Gregory eventually replaced Hyde as Yeats's guide through the Gaelic past and present.

A version of Yeats's story, "Costello the Proud, Oona Macdermott and the Bitter Tongue," first printed in 1896 and included in *The Secret Rose* (1897), may be found on pages 51–59 of Hyde's book.

D R. HYDE'S volume of translations, 'Love Songs of Connacht' (T. Fisher Unwin), is one of those rare books in which art and life are so completely blended that praise or blame become well nigh impossible. It is so entirely a fragment of the life of Ireland in the past that if we praise it we but praise Him who made man and woman, love and fear, and if we blame it we but waste our breath upon the Eternal Adversary who has marred all with incompleteness and imperfection. The men and women who made these love songs were hardly in any sense conscious artists, but merely people very desperately in love, who put their hopes and fears into simple and musical words, or went over and over for their own pleasure the deeds of kindness or the good looks of their sweethearts. One girl praises her lover, who is a tailor, because he tells her such pretty lies, and because he cuts his cloth as prettily as he tells them, and another cannot forget that hers promised her shoes with high heels. Nor is any little incident too slight to be recorded if only it be connected in some way with the sorrow or the hope of the singer. One poor girl remembers how she tossed upon her bed of rushes, and threw the rushes about because of the great heat.[1]

These poems are pieced together by a critical account, which is almost as much a fragment of life as are the poems themselves. Dr. Hyde wrote it first in Gaelic, of that simple kind which the writers of the poems must have thought, and talked, and then translated poems and

[1] This poem is "My Grief on the Sea." The passage paraphrased by Yeats is as follows:

> *On a green bed of rushes*
> *All last night I lay,*
> *And I flung it abroad*
> *With the heat of the day.*

prose together, and now we have both English and Gaelic side by side. Sheer hope and fear, joy and sorrow, made the poems, and not any mortal man or woman, and the veritable genius of Ireland dictated the quaint and lovely prose. The book is but the fourth chapter of a great work called "The Songs of Connacht." The preceding chapters are still buried in Irish newspapers. The third chapter was about drinking songs, and the present one begins: "After reading these wild, careless, sporting, airy drinking songs, it is right that a chapter entirely contrary[2] should follow. Not careless and light-hearted alone is the Gaelic nature, there is also beneath the loudest mirth a melancholy spirit, and if they let on (pretend) to be without heed for anything but sport and revelry, there is nothing in it but letting on (pretence). The same man who will today be dancing, sporting, drinking, and shouting, will be soliloquising by himself to-morrow, heavy and sick and sad in his poor lonely little hut, making a croon over departed hopes, lost life, the vanity of this world, and the coming of death. There is for you the Gaelic nature, and that person who would think that they are not the same sort of people who made those loud-tongued, sporting, devil-may-care songs that we have been reading in the last chapter, and who made the truly gentle, smooth, fair, loving poems which we will see in this part, is very much astray. The life of the Gael[3] is so pitiable, so dark and sad and sorrowful, and they are so broken, bruised, and beaten down in their own land and country that their talents and ingenuity find no place for themselves, and no way to let themselves out but in excessive, foolish mirth or in keening and lamentation. We shall see in these poems that follow, more grief and trouble, more melancholy and contrition of heart, than of gaiety or hope. But despite that, it is probably the same men, or the same class of men, who composed the poems which follow and the songs which we have read. We shall not prove that, and we shall not try to prove it, but where is the person who knows the Gaeldom of Erin and will say against (or contradict)[4] us in this? They were men who composed many[5] of the songs in the last chapter, but it is women who made many of the love-songs, and melodious and sorrowful they made them," and in like fashion the critical account flows on, a mountain stream of sweet waters. Here and there is some quaint or potent verse, like a moss-covered stone or jutting angle of rushes. Thus, for instance, lamented some girl long ago.[6] "My heart is as black as a sloe, or as a black coal that would be

---

[2] *chapter entirely contrary*: Hyde said "chapter entirely contrary to them should follow...."
[3] *life of the Gael*: Hyde's book reads "life of the Gaels."
[4] *say against (or contradict)*: Hyde reads "say against (*i.e.* contradict)."
[5] *composed many*: Hyde reads "composed all."
[6] This poem, "If I Were to Go West," was printed by Hyde in stanzaic form, even though Hyde's translation was not what Yeats considered a translation into English verse.

burnt in a forge, as the sole of a shoe upon white halls, and there is
great melancholy over my laugh. My heart is bruised, broken, like ice
upon the top of water, as it were a cluster of nuts after their breaking,
or a young maiden after her marrying. My love is of the colour of the
raspberry on a fine sunny day, of the colour of the darkest heath berries
of the mountain; and often has there been a black head upon a bright
body. Time it is for me to leave this town. The stone is sharp in it, and
the mould is cold; it was in it I got a voice (blame) without riches and a
heavy word from the band who backbite. I denounce love; woe is she
who gave it to the son of yon woman, who never understood it. My
heart in my middle, sure he has left it black, and I do not see him on the
street or in any place."

As the mournful sentences accumulate in our ears, we seem to see a
heart dissolving away in clouds of sorrow. The whole thing is one of
those "thrusts of power" which Flaubert has declared to be beyond
the reach of conscious art. Dr. Hyde is wise in giving it to us in prose,
and in giving, as he does, prose versions of all the poems, but one
would gladly have had a verse version also. He has shown us how well
he can write verse by his versions of some of the more elaborate poems,
especially of the wonderful "My love, O, she is my love":—[7]

> *She casts a spell, O, casts a spell,*
> *Which haunts me more than I can tell,*
> *Dearer, because she makes me ill,*
> *Than who would will to make me well.*
>
> *She is my store, O, she my store,*
> *Whose grey eye wounded me so sore,*
> *Who will not place in mine her palm,*
> *Who will not calm me any more.*
>
> *She is my pet, O, she my pet,*
> *Whom I can never more forget;*
> *Who would not lose by me one moan,*
> *Nor stone upon my cairn set.*
>
> *She is my roon, O, she my roon,*
> *Who tells me nothing, leaves me soon;*
> *Who would not lose by me one sigh,*
> *Were death and I within one room.*
>
> *She is my dear, O, she my dear,*
> *Who cares not whether I be here,*
> *Who would not weep when I am dead,*
> *Who makes me shed the silent tear.*

[7] Yeats changed each appearance of Hyde's "oh. . ." [no comma after it] to "O, . . ."

This translation, which is in the curious metre of the original, is, without being exactly a good English poem, very much better than the bulk of Walsh's[8] and beyond all measure better than any of Mangan's in "The Munster Poets."[9]

I have now given examples of Dr. Hyde's critical prose, and of his prose and verse translations, and must leave him to do the rest himself. As for me, I close the book with much sadness. Those poor peasants lived in a beautiful if somewhat inhospitable world, where little had changed since Adam delved and Eve span. Everything was so old that it was steeped in the heart, and every powerful emotion found at once noble types and symbols for its expression. But we—we live in a world of whirling change, where nothing becomes old and sacred, and our powerful emotions, unless we be highly-trained artists, express themselves in vulgar types and symbols. The soul then had but to stretch out its arms to fill them with beauty, but now all manner of heterogeneous ugliness has beset us. A peasant had then but to stand in his own door and think of his sweetheart and of his sorrow, and take from the scene about him and from the common events of his life types and symbols, and behold, if chance was a little kind, he had made a poem to humble generations of the proud. And we—we labour and labour, and spend days over a stanza or a paragraph, and at the end of it have made, likely as not, a mere bundle of phrases. Yet perhaps this very stubborn uncomeliness of life, divorced from hill and field, has made us feel the beauty of these songs in a way the people who made them did not, despite their proverb:

"*A tune is more lasting than the song of the birds,*
A word is more lasting than the riches of the world."

We stand outside the wall of Eden and hear the trees talking together within, and their talk is sweet in our ears.

W. B. Yeats

The Ainu

This review of *Life with Trans-Siberian Savages* by B. Douglas Howard, London, 1893, appeared unsigned in the *Speaker*, October 7, 1893. A clipping of it, corrected in Yeats's hand, is in the National Library of Ireland, MS

[8] Edward Walsh, translator of *Reliques of Irish Jacobite Poetry* (1844) and *Irish Popular Songs* (1847).
[9] James Clarence Mangan's collection was *Poets and Poetry of Munster* (1850).

12148. This book was certainly Yeats's strangest reviewing assignment. Yet, despite the exoticism of the topic, Yeats seems to have been informed about the Ainus of Japan as indeed he was interested in all primitive myth and religion. The last paragraph has the true "Celtic Twilight" ring.

IT is likely that the readers of this book will find themselves as utterly ignorant of the Shangalin[1] savages it describes as of the traveller who has written it. Yet both are memorable, for the first have preserved more perfectly than any other Asiatic race their primitive habits and beliefs, and the second can talk quietly of "leisurely meanderings" in Russia, Northern India, Thibet, Corea, and Siberia. Mr. Howard appears to be an English sportsman with a turn for religion and primitive life, and a double portion of that disposition which brings adventures. He travelled, he tells us, through Siberia bent on getting to the bottom of the Russian exile system, and on seeing how it worked in even the most out-of-the-way places. He came in this way to Vladivostock, the only Russian port upon the east coast of Siberia, and there heard shuddering mention of a terrible island where intractable exiles, great criminals, and recaptured fugitives were imprisoned. The name was rarely if ever mentioned but the description was plainly that of the long woody island Shangalin. He now met by good luck the governor of the island, and was invited to be his guest; and while with him saw in the hospital his first Ainu, a black, hairy creature tattooed and hideous, and had his curiosity so excited that he set out, with a convict for guide, to see the Ainus in their own forests. As soon as he found an Ainu village, he sent his convict home and threw himself upon the hospitality of its inhabitants, and was received with that courtesy which seems common to all ancient and primitive peoples. Though he could only talk to them in signs, he soon learnt to enter into their life, and to take part in their hunting and their fishing, in their ceremonies and their festivals. In time he was even made one of the two chiefs of the village, and taught the carefully-guarded secret of their arrow-poison. In this way he learnt more of the simple and kindly Ainus of Shangalin than any other traveller has learnt even of the far better known Ainus of Japan. Miss Bird[2] has done more than anybody else to make us know these latter, but her description is avowedly and obviously from without—the stray notes of a passer-by. Mr. Howard, on the other hand, needed little but some tattoo marks—and these he avoided, he tells us, with much difficulty—to make him a veritable Ainu; and when we lay

[1] Shangalin, now spelled "Sakhalin," is an island off the Pacific coast of the Soviet Union north of Japan.
[2] Isabella L. Bird [Mrs. J. F. Bishop], author of *Unbeaten Tracks in Japan*, New York, 1880.

down his book, we do so with something of reverent affection for those fishers and hunters, and, above all, for his old fellow-chief; and with no little admiration for that simple and beautiful creed which he holds to be the very crown of all the Ainu life, the very essence of all their being —a creed which would have seemed almost entirely admirable to most of the great European mystics.

The savage looks upon naked eternity, while we unhappy triflers have built about us a wall of odds and ends. Mr. Howard's friends affirm one supreme god the maker of gods and men, but hold that he has under him innumerable minor divinities, such as the god of running waters, the god of lakes, the god of the sea, the god of the waters as a whole, and as the great goddess of the sun's fire, and the minor and mediatorial goddess of the household flame. There is an ancient Catholic writer who holds that "The Most High set the borders of the nations after the number of the angels of God."[3] Are not fire and the waters more unchanging and mightier than any nations? There are, say the Ainu, three heavens—the supreme heaven of outer space where the supreme god lives, the star-bearing heaven, and the heaven of the clouds which is about us. The gods dwell in these heavens, but each has for his contrary an evil spirit, and these evil spirits are ruled over by one supreme evil deity and inhabit six hells. The souls of the dead whether of men or animals,[4] go either among the good or evil spirits after death, but are permitted to return at times, the animals to help and the old women to injure men. The Ainu worshipper has neither priest nor chapel, but whittles the end of a long stick into a kind of fringe and then thrusts the stick into the earth and prays beside it, and according to the place of the god prayed to in the celestial hierarchy is the place of the chip fringe upon the stick. The women are not permitted to pray for fear they might bring to the gods tittle-tattle about the men.

Mr. Howard tells all this so admirably and sympathetically that his concluding appeal to someone to go preach Christianity to his late subjects may excite surprise. If a member of the Women's Liberal Federation would go and talk to them of the rights of her sex they would be better off in the matter of religion than the bulk of us, and would at any rate have a more developed creed than many a captain in the Salvation Army. Should we not rather ask them to send us a tattooed and hairy missionary to help evangelise our own heathen? He cries out, too, for someone to do something for their material well-being. The Russians leave them alone, forbid anybody to sell them drink,

[3] In Yeats's second article on "Irish National Literature" (*Bookman*, August, 1895) he identifies this statement as "words put into the mouth of St. Dionysius." Yeats probably meant the mystical theologian Dionysius, the Pseudo-Areopagite (fl. 500).

[4] In National Library of Ireland, MS 12148, Yeats changed this sentence. The *Speaker* printing read "The good, whether they be men or animals. . . ."

and abandon to them the game of the island, and for these things Mr. Howard is fittingly grateful, and yet he calls out for the philanthropists. Has not the Ainu the great woods and the overwhelming mountains? and if the winter be cold and food scarce at times, how is he worse off than his fathers before him? He has his spear and his supplebow, and the delight of the long-followed trail, and love, and the talk about the fire, and at the end of all the heaven of stars or the heaven of cloud. Is our own life so much the better that we must needs give him of its abundance?

Interview with Mr. W. B. Yeats

This interview, published in the *Irish Theosophist*, Vol. II, no. 1 (October 15, 1893), deals mainly with Yeats's experiences in the Theosophical Society in London. Yeats joined the Blavatsky Lodge in London in 1887 and in 1888 he was admitted to the Esoteric Section. Around November, 1890, Yeats was asked to resign from this inner circle. In his autobiography he claimed that Madame Blavatsky was annoyed by his psychical experiments. From his letters, it seems that the cause of the trouble was a criticism of the Madame's magazine *Lucifer* which Yeats had written for another Theosophical magazine, *Weekly Review*, edited by his friend Charles Johnston (*Letters*, pp. 159–60).

Yeats's remarks on Madame Blavatsky supplement what he has to say about her in his autobiography. As a young man in 1886 he defended her against those who claimed that she was a charlatan. Even by 1893 he appears to have become skeptical. Yeats's interviewer, "D.N.D.," was probably D. N. Dunlop, the editor of *Irish Theosophist*. Although Yeats signed a contribution to this magazine with "D.E.D.I.," his occult initials, many articles were signed with name initials, such as "G.W.R." (George William Russell, who usually preferred "A.E.").

A FEW evenings ago I called on my friend, Mr. W. B. Yeats, and found him alone, seated in his arm-chair, smoking his cigarette, with a volume of Homer before him. The whole room indicated the style and taste peculiar to its presiding genius. Upon the walls hung various designs by Blake and other less well-known symbolic artists; everywhere books and papers, in apparently endless profusion.

In his usual genial way he invited me to have a cup of tea with him. During this pleasant ceremony little was said, but sufficient to impress me more than ever with the fact that my host was supremely an artist, much in love with his art. With a passion deep and entrancing he adores his art: "his bread is from her lips; his exhilaration from the taste of her." The Muse finds in him a tongue to respond to her most subtle beauties. In song was [*sic*] handed down the great Solar Religions that advanced the people of antiquity; in song those of a later day received that which caused them to emerge from their cold isolation and kiss "the warm lips of Helios"; and in these days, too, we look to the poets for that inspiration which will

> "*Overflow mankind with true desires,*
> *And guide new Ages on by flights of living lyres.*"

Tea over, I disclosed the object of my visit. "Mr. Yeats," I said, "I understand that you saw a great deal of Madame Blavatsky in the earlier days of the Theosophical movement in England, and so I thought you might have something to say regarding her, which would interest the readers of the IRISH THEOSOPHIST."

"Yes," replied Mr. Yeats, "I had the privilege of seeing Madame Blavatsky frequently at that time, and so many interesting little incidents crowd in upon me, that I find some difficulty in selecting what might be most interesting to your readers."

"Well," I replied, "suppose you begin by giving your personal impressions."

"Madame Blavatsky," said Mr. Yeats, "struck me as being a very strong character. In her ordinary moods, rather combative, and inclined to rub people's prejudices the other way. When depressed, she dropped her combativeness, and, thrown back on herself, as it were, became most interesting, and talked about her own life. A clever American, who was not a Theosophist, said to me once: 'Madame Blavatsky has become the most famous woman in the whole world, by sitting in her arm-chair, and getting people to talk to her.'"

"I have heard it stated," said I, "in connection with the Coloumb [*sic*][1] incidents, that Madame Blavatsky showed great lack of insight into character."

"For so powerful a personality," replied Mr. Yeats, "she did seem to lack something in that respect. I remember, for instance, on one occasion she introduced me to a French occultist, whom she spoke of very highly, and even urged me to read his books. Within a short time he

[1] Madame Coulomb (neé Emma Cutting), who exposed Madame Blavatsky in 1884, had been a friend of Madame Blavatsky since 1871. She arrived in Bombay in 1880 with her husband, a carpenter. The two, by their later admission, assisted Madame Blavatsky in spiritualistic hoaxes. They were left in charge of the society's headquarters at Adyar, outside Madras, and during a quarrel in 1884 they made public their accusations against the Madame. Their testimony was an important part of the report which Richard Hodgson completed for the London Society for Psychical Research in 1885.

was expelled from the Society for what appeared excellent reasons. 'I have had to expel him,' said Madame Blavatsky to me; 'he sold a love elixir for two francs; had it been forty francs I might have overlooked the fact.' On another occasion she told me, quite seriously, that I would have a severe illness within six months, and I am waiting for that illness still. Attempts are made by people very often," continued Mr. Yeats, "to wash humanity out of their leaders. Madame Blavatsky made mistakes; she was human, and to me that fact makes her, if possible, the more interesting. Another peculiarity was her evident lack of proportion. An attack on the Theosophical movement (she did not seem to mind personal attacks) in some obscure little paper,[2] was to her of as much importance as if it appeared in the *Times*."

In reply to another question, Mr. Yeats remarked that she had met Demussét [sic] a few times, and Balzac once. She had worked a little at occultism with George Sands [sic], but, to use her own words, both were "mere dabblers" at the time.

"What did you think of Madame Blavatsky as a talker?" I asked.

"It has been said of Dr. Johnson,"[3] replied Mr. Yeats, "that the effeminate reader is repelled by him; and the same might be said of Madame Blavatsky as a talker. She had that kind of faculty which repelled the weak, and attracted those of a stronger temperament. She hated paradox, and yet she gave utterance to the most magnificent paradox I ever heard."

"As you heard her talk a good deal, perhaps you will kindly relate to me any interesting sayings that occur to you," said I.

"With pleasure," replied Mr. Yeats, lighting another cigarette. "I called on Madame Blavatsky one day, with a friend—a T. C. D. man.[4] She was trying to explain to us the nature of the Akas,[5] and was entering into an exceedingly subtle metaphysical analysis of the difference between fore-knowledge and predestination—a problem which has interested theologians of ancient, as well as modern times— showing the way in which the whole question was mixed up with the question of the Akas, when suddenly she broke off—my friend not following, and said, turning round, and pointing to one of her followers who was present: 'You with your spectacles and your impudence, you will be sitting there in the Akas to all eternity—no not to all eternity, for a day will come

---

[2] The "obscure little paper" was the *Weekly Review*, now lost, edited by Charles Johnston. Yeats contributed, around November, 1890, an article critical of *Lucifer* (Madame's magazine) which led to his resignation from the Esoteric Section of the Blavatsky Lodge.

[3] In his autobiography Yeats called her "a sort of female Dr. Johnson."

[4] The Trinity College, Dublin, man may have been Charles Johnston, a friend of Yeats and a fellow occultist.

[5] Akas (or Akasha), a celestial ether, or astral light that fills all space. All thought and action is recorded in it and the seer can thus read the past through it (F. Gaynor, *Dictionary of Mysticism*, New York, 1953).

when even the Akas will pass away, and then there shall be nothing but God—Chaos—that which every man is seeking in his heart.' "

"At another time, when I called, she seemed rather depressed. 'Ah!' she said, 'there is no solidarity among the good; there is only solidarity among the evil. There was a time when I used to blame and pity the people who sold their souls to the devil, now I only pity them; I know why they do it; they do it to have somebody on their side.' 'As for me I write, write, write, as the Wandering Jew walks, walks, walks.' "

"On one occasion, too," said Mr. Yeats, continuing, "she referred to the Greek Church as the church of her childhood, saying: 'The Greek Church, like all true religions, was a triangle, but it spread out and became a bramble bush, and that is the Church of Rome; then they came and lopped off the branches, and turned it into a broomstick, and that is Protestantism.' "

In reply to a question, Mr. Yeats said, quoting her own words, with reference to Col. Olcott[6]: "Ah! *he* is an honest man; *I* am an old Russian savage"; and, referring to Mr. Old,[7] she said, with a hearty enthusiasm that, in certain respects, he was above all those about her at that time.

"Can you remember anything in the nature of a prophecy, Mr. Yeats, made by Madame Blavatsky, that might be of interest to record, notwithstanding the fact that you are yet awaiting your prophesied illness?" I asked.

"The only thing of that nature," replied Mr. Yeats, "was a reference to England." "The Master told me," said she, "that the power of England would not outlive the century, and the Master never deceived me."

"I am very much obliged to you, Mr. Yeats," said I, "for the kind manner in which you have responded to my enquiries regarding Madame Blavatsky; perhaps you will pardon me if I ask you one or two questions about your own work now. Do you intend, at any time, publishing a book on 'Mysticism'?"

"Yes; at no very distant date I hope to publish a work dealing with mystics I have seen, and stories I have heard, but it will be as an artist, not as a controversialist."[8]

"And what about your present work?" I asked.

" 'Celtic Twilight,' a work dealing with ghosts, goblins, and faeries,

[6] Colonel H. S. Olcott (1832–1907) founded, with Madame Blavatsky, the Theosophical Society.
[7] W. R. Old, author of *What is Theosophy*, London, 1891, was a sub-editor of the *Theosophist*. In 1894 he supplied F. E. Garrett with materials for a series of articles in *Westminster Gazette* exposing theosophy. Garrett published them in book form as *Isis Very Much Unveiled* (London, 1894). See A. B. Kuhn: *Theosophy, A Modern Revival of Ancient Wisdom*, New York, 1930, p. 317.
[8] This work on mysticism never appeared, unless *A Vision* can be said to be the ultimate result of that intention.

will be out shortly; also a small selection of 'Blake's Poems,'"⁹ he replied. "Then, I am getting ready for publication, next spring, a book of poems, which I intend calling, 'The Wind among the Reeds',¹⁰ and, as soon afterwards as possible, a collection of essays, and lectures dealing with Irish nationality and literature, which will probably appear under the title of the 'Watch Fire.'"¹¹

After due apologies for my intrusion, I bade my host good evening, and withdrew feeling more than satisfied with the result of my interview.

Mr. Yeats has often been spoken of as a dreamer, and many strange stories are afloat which go a long way to bear out such a statement. But, in my opinion, he combines the man of thought with the man of action; he is "whole of heart and sound of head," and Ireland may, indeed, be proud of one who promises to rank among her most worthy sons.

D. N. D.
[D. N. Dunlop]

Reflections and Refractions

This review of *Reflections and Refractions* by Charles Weekes, London, 1893, appeared in the *Academy*, November 4, 1893. Weekes was an old Dublin friend of Yeats. He had joined Yeats in 1885 in founding the Dublin Hermetical Society. Among the Yeats manuscripts in the National Library of Ireland is a note to Mr. Cotton, perhaps James Sutherland Cotton (1847–1918), the editor of the *Academy* from 1896 to 1903: "This is a book of poems by a young Dublin man 'Reflections and Refractions by Charles Weekes.' May I review it for you? Yours . . . W. B. Yeats."

Weekes was dissatisfied with the book or with its reception, for he withdrew it from circulation soon after publication. Copies of it are very rare.

A POEM cast into an impersonal artistic shape can be judged by recognised canons. But a poem taking nearly all its interest from the expression of personal idiosyncrasy comes before a very different court,

⁹ The small selection of Blake's poems, published in 1893, was a by-product of the Yeats-Ellis edition of Blake's complete works, also published in 1893.

¹⁰ Yeats published a collection of his poems in 1895. The title "The Wind Among the Reeds" was not used for a book of poems until 1899.

¹¹ The "Watch Fire" was never lit. It would certainly have included the lecture "Nationality and Literature" (*United Ireland*, May 27, 1893) as well as many of the pieces in the present collection.

and is liked, or disliked, from reasons as personal as its own inspiration, or as the reasons for which we like or dislike the people we meet in daily life; and if it be not more personal than difficult or rugged, our judgment is likely to be somewhat of the summary kind. A Tennyson, or a Mr. Swinburne, finds his public with a volume or two; while a Browning has for years to publish at his own expense, and a Whitman to be his own bookseller. A rugged, obscure personal book, if it be at all excellent, has, therefore, a double claim upon our hospitality: the claim to be received for its own sake, and the claim to be received because of the dangers and difficulties that beset its future.

Mr. Charles Weekes's uncouthly-named *Refractions and Reflections* [*sic*] is just such a book. It is as interesting as it is rugged and obscure. There is not a poem without some unusual thought or pleasant phrase, and there is scarcely one that can be taken apart from the rest and left to explain itself with security. One of the best and most intelligible is undoubtedly "Phthisical," as Mr. Weekes has horribly named a very beautiful description of the approach of dawn, supposed to be written by a dying man. I quote the central verses:—

> "Long before the dawn
>   Yesterday,
> Sleepless thro' the twilights fair,
> I was somehow drawn,
>   Unaware,
> Into love of this old earth—
>   Could I say!
>
> "First the stillness; then
>   Round the house
> Flew the owls a moment; and
> Silence once again:
>   All the land
> Lay in perfect twilight; stirred
>   Not a mouse.
>
> "Fallen thus on peace,
>   I awoke
> To that speechless thought of her;
> Gave me wondrous ease.
>   Not a stir
> Marked I till the mellow-tongued
>   Blackbird spoke.
>
> "Then returned the owls.
>   From the wall
> Dropped the plaster on the walk.

In the chimney-holes
Jackdaw-talk.
In the Herrick Farm the cock
Gave a call.

"Silence then. In haste
O'er the town
Thatched and steepled, every star,
By the morning chased,
Crowded far
With the copper-coloured moon
Going down.

"Shortly barked the fox;
And the cart
Rumbled on the market-road;
Then the choir of cocks
Hoarsely crowed;
Lastly, pulsed once more the whole
Eternal heart."

There is surely notable literary power of some kind in this massing of significant detail; but whether a prose power or a verse power is not yet perfectly clear. Most of the other poems halt likewise between the analytic method of prose, and the synthetic method of poetry; but here and there is a poem or a stanza which in its fashion and degree is pure poetry. "Hesperus," despite its slightness, is such a poem:

"Hesperus at milking time,
Is most beautiful of stars [:][1]
Well he likes our shepherd maids,
Well he likes our lowing herds,
Rumbling wheels and clink and chime,
Of our pails and milking cars.

"All our young men are made mild
When they see him in the sky;
And whenever he has smiled,
Simple mortals do not sigh:
Hesperus is friend to all,
Hesperus at milking time."

The bulk of the poems are, however, less expressions of mood and feeling than definitions or expositions of intricate arguments, subtle conceptions, detailed observations or obstinate questionings; and if but seldom these arguments, conceptions, observations, and questionings are expressed with enough precision of form and boldness of cadence to be absolutely poetry, they are well-nigh always poetical and

---

[1] Weekes placed a colon at the end of this line.

stimulating, and here and there put some fine or curious thought into really memorable shape, as in the little lyric called "Art"—

> *"Upon the mid-stream rushing hence,*
> *To hold those wild hot lips which burn*
> *Thy face, but never more return,*
> *Detached from every other sense.*
>
> *"Upon the stream that whirls along*
> *To hold that wondrous hue alone;*
> *Or that delightful undertone*
> *Detached from every other song.*
>
> *"At last, upon the flowing stream*
> *To hold, and with the inward sight,*
> *That thought within a blaze of light,*
> *Detached from every other dream."*

—or reset an ancient question in a new way, as in "That":

> *"What is that beyond this[2] life,*
> *And beyond all life around,*
> *Which, when this quick brain is still,*
> *Nods to thee from the stars?*
> *Lo, it says, thou hast found*
> *Me, the lonely, lonely one."*

Mr. Weekes is least successful in his longer poems, though in all there are fine stanzas and passages; for a big canvas or long discussion seems to absorb too much of his attention and make his style get out of control like a ship in a high wind. These longer poems are full of uncouth ejaculations and abbreviations, no less than of echoes from Browning, Arnold, and Omar Khayam [*sic*], strange in so original a writer. The book is, however, marked by daring—and in literature the prize falls to the bold sooner or later—and is, apart from its promise, both moving and interesting.

W. B. Yeats

The Silenced Sister

On December 8, 1893, Richard Ashe King delivered to the National Literary Society in Dublin a lecture entitled "The Silenced Sister." King attacked oratory and partisan politics as forces which had overwhelmed the finer

[2] *this*: Weekes's poem reads "thy."

literary arts in Ireland. There appeared in the December 16 *United Ireland* an editorial, "A Candid Critic," on the speech and a long letter from "Iris Olkryn" (pseudonym of Alice Milligan) which was critical of King's speech, T. W. Rolleston, and Yeats.

The following two letters, of December 23 and 30, 1893, were Yeats's reactions to the controversy. Yeats had denounced the arts of invective himself in his lecture "Nationality and Literature" (*United Ireland*, May 27, 1893). It is easy to see behind Yeats's unflattering portrait of the partisan orator the person of John F. Taylor, who had battled and bested Yeats over the editorship of the New Irish Library just the year before.

Richard Ashe King (1839–1932) wrote popular novels as well as works on Swift and Goldsmith. His *Swift in Ireland* was reviewed by Yeats in the June, 1896, *Bookman* (see below). In dedicating *Early Poems and Stories* (1925) to King, Yeats said, "A couple of days ago, while correcting the proofs of this book, I remembered a lecture you delivered in the year 1894 [?] to the Dublin National Literary Society; a denunciation of rhetoric, and of Irish rhetoric most of all; and that it was a most vigorous and merry lecture and roused the anger of the newspapers. Therefore I decided to offer the book to you . . ." (*Variorum Poems*, p. 854).

[December 23, 1893]

TO THE EDITOR OF *UNITED IRELAND*

DEAR SIR—The writer of the leading article called "A Candid Critic," admits that he was not present at the lecture which Mr. King gave last week under the auspices of the National Literary Society. This has been a double misfortune, for it has made him miss one of the most brilliant lectures I have ever heard, and be very unjust to Mr. King. Mr. King did not say that politics laid waste the Irish intellect, but only that partisan politics laid it waste. He went so far indeed as to affirm that everything which has been won for Ireland has been won by politics. It is, of course, difficult to say where the politics of the partisan end and the politics of the patriot begin but the line of division is thus, and the politician who does not find it brawls his way into chaos. It seems to my eyes, at any rate, that politics become partisan when the great principles of the national demand are made less visible than what are held to be the failings of opponents; and how perfectly this kind of thing ruins the sense of proportion upon which literature is built up, can be discovered by anyone who will read "Valentine McClutchy."[1] Carleton was a man of genius, but the habit of dividing men into sheep and goats for the purposes of partisan politics made havoc of what might have been a great novel. Carleton was so bedevilled by partisan vehemence that he forgot to remember how men ally themselves with

[1] *Valentine M'Clutchy* was William Carleton's attack on Irish landlords.

any and every cause for the best of motives. He forgot that the crusader, if he had anything of nobility, must be prepared to find many a fool and selfseeker among his allies, and many a wise and just person among his opponents. I think I may add that newspapers become partisan when they give columns to some heated and trivial gentleman who is explaining that his opponent, Mr. John Redmond, Mr. John Dillon or Colonel Saunderson,[2] as the case may be, is immensely deceitful and desperately wicked; while they can spare but a few lines at the utmost for a lecture upon some of the momentous problems in the life of a nation by one of the most eloquent and thoughtful of our men of letters. Nor can they repel the charge by pleading that the people hunger and thirst for the words of the most trivial of Town Councillors and most heated of MP's, and feel indifferent to the serious and careful thought of the man of letters, for it was they who fed the gaping mouths with the east wind until they had destroyed all taste for better food. *United Ireland* has, however, always done what it could, and kept up the good fight bravely.

"I Olkyrn"[3] wrote you a very beautiful letter, and her slight misunderstanding of my own speech would never have led me to break silence if I had not been forced to do so by your article upon Mr. King. I did not say the man of letters should keep out of politics, but I remember the examples of Hugo, and Milton, and Dante [,] but only that he should, no matter how strong be his political interests, endeavour to become a master of his craft, and be ever careful to keep rhetoric, or the tendency to think of his audience rather than of the Perfect and the True, out of his writing. It is, however, a pleasure to be misunderstood when the misunderstanding helps to draw out so beautiful a letter.—
Yours very truly,
W. B. Yeats.

[December 30, 1893]

TO THE EDITOR OF *UNITED IRELAND*

DEAR SIR—In my letter last week I dealt with Mr. King's attack upon partisan politics, but have still a few words to say about his no less vigorous condemnations of our national devotion to oratory.

[2] John Redmond (1856–1918) was a leader of the Home Rule party. He supported Parnell in 1890, and after Parnell's death he led the loyalist branch of the party.

John Dillon (1851–1927) was also a member of the Home Rule party. He opposed Parnell at the "split" in 1890 and later succeeded Justin McCarthy as leader of the anti-Parnellite party.

Edward Saunderson (1837–1906) was the leader of the Ulster party against Home Rule.

[3] "Iris Olkryn" was the pseudonym of the poet Alice Milligan (1866–1953). Her letter had appeared in the December 16 issue of *United Ireland*.

Mr. King has found an ally in Mr. Standish O'Grady, the first Irishman, I believe, who has tried to write Irish history which shall be no mere chronicle of bills and battles, or arid analysis of party dialectics. Mr. O'Grady, having told how the Irish gentry were bribed and wheedled into passing the Act of Union, continues as follows:—"I believe myself that they were stupified by too much oratory. For the last quarter of a century they had yielded themselves up to the intoxicating delight of fine speaking. This was the age of Grattan, Flood, Hussey Burgh,[1] and other famous rhetoricians, who charmed their ears and darkened their understandings with tropes and figures of ridiculous sublimity, so unlike the plain and honest speaking of Swift and Berkley [*sic*]. Oratory, like pride, comes before a fall, an assertion which universal history bears out."

Now, I have not sufficient knowledge of the period and of its oratory to know whether Mr. O'Grady speaks correctly or not, and I am certainly no more inclined to agree with his view than with Mr. King's description of oratory as a "mountebank art." But I do feel, upon the other hand, that historians like Mr. O'Grady do not make statements like this without weighty reasons. I believe that the reason in this case is, that Mr. O'Grady, like Mr. King, has seen that though fondness for oratory is inevitable and necessary in a country like Ireland, it is none the less a danger and a cause of many evils, and that he has allowed his fears for the present to colour his impressions of the past.

It is of the very nature of oratory that the orator should make his hearers feel he is convinced of what he is saying, and, therefore, he is forever tempted to assume, for the sake of effect, a show of sincerity and vehement conviction, or, what is worse, to become really sincere and vehemently convinced about things of which he has no adequate knowledge. In the world God made are none but probabilities, and, as the Persian poet sings, a hair divides the false and true;[2] but too often there are none but certainties in the world of the orator. If once a nation is thoroughly stupefied by oratory of this kind, she loses all sense of proportion, all sense of reality, for has she not discovered that her orators can convince themselves and her of anything at a few minutes' notice, and bring both, by the pleasant pathway of a few similes, a few vehement gestures, to that certainty which the scholar attains after years of research, and the philosopher after a lifetime of thought? Once set her upon that pathway and she will come to the fall Mr. O'Grady speaks of, for she will find no high and remote thing any-

---

[1] The famous statesmen and orators were Henry Grattan (1746–1820), Henry Flood (1732–1791), and Walter Hussey Burgh (1742–1783).

[2] "A Hair perhaps divides the False and True," from stanza 49 of FitzGerald's translation of *The Rubá'iyat of Omar Khayyám*.

where, nothing worth making herself really uncomfortably about. Convictions will be cheap and common in her world, and if a few be damaged or battered for a price, behold there are plenty of others to be had for the asking. We are a nation of orators, and must suffer the defects of our quality with good grace; but we would soon go headlong into unreality were there not men like Mr. King and Mr. O'Grady ever ready to raise the red flag before us. Has not oratory played the devil with us of late in public life, for have we not seen a number of our politicians affirm with every mark of passionate sincerity that Mr. Parnell was the only possible leader and then a few hours after, with equal passion that he was the one leader quite impossible? Do not our newspapers with their daily tide of written oratory, make us cry out, "O God, if this be sincerity, give us a little insincerity, a little of the self-possession, of the self-mastery that go to a conscious lie." Is not our social life ruined by the oratorical person? Whether his subject be the sins of the Parnellites or the anti-Parnellites, protection, the liquor laws, literature, or philosophy, all worthy and kindly converse dies when he enters a room. We all know his vehement intolerance—for how can he be tolerant whose world contains none but certainties?— his exaggerated opinions—for how can he be moderate who must always have a profound conviction?—his scorn of delicate half lights and quiet beauty—for how can he who is ever affirming and declaring understand that the gentle shall inherit the earth?[3]

But what is the remedy for all this? Must we give up oratory? Surely no! But let us respect the orator, not because he makes an effort, but because he tells a new, forgotten, or seasonable truth, and, above all, let us war upon the idea that the expedient is justifiable in public life. I have heard even Parnellites say that Mr. Healy[4] was justified from the point of view of his party, because his underbred and untruthful articles and speeches helped more than anything else to bring about the change which took place in Irish opinion. And, above all, let us attack the cause of these evils, and educate our people by philosophy and literature, for these teach there is a truth and a beauty which, not being made by hands, are above all expediencies, above all nations; and first, as a small help towards this education, let us cease to clamour and call out "West-Briton!" whenever a lecturer talks of our National dangers and weaknesses, do not let us be blind to what is true in his criticism because of some passing over-emphasis, some chance exaggeration of phrase.

—Yours very truly, W. B. Yeats

[3] This whole passage probably refers to the orator John F. Taylor.
[4] Timothy Healy (1855–1931), Home Rule politician, actively campaigned against Parnell after the 1890 break in the party.

P.S.—While thanking you for your kind review[5] of "The Celtic Twilight," I take this opportunity of saying it is not "founded upon fact," as your reviewer says, but, with the exception of one or two changes of name and place, literally true. Your reviewer doubts the existence of "sorcery" in Ireland. He should read a series of letters from a Dublin glass-stainer given in Dr. Adam Clark's [*sic*] memoirs.[6] He will find there far more "sensation" than anything in my work. They refer to events which came under the eyes of the glass-stainer, of whose good faith, Dr. Clark, a celebrated theologian, as you will remember, appears to have had no doubt whatever.

Michael Clancy, the Great Dhoul, and Death*

BY W. B. YEATS
Author of "The Countess Kathleen," etc.

This story is one of the very few in which Yeats attempted to reproduce Irish dialect. As originally printed in *The Old Country* (the version reprinted below), a Christmas annual for 1893, it was illustrated by Jack B. Yeats and had a photo of W. B. Y. at the end. When it was reprinted in the *Kilkenny Moderator*, Christmas number, 1898, it was prefaced by a letter from Yeats to the editor, Standish O'Grady. The letter, as reprinted in *Letters*, pp. 307–308, is as follows:

Dear Mr̃. O'Grady, You ask me to explain how I came to write anything so unlike the rest of my writings as this little bit of fooling. You know that a whole cycle of stories and poems were written about Reynard the Fox in the Middle Ages, and how the tricks Reynard played upon the wolf and the lion and other beasts was a cover for much fantastical satire of the lords and priests. When I was about eighteen I came upon a Connaught folk tale of a tinker and Death and the Devil; and a little later on I found that it existed in Russia, where it had gathered unto itself the man who crowed to shame St. Peter, and some other old tales. I began what was to be a long poem in octosyllabic verse, the verse of the Reynard poems, meaning to make the tinker a type of that kind of jeering, cheating Irishman called 'a melodious lying Irishman' in another folk tale; and to bring him through many typical places and adventures. I remember planning out a long conversation between him and a certain portentous professor of Trinity whom I changed into a lap

[5] This review, by J. M'Grath, appeared in the December 23 issue of *United Ireland*.

[6] *An Account of the Infancy, Religious and Literary Life of Adam Clarke* in three volumes, London, 1833. Adam Clarke (1762?–1832) was a famous Methodist preacher.

* Founded upon a legend I heard down in Sligo. [Yeats's note].

dog, and set to guard the gates of Hell, and I intended to have written many conversations with many portentous persons. Gradually the thought of the enemies I should make if I succeeded, and of the number of verses I should have to write even if I did not, damped my courage, and I gave up my epic and wrote this little tale instead. I do not think much of it, but it has amused people who do not care for my poems or my romantic stories, and it is all I have left of a good intention. I commend it to your tolerance—I wrote it long ago, and it does not mean anything in particular; but had that first book, of which it is in part the shrivelled remnant, brought on the other works, Death and Devil would probably have become fantastic images of the sterility and the fruitfulness of the world. There is humour and fantasy as well as miraculous poetry in our old legends, and one can find in them all kinds of meanings. They will some day be the themes of poets and painters in many countries, and the substance of a new romantic movement, which will have found its beginning in your own beautiful and paramount books. They are the greatest treasure the Past has handed down to us Irish people, and the most plentiful treasure of legends in Europe; and I have always considered that you yourself have done more than all others to dig away the earth that has so long lain upon their beauty.

Yours sincerely
                                                            W B Yeats

O NE July night the tinker, Michael Clancy, was hurrying along under that seaward point of Benbulben [*sic*] which juts out like the bow of an overturned ship. He had been mending cans beyond Ballyshannon[1], and was now hurrying home to mend the pots of his own neighbourhood. The mending of iron pots needed special preparation, and had, therefore, a day set apart for it every summer, and already he knew the neighbours would have brought forty or fifty to his cabin, and his wife would have set them round the wall ready for his return. The moonlight beat down upon the white road, upon his sandy hair and beard, upon the swinging blackthorn in his hand, upon his leather apron of which one corner was tucked up under his belt, and upon the great iron-bound and cloth-covered budget[2] that was strapped to his shoulders, and in which he carried his shears, brazier, punch, lap-anvil, hammers, pewter-sticks, resin, soldering-iron, and much loose tin, beside a bundle of herbs, such as plaintain, mug-wort, self-heal and the like, and a bottle of some unknown mixture to doctor men and cattle when broken cans and porringers fell short, and the coulter[3] of a plough for making red-hot in the hearth when witches and sheogues had made off with some vanathee's butter and a bundle of crimson ribbons for a girl over beyond Calery.

At first he kept smiling to himself, as this or that clever device came

---

[1] Ballyshannon is a town on the west coast of Ireland, north of Sligo, in Co. Donegal.
[2] A budget is a pouch or bag.
[3] A coulter is an iron blade fixed in front of the share in a plow.

up in his memory, how he had cured one Bridget Purcell of the head-
ache by making her say her prayers with a big iron pot on her head, so
that, when she took the pot off, her head seemed to be in heaven; and
how he had shown one Patrick Bruin a long red worm and made him
believe he had taken it out of his bad tooth. Presently, however, he
frowned, for he remembered that the apple-tree behind his cabin should
now be covered with red apples, but that in all likelihood the boys and
girls out of Carney had gone off with the bulk of them, as they had done
the year before. "I've got the betther of many a man an' woman," he
muttered to himself; "and no woman or man has ever got the betther
of me, barrin' the boys and' girls out of Carney, and barrin' thim I fear
neither God nor Dhoul." While thinking these things he came to a
place where the road was shaded by big beech trees, and, before he had
time to cross himself or mutter a paternoster, or what was much more
to his mind, one of the old rhymes against Dhouls and Sheogues which
he had picked up in his tramps, he heard something rustle in the leaves
over his head, and then fall into his budget with a horrible smoke and
odour. He ran as hard as he could go, and did not stop till he was out
in the moonlight again. When at last he looked over his shoulder he
saw that the budget was bulging and gaping a bit, and that two black
things were sticking out through the slit, and swinging about; and that
one was long and thin, the other thick and short. One was certainly a
forked tongue, and the other a cloven hoof. "I'm thinkin', sur," he said,
" 'tis more aisy you'd be if ye'd come out of that an' walk, for it must
be mortial onpleasant to have thim pewtershticks an' thim shears
mixin' thimsilves up wid one's inside." "Now run, me honey," a soft
voice, like a Corkman's, replied from the budget. "'Tis but a little
time I have to be squandherin', and it's not that used I am to aisy livin'
and shleepin' that I need mind a pewter shtick or two, or an odd shears
in me vitals, wanst in a while."

"If ye'd be for gettin' out a bit, sur, sure 'tis glad I'd be to light a fire
in the brazier, an' maybe it's more at home you'd be feelin' an the top
of it nor among them could irons; an' we could tell ould tales for a bit,
an' it's morthial bad the boys are beyant an' about Ballyshannon, an'
I could tell you things of thim that it behoves ye for to know, for,
begor, 'tis the Dhoul himself they'd desaive, bad luck to 'em."

"Run, run," said the voice, "or me an' me ould wife 'ill roast ye this
very night;" and the Dhoul made the loose tin rattle horribly. "Run,
for we've got to be in Dublin before mornin'."

Michael Clancy ran as he was bid, but kept thinking how he was to
get out of this fix. Every now and then he slackened his pace, meaning
to try persuasion again, but as soon as the pace grew slack, the voice
began to threaten. At last he saw the light of a forge streaming out on

the road, and he bethought him what to do. He rushed in, and suddenly unstrapping the budget, flung it on the anvil, and seizing a hammer began to belabour it with all his might, and bade the blacksmith do the same. Then began the most terrible uproar. The yells and oaths that came out of the budget were so loud that it was a wonder they did not shake the stars out of the sky. The budget was so strong that instead of breaking it merely flattened out, and settled down like a concertina, but no sweet music came out of it. The hammers rose and fell, and the most dreadful odour came up from under the blows, and rose up to the rafters, and half-suffocated the cocks, and hens, and chickens, and made them come tumbling down. At last the Dhoul could bear it no longer, and yelled out:

"What'll ye take to let me out of this?"

"Wan thing only will I take; the boys and girls out of Carney does be stealin' me little red apples, and I'm longing to get the betther of thim, for they are the only souls in the worruld, or out of the worruld, that iver got the betther of me. I'll let ye out if y'll grant me that anyone who cames shtalin' me apples 'ill shtick to the three till I comes round an' leathers thim wid me blackthorn, or lets them go free, as the whim takes me."

"I'll grant ye that," says the Dhoul; "an' now let me out, for all the bones in me body is broke an me."

They ceased hammering and the Dhoul went away with a rush and took half the roof with him. The blacksmith fell on the floor in a faint, and his face was the colour of a big pullet that lay on the floor beside him where it had fallen from the rafters. He was never the same man after, but sat with his head on his knees, as the people say, to the day of his death. Michael Clancy was not going to be scared at a Dhoul he had got the better of, but went to his own house, thinking of those little red apples, and wondering whether he would find a boy or a girl or two sticking to the leaves or branches. He turned into the fields when he got near home, and went round to the back of his garden, and got over the ditch, and came close up to the tree. Sure enough there was something sticking to it and swinging about, like an old petticoat hung out to dry in a good wind. He came near and poked at it with his black-thorn. It was a little grey figure of some kind with what looked like a skull on it with a few tufts of hair on the top.

"Are ye a gurrl," he said, "for if it's a gurrl ye are I'd pull ye're ears an let yees go; but if so be ye're a boy I'll leather yees." The only answer was a moan. "Do ye hear me talkin' to ye now, is it a gurrl or a boy ye are?" he repeated, and still there was no answer but a moan. "Ye are a boy!" with that he began to beat the figure with the blackthorn. "What are ye at all at all, for yees rattle like a bag of bones?"

"I am DEATH!" said a voice that was like a rumble of water under-ground. "And I have come for your wife. For yesterday when she was putting the pots round the wall, she fell and hit her head on one of them, and now she is near her end. I was slipping in quietly by the back way when I caught sight of a little red apple just ready to fall, and put out my hand for it, and here I am caught by some kind of bird-lime."

"And there ye'll shtay till I lets ye go."

"If you will let me go," said Death, "I will let your wife live on a bit longer."

"Tis the blessing of Providence to take the poor woman away from her bargin' an' fightin', an' I'm not the man to interfere with the decrees of the Maker, glory be to God! But whisht, now! an' I'll tell yees how we'll get yees out of that, for I met the ould fellow himself a bit down the road, an' his honour said I might have what I wished, and I, like a glugger-a-bunthaun, axed the weeshiest bit of a thing. But now I've me siven sinses agin, an' I remimber I'm a poor man wid sorra a penny to bless meself, an' a great thirst entirely to satisfy, an' a power of inimies to keep down. Sometimes whin broken cans an' porringers an' ould pots are scarce, I docthor cows an' horses an' pigs an' Christians an' the like; an' sometimes they die an me, an' that's bad for thrade. Now, Death, me honey, just you give me some thrick for knowin' whin Christians an' things is goin' to die, that I mayn't be wastin' me medicine an thim, but keep it an meself out of harm's way. I don't want to be throublin' poor dyin' sowls wid me cures at all."

"I always sit at the feet of those who are going to get better," said Death, "and at the head of them that are going to die."

"Thank ye kindly," said Michael Clancy, "an' now ye may be goin' an' gettin' to your work, for we're all mortial." And with that he sat down under the apple-tree and began to smoke, while Death went on into the cabin. Presently he saw two black things going through the air together, and shaking the tobacco out of his pipe muttered, "I wondher now if it's to Hell or Purgatory she's goin' poor sowl!"

He very soon gave up tinkering altogether, and took entirely to doctoring; and, as all his patients recovered, his fame went far and wide, and his purse grew heavy. He spent his money rapidly, however. He bought shawls and ribbons for all the pretty girls, and gave dances with four fiddlers apiece, and lots of whiskey for everybody, in all the villages along his old route. He was thought all the more of because some-times he would refuse altogether to doctor this or that person, now saying that the Fairies had forbidden him, now, that he had to go off to some distant place to doctor a great lord who had been given up by all the doctors of Ireland, Scotland, England and France. He and Death became quite familiar with each other from meeting so often; at last, however, he made Death very angry. A pretty girl up at Roughley O'Byrne fell ill, and her parents sent for him; but when he came he saw Death sitting at the head of the bed. "Death," says he, "ye might let this nice little gurrl get well; an' if ye do I'll show ye where there are two ould aunts of me own with tongues like the clapper of a bell, an' ye can have the two of thim."

"I don't want any of your relations."

Made really angry by this, the tinker took the girl up in his arms, and turned her round, so that her feet were to Death. She got well almost at once, and before evening he was able to go home driving a donkey with a keg of good poteen made in the Island of Innismurray (where the souls of the dead come up upon the shore in the shape of seals) in each creel by way of payment from her grateful parents.

When the tinker awoke next morning he saw Death sitting at his own head, perched up on the bedstead. "Ye've got to come now," said Death, "and it's no use trying to turn yourself round, for if ye so much as wriggle, I'll have the soul out of ye in a jiffey;" and with that he put his long, dry fingers close to the tinker's breast.

"Will ye let me say wan Pather-Nosther afore I die for ould friendship's sake, for I've a lot of dhrink an' divilry an me con-science?"

"For ould friendship's sake," replied Death, "I won't take you till you have said your Pater-Noster."

"Then I'll never say another Pather-Nosther as long as I live, but make me sowl an Hail Marys."

Death got up with a moan, and, looking very old and feeble, went out through the window; but before he disappeared, turned round and cried: "The mischief take you, ye thief o' the world, that 'ud steal the cross off an ass's back, for I wash my hands of ye for good and all. Do as ye like, do as ye like; an' if ye want me ye'll have to send after me; I'm done with ye. Oh, that I should have lived to see this!" and he went off like a black cloud through the sky.

After this the tinker made a regular practice of turning patients round with their feet to Death, and he let nobody die in the whole country, unless they were very ugly or very cross. He lived on for scores upon scores of years, and began to get tired of things. He had fallen in and out of love dozens of times, and drunk poteen in every still in Con-naught, and nothing more remained to be done or seen. He went to the top of Benbulben to the pool where Dermod[4] was killed, and sent one of the fairies who lived there to fetch Death, and the fairy led Death to

---

[4] Dermod (variously spelled), a great hero of Irish legend, was slain by the wild boar of Ben Bulben.

him. Michael Clancy told Death that he wanted to die, and Death took
him away through the air until they came to a great grassy road. Death
told him that it led from Ireland to Heaven, and Hell, and Purgatory;
that it was grass-grown because hardly anyone had passed that way for
many a year now. Having said this he left him, and hurried off muttering
to himself. The tinker walked on slowly, stopping every now and then
to poke with his stick at the glittering things that lay about in the grass.
These were the earthly loves and hopes which kings and queens and
warriors had flung away there aforetime. Presently he came to a place
where the road divided into three, and saw a signboard with three
arms, and on the first arm was written "TO HEAVEN," upon the second
"TO HELL," and upon the third "TO PURGATORY."

"I like me whiskey either hot or could, an' I'll keep clear of Purgatory
anyhow," he said. "I'll thry Heaven for a turn." He went on until he
came to a little door in a big wall, with a square barred hole in the door
for talking through. He looked in and saw Death shooting arrows at a
butt a good way off among the trees, but could not see St. Peter anywhere. He therefore put his mouth to the square hole and crowed like a
cock as loud as ever he could. Presently he heard St. Peter running up
to the gate, calling out "Whisht! now, whisht!" Michael Clancy stopped
crowing, and St. Peter whispered through the hole, "If ye'll shtop that,
an' don't be disgracin' me afore the blessed Archangels an' all the Holy
Innocents, I'll go straight and bring your case before the authorities."
He went away, but after a little returned and said, "It's no use at all at
all; we've got to make an example of somebody. There are too many the
very shpit of ye in the place ye come from. And now begone wid yees,
for the sight of ye has given the poor ould gintleman over there a turn.
He hasn't been the same this many a day, and keeps practising wid thim
arrows of his, for it's a long shot he'll be takin' at the people from this
out."

"Thank ye kindly," said the tinker; "it's all wan to me so as I can get
a roof over me, and a sate though it 'ud be but a bit of a creepy-stool to
sit down on; for it's famished I am for a dhraw of the pipe. I'll thry
Hell for I'll be meetin' friends there I'm thinkin'."

He went back to the cross roads and took the way to Hell. The Great
Dhoul was sitting on an iron throne, and his wife, who by her first
husband, Adam, who had not then met with Eve, had borne all the
fairies, and by her present husband, all the evil spirits in the world, was
sitting at his side with their children at their feet. The Dhoul saw
Michael Clancy, coming, and remembering the anvil, began to rub
himself all over; but his wife caught her youngest by the hair, and flung
him with all her might at the tinker, and striking him on the mouth,
knocked him clean away beyond the grassy road, and down through

the air and into the river at Ballisodare; and there her eldest children found him and turned him into a salmon. He still wanders through the water, but, if anyone catch him with a fly, he breaks the tackle or goes off, maybe, with half the rod.

Seen in Three Days

Yeats reviewed *Seen in Three Days*, a long poem written, engraved, and illustrated by Edwin J. Ellis, London, 1893, in the *Bookman* issue of February, 1894.

After spending almost five years with Ellis in puzzling out the symbolism of Blake, Yeats seems to have been unwilling to spend very much time puzzling out the symbolism of E. J. Ellis. Yeats had given Ellis's first book of poems, *Fate in Arcadia*, a good review, but *Seen in Three Days* was intractable to all but summary. Yeats and Ellis seem to have drifted apart after completing their edition of Blake. When Yeats included some of his friend's poems in his *Oxford Book of Modern Verse*, he could not locate Ellis's literary executors.

I T will ever be a matter of argument how far a poet may be obscure. I myself hold he cannot be obscure from imperfect expression except at his peril, but that obscurity born of subtle and unusual thought must often be inevitable, unless we are to lack a whole class of poetry. No wise man rails at the great Persian poet because he was called the tongue of the secret, for we know his obscurity to have been inherent in his subjects. The average man reads poetry for amusement, or as a mere rest after the day's work, and to him there naturally seems nothing more absurd and abominable than a poem which gave him a great deal of trouble. Yet even the poetry which mingles something of the illegitimate obscurity with the legitimate is often very powerful and desirable, for poetry is not an amusement and a rest, but a fountain of ardour and peace, whither we must force our way even through briar and bramble.

Mr. Ellis's 'Seen in Three Days' has a good deal of both obscurities, or this review would not be as belated as it is. The greatest difficulty in the way of a clear comprehension of its strange pages of mingled verse and picture is the lack of any very visible story or sequence. One is tempted to think that its pages, like the leaf-inscribed oracles of the sybil of old, were tossed hither and thither by the wind, and then bound together in the order in which the wind left them. I have at last, however, puzzled out what is, I imagine, pretty nearly the correct story.

Errors I may have made, for Mr. Ellis does not, like Blake, use a technical language in which every word has the same invariable interpretation.

The poem is in blank verse, with the exception of an opening sonnet describing the being of whose wanderings it is the history.

> "The great sun laughs in his eternal home
>   At this poor earth, still circling round in pain,
>   Yet in each little drop of rainbow'd rain,
> In each small bublet of the soft sea-foam,
> The same sun in a tiny crystal dome,
>   From milky morning to red evening stain
>   Rises and labours, shines and sets again.
> So, though not now we look to witness come
>   The angel of the Presence Divine to earth,
>   Yet in each heart there is a Presence Divine,
>   And in each Presence has an angel birth.
> If mine has wandered, has not also thine?
>   As mine returns, lo, thine returns as well,
>   Interpreting before what we would tell."

This angel of the heart enters the heart of the poet by the doorway of a dream, lifting the moon-shaped knocker.

> "Three moons had made her beauty. The sea moon
> Had given the gleam in darkness to her eyes,
> The moon that drives the milky flocks had woven
> Of whiter mist than theirs the slender breast
> Through which her childhood shone. The morning moon
> That looks on sunrise taught her wind-blown hair
> The tender secret of its dewy gold."

She has wandered for three days and two nights, and is shrinking in fear from the third night. "A chain of strange learning," the memory of what she has seen and heard, encircles her. The poet asks her history, and the chain wraps him round. Every link is an incident and a symbol. After a vision of dumb show and blind words, painting and poetry, he listens to the story of the angel. She first saw a girl dragged from a cave by two men upon one horse, and by this is typified the alternation throughout the poem of certain opposites, love and time, sacrifice and selfishness, innocence and experience, and so on. She then saw a vision of Fate parting lovers, for this first day is to be taken up chiefly with ill-starred love. She next saw a youth dragging a stone to the edge of a precipice. He is chained to the stone, and struggles to end his life and his captivity. This is a symbol of "sacrificial victory," of life struggling towards death, driven on by some great enthusiasm. Immediately its opposite rises, and she sees a youth driving a spear into the breast of a maiden, because she had asked his eyes, and so releasing himself.

> *"But with defeat in sacrifice, for now*
> *He saved himself to die for Death alone,*
> *Who might have died for her."*

Near at hand her sister has asked the eagle for his wing—

> *"Who dares to blame the red lips of the maid*
> *For asking gifts? Why did God make the world,*
> *If not as gift-house for a maid?"*

The eagle, who is a minor type of sacrificial victory, gave the wing and died. After that she saw the maiden mourning for the death of the eagle, and in a little, amid the coming on of night, descends, like the figure in one of Blake's designs to Blair's "Grave," into the caverns of the grave, "love's home in error," and sees therein the upas tree under which are those who have wedded unhappily. The night is now upon her, and in the night she sees Life typified in a young girl wandering, with a panther, her incarnate fear, looking for Death to slay him with a look of abhorrence. The angel sees Death in the shape of four men, who typify human life, one full of pride about to begin the contest of life, another chained to him and crawling feebly towards an open grave, another digging the grave, and another, divine and beautiful, flying in the air. The last is the Death that "chills the blood," but "warms the wondering, exultant soul." The sun rises and the second day begins. The first day was devoted to love, but this is given to Time. Life, the young girl, comes out of the wood, but Fear is now in her arms disguised as a child, who apparently typifies Hope. Presently the angel sees Time changing innocence into experience. He is flinging serpents among a group of young girls who sail in a boat along a stream, which is perhaps the river of dreams. While looking at them the angel finds the child Pity in her arms. She ascends into a world of exalted contemplation, and Pity leaves her, for Pity cannot live there. She sees Beauty, "the first of all the storms Eternity let loose," defying time by the right of her immortality. Fate, "silently parting lovers," brooded over the first day, the day of love, and Beauty broods over the second day, the day of time. The angel asks Beauty for "the stone of choice." He who lives for Beauty lives in the free will, choosing and rejecting. Beauty says that "choice" and "fear" are one, and will not give the stone. The angel flies, and sees for a moment a pastoral people at peace with time, and then a youth running along the seashore with a torch. He falls and dies, and another lights a new torch from his, and begins in his turn to run. This is the defeat of Time. Then the night begins to gather, and in the twilight she sees a woman with a child and two men who are friends, and these, with another man and woman and child who join them later, form a group and talk splendidly of love and friendship. This second night is ushered in, not by the vision of the upas tree, but by peace and love. Then the beneficent night comes, and "Mother Night put off old age and raised her love lamp high." The two nights are among the opposites typified by the two horsemen, as are also the two days, the day of love and the day of time, the day of that which desires steadfastness and the day of that which is eternal change. The third day now dawns, and combines the nature of the first and second days. The angel sees the unchanging and change typified, respectively, by the wandering Jew, who sees all things pass away, but is himself ever the same, and Pythagoras, who remembers a thousand lives and a thousand deaths. They talk together magnificently for many pages.

This abstract and partial interpretation will, in spite of its inadequacy, help the reader, I think, to read with pleasure one of the most singular poems of our time. I feel there are oppositions and correspondences in plenty which I do not understand, for the mystics cannot, or will not, let any quite pluck out the heart of their mystery. Though not equal to Mr. Ellis's 'Fate in Arcadia,' it is full of music and beauty, and the illustrations are a considerable advance upon those in the previous book. The method, too, which Mr. Ellis has adopted of writing and then lithographing his verse, instead of printing it in the ordinary way, has reduced the merely mechanical part to a minimum, and helps to make the whole vivid with personality.

The subject of the design given above[1] is Moonrise—

> "*Laughing stars*
> *Gathered and showed their playthings. Mother Night*
> *Put off old age, and raised her love-lamp high,*
> *And the world saw, and under her dark trees*
> *Smiled well content, and closed her flowers and slept.*"

W. B. Yeats

A Symbolical Drama in Paris

Yeats's review of a performance of Villiers de l'Isle-Adam's *Axël* appeared in the *Bookman* of April, 1894, and it was the result of Yeats's trip to Paris in February, 1894.

[1] Yeats's review in the *Bookman* was accompanied by the reproduction of one of Ellis's engraved pages to be seen on the facing page.

Gathered and showed their playthings. Mother Night
Put off old age and raised her love-lamp high
And the world saw, and under her dark trees
Smiled well content, and closed her flowers & slept.

This page of Ellis's *Seen in Three Days* was reproduced in the *Bookman* of February, 1894, to accompany Yeats's review.

He had gone to see *Axël* with Maud Gonne, who must have been able to translate some of the play for him. About this time he was slowly making his way through the play in French and his difficulties with the language made the philosophy of the play seem more profound (*Autobiography*, p. 213). During this visit to Paris he lived with his fellow-adept Macgregor Mathers. He called on Verlaine and turned that visit into a short article for the April, 1896, issue of the *Savoy*.

Axël was a powerful influence on Yeats in the later nineties. One has only to repeat the lines quoted by Yeats, "Oh, to veil you with my hair, where you will breathe the spirit of dead roses," to evoke many poems from the collection *The Wind Among the Reeds* (the title of this book is even mentioned in the review) as well as the final lines of Dectora in *The Shadowy Waters*, "Bend lower, that I may cover you with my hair,/ For we will gaze upon this world no longer."

Yeats contributed a preface to H. P. R. Finberg's translation of *Axël* published in 1925 and used three passages from this 1894 review, which I have enclosed in brackets.

THE scientific movement which has swept away so many religious and philosophical misunderstandings of ancient truth has entered the English theatres in the shape of realism and Ibsenism, and is now busy playing ducks and drakes with the old theatrical conventions. We no longer believe that the world was made five thousand years ago, and are beginning to suspect that Eve's apple was not the kind of apple you buy at the greengrocer's for a penny, but we have still a little faith in the virtuous hero and the wicked villain of the theatre, and in the world of tricks and puppets which is all that remains of the old romance in its decadence. Outside the theatre[,] science[,] having done its work, is beginning to vanish into the obscurity of the schools, but inside there is still so much for it to do that many forget how impermanent must be its influence, and how purely destructive its mission there, and write and talk as if the imaginative method of the great dramatists, of Kaladasa,[1] of Sophocles, of Shakespeare, and of Goethe was to let its house on a lease for ever to the impassioned realisms of M. Zola and of Dr. Ibsen in his later style, or to the would-be realisms of Mr. Pinero or Mr. Jones. The barricades are up, and we have no thought for anything but our weapons—at least here in England. In France they had their Independent Theatre before we had ours, and the movement which must follow the destructive period has come, it seems, to them already. Those among the younger generation whose temperament fits them to receive first the new current, the new force, have grown tired of the photographing

[1] Kaladasa, usually spelled "Kalidasa," lived in the fourth century, A.D. India's greatest dramatist, he is best known for the play *Sakuntala*.

of life, and have returned by the path of symbolism to imagination and
poetry, the only things which are ever permanent. [The puppet plays[2]
of M. Maeterlinck have been followed by a still more remarkable
portent. Thirty thousand francs and enthusiastic actors have been found
to produce the 'Axel'[3] of his master, Villiers De L'isle Adam.[4] On
February the 26th a crowded audience of artists and men of letters
listened, and on the whole with enthusiasm, from two o'clock until ten
minutes to seven to this drama, which is written in prose as elevated as
poetry, and in which all the characters are symbols and all the events
allegories. It is nothing to the point that the general public have since
shown that they will have none of 'Axel,' and that the critics have
denounced it in almost the same words as those in which they denounce
in this country the work of Dr. Ibsen, and that they have called the
younger generation both morbid and gloomy.] That they would do so
was obvious from the first, for to them the new dramatic art is "like
a lawyer serving a writ," and must be for a good while to come. [One
fat old critic who sat near me, so soon as the Magician of the Rosy-
Cross, who is the chief person of the third act, began to denounce the
life of pleasure and to utter the ancient doctrine of the spirit, turned
round with his back to the stage and looked at the pretty girls through
his opera-glass. One can well imagine his feelings, at least if they were
at all like those which an elderly English critic would feel under like
circumstance. Have we not proved, he doubtless thought, that nothing
is fit for the stage except the opinions which everybody believes, the
feelings which everybody shares, the wit which everybody understands?
and yet, in spite of all we have done, they have brought Dr. Ibsen and
the intellect onto the boards, and now here comes Villiers De L'isle
Adam and that still more unwholesome thing the soul.][5] I don't know
which of the criticisms that I have read was by my fat old neighbour,
but really he might have written any of them, even those by men supposed to be "advanced." Revolutions have notoriously eaten their
own children, and the imaginative movement can do no other than be
the death of the merely analytic and rationalistic critics who have
made it possible by clearing away the rubbish and the wreckage of
the past.

M. Paul Verlaine says of a type of woman common in the works of
Villiers De L'isle Adam, "Villiers conjures up the spectre of a mysterious
woman, a queen of pride, who is mournful and fierce as the night when
it still lingers though the dawn is beginning, with reflections of blood

[2] This passage in brackets was quoted by Yeats in his preface to Finberg's translation of
Axël, pp. 9–10.
[3] Yeats used the English spelling, "Axel," rather than the French "Axël."
[4] *De L'isle Adam*: usually spelled "de l'Isle-Adam."
[5] Quoted by Yeats in Finberg, p. 10.

and of gold upon her soul and her beauty."[5] In the play Sara, a woman
of this strange Medusa-like type, comes to the castle of a Count Axel,
who lives in the Black Forest studying magic with Janus, a wizard
ascetic of the Rosy Cross. When she arrives he has already refused first
the life of the world, typified by the advice of a certain "commander"
his cousin, the life of the spiritual intellect labouring in the world but
not of it, as symbolized by the teaching and practice of the adept
Janus; and she herself has refused the religious life as symbolized by the
veil of the nun. In a last great scene they meet in a vault full of treasure
—the glory of the world—and avow their mutual love. He first tries to
kill her because the knowledge that she is in the world will never let
him rest. She throws herself upon his neck and cries, "Do not kill me;
what were the use? I am unforgettable. Think what you refuse. All the
favour of other women were not worth my cruelties. I am the most
mournful of virgins. I think that I can remember having made angels
fall. Alas, flowers and children have died in my shadow. Give way to
my love. I will teach you marvellous words which intoxicate like the
wine of the East. . . . I know the secrets of infinite joys, of delicious
cries, of pleasures beyond all hope . . . Oh, to veil you with my hair,
where you will breathe the spirit of dead roses." The marvellous scene
prolongs itself from wonder to wonder till in the height of his joyous
love Axel remembers that this dream must die in the light of the common world, and pronounces the condemnation of all life, of all pleasure,
of all hope. The lovers resolve to die. They drink poison, and so complete the fourfold renunciation—of the cloister, of the active life of the
world, of the labouring life of the intellect, of the passionate life of love.
The infinite is alone worth attaining, and the infinite is the possession of
the dead. Such appears to be the moral. Seldom has utmost pessimism
found a more magnificent expression.

The final test of the value of any work of art to our particular needs,
is when we place it in the hierarchy of those recollections which are our
standards and our beacons. At the head of mine are a certain night
scene long ago, when I heard the wind blowing in a bed of reeds by the
border of a little lake, a Japanese picture of cranes flying through a blue
sky, and a line or two out of Homer. I do not place any part of 'Axel'
with these perfect things, but still there are lines of the adept Janus, of
the Medusa Sara, which are near them in my hierarchy. Indeed the play
throughout gives a noble utterance to those sad thoughts which come

[5] I have been unable to locate this remark in Verlaine's critical writings. Yeats may have
remembered such a statement from his February, 1894, interview with Verlaine. In his
memoir printed in the *Savoy* of April, 1896, Yeats included an opinion of Verlaine's on *Axël*
which he omitted from the version printed in his autobiography: ". . . 'Axël' he interpreted
and somewhat narrowly, as I could but think, as meaning that love was the only important
thing in the world. . . ."

to the most merry of us, and thereby robs them of half their bitterness. We need not fear that it will affect the statistics of suicide, for the personages of great art are for the most part too vast, too remote, too splendid, for imitation. They are merely metaphors in that divine argument which is carried on from age to age, and perhaps from world to world, about the ultimate truths of existence. It is not 'Ecclesiastes,' but the sordid and jangled utterance of daily life which has saddened the world. In literature, moreover, it is seldom the sad book, the sad play which corrupts, but rather the cheap laughter, the trivial motive of books and plays which give the mind no trouble. In a decade when the comic paper and the burlesque are the only things sure to awaken enthusiasm, a grim and difficult play by its mere grimness and difficulty is a return to better traditions, it brings us a little nearer the heroic age.

I hear that there is a chance of 'Axel' being performed in London; if so, I would suggest that the second and third acts be [enormously reduced in length. The second act especially dragged greatly. The situation is exceedingly dramatic, and with much of the dialogue left out would be very powerful. The third act, though very interesting, to anyone familiar with the problems and philosophy it deals with, must inevitably as it stands bore and bewilder the natural man, with no sufficient counterbalancing advantage. There was no question of the dramatic power of the other acts. Even the hostile critics have admitted this.][6] The imaginative drama must inevitably make many mistakes before it is in possession of the stage again, for it is so essentially different to the old melodrama and the new realism, that it must learn its powers and limitations for itself. It must also fail many times before it wins the day, for though we cannot hope to ever again see the public as interested in sheer poetry, as the audiences were who tolerated so great a poet, so poor a dramatist as Chapman, it must make its hearers learn to understand eloquent and beautiful dialogues, and to admire them for their own sake and not as a mere pendent to the action. For this reason its very mistakes when they are of the kind made by the promoters of 'Axel' help to change the public mind in the right direction, by reminding it very forcibly that the actor should be also a reverent reciter of majestic words.

W. B. Yeats

[6] Quoted by Yeats in Finberg, p. 11.

The Evangel of Folk-Lore

This review of William Larminie's *West Irish Folk Tales*, London, 1894, appeared in the *Bookman*, June, 1894. The years 1893–1894 represented the height of Yeats's interest in folk lore. His own *Celtic Twilight* had appeared in 1893. In such essays as "The Message of the Folk-Lorist" (*Speaker*, August 19, 1893) Yeats had claimed, as he does here, that the greatest writers of the world were dependent upon folklore for their inspiration.

Larminie (1849–1900) was a poet as well as a folklorist. A book of his poems, *Fand*, was reviewed by Yeats in *United Ireland*, July 23, 1892. Larminie contributed, with Yeats, to the symposium *Literary Ideals in Ireland* (Dublin, 1899).

THE recent revival of Irish literature has been very largely a folk-lore revival, an awakening of interest in the wisdom and ways of the poor, and in the poems and legends handed down among the cabins. Past Irish literary movements[1] were given overmuch to argument and oratory; their poems, with beautiful exceptions, were noisy and rhetorical, and their prose, their stories even, ever too ready to flare out in expostulation and exposition. So manifest were these things that many had come to think the Irish nation essentially rhetorical and unpoetical, essentially a nation of public speakers and journalists, for only the careful student could separate the real voice of Ireland, the song which has never been hushed since history began, from all this din and bombast. But now the din and bombast are passing away, or, at any rate, no longer mistaken for serious literature, and life is being studied and passion sung not for what can be proved or disproved, not for what men can be made do or not do, but for the sake of Beauty "and Time's old daughter Truth." Let us be just to this din and bombast; they did good in their day, helped many an excellent cause, made the young more patriotic, and set the crooked straight in many ways, but they were of practical and not poetical importance. Compare the method of the older writers with the method of the new, and lay the difference at the door of the folk-lorist, for it is practically with his eyes that Miss Barlow, Miss Lawless, Mr. Standish O'Grady, and Mrs. Hinkson[2] in her later work, look at Irish life and manners, and it is he who has taught them to love the wisdom and ways of the poor, the

---

[1] Yeats meant primarily the Young Ireland movement of the 1840s.

[2] Jane Barlow (1857–1917) wrote *Bogland Studies* (1892) and *Irish Idylls* (1892). Emily Lawless (1845–1913) wrote the novels *Grania* (1892) and *Maelcho* (1895). Mrs. Hinkson was the married name of Katharine Tynan.

events which have shaped those ways and that wisdom, and the kings and heroes of the phantasies of the cabin with so simple a love, such a quiet sincerity. There is indeed no school for literary Ireland just now like the school of folk-lore; and, lest the school should lack teachers, every year brings us some new collection. Mr. Curtin, Lady Wylde [*sic*], Dr. Hyde, Mr. MacAnally, Mr. Fitzgerald[3] have already given us a goodly parcel of the ancient romance, and now comes Mr. Larminie with as fine a book as the best that has been.

Is not the evangel of folk-lore needed in England also? For is not England likewise unduly fond of the story and the poem which have a moral in their scorpion tale. These little stories of Mr. Larminie's have no moral, and yet, perhaps, they and their like are the only things really immortal, for they were told in some shape or other, by old men at the fire before Nebuchadnezzar ate grass, and they will still linger in some odd crannie or crevice of the world when the pyramids have crumbled into sand. Their appeal is to the heart and not to the intellect. They take our emotions and fashion them into forms of beauty as a goldsmith fashions gold, as a silversmith fashions silver. Our love for woman's beauty is for ever a little more subtle once we have felt the marvel of that tale of a boy who, finding on the road a little box containing a lock of hair which shone with a light like many candles, travelled through numberless perils to find her from whose head it had been shorn; our sense of pity is ever a little more poignant once we have understood the charm of that tale of the woman who dwelt seven years in hell to save her husband's soul, keeping—for such was her appointed work—the ever-bobbing souls of the lost from getting out of a great boiler, and then another seven years that she might have the right to take all she could carry, and bring the souls away clinging to her dress. Nor can our power of wonder be other than a little more transcendent when we have dreamed that dream of "the place where were seals, whales, crawling, creeping things, little beasts of the sea with red mouths, rising on the sole and palm of the oar, making faery music and melody for themselves, till the sea, arose in strong waves, hushed with magic, hushed with wondrous voices;"[4] or of the magical adventurer

---

[3] Jeremiah Curtin, author of *Myths and Folk-Lore of Ireland* (1890) and *Hero Tales of Ireland* (1894); Lady Wilde, author of *Ancient Legends, Mystic Charms, and Superstitions of Ireland* (1887), and *Ancient Cures, Charms and Usages of Ireland* (1890); Douglas Hyde, author of *Beside the Fire* (1890); D. R. McAnally, Jr., author of *Irish Wonders* (1887); and David Fitzgerald, who, Yeats said in a review of Hyde's *Beside the Fire* (*National Observer*, February 28, 1891), was contributing folklore to *Revue Celtique*.

[4] This passage from "The Story of Bioultach" reads in Larminie as follows: ". . . in the place where there were seals, whales, crawling, creeping things, little beasts of the sea with red mouth, rising on the sole and the palm of the oar, making fairy music and melody for themselves, till the sea arose in strong waves, hushed with magic, hushed with wondrous voices."

who became for a year a grey flagstone covered with heaps of ice and
snow, and yet died not wholly, but awoke again and turned to his
adventures as before.

And there are a plenty of such things in Mr. Larminie's book, more,
perhaps, than in any book of Irish folk-lore since Lady Wylde's [*sic*]
'Ancient Legends.' Dr. Hyde is by far the best Irish folk-lorist by the
right of his incomparable skill as a translator from the Gaelic, and
among the first of Irish story-tellers by the right of 'Teig O'Kane,'
well nigh as memorable a masterpiece as 'Wandering Willie's Tale';[5]
but his 'Beside the Fire' is no such heaped-up bushel of primeval
romance and wisdom as 'West Irish Folk Tales.' Mr. Larminie
gathered his store in remote parts of Donegal, Roscommon and
Galway, and his book has the extravagance and tumultuous movement
as of waves in a storm, which Mr. Curtin had already taught us to
expect from the folk tale of the extreme west. When such tales are well
understood; when the secret of their immortality is mastered; when
writers have begun to draw on them as copiously as did Homer, and
Dante, and Shakespeare, and Spenser, then will the rhetorician begin
to wither and the romance maker awake from a sleep as of a grey flagstone, and shake off the ice and snow and weave immortal woofs again.

W. B. Yeats

The Rose of Shadow

This story, originally entitled "Those Who Live in the Storm," first appeared
in the *Speaker*, July 21, 1894. It was reprinted in *The Secret Rose* (the version
included here) but not in the collected works of 1908, nor thereafter. It is not
as thoroughly rewritten as "The Binding of the Hair" (see pp. 390–93), a story
which had a similar fate. The major changes are recorded in the footnotes.

Oona Herne resembles Mary Bruin, the heroine of *The Land of Heart's
Desire*, a play which Yeats also wrote in 1894. One woman is called "away"
by the fairies, and the other is claimed by her demon lover. The program for
the play had the sentence "The characters are supposed to speak in Gaelic."
At one point in this story Peter Herne "said in Gaelic." In the revised version
he simply "said." Perhaps between 1894 and 1897 Yeats had become sensitive
to the criticism that telling one's audience that Gaelic is being spoken does
not increase the impression of folk integrity.

---

[5] "Wandering Willie" is a blind fiddler named Willie Steenson in Sir Walter Scott's
Redgauntlet.

A VIOLENT gust of wind made the roof shake and burst the door open, and Peter Herne got up from his place at the table and shut it again, and slipped the heavy wooden bolt; saying, as he did so: 'One would almost think the house was about to fall upon our heads.' His father and mother were at the table, but his sister, Oona, unmindful of her mother's call to supper, was sitting near the door listening to the wind among the fir-trees upon the mountain. Peter Herne, made lonely by a glimpse of the dishevelled night sky through the open door, turned toward her and said:[1] 'It is the blackest storm that ever came out of the heavens.'

'Twelve months ago this night,' answered the girl, 'it was as black and as bitter, and the wind blew then as now, along the Mountain of Bulben[2] and out to sea.'

Peter Herne and Simon Herne started and looked at each other, and the hand of old Margaret Herne began to tremble. A year that night Peter Herne had killed, with a blow from a boat-hook, one Michael Creed, the master of a coasting smack, who had long been the terror of the little western ports because of his violence and brutality, and the hatred of all peaceful households, because of his many conquests among women, whom he subdued through that love of strength which is deep in the heart of even the subtlest among them.

Until this moment Oona had never alluded, even indirectly, to this quarrel and the blow, and they had hoped she had half forgotten, or even come to think of that night as a night of deliverance.

'Mother,' she went on, speaking in a low voice, 'when those who have done crimes, when those who have never confessed, are dead, are they put in a place apart, or do they wander near to us?'

'Child,' replied the old woman, 'my mother told me that some are spitted upon the points of the rocks, and some upon the tops of the trees,[3] but that others wander with the season in the storms over the seas and about the strands and headlands of the world. But, daughter, I bid you think of them no more, for when we think of them they draw near.'

'Mother,' said the girl, with a rapt light in her eyes, 'last night when you had all gone to bed, I put my cloak over my night-gown and slipped out, and brought in a sod from his grave and set it on the chair beside my bed; and after I had been in bed a while, I heard it whisper and then speak quite loudly. "Come to me, alanna,"[4] it said; and I

[1] In the *Speaker* version, he "said in Gaelic. . . ."

[2] The *Speaker* version read "Bulber." *The Secret Rose* read "Gulben." For some reason *The Secret Rose*, 1897, printing read in every instance of "Bulben" "the mountain of Gulben." The stories containing this phrase which were reprinted in the 1908 collected edition of Yeats's works all have "mountain of Gulben" changed to "Ben Bulben."

[3] Yeats learned that the souls of the damned were spitted upon rocks from D. R. McAnally's *Irish Wonders, The Ghosts, Giants . . . and other Marvels of the Emerald Isle*, a book Yeats reviewed twice.   [4] "Alanna" is Gaelic for "child."

answered, "How can I come?" And it said, "Come with me when the wind blows along the Mountain of Bulben and out to sea." Then I was afraid, and I put it outside on the window-sill.'

The old woman went over to the little china font which hung upon a nail by the window, and dipped her fingers into it and sprinkled the holy water over the girl, who thanked her in a low voice. For a moment the brooding look went out of her face, and then the eyes clouded with dreams once more.

'Put such things out of your head,' said Simon Herne angrily. 'Had not Peter struck a straight blow the devils had been one less, but the disgraced and shamefaced of the earth one more. I bid you know, colleen, that it is not this house but the bare highway that had been your home on the day when your brawler had tired of you!'

The girl did not seem to hear; she seemed to be wholly absorbed in listening to the storm in the fir-trees.

'Come to the table,' cried Peter Herne, 'and eat your supper like another.'

The girl made no answer, but gazed upon the smoke-blacked wall as though she could see through it. With an oath the old man began his supper, and Peter Herne busied himself filling his father's noggin and his own from a jug of Spanish wine out of a recently-smuggled cargo. Margaret Herne kept glancing at the girl from time to time. Meanwhile the wind roared louder and louder, and set the hams that hung from the rafters swaying to and fro. Presently the old woman saw by the girl's moving lips that she was speaking, but the wind drowned her words. Slowly, however, the wind became still, as though the beings that controlled it were listening also.

The girl was singing a fitful, exultant air in a low voice. The words were inaudible, but the air they knew well.

'Be silent!' cried the old man, going over and striking her on the mouth with his open hand; 'that is an evil air, and no daughter of mine shall ever sing it. Hanrahan the Red[5] sang it after he had listened to the singing of those who are about the faery Cleena of the Wave[6], and it has lured, and will lure, many a girl from her hearth and from her peace.'

'Good colleen,' said her mother, 'the host of Cleena sang of a love too great for our perishing hearts, and from that night Hanrahan the Red is always seeking with wild tunes and bewildered words to answer their voices, and a madness is upon his days and a darkness before his

[5] Hanrahan the Red is the hero of a group of Yeats's stories. In the *Speaker* version, it was "O'Sullivan the Red" who was Owen Roe O'Sullivan (1748–1784), a wandering Gaelic bard, killed in a duel.

[6] Cleena is the queen of the faeries of south Munster. Her palace is Carrig-Cleena, near Mallow.

feet. His songs are no longer dear to any but to the coasting sailors and to the people of the mountain, and to those that are ill-nurtured and foolish. Look, daughter, to the spinning-wheel, and think of our goods that, horn by horn and fleece by fleece, grow greater as the years go by, and be content.'

The girl heard and saw nothing of the things about her, but sang on as if in a trance. And now some wild words of love became audible from time to time, like a torch in a dim forest, or a star among drifting clouds; and the others could not help themselves but listen while she sang, an icy feeling beginning to creep about the room and into their hearts, as though all the warmth of the world was in that low, exultant song.

'It is very cold,' said Peter Herne, shivering; 'I will put more turf upon the fire.' And going over to the stack in the corner he flung an armful upon the flickering hearth, and then stooped down to stir the embers. 'The fire is going out,' he said; 'I cannot keep it alight. My God! the cold has numbed my feet;' and, staggering to his chair, he sat down. 'One would half think, if one did not know all such things to be but woman's nonsense, that the demons,[7] whose coming kills the body of man, were in the storm listening to this evil song.'

'The fire has gone out,' said the old man.

The eyes of the girl brightened, and she half rose from her chair, and sang in a loud and joyous voice:—

> O, what to me the little room,
>> That was brimmed up with prayer and rest?
> He bade me out into the gloom,
>> And my breast lies upon his breast.[8]
>
> O, what to me my mother's care,
>> The home where I was safe and warm?[9]
> The shadowy blossom of my hair
>> Will hide us from the bitter storm.
>
> O, hiding hair and dewy eyes,
>> I am no more with life and death!
> My heart upon his warm heart lies;
>> My breath is mixed into his breath.

While she had been singing, an intense drowsiness had crept into the room, as though the gates of Death had moved upon their hinges. The

---

[7] The *Speaker* version had "seabar" for "demons."
[8] In the *Speaker* the first stanza read:
> O, what to me the firelit room,
>> Where I have laughed and spun and played[9]
> He bade me out into the gloom,
>> And my white breast on his he laid.
[9] In the *Speaker* this line read "*The milking-place, the sheltered farm?*"

old woman had leaned forward upon the table, for she had suddenly understood that her hour had come. The young man had fixed his eyes fiercely on the face of the girl, and the light died out of them. The old man had known nothing, except that he was very cold and sleepy, until the cold came to his heart.[10] At the end of the song the storm began again with redoubled tumult, and the roof shook. The lips of the girl were half-parted in expectation, and out of her eyes looked all the submission which had been in the heart of woman from the first day.

Suddenly the thatch at one end of the roof rolled up, and the rushing clouds and a single star flickered before her eyes for a moment, and then seemed to be lost in a formless mass of flame which roared but gave no heat, and had in the midst of it the shape of a man crouching on the storm. His heavy and brutal face and his partly naked limbs were scarred with many wounds, and his eyes were full of white fire under his knitted brows.[11]

W. B. Yeats

Some Irish National Books

In this article for the *Bookman*, August, 1894, Yeats reviewed *The New Spirit of the Nation*, edited by Martin McDermott, London and Dublin, 1894; *A Parish Providence* by E. M. Lynch, London and Dublin, 1894; and *The Jacobite War in Ireland*, 1688–1691, by Charles O'Kelly, edited by George Noble Count Plunkett and the Rev. Edm. Hogan, S.J., Dublin, 1894.

This review was Yeats's sweet revenge for his defeat two years before by Sir Charles Gavan Duffy in their battle for the editorship of the New Irish Library series, a publishing venture which grew out of the inauguration in 1892 of the National Literary Society. Yeats had predicted that Sir Charles, in his old age, would choose books according to an outmoded taste, and he was not slow in pronouncing the same opinion over the books as they appeared. Some of his reviews of later volumes were more favorable.

LORD BEACONSFIELD[1] once said that the way to give a successful supper party was never to ask anybody who had to be explained, and the advice is good for more important matters. The members of "The Irish Literary Society" of London and "The National

[10] In the *Speaker* this sentence concludes "and his head fell backwards, convulsed."

[11] This ending is an improvement upon the *Speaker* version, which continued: "The rest of the roof rolled up and then fell inward with a crash, and the storm rushed through the house.

The next day the neighbors found the dead in the ruined house, and buried them in the barony of Amharlish, and set over them a tombstone to say they were killed by the great storm of October, 1765."   [1] Benjamin Disraeli, First Earl of Beaconsfield.

Literary Society" of Dublin, and the other persons responsible for the present Irish literary movement, had done well to have taken it to heart and avoided anything so desperately in need of explanation as three out of the four books already published in this "New Irish Library." Their first volume, 'The Patriot Parliament,'[2] was an historical tractate which, if modified a little, had done well among the transactions of a learned society, but it bored beyond measure the unfortunate persons who bought some thousands of copies in a few days, persuaded by the energy of the two societies, and deluded by the names of Sir Charles Gavan Duffy and Thomas Davis upon the cover. Pages upon pages of Acts of Parliament may be popular literature on the planet Neptune, or chillier Uranus, but our quick-blooded globe has altogether different needs. The admirable and picturesque book by Mr. O'Grady,[3] which followed, did well, I understand, despite the vehement refusal of numbers of the peasantry to take anything from a series which had already beguiled them outrageously; but I cannot believe that the most skilful advertising, the most eloquent appeals to patriotism, the most energetic canvassing will make the Irish people read 'The New Spirit of the Nation' or 'The Parish Providence.'

'The New Spirit of the Nation' is a gleaning from the same fields from which the editors of 'The Spirit of the Nation'[4] reaped their not too golden sheaves. If, however, one except three or four songs of excellent oratory by D'Arcy McGee,[5] and an interesting fragment by Davis called "Maurye Nangle," it contains nothing good which cannot be found with better company in several other collections. If one desire to possess "The Dark Rosaleen," or "O'Donovan's Daughter"—and this about exhausts the list of desirable things—one had best give nine pence for Mr. Sparling's[6] 'Irish Minstrelsy.'

The editor of this series, Sir Charles Gavan Duffy, should have given us a book which, while containing the best work of Callanan, Walsh, and Davis, and the other ballad makers, would have drawn more largely and carefully than Mr. Sparling's from the masters of Irish song— Ferguson, Mangan, Allingham, and De Vere—and, unlike his, have taken up whatever well-wrought fragments remain of Tom Moore's ruined house. Such a book would have won the enthusiastic admiration of every class in Ireland, and could have been put into the hands of a

---

[2] Thomas Davis, *The Patriot Parliament of 1689*, edited by Sir C. G. Duffy, London and Dublin, 1893.

[3] *The Bog of Stars and Other Stories and Sketches*, in the New Irish Library, London and Dublin, 1893. [4] *The Spirit of the Nation*, edited by Thomas Davis.

[5] Thomas D'Arcy McGee (1825–1868), poet of the Young Ireland movement. He emigrated to Canada and was assassinated by the Fenians in 1868.

[6] Herbert Halliday Sparling, son-in-law of William Morris. Yeats knew Sparling in the later eighties in London, and he is frequently mentioned in Yeats's correspondence of that period. *Irish Minstrelsy* appeared in 1887.

cultivated man of any country without need of explanation. But what educated person, even when you have explained its political value, its moral earnestness, its practical utility, can take pleasure in

> *"Come, Liberty, come! we are ripe for thy coming;*
> *Come freshen the hearts where thy rival has trod;*
> *Come, richest and rarest! come, purest and fairest,*
> *Come, daughter of science! come, gift of the god!"*[7]

Such jigging doggrel [*sic*]—I regret I have no gentler word—is in its place upon a broadsheet, or in one of Cameron and Ferguson's little Irish song-books, but how can it do other than hinder a literary movement which must perish, or dwindle into insignificance if it do not draw into its net the educated classes? You may persuade the half-educated country clerk or farmer's son that "Come richest and rarest, come purest and fairest" is noble rhythm and shining poetry, but the wholly uneducated peasant of the mountains and the wholly educated professional man of the cities will have none of it, for the one has his beautiful Gaelic ballads and his tumultuous world-old legends, while the gleaming city of English literature flings wide its doors to the other.

The truth of the matter is that Sir Charles Gavan Duffy has let that old delusion, didacticism, get the better of his judgment, as Wordsworth did when he wrote the Ecclesiastical Sonnets, and has given us a library which, however pleasing it be to "the daughter of science, the gift of the god," is, if we except Mr. O'Grady's stories, little but a cause of blaspheming to mere mortals, who would gladly see the Irish reading classes discovering the legends and stories and poems of their own country, instead of following at a laborious distance the fashions of London.

To make it wholly clear that he has some other intention than to gather into one series the best works of the Irish writers of the past and present, Sir Charles Gavan Duffy has made a book out of one of the poorest of Balzac's novels,[8] not improved by having the French names turned into English ones; an introduction on agriculture and local industries forty pages long, and made up mostly out of a fifty-year old article of his own, and an appendix full of quotations from a blue book. We might, it seems, have taken even a bad Balzac for that impracticable thing, "mere literature," and so must needs suffer the blue books and the agricultural information with what grace we may. Not that Sir Charles Gavan Duffy has compiled this queer piece of "Irish literature" altogether without wisdom; on the contrary, he has been careful to issue his wares as an innocent "country tale" by "E. M. Lynch," and suppresses upon cover and title-page alike all mention either of Balzac

[7] "Come, Liberty, Come!" is by Denis Florence MacCarthy, and it reminds the editor of Schiller's "An die Freude."   [8] The Balzac novel was *Médecin de campagne*.

or of agriculture; they spring on you together in the introduction. He
has been always, the fact is, an influence making for didacticism, rather
than literature—for his great qualities are essentially practical. William
Carleton, after a succession of masterpieces, contributed three stories
to his "Library of Ireland," and in them departed from his own admirable manner, and, instead of creating new masterpieces of pity and
humour, wrote three tracts against intemperance, sloth, and the secret
societies, and never after quite got the beam out of his eyes. Yet it is no
way clear why it should be held for righteousness in any man to over-
balance the right proportions of nature and caricature humanity to
make some commonplace moral shine out with artificial distinctness;
or that a wiser age would do other than hold all such works for the
creation of the Father of Lies.

The first volume of "The Irish Home Library," the Dublin rival to
"The New Irish Library," is a good book of its kind, being an account
of the war of William and James in Ireland by a man who was in the
thick of it, but one has some doubt whether it be of a good kind to
start a popular library. Surely one needs something more picturesque,
more vivid, if one would catch the general taste. For instance, we have
famous figures flitting about the pages—Sarsfield, Schomberg, William,
James, Tirconnell—but not one is ever described or made live as a man
before us. O'Kelly wrote for historians who had them already before
their eyes, or for comrades who had seen them in the flesh, and did all
needful for his purpose. Yet it is a good book, edited carefully by two
excellent scholars—Father Hogan and Count Plunkett—and cannot be
recommended too strongly to one already interested in the period of
which it treats. It is, however, books which can create an interest where
there is none which are needed for a series of this kind, and if any
publisher would set Mr. O'Grady, Dr. Hyde, Miss Lawless, Miss
Barlow, Dr. Todhunter, Mrs. Bryant, and Mrs. Hinkson,[9] to the
making of such books, he would probably prosper.

W. B. Yeats

A New Poet

Yeats's first review of A.E.'s *Homeward Songs by the Way*, Dublin, 1894,
appeared in the *Bookman*, August, 1894.

A.E., the first two letters of the Gnostic word "AEON," meaning heavenly

---

[9] See footnote 2 to "The Evangel of Folklore" (*Bookman*, June ,1894), p. 326, for information on some of these authors. For Mrs. Bryant, see review of *Celtic Ireland*, pp. 162–66
above.

spirit, was the pen name of George William Russell (1867–1935), one of Yeats's oldest friends. Their acquaintance began when they studied together at the Dublin School of Art. Yeats took part in the activities of the Dublin lodge of the Theosophical Society in Ely Place where Russell lived until his marriage. Russell printed an article by Yeats in his magazine *Irish Theosophist*.

This present review was part of a publicity campaign which Yeats told John O'Leary (*Letters*, p. 231) he would organize in London for A.E.'s first volume of poems. Yeats was unceasing in his praise of Russell until the end of the century.

In his autobiography Yeats said of Russell, "We are never satisfied with the maturity of those whom we have admired in boyhood . . ." (*Autobiography*, p. 165). Although Yeats and A.E. remained good friends, their disillusionment was mutual.

Yeats wrote a notice of the American edition of this book in the May, 1895, *Bookman*.

A YOUNG Englishman of literary ambition is usually busy with details of rhythm, the advantages of opposing methods, and the like, and is content to leave problems of government to the journalists, and questions of fate, free-will, foreknowledge absolute,[1] to the professors and the devils. In Ireland we go into the other extreme, and our literature has sprung generally from some movement in public affairs, and, but for the lack of education and the belief that all such matters have been settled out of hand by the Catholic Church, would, I doubt not, have sprung also from philosophical movements, for an Irishman cut adrift from his priest is exceedingly speculative. A little school of transcendental writers has indeed started up in the last year or two, as it is, and made many curious and some beautiful lyrics. I make no excuse for telling its history, for not one moment is trivial among the million ages which Blake says go to the making of a flower. About twelve years ago seven youths[2] began to study European magic and Oriental mysticism, and because, as the Gaelic proverb puts it, contention is better than loneliness, agreed to meet at times in a room in a dirty back street and to call their meetings "The Dublin Hermetic Society." They gradually accumulated a set of convictions for themselves, of which a main part was, I think, that the poets were uttering,

---

[1] *fate, free will, foreknowledge absolute*: Yeats paraphrases *Paradise Lost*, Book II, ll. 559–60.
[2] Among these seven were Yeats, Charles Johnston, Charles Weekes, and Claude Wright (the last on the authority of Richard Ellmann in *Yeats—The Man and The Masks*, New York, 1958, p. 41). Yeats told Ernest Boyd that A.E. was not a member of the Dublin Hermetic Society (*Letters*, p. 592). A.E. probably first joined the Dublin Lodge of the Theosophical Society, founded about 1886. According to the *Dublin University Review* issue of July, 1885 (p. 155), the first meeting of the Dublin Hermetic Society was held on June 16 at Trinity College. Papers were delivered by Yeats, Charles Johnston, and Mr. Smeeth.

under the mask of phantasy, the old revelations, and that we should
truly look for genii of the evening breeze and hope for the final con-
summation of the world when two halcyons might sit upon a bough and
eat once-poisonous herbs and take no harm. As for the rest, they spent
their days in battles about the absolute and the alcahest,[3] and I think
that none read the newspapers, and am sure that some could not have
told you the name of the viceroy. These periodical meetings started a
movement, and the movement has begun to make literature. One of the
group[4] published last year a very interesting book of verse which he
withdrew from circulation in a moment of caprice, and now "A.E.,"
its arch-visionary, has published 'Homeward: Songs by the Way' [*sic*], a
pamphlet of exquisite verse. He introduces it with this quaint preface:
"I moved among men and places and in living I learned the truth at last.
I know I am a spirit, and that I went forth[5] from the self-ancestral to
labours yet unaccomplished; but, filled ever and again with homesickness, I made these songs by the way." The pamphlet is in no sense,
however, the work of a preacher, but of one who utters, for the sake of
beauty alone, the experience of a delicate and subtle temperament. He
is a moralist, not because he desires, like the preacher, to coerce our
will, but because good and evil are a part of what he splendidly calls
"the multitudinous meditation" of the divine world in whose shadow
he seeks to dwell. No one who has an ear for poetry at all can fail to
find a new voice and a new music in lines like these:

> "*What of all the will to do?*
> *It has vanished long ago,*
> *For a dream-shaft pierced it through*
> *From the Unknown Archer's bow.*
>
> *What of all the soul to think?*
> *Some one offered it a cup*
> *Filled with a diviner drink,*
> *And the flame has burned it up.*
>
> *What of all the hope to climb?*
> *Only in the self we grope*
> *To the misty end of time:*
> *Truth has put an end to hope.*

---

[3] *alcahest*: Yeats in his review of Ibsen's *Brand* (*Bookman*, October, 1894) defines alcahest
as follows: "Certain alchemical writers say that the substance left over in the retort is the
philosopher's stone, and the liquid distilled over, the elixir or alkahest; and all are agreed
that the stone transmutes everything into gold, while the elixir dissolves everything into
nothing, and not a few call them the fixed and the volatile."

[4] Charles Weekes, whose book *Reflections and Refractions* was reviewed by Yeats in the
Academy, November 4, 1893. A.E. dedicated *Homeward Songs by the Way* to Weekes.

[5] A.E. reads "went forth in old time from. . . ."

> *What of all the heart to love?*
> *Sadder than for will or soul,*
> *No light lured it on above;*
> *Love has found itself the whole."*

Such poetry is profoundly philosophical in the only way in which
poetry can be; it describes the emotions of a soul dwelling in the
presence of certain ideas. Some passionate temperaments, amorous of
the colour and softness of the world, will refuse the quietism of the
idea in a poem like "Our Throne's[6] Decay," but they can do no other
than feel the pathos of the emotion:

> *"I said my pleasure shall not move;*
> *It is not fixed in things apart;*
> *Seeking not love—but yet to love—*
> *I put my trust in my[7] own heart.*
>
> *I know[8] the fountain of the deep*
> *Wells up with living joy, unfed:*
> *Such joys the lonely heart may keep,*
> *And love grow rich with love unwed.*
>
> *Still flows the ancient fount sublime;*
> *But, ah, for my heart, shed tears, shed tears;*
> *Not it but love has scorn of time;*
> *It turns to dust beneath the years."*

Nor would A.E. be angry with one who turned away from his ideas,
for he himself knows well that all ideas fade or change in passing from
one mind to another, and that what we call "truth" is but one of our
illusions, a perishing embodiment of a bodiless essence:

> *"The hero first taught[9] it:*
> *To him 'twas a deed;*
> *To those who retaught it*
> *A chain on their speed.*
>
> *The fire that we kindled—*
> *A beacon by night—*
> *When darkness has dwindled*
> *Grows pale in the light.*
>
> *For life has no glory*
> *Stays long in one dwelling,*
> *And time has no story*
> *That's true twice in telling.*

---

[6] *Throne's*: A.E.'s title reads "Thrones."   [7] *my*: A.E. reads "mine."
[8] *know*: A.E. reads "knew."   [9] *taught*: A.E. reads "thought."

And only the teaching
That never was spoken
Is worthy thy reaching
The fountain unbroken."

There are everywhere such memorable lines as "Come earth's little children, pit pat from their burrows in the hill," "White for Thy whiteness all desires burn," "Withers once more the old blue flower of day," "The fiery dust of evening shaken from the feet of light," "We are but embers wrapped in clay," "Make of thy gentleness thy might," "Be thou thyself that goal in which the wars of time shall cease," and "No image of the proud and morning stars looks at us from their faces."

The book has faults in plenty, certain rhymes are repeated too often, the longer lines stumble now and again, and here and there a stanza is needlessly obscure; but, taken all in all, it is the most haunting book I have seen these many days. Books published in Ireland are only too often anything but comely to look at, but this little pamphlet makes us hope much from the new house of Whaley, for it is beautifully printed upon excellent paper.

                                                        W. B. Yeats

[The New Irish Library]

In *United Ireland*, August 18, 1894, the editor, John McGrath, commented on Yeats's review of three New Irish Library volumes (*Bookman*, August, 1894, see p. 332). McGrath agreed with Yeats in general, but he thought that *The Patriot Parliament* was a suitable choice for the New Irish Library, and he stated in its defense that it had "a bigger sale than any Irish book of our time." Yeats's reply was printed in the September 1 issue.

In November, 1894, Yeats had another difference of opinion with McGrath. In a review of a book of poems by an Irishman, McGrath said that Irish writers should ignore the opinions of any critics outside Ireland. Yeats replied that "the true ambition is to make criticism as international, and literature as national, as possible", a maxim that served as the aesthetic basis for most of the criticism in this book (reprinted in *Letters*, pp. 238–39).

                                                   [September 1, 1894]

M R. W. B. YEATS sends me the following with reference to some paragraphs which appeared in this column a fortnight ago on the New Irish Library:

"Dear Sir—It is no manner of use our deceiving ourselves about the sale of the 'Patriot Parliament.' It is perfectly well known that the first volume of any much-talked of series is certain of a large sale, quite independent of its merits, and the ten or fifteen thousand sold is not exceptional. The question is whether it did or did not help the other volumes, and I have reason to know that numbers of the peasantry refused to buy 'The Bog of Stars'[1] because of the dullness of its predecessor. Believing, as I do, that literature is almost the most profound influence that ever comes into a nation, I recognize with deep regret, and not a little anger, that the 'New Irish Library' is so far the most serious difficulty in the way of our movement, and that it drives from us those very educated classes we desire to enlist, and supplies our opponents with what looks like evidence of our lack of any fine education, of any admirable precision[2] and balance of mind, of the very qualities which make literature possible. Perhaps honest criticism, with as little of the 'great day for Ireland' ritual as may be can yet save the series from ebbing out in a tide of irrelevant dulness, and keep the best opportunity there has been these many decades from being squandered by pamphleteer and amateur. We require books by competent men of letters upon subjects of living national interest, romances by writers of acknowledged power, anthologies selected from men like De Vere, and Allingham, and Fergusson [*sic*], and impartial picturesque lives of Emmet, Wolfe Tone, Mitchel, and perhaps O'Connell, and, if they are not to be obtained, let us bow our heads in silence and talk no more of a literary renaissance, for we can, at least, cease to be imposters.

If you re-read my remarks in the *Bookman* upon 'The Patriot Parliament' you will find that instead of criticising its historical merits I assumed them and called it a good book for the proceedings of a learned society. I made no other criticism than that it was 'dull,' whereas, you prefer the words 'not brilliant' or 'particularly readable'. I accept your amendations [*sic*] with pleasure, and we are at one again.—Yours sincerely,

W. B. Yeats."

By-the-way, I hear Mr. Yeats is working on a new Irish poem, which he expects to publish before Christmas. One of Mr. Yeats's latest admirers is Mr. Robert Louis Stevenson, the celebrated novelist, who has just written him from his far-away home in Samoa to say that his poetry has taken him "captive." This is a remarkable tribute from such a critic. Mr. Stevenson was taken captive by Swinburne when a boy, and ten years ago by the verses of George Meredith. Our Irish bard, you see, is climbing up into high company.

J. M'G. [John McGrath]

[1] *The Bog of Stars* by Standish O'Grady was the second volume in the New Irish Library series.　　[2] *precision*: *United Ireland* printed "precession."

An Imaged World

This anonymous review of Edward Garnett's *An Imaged World: Poems in Prose*, London, 1894, appeared in the *Speaker* issue of September 8, 1894.

Edward Garnett (1868–1937) was the son of Richard Garnett (1835–1906), the Keeper of Printed Books at the British Museum, and the father of David Garnett, the author. As a reader for the firm of T. Fisher Unwin, Garnett was influential in having this firm publish some of Yeats's early works. During the controversy over the management of the New Irish Library, Yeats appealed to Garnett to help save this projected series of books from the editorship of Sir Charles Gavan Duffy (the firm of Unwin was to publish the books in England). Garnett may have used his influence but the forces combined against Yeats were too strong, and Duffy became the editor of this project.

In October, 1892, Yeats asked Garnett: "How does the *Imaged World* thrive? Please let me know before any work of yours comes out as I am now reviewing on the Bookman and may be able to be of use" (*Letters*, p. 214). *An Imaged World, Poems in Prose* was given a bad review in the *Bookman* of August, 1894. There is no strong indication that Yeats wrote this review. Although he may have used his influence to get the book reviewed, he could not control the decision of the reviewer. Yeats previously had solicited reviews for friends only to have the reviews turn out badly.

This *Speaker* review has many signs of Yeats's authorship: the references to Vaughan the Silurist, an alchemist named Dr. Rudd, and the quotation from Blake. We know from other reviews that Yeats was familiar with *The Bard of the Dimbovitza*, referred to in the phrase "the peasant poets of Roumania." He did not like prose poems and this attitude is made plain in this review in spite of the friendliness shown to Garnett. The misquotations, in contrast to the letter-perfect *Bookman* review, are usual in Yeats's reviews. For a fuller discussion of my attribution, see Introduction, pp. 28–30.

Yeats quarrelled with Garnett in 1903 over Lady Gregory's translation of Irish sagas, *Cuchulain of Muirthemne*. Yeats had claimed in his introduction to it that the book was the finest to come out of Ireland in his time. In an article in the *Academy* of February 14, 1903, Garnett argued that the book was hardly that. The two men were never reconciled. (See *The Garnett Family* by Carolyn G. Heilbrun, London and New York, 1961, p. 106.)

W HEN Vaughan the Silurist[1] said that man was a world and had another to attend him, he but expressed the faith of those mediaeval mystics who held the soul to correspond exactly to the universe, and its emotions to the stars and the forest, the seas and the

---

[1] *Vaughan the Silurist*: The poet Henry Vaughan (1621–1695) called himself "Silurist" after the Latin name for the part of Wales in which he was born.

storms. Man had Nature for his friend or foe, they held, and must study her whims and phantasies, or she would pelt him with hail and rain or affright him with choleric meteors, and some of the wisest among them were so privileged as to behold her in human shape, like the alchemist, Dr. Rudd, who met her walking, "black but comely," in his garden in Devonshire, and when she departed after much wise conversation, noted down that she went, "half smiling and half sad," in a way that was "very pretty," for she was loth to fade from him and be disguised in the noisy elements again.

Mr. Garnett has cultivated this ancient intimacy with tact and patience, and the images of his "Imaged World" are but the haphazard shapes and shadows which Nature casts upon the "glass of imagination;" and through his whole work runs a sense of union with her and hers which lacks only the hard touch of philosophy to become mediaeval and mystical. It is supposed to be written by a lover who finds in every change of weather, in every passing face, a symbol of his own joy or trouble, an adherent or an enemy of his hopes. Now it is the path in the wood which shares his longing: "O Hyld! down there in the woods my feet have bruised a tiny path amid the autumn grass, as I went, thinking of thee; a little path amid nut-bushes winding. It has not led me to an end; O girl, have pity on that poor bruised path, which cannot speak its heart, and come and pass by it." And now the night holds his love from him, and he calls out to the storms: "Tear the swart twilight, O[2] rushing white rain-storm; tear the edge of the fast-travelling night, and let my love through to me! Yes, all the sombre horizon is ravelling with a foam edge of light in the dying west—ah, if I could get there, if I could get there, thou and my fate would meet me! Art thou jeering at me, O storm-wind? Ah! wait a little, O lone night, and thou shalt hear us whispering our secrets together! O streaming leaves, when the wind has flung ye dying on earth's cold bosoms, I shall be lying on my love's warm breasts." And yet, again, it is the faces in the street that keep her from him: "Faces, faces; everywhere I see[3] fresh faces, yet I could not see her gentle face. Faces, faces; fixed and serious faces all keep passing in long procession,[4] yet I could not find her frightened face. It is you, you thousand secret-hiding faces, that she feared, your curious eyes and sneering looks, if you had guessed her secret." Sometimes he broods over other things than love, but always as a lover—always as one who seeks to be alone, always as one filled with a consuming idealism which makes every imperfect thing dreadful; and through all his meditations is the recurring thought that men and women have fallen for ever from beauty and happiness. His final word is: "O young earth, fresh earth,

---

[2] *O*: Garnett has "oh."   [3] *see:* Garnett reads "saw."
[4] *in long procession*: Garnett has "in a long procession."

earth of ecstasy, would that we, the grey multitudes with our pale pleasures, had never[5] been born in thy green lap! O[6] grant that memory of us be lost when to the young[7] clear-eyed race shalt pass thy mountains, plains, and forests. Grant then that our cities lie buried deep, and thy heart, O earth, betray[8] us not when the surf-waves break athwart the dance of the twining, laughing girls, at purple eve, on the great sea's windy shore."

There is enough of poetry in this remarkable book for many poems, and yet it seldom perfectly satisfies the artistic conscience or quite lays asleep the thought that we will forget it when it is thrust into the shelf. It is almost impossible to open it without finding beauty, but in the midst of the most beautiful passages will come a word without precision[9] or a phrase without music, and the impression of the whole is a little vapoury. Here and there, too, Mr. Garnett's own thoughts and methods struggle for mastery with a mannerism from Walt Whitman or Richard Jefferies, or the peasant poets of Roumania.[10] The truth is that Mr. Garnett has discovered a medium which suits him and which, despite the general prejudice against everything called "a poem in prose," is as legitimate as any other, but can, as yet, only at times fulfil the ideal of the inevitable words in the inevitable order; and that he has gathered many pathetic and lovely impressions and moods, but has not yet amassed them into a coherent image of the world and marked them round with what Blake called "the outline of the Almighty." The more emotional and ideal a writer's manner and material the more firm must be his hand, the more orderly the procession of his moods, if he would have his book draw us out of our common interests and linger in the memory when we have returned to them again. Despite all defects, however, "An Imaged World" is full of delightful things; nor is it other than delightful to look upon, for Mr. William Hyde,[11] who has no equal within his limits, has made for it five illustrations full of the exultation of wind and sea, of the triumph of moon and stars, and two designs of barbed leaves for the cover and margins, which, though less memorable and though one is repeated too often, are comely and pleasant to the fancy.

---

[5] *never*: Garnett has "ne'er."   [6] Garnett has "Oh."

[7] *the young*: Garnett has "the strong young."   [8] *betray*: Garnett reads "betrays."

[9] *precision*: Yeats says elsewhere (*Bookman*, April, 1896) that Blake's great word was "precision."

[10] *peasant poets of Roumania*: Yeats meant *The Bard of the Dimbovitza*, a collection of Roumanian folk poems translated into French by Hélène Vacaresco and into English by Carmen Sylva (Elizabeth, Queen of Roumania) and Alma Strettell, first series in 1892, second series in 1894. Yeats quoted passages from the second volume in his review of Lucy Garnett's collection *Greek Folk Poesy* (*Bookman*, October, 1896).

[11] William Hyde illustrated Yeats's article "Popular Ballad Poetry of Ireland," *Leisure Hour*, November, 1889.

The Stone and the Elixir

Yeats reviewed Ibsen's *Brand*, in a verse translation by F. E. Garrett, London, 1894, in the *Bookman* issue of October, 1894.

Yeats deplored the influence of Ibsen on the English stage. He tells in his autobiography of his dislike for a performance of *A Doll's House*. *Rosmersholm* is described as a play ". . . where there is symbolism and a stale odour of spilt poetry" (*Autobiography*, p. 185). Yeats could neither agree with the "clever young journalists" who admired Ibsen's realism nor adopt the views of conventional people who were shocked by Ibsen's themes.

Yeats liked *Brand* and *Peer Gynt*, after his fashion. This review gave him an opportunity to raise poetry above didactic art and the early verse plays of Ibsen over his later problem plays.

C ERTAIN alchemical writers say that the substance left behind in the retort is the philosopher's stone, and the liquid distilled over, the elixir or alkahest; and all are agreed that the stone transmutes everything into gold, while the elixir dissolves everything into nothing, and not a few call them the fixed and the volatile. One might take these contraries as symbols of the minds of Brand and Peer Gynt. Peer Gynt lets sheer phantasy take possession of his life, and fill him with the delusion that he is this or that personage, now a hunter, now a troll, now a merchant, now a prophet, until the true Peer Gynt is well-nigh dissolved. Brand, upon the other hand, seeks to rise into an absolute world where there is neither hunter, nor troll, nor merchant, nor prophet, but only God and his laws, and to transmute by the force of his unchanging ideal everything about him into imperishable gold, only to perish amid ice and snow with the cry in his ears, "Die! the earth[1] has no use for thee!" His mistake is not less disastrous, though immeasurably nobler, than the mistake of Peer Gynt, for the children of the earth can only live by compromise, by half measures, and by disobedience to his impassioned appeal:

> *"Grant you are slaves to pleasure; well,*
> *Be so, from curfew-bell to bell;*
> *Don't be some special thing one minute*
> *And something else the next, by fits!*
> *Whate'er you are be whole soul[2] in it,*
> *Not only piecemeal and in bits!*
> *There's beauty in a true Bacchante;*
> *But in your toper's headache, scanty.*

[1] Garrett's translation reads "the world" instead of "the earth."
[2] *whole-soul*: Garrett reads "whole-souled."

Silenus still is picturesque;
A tippler is the god's grotesque.
Go round the country, do but fling
A watchful glance at folks; you'll see
That every one has learned[3] to be
A little bit of everything.
A little smug (on holy days);
A little true to old-time ways;
A little sensual when he sups—
(His fathers were so in their cups)."

Poetry has ever loved those who are not "piecemeal," and has made of them its Timons and its Lears, but Nature, which is all "piecemeal," has ever cast them out.

Dr. Jaeger and Mr. Boyesen[4] will have it that 'Peer Gynt' is a description of what Ibsen believes his countrymen to be, and 'Brand' of what he would have them become, while Mr. Bernard Shaw reads 'Brand' as a satire upon ideals of all kinds. These various readings are but so many proofs that the poem is not an argument, but a work of art; not criticism, but the substance of life; not propaganda, but poetry. Ibsen saw two types underlying all others; he saw everywhere the old duality of the alchemist, the fixed and the volatile, and created two characters to embody them, and having carried each character to its moment of perfect expression, the one amid overwhelming and lifeless snow, the other face to face with the button moulder who would melt him down to make new buttons, new personalities, passed on to fresh creations. It is our business and not his to judge and measure and condemn, for the work of the poet is revelation, and the work of the reader is criticism. If he turned aside from his office he would enslave us instead of liberating us, and his work would be as ephemeral as the newspaper, or the last invention.

Ibsen is, however, a man of his age, and to him individual character, instead of being an end in itself, as it was to the Elizabethan dramatist, is but a means for the expression of broad generalisations and classifications, and of the pressure of religion and social life upon the soul; and it is his peculiar glory that he makes us share his interest in these things, and makes them move us as they move him, and yet never sinks the artist in the theorist or the preacher. But because he writes of things of which the theorist makes his theories, the preacher his commandments, he has been caught up by all manner of propagandists, who dream him

[3] *learned*: Garrett reads "learnt."

[4] Henrik Bernhard Jaeger (1854–1895) was a biographer of Ibsen. An English translation of his life of Ibsen appeared in 1890. Hjalmar Hjorth Boyesen (1848–1895) was a critic of German and Scandinavian literatures.

one of themselves. And because prose is more syllogistic than poetry, and because the theorist and the preacher have devoured the land like the locust, the later and less imaginative though profoundly interesting plays have been acted and expounded to the neglect of the works of his prime, and until two or three years ago neither 'Brand' nor 'Peer Gynt' had been translated. Now, however, we have one, presumably literal though not over poetical, translation of 'Peer Gynt,' and three of 'Brand,' one in prose and two in verse, and have seen a pathetic and incomparable fragment of 'Brand' upon the stage. This last 'Brand' by Mr. Garrett is rather more vigorous than its immediate predecessor by Dr. Herford, and on the whole more satisfactory than Mr. Wilson's prose version. A poem when robbed of its metrical architecture seems vague and rhetorical, just as the best prose if put into rhyme and metre would seem incredibly flat and long drawn out. Prose translations are of infinite use as books of reference, but can never be final. On the other hand, neither Dr. Herford nor Mr. Garrett can claim to have given us a definitive translation, but then definitive translations are even rarer than works of original genius.

W. B. Yeats

Professor Dowden and Irish Literature—I

On January 14, 1895, a lecture on Sir Samuel Ferguson by Roden Noel, then recently deceased, was read by Miss Emily H. Hickey in the Leinster Lecture Hall, Dublin. Among those who commented on Ferguson's poetry after the lecture was Edward Dowden, the famous professor of English literature at Trinity College.

Dowden, as quoted in the *Dublin Daily Express*, January 15, 1895, said that "he did not take the enthusiastic view of Irish poetry expressed by Sir Wm. Stokes [who had spoken before him]." He thought that Davis, Mangan, and other names mentioned were poets not of the first, second, or perhaps even third rank. Yeats would have agreed with him about Thomas Davis but not about James Clarence Mangan. Of Irish poetry as a whole, Dowden said that its typical defects, from which Ferguson was free, were an "undue tendency to rhetoric . . . sentimentality, . . . and deficiency of technique." He praised British writers by way of comparison. That Ferguson was not esteemed highly in England had nothing to do with his being Irish. Dowden claimed that "there was no prejudice against Irishmen in England when they proved themselves worthy of being received (applause)." For a student of British, or any, prejudices, that slight qualification is particularly laughable.

Ferguson was not popular, said Dowden, because he had been born out of his proper time. He belonged to an age of faith and the nineteenth century had been an age of doubt. Dowden said that "they could not expect people who were asking questions about the existence of God to interest themselves in Cuculain." It was not for nothing that Dowden taught rhetoric among other things at Trinity.

An account of Dowden's remarks was printed in the *Irish Times* on January 15, and the following day was printed a letter from Dowden complaining of misquotation, but this quarrel only involved whether Dowden had said Ferguson "was" or "was not" born in an age of faith. The *Daily Express* later printed letters by T. W. Rolleston and Standish O'Grady as well as Yeats, whose letters appear below.

Yeats was in an ambiguous position in this controversy. He had been denouncing the same faults in Irish writing as Dowden had, yet he could not seem to be agreeing with Dowden. On Ferguson's poetry, Yeats had castigated Dowden for allowing English critics to ignore Ferguson as long ago as 1886. On a wider scale, the members of the "Irish literary movement" took this opportunity to debate as loudly and as long as they could the merits of past and present Irish writers. The debate had a second round in March, 1895 (see letters on pp. 351–53)

[January 26, 1895]

TO THE EDITOR OF THE *DAILY EXPRESS*

SIR—Prof Dowden says that Irish literature has many faults, and this is indeed obvious; nor could it well be otherwise in a young literature, an experimental literature, a literature preoccupied with hitherto unworked material, and compelled to seek an audience for the most part among the poor and the ignorant. The only question at issue is whether we can best check these faults by carefully sifting out and expounding what is excellent, as Mr. Stopford Brooke, Mr. Rolleston, Dr. Hyde, Mr. Ashe King, Mr. Alfred Perceval Graves, Mr. Lionel Johnson, and the other leaders of "the Irish literary movement" are endeavoring to do; or by talking, like Professor Dowden, occasional vague generalities about rhetoric and sentimentality and bad technique. It does not seem to me a question for us whether this literature be important or unimportant, but only whether it be new or not new. If it be new no man living can measure its importance, or say what sails may be filled by it in the future, not merely in Ireland but out of Ireland. And I think that the man who cannot find a distinct character in Callahan's "Outlaw of Loch Lene," in Walsh's "Mairgreod Ni Chelleadu," in Davis' "Marriage" and "Plea for Love," in Mangan's "Ode to The Maguire" and "Woman of Three Cows," in Doheney's "A Cushla Gal ma Chree," in Allingham's "Winding Banks of Erin" [*sic*],¹ in Ferguson's "Conary," in de Vere's "Wedding of the Clans," and in countless other poems, which are neither rhetorical nor sentimental, nor of flaccid technique, must be either prejudiced or a little lacking in artistic sensitiveness. I am sure that if Professor Dowden does not perceive this distinct character it can only be because he has given the subject too little attention; and if he does perceive it I ask him does he think he has quite done his duty by this new creative impulse. It is not possible to separate out Ferguson and say that he alone has it, for the men I have named have each written something as distinguished, as pathetic, as characteristic as any of his poems. They fall short of his epic aim and of his sustained excellence, but at times excel him in delicacy and in mastery over what Blake² has called "minute appropriate words." Professor Dowden has been for years our representative critic, and during that time he has done little for the reputation of Ferguson, whom he admires, and nothing for the reputation of these others, whom Ferguson admired. Our "movement," on the other hand, has only existed three or four years, and during that time it has denounced rhetoric with more passionate vehemence than he has ever done. It has exposed sentimentality and flaccid technique with more effect than has been possible to his imperfect knowledge of Irish literature, but, at the same time, it has persuaded Irish men and women to read what is excellent in past and present Irish literature, and it has added to that literature books of folk-lore, books of history, books of fiction, and books of verse, which, whatever be their faults, are yet the expression of the same dominant mood, the same creative impulse which inspired Ferguson and the poets I have named. Nor is it a self-conscious endeavor to make a literature, but the spontaneous expression of an impulse which has been gathering power for decades, and which makes itself heard in the lull of our political tumults. I have not seen any mention in the reports of the Hon. Roden Noel's lecture of the fact that it was originally delivered before the Irish Literary Society, London, and is therefore itself a specimen of our work.—Yours truly,

W. B. Yeats

February 7, 1895

TO THE EDITOR OF THE *DAILY EXPRESS*

Sir,—A very amusing proof of the unfounded nature of one of Professor Dowden's charges against the Irish literary movement has just reached me. At the very time Professor Dowden was sending to

¹ Allingham's poem is "The Winding Banks of Erne."
² *Blake*: *United Ireland* printed "Bake."

the Press an introduction,[1] saying that we indulged in indiscriminate praise of all things Irish, and went about "plastered with shamrocks and raving of Brian Boru," a certain periodical was giving the hospitality of its pages to a long anonymous letter making a directly contrary charge. The writer of the letter accused some of the members of the Irish Literary Society of discouraging "worthy workers in the field," of endeavouring to substitute the pursuit of what he called "high art" for the old, easy-going days when every patriotic writer was as good as his neighbour, and even of making allegations against the literary merits of the Young Ireland Party. His feelings about one member, who had been rather active in criticism, so completely overpowered him that he could only say this member's walk was ungainly, his personal habits objectionable, and his face dirty, but then he said these things with an exuberant eloquence which I cannot even try to rival. I will not advertise this periodical by naming it, but I shall be delighted to send Professor Dowden my own copy, though it is one of my most precious possessions, and with a little industry I can find him, I dare say, much more of the same kind in other periodicals. If proof were required of the extent to which Dublin is dominated by scholastic —perhaps I should say school room—ideals, Mr. Colles[2] gives that proof by finding it "ludicrous" that a young writer like myself should make "an earnest protest" against some of the opinions and methods of an older and better known man of letters. Has Mr. Colles forgotten that every literary revolution the world has seen has been made because of the readiness of the young to revolt against what Walt Whitman has called "the endless audacity of elected persons?"—Yours sincerely,

W. B. Yeates [*sic*]

[1] Introduction to *New Studies in Literature* by Edward Dowden, London, 1895. Dowden said, "Let an Irish prose writer show that he can be patient, exact, just, enlightened, and he will have done better service for Ireland, whether he treats of Irish themes or not, than if he wore shamrocks in all his buttonholes and had his mouth for ever filled with the glories of Brian the Brave." In a letter to the *Dublin Daily Express*, January 29, 1895, Dowden, answering insinuations by Standish O'Grady, said that the introduction was written before Yeats began to write and hence had no reference to him. Dowden's adversaries made much of the use of an introduction more than a decade old to represent Dowden's current opinions on Irish literary nationalism.

[2] Ramsay Colles wrote a letter in support of Dowden, which was printed in the *Dublin Daily Express* on February 2, 1895.

Battles Long Ago

This review of Standish O'Grady's *The Coming of Cuculain*, London, 1895, is from the *Bookman*, February, 1895.

EVERY one of the great European legend cycles has inspired the poets and musicians of our time, except, curiously enough, the one which is probably the most copious and ancient. The German and Scandinavian lives again in Wagner and Morris, the Welsh delights thousands in 'The Idylls of the King,' and in Mr. Swinburne's 'Tristram and Iseult'; but the Irish was until yesterday the exclusive possession of Professor Dryasdust and his pupils. That it is becoming again an imaginative existence is due almost wholly to Mr. Standish O'Grady, whose 'History of Ireland, Heroic Period,' published in 1878, was the starting point of what may yet prove a new influence in the literature of the world. A couple of years ago, after a long devotion to mediaeval Ireland, he returned to his old studies, and wrote his delightful 'Finn and his Companions,' and now he has just issued 'The Coming of Cuchullin,'[1] the memorable first part of a kind of prose epic. It is probable that no Englishman can love these books as they are loved by the many Irishmen who date their first interest in Irish legends and literature from the 'History.' There is perhaps, too, something in their tumultuous vehemence, in their delight in sheer immensity, in their commingling of the spirit of man with the spirit of the elements, which belongs to the wild Celtic idealism rather than to the careful, practical ways of the Saxon. The heroes of 'The Idylls of the King' are always merely brave and excellent men, calculable and measurable in every way; but the powers of Cuchullin are as incalculable and immeasurable as the powers of nature. When he leaps, for instance, into his chariot, after his knighting, the spirits of the glens and the demons of the air roar about him; the gods shout within the armoury, and clash the swords and shields together; the god "Lu, the Long-handed," "the maker and decorator of the firmament," whose hound was the sun, thunders; the god of the sea, Mananan Mac Lir, passes "through the assembly with a roar of innumerable waters";[2] and the goddess of Battle, "the Mor Rega,"[3] stands with a foot on each side of the plain, and shouts with "the voice of a host."[4]

[1] Yeats differed from O'Grady in his spelling of this name.
[2] O'Grady wrote "with a roar of far-off innumerable waters. . . ."
[3] O'Grady spelled this name "Mor Reega."
[4] O'Grady wrote "the shout of a host."

Mr. O'Grady does not attempt to give the old stories in the form they have come down to us, but passes them through his own imagination. Yet so familiar is he with the old legends, so profound a sympathy has he with their spirit, that he has made the ancient gods and heroes live over again their simple and passionate lives. The Red Branch feasting with Cullan the smith, Cuchullin taming the weird horses, Cuchullin hunting down in his chariot the herd of enchanted deer, whose horns and hoofs are of iron, belong in nothing to our labouring noontide, but wholly to the shadowy morning twilight of time.

W. B. Yeats

Professor Dowden and Irish Literature—II

This letter is the product of two events. As an outgrowth of the Dowden controversy on Irish literature, Yeats wrote a letter to the *Dublin Daily Express* (printed on February 27, 1895), that contained a list of the thirty best Irish books (*Letters*, pp. 246–51). On February 28 the *Daily Express* printed a letter from D. F. Hannigan with a better list of thirty Irish books. Hannigan especially objected to the inclusion of six books by Standish O'Grady.

The other event was a debate at the Trinity College Historical Society, on February 27, 1895, on the motion "that the movement for the revival of Irish literature deserves our support." Dowden presided and the motion carried by a large majority. Dowden's remarks, generally sympathetic to the motion, were given in short summary in the *Dublin Daily Express* of February 28, 1895. A much more detailed account was given in the *Saturday Herald* on March 2, 1895.

In a letter in the *Daily Express*, March 9, 1895, Dowden said, "Mr. Yeats tilts against a windmill." Dowden claimed that the *Herald* account was the work of an auditor, not a reporter, and that his views had been distorted or misstated.

March 8, 1895

TO THE EDITOR OF THE *DAILY EXPRESS*

Sir—I should have replied before to my critics[1] but for my difficulty in finding out what the most important of them—Professor Dowden—did or did not say. The reports of his speech at "The Historical" which

---

[1] D. F. Hannigan, in a letter printed in the *Daily Express* on February 28, 1895, and Dowden.

I found in the morning papers[2] were too meagre to reply to. A friend
has, however, just sent me Saturday's Herald[3] with a full and manifestly
fair exposition of his argument. He began by accusing us of telling
people "to boycott English literature," and built up much elaborate
and irrelevant eloquence upon this absurd charge, and then, becoming
for a moment the serious critic we are accustomed to, gave an admirable
definition of an Irish national literature, and after making some comments on my list,[4] which showed, I cannot but think, less than his old
scrupulous accuracy, passed on to expound a list of his own. He said
that a national Irish literature "must be based on the old Celtic legends,
must come from the Celtic people of the country, must have the basis
and inspiration of race and racial tradition and must not and cannot be
divorced from the philosophy and influences of the Catholic religion."
With the obvious corrections, which Prof. Dowden will at once accept,
this Ireland is not wholly Celtic any more than England is wholly
Saxon, or wholly Catholic any more than England is wholly Protestant,
I agree with this definition, and affirm that it covers every book upon
my list. Are not "Beside the Fire," "The Coming of Cuchullin," and
"Fin and his Companions"[5] "based on the old Celtic literature and
legends?" Are not "the ballads and lyrics" of Mrs. Hinkson[6] "full of the
philosophy and influence and inspiration of the Catholic religion?"
Are not "Fardarougha the Miser," "The Nolans," and "Castle Rackrent"[7] informed with the inspiration of our "racial tradition?" On the
other hand, does his definition cover a single one of the books selected
from Ussher and Swift and Berkeley, which he desired us to consider
our national literature? He named none but admirable books, certainly,
but "Gulliver's Travels" and "Tristram Shandy" will be substitutes
for the books I have named only when the books of Hume are considered Scotch literature in the same sense as the books of Burns and
Barrie, or when the writings of Welshmen like Mr. George Meredith
and Mr. William Morris are thought as full of the spirit of Wales as the
triads of Taliesin. Professor Dowden must have been dreaming, or very
eloquent, which comes to much the same thing, or he would never have
included in the same speech so admirable a definition, so irrelevant a
list. He also stated that all Mr. Yates' [sic] books had been produced

[2] The *Daily Express* account on February 28 was very short.

[3] *Saturday Herald*, March 2, 1895.

[4] Yeats's list of the thirty best Irish books was contained in a letter to the *Daily Express*,
February 27, 1895.

[5] *Beside the Fire* is a collection of folk tales by Douglas Hyde. *The Coming of Cuculain* (not
"Cuchullin") and *Finn* (not "Fin") *and his Companions* are a retelling of bardic tales by
Standish O'Grady.

[6] Mrs. Hinkson was better known by her maiden name, Katharine Tynan.

[7] *Fardarougha the Miser* is a novel by William Carleton. John Banim wrote the novel
The Nolans and Maria Edgeworth wrote *Castle Rackrent*.

during the present century, and founded upon this supposed fact some argument which the reporter appears to have forgotten. If he referred to the print and paper, or even to the editor's comment and the like, he was accurate; but if he referred, as I think he must, to the contents, inaccurate, for "Beside the Fire," "The Love Songs of Connaught," and the "Silva Gadelica,"[8] a collection of many books under our ample cover, are translations of stories and verses all older than this century and some of great antiquity. I could, as Professor Dowden must have known, have added indefinitely to these translations, but translations are seldom satisfactory literature. By insisting on the modernness of the works I named, he wished I suppose, to show that Irish literature grew from a shallow soil, and yet it is obvious that the literature of a country which has recently changed its language must be very modern. I have now, I think, dealt with every argument of Professor Dowden's which was quoted in the Press, and I have done so, because it is important to show that "our acknowledged authority" brings to a merely Irish literary matter something less than that careful logic, that scrupulous[9] accuracy, that sympathetic understanding, which he brings to all English literary questions; in fact that he is no authority at all when he speaks of Irish verse or Irish legend, but a partisan ready to seize upon any argument which promises a momentary victory. He has indeed made that fatal mistake which critics who have more knowledge than impulse are ever prone to, he has set himself upon the side of academic tradition in that eternal war which it wages on the creative spirit.

Others object to my giving six books of Mr Standish O'Grady's,[10] and would have me set Haverty's "History of Ireland," Lefanu's novels, or Griffin's verses[11] in their place. I could do no other than give Mr O'Grady the lion's share, because his books have affected one more powerfully than those of any other Irish writer, and I know of no other criticism than a candid impressionism. I believe them to be ideal books of their kind, books of genius, but even if they were not, they would still contain more of ancient legend and circumstance than any other.— Yours, &c,

W. B. Yeats.

[8] *The Love Songs of Connacht* (not "Connaught") was a collection of folk poems translated by Douglas Hyde. *Silva Gadelica* was a collection of translations from the Gaelic by Standish Hayes O'Grady.
[9] *scrupulous*: *Daily Express* printing read "scrupulousness."
[10] D. F. Hannigan had so objected.
[11] Yeats refers to Martin Haverty's *History of Ireland, Ancient and Modern*, the novels of Joseph Sheridan Le Fanu, and the poems of Gerald Griffin.

An Excellent Talker

Yeats's review of *A Woman of No Importance*, a comedy by Oscar Wilde, London, 1894, appeared in the *Bookman* issue of March, 1895.

After a brief period of friendship in 1888–1889, Yeats and Wilde ceased to be close friends. Wilde regarded the Rhymers' Club, especially when it met at the Cheshire Cheese, as too bohemian.

Yeats never reviewed the early works of Wilde, which he admired. In his review of *Lord Arthur Savile's Crime and Other Stories* (*United Ireland*, September 26, 1891) Yeats looked, as he did in the present review, to a better Wilde, the author of *The Picture of Dorian Gray* and the essays collected in *Intentions*.

This review appeared shortly before the scandal that resulted in Wilde's imprisonment. In his autobiography, Yeats expressed his admiration of Wilde's decision to remain in England and face the vengeance of society.

MR. PATER once said that Mr. Oscar Wilde wrote like an excellent talker,[1] and the criticism goes to the root. All of 'The Woman of no Importance' [*sic*] which might have been spoken by its author, the famous paradoxes, the rapid sketches of men and women of society, the mockery of most things under heaven, are delightful; while, on the other hand, the things which are too deliberate in their development, or too vehement and elaborate for a talker's inspiration, such as the plot, and the more tragic and emotional characters, do not rise above the general level of the stage. The witty or grotesque persons who flit about the hero and heroine, Lord Illingworth, Mrs. Allonby, Canon Daubeney,[2] Lady Stutfield, and Mr. Kelvil, all, in fact, who can be characterised by a sentence or a paragraph, are real men and women; and the most immoral among them have enough of the morality of self-control and self-possession to be pleasant and inspiriting memories. There is something of heroism in being always master enough of one-self to be witty; and therefore the public of to-day feels with Lord Illingworth and Mrs. Allonby much as the public of yesterday felt, in a certain sense, with that traditional villain of melodrama who never laid aside his cigarette and his sardonic smile. The traditional villain had self-control. Lord Illingworth and Mrs. Allonby have self-control and intellect; and to have these things is to have wisdom, whether you obey it or not. "The soul is born old, but grows young. That is the comedy of life. And the body is born young and grows old. That is

---

[1] Walter Pater said this in his review of *The Picture of Dorian Gray*, printed in the November, 1891, issue of the *Bookman*.

[2] *Daubeney*: in Wilde's play this character's name is spelled "Daubeny."

life's tragedy."[3] Women "worship successes," and "are the laurels to hide their baldness." "Children begin by loving their parents. After a time they judge them. Rarely if ever do they forgive them." And many another epigram, too well known to quote, rings out like the voice of Lear's fool over a mad age. And yet one puts the book down with disappointment. Despite its qualities, it is not a work of art, it has no central fire, it is not dramatic in any ancient sense of the word. The reason is that the tragic and emotional people, the people who are important to the story, Mrs. Arbuthnot, Gerald Arbuthnot, and Hester Worsley, are conventions of the stage. They win our hearts with no visible virtue, and though intended to be charming and good and natural, are really either heady and undistinguished, or morbid with what Mr. Stevenson has called "the impure passion of remorse." The truth is, that whenever Mr. Wilde gets beyond those inspirations of an excellent talker which served him so well in 'The Decay of Lying' and in the best parts of 'Dorian Grey' [sic], he falls back upon the popular conventions, the spectres and shadows of the stage.

W. B. Yeats

The Thirty Best Irish Books

This letter was in reply to criticism in the March 9, 1895, issue of *United Ireland* in which Yeats's list of the thirty best Irish books was reprinted from the *Daily Express*. See p. 351 for further clarification of this imbroglio In this same issue appeared D. F. Hannigan's alternate list of thirty best Irish books. That list had already appeared in the *Dublin Daily Express* of February 28, 1895. It is no wonder that by the end of this decade Yeats developed a hatred of such lists. His longest list, printed in the *Bookman*, October, 1895, still lay ahead of him.

[March 16, 1895]

TO THE EDITOR OF *UNITED IRELAND*

DEAR SIR—I perfectly agree with you about the unwisdom of including an unpublished book in a list of "The Best Thirty Irish Books." The fact is that I saw "advanced sheets" of Dr. Hyde's "Story of Early Gaelic Literature" some little time ago, and when writing my

---

[3] Not only "life's tragedy," but, one is tempted to add, the burden of "Sailing to Byzantium" and much of Yeats's later poetry.

letter to the *Express*[1] was deceived by a paragraph in the papers into the belief that it was already out. The historical section of my list is, as you say, rather meagre, but is less eccentric when read with the explanatory comment. Had I not avowedly excluded all books of strong political feeling, and all books which are neither works of imagination, or books of research, helping one to understand the imaginations of Ireland, it would probably have been as follows—

Lecky's "History of Ireland in the Eighteenth Century."
O'Grady's "Red Hugh"[2] and "Story of Ireland."
Joyce's "Short History of Ireland."
Bagwell's "Ireland under the Tudors."
Mitchel's "Jail Journal."
Wolfe Tone's "Autobiography."

You make no comment on the poetic section, but will permit me to say that I omit some of the best of our poets merely because the editions of their poems are too uncritical to rank among our best books. I trouble you with this letter because I would rather be held possessed by any fiend, even by "Modo" or "Mahu," than by "the foul fiend Flibberti-gibbert [*sic*]."[3]

Yours truly, W. B. Yeats.

Dublin Mystics

This review from the *Bookman* of May, 1895, deals with the second edition of A.E.'s *Homeward Songs by the Way*, 1895, and an American pirated edition, with additional poems, issued by T. B. Mosher, Portland, Maine, 1895, as well as John Eglinton's *Two Essays on the Remnant*, Dublin, 1895. Yeats had reviewed the first printing of *Homeward Songs by the Way* in the *Bookman* issue of April, 1894. To John O'Leary, Yeats had promised to organize a reception of A.E.'s book, and he was faithful to his word.

John Eglinton was the pen name of W. K. Magee, a member with A.E. of the Dublin Theosophical Society. In 1898 Yeats became involved with Eglinton in a newspaper controversy on the question of whether the ancient Irish myths were suitable subjects for the dramas of the Irish Literary Theatre. The articles of Yeats and Eglinton as well as contributions of A.E.

[1] Yeats's list was in a letter in the *Dublin Daily Express*, printed on February 27, 1895. It is reprinted in *Letters*, pp. 246–47.

[2] Standish O'Grady's *Red Hugh's Captivity*, London, 1889.

[3] *King Lear*, Act IV, Scene 1: "Bless thee, good man's son, from the foul fiend! Five fiends have been in poor Tom at once; . . . Mahu, of stealing; Modo, of murder; Flibber-tigibbet, of mopping and mowing, who since possesses chambermaids and waiting women. . . ." (quoted from G. L. Kittredge edition, New York, 1958).

and William Larminie were reprinted in a pamphlet entitled *Literary Ideals in Ireland*. Eglinton was for many years assistant librarian of the National Library of Ireland, where one may observe him in the "Scylla and Charybdis" section of Joyce's *Ulysses*, discussing Shakespeare with A.E. and Stephen Dedalus.

Yeats selected passages from Eglinton's prose for a collection printed by the Dun Emer press in 1905. Eglinton's account of Yeats appeared in *Irish Literary Portraits*, London, 1935, a book wherein Eglinton was generous to his subjects, even to Edward Dowden.

THE success of these little books is certainly one of the significant things in the imaginative awakening of our time. 'Homeward: Songs by the Way' [*sic*] has been reprinted in America in an edition of 975 copies, as well as running into its second five hundred at home; while 'Two Essays on the Remnant,' though published much later, is already in its second edition. Yet both books bear the imprint of an unknown publisher, and are issued in a city which has long published little but school-books and prayer-books, and both are full of unfamiliar ideas. They owe their success to a kind of charm rare in an age when artists and writers obey only too much the command of the Elizabethan painter who bade his pupils grind the whole world into paint. One feels that the thoughts they contain were thought out for their own sake, and not for the sake of literature; that their writers could become silent to-morrow without a pang, and that their silence would be no mere refuge from thought, no mere laying down of a burden. Other writers may celebrate life and joy and love, or set their hearts on fame, or in the sheer delight of writing, but these men write to hearten the pilgrims to the eternal city, and to keep them from forgetting the day A.E. sings of:

> "*When the shepherd of the Ages draws his misty herds[1] away*
> *Through the glimmering deeps to silence, and within the awful fold*
> *Life and joy and love for ever vanish as a tale is told.*"

A.E. is always the visionary and the poet, and like all purely creative forces, is unanalysable and incalculable; but John Eglington [*sic*] is none the less a theorist and a thinker because he wraps his theories and his thoughts in sentences which are rich and elaborate as old embroidery. We live, he tells us, at a period when we must "perpetuate the onward impulse in our own individual lives," or "content ourselves with maintaining a decadent literature, art and science";[2] and his book is a passionate and lofty appeal to the "idealists" to come out of the modern world as the children of Israel came out of Egypt. His appeal is no mere literary method of giving weight and emphasis to his subtle criticisms

[1] *herds*: A.E. reads "hordes." [2] *science*: *Bookman* printing reads "sience."

of men and books, for it is born of the influence and doctrines of a little group of men and women who have been for years living the life he preaches, as best they can under modern disabilities, and setting themselves in "league," as he would have them, "with the green hosts³ of trees" "and the countless horde of grass that springs in the breaches of ruins and in the interstices of depopulate pavements."

W. B. Yeats

The Story of Early Gaelic Literature

This review of *The Story of Early Gaelic Literature* by Douglas Hyde, London, 1895, from the *Bookman*, June, 1895, marks a parting of the ways for Yeats and Hyde. Yeats had enthusiastically greeted Hyde's earlier works of folklore, but he had ever been suspicious of the nationalism inherent in Hyde's efforts to revive the Gaelic language. By 1895 Yeats seems to have realized that the scholar and linguist in Hyde had overwhelmed whatever there had been of the imaginative artist in him. Yeats does not mention it, but this volume was from the New Irish Library. For personal reasons, Yeats usually had a negative reaction to this series. See letters above on the New Irish Library controversy (September, 1892), pp. 249-44.

D R. DOUGLAS HYDE is probably the most successful of all that little group of men of letters who are trying to interest the Irish people in their history and literature. His lectures in English to the National Literary Society and in Gaelic to "The Gaelic League" have had the most extraordinary effect in awakening interest in the Irish language. In towns where three or four years ago there was not a single Gaelic-speaking person there are now hundreds, and the movement is growing every day. The present book is probably intended as a textbook for these groups of enthusiasts; and though too full of exposition and appeal to have the haunting charm of the 'Connaught Love Songs,'¹ and too full of crowded facts to touch the imagination like 'Beside the Fire,'² it is certainly moving and excellently readable. It describes the great legend cycles, the mythological, the Cuchullain, the Fenian, and discusses the views, as to their antiquity and origin, held by Nutt,

---

³ *hosts*: *Bookman* printing reads "hostes."
¹ *The Love Songs of Connacht*, a collection of folk poetry translated by Douglas Hyde.
² *Beside the Fire*, a translation of Gaelic folk tales by Douglas Hyde, Dublin, 1890.

Rhys, Joubainville,[3] and others, in short but sufficient chapters. In the great controversy which divides Irish scholars as to whether Finn and Cuchullain, their friends and their followers, their battles and their huntings, are legend coloured by history or history coloured by legend, Dr. Hyde throws in his lot with those who hold them historical in the main; and this choice seems to an obstinate upholder of the other theory but a part of the one capital defect of his criticism. He is so anxious to convince his little groups of enthusiasts of the historical importance of the early Irish writings, of the value to modern learning of the fragments of ancient customs which are mixed up with their romance, that he occasionally seems to forget the noble phantasy and passionate drama which is their crowning glory. He does not notice at all, for instance, "The Death of Cuchullin," which is among the greatest things of all legendary literature; and gives an entire chapter to "The Feast of Brian," which is among the least; and all because "Posidonius, who was a friend of Cicero, and wrote some hundred years before Christ, mentions that there was a custom in Gaul"[4] which is also in "The Feast." This defect is probably caused to some extent by the traditions of Irish learning which are hopelessly dry-as-dust, but if our own profoundly imaginative Irish scholar cannot throw off the ancient chains we are indeed lost.

W. B. Yeats

Irish National Literature, I: From Callanan to Carleton

This article is the first of four pieces on Irish national literature which Yeats contributed to the *Bookman* from July to October, 1895. They represent the most extended critical exposition of the Irish literary movement of which Yeats was the leader, and the most concerted effort on Yeats's part to place that movement in the perspective of past Irish literature.

Yeats wanted to have these articles preserved in more permanent form. He wrote to the publisher T. Fisher Unwin on November 3, 1895:

I have been so busy that I have only just found time to find and tear out the articles on Irish Literature which I want you to publish in a pamphlet under

---

[3] Alfred Nutt was a writer and publisher of folklore. John Rhys wrote *Lectures on the Origin and Growth of Religion as Illustrated by Celtic Heathendom*, London, 1888. H. D'Arbois de Jubainville was Professor of Celtic at the Collège de France. Among his many important books, one, *The Irish Mythological Cycle and Celtic Mythology*, was translated into English and published in Dublin in 1903.   [4] Hyde wrote "that there was a custom at that time in Gaul."

the title *What to Read in Irish Literature.* When I have restored certain quotations cut out by the *Bookman* people for lack of space, and written half a
dozen pages or so of introduction on the relation of such literature to general
literature and culture and to contemporary movements, there should be
material enough for a decent shilling's worth. (*Letters*, p. 258.)

The proposal came to nothing. The only subsequent use of these articles was
the reprinting of the opening paragraphs of the second and third articles in
Ideas of Good and Evil.

In this same year Yeats's other attempt to mold the Anglo-Irish literary
past was his *Book of Irish Verse*, which was, as he said in his introduction,
". . . intended only a little for English readers, and not at all for Irish
peasants. . . ." The first article in the present series molded the Irish literary
past by omitting the Anglo-Irish Augustans—Swift, Berkeley, Burke—and
by attempting to diminish the importance and influence of the Young
Ireland movement of the 1840s. The remaining writers whom Yeats found
attractive—Callanan, Carleton, and John Mitchel—he liked for their rude
strength, evidence of a creative vitality which Yeats and his co-revivalists
wished to match with craftmanship in order to make a high art.

SOME of my countrymen include among national writers all writers
born in Ireland,[1] but I prefer, though it greatly takes from the
importance of our literature, to include only those who have written
under Irish influence and of Irish subjects. When once a country has
given perfect expression to itself in literature, has carried to maturity its
literary tradition, its writers, no matter what they write of, carry its
influence about with them, just as Carlyle remained a Scotsman when
he wrote of German kings or French revolutionists, and Shakespeare
an Elizabethan Englishman when he told of Coriolanus or of Cressida.
Englishmen and Scotsmen forget how much they owe to mature traditions of all kinds—traditions of feeling, traditions of thought, traditions
of expression—for they have never dreamed of a life without these
things. They write or paint or think or feel, and believe they do so to
please no taste but their own, while in reality they obey rules and
instincts which have been accumulating for centuries; their wine of life
has been mellowed in ancient cellars, and they see but the ruby light
in the glass. In a new country like Ireland—and English-speaking
Ireland is very new—we are continually reminded of this long ripening
by the immaturity of the traditions about us; if we are writers, for
instance, we find it takes longer to learn to write than it takes an
Englishman, and the more resolute we are to express the national
character, and the more we understand the impossibility of putting our
new wine into old bottles, the longer is our struggle with the trivial,

[1] Edward Dowden, in a controversy the previous winter, had claimed a place in Irish
literature for Archbishop Ussher, Sterne, Swift, and Berkeley.

the incoherent, the uncomely. A young Englishman of little knowledge or power may write with considerable skill and perfect good taste before he leaves his university, while an Irishman of greater power and knowledge will go through half his life piling up in the one heap the trivial and the memorable, the incoherent and the beautiful, the commonplace and the simple.

The Irish national writers who have bulked largest in the past have been those who, because they served some political cause which could not wait, or had not enough of patience in themselves, turned away from the unfolding and developing of an Irish tradition, and borrowed the mature English methods of utterance and used them to sing of Irish wrongs or preach of Irish purposes. Their work was never quite satisfactory, for what was Irish in it looked ungainly in an English garb, and what was English was never perfectly mastered, never wholly absorbed into their being. The most famous of these men was Thomas Moore, who quenched an admirable Celtic lyricism in an artificial glitter learned from the eighteenth century; the most noble was Thomas Davis, who borrowed a manner from Macaulay and Scott and Lockhart, and with this strange help sang "a new soul into Ireland"; and the most inspired was John Mitchel, who thundered from his convict hulk a thunder that was half Carlyle's against England and the gods of his master. These were the most influential Irish voices of the first half of the century, and their influence was not at all the less because they had not a native style, for the one made himself wings out of the ancient Gaelic music, and the other two were passionate orators, expounding opinions which were none the less true because the utterance was alien; and not poets or romance-writers, priests of those Immortal Moods[2] which are the true builders of nations, the secret transformers of the world, and need a subtle, appropriate language or a minute, manifold knowledge for their revelation. John Mitchel, by the right of his powerful nature and his penal solitude, communed indeed with the Great Gods, now as always none other than the Immortal Moods, and set down his communings in that marvellous "Jail Journal,"[3] but he could give them no lengthy or perfect devotion, for he belonged to his cause, to his opinions, to his oratories.

> *"A dreamer born,*
> *Who with a mission to fulfil,*
> *   Left the muses' haunts to turn*
> *   The crank of an opinion mill."*

[2] Yeats explained this doctrine of the "Immortal Moods" in the second of this series of articles.

[3] Mitchel wrote his jail journal in British convict hulks to which he was sentenced for sedition in 1848. In 1853 he escaped to America, where the journal was published in 1854.

Meanwhile Callanan, a wastrel who wandered from place to place, from trade to trade, and was now a schoolmaster, now a common soldier, had begun, or rather had expressed for the first time in English, the traditions which have moulded nearly all of modern Irish literature. While Moore's sentimental trivialities were in their first fame, he printed in Irish periodicals four translations from the Gaelic of great simplicity and charm, "The Outlaw of Loch Lene," a wild love song like those in Dr. Hyde's 'Connaught Love Songs'; "The Convict of Clonmel," the lament of a peasant condemned to death for some unknown offence; "The Dirge of O'Sullivan Bere,"[4] a fragment of barbaric cursing; and "Felix M'Carthy," the complaining of an old man whose children have been killed by the fall of a house. It is very difficult to describe the peculiar quality of these verses, for their quality is a new colour, a new symbol, rather than a thing of thought or form. Despite their constant clumsiness and crudity, they brought into the elaborate literature of the modern world the cold vehemence, the arid definiteness, the tumultuous movement, the immeasurable dreaming of the Gaelic literature. Generations may pass by before this tradition is mature enough in the new tongue for any to measure its full importance, but its importance to Ireland needed and needs no measuring.

Callanan was followed immediately by other translators, of whom Edward Walsh, a village schoolmaster, was the best, and these in turn by countless ballad-writers, who combined a little of Gaelic manner with a deal of borrowed rhetoric, and created that interesting, unsatisfying, pathetic movement which we call in Ireland "the poetry of Young Ireland." This movement, if we leave out one or two patriotic songs like "The Memory of the Dead," a few love songs like "The Marriage," and a single poignant lament over the failure of the rebellion called "Cashla Gal Mo Chre,"[5] was of little literary importance, but it helped to build up an audience for four important poets—Mr. Aubrey De Vere, William Allingham, Clarence Mangan, and Sir Samuel Ferguson. Mr. Aubrey De Vere has more often written under English than Irish influence, but the most desirable of his poems are those in which the immature tradition of Callanan and the ancient poets, modified and expanded to express the moods and passions that interest men to-day, has taken the place of the grave, impersonal Wordsworthian manner in which he tells of English kings and Saxon saints. William Allingham has written out in verse full of emotional subtlety and intellectual simplicity the customs and accidents of his native Ballyshannon.

---

[4] *Bere*: in Callanan's title the word is spelled "Bear."

[5] "A Cushla Gal Mo Chree" (Bright Vein of my Heart) by Michael Doheney (1805–1863).

"A wild West coast, a little town
Where little folk go up and down,[6]
Human will and human fate,
What is little, what is great,
Howso'er the answer be,
Let me sing of what I know."

In him for the first time the slowly ripening tradition reached a perfect utterance; and the Immortal Moods, which are so impatient of rhetoric, so patient of mere immaturity, found in his poetry the one perfect ritual fashioned for their honour by Irish hands. The most perfect, but not the most passionate or most powerful, for the most passionate was made by Clarence Mangan, that strange visionary, ruined by drink and narcotics, who wrought some half-dozen lyrics of indescribable, vehement beauty; and the most powerful by Sir Samuel Ferguson, who has retold so many ancient tales of Deirdre, of Conary, of Concobar, of the "Tain Bo,"[7] that younger Ireland believes him, and I think rightly, the most Irish of poets. At his worst he is monotonous in cadence and clumsy in language; at his best a little like Homer in his delight in savage strength, in tumultuous action, in overshadowing doom. He had no deliberate art, and the tradition is often very immature in him, but in his moments of inspiration he is full of massy strength or tranquil beauty.

"A plenteous place is Ireland for hospitable cheer,
Uileacan dubh O![8]
Where the wholesome fruit is bursting from the yellow barley ear;
Uileacan dubh O!
There is honey in the trees when[9] *her misty vales expand,*
And her forest paths in summer are by falling waters fanned;
There is dew at high noontide there, and springs i' the yellow sand,
On the fair hills of holy Ireland."

The tradition expressed by these poets was that of the bards and the Gaelic ballad-writers, but there was still another tradition, another expression of the same dominant moods, that which was embodied in the customs of the poor, their wakes, their hedge-schools, their factions, their weddings, their habits of thought and feeling, and this could best be described in prose. Miss Edgeworth had called up for a moment this ancient life in the mournful humour of Thady Quirk,[10] but it was not until the brothers Banim and William Carleton began to write that it

---

[6] Yeats omits two lines after this one: "Tides flow and winds blow:/Night and Tempest and the Sea, . . ."
[7] *Táin Bó Cúailgne: The Cattle Raid of Cooley*, Irish epic of the seventh or eighth century.
[8] The refrain means "O sad lament!"   [9] *when*: Ferguson's poem reads "where."
[10] Thady Quirk is the old family servant who is Maria Edgeworth's narrator in *Castle Rackrent*.

found adequate historians. Michael Banim was excellent in much of "Father Connell," and John Banim in the first half of "The Nolans," and in the opening chapters of "Crohore of the Billhook,"[11] and at odd moments in all his books; but only Carleton, born and bred a peasant, was able to give us a vast multitude of grotesque, pathetic, humorous persons, misers, pig-drivers, drunkards, schoolmasters, labourers, priests, madmen, and to fill them all with an abounding vitality. He was but half articulate, half emerged from Mother Earth, like one of Milton's lions,[12] but his wild Celtic melancholy gives to whole pages of "Fardarougha"[13] and of "The Black Prophet" an almost spiritual grandeur. The forms of life he described, like those described with so ebullient a merriment by his contemporary Lever, passed away with the great famine, but the substance which filled those forms is the substance of Irish life, and will flow into new forms which will resemble them as one wave of the sea resembles another. In future times men will recognise that he was at his best a true historian, the peasant Chaucer of a new tradition, and that at his worst he fell into melodrama, more from imperfect criticism than imperfect inspiration. In his time only a little of Irish history, Irish folk-lore, Irish poetry had been got into the English tongue; he had to dig the marble for his statue out of the mountain side with his own hands, and the statue shows not seldom the clumsy chiselling of the quarryman. W. B. Yeats

The Three Sorrows of Story-telling

This unsigned review of *The Three Sorrows of Story-Telling, and Ballads of Columkille*, translated by Douglas Hyde, London, 1895, is from the *Bookman*, July, 1895. Allan Wade in his bibliography attributed it to Yeats.

THE stories known traditionally by this name are "Deirdre," "The Children of Lir," and "The Fate of the Children of Tuireann." Dr. Hyde has put them into verse to make them popularly known as they once were in Gaelic-speaking lands. His is by no means the first attempt. Dr. Joyce included two of them in his "Old Celtic Romances," and his brother[1] wrote a metrical version of "Deirdre." We can find them also in Mr. Jacobs' "Celtic Fairy Tales."[2] There is an obvious

---

[11] The titles of these novels are *The Nowlans* and *Crohoore of the Billhook*.
[12] *Paradise Lost*: VII, 463–65.   [13] *Bookman* printed "Fardaroughu."
[1] Robert Dwyer Joyce. Yeats wrote a two-part article on this Joyce for the *Irish Fireside* (November 27 and December 4, 1886). See pp. 104–14 above.
[2] *Celtic Fairy Tales*, selected and edited by Joseph Jacobs, London, 1891.

advantage in setting them, for popular reading, to metre; and of all the popular versions Dr. Hyde's seems to us, on the whole, the best. Our first feeling on reading them was irritation, but second thoughts modified that. Perhaps he knew what he was about in treating them in the style he has done. A failure in any high poetic attempt, or a miss in the endeavour to express more nearly their native Celtic spirit, would have landed him in obscurities or unfamiliarities which the English reader would have laughed or yawned over. Whether or not he was right in thinking such an attempt on his part would have ended in failure, we are not assured. The translator of "Connacht Love-Songs"[3] is a great deal more of a poet than anyone would guess, judging him from the metrical stories before us. But, at least the simplicity he has aimed at and achieved, the very want of ambition in his rendering—one might almost say, were it not gross ingratitude, the laziness that has left them as they are—have ended in their being models of clearness. The English mind, and what is much to the purpose, the English child's mind, will grasp these stories in their present form with easy understanding, may guess little of their mystic glamour, but cannot fail to recognise in the bare outlines the great beauty and the tragedy. There are passages of fine vigour in Dr. Hyde's version—it is far less lumbering and prosaic than Dr. Joyce's. The coming home of Brian and his brothers, all the tasks of the eric[4] accomplished, but with Death at their hearts as they near the coast of Erin and the hill of high Ben Edar, is told with much dignity. And to the beauty of Deirdre's death-song he has done no wrong.

> "*The cluster all is fallen, and I am left*,[5]
> *The fibres snap that hold me; thus I shake*
> *And tremble fast upon the withered stem*,
> *And quit my hold upon it—see, I fall*
> *Down from this cold and dismal bough of life.*"

And where the stories go clumsily along, it is but well to remember that Dr. Hyde confidingly tells in his preface that two of them were sent to press in mistake for another manuscript.

With all due allowances, then, let us accept gratefully what we have got, one more lucid, popular version of these legends. But it stirs a longing for what we have not. "Deirdre," "The Children of Lir," and "The Children of Tuireann" are three of the most beautiful stories in the whole world. Interfered with, patched, and mangled as they may

[3] *The Love Songs of Connacht*, which Yeats reviewed in the *Bookman*, October, 1893 (see p. 292 above).

[4] An eric was a fine paid by the ancient Irish as compensation for a homicide. Brian and the other sons of Tuireann perform heroic tasks as payment to Lugh for the slaying of his father, Cian.

[5] This passage begins with the line "I am the lonely apple on the tree, . . ."

have been, they have even now a central wholeness, and a haunting melancholy loveliness that is their very own. "Deirdre" is one of the many legends of princesses shut up in lonely towers on account of a prophecy that they will bring hurt to those they consort with. "The Children of Lir" is of the great family of transformation legends; and the "Children of Tuireann," with their burden of tasks, have as numerous a kin in folk-lore. But they keep their own tragic complexion. For the Celtic fairy-story has this distinction, that, removed as it is far from the region of average human habitation, remote, ethereal, and, other peoples say, too often inhuman, yet no other has so sternly dared to face inexorable human fate—sorrow, decay, and death. Beauty, valour, pure happiness, are all with Deirdre, but she and hers are conquered by the strong hand of the wicked. After ages of wandering and suffering, the swan-children of Lir gain back their human shape, but with it the feebleness and the palsy of old age, and at the touch of the holy water they drop dead. All the impossible tasks of the eric are fulfilled by Brian and his brethren; their fulfillment has been bought by death, and they come home great matchless heroes, but doomed. With Death alone they cannot fight. Here are high themes for high imaginations. But as yet they wander lost in unhappy transformation like Lir's children. Where is the spiritual poet who shall make these Three Sorrows fast in the world's great treasure-house?

Irish National Literature, II: Contemporary Prose Writers—Mr. O'Grady, Miss Lawless, Miss Barlow, Miss Hopper, and the Folk-Lorists

This is the second of Yeats's articles on Irish national literature; it appeared in the *Bookman*, August, 1895. Of all the literary genres, Yeats seems to have understood prose fiction least, and he had little success in writing it. As impresario of the literary revival, he had less success in calling forth novelists than poets or playwrights. (The greatest Irish prose writer was notably hostile to him and the movement.) This article reflects Yeats's discontent and impatience with Irish prose writers of that decade, but, as a good propagandist, Yeats makes the best of his resources.

In the opening paragraph (later reprinted as "The Moods" in *Ideas of Good and Evil*), Yeats sets forth most extensively his doctrine of the immortal moods as the bearers, through literature, of a transcendental revelation. Yet, spiritual as it seems, the imaginative process is material—angels and demons rising and falling in a manner particularly Yeatsian. The doctrine is an amalgam of Yeats's readings in Jacob Boehme (assisted by Coleridge), Swedenborg, William Blake, and his own visions. We may blame or thank this theory for much of Yeats's poetry on the nineties, but the impulse to create "The Secret Rose" and "To the Rose upon the Rood of Time" may have been prior to theory and demanded in turn an aesthetic to justify the mannerism. In any case, this essay makes an abrupt descent from the divine moods to Standish O'Grady.

LITERATURE differs from explanatory and scientific writing in being wrought about a mood, or a community of moods, as the body is wrought about an invisible soul; and if it uses argument, theory, erudition, observation, and seems to grow hot in assertion or denial, it does so merely to make us partakers at the banquet of the moods. It seems to me that these moods are the labourers and messengers of the Ruler of All, the gods of ancient days still dwelling on their secret Olympus, the angels of more modern days ascending and descending upon their shining ladder; and that argument, theory, erudition, observation, are merely what Blake called "little devils who fight for themselves," illusions of our visible passing life, who must be made serve the moods, or we have no part in eternity. Everything that can be seen, touched, measured, explained, understood, argued over, is to the imaginative artist nothing more than a means, for he belongs to the invisible life, and delivers its ever new and ever ancient revelation. We hear much of his need for the restraints of reason, but the only restraint he can obey is the mysterious instinct that has made him an artist, and that teaches him to discover immortal moods in mortal desires, an undecaying hope in our trivial ambitions, a divine love in sexual passion.

The writer of history or very historical romance can never perhaps be wholly an imaginative artist, for he must reason and compare and argue about mere accidents and chances, and so be bound upon the wheel of mortality; but if he reason and compare and argue only, he belongs to those who record and not to those who reveal, to science and not to literature, for none but the Divine Brotherhood can tell him how men loved and sorrowed, and what things are memorable and what things are alms for oblivion.

Ireland has but one historian who is anything of an artist, Mr. Standish O'Grady, and multifarious knowledge of Gaelic legend and Gaelic history and a most Celtic temperament have put him in communion with the moods that have been over Irish purposes from the hour when, in the words put into the mouth of St. Dionysius,[1] "The

[1] Yeats means the mystical writer, Dionysius the Pseudo-Areopagite (c. 500).

Most High set the borders of the Nations according to the angels of God." His "History of Ireland: Heroic Period," which was published in 1878, has done more than anything else to create that preoccupation with Irish folk-lore and legend and epic which is called the Irish literary movement. Ferguson had indeed been long busy with Irish folk-lore and legend and epic, but almost wholly in detached ballads, and always with an old-fashioned rigour of style which repels readers accustomed to the deep colour and emotional cadence of modern literature; but this book retold nearly every great legend, and traced the links that bound them one to another in a chaotic but vehement and lyrical prose. Every character was full of passion to the lips, and half a savage and half a god, like those persons whom the ancients celebrated in the stars, Boötes, Arcturus, the hunter Orion, and their innumerable comrades; and Celtic as the heroes of MacPherson's [*sic*] 'Ossian,'[2] with the something added that made them Irish also; and love tales and battle tales that had long been the prey of Dr. Dry-as-Dust and his pupils, started up clothed in the colour and music of a temperament which needed only a passion for precision of phrase and for delicacy of cadence to be the temperament of the great poets. Since then he has retold separate legends and groups of legend with more detail in 'Fin and his Companions,' his masterpiece, and in 'The Coming of Cuchullin,'[3] the beautiful but unequal opening of an epic in prose. He has also written a most vivid little book of Elizabethan tales and historical fragments called 'The Bog of Stars,' which has had a considerable success in Ireland, and among the Irish in England; 'Red Hugh's Captivity,'[4] the only historical book about Elizabethan Ireland which is more than dates and dialectics; and 'The Story of Ireland,' an impressionist narrative of Irish affairs from the coming of the gods to the death of Parnell, which has aroused acrimonious controversy, and is still something of a byword, for Ireland is hardly ready for impressionism, above all for a whimsical impressionism which respects no traditional hatred or reverence, which exalts Cromwell and denounces the saints, and is almost persuaded that when Parnell was buried, as when Columba died, "the sky was alight with strange lights and flames." In Ireland we are accustomed to histories with great parade of facts and dates, of wrongs and precedents, for use in the controversies of the hour; and here was a man who let some all-important Act of Parliament (say) go by without a mention, or with perhaps inaccurate mention, and for no better reason

[2] Perhaps not the best comparison, considering the doubts cast upon the authenticity of Macpherson's *Ossian*.

[3] *Finn and His Companions* and *The Coming of Cuculain*. Yeats reviewed the latter in the *Bookman*, February, 1895 (see p. 350).

[4] This book was reissued in 1897 as *The Flight of the Eagle* and Yeats reviewed it in the *Bookman*, August, 1897.

than because it did not interest him, and who recorded with careful vividness some moment of abrupt passion, some fragment of legendary beauty, and for no better reason than because it did interest him profoundly. "The effect" of his books, as Mill said of Michelet's 'History of France,' "is not acquiescence, but stir and ferment,"[5] and I disagree with his conclusions too constantly, and see the armed hand of nationality in too many places where he but sees the clash of ancient with modern institutions, to believe that he has written altogether the true history of Ireland; but I am confident that, despite his breathless generalisations, his slipshod style, his ungovernable likings and dislikings, he is the first man who has tried to write it, for he is the first to have written not mainly of battles and enactments, but of changing institutions and changing beliefs, of the pride of the wealthy and the long endurance "of the servile tribes of ignoble countenance."

Miss Lawless[6] is probably, like Mr. Standish O'Grady, on the unpopular side in Irish politics, but, unlike Mr. O'Grady, is in imperfect sympathy with the Celtic nature, and has accepted the commonplace conception of Irish character as a something charming, irresponsible, poetic, dreamy, untrustworthy, voluble, and rather despicable, and the commonplace conception of English character as a something prosaic, hard, trustworthy, silent, and altogether worshipful, and the result is a twofold slander. This bundle of half-truths made her describe the Irish soldiers, throughout 'Essex in Ireland,' as a savage, undisciplined, ragged horde, in the very teeth of Raleigh's letters, which prove them among the best armed and best disciplined in Europe; and made her in 'Grania' magnify a peasant type which exists here and there in Ireland, and mainly in the extreme west, into a type of the whole nation; and in 'Maelcho' set before us for a typical Englishman the absolute genius of exemplary dulness and triumphant boredom; and it fetters her imagination continually, and comes between her and any clear understanding of Irish tradition. Despite her manifest sincerity and her agile intellect, one would perhaps pass her by with but few words, did she not escape from her theory of England and Ireland when she describes visions and visionaries, as in the chapter upon the rise of the dead multitudes in 'Essex in Ireland,' and in the description of the chaunting of Cormac Cass in 'Maelcho,' though there is nothing of Ireland in the chaunt that he makes; and in the madness of Maelcho and in his last days in the

[5] John Stuart Mill reviewed Michelet's *History of France* in the *Edinburgh Review*, January, 1844. The review was reprinted in *Dissertations and Discussions*, London, 1859, in volume two. Mill said, "Michelet's are not books to save a reader the trouble of thinking, but to make him boil over with thought. Their effect on the mind is not acquiescence, but stir and ferment."

[6] Emily Lawless (1845–1913) was a writer of poetry, novels, and historical studies. This essay contains Yeats's only extended comment on her.

cavern with the monks. There is a kind of greatness in these things, and if she can cast off a habit of mind which would compress a complex, incalculable, indecipherable nation into the mould of a theory invented by political journalists and forensic historians, she should have in her the makings of a great book, full of an arid and half spectral intensity.

The only contemporary Irish novelist who has anything of Miss Lawless's popularity is undoubtedly Miss Barlow,[7] and it were hard to imagine a greater contrast, for 'Irish Idylls,' 'Kerrigan's Quality,' and 'Maureen's Fairing' are without theory of any kind. She is master over the circumstances of peasant life, and has observed with a delighted care no Irish writer has equalled, the coming and going of hens and chickens on the door-step, the gossiping of old women over their tea, the hiding of children under the shadow of the thorn trees, the broken and decaying thatch of the cabins, and the great brown stretches of bogland; but seems to know nothing of the exultant and passionate life Carleton celebrated, or to shrink from its roughness and its tumult. Her labourers and potato diggers and potheen makers and cockle pickers are passive, melancholy, and gentle, while the real labourers and potato diggers and potheen makers and cockle pickers are often as not grim as their limestone walls, or fiery as a shaken torch.

Miss Nora Hopper[8] is the latest of Irish romance writers, and the one absolute dreamer of Irish literature. Mr. O'Grady is interested in heroic and ungovernable men; Miss Lawless in theories about character and in visions elaborated out of character; Miss Barlow in a poor who are half observed, and half fashioned out of her own gentleness and benevolence; but Miss Hopper is only interested in so much of life as you can see in a wizard's glass. She has less strength than those whose interests are more earthy, but more delicacy of cadence and precision of phrase, a more perfect lyric temperament. Her little book, 'Ballads in Prose,' has the beauty of a dim twilight, and one praises it with hardly a reservation, except perhaps that here and there is too much of filmy vagueness, as in visions in the wizard's glass, before the mystical sweeper has swept the clouds away with his broom. The poetry is perhaps the better part, but my concern for the present is with the prose, and I have been haunted all the winter by "Daluan," "The Gifts of Aodh and Una," "The Four Kings," and "Aonan-na-Righ," and more than all by the sacrifice of Aodh in the temple of the heroes, that the land might be delivered from famine. "Then the door at which he was striving opened wide, and from the dark shrine swept out a cloud of fine grey dust. The door clanged to behind him, and he went up the

---

[7] Jane Barlow (1857–1917). Her best known work was *Irish Idylls* (1892).

[8] Yeats contributed a piece on Nora Hopper (1871–1906) to S. A. Brooke and T. W. Rolleston's *A Treasury of Irish Poetry*, London, first published in 1900.

aisle, walking ankle deep in the fine dust, and straining his eyes to see through the darkness if indeed figures paced beside him, and ghostly groups gave way before him, as he could not help but fancy. At last his outstretched hands touched a twisted horn of smooth cold substance, and he knew that he had reached the end of his journey. With his left hand clinging to the horn he turned towards the dark temple, saying aloud, 'Here I stand, Aodh, with gifts to give the Fianna and their gods. In the name of my mother's god, let them who desire my gifts come to me.' 'Aodh, son of Eochaidh,' a shivering voice cried out, 'give me thy youth.' 'I give,' Aodh said quietly. 'Aodh,' said another voice, reedy and thin, but sweet, 'give me thy knowledge. I, Grania, loved much and knew little.' There was a grey figure at his side, and without a word Aodh turned and laid his forehead on the ghost's cold breast. As he rested thus, another voice said, 'I am Oisin; give me thy death, O Aodh.' Aodh drew a deep breath, then he lifted his head, and clasped a ghostly figure in his arms, and holding it there, felt it stiffen and grow rigid and colder yet. 'Give me thy[9] hope, Aodh.' 'Give me thy faith, Aodh.' 'Give me thy courage, Aodh.' 'Give me thy dreams, Aodh.' So the voices called and cried, and to each Aodh[10] gave the desired gift. 'Give me thy[11] heart, Aodh,' cried another. 'I am Maive, who knew much and loved little,' and with a shrinking[12] sense of pain Aodh felt slender, cold fingers scratching and tearing their way through flesh and sinew till they grasped his heart, and tore the fluttering thing away. 'Give me thy love, Aodh,' another implored. 'I am Angus, Master of Love, and I have loved none.' 'Take it,' Aodh said faintly, and there was a pause. But soon the shivering voices began again, and the cold fingers clutched at his bare arms and feet, and the breath of ghostly lips played on his cheek as the cloudy figures came and went, and struggled and scrambled about him."

There are other Irish novelists of note, such as Mrs. Esler, who writes charmingly of Presbyterian life in Ulster, Mr. Frank Mathew, who has done excellent short stories and promises to do better, Mr. William O'Brien, who has written an able but inchoate political novel, Mr. Downey, who has done one piece of excellent fooling, the authors of "The Real Charlotte," who have described with unexampled grimness our middle-class life, Mrs. Hinkson, who has written a couple of books of kindly and picturesque sketches of Irish life and people,[13] and

---

[9] *thy*: *Ballads in Prose* reads "thine."

[10] *Ballads in Prose* reads "Aodh answered, and gave . . ."

[11] *thy*: *Ballads in Prose* reads "thine."

[12] *and with a shrinking*: In *Ballads in Prose*, "and" begins a new sentence, and it reads "sickening" instead of "shrinking."

[13] These authors are Erminda Esler (c. 1860–?); Frank Mathew (1865–1924); William O'Brien (1852–1928), author of *When We Were Boys* (1890); Edmund Downey (1856–1937),

various pleasant storytellers who are neither literature nor the promise
of literature, and one or two young men who have the promise but are
not yet pleasant storytellers. We have also a number of men of letters
busy with our history and folk-lore. One of these, Mr. Lecky, is so
famous that even if his methods were not those of historical science,
rather than of historical literature, and wholly apart from any Irish
tradition, it were useless to consider him here; another, Dr. Joyce,[14]
has written the most satisfactory of short Irish histories that are not in
the manner of literature, and a rather unsatisfactory book of 'Old Celtic
Romances' that is. Dr. Hyde, on the other hand, though at his worst he
is shapeless enough, is at his best an admirable artist, and the manner of
his 'Beside the Fire' is the ideal manner for a book of folk-lore, because
it is the manner of the peasants' talk by the glowing turf, and 'Teig
O'Kane,' which he has reshaped and made his own is nearly worthy
to be bound up with 'Wandering Willie's Tale,'[15] while the prose of his
'Connaught Love Songs' is perfect after its kind. Lady Wilde has told
inaccurately, but charmingly, innumerable tales which one cannot come
by elsewhere; while Mr. Larminie and Mr. Curtin are recording the
tales of the western peasantry with the industrious accuracy of Campbell of Islay; and Mr. Standish Hayse [*sic*] O'Grady, despite a hateful
Latin style, has a place in literature because of the magnificence of much
he has translated out of the Gaelic in "Silva Gadelica."[16] All these
scholars are better workmen, have more skill in arrangement and selection, and a more perfect criticism than the most important of their
predecessors; just as Mr. O'Grady, Miss Lawless, Miss Barlow, and
Miss Hopper outdo in the things that can be learned most of the earlier
novelists. Our public, too, is a little more exacting, a little more conscious of excellence and of what is Irish as apart from what is English
or Scottish than it was a few years ago; in the main through the tendency of all traditions of thought and feeling to grow less gross and
crude through the sheer boredom of grossness and crudeness; but
partly because Dr. Hyde, Mr. Larminie, Dr. Sigerson, Mr. Johnson,
Mr. Ashe King,[17] and others, whose names would carry no meaning,
have been busy denouncing rhetoric, and interpreting Gaelic history or

author of *Anchor-Watch Yarns* (1893), *Merchant of Killogue* (1894), and many other books.
The Real Charlotte (1894) was by Edith Œ. Somerville (1858–1949) and Martin Ross
(pseudonym of Violet F. Martin, 1865–1915). Mrs. Hinkson was better known by her
maiden name, Katharine Tynan.

[14] Patrick Weston Joyce (1827–1914), brother of Robert Dwyer Joyce, the poet, and no
relation of James Joyce.

[15] Yeats included "Teig O'Kane" in his *Fairy and Folk Tales of the Irish Peasantry.*
"Wandering Willie's Tale" is from Sir Walter Scott's romance *Redgauntlet.*

[16] The *Bookman* misprinted "Silex Godaelica." O'Grady's middle name was Hayes.

[17] Richard Ashe King had denounced rhetoric in a speech entitled "The Silenced Sister."
Yeats took part in the ensuing controversy (see 305–10).

modern romance in lectures and speeches. Whatever be the cause, we have for the first time in Ireland, and among the Irish in England, a school of men of letters united by a common purpose, and a small but increasing public who love literature for her own sake and not as the scullery-maid of politics; and may hope some day, in the maturity of our traditions, to fashion out of the world about us, and the things that our fathers have told us, a new ritual for the builders of peoples, the imperishable moods.

W. B. Yeats

That Subtle Shade

Yeats reviewed Arthur Symons's book of poems *London Nights*, London, 1895, in the August, 1895, issue of the *Bookman*.

Yeats had met Symons in the early nineties, and he depended much on Symons's knowledge of French to guide him through the French symbolists. When Yeats visited Paris in 1894, Symons may have supplied him with his introduction to Verlaine, which resulted in an article contributed to Symons's magazine, *The Savoy*, two years later (pp. 397–99).

Yeats's defense of the erotic realism of Symons is so much based on Yeats's spiritual aesthetic that he gives a rather chaste impression of this book. For its day and city, *London Nights* was a daring book.

A FAMOUS Hindu philosopher[1] once told me that one day, when he was a very young man, he walked on the bank of a great Indian river, reading a volume of erotic Sanscrit verse. He met a Hindu priest, and showed him the book, with the remark, "A book like this must be very bad for the world." "It is an excellent book, a wonderful book," said the priest, taking it from him, "but your calling it bad for the world shows it is bad for you," and thereupon dropped the book into the great river. Before the reviewing of Mr. Symons' 'London Nights' has come to an end, it is probable that a number of people will, if the Hindu priest spake truth, have borne witness against themselves, for the bulk of it is about musical halls, and what its author names "Leves Amores," and a little is a degree franker than Mr. Swinburne's 'Poems and Ballads'; and yet, though too unequal and experimental to be called "an excellent book, a wonderful book," it contains certain poems of an "excellent" and "wonderful" beauty peculiar to its author's muses. A great many of the poems are dramatic lyrics, and Mr. Symons' muses

---

[1] *famous Hindu philosopher*: probably Mohini Chatterjee, whom Yeats met in Dublin in 1885 and who served as source for many of Yeats's Indian anecdotes.

have not enough of passion, or his rhythms enough of impulse, to fuse
into artistic unity the inartistic details which make so great a part of
drama; he is at his best when simply contemplative, when expounding
not passion, but passion's evanescent beauty, when celebrating not the
joys and sorrows of his dancers and light o' loves, but the pathos of
their restless days. But in either mood he is honest and sincere, and
honesty and sincerity are so excellent, that even when about immoral
things, they are better for the world than hectic and insincere writing
about moral things. It is sometimes well for poetry to become a judge
and pronounce sentence, but it has always done all we have the right to
demand, when it has been an honest witness, when it has given the true
history of an emotion; and if it do so it serves beneficence not less than
beauty, because every emotion is, in its hidden essence, an unfallen
angel of God, a being of uncorruptible flame. It may have been some
idea of this kind, though more probably it was but the fascination of a
delightful phrase, which induced Mr. Symons to put into the mouth of
"an angel of pale desire" verses which at once describe and embody his
more admirable inspiration:—

> "*An angel of pale desire*
> *Whispered me in the ear*
> *(Ah me, the white-rose mesh*
> *Of the flower-soft, rose-white flesh!)*
> *'Love, they say, is a fire,*
> *Lo, the soft love that is here.*
>
> *'Love, they say, is a pain*
> *Infinite as the soul,*
> *Ever a longing to be*
> *Love's to infinity,*
> *Ever a longing in vain*
> *After a vanishing goal.*
>
> *'Lo, the soft joy that I give*
> *Here in the garden of earth;*
> *Come where the rose-tree grows;*
> *Thine is the garden's rose,*
> *Pluck thou, eat and live*
> *In ease, in indolent mirth.'*"[2]

At once the charm and defect of the book is that its best moments
have no passion stronger than a "soft joy" and a "pale desire"; and that
their pleasure in the life of sensation is not, as in Mr. Davidson's
music-hall poems, the robust pleasure of the man of the world, but the
shadowy delight of the artist. When it broods, as it does far too often,

---

[2] This quotation is the first three stanzas of Symons's "*Rosa Mundi.*"

upon common accidents and irrelevant details, it is sometimes crude, sometimes not a little clumsy; but it is wholly distinguished and beautiful when it tells of things an artist loves—of faint perfume, of delicate colour, of ornate and elaborate gesture.

> *"Olivier Metra's Waltz of Roses*
> *Sheds in a rhythmic shower*
> *The very petals of the flower;*
> *And all is roses,*
> *The rouge of petals in a shower.*
>
> .   .   .   .   .
>
> *Alone apart, one dancer watches*
> *Her mirrored, morbid grace;*
> *Before the mirror face to face*
> *Alone she watches*
> *Her morbid, vague, ambiguous grace.*
>
> *Before the mirror's dance of shadows*
> *She dances in a dream,*
> *And she and they together seem*
> *A dance of shadows;*
> *Alike the shadows of a dream."*[3]

On the whole, then, Mr. Symons must be congratulated upon having written a book which, though it will arouse against him much prejudice, is the best he has done; and none who have in their memory Shelley's 'Defence of Poetry' will condemn him because he writes of immoral things, even though they may deeply regret that he has not found an ampler beauty than can be discovered under "that subtle shade."

W. B. Yeats

Irish National Literature, III: Contemporary Irish Poets—Dr. Hyde, Mr. Rolleston, Mrs. Hinkson, Miss Nora Hopper, A.E., Mr. Aubrey de Vere, Dr. Todhunter, and Mr. Lionel Johnson

This is the third of Yeats's four articles on Irish national literature; it appeared in the *Bookman*, September, 1895. Here Yeats did better than in the preceding article on prose, for he had many of his talented friends to praise. Yet there

---

[3] Yeats described this same lyric in his 1897 review of Symons's *Amoris Victima* as "one of the most perfect lyrics of our time. . . ."

is a large distortion in this article, which stems from Yeats's inability to talk about himself. Without the master, the poetry of A.E., Lionel Johnson, Katharine Tynan, and T. W. Rolleston seems small beer indeed.

The first paragraph was reprinted by Yeats under the title "The Body of the Father Christian Rosencrux" in *Ideas of Good and Evil*.

THE followers of the Father Christian Rosencrux,[1] says the old tradition, wrapped his imperishable body in noble raiment and laid it under the house of their order, in a tomb containing the symbols of all things in heaven and earth, and in the waters under the earth, and set about him inextinguishable magical lamps, which burnt on generation after generation, until other students of the order came upon the tomb by chance. It seems to me that the imagination has had no very different history during the last two hundred years, but has been laid in a great tomb of criticism, and had set over it inextinguishable magical lamps of wisdom and romance, and has been altogether so nobly housed and apparelled that we have forgotten that its wizard lips are closed, or but opened for the complaining of some melancholy and ghostly voice. The ancients and the Elizabethans abandoned themselves to imagination as a woman abandons herself to love, and created great beings who made the people of this world seem but shadows, and great passions which made our loves and hatreds appear but ephemeral and trivial phantasies; but now it is not the great persons, or the great passions we imagine, which absorb us, for the persons and passions in our poems are mainly reflections our mirror has caught from older poems or from the life about us, but the wise comments we make upon them, the criticism of life we wring from their fortunes. Arthur and his Court are nothing, but the many-coloured lights that play about them are as beautiful as the lights from cathedral windows; Pompilia and Guido[2] are but little, while the ever-recurring meditations and expositions which climax in the mouth of the Pope are among the wisest of the Christian age. It seems to a perhaps fanciful watcher of the skies like myself that this age of criticism is about to pass, and an age of imagination, of emotion, of moods, of revelation, about to come in its place; for certainly belief in a supersensual world is at hand again; and when the notion that we are "phantoms of the earth and water" has gone down the wind, we will trust our own being and all it desires to invent; and when the external world is no more the standard of reality, we will learn again that the great Passions are angels of God, and that to

[1] Christian Rosencreutz (pseudonym of Johann Valentin Andraeae, 1586–1654) was the modern founder of Rosicrucianism. Among his works were *Fama fraternitatis*, 1614, *Confessio rosae*, 1615, and *Chymische Hochzeit*, 1616.

[2] Browning's *The Ring and the Book*.

embody them "uncurbed in their eternal glory," even in their labour
for the ending of man's peace and prosperity, is more than to comment,
ever so wisely, upon the tendencies of our time, or to express the social-
istic, or humanitarian, or other forces of our time, or even "to sum up"
our time, as the phrase is; for Art is a revelation, and not a criticism,
and the life of the artist is in the old saying, "The wind bloweth where
it listeth, and thou hearest the sound thereof, but canst not tell whence
it cometh and whither it goeth; so is every one that is born of the
spirit."[3]

This revolution may be the opportunity of the Irish Celt, for he has
an unexhausted and inexhaustible mythology to give him symbols and
personages, and his nature has been profoundly emotional from the beginning. An old Gaelic writer describes him as "celebrated for anger and
for amouresness [sic]," and an old English writer tells of his playing
"hastily and swiftly" upon the harp and the timbre, and a chronicler of
Queen Elizabeth's time has no better word for wild sorrow than "to
weep Irish"; while Dr. Hyde says of him, as he is in our own time, that
"he will to-day be dancing, sporting, drinking, and shouting, and will
be soliloquising by himself to-morrow, heavy and sick and sad in his
poor lonely little hut, making a croon over departed hopes, lost love,
the vanity of this world, and the coming of death";[4] and from such a
temperament must come a literature which, whether important or
unimportant, will yet be built after the ancient manner. The "Love
Songs of Connaught," translated by Dr. Douglas Hyde, express this
emotional nature in its most extreme form, for, though they have
nothing of the verbal extravagance of the bards, they seem to be continually straining to express a something which lies beyond the possibility of expression, some vague, immeasurable emotion. One understands
this better from the prose than from the verse translations,[5] good as
these often are; from such passages as: "It is happy for thee, O blind
man, who dost not see much of women. Och, if thou wert[6] to see what
we see, thou wouldst be sick even as I am. It is a pity, O God, that it is[7]
not blind I was before I saw her twisted cool (hair) and her snowy
body.[8] . . . I always thought the blind pitiable until my calamity waxed
beyond the grief of all; then, though it is a pity, my pity I turned into
envy. . . . It is woe for whoever saw her, and it is woe for him who sees
her not each day. It is woe for him on whom the knot of her love is tied,
and it is woe for him who is loosened out of it. It is woe for him who

---

[3] John 3 : 8.

[4] This quotation is from the introduction to Hyde's *The Love Songs of Connacht*.

[5] Hyde gives verse translations of the two following poems but Yeats quotes from the
prose versions.

[6] *thou wert*: Hyde reads "you were." [7] *is*: Hyde reads "was."

[8] This passage reads in Hyde "cool. Her snowy body . . . ."

goes to her, and it is woe to him who is not with her constantly. It is woe for a person to be near her, and it is woe[9] for him who is not near her"; or from such a wild outburst as, "My love, O she is my love, the woman who is most for destroying me; dearer is she for [10] making me ill than the woman who would be for making me well. She is my treasure, O she is my treasure, the woman of the grey eye . . . a woman who would not place a hand beneath my head . . . She is my affection, O she is my affection, the woman who left no strength in me; a woman who would not breathe a sigh after me, a woman who would not raise a stone at my tomb." Almost all we have had translated out of the Gaelic is as purely lyrical in spirit, though not always as passionate as this. Mr. Rolleston's translation from a very old original, "The Dead of Clonmacnois,"[11] though [it?] does not strain to express anything which lies beyond the possibility of expression, is so purely emotional that it must stand an example of the Gaelic lyric come close to perfection.

> *In a quiet watered land, a land of roses,*
> *Stands Saint Kieran's city fair;*
> *And the warriors of Erin in their famous generations*
> *Slumber there*
>
> *There beneath the dewy hillside sleep the noblest*
> *Of the clan of Conn,*
> *Each below his stone with [12] name in branching Ogham,*
> *And the sacred knot thereon.*
>
> *There they laid to rest the seven Kings of Tara,*
> *There the sons of Cairbre sleep—*
> *Battle-banners of the Gael, that in Kieran's plain of crosses*
> *Now there final hosting keep*
>
> *And in Clonmacnois they laid the men of Teffia,*
> *And right many a lord of Breagh;*
> *Deep the sod above Clan Creide and Clan Conaill,*
> *Kind in hall and fierce in fray*
>
> *Many and many a son of Conn the Hundred Fighter*
> *In the red earth lies at rest;*
> *Many a blue eye of Clan Colman the turf covers,*
> *Many a swan-white breast.*

No living Irish poet has learned so much from the translators as Mrs. Hinkson, and the great change this knowledge has made in her verse is an example of the necessity for Irish writers to study the native

---

[9] *woe*: Hyde reads "a woe."　　　　　[10] *for*: Hyde reads "from."
[11] "The Dead of Clonmacnois" is translated from the Irish of Angus O'Gillan. It is reprinted in Rolleston's *Sea Spray: Verses and Translations*, Dublin, 1909.
[12] *with*: Rolleston reads "his."

tradition of expression. Her first two books, "Louise de Vallière"[13] and "Shamrocks," contained here and there a moving lyric, but were on the whole merely excellent in promise, for the political turmoil of the time, and perhaps her own work for "the Ladies' Land League," continually drew her into rhetoric, while her own haste and inexperience kept her in a bondage of imitation of contemporary English poets. The work of the Irish folklorists, and the translations of Dr. Hyde and of an earlier poet, the village schoolmaster, Edward Walsh, began to affect her, however, soon after the publication of "Shamrocks"; and the best of "Ballads and Lyrics" and cuckoo songs[14] have the freedom from rhetoric, the simplicity and the tenderness, though not the passion, of the Gaelic poets. Such avowed imitations as "The Red Haired Man's Wife" and "Gramachree" are interesting, but scarcely so interesting as the poems in which she has assimilated the spirit, without copying the letter, of folk-song, and of these none are more touching than "Sheep and Lambs" from "Legends and Lyrics."

> *"All in the April evening,*
> *April airs were abroad,*
> *The sheep with their little lambs*
> *Passed me by on the road.*
>
> *The sheep with their little lambs*
> *Passed me by on the road;*
> *All in the April evening*
> *I thought on the Lamb of God.*
>
> *The lambs were weary, and crying*
> *With a weak, human cry.*
> *I thought on the Lamb of God*
> *Going meekly to die.*
>
> *Up in the blue, blue mountains,*
> *Dewy pastures are sweet,*
> *Rest for the little bodies,*
> *Rest for the little feet.*
>
> *But for the Lamb of God,*
> *Up on the hill-top green,*
> *Only a cross of shame,*
> *Two stark crosses between.*
>
> *All in the April evening,*
> *April airs were abroad,*
> *I saw the sheep with their lambs,*
> *And thought of*[15] *the Lamb of God."*

[13] Katharine Tynan's title was *Louise de la Vallière and other poems* (1885).
[14] *Cuckoo Songs* (1894) was the title of a book of Katharine Tynan's poems.
[15] *of*: Tynan reads "on."

Her best and her most popular book will probably be the forthcoming "Miracle Plays,"[16] for her best inspiration has ever come from Catholic belief, and to give an excellent expression to the ancient symbols is to be for a delight and a comfort to many ardent and dutiful spirits.

The work of the two latest of Irish poets, Miss Nora Hopper and A.E., is, upon the other hand, wholly without any exclusively Catholic, or even Christian feeling. The little songs between the stories in Miss Hopper's "Ballads in Prose" sing, with a symbolism drawn from mythology and folklore, of a pagan fairy world where good and evil, denial and affirmation, have never come, are full of a perception of the spirit without any desire for union with the spirit, have at all times a beautiful, alluring, unaspiring peace; and there is no better mood and manner for songs of the fairies, who must sing in a like fashion themselves. A.E.'s "Homeward: Songs by the Way"[17] embody, upon the other hand, a continual desire for union with the spirit, a continual warfare with the world, in a symbolism that would be wholly personal but for an occasional word out of his well-loved "Upanishads." No voice in modern Ireland is to me as beautiful as his; and this may well be because the thoughts about the visible and invisible, and the passionate sincerity, of the essays and stories, had long held me under their spell when his poems came as a delight and a surprise; but I am nearly convinced that it is because he, more than any, has a subtle rhythm, precision of phrase, an emotional relation to form and colour, and a perfect understanding that the business of poetry is not to enforce an opinion or expound an action, but to bring us into communion with the moods and passions which are the creative powers behind the universe; that though the poet may need to master many opinions, they are but the body and the symbols for his art, the formula of evocation for making the invisible visible. The spirit, he writes in the last number of that little Dublin mystical magazine[18] which publishes his poems and his coloured symbolic pictures, "cannot be argued over" or spoken "truly of from report." "It will surely come to those who wait in trust, a glow, a heat in the heart announcing the awakening of the fire. And as it blows with its mystic breath into the brain, there is a hurtling of visions, a brilliance of lights, a sound of great waters vibrant and musical in their flowing, and murmurs from a single yet multitudinous being." He is describing a mystical state, but one which differs in degree, and not in kind, from the state of poetical inspiration. He says also, and this time thinking probably more of poetic utterance in the ordinary sense, "every word which really inspires is spoken as if the golden age had never passed away," and surely criticism, even criticism

---

[16] *Miracle Plays: Our Lord's Coming and Childhood* appeared in 1895.   [18] *Irish Theosophist*.
[17] A.E.'s title has no colon. Yeats seems always to have spelled it with one.

of life, is of the fall and the fatal tree; and bids all believers cast away "the mood of the martyr," and put on "a mood at once gay and reverent, as beseems those who are immortal"; and his own songs, but for a little sadness, were no other than like his precept. Certainly he often sings of that energy "which is eternal delight," as in this from among the new poems in the American edition (published by Thomas B. Mosher) of "Homeward: Songs by the Way."

> *"We must pass like smoke or live within the spirit's fire,*
>   *For we can no more than smoke unto the flame return,*
> *If our thought has changed to dream or will unto desire.*
>   *As smoke we vanish, though the fire may burn.*
>
> *Lights of infinite pity star the grey dusk of our days;*
>   *Surely here is soul; with it we have eternal breath:*
> *In the fire of love we live or pass by many ways,*
>   *By unnumbered ways of dream to death."*

Dr. Todhunter and Mr. Aubrey De Vere are but slightly related to the Irish lyrical movement of to-day, for the bulk of their work is of a past time, and but little of it is Irish in subject or temperament, or written under an Irish influence. In the case of the elder man, Mr. Aubrey De Vere, the part that is Irish in subject is often alien in form. His "Red Branch Heroes" are knights and wear armour, while his telling of "Naisi's Wooing" and of "The Children of Lir" is of a Tennysonian-Wordsworthian elaboration which lets most of the old wine flow out. "The Bard Ethell" and "The Wedding of the Clans" are, however, a perfect marriage of meaning and form, and here and there a lyric like "The Little Black Rose" is at once quaint and beautiful.

The alien manner of much of the rest is perhaps due mainly to the small number of the old epics, lyrics, and folk-tales which were translated, and the small amount of old custom which was expounded when Mr. De Vere was forming his style; but something may be due to a defect of genius, for he seems to me, despite his noble placidity, his manifold and moving exposition of Catholic doctrine and emotion, but seldom master of the inevitable words in the inevitable order, and I find myself constantly distinguishing, when I read him, between that calculable, considered, intelligible and pleasant thing we call the poetical, and that incalculable, instinctive, mysterious, and startling thing we call poetry. Dr. Todhunter, writing later than Mr. De Vere, and with plentiful epics and lyrics and folktales to inspire him, has thought out a couple of curious metres, and with their help retold "The Children of Lir" and "The Sons of Turaun,"[19] with little loss of

----

[19] Todhunter spelled this name "Turann."

meaning, but also with little rhythmical impulse. His "Banshee," a personification of Ireland, in some sixty irregular, rhymeless lines, is still his best.

"An aged desolation,
She sits by old Shannon's flowing,
A mother of many children,
Of children exiled and dead;
In her home, with bent head, homeless,
Clasping her knees she sits,
Keening, keening!

And at her keene the fairy-grass
Trembles on dun and barrow;
Around the foot of her ancient crosses
The grave-grass shakes and the nettle swings;
In haunted glens the meadow-sweet
Flings to the night-wind
Her mystic mournful perfume;
The sad spearmint by holy wells
Breathes melancholy balm."

Mr. Lionel Johnson also has written a few Irish poems of distinguished beauty, but, unlike Mr. De Vere and Dr. Todhunter, is best when he writes on subjects, and under influences, which have no connection with Ireland. All these writers, however—for even A.E. has begun to dig for new symbols in the stories of Fin and Oisin, and in the song of Amergin—are examples of the long continued and resolute purpose of the Irish writers to bring their literary tradition to perfection, to discover fitting symbols for their emotions, or to accentuate what is at once Celtic and excellent in their nature, that they may be at last tongues of fire uttering the evangel of the Celtic peoples.

W. B. Yeats

Irish National Literature, IV: A List of the Best Irish Books

This is the fourth and last of Yeats's articles on Irish national literature; it appeared in the *Bookman*, October, 1895. Yeats adopted here the most combative tone of the series, for several reasons. The article is an extension of his quarrel the previous winter with Edward Dowden over the quality and validity of the Irish literary revival (see "Professor Dowden and Irish Literature", pp. 346–49, 351–53). During that controversy Yeats had assembled a list of the thirty best Irish books (in a letter to the *Dublin Daily Express,* published February 27, 1895; *Letters,* pp. 246–51). His defense of his choice of books is reflected in his comments in this article. And lastly, the fighting stance was intended to sell books, or to force publishers into reprinting them. The latter purpose was promoted by including four out-of-print volumes in his list.

L ISTS of "the best hundred books"[1] and the like are commonly among the most futile of things, for they would erect mere personal liking into a general law, forgetting that "the same law for the lion and the ox is oppression." In a literature like the Irish, however, which is not only new, but without recognised criticism, any list, no matter how personal, if it be not wholly foolish, is a good deed in a disordered world. The most that read Irish national literature read from patriotism and political enthusiasm, and make no distinction between literature and rhetoric. Allingham is but a name, while "The Spirit of the Nation" is on the counter of every country stationer;[2] Carleton's great novel, "Fardorougha," has but now gone to its second edition, and his scarce less impressive "Black Prophet" is still out of print, while his formless and unjust "Valentine McClutchy" and his feeble "Willy Reilly" have gone to numberless editions; for this zealous public loves vehement assertion better than quiet beauty and partisan caricature better than a revelation of reality and peace. This public is of no disadvantage to Ireland, for it is mainly drawn from a class who read a worse literature elsewhere, while its enthusiasm has kept Irish literature alive for better fortune; but it has none the less persuaded some of our best writers to immense stupidities, as when it set Carleton writing stories now against intemperance, now against landlords, and it has created out of itself, besides, some few of genius, a multitude of bad writers who fare better than the best. It had done no permanent mischief were it not that our educated classes are themselves full of a different, but none the less noisy, political passion, and are, with some admirable exceptions, too anti-Irish to read an Irish book of any kind, other than a book of jokes or partisan argument.

The professor of literature at Trinity College, Dublin, is one of the most placid, industrious, and intelligent of contemporary critics when he writes on an English or a German subject, but the "introduction" to

---

[1] Yeats probably referred to *The Best Hundred Irish Books,* originally printed in the *Freeman's Journal* and reprinted as a separate pamphlet in Dublin, 1886.

[2] William Allingham (1824–1889) was a prolific poet, of whose works Yeats liked best the Irish songs and ballads of Allingham's native Ballyshannon. *The Spirit of the Nation* was a collection of patriotic songs by contributors to the *Nation* magazine.

his last book of essays[3] is a perfect example of this prejudice. It was written twelve years ago, when scarcely a writer, prominent in Irish literature in our time, was before the public, and at a moment of political excitement, and accused Irish writers with great heat of "raving of Brian Beru [*sic*]," of "plastering" themselves "with shamrocks," and of having neither "scholarship" nor "accuracy," and is reprinted to-day with nothing changed, except that the words, "Irish Literary Movement," are inserted here and there to make it apply to Mr. Rolleston, Mr. Graves, Dr. Hyde, Mr. Larminie, Mr. Lionel Johnson, Mr. King, Mr. O'Grady, Mrs. Hinkson, Miss Barlow, and Miss Lawless, writers of whom some are not less eminent than Prof. Dowden himself. I quote this criticism not because I have any special quarrel with Prof. Dowden, who is less prejudiced than many, but because his offence is new and flagrant, and because like criticism has done and is doing incalculable harm. It is too empty of knowledge and sympathy to influence to any good purpose the ignorant patriotic masses, and it comes with enough of authority to persuade the undergraduates and the educated classes that neither the history, nor the poetry, nor the folklore, nor the stories which are interwoven with their native mountains and valleys are worthy of anything but contempt. This would perhaps be no great matter if it drove them to read Goethe and Shakespeare and Milton the more and the better. It has no such effect, however, but has done much to leave them with no ideal enthusiasm at all by robbing them of the enthusiasm which lay at their own doors. Year after year the graduates and undergraduates of Trinity College compose vacant verses, and how vacant their best are can be seen from a recent anthology;[4] and young ladies from Alexandra College gather in little groups and read Shakespeare, and common-place is the abundant fruit. It is only when some young man or young girl is captured by a despised enthusiasm that the vacancy is peopled and the common made uncommon; and to make such captures and at length overthrow and sack Dublin scholasticism is one half the business of "The Irish Literary Movement." Its methods are at times artificial, for it has to mend an artificial state of things, and this must be my excuse for making anything so apparently futile as a list of some forty best Irish books. The list is in a sense an epitome of my preceding articles, and, like them,

[3] Yeats refers to the introduction to Edward Dowden's *New Studies in Literature*, London, 1895. I have been unable to trace the twelve-year-old version of this introduction. The 1895 version does not read as Yeats quotes. In it Dowden said, "Let the Irish prose writer show that he can be patient, exact, just, enlightened, and he will have done better service for Ireland, whether he treats of Irish themes or not, than if he wore shamrocks in all his buttonholes and had his mouth for ever filled with the glories of Brian the Brave."

[4] *Dublin Verses. By Members of Trinity College*, London, 1895, was edited by Henry Hinkson, Katharine Tynan's husband.

confines itself to literature and the material for literature, and takes no stock of historical science, even though it lose thereby Mr. Lecky's great history; and it includes no book not upon an Irish subject, or written under some obvious Irish influence. The time has not yet come for Irishmen, as it has for Scotsmen, to carry about with them a subtle national feeling, no matter when, or of what they write, because that feeling has yet to be perfectly elaborated and expounded by men of genius with minds as full of Irish history, scenery, and character as the minds of Burns and Scott were full of Scottish history, scenery, and character. For a like reason it contains many imperfect books, which seem to me to hide under a mound of melodrama or sheer futility a smouldering and fragrant fire that cannot be had elsewhere in the world; and even some few poems which, like "The Lament of Moria Shehone for Miss Mary Bourke" in "The Book of Irish Verse,"[5] are precious because of a single line that is the signature of an ancient and Celtic emotion.

I will anticipate one other criticism of a more purely personal nature, and then have done. Some of the Irish papers have been kind enough to quote and criticise my articles,[6] and one or two have complained that I have "log-rolled," and to them I would say that, with the exception of A.E., who was a fellow student of mine,[7] there is no writer in this list whose work I did not admire before ever I set eyes upon him, and whose friendship I have sought for any reason but admiration of his work. I must apologise for mentioning these personal facts, which are necessary mainly because my praise of Mr. O'Grady,[8] whom I believe to be the most important of living Irish prose writers, is described as mere friendship by Irish Nationalists, who dislike his often anti-national opinions; and I would have my praise, no matter how small be its intrinsic value, carry at any rate the weight of its sincerity.

NOVELS AND ROMANCES

Castle Rackrent. By Miss Edgeworth.
The Nolans. By John Banim. (Out of print.)
John Doe. By John Banim. (Bound up with "Crohore[9] of the Bill-hook".)
Father Connell. By Michael Banim. (Out of print.)

[5] The title of this anonymous song as given in Yeats's A Book of Irish Verse is "Lament of Morian Shehone for Miss Mary Rourke."
[6] United Ireland did so on August 17, 1895.
[7] Yeats and A.E. were fellow students at the Metropolitan School of Art in Dublin.
[8] D. F. Hannigan, a critic of Yeats's previous list of the best Irish books, had complained that six out of thirty books on the list were by Standish O'Grady.
[9] In Banim's title, the name is spelled "Crohoore."

Barny O'Reirdan. By Samuel Lover (in "Tales and Stories").
The Collegians. By Gerald Griffen.[10]
Father Tom and the Pope. By Sir Samuel Ferguson (in "Tales from Blackwood.")
Traits and Stories. By William Carleton.
Fardarougha. By William Carleton.
The Black Prophet. By William Carleton. (Out of print.)
Charles O'Malley. By Charles Lever.
Flitters, Tatters, and the Councillor. By Miss Laffan. (Out of print.)
Maelcho. By Miss Lawless.
Irish Idylls. By Miss Barlow.
The Bog of Stars. By Standish O'Grady. (New Irish Library.)
The Coming of Cuchullin. By Standish O'Grady.
Finn and his Companions. By Standish O'Grady.
Ballads in Prose. By Miss Hopper.

FOLKLORE AND LEGEND

Old Celtic Romances. By P. W. Joyce.
History of Ireland. Two vols. By Standish O'Grady.
Ancient Legends. By Lady Wilde.
Beside the Fire. By Dr. Douglas Hyde.
West Irish Folk Tales. By William Larminie.
Hero Tales of Ireland. By Jeremiah Curtin.
Myths and Folklore of Ireland. By Jeremiah Curtin.
Tales of the Irish Fairies. By Jeremiah Curtin.
Fairy Legends of the South of Ireland. By Crofton Croker.
Teig O'Kane. By Dr. Douglas Hyde (in "Fairy and Folk Tales of the Irish Peasantry").[11]
Silva Gadaelica. By Standish Hayse [*sic*] O'Grady. (Two vols. of Translations.)
Manuscript Materials.[12] By Eugene O'Curry.

HISTORY

A Short History of Ireland. By P. W. Joyce.
The Story of Ireland. By Standish O'Grady.
Red Hugh. By Standish O'Grady. (Out of print.)[13]
The Jail Journal. By John Mitchell.[14]

[10] This name is spelled "Griffin."
[11] This is Yeats's own compilation.
[12] *Lectures on the Manuscript Materials of Ancient Irish History* by Eugene O'Curry, Dublin, 1861.
[13] *Red Hugh's Captivity* was reprinted in 1897 as *The Flight of the Eagle*. Yeats reviewed it in the August, 1897, *Bookman* (see above).   [14] This name is usually spelled "Mitchel."

The Autobiography of Wolfe Tone (in Mr. Barry O'Brien's edition).
The Story of Early Gaelic Literature. By Dr. Douglas Hyde. (New
  Irish Library.)

POETRY

Irish Poems. By William Allingham.
Lays of the Western Gael. By Sir Samuel Ferguson.
Conary. By Sir Samuel Ferguson (in his "Poems").
Selections from the Poems of Aubrey De Vere. Edited by G. E. Wood-
  berry.
Legends and Lyrics. By Mrs. Hinkson.
Homeward: Songs by the Way.[15] By A.E.
The Love-Songs of Connaught. By Dr. Douglas Hyde (and to this
  should be added his "The Religious Songs of Connaught," as soon
  as it is reprinted from the Irish magazine in which it is now appear-
  ing).
The Irish Song Book. By A. P. Graves. (New Irish Library.)
Irish Love Songs. Edited by Mrs. Hinkson.
A Book of Irish Verse.

  The last book on my list was edited by myself, and my excuse for
including it is that some anthology was necessary; and that I compiled
"A Book of Irish Verse" because I disliked those already in existence.
If Mr. Graves' and Mr. Stopford Brooke's promised anthology were
out,[16] I would probably escape the necessity of pushing my own wares.
There is one book, "Mythologie Irlandais," by D'Arbois Joubainville
[sic], which could not be included in my list, as it is by a foreign writer,
but is so important that no right knowledge of Irish legend is possible
without it.[17]

W. B. Yeats

The Life of Patrick Sarsfield

This is a review of The Life of Patrick Sarsfield by John Todhunter, London,
1895, from the Bookman, November, 1895. Todhunter's book was one of the
few New Irish Library series which Yeats praised. He had wanted to edit that
series when it began in 1892, and when he was pushed out by the supporters

  [15] A.E.'s title was Homeward Songs by the Way.
  [16] This volume appeared in 1900 as A Treasury of Irish Poetry in the English Tongue, edited
by S. A. Brooke and T. W. Rolleston. Yeats contributed several biographical introductions
to it.
  [17] This book appeared in an English translation by Richard Irvine Best as The Irish
Mythological Cycle and Celtic Mythology, Dublin and London, 1903. The author, whose name
Yeats most persistently misspelled, was H. D'Arbois de Jubainville.

of Sir Charles Gavan Duffy, he left with many prophecies of publishing disaster.

Yeats would hardly have treated a book by Todhunter harshly. A doctor and a poet, he had been an old friend of Yeats's father, and Yeats had been praising his books for almost a decade. Todhunter had been a neighbor of the Yeats family in the Bedford Park section of London in the later 1880s, and Yeats had his first contact with the production of plays when Todhunter's *A Sicilian Idyll* was put on in the Bedford Park playhouse.

The subject of Todhunter's book, Patrick Sarsfield, was one of James II's generals in the campaign of 1689. William of Orange's victory over James at the battle of the Boyne river had determined Protestant ascendancy over Catholic Ireland for more than two hundred years. The subject was therefore delicate. Yeats, himself, was somewhat neutral. He did not know or could not remember on which side of the battle of the Boyne his ancestors had fought, and the resulting confusion made necessary some awkward changes in the poem "Pardon, Old Fathers."

IRELAND has always had a literary history quite separate from the literary history of England; and week after week young men gather together in "Young Ireland," "Celtic," and "National Literary" societies, and discuss, often with as much heat as though there were no other literary history in the world, books and movements of which the greater number are not even names out of Ireland. Few of these books and movements are of great importance, if measured by merely literary standards, but as stages in the development of a national culture, nearly all are as important as they are interesting. When a few years have frozen the changing present into a changeless memory that it may be studied with deliberate care, young men in Dublin and Limerick and Belfast will be reading essays to each other about the great transformation of Irish opinion which marked the early nineties; and whether those who made it or expressed it be forgotten or remembered by the world at large, it will seem to them a momentous and memorable transformation. A few years ago Irish history, if written by Irishmen and with Irish sympathies, did not seek to discover neglected truths, or illustrate novel points of view, but only to blacken some national enemy more perfectly, or to set a finer glory about some national hero; for a conventional patriotism had killed honest research and over-thrown imaginative freedom. The result was that one had to go to Englishmen, whose sympathies were naturally with their own country, for any history not wholly empty of the historical spirit; for no educated Irishman, not even among the young men in the literary societies, believes in the mystery play of devils and angels which we call our national history, though even to-day the Irish press and the penny story papers, despite Mr. O'Grady and others of a less genius, keep up the pretence with admirable courage. A few months ago one of the Dublin societies of Catholic young men failed to organise a debate on the character of Oliver Cromwell, because all its members who could speak had forgotten "the curse of Cromwell" in the study of Carlyle; and this was from no lack of national spirit, for the most were only not Fenians because the Fenians are not the party of the moment. I labour this point, because I believe it is most important for the management of "The New Irish Library" to understand this transformation and give us more books like this admirably sincere "Life of Patrick Sarsfield," and less books like some of its rhetorical and conventional predecessors; and help thereby to set a new national history in place of the old. I doubt if Dr. Todhunter writes with a sufficiently decided point of view, or generalizes his conclusions often enough or vividly enough, to be very widely read, but his careful scholarship is above praise, and can only do good to our people. His patriotism has found expression not in vehement assertion or denial, but in care for the exact truth and in love for all things which counted, whether for good or evil, in the national and religious quarrel he is describing. Both Macaulay and Froude,[1] for instance, writing of events which did not concern them very deeply, accepted with too little examination the French account of the Battle of the Boyne, and did, the one regretfully, the other gleefully, a deep injustice to the courage of the Irish peasantry who fought there; but here the whole story is set out for the first time and every statement proved from contemporary writers, and no rhetoric could so well serve Irish self-respect, for "raw Irish levies, badly disciplined, half armed, without artillery," "left to face some of the best troops of Europe, by whom they were outnumbered three to one,"[2] are proved to have made an "heroic" defence of their fords. Irish historians and poets and story-makers, on the other hand, have ever declared Sarsfield the immaculate genius of that time, but here we have it on the word of a friend that, the battle over, the great soldier made confusion "in civil affairs" by giving out "many orders," and helped on the plundering of the troops by being "so easy that he would sign any paper[3] that was laid before him." One only regrets that the countenance he gave in his more youthful days to a certain rather mercenary elopement were recorded also, for the personal facts about his gallant, alluring personality are of the fewest, and it were a good deed besides to drag him even a little forth from the mystery play.

W. B. Yeats

[1] Thomas Babington Macaulay in his *History of England*; James Anthony Froude in his *The English in Ireland in the Eighteenth Century*.
[2] Todhunter wrote "outnumbered by about three to one."
[3] The quotation in Todhunter reads "that he would not deny signing papers. . . ."

The Binding of the Hair

This story, first printed in the *Savoy*, January, 1896, was reprinted in *The Secret Rose* (1897), Yeats's most ineffable prose collection. It was omitted from the 1908 collected works and not reprinted thereafter. The version reprinted here is *The Secret Rose* version. It is considerably rewritten and in most cases expanded from the *Savoy* version. I have given some examples of the first, *Savoy*, version in footnotes.

The obsession with hair matches that of many of the poems in *The Wind among the Reeds*. The decapitation pleased a decade in which Wilde's *Salome* led a procession of severed heads. The lyric at the end, to which the story serves as prologue, was titled "He gives his Beloved certain Rhymes" in *The Wind among the Reeds*.

The Secret Rose was illustrated by Jack B. Yeats. The frontispiece illustration is of Aodh's head hanging from the branch; the face does not resemble W. B. Y. The story is overstuffed to the point of self-parody. But as an introduction to the poem, it redeems itself and makes a typical lyric of *The Wind Among the Reeds* seem extraordinary.

T HE men-at-arms of the young and wise Queen Dectira,[1] and of the old and foolish King Lua, had lighted a line of fires from the mountain of Bulben[2] to the sea and set watchmen by every fire; and built close to the place where the Liss of the Blindman was built in later times, a large house with skin-covered wattles for the assembly, and smaller houses to sleep in, and dug round all a deep ditch: and now they sat in the large house, waiting the attack of certain nations of the People of the Bag coming up out of the south, and listened to the bard Aodh, who spoke to them a story of the wars of Heber and Heremon.[3] The tale was written upon thin slips of wood, which the bard held before him like a fan, grasping them above the brazen pivot, and only laid down when he would take up the five-stringed cruit from the ground and chaunt hastily, and with vehement gesture, one of the many songs woven into the more massive measure of the tale. Though the bard was famous, and claimed to be descended from the bard for whom the nations of Heber and Heremon cast lots at the making of the world, the old and foolish king did not listen, but leaned his head upon the middle pillar and snored fitfully in a wine-heavy sleep; but the young queen sat among her women, straight and still like a white candle, and listened as

[1] Queen Dectira is the mother of Cuchulain.

[2] *Bulben*: *Savoy* printing read "from Bulben." For some reason *The Secret Rose*, 1897, printing read in every instance of "Bulben" "the mountains of Gulben." The stories containing this phrase which were reprinted in the 1908 collected edition of Yeats's works all have "mountain of Gulben" changed to "Ben Bulben."

[3] According to a note by Yeats to his early poems, "'Heber and Heremon' were the ancestors of the merely human inhabitants of Ireland."

though there was no tale in the world but this tale of Aodh's, for the enchantment of his dream-heavy[4] voice was in her ears; the enchantment of his dream-distraught[5] history in her mind: how he would live now in the raths of kings, now alone in the great forest; how, despite the grey hairs mingling before their time with the dark of his beard, he was blown hither and thither by love and anger; how, according to his mood, he would fly now from one man and with blanched face, and would now show an extreme courage one man against many; and, above all, how he had sat continually by her great chair telling of forays and battles, to hearten her war-weary men-at-arms, or chanting histories and songs laden with gentler destinies for her ears alone, or, more often still, listening in silence to the rustling of her dress.

He sang now of anger and not of love, for it was needful to fill the hearts of her men-at-arms with thirst of battle that her days might have peace; yet over all the tale hovered a mournful beauty not of battle, and from time to time he would compare the gleam of a sword to the brightness of her eyes; or the dawn breaking on a morning of victory to the glimmering of her breast. As the tale, and its songs, which were like the foam upon a wave, flowed on, it wrapped the men-at-arms as in a tide of fire, and its vehement passages made them clash their swords upon their shields and shout an always more clamorous approval. At last it died out in a chaunt of triumph over battle-cars full of saffron robes and ornaments of gold and silver, and over troops of young men and young girls with chains of bronze about their ankles; and the men shouted and clashed their swords upon their shields for a long time. The queen sat motionless for a little, and then leaned back in her chair so that its carved back made one dark tress fall over her cheek. Sighing a long, inexplicable sigh, she bound the tress about her head and fastened it with a golden pin. Aodh gazed at her, the fierce light fading in his eyes, and began to murmur something over to himself, and presently, taking the five-stringed cruit from the ground, half knelt before her, and softly touched the strings. The shouters fell silent, for they saw that he would praise the queen, as his way was when the tales were at an end; and in the silence he struck three notes, as soft and sad as though they were the cooing of doves over the Gates of Death.

Before he could begin his song, the door which led from the long room into the open air burst open and a man rushed in, his face red with running, and cried out:

'The nations with ignoble bodies and ragged beards[6] have driven us from the fires and have killed many!'

[4] *dream-heavy*: *Savoy* version had simply "dreamy."
[5] *dream-distraught history*: *Savoy* version had "changing history."
[6] This improbably long cry was made longer in the *Savoy* version by the phrase at this point "from beyond the Red Cataract."

The words were scarcely from his mouth before another man struck against him, making him reel from the door, and this man was followed by another and another and another, until all that remained of the watchmen stood in the middle of the hall, muddy and breathless, some pouring wine into horns from the great stone flagon that stood there, and some unhooking their bronze helmets and shields and swords from the wall and from the pillars, and all cursing the nations of the People of the Bag. The men about the queen also unhooked their bronze helmets and shields and swords from the walls and from the pillars: but the queen sat there straight and still; and Aodh half knelt before her, with bowed head, and slowly touched the five-stringed cruit as though he were half sunk into a Druid sleep.[7]

At last he rose with a sigh, and was about to pass into the crowd of the men-at-arms when the queen leaned forward, and, taking him by the hand, said, in a low voice:

'O Aodh, promise me to sing the song out before the morning, whether we overcome them or they overcome us.'

He turned, with a pale face, and answered:

'There are two little verses in my heart, two little drops in my flagon, and I swear by the Red Swineherd that I will pour them out before the morning for the Rose of my Desire, the Lily of my Peace,[8] whether I live or be with Orchil and her faded multitude!'[9]

Then he took down from a pillar his shield of wicker and hide, and his bronze helmet and sword, and passed among the crowd that went, shouting, through the wide door; and there was no one left in the room except the queen and her women and the foolish king, who slept on, with his head against a pillar.

After a little, they heard a far-off ringing of bronze upon bronze, and the dull thud of bronze upon hide, and the cries of men, and these continued for a long time, and then sank into the silence. When all was still, the queen took the five-stringed cruit upon her knees and began touching the strings fitfully and murmuring vague words out of the love songs of Aodh; and so sat until about two hours before dawn, when she heard the trampling of the feet of the men-at-arms. They came in slowly and wearily, and threw themselves down, clotted with blood as they were, some on the floor, some on the benches.

[7] In the *Savoy* version, he touches "the five-stringed cruit slowly and dreamily."

[8] Compare these phrases with the lines from "The Travail of Passion":

We will bend down and loosen our hair over you,
That it may drop faint perfume, and be heavy with dew,
Lilies of death-pale hope, roses of passionate dream.

[9] In the *Savoy* version, this clause read "whether I have living lips or fade among the imponderable multitudes." In a note to his early poems, Yeats described Orchil as "a Fomorian sorceress." In a later edition he said, "I forget whatever I may have once known about her."

'We have slain the most, and the rest fled among the mountains,' said the leader; 'but there is no part of the way where there was not fighting, and we have left many behind us.'

'Where is Aodh?' said one of the women.

'I saw his head taken off with a sword,' said the man.

The queen rose and passed silently out of the room, and, half crossing the space within the ditch, came where her horses were tethered, and bade the old man, who had charge of their harness and chariot, tell none, but come with her and seek for a dead man. They went along the narrow track in the forest that had been trod by marauders, or by those sent to give them battle, for centuries; and saw the starlight glimmer upon the helmets and swords of dead men, troubling a darkness which seemed heavy with a sleep older than the world. At last they came out upon the treeless place where the nations of the People of the Bag[10] had fought desperately for the last time before they were scattered. The old man tied the reins to a tree and lit a torch, and the old man and the queen began to search among the dead. The crows, which had been tearing the bodies, rushed up into the air before them with a loud cawing, and here and there the starlight glimmered upon a helmet or a sword, or in pools of blood, or in the eyes of the dead.

Of a sudden, a sweet, tremulous song came from a bush near them. They hurried towards the spot, and saw a head hanging from the bush by its dark hair; and the head was singing, and this was the song it sung;

> *Fasten your hair with a golden pin,*
>   *And bind up every wandering tress;*
>   *I bade my heart build these poor rhymes:*
> *It worked at them, day out, day in,*
>   *Building a sorrowful loveliness*
>   *Out of the battles of old times.*

> *You need but lift a pearl-pale hand,*
>   *And bind up your long hair and sigh;*
>   *And all men's hearts must burn and beat;*
> *And candle-like foam on the dim sand,*
>   *And stars climbing the dew-dropping sky,*
>   *Live but to light your passing feet.*

And then a troop of crows, heavy like fragments of that sleep older than the world, swept out of the darkness and, as they passed, smote those ecstatic lips with the points of their wings; and the head fell from the bush and rolled over at the feet of the queen.

W. B. Yeats

[10] In the *Savoy* version, the "People of the Bag" were "the servile tribes."

William Carleton

This review of *The Life of William Carleton* appeared in the *Bookman*, March, 1896. The book is Carleton's incomplete autobiography, completed and edited by D. J. O'Donoghue, in two volumes, London, 1896.

Yeats had shown much interest in William Carleton's work around 1890. He had edited the selection *Stories from Carleton* and had included excerpts from Carleton in his *Representative Irish Tales*, New York, 1891. By the later nineties his interest in Carleton had faded somewhat. He wrote in John Quinn's copy of *Stories from Carleton* in 1904, "I thought no end of Carleton in those days & would still I dare say if I had not forgotten him."

WILLIAM BLAKE expounds the history of inspiration by a very curious and obscure symbol. A lark, he says, mounts upward into the heart of the heavens, and there is met by another and descending lark, which touches its wings to its wings; and he would have us understand, if I remember the passage and its context rightly—for I have not the prophetical book "Milton" by me[1]—that man attains spiritual influence in like fashion. He must go on perfecting earthly power and perception until they are so subtilised that divine power and divine perception descend to meet them, and the song of earth and the song of heaven mingle together. Every literary current and tradition goes, I believe, through something like this development, coming only very late to its Shelleys and Wordsworths. Whether Irish prose literature be or be not to-day awaiting the celestial lark, and though no living Irish romance writer, with the exception of Mr. Standish O'Grady, has anything of Carleton's genius, it is certainly much more subtle, much more spiritual than before. The author of "The Traits and Stories"[2] was not an artist, as those must needs be who labour with spiritual essences, but he was what only a few men have ever been or can ever be, the creator of a new imaginative world, the demiurge of a new tradition. He had no predecessors, for Miss Edgeworth wrote by prefer-

[1] *Milton*, Book II, p. 512, Vol. I in *The Poetical Works of William Blake*, edited by Edwin J. Ellis, London, 1906:

> *When on the highest lift of his [the lark's] light*
> *pinions he arrives*
> *At that bright Gate, another Lark meets him, and*
> *back to back*
> *They touch their pinions, tip tip, and each descend*
> *To their respective Earths, and there all night*
> *consult with Angels. . . .*

[2] Carleton's most famous collection was *Traits and Stories of the Irish Peasantry*, first series in 1830, second series in 1833.

ence of that section of Irish society which is, as are the upper classes everywhere, the least national of all, and was, as the upper classes have seldom been anywhere, ashamed of even the little it had of national circumstance and character; and when she did take a man out of the Gaelic world and put into his mouth the immortal "Memoirs of the Rackrent Family," it was a poor man living in great men's houses, and not a poor man at his hearth and among his children. She could not have done otherwise, for she was born and bred among persons who knew nothing of the land where they were born, and she had no generations of historians, Gaelic scholones, and folk-lorists behind her, from whom to draw the symbols of her art. Carleton, on the other hand, came from the heart of Gaelic Ireland, and found there the symbols of his art. His description of his peasant father and mother in this unique autobiography would alone prove how strange a race had at length found a voice, and how potent and visionary a power had begun in the world's literature. His father, he writes, "was unrivalled" "as a narrator of old tales, legends, and historical anecdotes," "and his stock of them was inexhaustible. He spoke the Irish and English languages with equal fluency. With all kinds of charms, old ranns, or poems, old prophecies, religious superstitions, tales of pilgrims, miracles and pilgrimages, anecdotes of blessed priests and friars, revelations from ghosts and fairies, he was thoroughly acquainted." In a later part of the book he tells of his father's supernatural terrors, and of his continual praying, often with a "round rod, about as thick as the upper end of a horse-whip," under his knees for a penance. His mother "possessed the sweetest and most exquisite of voices, in her early life,[3] I have often been told by those who have[4] heard her sing, that any previous intimation of her presence at a wake, dance, or other festive occasion, was sure to attract crowds of persons, many from a distance of several miles, in order to hear from her lips the touching old airs of the country." "Her family had all been imbued with a poetical spirit, and some of her immediate ancestors composed in the Irish tongue several fine old songs and airs, just as Carolan did[5]—that is, some in praise of a patron or a friend and others to celebrate rustic beauties who had been long sleeping in the dust. For this reason she had many old compositions that were peculiar to her family." "I think her uncle, and I believe her grand-father, who were long dead before my time, were the authors of several Irish poems and songs." "Perhaps there never lived a human being capable of giving the Irish cry or *keen* with such exquisite effect or of pouring into its wild notes a spirit of such irresistible pathos and

3 In Carleton, this passage reads "most exquisite of human voices. In her early life, ..."
4 *have*: Carleton reads "had."
5 Turlough Carolan (1670–1738) was one of the last of the Gaelic bards.

sorrow. I have often been present when she has *'raised the keen'*—as it is called—over the corpse of some relative or neighbour, and my readers may judge of the melancholy charm which accompanied this expression of her sympathy when I assure them that the general clamour of violent grief was gradually diminished by admiration, until it became ultimately hushed, and no voice was heard but her own wailing, in sorrowful but solitary beauty."

I have quoted these passages at length because they show more than anything how this strange Gaelic race lives between two worlds, the world of its poverty, and a world of wild memories and of melancholy, beautiful imaginations. Carleton lived only just in time to describe its manners and customs as they had been left by centuries of purely Gaelic influence, for the great famine changed the face of Ireland, and from that day a hundred influences which are not Gaelic began to mould them anew. His autobiography describes the actual wakes and faction fights and conspiracies and hedge schools and pilgrimages out of which he fashioned the half imaginary adventures of the "Traits and Stories," and describes them not as one who observes with the philosophic indifference of the historian, but with the moving sympathy of one who has himself mourned and conspired and learnt and taught and gone on pilgrimage, and to whom all these things seem natural and inevitable. He also lived between two worlds, and has set down here the story of a love which touched the very height of passion, and which in old age was still the greatest of his memories, though he and his beloved never spoke, but only gazed at each other on the "chapel green"; and to him also this solid world and its laws seemed somewhat of a shadow and a dream; so much so indeed that when more than nineteen years old and able to talk Latin like English, he was so greatly excited by a folk-tale of a priest who saved himself from drowning by walking on the water that he resolved to try and walk on a pool in an old marl pit, and so be ready for any mischance. "After three days' fasting and praying for the power of not sinking in water, I stepped[6] very quietly down to the pit, and after reconnoitring the premises, to be sure there was no looker-on, I approached the brink. . . . At the edge of the pit grew large water-lilies, with their leaves spread over the surface. . . . I am ashamed[7] even while writing of this of the confidence I put for a moment in a treacherous water-lily, as its leaf lay spread so smoothly and broadly over the surface of the pond. . . . After[8] having stimulated myself afresh with a

[6] *stepped*: Carleton reads "slipped."   [7] Carleton reads "I am really ashamed. . . ."
[8] This sentence is so greatly changed that I quote the original: . . . "after having stimulated myself by a fresh *pater* and *ave*, I advanced—my eyes turned up enthusiastically to heaven . . . my whole soul strong in confidence . . . I made a tremendous stride, planting my right foot exactly in the middle of the treacherous water-lily leaf, and the next moment was up to my neck in water."

pater and an *ave*, I advanced—my eyes turned up to heaven . . . my soul strong in confidence, I made a tremendous stride, planting my foot exactly in the middle of the treacherous water-lily leaf, and the next moment was up to my neck in the water."

The autobiography, the discovery of which we owe to its editor, Mr. O'Donohue [*sic*],⁹ does not come beyond his youth and early manhood. The rest of his life is told, and told admirably, by Mr. O'Donohue with the help of an immense correspondence which Carleton carried on with peasants in the country, and with journalists and men of letters in London and Dublin; but the interest of the book is necessarily in the earlier part. Even had Carleton lived to write it all with his own hand, it had hardly been otherwise, for the further we get from that strange, wild Gaelic life, the further we get from all that made Carleton a great voice in modern romance and the founder of Irish prose literature. The publisher has attached to the book a critical essay by Mrs. Cashel Hoey,¹⁰ which scarcely seems relevant or excellent in any way. Mrs. Cashel Hoey has, I understand, done much useful work, but she is not a critic; and it is only in Irish literature, which has always been at the mercy of the first comer—priest, leisured amateur, town councillor, member of parliament, or casual jack of all trades—that she would be set to so uncongenial a task. To treat in this way, so important a book as this, is to continue the tradition which has allowed much of the best work of Carleton to drop out of print, while absolute rubbish like "The Evil Eve," and readable but empty melodrama like "Willy Reilly," and dull moralising like "Paddy go Easy," are reprinted continually.

W. B. Yeats

Verlaine in 1894

This sketch of Verlaine appeared in the *Savoy* in April, 1896. Verlaine had died in January, 1896, and this piece was the second of three articles about or by him. The opening reminiscence was Edmund Gosse's "A First Sight of Verlaine," and the third was Verlaine's recollection of "My Visit to London (November, 1893)," translated by Arthur Symons.

On his first visit to Paris in February, 1894, Yeats had stayed with Mac-Gregor Mathers, his fellow member in the occult "Order of the Golden Dawn." His introduction to Verlaine was probably through a note from

---

⁹ This name is spelled "O'Donoghue."

¹⁰ Frances Cashel Hoey (1830–1908) was the author of many novels in serial form. She wrote occasionally under the name of Edmund Yates, the editor of *The World* magazine.

Arthur Symons. This visit to Paris was momentous in another way. Accompanied by Maud Gonne, he attended the premiere of Villiers de L'Isle Adam's *Axël*, a play which was to have a profound effect on Yeats. He wrote a review of *Axël* for the *Bookman* (April, 1894. See pp. 320–25).

The first paragraph of this article was reprinted in "The Tragic Generation" section of his autobiography. There he introduced the anecdote with his usual fuzziness about dates—"In what month was it that I received a note . . .?"

IN the spring of 1894 I received a note in English, inviting me to "coffee and cigarettes plentifully," and signed "yours quite cheerfully, Paul Verlaine." I found him in a little room at the top of a tenement house in the Rue St. Jacques, sitting in an easy chair, with his bad leg swaddled in many bandages. He asked me, and in English, for I had explained the poverty of my French, if I knew Paris well, and added, pointing to his leg, that it had "scorched" his leg, for he knew it "well, too well," and lived in it like "a fly in a pot of marmalade;" and taking up an English dictionary, one of the very few books in his room, began searching for the name of the disease, selecting, after much labour, and with, I understand, imperfect accuracy, "erysipelas." Meanwhile, his homely and middle-aged mistress, who had been busy when I came, in dusting, or in some other housewife fashion, had found the cigarettes, and made excellent coffee. She had obviously given the room most of its character: her canary birds, of which there were several cages, kept up an intermittent tumult in the open window, and her sentimental chromolithographs scattered themselves among the nude drawings, and the caricatures of himself as a monkey, which M. Verlaine had torn out of the papers and pinned against the wall. She handed me a match to light my cigarette, with the remark, in English, "A bad match, a French match," and I saw by the way her face lighted up when my reply, "They have the best matches in England, but you have the best poets," was translated to her, that she was proud of her ungainly lover. While we were drinking our coffee she drew a box towards the fire for a singular visitor, a man, who was nicknamed Louis XI., M. Verlaine explained, because of a close resemblance, and who had not shaved for a week, and kept his trousers on with a belt of string or thin rope, and wore an opera hat, which he set upon his knee, and kept shoving up and down continually while M. Verlaine talked. M. Verlaine talked of Shakespeare, whom he admired, with the reservations of his article in the "Fortnightly";[1] of Maeterlinck, who was "a dear good fellow," but in his work "a little bit of a mountebank"; of Hugo, who was "a

[1] Verlaine's article "Shakespeare and Racine" appeared in the *Fortnightly Review*, September, 1894.

volcano of mud as well as of flame," but always, though "not good enough for the young messieurs," a supreme poet; and of Villiers de l'Isle Adam, who was "exalté," but wrote "the most excellent French," and whose "Axël" he interpreted, and somewhat narrowly, as I could but think, as meaning that love was the only important thing in the world; and of "In Memoriam," which he had tried to translate and could not, because "Tennyson was too noble, too *Anglais,* and when he should have been broken-hearted had many reminiscences."

No matter what he talked of, there was in his voice, in his face, or in his words, something of the "voluminous tenderness" which Mr. Bain[2] has called, I believe, "the basis of all immorality," and of the joyous serenity and untroubled perception of those who commune with spiritual ideas. One felt always that he was a great temperament, the servant of a great daimon, and fancied, as one listened to his vehement sentences that his temperament, his daimon, had been made uncontrollable that he might live the life needful for its perfect expression in art, and yet escape the bonfire. To remember him is to understand the futility of writing and thinking, as we commonly do, as if the ideal world were the perfection of ours, a blossom rooted in our clay; and of being content to measure those who announce its commandments and its beauty by their obedience to our laws; and of missing the wisdom of the Hebrew saying, "He who sees Jehovah dies." The ideal world, when it opens its fountains, dissolves by its mysterious excitement in this man sanity, which is but the art of understanding the mechanical world, and in this man morality, which is but the art of living there with comfort; and, seeing this, we grow angry and forget that the Incarnation has none the less need of our reverence because it has taken place in a manger of the dim passions,[3] or bring perhaps our frankincense and myrrh in secret, lest a little truth madden our world.

W. B. Yeats

---

[2] Perhaps Francis William Bain (1863–1940), romancer and translator of Indian tales. One suspects that Bain said "immortality" rather than "immorality," although both might apply to Verlaine.

[3] Yeats introduced his Verlaine anecdote in his autobiography with the following sentence, related in thought to "manger" and "Incarnation": "Paul Verlaine alternated between the two halves of his nature with so little apparent resistance that he seemed like a bad child, though to read his sacred poems is to remember perhaps that the Holy Infant shared His first home with the beasts."

Compare also these lines from "The Magi":

> *And all their eyes still fixed, hoping to find once more*
> *Being by Calvary's turbulence unsatisfied,*
> *The uncontrollable mystery on the bestial floor.*

William Blake

This review of Richard Garnett's *William Blake*, London, 1896, is from the *Bookman*, April, 1896. Blake, whom Yeats referred to as "my master," was the author about whom he was best equipped to do scholarly and critical battle. Garnett was lucky to get off as easily as he did; Laurence Housman's edition in 1893 had been treated more roughly. There is a note of resignation at the end of this review as if Yeats had realized that his and Ellis's edition of Blake, published in 1893, had not changed public ignorance on the mystical aspect of his "master."

IF the saying, that to be representative is to be famous, have anything of truth, the fame of William Blake should overspread the world; for, just as Shelley is the example from which most men fashion their conception of the poetic temperament, Blake is, to the bulk of students, the most representative of seers, the one in whom the flame is most pure and most continual. Swedenborg had perhaps as great an original genius, but he commingled Biblical commentary and moral argument with his vision; while Boehme, who had possibly a greater genius, was much of a theologian and something of an alchemist; and neither Swedenborg nor Boehme had an exterior life perfectly dominated and moulded by the interior spirit. I have said that Boehme had possibly a greater original genius, not because he seems to me so important to our time, but because he first taught in the modern world the principles which Blake first expressed in the language of poetry; and of these the most important, and the one from which the others spring, is that the imagination is the means whereby we communicate with God. "The word image," says "The Way of Christ," a compilation from Boehme and Law's interpretations of Boehme,[1] published at Bath when Blake was eighteen, "meaneth not only a creaturely resemblance, in which sense man is said to be the Image of God; but it signifieth also a spiritual substance, a birth or effect of a will, wrought in and by a spiritual being or power. And imagination, which we are apt erroneously to consider an airy, idle, and impotent faculty of the human mind, dealing in fiction and roving in phantasy or idea without producing any[2] powerful or permanent, is the magia or power of raising and forming such images or substances, and the greatest power in nature." The proud and lonely

[1] The words quoted are by William Law, the commentator of *The Way to Christ* by Jacob Behmen (Bath, 1775), pp. 425-26. The quotation is therein cited as taken from "*Law's* appeal to all that doubt, etc., p. 169."
[2] *any*: This passage is unclear. Law may have meant "producing any*thing* powerful or permanent."

spirit of Blake was possessed and upheld by this doctrine, and enabled to face the world with the consciousness of a divine mission, for were not the poet and the artist more men of imagination than any others, and therefore more prophets of God? Boehme taught that prayer was the great power which acts upon imagination, and therby "forms and transforms" the souls of men "into everything that its desires reach after." But Blake held the creation of beautiful thoughts or forms or acts to be the greater power, and affirmed that "Christ's apostles were artists," that "Christianity is art," that "the whole business of man is the arts,"³ that the beautiful states of being which the artist in life or thought perceives by his imagination and tries to call up in himself or others "are the real and eternal world of which this vegetable universe is but a faint shadow," and that "the Holy Ghost" is "an intellectual fountain.⁴ "The old mystics had the words "goodness" and "holiness" much in their mouths, and strained out of its true meaning the saying that "the wisdom of this world is foolishness"; but his cry was, "I care not whether a man is good or bad; all I care is whether he is a wise man or a fool. Go, put off holiness, and put on intellect," and by intellect he meant his reason, his imagination. He was the first to claim for imagination the freedom which, Mr. Pater has told us, was won for the heart by the Renaissance, and through his unlearned and obscure voice spoke the unborn learning and glory of the modern world. There are some who hold that he who wrote, "grandeur of ideas is founded upon precision of ideas,"⁵ and whose great word was, according to Palmer, "precision," was a mere child delighting in meaningless words out of sheer love of their sound or their momentary charm; and there are others, and these are perhaps the bulk of idle readers, who will have it that it does not matter whether the "Prophetic Books" had or had not a meaning, for his more charming lyrics are all we need know, as though a philosophy which has blossomed in so many a vivid aphorism had not its separate interest. It is to Dr. Garnett's credit that he does not, like some of his predecessors, definitely commit himself to the first theory, though such sentences as, he "could manifestly be as transparent as a crystal when he knew exactly what he wished to say—a remark which may not be useless to the student of mystical and prophetical

---

³ From notes to "The Laocoon" (engraved about 1820). Blake said, "Jesus & his apostles & Disciples were all artists . . . The Whole Business of Man Is The Arts, & All Things Common . . . Christianity is Art & not Money" (*The Writings of William Blake*, edited by Geoffrey Keynes, London, 1925, Vol. III, pp. 359–60).

⁴ Quoted from the introduction to the fourth chapter of Blake's *Jerusalem*:
   . . . *Imagination, the real & eternal World of which this*
   Vegetable Universe is but a faint shadow . . . .
   is the Holy Ghost any other than an Intellectual Fountain?
In Keynes edition cited in previous note, Vol. III, p. 284.

⁵ Note on Discourse III of *The Discourses of Sir Joshua Reynolds*, quoted on p. 328, Vol. II, of Yeats-Ellis edition of Blake's works.

writings," which is as though one should say, "the songs of Shake-speare are very clear, let us therefore trouble no more over the mystery of Hamlet, for all that was writ at haphazard," is very nearly a committal. He has, however, very definitely pronounced for the second and greater folly by affirming that if Hayley "thought that one page of the 'Poetical Sketches' or the 'Songs of Innocence' was worth many pages of 'Urizen,'[6] apart from the illustrations, he had reason for what he thought," as though one could judge of the value of a book without understanding what it is about; and if the truth be told, Mr. Garnett, like Mr. Gilchrist, Mr. Rossetti, and almost every one who has ever written on the subject, does not show evidence of having ever given so much as a day's study to any part of Blake's mystical writing, or of having anything of the knowledge necessary to make even prolonged study fruitful. This very book of "Urizen" would alone convict com-mentators, for they have not even discovered the fact lying upon its threshold, that it is page by page a transformation, according to Blake's peculiar illumination, of the doctrines set forth in the opening chapters of the "Mysterium Magnum" of Jacob Boehme; yet none so certain of their opinion as they, none so sweeping in statement.

These follies, for which he has distinguished precedents, apart, Dr. Garnett has worked modestly and carefully, and produced an essay, which pleasantly accompanies some admirable reproductions, of which two are in colour, and which, though it certainly neither throws nor tries to throw new light on anything, yet tells gracefully enough the essential facts of a beautiful life, and enumerates and describes accurately many famous pictures and poems. There is, however, one curious slip which is several times repeated. Dr. Garnett speaks of "Sampson" as a blank verse poem, and regrets that Blake did not write his "Prophetic Books" in a like regular metre, instead of in a loose chant, to the fashioning of which he "may have been influenced by Ossian." "Sampson" was written at a time in which Blake was manifestly "influenced by Ossian," and both written and printed as prose in the "Poetical Sketches." Mr. Garnett has evidently seen the poem in Mr. Rossetti's edition, where it is printed as a kind of irregular blank verse, to show how the cadence of verse clung to Blake's mind even in prose, and has confused it with the fairly regular verse of "Edward the Third"; and if he reads it again he will find that it bears no comparison with the beautiful fluid rhythms of "Thell,"[7] and of the best parts of "Vala" and of "The Daughters of Albion." The pity is, not that Blake did not write the "Prophetic Books" in blank verse, but that he did not sustain the level of their finest passages. Despite these and some mis-

---

[6] *Urizen: Bookman* printed "Urigen." I cannot believe that Yeats would make this mistake.
[7] *"Thell"*: Usually spelled "Thel."

understandings beside, Dr. Garnett's book may be cordially recommended to all who would learn a little of one of the most creative minds of modern days, for its futilities are wholly, and its errors almost wholly, in the parts where it touches mysticism, and for mysticism the general reader cares naught, nor is it dreadful that he should.

W. B. Yeats

An Irish Patriot

Yeats had begun his career as a prose writer in 1886 with articles on Samuel Ferguson. In this review of Lady Ferguson's biography *Sir Samuel Ferguson in the Ireland of his Day* (from the *Bookman*, May, 1896) Yeats expressed his afterthoughts of a decade later. He still admired the poems of Ferguson, but this biography aroused his scorn for the society of Unionist bishops to which Ferguson belonged. Yeats, the grandson of a Church of Ireland clergyman, might have entered those same social circles. In the catalog of that group's faults, Yeats gave greatest emphasis to the charge ". . . and into whose churches no joyous and mystical fervour has ever come."

Lady Ferguson in this biography had quoted Yeats's words of praise for her husband expressed in his *Dublin University Review* article of November, 1886 (see second article in this book), but she found his remarks on Thomas Moore in his *Book of Irish Verse* to be "caustic."

ONE night about twelve years ago I was standing on the doorstep of a man[1] who had spent several years in prison, and more in exile, for Fenianism, and at whose house met from time to time most of the men and women who now make up what is called "The Irish Literary Movement." I had prolonged my "good-night" to ask my host's opinion of Sir Samuel Ferguson, whose verse I was reading for the first time and with boyish enthusiasm. I was so accustomed to find Unionist hating Nationalist, and Nationalist hating Unionist, with the hatreds of Montagu and Capulet, that his answer is impressed on my memory with a distinctness which may seem inexplicable to those who live in more placid lands. "Sir Samuel Ferguson," he replied, "is, I understand, a Unionist, but he is a better patriot than I am; he has done more for Ireland than I have done or can ever hope to do." Enthusiasm for the poetry of Sir Samuel Ferguson was indeed the common possession of the Irish writers and students under whose influence or among whom I grew out of my teens—I but mention myself as typical of the

[1] John O'Leary.

new literary generation in Ireland. So soon as they found any to listen they wrote and talked and, I think, lectured on his writing, and with so much success that a few months ago, when one of the largest of the young men's societies debated the question, "Who is the national poet of Ireland?" Ferguson was voted the place long held by Davis or Moore. I have not read the debate, and so know nothing of the arguments, but ours would have been that Mangan had a more athletic rhythm, a more lyrical temperament, Allingham a more delicate ear, a more distinguished mastery over words, but that the author of "The Vengeance of the Welshmen of Tirawley" alone had his roots in no personal idiosyncrasy, but in Irish character and Irish history, and that he alone foreshadowed the way of the poets who would come after him. We forgave his failures readily, and, like all Irish poets, his power of self-criticism was small and his failures many, because his faults were faults of hardness and heaviness, and not the false coin of a glittering or noisy insincerity which Moore and the rhetoricians had made current in Ireland. Davis, Mangan, D'Arcy Magee, Kickham, Carleton, Banim—almost every story-writer or poet who had taken the popular side in Ireland had ruined a part of his work by didactic writing, and even when they had written with a purely artistic purpose they had often failed to shake off habits of carelessness and commonness acquired in thinking of the widest rather than of the best audience; they had made themselves, and for the most generous of reasons, a mirror for the passions and the blindness of the multitude. Lady Ferguson's life of her husband makes one understand, however, with a new vividness, that Capulet is no better than Montagu for a poet. Sir Samuel Ferguson lived entirely among dignitaries, professional condemners of the multitude, archbishops and bishops, deans and archdeacons, professors and members of learned societies, Lord Chancellors and leaders of the Bar, and he who will may read in this book of their opinions and their actions, and try to read their letters, and when he has laid it down it will be as though he had wandered, and not without a certain curious interest, in that fabled stony city of Arabia or in that circle of outer space where Milton saw "cowls, hoods, and habits with their wearers, tossed and fluttered into rags"[2] before melancholy winds. Consumed with one absorbing purpose, the purpose to create an Irish school of literature, and overshadowed by one masterful enthusiasm, an enthusiasm for all Gaelic and Irish things, he wrote and talked through a long life; and, as he wrote and talked, a hardness and heaviness crept into his rhythm and his language from the dead world about him, marring the barbaric power of "Conary," still, with all its defects, the most characteristic of Irish poems, and making, as I can but think, the Homeric imagination

[2] *Paradise Lost*, Book III, 490–91.

of "Congal" without avail. This, which could not but have been accompanied by some diminution of his delight in beauty, had mattered less to him had he found ready sympathy for his love for the earth and stones of the land, and for his belief in its ultimate welfare; but even this poor sympathy was so rare that when a dignitary, an archbishop of the Irish Church, sent him some incredibly feeble verses inspired by an amiable but conventional patriotism—

> *"Go point me out on any map*
> *A match for green Killarney,*
> *Or Kevin's bed, or Dunlo's gap,*
> *Or mystic shades of Blarney,*
> *Or Antrim's caves, or Shannon's waves—*
> *Ah me! I doubt if ever*
> *An Isle so fair you'll find elsewhere,*
> *Oh! never, never, never"*—[3]

he hailed them as giving him more[4] "hope and pleasure than any other expression of cultivated Irish sentiment that he had seen" for many years.[5] He lived in a class which, through a misunderstanding of the necessities of Irish Unionism, hated all Irish things, or felt for them at best a contemptuous and patronising affection, and which through its disgust at the smoky and windy fires of popular movements had extinguished those spiritual flames of enthusiasm that are the substance of a distinguished social and personal life, a class at whose dinner-tables conversation has long perished in the stupor of anecdote and argument, and on whose ears the great names of modern letters fall to awaken no flutter of understanding, or even of recognition, and into whose churches no joyous and mystical fervour has ever come. When the new school of Irish literature and criticism was founded; a school whose declared purpose is to create in Ireland a true, cultivated, patriotic class, and which for the first time unites Montagu and Capulet in the one movement; Ferguson, a very old man, was without fame, and, but for the popular ballad books, which had always a few of his verses, without readers. To-day there are hundreds whom the ballad books could never have reached, who have made his "Fair Hills of Holy Ireland" an expression of their hearts.

> *"A plenteous place is Ireland for hospitable cheer,*
> Uileacan dubh O![6]
> *Where the wholesome fruit is bursting from the yellow barley ear;*
> Uileacan dubh O!

[3] This poem is "A Patriot's Rebuke," by Lord Plunket, Archbishop of Dublin.
[4] *more*: Ferguson's statement reads "hope and pleasure more than . . . ."
[5] In Lady Ferguson, this sentence ends as follows: "that I have seen for many years."
[6] The Gaelic refrain means "O black lament."

There is honey in the trees where her misty vales expand,
And her forest paths in summer are by falling waters fanned;
There is dew at high noontide there, and springs i' the yellow sand.
    On the fair hills of holy Ireland.

Curled he is and ringleted, and plaited to the knee,
        Uileacan dubh O!
Each captain who comes sailing across the Irish sea;
        Uileacan dubh O!
And I will make my journey, if life and health but stand,
Unto that pleasant country, that fresh and fragrant strand,
And leave your boasted braveries, your wealth and high command,
    For the fair hills of holy Ireland."

W. B. Yeats

The New Irish Library

This review of *Swift in Ireland* by Richard Ashe King, Dublin and London, 1896; *Owen Roe O'Neill* by John F. Taylor, Dublin and London, 1896; and *Short Life of Thomas Davis* by Sir Charles Gavan Duffy, Dublin, London, and New York, 1895—all published by T. Fisher Unwin in the New Irish Library series—is from the *Bookman*, June, 1896.

Yeats dealt in this review with one friend and two enemies. He had quarreled with Taylor and Duffy in 1892 over the editorship of the New Irish Library and lost. He had been continually fighting with the orator Taylor over the respective virtues of oratory and literature. His friend in this group of authors was King, whom he had defended three years before after King had maintained that in Ireland partisan oratory had overwhelmed literature.

Yeats treated Duffy here more kindly than he had in the past. And his gentle reminder to Taylor that his work was good but not literature was mild indeed after the insults Yeats had received from Taylor four years before.

Yeats shows here an admiration for Swift as a man but a disdain for the eighteenth century. Twenty-five years later Yeats was to become obsessed with Swift and to make his peace with that century which he here accused of setting "chop-logic in the place of the mysterious power, obscure as a touch from behind a curtain, that had governed 'the century of poets.'"

THE last time I reviewed a bundle of new Irish Library books I had little good to say of them. The series had all the faults of that "Young Ireland" literature which, like so many things that did excellent service in their own time, has become a difficulty in the way of good literature and good criticism. It had printed a politico-historical pamphlet of some value,[1] and called it a model of historical writing; a mass of political rhymes of nearly no value,[2] and called it great poetry; and it had debased the coinage of imagination by turning a story of Balzac's into a sermon on village industries.[3] The best of the Irish public, however, having outlived the false ideals of Young Ireland, scouted prose and rhyme alike, and the library suddenly transformed itself and became vivid and scholarly. I praised, at the times of their appearance "The Irish Song Book,"[4] "The Story of Early Gaelic Literature," and "The Life of Patrick Sarsfield," and the new volumes keep the same high level. "Swift in Ireland," certainly one of the most useful and readable books of its kind in contemporary literature, discusses the life of Swift from the point of view of Ireland with unfailing witty and wise comment, and is a beginning of that scholarly criticism of men and things which is needed in Ireland even more perhaps than creative literature, for until it come we are perforce at the mercy of our rhetoricians and our newspaper hacks. Its only serious defect is that it does not contain enough of purely literary criticism, and makes no serious endeavour to consider the value of Swift's writings taken apart from the light they throw upon his actions and opinions, and in opinion-ridden Ireland some such estimate had been useful.

The recognition of the expression of a temperament as an end in itself, and not merely as a means towards a change of opinion, is the first condition of any cultivated life, and there is no better text than Swift for preaching this. He did not become, like the subject of Sir Charles Gavan Duffy's volume, a great light of his time because of the utility of his projects or of any high standard of honest thinking—for some of his most famous projects were mere expressions of a paradoxical anger, while others he defended with arguments which even he could not have believed—but because he revealed in his writings and and in his life a more intense nature, a more living temperament, than any of his contemporaries. He was as near a supreme man as that fallen age could produce, and that he did not labour, as Blake says the supreme man should, "to bring again the golden age" by revealing it in his work and his life, but fought, as with battered and smoke-blackened armour in the mouth of the pit, was the discredit of "the century of

---

[1] *The Patriot Parliament*, edited by Thomas Davis, a collection of historical documents from 1689. This volume had been the first in the New Irish Library series.
[2] *The New Spirit of the Nation*, edited by Martin MacDermott.
[3] *A Parish Providence* by "E. M. Lynch," actually a translation of Balzac's *Médecin de campagne*. Yeats had given a bad review to this and the previously mentioned volume in the *Bookman*, August, 1894 (see above).
[4] There is no record of Yeats's reviewing *The Irish Song Book*, but such a review may very well exist.

philosophers": a century which had set chop-logic in the place of the mysterious power, obscure as a touch from behind a curtain, that had governed "the century of poets." Some pages of Sir Thomas Brown [*sic*] are, one doubts not, of a greater kind, as pure literature, than any he wrote, but he has given the world an unforgettable parable by building an over-powering genius upon the wreckage of the merely human faculties, of all that the Herr Nordaus[5] of ours and other times have acclaimed and preached; and it is because the most ignorant feel this in some instinctive way that his throne is unassailable. Ireland seems to me to especially need this parable, for she is so busy with opinions that she cannot understand that imaginative literature wholly, and all literature in some degree, exists to reveal a more powerful and passionate, a more divine world than ours; and not to make our ploughing and sowing, our spinning and weaving, more easy or more pleasant, or even to give us a good opinion of ourselves by glorifying our past or our future.

Mr. Taylor's and Sir Charles Gavan Duffy's books, though not literature and the interpretation of literature, are excellently useful so long as our Irish readers do not think them one or the other. Mr. Taylor has explored an obscure historical period with an industry above all praise, and with a strong national enthusiasm, but—and I must apologise for judging him by a standard by which he has never desired to be judged—his book is not literature, because he does not, as Mr. King does occasionally, reveal the actions and persons of his story in the mirror of a temperament, because he has not what Matthew Arnold called "the literary consciousness." Sir Charles Gavan Duffy is always interesting on the friends of his youth, and there is no book of his so valuable for Irish purposes as his life of Davis, already well known in its more expensive form. One regrets, however, to find that he still persists in calling Davis—the maker of three or four charming songs that were not great, and of much useful political rhyme that was not poetry—a great poet, and in seeking to prove it by quoting "Fontenoy" and other savourless imitations of Macaulay. No one who does not know literary Ireland can understand the harm done by such criticism, and the barren enthusiasm for the second-hand and the second-rate it prolongs. Let us sing our political songs with ardour, shouldering our pikes while we sing if we be so minded, but do not let us always call them great poetry.

W. B. Yeats

[5] Max Simon Nordau (1849–1923) had attempted to prove in *Entartung*, 1892 (English translation, *Degeneration*, 1895) a relationship between genius and degeneracy.

Greek Folk Poesy

This review of *New Folklore Researches*, *Greek Folk Poesy*, translated by Lucy M. J. Garnett, with Essays on Folklore by J. S. Stuart-Glennie, in two volumes, London, 1896, is from the *Bookman*, October, 1896.

Yeats's exposition of Stuart-Glennie's theory is particularly interesting for the study of his characteristic attitudes on race and class. Glennie said that civilization was born out of the meeting and conflict of a superior race and an inferior one. Such a theory supported Yeats's aristocratic ideals as well as his absorption with folklore. In his ideal world, the Anglo-Irish ascendancy were in the "great house," dispensing the benefits of civilization to the peasants in their cottages, and receiving in turn a rich wealth of folklore.

Yeats thought Miss Garnett's translations without value, yet he seems to have gained something from reading this book. He tells us in a note (*Variorum*, p. 806) that his poem "The Song of Wandering Aengus" was suggested by a Greek folk song. Perhaps it was Miss Garnett's translation of "The Lover's Return," in which the lover is "a wanderer o'er the hills" and there is much gold, silver, and apple images. Or perhaps "The Fruit of the Apple Tree," which ends:

> "*Come, gather, youth! Come, gather them, the apples of my fruit tree;*
> *And gather them again, again, and stoop again and again!*"

R. K. Alspach in "Two Songs of Yeats," *Modern Language Notes*, lxi, 395–400, thinks that Yeats's source was "The Three Fishes" (cited in A. Norman Jeffares, *A Commentary on the Collected Poems of W. B. Yeats*, London, 1968, pp. 61–62).

M ISS LUCY M. J. GARNETT has translated in "Greek Folk Poesy" about four hundred pages of Greek folk poetry, a part newly collected, and a part translated from Greek collections; and Mr. J. S. Stuart Glennie has prefaced the book with certain essays on a new theory of the origin of civilisation. Anthologies of Greek folk prose and of Gaelic folk poetry are to follow, and the introductions and notes, etc., of these books are to be Mr. Stuart Glennie's final proof of his theory. One reads him at first with difficulty and reluctance because of the barbarism of his style. He uses the longest and most unmusical words, and, even when he has a simple word like "records" ready to his hand, delights in such fruit of his own fancy as "recordations"; while his misuse of capitals passes belief. One gradually, however, becomes aware of a certain force of imagination and lucidity of intellect in the midst of this verbiage; and presently one is mastered by a strong curiosity. For the accepted theories of a spontaneous development of civilisation out of savagery he substitutes what he calls "the general

conflict theory," and suggests that "civilised" or "progressive com-
munities" began when a race of superior intellectual power compelled
or persuaded a race of lesser intellectual power to feed it and house it,
in return for the religion and science which it had thus found the leisure
to make, and to pass on from generation to generation in always growing complexity. This contest, the contest of subtlety against force, the
subtlety often of a very few against the force of a multitude, gradually
changed from a contest between men of different races to a compact
between men of different classes, and so created the modern world. He
supports this theory with an elaborate array of arguments, which I have
not enough of science to apprise, among the rest with arguments based
on the existence "at the very earliest ages of which we have anthropo-
logical evidence" of "at least two different or intellectually unequal
Species or Races of Primitive Man," differing from each other "in
cranial type as well as in stature, even more than whites differ from
blacks." This theory, if established, Mr. Stuart Glennie points out, will
reconcile the theories of writers like Professor Max Müller,[1] who
believes the great ancient mythologies, to have a profound and complex meaning, with the theories of writers like Mr. Andrew Lang,[2]
who believes them a survival of the beliefs of savages; for the men of
the higher race could invent no more certain way of prolonging their
own rule than to change the childish beliefs about them into a complex
mystery of which they were themselves the prophets and guardians: all
that was merely instinctive and spontaneous coming from the many and
from the dominant few all that was intellectual and deliberate. I find
this theory, which affirms the supremacy of the intellect, much more
plausible than any of those theories which imply the origin, by a vague
process which no one has explained, of the most exquisite inventions of
folk-lore and mythology from the imaginations of everybody and
nobody; but only scientific folk-lorists and mythologists can say whether
it is consistent with the facts. I am, however, convinced that some such
theory will be established in the long run; being no democrat in intellectual things, and altogether persuaded that elaborate beauty has never
come but from the mind of a deliberate artist writing at leisure and in
peace.

Mr. Stuart Glennie gives certain pages to a destructive analysis of the
accepted classifications and definitions of the science of folk-lore, and
suggests classifications and definitions in accordance with his new
theory. All his definitions appear to me to be excellent, except perhaps

[1] Max Müller (1823–1900) was a German philologist and orientalist. His major work was
his edition of *Sacred Books of the East*, a 51-volume collection of oriental non-Christian
religious writings.

[2] Andrew Lang (1844–1912), poet and essayist, was one of the translators of the famous
prose versions of the *Iliad* and the *Odyssey*. He wrote many books on folklore and mythology.

his definition of religion, which makes religion too exclusively a matter of conduct; and his classifications would perhaps be as useful as they are certainly interesting, but for his lack of any instinct for the right word. "Zoonist" is not English, and to make an arbitrary distinction between "tales" and "stories" in order to distinguish between the folk-lore of cosmical and the folk-lore of moral ideas is not good sense. As he is not worse in this matter than certain other folk-lorists, one had been content perhaps to forget his style out of respect for his theory had he not taken to himself a collaboratress who writes seven times worse than himself. A scientific theory can but suffer a temporary injury from the language of its exposition, but a folk song put into bad verse loses the half of its scientific and nearly all its literary interest. Miss Garnett would perhaps have made a beautiful book had she been content to write it in prose. Leconte de Lisle's translations of Homer, Virgil and Aeschylus, Mr. Lang's, Mr. Butcher's, and Mr. Leaf's translation of Homer, Mr. Lang's translation of Theocritus, and the recent trans-lations of Roumanian folk songs,[3] were surely a sufficient precedent. There can be no justification of the writing of verse except the power to write as a poet writes; and such lines as

> "I hear my heart a-sighing, a-grieving with its smart,
> And my nous which calls in answer, 'Have patience, O dear heart'";

and such lines as

> "A flower I took thee to my heart, and there a thorn art thou;
> And marvels all the world to see that lost our love is now";

and such lines as

> "Vlachopoulo,[4] thee I love;
> This I've come to tell my dove."
>
> "Goumene, if thou lov'st true,
> Go and fetch a boat, now do."
>
> "Handsome let its boatman be,
> To pull the oars for thee and me,"

are not written as a poet writes.

Miss Garnett's translations are indeed so lifeless that it is impossible to form any judgment of the poetical value of the originals, or get more than a few rare and faint emotions from all her four hundred pages. Greek folk poetry is apparently a very civilised poetry, with little of the superhuman preoccupations and extravagant beauty of Roumanian and Gaelic folk poetry. It mentions, for instance, a five hundred years

[3] *The Bard of the Dimbovitza, Roumanian Folk-Songs*, second series, gathered by Hélène Vacaresco and translated by Carmen Sylva and Alma Strettell, London, 1894.
[4] In Miss Garnett's translation this name is "Vlachopoula."

old witch, but takes no pleasure in her age such as the Gaelic folk poet took when he made her cry, "Who has carried away my gold, which I was for five hundred years gathering in the waste places of the earth?"[5] And its expression of love is prudent, temperate, almost calculating, beside the ungovernable passion of more primitive verse. It has nothing of that search for some absolute of emotion, some mysterious infinite of passion which is in so much of Gaelic poetry. There is never anything like that wild lyrical outburst translated by Dr. Hyde: "She is my treasure, O, she is my treasure, the woman of the gray eyes, a woman who would not place a hand under my head. She is my love, O she is my love, a woman who left no strength in me, a woman who would not breathe a sigh after me, a woman who would not raise a stone at my tomb. She is my secret love, O she is my secret love, a woman who tells me nothing . . . a woman who does not remember when I am out, a woman who would not weep at my death."[6] Its emotion is weighted and measured with a nice sense of occasions and circumstances; one feels that the poets who wrote it were well aware of a great civilised literature somewhere behind them, and trod carefully in the footsteps of men preoccupied with the state and with the world. Nor has it that marvellous sense of a subtle union between an emotion and outer things which is in such songs as this Roumanian love song: "Take which ever way thou wilt, for the ways are all alike; but do thou only come—I bade my threshold wait thy coming. From out my window one can see the graves—and on my life the graves too keep a watch."[7] It is indeed as unlike such a song as possible, being always definite, lucid, reasonable, having the clear light of the day of work and thought, and not the vague magnificence of sunrise or of sunset. It lacks, in other words, those very characteristics which written literature is continually absorbing from unwritten literature, that it may escape the old age of many reasons, the frailty of feet that tread but upon smooth roads; an absorption which is itself an illustration of Mr. Stuart Glennie's theory. It seems less like a folk literature than an imperfect literature of culture, and if one judged it by its literary characteristics alone, one would class it, not with primitive poetry like the poetry of Gaelic Ireland and Scotland, but with such half-cultivated, half-instinctive verse as that written by men like Walsh, Callanan, and the "Young Ireland" writers, in Ireland in this century.

W. B. Yeats

[5] This quotation is from "Paudeen O'Kelly and the Weasel," a folktale in Douglas Hyde's *Beside the Fire*. See Yeats's review in this collection, p. 186.
[6] From Douglas Hyde's *Love Songs of Connacht*.
[7] From the poem "At the House" from *The Bard of the Dimbovitza*.

The Cradles of Gold

This story of the peasant wife who was taken "away" by the fairies appeared in the *Senate*, November, 1896. Yeats gathered other such stories in *The Celtic Twilight*, and with Lady Gregory he assembled enough legends like it to make the long quarterly article "Away" (*Fortnightly Review*, April, 1902). The lullaby "The fairy children laugh in cradles of wrought gold" had appeared previously in the *Savoy* (April, 1896) and was included in *The Wind among the Reeds* (1899). The geography of the poem is that Sligo landscape made famous by Yeats's poetry.

NOT so long ago as when herons built their nests in old men's beards, but long ago, one Michael Hearne leaned over his half-door and looked down the borreen that led from his wind-beaten cot on one of the more easterly of the Ox Mountains to the Sligo and Ballina Road. He lived alone, because the many scars left by the fights at patterns and on fair days, and his reputation for grimness and violence, had kept him from getting a wife. He was often lonely, and was lonely to-night, and saw with pleasure Peter Hearne, his brother, whom he had not seen for years, coming along the borreen. The Hearnes were not at all adventurous, and, except for patterns and fair days, had not strayed for years, the one from the shore of Lough Gill about Dooney,[1] and the other from the mountainous barony of Skreen; and neither could have told you anything of the world beyond the mountains that rose behind their cots, except that it contained monsters, and marvels, and perils. "God be with you, Peter, and how is Whinny," he cried, when Peter Hearne was within earshot; but Peter Hearne did not answer until his slow dejected feet had brought him to the thorn-tree a little way from the door of the cabin. "I have come to speak about Whinny," he said, stopping by the thorn-tree, "for she has gone from me; but she is not dead. Oh, no, she is not dead at all. Whinny is gone among the Shee.[2] God be between us and harm."

"Be quiet now," replied the other, "you are standing by the old thorn where they gather at night." And with this he led the way into the house, and drew a chair over to the fire for his brother, driving away a white hen that had made it her perch, and cleaning it with a bit of rag. He sat a creepy stool before it for himself, and began filling his

[1] Lough Gill, which contains the lake isle of Innisfree, flows westward through the river Garavogue past the town of Sligo into Sligo bay. The promontory of Dooney Rock, jutting out into Lough Gill, is the locale of Yeats's "The Fiddler of Dooney."

[2] "Shee," the Irish word for fairies, is sometimes spelled "Sidhe."

pipe. The other told, with many repetitions and with many loud lamentations, how Whinny, his wife, had been queer, distraught, low-voiced, and pale-faced for the three years of their married life, and went often, and particularly when the moon was up, to the edge of the Lough, and lingered there, whispering ancient songs to herself, and gazing out over the water. Even after their child was born she would leave it in its cradle and go down to the stream and be walking up and down there half the night, and one night she came in and said she had seen cradles of gold hanging between the trees and bushes on a little island that is under Sleuth Wood. The next night she did not come in at all, nor any night after this for a long time, and so he went to the wise man of Cairns Foot, who came to the shore and looked out over the lake through a hole in the bone of a hare, and saw her sweeping over the water among the Shee, tossing out her hair, and laughing at her image in the water. A few nights after this Peter Hearne saw from where he lay in the big bed, the door open slowly and Whinny come in and sit down by the cradle, and take the child out and suckle it awhile, and then put it back in the cradle and rock it and croon over it; and all the while he heard the Shee talking out on the Lough side. He could have spoken to her, and taken hold of her, and held her, he said, but he was in a great dread of the Shee, and could only lie there keeping his eyes upon her. She stopped there rocking and crooning for a good hour, and then went out, and he heard the talking grow fainter and fainter as though the Shee were going away over the water, and when she had gone the child was so soundly and sweetly asleep and slept so long, and woke so like a bird that he knew she must have crooned some druid song over its sleep. The next night it was the same, and the night after, and the night after, and the night after, and on till the very night that was last gone, and he never stirred nor spoke, for he was always, and Michael knew that he spoke truth, a timid man.

"You were always," said Michael Hearne when he had finished, "a poor spirited peaceful man, and you will want me now to go to Dooney and speak to her, and take hold of her, and let none of them pull her away."

It was afternoon before the two men set out, and the sun had gone down behind the barrow of Maeve[3] a good hour when they reached the cot at the end of the bay that runs in between Sleuth Wood and the woods about Dooney Rock. The wooded islands and the wooded mountainous headlands mirrored in the still waters of the lake, seemed to Peter Hearne full of that mysterious stillness which falls upon the exterior when the interior world is about to open its gates, and it was with relief that he closed the door, and stirred the turf to a blaze and

[3] Legend has it that Queen Maeve is buried under a cairn of stones upon Knocknarea.

thrust an old coat into the little window. He drew a settle to where his ancestral four post bed threw a shadow on the fire-lit floor, that Michael Hearne might watch in comfort and unseen, and set the cradle and a chair well in the fire-light; then he undressed and got into bed and drew the moth-eaten curtains and pulled his night-cap over his ears. Michael Hearne lay down on the settle and covered himself with his great frieze coat, and waited with his eyes on the door. Two hours passed before he heard a faint whispering somewhere in the distance, and this grew nearer and nearer becoming at last a confused talking, mixed with a fitful music from stringed instruments. Then he heard the latch lifted and saw the door open, and Whinny, his brother's wife, came in with the indecisive steps, and the pale face in which the beauty was fading, early, as the way is with peasant women, which he had seen occasionally on market days at Sligo. She sat down with a sigh and lifted the child, which had begun to cry feebly, out of the wooden cradle, covered it with kisses, and began to suckle it, gazing on it the while with a profound tenderness. Presently the music and voices outside the door seemed to catch her ear, for she looked towards them, and Michael Hearne looked too and saw between the open door and the lake a multitude of tall, slender forms dressed in a saffron raiment, and having torques of silver and gold, and coolleens of ruddy curls, moving hither and thither, full of a restless life, and holding stringed instruments of a shape he had never seen before, which they played by striking little wands of silver against the strings. Then she looked at the child again, and pressed it passionately against her breast, and did this again and yet again, and then she laid it in the cradle and began rocking the cradle and singing. He recognised the air and the words of "The winds from beyond the world," a very ancient cradle-song, made for her only child by the wicked wife of that wizard Garreth, who rides hither and thither over the hills of Munster, awaiting the time when the shoes of his horse, now thin as a cat's ear, shall be worn through, and the deliverance of Ireland at hand. He listened with a shudder to the wild air, at whose sound all wholesome desires and purposes were thought to weaken and dissolve, and to the unholy words which pious mothers had ever forbid their daughters to sing:

> "*The fairy children laugh in cradles of wrought gold,*
> *And clap their hands together and half close their eyes,*
> *For they will ride the winds when the gier-eagle flies*
> *With heavy, whitening wings, and a heart fallen cold:*
> *I kiss my wailing child and press it to my breast*
> *And hear the narrow graves calling my child and me:*
> *Desolate winds that cry over the wandering sea,*
> *Desolate winds that hover in the flaming West,*

Desolate winds that beat the doors of Heaven, and beat
The doors of Hell, and blow there many a whimpering ghost,
And hear the winds have shaken, the unappeasable host
Is comelier than candles before Maurya's feet."4

When the song had ended, he rose and went silently and carefully towards the singer, who did not hear, for now her eyes rested again upon the tall, slender, saffron-robed figures. He seized her by the arm with the right hand, and shaking his left hand towards the door, cried out, "Children of the Goddess, children of Dana, faeries of the Hill, take her from me if you dare." She turned her eyes upon him, and they were like the eyes of a hare taken in a trap. "Let me go, Michael Hearne," she said, "for I am nurse to the child of Finivaragh, the King,5 and it will cry if I do not go." And then, seeing that he still held her, she began calling for help. At once a clamour broke out among the saffron-robed figures, and they began crowding through the door; and in a moment Michael Hearne felt a hundred hands trying to pull her away or beating him with closed fists, and heard many voices denouncing him with words that seemed at once very near and very far off. They might as well have pulled and beaten the boulders on the Bird Mountains overhead as try to pull her from those fingers, hardened with clasping the alpeen in a hundred faction fights, or try to trouble over greatly that head upon which so many alpeens had descended in vain. Every moment their struggles were becoming more violent and their voices shriller, when suddenly he heard an imperious voice by the door saying, "Did I not tell you to be silent, that I might meditate upon the wisdom that Mongan raved out after he had drunk from the seven vats of wine!"6

All was silent in a moment, and the fingers released their hold and the hands ceased to smite. A tall person, with a pale, proud face, and eyes which seemed to burn with some unquenchable desire, wearing a much-pointed and flame-like crown of red gold, and looking all of fire in his straight robe of saffron, was standing in the door, against the dark and vaporous blue of the lake.

"He has taken hold of Whinny Hearne," said a voice, close by Michael's elbow, "and will not let her go."

4 This poem appeared in the *Savoy* of April, 1896, as "A Cradle Song." Its final title in the collected poems is "The Unappeasable Host." For changes in this poem see *Variorum*, pp. 146–47.

5 Yeats identified Finivaragh as "the king of the faeries of Connaught" (notes to *Poems*, London, 1908).

6 Mongan, legendary king of Ulster and the son of the sea god Manannan mac Lir, returns from the Land of Youth, and his adventures, as he tells them to Colum Cille, are given in the *Tain Bo Cuailgne*. Yeats's poem "Song of Mongan" (later called "He thinks of his Past Greatness when a Part of the Constellations of Heaven") opens, "I have drunk ale from the Country of the Young./And weep because I know all things now. . . ."

The tall person strode over the threshold, and stood for a moment looking down at Michael Hearne and Whinny with something of impatience in his eyes, and then spoke in the same imperious voice, "I am Finivaragh, the King, and understand many things that even the archangels do not understand, and out of my knowledge I bid you let her go. There are those in the world for whom no mortal kiss has more than a shadowy comfort, nor the rocking of any mortal cradle, but a fragile music, and she is of them; but now, when the moon has crumbled a little longer, the last affection will die out of her heart and she will become a crowned flame, dancing on the bare hills and in the darkness of the woods."

But Michael Hearne still held Whinny by the arm, looking at Finivaragh with a mingled fear and anger and reverence.

"If you will let her go, I will be a friend to you and to your brother over there in the bed, and keep your cattle safe from the arrows of the Shee, and your milk from the spells of witches."

Michael Hearne half bowed his head as became him in so famous and royal a presence, but his fingers did not open.

"We have let her come among the wooden cradles for we are always pitiful to the young, knowing that the young have never dug in our raths or torn up our thorn-trees. She sings every night over her cradle, a song as heavy with sleep as the white hair of Partholan,[7] a song that we taught to the most subtle of women many years ago. And see, her child lies in the sweet sleep of the children of Dana, and even though the death Mocha and Black Scanlan were to beat their hoofs upon the thatch its eyelids would not quiver. But, most witless of the children of Mil,[8] it will be as you will have it be, and she shall go and live among you again and have a chill touch and a low voice. When my child has been weaned it will be the full of the moon, and then she will go to you again; Finivaragh the son of Feval has promised."

Then Michael Hearne began to smile, and he opened his hand, and the saffron crowd caught up Whinny and began rushing round about her in a tumult of joy; and the King turned towards the lake and went out, and all the crowd followed, and Michael Hearne saw them sweep away with Whinny in the midst of them over the still waters like a rushing flame, their reflection gleaming underneath them, and at so great speed that he understood how much it had irked their passionate natures to stand still in one place for a long while. When they had vanished into the darkness beyond Sleuth Wood, he turned towards the bed, and drawing back its curtains shook Peter Hearne until he sat up

---

[7] Partholan was one of the prehistoric settlers of Ireland.

[8] The sons of Mile emigrated from Spain and colonized Ireland. They formed the race of Milesians.

and drew the night-cap off his ears; and he said: "She will come in at the door at a full moon and stay with you till she dies, for Finivaragh has promised, and since the time of Eoha of the heavy sighs, when first he began going to and fro between the Ox and the Bird Mountains, he has never broken his word, and that is for twelve hundred years."

For nearly a month Peter Hearne saw Whinny rocking the cradle in the night, and lay watching her and trembling; and at last it was the night of the full moon. That night he heard no voices, and no faint footsteps, but a rustling in the bushes on the lake-side, and a low moan- at his door. When it was broad daylight his courage came to him, and he opened the door and found Whinny, crouched with her head against the wall, and sound asleep. He shook her until she awoke, and asked her why she had gone away. She had gone out the night before, she said, with a great desire to wander along the edge of the Lough, and while she was wandering, a grey mist covered her, and she did not know any more until she felt his hand upon her shoulder. He told her how many nights she had been gone, and sent her to the chapel to pray against the power of the Shee, and when she came back, brought her into the room and set her by the cradle. She lived with him many years, and never saw the children of Dana again; but always, when the moon was at full, a desire to be far away came upon her, and she would stand at the door watching the wild ducks flying in long lines over the water, and would move restlessly hither and thither, and talk excitedly until the moon had begun to crumble a little at one side; but at all the other times her voice was low and her touch chill, as Finivaragh had said.

W. B. Yeats

The Well at the World's End

Yeats reviewed William Morris's romance *The Well at the World's End*, Kelmscott Press, Hammersmith, and London, 1896, in the *Bookman* issue of November, 1896.

Yeats had known William Morris and his family well in 1888–1890. He attended some meetings of the Socialist League at Morris's home. After a time, he found this group's indifference to religion so annoying that he left the circle for good.

This review appeared shortly after Morris's death. Yeats gave an extended characterization of Morris in the "Four Years: 1887–91" section of his auto-biography. In another essay on Morris (reprinted in *Ideas of Good and Evil*) he admitted that Morris was not one of the greatest of poets but "he was among the greatest of those who prepare the last reconciliation when the Cross shall blossom with roses."

THAT Mr. William Morris was the greatest poet of his time one may doubt, remembering more impassioned numbers than his, but one need not doubt at all that he was the poet of his time who was most perfectly a poet. Certain men impress themselves on the imagination of the world as types, and Shelley, with his wayward desires, his unavailing protest, has become the type of the poet to most men and to all women, and perhaps because he seemed to illustrate that English dream, which holds the poet and the artist unfitted for practical life: laughable and lovable children whose stories and angers one may listen to when the day's work is done. If, however, a time come when the world recognises that the day's work, that practical life, become noble just in so far as they are subordinated to the sense of beauty, the sense of the perfect, just in so far as they approach the dream of the poet and the artist, then Mr. William Morris may become, instead of Shelley, the type of the poet: for he more than any man of modern days tried to change the life of his time into the life of his dream. To others beauty was a solitary vision, a gift coming from God they knew not how; but to him it was always some golden fleece or happy island, some well at the world's end, found after many perils and many labours in the world, and in all his later books, at any rate, found for the world's sake. Almost alone among the dreamers of our time, he accepted life and called it good; and because almost alone among them he saw, amid its incompleteness and triviality, the Earthly Paradise that shall blossom at the end of the ages.

When Ralph, the pilgrim to the well at the world's end, is setting out upon his journey, he meets with a monk who bids him renounce the world. "'Now, lord, I can see by thy face that thou art set on beholding the fashion of this world, and most like it will give thee the rue.'

"Then came a word into Ralph's mouth, and he said: 'Wilt thou tell me, father, whose work was the world's fashion?'

"The monk reddened, but answered nought, and Ralph spake again: 'Forsooth, did the craftsman of it fumble over his work?'

"Then the monk scowled, but presently he enforced himself to speak blithely, and said, 'Such matters are over high for my speech or thine, lord; but I tell thee, who knoweth, that there are men in this House who have tried the world and found it wanting.'

"Ralph smiled and said, stammering: 'Father, did the world try them, and find them wanting perchance?'"

And later on it is said to the seekers of the well, "If you love not the earth and the world with all your souls, and will not strive all ye may to be frank and happy therein, your toil and peril aforesaid shall win you no blessing, but a curse."

In the literal sense of the word, and in the only high sense, he was a prophet; and it was his vision of that perfect life, which the world is always trying, as Jacob Behmen[1] taught, to bring forth, that awakened every activity of his laborious life—his revival of mediaeval tapestry and stained glass, his archaic printing, his dreams of Sigurd and of Gudrun and of Guinevere, his essays upon the unloveliness of our life and art, his preaching in parks and at the corners of streets, his praise of revolutions, his marchings at the head of crowds, and his fierce anger against most things that we delight to honour. We sometimes call him "melancholy," and speak of the "melancholy" of his poems, and I know not well why, unless it be that we mistake the pensiveness of his early verse, a pensiveness for noble things once had and lost, or for noble things too great not to be nearly beyond hope, for his permanent mood, which was one of delight in the beauty of noon peace, of rest after labour, of orchards in blossom, of the desire of the body and of the desire of the spirit. Like Blake, he held nothing that gave joy unworthy, and might have said with Ruysbroeck,[2] "I must rejoice without ceasing, even though the world shudder at my joy," except that he would have had the world share his joy. There is no picture of him more permanent in my mind than that of him sitting at one of those suppers at Hammersmith to which he gathered so singular a company of artists and workmen, and crying out on those who held it unworthy to be inspired by a cup of wine: for had not wine come out of the sap and out of the leaves and out of the heat of the sunlight? It was this vision of happiness that made him hate rhetoric, for rhetoric is the triumph of the desire to convince over the desire to reveal. His definition of good writing would have been writing full of pictures of beautiful things and beautiful moments. "My masters," he said once, "are Keats and Chaucer, because Keats and Chaucer make pictures." Dante he held for a like reason to be more a poet than Milton, who, despite his "great, earnest mind, expressed himself as a rhetorician." These pictures were not, I imagine, to be so much in great masses as in minute detail. "The beauty of Dante," he said to me once, "is in his detail"; and in all his art one notices nothing more constant than the way in which it heaps up, and often in the midst of tragedy, little details of happiness. This book is full of them, and there is scarcely a chapter in which there is not some moment for which one might almost give one's soul.

W. B. Yeats

---

[1] *Behmen*: usually spelled "Boehme" or "Böhme."

[2] Jan van Ruysbroeck (1293–1381), Flemish mystic. Maurice Maeterlinck translated his *De Gheestelike Brulocht* into French (*L'Ornement des noces spirituelles*, 1891) and a translation of selections of this work appeared in London, in 1894, as *The Adornment of the Spiritual Marriage*.

Miss Fiona Macleod as a Poet

Yeats reviewed Fiona Macleod's *From the Hills of Dream: Mountain Songs and Island Runes*, Edinburgh, 1896, in the December, 1896, issue of the *Bookman*.

Scottish Celticism seems to lend itself to literary double identities bordering on the fraudulent. With the example of Macpherson's *Ossian* to guide him, William Sharp, a successful literary journalist, created a second identity —that of Fiona Macleod—with a separate literary style and handwriting. Yeats had known Sharp since 1888 and then ". . . hated his red British face of flaccid contentment" (*Letters*, p. 43). He came to know of Fiona Macleod during the mid-nineties.

Yeats admired Sharp's psychic powers. The two men joined in experiments in vision and trance until Sharp, complaining that his health was injured, resumed his private vision. For a time Yeats believed Fiona Macleod to be a real person, wrote her letters, and received answers in Sharp's special "Macleod" handwriting. He may have discovered the secret before Sharp's death. Yeats believed that the writings of Fiona Macleod were the genuine products of trance-like visions in which a separate personal identity spoke through Sharp.

At first Yeats thought Fiona Macleod was a writer of great promise, especially since her writings seemed a perfect example of the decline of realistic and the coming of symbolic art. Her work was all the more important to Yeats in that she was a Scottish Celt and hence proved the universality of Celtic traits. With Irish, Welsh, Scottish, and, as he hoped, Breton Celticism in full renaissance, the Saxon empire of realism and materialism might be encircled and destroyed. Despite his wish to be pleased, Yeats's three reviews of "her" work mark an increasing impatience with the careless, overblown verbiage of Sharp in his Macleod phase.

The section of *From the Hills of Dream* entitled "Foam of the Past" was dedicated to Yeats as a kindred Celtic seer. Miss Macleod told Yeats in this dedication, "So you, perhaps, may say of some of these lines in 'From the Hills of Dream' and 'Foam of the Past' that they come familiarly to you in other than the sense of mere acquaintance." Sharp meant a community of experience, but these lines from "The Bugles of Dreamland" may have seemed familiar to Yeats for other reasons:

> Come away from the weary old world of tears,
> Come away, come away to where one never hears
> The slow weary drip of the slow weary years,
> But Peace and deep rest till the white dews are falling
> And the blithe bugle-laughters through Dreamland are calling.

IN France, where every change of literary feeling brings with it a change of literary philosophy, the great change of our time is believed to be a return to the subjective. We no longer wish to describe nature like the "nature poets," or to describe society like the "realists," but to make our work a mirror, where the passions and desires and ideals of our own minds can cast terrible or beautiful images.[1] If the French are right—and every new book which seems at all of our time is, I think, a proof that they are—we are at the beginning of a franker trust in passion and in beauty than was possible to the poets who put their trust in the external world and its laws. Some of the poems in "From the Hills of Dream" would have been almost impossible ten years ago. For ten years ago Miss Macleod would have asked herself, "Is this a valuable and a sober criticism upon life?"[2] and we should probably have lost one of the most inspired, one of the most startling, one of the most intense poems of our time, her incomparable "Prayer of Women."[3]

> "O Spirit that broods upon the hills,
> And moves upon the face of the deep,
> And is heard in the wind,
> Save us from the desire of men's eyes.
>
> .   .   .   .   .
>
> Ah, hour of the hours,
> When he looks at our hair and sees it is grey;
> And at our eyes and sees they are dim;
> And at our lips, straightened out with long pain;
> And at our breasts, fallen and seared like a barren hill;[4]
> And at our hands, worn with toil!
> Ah, hour of the hours,
> When, seeing, he seeth all the bitter ruin and wreck of us—
> All save the violated womb that curses him—
> All save the heart that forbeareth . . . for pity—
> All save the living brain that condemneth him.
>
> .   .   .   .   .
>
> O spirit and the nine angels who watch us,
> And Thy Son and Mary Virgin,[5]
> Heal us of the wrong of man:
> We whose breasts are weary with milk
> Cry, cry to Thee, O Compassionate."

This poem was, I understand, first written in Gaelic,[6] and Miss Macleod is always best when she writes under a Gaelic and legendary

[1] *a mirror*: Shelley in the peroration of his "Defence of Poetry" called Poets ". . . the mirrors of the gigantic shadows which futurity casts upon the present. . . ."

[2] *criticism upon life*: Yeats echoes Arnold's famous dictum that poetry was ". . . a criticism of life under the conditions fixed for such a criticism by the laws of poetic truth and poetic beauty" (Arnold's essay "The Study of Poetry").

[3] *"Prayer of Women"*: Yeats shortened this poem by 23 lines.

[4] *like a barren hill*: Sharp reads "as a barren hill."

[5] This line read in Sharp "And Thou, White Christ, and Mary Mother of Sorrow. . . ."

[6] *From the Hills of Dream* contains translations from the Gaelic.

and mythological influence. Emotions which seem vague or extravagant when expressed under the influence of modern literature, cease to
be vague and extravagant when associated with ancient legend and
mythology, for legend and mythology were born out of man's longing
for the mysterious and the infinite. When Miss Macleod writes of "the
white Peace"[7] which "lies not on the sunlit hill," nor "on the sunlit
plain," nor "on any running stream," but comes sometimes into the
soul of man as "the moonlight of a perfect Peace," I find her thought
too vague greatly to move or impress me; but when she writes of "the
four white winds of the world,[8] whose father the golden sun is, whose
mother the wheeling moon is, the north and the south and the east and
the west," and of "the three dark winds of the world; the chill breath
of the grave, the breath from the depth of the sea," and "the breath of
to-morrow," I am altogether moved and impressed. I feel, indeed,
throughout this book two influences—a Gaelic influence, which Miss
Macleod has mastered and remoulded, and an influence from modern
literature which she has not yet been able to master and mould; and
this is, perhaps, why "From the Hills of Dream" seems to me so much
more unequal, so much more experimental, than "The Sin Eater" or
"The Washer of the Ford." Many of the poems which have the
strongest Gaelic influence, and therefore the most authentic inspiration,
are in wild and irregular measures; and this is a pity, because the best
critics are not convinced that wild and irregular measures are perfectly
legitimate. The poems in rhyme and in regular measures which seem
to be latest in date are, however, a great advance upon their fellows,
and have occasional passages of a charming phantasy, like the second,
third, fourth, and fifth stanzas in "The Moon Child," or of a beautiful

---

[7] Yeats quoted phrases out of context and distorted by so doing the poem "The White
Peace":

> *It lies not on the sunlit hill*
> *Nor on the sunlit plain:*
> *Nor ever on any running stream*
> *Nor on the unclouded main—*
> *But sometimes, through the Soul of Man,*
> *Slow moving o'er his pain*
> *The moonlight of a perfect peace*
> *Floods heart and brain.*

[8] These passages from "The Rune of the Four Winds" are as follows in Sharp:

> *By the four white winds of the world,*
> *Whose father the golden Sun is,*
> *Whose mother the wheeling Moon is,*
> *The North and the South and the East and the West: . . .*

And,

> *By the three dark winds of the world;*
> *The chill dull breath* ["dull" is omitted by Yeats] *of the Grave,*
> *The breath from the depths* ["depth" in Yeats] *of the Sea,*
> *The breath of To-morrow: . . .*

intensity, like this passage, which expresses something almost beyond the range of expression.

> *"She had two men within the palm, the hollow of her hand;*
> *She takes their souls and blows them forth as idle drifted sand;*
> *And one falls back upon her breast that is his quiet home,*
> *And one goes out into the night and is as wind-blown foam,*
> *And when she sees the sleep of one, ofttimes she riseth there,*
> *And looks into the outer dusk and calleth soft and fair."*[9]

W. B. Yeats

[9] There is a stanza break after the fourth line of this quotation of Sharp's "In the Shadow." Other variants are:

1st line—Sharp reads "She has two men . . ."
5th line—Sharp reads "she rises there,"
6th line—Sharp reads "outer dark".

Bibliography

An asterisk before an entry means that a review by Yeats of that book is included in this collection. A general index will be included in volume two. To assist the reader in finding a review of a particular book, I have included after the entry the page on which Yeats's review of that book appears.

The Yeats section is divided into two groups, one for books and another for articles, reviews, and letters. An asterisk before a magazine review in this section means that the review may be found in this collection, and the page number is given after the entry.

GENERAL LIST OF WORKS CONSULTED

A.E. [George William Russell]. *The Earth Breath and Other Poems*. London, 1897. (*Sketch*, April 6, 1898)

*———. *Homeward Songs by the Way*. Dublin, 1894. (*Bookman*, August, 1894, and May, 1895)   [p. 335, p. 356]

———. *Letters to AE*, edited by Alan Denson. New York, 1961.

*Allingham, William. Collected poems in six volumes. London, 1887–1891. (*United Ireland*, December 12, 1891)   [p. 208]

Anne Boleyn: A Historical Drama in Five Acts. London, 1893. (*Speaker*, July 22, 1893)   [p. 276]

Arbois de Jubainville, H. d'. *Le Cycle mythologique irlandais, et la mythologie celtique*, Vol. II of *Cours de littérature celtique*. Paris, 1884.

———. *The Irish Mythological Cycle and Celtic Mythology*, translated by Richard Irvine Best. Dublin and London, 1903.

Arnold, Matthew. *The Study of Celtic Literature*. London, 1905.

Arts and Crafts Essays, by Members of the Arts and Crafts Exhibition Society, with a preface by William Morris. London, 1893.

Barrington, Sir Jonah. *Personal Sketches of His Own Times*, 2 vols. London, 1869.

Bechhofer-Roberts, C. E. *The Mysterious Madame, Helena Petrovna Blavatsky*. New York and London, 1931.

Behrman, S. N. *Portrait of Max*. New York and London, 1960. British title: *Conversations with Max*.

The Best Hundred Irish Books. Dublin, 1886. Originally printed in *The Freeman's Journal*.

Blake, William. *Poems of William Blake*, edited by W. B. Yeats. New York, Modern Library, n.d.

*———. *Selections from the Writings of William Blake*, edited by Laurence Housman. London, 1893. (*Bookman*, August, 1893)   [p. 280]

Blake, William. *The Works of William Blake*, edited by Edwin J. Ellis and W. B. Yeats, 3 vols. London, 1893.
———. *The Writings of William Blake*, edited by Geoffrey Keynes, 3 vols. London, 1925.
Blunt, Lady Anne. *Bedouin Tribes of the Euphrates*, 2 vols. London, 1879.
———. *A Pilgrimage to Nejd, the Cradle of the Arab Race*. London, 1881.
*Blunt, Wilfred Scawen. *Love Sonnets of Proteus*. London, 1885. (*United Ireland*, January 28, 1888)   [p. 122]
———. *My Diaries*, Part I. London, 1919.
[Boehme] Behmen, Jacob. *The Way to Christ*. Bath, 1775.
———. *The Works of Jacob Behmen*, 4 vols. London, 1772.
Boyd, Ernest A. *Ireland's Literary Renaissance*. New York and London, 1916.
*Bryant, Sophie. *Celtic Ireland*. London, 1889. (*Scots Observer*, January 4, 1890)   [p. 162]
———. *The Genius of the Gael, a Study in Celtic Psychology and Its Manifestations*. London, 1913.
Buchanan, Robert. *Look Round Literature*. London, 1887.
*———. *The Wandering Jew*. London, 1893. (*Bookman*, April, 1893)
                      [p. 263]
Butler, E. M. *The Myth of the Magus*. New York and London, 1948.
*Carleton, William. *The Life of William Carleton*, completed and edited by D. J. O'Donoghue, 2 vols. London, 1896. (*Bookman*, March, 1896)
                      [p. 394]
*———. *The Red-Haired Man's Wife*. Dublin, 1889. (*Scots Observer*, October 19, 1889)   [p. 141]
*———. *Stories from Carleton*, compiled by W. B. Yeats. London, 1889. (*Scots Observer*, October 19, 1889)   [p. 141]
Cleeve, Brian. *Dictionary of Irish Writers*. First series—Fiction. Cork, 1967.
Colum, Padraic and Mary. *Our Friend James Joyce*. New York, 1958; London, 1959.
Coxhead, Elizabeth. *Daughters of Erin, Five Women of the Irish Renascence*. London, 1965.
Crone, John S. *A Concise Dictionary of Irish Biography*. New York and Dublin, 1928.
*D.N.D. [D. N. Dunlop?]. "Interview with W. B. Yeats," *Irish Theosophist*, October 15, 1893.   [p. 298]
Dowden, Edward. *Letters of Edward Dowden and Correspondents*. London, 1914.
———. *New Studies in Literature*. London, 1895.
*Duffy, Sir Charles Gavan. *Short Life of Thomas Davis*. In "New Irish Library" Series. London, Dublin, New York, 1895. (*Bookman*, June, 1896)   [p. 406]
———. *Young Ireland*. In "New Irish Library" Series. Dublin and London, 1896. (*Bookman*, January, 1897)
*Dyer, T. F. Thistelton. *The Ghost World*. London, 1893. (*Speaker*, August 19, 1893)   [p. 283]
Eglinton, John [W. K. Magee]. *Irish Literary Portraits*. London, 1935.
———. *A Memoir of A.E.: George William Russell*. London, 1937.

Eglinton, John [W. K. Magee]. *Two Essays on the Remnant*, 2nd ed. Dublin, 1895. (*Bookman*, May, 1895)   [p. 356]
*——. W. B. Yeats, A.E., W. Larminie. *Literary Ideals in Ireland*. London, 1899.
Eliot, T. S. *Selected Essays*, new ed. New York, 1950.
*Ellis, Edwin J. *Fate in Arcadia*. London, 1892. (*Bookman*, September, 1892)   [p. 234]
*——. *Seen in Three Days*. London, 1893. (*Bookman*, February, 1894)
                    [p. 317]
Ellmann, Richard. *Yeats—the Man and the Masks*, paper bound ed. New York, 1958.
Engelberg, Edward. *The Vast Design: Patterns in W. B. Yeats's Aesthetic*. Toronto, 1964.
Faulkner, Peter. *William Morris and W. B. Yeats*. Dublin, 1962.
*Ferguson, Mary Catharine, Lady. *Sir Samuel Ferguson in the Ireland of His Day*. London, 1896. (*Bookman*, May, 1896)   [p. 403]
——. *The Story of the Irish before the Conquest. From the Mythical Period to the Invasion under Strongbow*, 3rd ed. Dublin, London, Edinburgh, 1903.
Ferguson, Sir Samuel. *Poems of Sir Samuel Ferguson, with an Introduction by Alfred Perceval Graves*. In "Every Irishman's Library." Dublin and London, n.d.
*Field, Michael [Katharine Harris Bradley and Edith Emma Cooper]. *Sight and Song*. London, 1892. (*Bookman*, July, 1892)   [p. 225]
——. *Works and Days, from the Journal of Michael Field*. London, 1933.
Finch, Edith. *Wilfred Scawen Blunt, 1840–1922*. London, 1938.
Flanagan, Thomas. *The Irish Novelists, 1800–1850*. New York, 1959; London, 1960.
*Garnett, Edward. *An Imaged World: Poems in Prose*. London, 1894. (*Speaker*, September 8, 1894)   [p. 341]
*Garnett, Lucy M. J. *New Folklore Researches. Greek Folk Poesy*. Translated by Lucy Garnett, with Essays on Folklore by J. S. Stuart-Glennie, 2 vols. London, 1896. (*Bookman*, October, 1896)   [p. 409]
*Garnett, Richard. *William Blake*. London, 1896. (*Bookman*, April, 1896)
                    [p. 400]
Gaynor, F. *Dictionary of Mysticism*. New York, 1953.
Gilchrist, Alexander. *Life of William Blake,* 2 vols. London, 1880.
Goethe, Johann Wolfgang von. *Goethe und Werther, Briefe Goethes,* edited by A. Kestner. Stuttgart and Augsburg, 1855.
Gourmont, Rémy de. *Pages choisies*. Paris, 1922.
Gregory, Isabella Augusta, Lady. *Cuchulain of Muirthemne*, with an introduction by W. B. Yeats. London, 1903.
——. *Poets and Dreamers: Studies and Translations from the Irish*. Dublin, 1903. (*Bookman*, May, 1903)
*Haig, Fenil [Ford Madox Ford]. *The Questions at the Well*. London, 1893. (*Speaker*, August 26, 1893)   [p. 288]
*Hallam, Arthur Henry. *The Poems of Arthur Henry Hallam, Together with His*

Essay on the Lyrical Poems of Alfred Tennyson. London, 1893. (*Speaker*, July 22, 1893) [p. 276]

Heilbrun, Carolyn G. *The Garnett Family.* New York and London, 1961.

Hone, Joseph. *W. B. Yeats, 1865–1939.* London, 1942.

Hopper, Nora. *Ballads in Prose.* London, 1894.

*Hosken, James Dryden. *Verses by the Way.* London, 1893. (*Speaker*, August 26, 1893) [p. 288]

*Howard, B. Douglas. *Life with Trans-Siberian Savages.* London, 1893. (*Speaker*, October 7, 1893) [p. 295]

Hueffer [Ford], Ford Madox. *Collected Poems.* London, 1914.

*Hyde, Douglas. *Beside the Fire: a Collection of Irish Gaelic Folk Stories*, translated by Douglas Hyde. London, 1890. (*National Observer*, February 28, 1891) [p. 186]

*———. *Love Songs of Connacht.* London, 1893. (*Bookman*, October, 1893) [p. 292]

*———. *The Story of Early Gaelic Literature.* In "New Irish Library" Series. Dublin and London, 1895. (*Bookman*, June, 1895) [p. 358]

*———. *The Three Sorrows of Story-Telling, and Ballads of St. Columkille.* London, 1895. (*Bookman*, July, 1895) [p. 364]

*Ibsen, Henrik. *Brand*, translated by F. E. Garrett. London, 1894. (*Bookman*, October, 1894) [p. 344]

Irish Minstrelsy, Being a Selection of Irish Songs, Lyrics and Ballads, edited by H. H. Sparling. London, 1887.

Jeffares, A. Norman. *A Commentary on the Collected Poems of W. B. Yeats*, London, 1968.

———. *W. B. Yeats, Man and Poet.* New Haven and London, 1949.

Jochum, K. P. S. *W. B. Yeats's Plays. An Annotated Checklist of Criticism.* Saarbrücken, 1966.

Johnson, Lionel. *Ireland, with Other Poems.* London, 1897. (*Bookman*, February, 1898)

Joyce, James. *The Critical Writings of James Joyce*, edited by Ellsworth Mason and Richard Ellmann. New York and London, 1959.

———. *Dubliners.* New York, Modern Library, 1926.

———. *Finnegans Wake.* New York, 1959.

———. *Ulysses.* New York, 1961.

Joyce, Patrick Weston. *Old Celtic Romances*, translated from the Gaelic by P. W. J. London, 1879.

Joyce, Robert Dwyer. *Ballads of Irish Chivalry; Songs and Poems.* Boston, 1872.

Keynes, Geoffrey. *A Bibliography of William Blake.* New York, 1921.

*King, Richard Ashe. *Swift in Ireland.* In "New Irish Library" Series. Dublin and London, 1896. (*Bookman*, June, 1896) [p. 406]

Kuhn, Alvin Boyd. *Theosophy, a Modern Revival of Ancient Wisdom.* New York, 1930.

La Motte-Fouqué, Friedrich, Baron de. *Undine, and Other Tales*, translated by F. E. Bunnett. Leipzig, 1867.

*Larminie, William. *Fand.* Dublin, 1892. (*United Ireland*, July 23, 1892) [p. 228]

*Larminie. William. *West Irish Folk Tales.* London, 1894. (*Bookman*, June, 1894) [p. 326]

Lewes, George Henry. *The Life and Works of Goethe.* Boston, 1856.

Loftus, Richard J. *Nationalism in Modern Anglo-Irish Poetry.* Madison, 1964.

*Lynch, E. M. *A Parish Providence.* [This is a translation of Balzac's *Le Médecin de campagne.*] In "New Irish Library" Series. Dublin and London, 1894. (*Bookman*, August, 1894) [p. 332]

*McAnally, Jr., David Rice. *Irish Wonders, The Ghosts, Giants, Pookas, Demons, Leprechawns, Banshees, Fairies, Witches, Widows, Old Maids and Other Marvels of the Emerald Isle.* Boston and New York, 1888. (*Scots Observer*, March 30, 1889) [p. 138]

MacBride, Maud Gonne. *A Servant of the Queen.* London, 1938.

Macleod, Fiona [William Sharp]. *The Dominion of Dreams.* Westminster, 1899. (*Bookman*, July, 1899)

*———. *From the Hills of Dream: Mountain Songs and Island Runes.* Edinburgh, 1896. (*Bookman*, December, 1896) [p. 421]

———. *Spiritual Tales.* Edinburgh, 1897. (*Sketch*, April 28, 1897)

Maeterlinck, Maurice. *Aglavaine and Selysette, a Drama in Five Acts*, translated by Alfred Sutro. London, 1897. (*Bookman*, September, 1897)

———. *The Treasure of the Humble*, translated by Alfred Sutro. London, 1897. (*Bookman*, July, 1897)

Mangan, James Clarence. *The Poets and Poetry of Munster*, edited by John O'Daly. Dublin, 1849.

Mercier, Vivian. *The Irish Comic Tradition.* Oxford, 1962.

Mill, John Stuart. *Dissertations and Discussions.* London, 1859.

Monroe, Harriet. *A Poet's Life.* New York, 1938.

Moore, Thomas. *The Poetical Works of Thomas Moore*, edited by A. D. Godley. London, 1929.

Moore, Virginia. *The Unicorn, William Butler Yeats' Search for Reality.* New York, 1954.

*Morris, William. *The Well at the World's End.* Kelmscott Press, Hammersmith, and London, 1896. (*Bookman*, November, 1896) [p. 418]

The New Spirit of the Nation, or Ballads and Songs by the Writers of "The Nation", edited by Martin MacDermott. In "New Irish Library" Series. Dublin and London, 1894. (*Bookman*, August, 1894) [p. 332]

O'Donoghue, D. J. *The Poets of Ireland.* Dublin, 1912.

*O'Grady, Standish. *The Coming of Cuculain.* London, 1895. (*Bookman*, February, 1895) [p. 350]

———. *History of Ireland*, 2 vols. London, 1878–1880.

*O'Kelly, Charles. *The Jacobite War in Ireland 1688–1691.* Edited by George Noble, Count Plunkett and Rev. Edm. Hogan. In "Irish Home Library." Dublin, 1894. (*Bookman*, August, 1894) [p. 332]

O'Leary, John. *Recollections of Fenians and Fenianism*, 2 vols. London, 1896.

Orel, Harold. *The Development of William Butler Yeats: 1885–1900.* Lawrence, 1968.

Oxford Book of Modern Verse, chosen by W. B. Yeats. Oxford, 1936.

Patrick, Arthur W. *Lionel Johnson, poète et critique*. Paris, 1939.
*Piatt, Sarah. *An Enchanted Castle*. London, 1893. (*Speaker*, July 22, 1893)
[p. 276]
Poems and Ballads of Young Ireland. Dublin, 1888.
The Poets and the Poetry of the Century, edited by Alfred Miles. London, 1892.
Quinet, Edgar. *Génie des religions*. Paris, 1842.
*Reilly, Robert J. *Songs of Arcady*. Dublin, 1892. (*United Ireland*, July 23, 1892)
[p. 228]
The Revival of Irish Literature. Addresses by Sir C. G. Duffy, Dr. G. Sigerson, and Dr. D. Hyde. London, 1894.
Reynolds, Horace. *A Providence Episode in the Irish Literary Renaissance*. Providence, 1929.
Rhys, Sir John. *Lectures on the Origin and Growth of Religion as Illustrated by Celtic Heathendom*. [The Hibbert Lectures, 1886.] London, 1888.
Rolleston, T. W. *Sea Spray: Verses and Translations*. Dublin, 1909.
*Savage-Armstrong, George. Collected Works, 9 vols. London, 1891–1892. (*United Ireland*, July 23, 1892, and *Bookman*, September, 1892)
[p. 228, p. 237]
*Sayle, Charles. *Musa Consolatrix*. London, 1893. (*Speaker*, July 22, 1893)
[p. 276]
Sharp, Elizabeth. *William Sharp* (*Fiona Macleod*), *a Memoir*, 2 vols. London, 1912.
Shaw, Bernard. *Fabian Essays*. London, 1889.
Shelley, Percy Bysshe. "A Defence of Poetry" in *The Percy Reprints*, No. 3. Edited by H. F. B. Brett-Smith. Oxford, 1937.
Swedenborg, Emanuel. *The Spiritual Diary of Emanuel Swedenborg*, translated by J. H. Smithson, Vol. I. London, 1846.
Symons, Arthur. *Amoris Victima*. London, 1897. (*Bookman*, April, 1897)
*———. *London Nights*. London, 1895. (*Bookman*, August, 1895)
[p. 373]
———. *The Symbolist Movement in Literature*. London, 1899; New York, 1919.
*Taylor, John F. *Owen Roe O'Neill*. In "New Irish Library" Series. Dublin and London, 1896. (*Bookman*, June, 1896)   [p. 406]
*Tennyson, Alfred, Lord. *The Death of Oenone, Akbar's Dream, and Other Poems*. London, 1892. (*Bookman*, December, 1892)   [p. 251]
*Todhunter, John. *The Banshee and other poems*, 2nd ed. Dublin, 1891. (*United Ireland*, January 23, 1892)   [p. 215]
*———. *The Life of Patrick Sarsfield*. In "New Irish Library" Series. London, 1895. (*Bookman*, November, 1895)   [p. 387]
Torchiana, Donald T. *Yeats and Georgian Ireland*. Evanston, 1966.
A Treasury of Irish Poetry in the English Tongue, edited by S. A. Brooke and T. W. Rolleston. New York, 1923.
Tylor, Sir Edward. *Primitive Culture*, 2 vols. London, 1871; New York, 1883.
*Tynan, Katharine. *Shamrocks*. London, 1887. (*Irish Fireside*, July 9, 1887)
[p. 119]
———. *Twenty-five Years, Reminiscences*. London, 1913.
———. "W. B. Yeats," *The Bookman*, October, 1893.

Vacaresco, Hélène. *The Bard of the Dimbovitza*, translated by Carmen Sylva and Alma Strettell. London, first series, 1891; second series, 1894.

Villiers de l'Isle-Adam, Jean Marie Mathias Philippe Auguste, Comte de. *Axel*, translated by H. P. R. Finberg, with a Preface by W. B. Yeats. London, 1925.

The Vision of MacConglinne, edited by Kuno Meyer. London, 1892. (*Bookman*, February, 1893) [p. 261]

The Voyage of Bran, edited by Kuno Meyer and Alfred Nutt. London, 1897. (*Bookman*, September, 1898)

Wade, Allan. *A Bibliography of the Writings of W. B. Yeats*, 3rd ed. rev. London, 1968.

Walkley, Arthur Bingham. *Drama and Life*. London, 1907; New York, 1908.

Walsh, Edward. *Irish Popular Songs*. Dublin, 1883.

Walsh, John Edward. *Ireland Sixty Years Ago*. Dublin, 1861.

*Weekes, Charles. *Reflections and Refractions*. London, 1893. (*Academy*, November 4, 1893) [p. 302]

Whittington-Egan, Richard, and Smerdon, Geoffrey. *The Quest of the Golden Boy, the Life and Letters of Richard Le Gallienne*. London, 1960.

*Wilde, Jane Francesca, Lady. *Ancient Cures, Charms, and Usages of Ireland*. London, 1890. (*Scots Observer*, March 1, 1890). [p. 169]

Wilde, Oscar. *A Critic in Pall Mall, Being Extracts from "Reviews and Miscellanies"*. Selection made by E. V. Lucas. London, 1919.

———. *Intentions*. London, 1891.

*———. *Lord Arthur Savile's Crime and Other Stories*. London, 1891. (*United Ireland*, September 26, 1891) [p. 202]

*———. *A Woman of No Importance*. London, 1894. (*Bookman*, March, 1895) [p. 354]

Yeats, John Butler. *Letters to his Son, W. B. Yeats, and Others, 1869–1922*, edited by Joseph Hone. London 1944; New York, 1946.

Young, Ella. *Flowering Dusk, Things Remembered Accurately and Inaccurately*. New York, 1945.

BOOKS WRITTEN OR EDITED BY W. B. YEATS

Yeats, W. B. *The Autobiography of W. B. Yeats*. New York, 1965.

———. *A Book of Irish Verse, Selected from Modern Writers*, with an Introduction and Notes by W. B. Yeats. London, 1895.

———. *The Celtic Twilight, Men and Women, Dhouls and Faeries*. London, 1893.

———. *The Collected Plays of W. B. Yeats*, new ed., with five additional plays. New York, 1953.

———. *The Collected Works in Verse and Prose of William Butler Yeats*, 8 vols. Stratford on Avon, 1908.

———. *Essays and Introductions*. New York and London, 1961.

———. *Explorations*. New York and London, 1962.

———. *Fairy and Folk Tales of the Irish Peasantry*. London, 1888.

Yeats, W. B.. *Irish Fairy Tales*. In "The Children's Library." London, 1892.
———. *John Sherman and Dhoya* [published under the pseudonym "Ganconagh"]. London, 1891.
———. *The Letters of W. B. Yeats*, edited by Allan Wade. New York, 1955.
———. *Letters on Poetry from W. B. Yeats to Dorothy Wellesley*. London, 1964.
———. *Letters to Katharine Tynan*, edited by Roger McHugh. New York, 1953.
———. *Letters to the New Island*, edited by Horace Reynolds. Cambridge, Mass., 1934.
———. *Mythologies*. New York and London, 1959.
———. *Poems of William Blake*, edited by W. B. Yeats. New York, Modern Library, 1893.
———. *Representative Irish Tales*. Compiled with an introduction and notes by W. B. Yeats. 2 vols. New York, 1891.
———. *The Secret Rose*. London, 1897.
———. *Selected Criticism*, edited by A. Norman Jeffares. London, 1964.
———. *Selected Prose*, edited by A. Norman Jeffares. London, 1964.
———. *The Variorum Edition of the Plays of W. B. Yeats*, edited by Russell K. Alspach. London, 1966.
———. *The Variorum Edition of the Poems of W. B. Yeats*, edited by Peter Allt and Russell K. Alspach. New York and London, 1957.
———. *A Vision, a Reissue with the Author's Final Revisions*. New York, 1956.

ARTICLES, REVIEWS, AND LETTERS TO NEWSPAPERS BY W. B. YEATS

Articles and reviews included in this book are marked by an asterisk, and the page number is given at the end of the entry.

Yeats, W. B. "'A.E.'s' Poems." Review of A.E.'s *The Earth Breath*. *The Sketch*, April 6, 1898.
———. "Aglavaine and Selysette." Review of Maurice Maeterlinck's play *Aglavaine and Selysette*, translated by Alfred Sutro. *The Bookman*, September, 1897.
*———. "The Ainu." Unsigned review of B. Douglas Howard's *Life with Trans-Siberian Savages*. *The Speaker*, October 7, 1893.   [p. 295]
*———. "Bardic Ireland." Review of Sophie Bryant's *Celtic Ireland*. *Scots Observer*, January 4, 1890.   [p. 162]
*———. "Battles Long Ago." Review of *The Coming of Cuculain* by Standish O'Grady. *The Bookman*, February, 1895.   [p. 350]
*———. "The Binding of the Hair," *The Savoy*, January, 1896. In 1897 reprinted in *The Secret Rose*.   [p. 390]
*———. "A Bundle of Poets." Unsigned review of *The Poems of A. H. Hallam, Anne Boleyn, Musa Consolatrix* by Charles Sayle, and *An Enchanted Castle* by Sarah Piatt. *The Speaker*, July 22, 1893.   [p. 276]
———. "A Canonical Book." Review of Lady Gregory's *Poets and Dreamers*. *The Bookman*, May, 1903.

*Yeats, W. B. "Celtic Beliefs about the Soul." Review of *The Voyage of Bran*, edited by Kuno Meyer and Alfred Nutt. *The Bookman*, September, 1898.

*———. "Clarence Mangan," *The Irish Fireside*, March 12, 1887. [p. 114]

*———. "Clarence Mangan's Love Affair," *United Ireland*, August 22, 1891. [p. 194]

*———. "Clovis Huges on Ireland," *United Ireland*, January 30, 1892. [p. 218]

*———. "The Cradles of Gold," *The Senate*, November, 1896. [p. 413]

*———. "The Death of Oenone." Review of Tennyson's *The Death of Oenone*. *The Bookman*, December, 1892. p. 251]

*———. "Dr. Todhunter's Irish Poems." Review of John Todhunter's *The Banshee and other poems*. *United Ireland*, January 23, 1892. [p. 215]

———. "The Dominion of Dreams." Review of Fiona Macleod's *The Dominion of Dreams*. *The Bookman*, July, 1899.

*———. "Dublin Mystics." Review of A.E.'s *Homeward Songs by the Way*, 2nd ed., and John Eglinton's *Two Essays on the Remnant*. *The Bookman,* May, 1895. [p. 356]

*———. "Dublin Scholasticism and Trinity College," *United Ireland*, July 30, 1892. [p. 231]

*———. "Ellen O'Leary." Biographical sketch which accompanied a selection of Miss O'Leary's poetry in Alfred Miles's anthology *The Poets and the Poetry of the Century*, London, 1892. [p. 256]

*———. "The Evangel of Folk-Lore." Review of William Larminie's *West Irish Folk Tales*. *The Bookman*, June, 1894. [p. 326]

*———. "An Excellent Talker." Review of Oscar Wilde's *A Woman of No Importance*. *The Bookman*, March, 1895. [p. 354]

*———. "An Exhibition at William Morris's," *Providence Sunday Journal*, Providence, R.I., October 26, 1890. [p. 182]

*———. "Greek Folk Poesy." Review of *Greek Folk Poesy*, translated by Lucy Garnett. (*The Bookman*, October, 1896. [p. 409]

*———. "Hopes and Fears for Irish Literature," *United Ireland*, October 15, 1892. [p. 247]

———. "An Imaged World." Unsigned review of Edward Garnett's *An Imaged World*. *The Speaker*, September 8, 1894. [p. 341]

*———. "Invoking the Irish Fairies" by D.E.D.I. ("Demon Est Deus Inversus," Yeats's motto in the Order of the Golden Dawn), *The Irish Theosophist*, October, 1892. [p. 245]

*———. "Irish Fairies," *The Leisure Hour*, October, 1890. [p. 175]

*———. "Irish Fairies, Ghosts, Witches, Etc.," *Lucifer*, January 15, 1889. [p. 130]

———. "Irish Fairy Beliefs." Review of Daniel Deeney's *Peasant Lore from Gaelic Ireland*. *The Speaker*, July 14, 1900.

*———. "Irish Folk Tales." Review of Douglas Hyde's *Beside the Fire*. *National Observer*, February 28, 1891. [p. 186]

*———. "Irish National Literature, I: From Callanan to Carleton," *The Bookman*, July, 1895. [p. 359]

*———. "Irish National Literature, II: Contemporary Prose Writers—

Mr. O'Grady, Miss Lawless, Miss Barlow, Miss Hopper, and the
Folk-Lorists," *The Bookman*, August, 1895.   [p. 366]

*————. "Irish National Literature, III: Contemporary Irish Poets—Dr.
Hyde, Mr. Rolleston, Mrs. Hinkson, Miss Nora Hopper, A.E., Mr.
Aubrey De Vere, Dr. Todhunter, and Mr. Lionel Johnson," *The
Bookman*, September, 1895.   [p. 375]

*————. "Irish National Literature, IV: A List of the Best Irish Books,"
The Bookman, October, 1895.   [p. 382]

*————. "An Irish Patriot." Review of Lady Ferguson's *Sir Samuel Ferguson
in the Ireland of his Day. The Bookman*, May, 1896.   [p. 403]

*————. "Irish Wonders." Unsigned review of D. R. McAnally, Jr.'s *Irish
Wonders, The Ghosts, Giants . . . of the Emerald Isle. Scots Observer*, March
30, 1889.   [p. 138]

————. "John O'Leary." Review of John O'Leary's *Recollections of Fenians
and Fenianism. The Bookman*, February, 1897.

*————. Letter to *The Academy*, "Poetry and Science in Folk-Lore," October
11, 1890.   [p. 173]

*————. Letters to the *Dublin Daily Express*, "Professor Dowden and Irish
Literature," January 26, February 7, 1895.   [p. 346]

*————. Letter to the *Dublin Daily Express*, "Professor Dowden and Irish
Literature," March 8, 1895.   [p. 351]

*————. Letters to the *Freeman's Journal*, "The National Publishing Company," September 6, 1892, September 8, 1892, September 10, 1892.
                                                          [p. 239]

————. Letter to the *Leader*, September 1, 1900.

*————. Letter to *The Nation* (Dublin), "Carleton as an Irish Historian,"
dated January 3, 1890, printed January 11, 1890.   [p. 166]

*————. Letter to *United Ireland*, "The Irish Intellectual Capital: Where Is
It?—The Publication of Irish Books," May 14, 1892.   [p. 222]

*————. Letter to *United Ireland*, "The Irish Literary Society, London,"
July 30, 1892.   [p. 230]

*————. Letter to *United Ireland*, "Libraries Scheme," September 24, 1892.
                                                          [p. 244]

*————. Letter to *United Ireland*, "The De-Anglicising of Ireland," December
17, 1892.   [p. 254]

*————. Letter to *United Ireland*, "The Silenced Sister," December 23 and
30, 1893.   [p. 305]

*————. Letter to *United Ireland*, [The New Irish Library], September 1, 1894.
                                                          [p. 339]

*————. Letter to *United Ireland*, "The Thirty Best Irish Books," March 16,
1895.   [p. 355]

*————. "The Life of Patrick Sarsfield." Review of John Todhunter's *The
Life of Patrick Sarsfield. The Bookman*, November, 1895. [p. 387]

*————. "The Message of the Folk-lorist." Review of T. F. Thistelton Dyer's
The Ghost World. The Speaker, August 19, 1893.   [p. 283]

*————. "Michael Clancy, the Great Dhoul and Death," *The Old Country*
(a Christmas annual), 1893.   [p. 310]

*Yeats, W. B. "Miss Fiona Macleod." Review of Fiona Macleod's *Spiritual Tales. The Sketch*, April 28, 1897.

*———. "Miss Fiona Macleod as a Poet." Review of Fiona Macleod's *From the Hills of Dream. The Bookman*, December, 1896.   [p. 421]

*———. "Miss Tynan's New Book." Review of Katharine Tynan's *Shamrocks. The Irish Fireside*, July 9, 1887.   [p. 119]

———. "Mr Arthur Symons' New Book." Review of Arthur Symons's *Amoris Victima. The Bookman*, April, 1897.

———. "Mr. Lionel Johnson's Poems." Review of Lionel Johnson's *Ireland and Other Poems. The Bookman*, February, 1898.

———. "Mr. Rhys' Welsh Ballads." Review of Ernest Rhys's *Welsh Ballads. The Bookman*, April, 1898.

*———. "Nationality and Literature." Lecture. *United Ireland*, May 27, 1893.   [p. 266]

*———. "The New Irish Library." Review of Richard Ashe King's *Swift in Ireland*, John F. Taylor's *Owen Roe O'Neill*, and Sir Charles Gavan Duffy's *Short Life of Thomas Davis. The Bookman*, June, 1896.   [p. 406]

*———. "A New Poet." Review of A.E.'s *Homeward Songs by the Way. The Bookman*, August, 1894.   [p. 335]

*———. "A New Poet." Review of Edwin J. Ellis's *Fate in Arcadia. The Bookman*, September, 1892.   [p. 234]

*———. "The New 'Speranza,'" *United Ireland*, January 16, 1892.   [p. 212]

*———. "'Noetry' and Poetry." Review of the collected verse of George Savage-Armstrong. *The Bookman*, September, 1892.   [p. 237]

*———. "Old Gaelic Love Songs." Review of Douglas Hyde's *Love Songs of Connacht. The Bookman*, October, 1893.   [p. 292]

*———. "Oscar Wilde's Last Book." Review of *Lord Arthur Savile's Crime and Other Stories* by Oscar Wilde. *United Ireland*, September 26, 1891.   [p. 202]

*———. "Plays by an Irish Poet." Review of performances of John Todhunter's *A Sicilian Idyll* and *The Poison Flower. United Ireland*, July 11, 1891.   [p. 190]

*———. "A Poet We Have Neglected." Review of the works of William Allingham. *United Ireland*, December 12, 1891.   [p. 208]

*———. "The Poetry of R. D. Joyce," *The Irish Fireside*, November 27 and December 4, 1886.   [p. 104]

*———. "The Poetry of Sir Samuel Ferguson," *Dublin University Review*, November, 1886.   [p. 87]

*———. "The Poetry of Sir Samuel Ferguson," *Irish Fireside*, October 9, 1886.   [p. 81]

*———. "Popular Ballad Poetry of Ireland," *The Leisure Hour* (London), November, 1889.   [p. 146]

*———. "The Prose and Poetry of Wilfred Blunt." Review of Wilfred Scawen Blunt's *Love Sonnets of Proteus. United Ireland*, January 28, **1888.**   [p. 122]

*Yeats W. B. "A Reckless Century. Irish Rakes and Duellists," *United Ireland*, September 12, 1891. [p. 198]

*———. "Reflections and Refractions." Review of Charles Weekes's book of verse by that title. *The Academy*, November 4, 1893. [p. 302]

*———. "The Rose of Shadow." Reprinted in *The Secret Rose*, London, 1897. This story originally appeared in the *Speaker*, July 21, 1894, as "Those Who Live in the Storm." [p. 328]

*———. "Seen in Three Days." Review of E. J. Ellis's *Seen in Three Days*. *The Bookman*, February, 1894. [p. 317]

*———. "Sight and Song." Review of Michael Field's *Sight and Song*. *The Bookman*, July, 1892. [p. 225]

*———. "Some Irish National Books." Review of *The New Spirit of the Nation*, *A Parish Providence*, and *The Jacobite War in Ireland*. *The Bookman*, August, 1894. [p. 332]

*———. "Some New Irish Books." Unsigned review of the works of George Savage-Armstrong, *Fand* by William Larminie, and *Songs of Arcady* by Robert J. Reilly. *United Ireland*, July 23, 1892. [p. 228]

*———. "The Stone and the Elixir." Review of Ibsen's *Brand*, translated by F. E. Garrett. *The Bookman*, October, 1894. [p. 344]

*———. "The Story of Early Gaelic Literature." Review of Douglas Hyde's *The Story of Early Gaelic Literature*. *The Bookman*, June, 1895. [p. 358]

*———. "A Symbolical Drama in Paris." Review of a performance of Villiers de l'Isle-Adam's *Axël*. *The Bookman*, April, 1894. [p. 320]

*———. "Tales from the Twilight." Review of Lady Wilde's *Ancient Cures, Charms, and Usages of Ireland*. *The Scots Observer*, March 1, 1890. [p. 169]

*———. "That Subtle Shade." Review of Arthur Symons's *London Nights*. *The Bookman*, August, 1895. [p. 373]

———. "Three Irish Poets." Article on A.E., Lionel Johnson, and Nora Hopper in a special supplement to the *Irish Homestead* entitled "A Celtic Christmas," December, 1897.

*———. "The Three Sorrows of Story-Telling." Review of Douglas Hyde's *The Three Sorrows of Story-Telling and Ballads of St. Columkille*. *The Bookman*, July, 1895. [p. 364]

———. "The Treasure of the Humble." Review of Maurice Maeterlinck's *The Treasure of the Humble*. *The Bookman*, July, 1897.

*———. "Two Minor Lyrists." Unsigned review of J. D. Hosken's *Verses by the Way* and Fenil Haig's [Ford Madox Ford's] *The Questions at the Well*. *The Speaker*, August 26, 1893. [p. 288]

*———. "Verlaine in 1894," *The Savoy*, April, 1896. [p. 397]

*———. "The Vision of MacConglinne." Review of book by that title, edited by Kuno Meyer. *The Bookman*, February, 1893. [p. 261]

*———. "The Wandering Jew." Review of Robert Buchanan's book by that title. *The Bookman*, April, 1893. [p. 263]

*———. "The Well at the World's End." Review of William Morris's book by that title. *The Bookman*, November, 1896. [p. 418]

*Yeats, W. B. "William Allingham." Biographical sketch Yeats contributed to Alfred Miles's anthology *The Poets and the Poetry of the Century,* London, 1892.   [p. 258]

*———. "William Blake." Review of Richard Garnett's *William Blake. The Bookman,* April, 1896.   [p. 400]

*———. "William Carleton." Review of Carleton's autobiography, *The Life of William Carleton,* completed and edited by D. J. O'Donoghue. *The Bookman,* March, 1896.   [p. 394]

*———. "William Carleton." Unsigned review of *Stories from Carleton* and Carleton's *The Red-Haired Man's Wife. The Scots Observer,* October 19, 1889.   [p. 141]

*———. "The Writings of William Blake." Review of Laurence Housman's *Selections from the Writings of William Blake. The Bookman,* August, 1893.
                                                              [p. 280]

———. "Young Ireland." Review of Sir Charles Gavan Duffy's *Young Ireland. The Bookman,* January, 1897.

*———. "The Young Ireland League," *United Ireland,* October 3, 1891.
                                                              [p. 206]